what we call "civilization" is relatively recent, indeed, with the first permanent settlements occurring in the Middle East a scant 12,000 years ago. But the written record of our species' existence extends back only half this long, to the time humans invented writing and first farmed with animal-driven plows some 5,000 years B.P.

Sociology came into being in the wake of the many changes to society wrought by the Industrial Revolution over the last few centuries—just the blink of an eye in evolutionary perspective. The lower time line provides a close-up look at the events and trends that have defined **The Modern Era**, most of which are discussed in this text. Innovations in technology are charted in the _____ provide a useful backdrop _____ progress highlighted in t _____ major contributions to the dev _____ are traced along the very bo _____

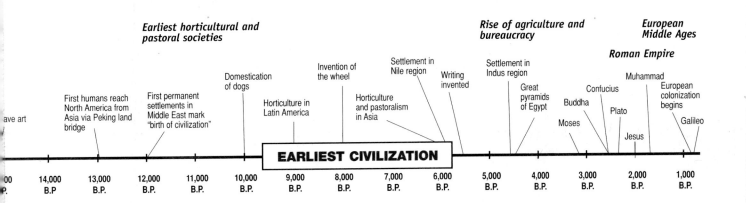

**Earliest horticultural and pastoral societies**

**Rise of agriculture and bureaucracy**

**European Middle Ages**

**Roman Empire**

Invention of the wheel

Settlement in Nile region

Writing invented

Settlement in Indus region

Muhammad

European colonization begins

Domestication of dogs

First humans reach North America from Asia via Peking land bridge

First permanent settlements in Middle East mark "birth of civilization"

Horticulture in Latin America

Horticulture and pastoralism in Asia

Great pyramids of Egypt

Buddha

Confucius

Plato

Jesus

Galileo

Moses

ave art

**EARLIEST CIVILIZATION**

| 00 P. | 14,000 B.P. | 13,000 B.P. | 12,000 B.P. | 11,000 B.P. | 10,000 B.P. | 9,000 B.P. | 8,000 B.P. | 7,000 B.P. | 6,000 B.P. | 5,000 B.P. | 4,000 B.P. | 3,000 B.P. | 2,000 B.P. | 1,000 B.P. |

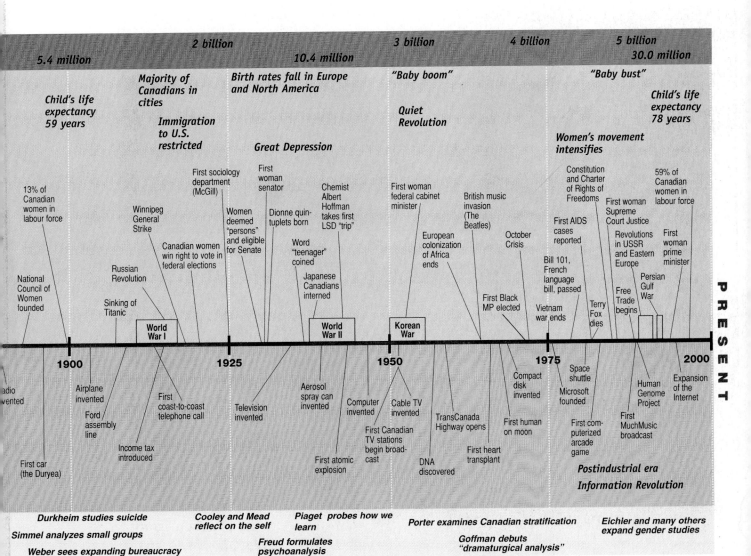

5.4 million

2 billion

10.4 million

3 billion

4 billion

5 billion

30.0 million

**Child's life expectancy 59 years**

**Majority of Canadians in cities**

**Immigration to U.S. restricted**

**Birth rates fall in Europe and North America**

**Great Depression**

**"Baby boom"**

**Quiet Revolution**

**"Baby bust"**

**Women's movement intensifies**

**Child's life expectancy 78 years**

13% of Canadian women in labour force

Winnipeg General Strike

First sociology department (McGill)

First woman senator

Chemist Albert Hoffman takes first LSD "trip"

First woman federal cabinet minister

British music invasion (The Beatles)

October Crisis

Constitution and Charter of Rights of Freedoms

First woman Supreme Court Justice

59% of Canadian women in labour force

National Council of Women founded

Russian Revolution

Canadian women win right to vote in federal elections

Women deemed "persons" and eligible for Senate

Dionne quintuplets born

Word "teenager" coined

European colonization of Africa ends

First AIDS cases reported

Revolutions in USSR and Eastern Europe

First woman prime minister

Sinking of Titanic

Japanese Canadians interned

First Black MP elected

Bill 101, French language bill, passed

Vietnam war ends

Terry Fox dies

Free Trade begins

Persian Gulf War

**World War I**

**World War II**

**Korean War**

adio vented

1900

1925

1950

1975

2000

Airplane invented

Aerosol spray can invented

Compact disk invented

Space shuttle

Expansion of the Internet

Ford assembly line

First coast-to-coast telephone call

Television invented

Computer invented

Cable TV invented

TransCanada Highway opens

First human on moon

Microsoft founded

Human Genome Project

Income tax introduced

First Canadian TV stations begin broadcast

First computerized arcade game

First MuchMusic broadcast

First car (the Duryea)

First atomic explosion

DNA discovered

First heart transplant

**Postindustrial era**

**Information Revolution**

P R E S E N T

Durkheim studies suicide

Simmel analyzes small groups

Weber sees expanding bureaucracy

Cooley and Mead reflect on the self

Freud formulates psychoanalysis

Piaget probes how we learn

Porter examines Canadian stratification

Goffman debuts "dramaturgical analysis"

Eichler and many others expand gender studies

*This book is offered to teachers of sociology in the hope that it will help our students understand their place in today's society and, more broadly, tomorrow's world.*

SECOND CANADIAN EDITION 2

# SOCIETY

## *the basics*

**John J. Macionis**
Kenyon College

**S. Mikael Jansson**
University of Western Ontario

**Cecilia M. Benoit**
University of Victoria

Prentice
Hall

Toronto

**National Library of Canada Cataloguing in Publication Data**

Macionis, John J.

      Society : the basics

2nd Canadian ed.

Includes bibliographical references and index.

ISBN 0-13-060206-X

1. Sociology.  I. Jansson, Mikael, 1959–  .  II. Benoit, Cecilia, 1954–  .  III. Title.

HM586.M32 2002              301             C2001-930221-5

Original edition published by Prentice Hall Inc., a division of Pearson Education, Upper Saddle River, New Jersey. Copyright ©2002, 1998,1996,1994,1992 by Prentice Hall, Inc.

This edition is authorized for sale only in Canada.

ISBN 0-13-060206-X

Vice President, Editorial Director: Michael Young
Editor-in-Chief: David Stover
Acquisitions Editor: Jessica Mosher
Marketing Manager: Judith Allen
Developmental Editor: Dawn du Quesnay
Senior Production Editor: Sherry Torchinsky
Copy Editor: Allyson Latta
Production Coordinator: Peggy Brown
Page Layout: Christine Velakis
Photo Research: Patricia Buckley
Art Director: Julia Hall
Interior Design: Alex Li
Cover Design: Liz Harasymczuk
Cover Image: Stock Illustration Source/Noma

The credits appear on pages 467–468. They should be considered an extension of the copyright page. Statistics Canada information is used with permission of the Minister of Industry, as Minister responsible for Statistics Canada. Information on the availability of the wide range of data from Statistics Canada can be obtained from Statistics Canada's Regional Offices, its World Wide Web site at http://www.statcan.ca, and its toll-free access number 1-800-263-1136.

1 2 3 4 5     05 04 03 02

Printed and bound in the United States of America.

# BRIEF CONTENTS

# CONTENTS

6

7

13

# 16

# WINDOW ON THE WORLD

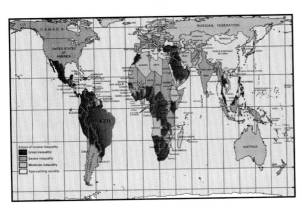

# SEEING OURSELVES

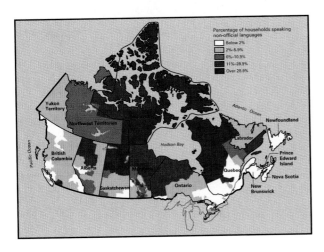

# BOXES

## GLOBAL SOCIOLOGY

## SOCIAL DIVERSITY

# APPLYING SOCIOLOGY

# CRITICAL THINKING

# CONTROVERSY & DEBATE

# PREFACE

It was just five or six years ago that people were beginning to talk about the Internet and the Information Revolution. Today, computers and other new technology already play a part in how people entertain themselves, stay in touch with others, shop for everything from gadgets to groceries, teach classes, and study for exams. One can only imagine the extent of the transformation that will unfold over the course of this new century.

Yet there remains a contradiction in calling this the "information age." No one doubts that we have more information available to us than ever before. But it is also the case that many of us know amazingly little about our own society and even less about the larger world. Students are no exception; and it is here that sociology has a crucial part to play. By developing students' sociological imagination, we help them see the shape of the society that guides their lives, learn to apply it to their own lives, and at the same time come to appreciate ever-present forces of change brought about by forces within and beyond their influence. This same imagination also lets them place this society in a global context, highlighting the worldwide structures and systems that affect us all.

In this spirit, we are delighted to offer this second Canadian edition of *Society: The Basics*, the discipline's most popular text, and a book that never stands still. As in the past, this edition of *Society* is authoritative, comprehensive, stimulating, and—as student e-mail messages testify—fun to read. This major revision elevates sociology's most popular text to a still higher standard of excellence, and offers an unparalleled resource to today's students as they learn about both our diverse society and the changing world.

In addition to the text, students using *Society: The Basics, Second Canadian Edition* can log on to a full-featured Web site, **http://www.pearsoned.ca/macionis** also at no cost to them, using the access code that will be provided to instructors. From the main page, simply click on the cover of this text to reach a fully-featured learning site, including chapter overviews and learning objectives, Critical Thinking and Applying Sociology exercises, as well as multiple-choice and true-false questions that the server will grade, chapter-relevant Web destinations, and a chat room where students can share experiences and opinions with others taking the course. Faculty will find a full complement of resources as well, including a Windows version of the Instructor's Manual, PowerPoint slides, and the syllabus manager system that allows posting a course syllabus to the

Internet without having to learn hypertext markup language (HTML); the server does the work for you.

Prentice Hall and EBSCO, the world leader in online journal subscription management, have come together to develop an innovative new feature of our *Companion Website™—ContentSelect*. With database access to more than 100 academic journals and leading popular sources, *ContentSelect* provides a twenty-four-hour-a-day window into the most reputable content in the discipline of sociology.

## ORGANIZATION OF THIS TEXT

*Society: The Basics* carries students through sociology's basic ideas, research, and insights in sixteen logically organized chapters. Chapter 1 ("Sociology: Perspective, Theory, and Method") explains how the discipline's distinctive point of view illuminates the world in a new and exciting way. In addition, the first chapter introduces major theoretical approaches and explains the key methods sociologists use to test and refine their knowledge. The next six chapters examine core sociological concepts. Chapter 2 ("Culture") explores the fascinating diversity of human living in our world. Chapter 3 ("Socialization: From Infancy to Old Age") investigates how people everywhere develop their humanity as they learn to participate in society. While highlighting the importance of the early years to the socialization process, this chapter describes significant transformations that occur over the entire life course, including old age. Chapter 4 ("Social Interaction in Everyday Life") takes a micro-level look at how people construct the daily realities that we often take for granted. Chapter 5 ("Groups and Organizations") focuses on social groups, within which we have many of our most meaningful experiences. It also highlights the expansion of formal organization and points up some of the problems of living in a bureaucratic age. Chapter 6 ("Deviance") analyzes how the routine operation of society promotes deviance as well as conformity. Chapter 7 ("Sexuality"), new to this edition, explains the social foundations of human sexuality. Based on recent research, this chapter surveys sexual patterns in Canada and also explores variations in sexual practices through history and around the world today.

The next four chapters provide more coverage of social inequality than is found in any other brief text. Chapter 8 ("Social Stratification") introduces basic concepts that describe dimensions of social stratification throughout human history and around the world today. The chapter then highlights dimensions of social difference in present-day Canada. Chapter 9 ("Global Stratification") extends this text's commitment to global education by analyzing the social ranking of nations themselves. Why, in other words, do people in some societies have abundant wealth while, in others, people struggle every day just to survive? *Society: The Basics* also provides full-chapter coverage of two additional dimensions of social difference. Chapter 10 ("Gender Stratification") describes how gender is a central element of social stratification in Canada, as it is worldwide. Chapter 11 ("Race and Ethnicity") explores racial and ethnic diversity in our country, explaining how societies use physical and cultural traits to construct and rank categories of people in a hierarchy.

Next are three chapters that survey social institutions. Chapter 12 ("Economics and Politics") looks at the economy of Canadian society, beginning with how the Industrial Revolution transformed the Western world. This chapter contrasts capitalist and socialist economic models, and investigates how economic systems are linked to a society's distribution of power. This chapter also contains coverage of the military and the important issues of war and peace.

Chapter 13 ("Family and Religion") spotlights two institutions central to the symbolic organization of social life. The chapter begins by focusing on the variety of family forms in Canada, making frequent comparison to kinship systems in other parts of the world. Basic elements of religious life come next, with an overview of recent religious trends.

Chapter 14 ("Education and Medicine") examines two institutions with special importance in the new century. The chapter looks first at the historical expansion of schooling, noting many ways in which the scope and kind of education are linked to other social institutions. Next, we look at health, which also has become a central institution during the last century and a half. The chapter concludes by explaining the distinctive strategies various countries—including our own—employ to promote access to high quality health care and also highlights the tensions in the Canadian health care system as it grapples with demographic and other societal shifts.

The final two chapters of the text focus on dimensions of social change. Chapter 15 ("Population, Urbanization, and Environment") is a new synthesis that begins by spotlighting the growth of population in the world. Our attention then turns to the rise of cities in Canada and the United States and to the urban explosion now taking place in low-income countries around the world. Finally, the chapter explains how the state of the natural environment reflects social organization. Chapter 16 ("Social Change: Modern and Postmodern Societies") concludes the text with summaries of major theories of social change, a look at how people forge social movements to encourage or resist change, analysis of various benefits and liabilities of modern social patterns, and the emergence of a "postmodern" way of life.

## CONTINUITY: ESTABLISHED FEATURES OF *SOCIETY: THE BASICS*

The extraordinary success of *Society: The Basics*, as well as *Sociology*—the market leader among comprehensive hardback texts—results from a combination of the following distinctive features.

**The best writing style.** Most important, this text offers a writing style widely praised by students and faculty alike as elegant and inviting. Society is an enjoyable text that encourages students to read—even beyond their assignments. No one says it better than the students themselves, whose recent e-mail includes testimonials such as these:

Thanks for writing such a brilliant book. It has sparked my sociological imagination. This was the first textbook that I have ever read completely and enjoyed. From the moment that I picked the book up I started reading nonstop.

I have read four chapters ahead; it's like a good novel I can't put down! I just wanted to say thank you.

Your book is extremely well written and very interesting. I find myself reading it for pleasure, something I have never done with college texts. It is going to be the only collegiate textbook that I ever keep simply to read on my own. I am also thinking of picking up sociology as my minor due to the fact that I have enjoyed the class as well as the text so much. Your writing has my highest praise and utmost appreciation.

I am taking a Sociology 101 class using your text, a book that I have told my professor is the best textbook that I have ever seen, bar none. I've told her as well that I will be more than happy to take more sociology classes as long as there is a Macionis text to go with them.

**A global perspective.** *Society* was the first brief text to mainstream global content, introduce global maps, and offer comprehensive coverage of global topics like stratification and the environment. No wonder this text has been adapted and translated in half a dozen languages for use around the world. Each chapter explores the social diversity of the entire world as well as explaining why social trends and issues in Canada—from changing family patterns, increasing ethnic and racial diversity, urban sprawl, to the growing disparity of income—are influenced by what happens elsewhere. Just as important, students will learn ways that social patterns and policies at home impact low-income nations around the world.

**A celebration of social diversity.** *Society: The Basics* invites students from all social backgrounds to discover a fresh and exciting way to see themselves within the larger social world. Readers will discover in this text the diversity of Canadian society—people of a multitude of backgrounds ranging from Aboriginal, Asian, European, and African and other ancestries, as well as women and men of various class positions and at all points in the life course. Just as important, without flinching from the problems that marginalized people confront, this text does not treat minorities as social problems but highlights their agency and recognizes their significant achievements.

**Emphasis on critical thinking.** Critical-thinking skills include the ability to challenge common assumptions by formulating questions, to identify and weigh appropriate evidence, and to reach reasoned conclusions. This text not only teaches but also encourages students to discover on their own.

**Engaging and instructive chapter openings.** One of the most popular features of the first Canadian edition of *Society* was the engaging vignettes that begin each chapter. These openings—for instance, using the tragic sinking of the Titanic to illustrate the life and death consequences of social inequality, the story of Anna, a little girl who grew up tied to a chair in the attic, to show the importance of socialization, or the story of the wrongful convictions of David Milgaard and Thomas Sophonow to open the chapter on deviance— spark the interest of readers as they introduce important themes. This revision retains eight of the best chapter-opening vignettes found in earlier editions and offers eight new ones as well.

**Inclusive focus on women and men.** Beyond devoting two full chapters to the important concepts of sex and gender, *Society* mainstreams gender into every chapter, showing how the topic at hand affects women and men differently, and explaining how gender operates as a basic dimension of social organization.

**Theoretically clear and balanced.** This text makes theory easy. The discipline's major theoretical approaches are introduced in Chapter 1 and are carried through later chapters. The text highlights the social-conflict, structural-functional, and symbolic-interaction paradigms, and also incorporates other theoretical approaches including feminism, social-exchange analysis, ethnomethodology, and sociobiology.

**Recent research and the latest data.** *Society: The Basics, Second Canadian Edition*, blends classic sociological statements with the latest research, as reported in the leading publications in the field. More than 1000 research citations support this revision, more than one-third of them published since 1990. We have used the latest government and other reputable sources to ensure that—chapter to chapter—the text's content and statistical data are the most recent available.

**Learning aids.** This text has many features to help students learn. In each chapter, **Key Concepts** are identified by boldfaced type, and following each appears a *precise, italicized definition.* A listing of key concepts with their definitions appears at the end of each chapter, and a complete **Glossary** is found at the end of the book. Each chapter also contains a numbered **Summary** and four **Critical-Thinking Questions** that help students review material and assess their understanding. Following these are a number of **Applications and Exercises,** which provide students with activities to do on or near the campus. Finally, each chapter ends with an annotated listing of worthwhile **Sites to See** on the Internet.

**Outstanding images: photography and fine art.** *Society: The Basics, Second Canadian Edition*, offers the finest and most extensive program of photography and artwork available in any comparable book. We search extensively to obtain the finest images of the human condition and present them with thoughtful captions, often in the form of questions.

**Thought-provoking theme boxes.** Although boxed material is common to introductory texts, *Society: The Basics, Second Canadian Edition*, provides a wealth of uncommonly good boxes. Each chapter typically contains three boxes, which fall into five types that amplify central themes of the text. **Global Sociology** boxes provoke readers to think about their own way of life by examining the fascinating social diversity that characterizes our world. **Social Diversity** boxes focus on multicultural issues and present the voices of women and other minorities. **Critical Thinking** boxes teach students to ask sociological questions about their surroundings, and help them evaluate important, controversial issues. Each Critical-Thinking box is followed by three "What do you think?" questions. **Controversy & Debate** boxes present several points of view on hotly debated issues and conclude with "Continue the debate" questions to stimulate thought and generate spirited class discussion. **Applying Sociology** boxes, new to this edition, show the value of applying the sociological perspective to the world around us— especially the work we do.

Society contains fifty-six boxes in all, including twenty-five that are new to this edition. A complete listing of this text's boxes appears after the table of contents.

**An unparalleled program of thirty-two global and national maps.** Another popular feature of *Society: The Basics* is the program of global and national maps. Window on the World global maps—twenty in all—

are truly sociological maps offering a comparative look at income disparity, favoured languages and religions, the extent of prostitution, permitted marriage forms, the degree of political freedom, the incidence of HIV infection, and a host of other issues. The global maps use the non-Eurocentric projection devised by cartographer Arno Peters that accurately portrays the relative size of all the continents.

Seeing Ourselves national maps—twelve in all—help to illuminate the social diversity of Canada. Most of these maps are broken down into the 288 national census divisions, with the result that they illustrate the important differences that exist within provinces much more accurately than is possible with just provincial averages. They present at a glance the national picture on such topics as the percentage of families below the poverty line, and the percentage of single-parent families across Canada, and much more. A complete listing of the Seeing Ourselves national maps as well as the Window on the World global maps follows the table of contents.

## INNOVATION: CHANGES IN THE SECOND CANADIAN EDITION

The first Canadian edition of *Society: The Basics* and three Canadian editions of *Sociology* have each broken new ground, one reason that almost 87 000 students have learned from these sociological best-sellers. A revision raises high expectations, but, after two years of planning and hard work, we are pleased to offer a major revision that sets a new standard for brief texts. Here is a brief overview of the innovations that define *Society: The Basics, Second Canadian Edition.*

**A new chapter on sexuality.** This revision offers a new chapter. Chapter 7 ("Sexuality") is a sociological look at a central dimension of human existence. The chapter begins by explaining the biological and cultural foundations of sexuality, surveys changing sexual attitudes in Canada, explores the myths and realities surrounding sexual orientation, and then provides balanced discussion of sexual controversies including teen pregnancy, pornography, prostitution, and sexual violence. The chapter concludes with various theoretical analyses of sexuality.

**A new synthesis: population, urbanization, and the environment.** This revision draws three closely-related issues together into a new synthesis. Chapter 15 begins by outlining the study of population, moves to the steady rise in the share of humanity residing in cities, and then links both topics to the state of the physical environment.

**A greater emphasis on social diversity.** A long-time strength of this text is its emphasis on social diversity. In this revision, from chapter to chapter, race, class, and gender receive even more attention, with more discussions, and more Social Diversity boxes.

**A greater emphasis on applications.** This text helps students apply the power of sociology to their present lives and future careers. We've added a set of Applying Sociology theme boxes (nine in all). Moreover, at the end of each chapter is a listing of Applications and Exercises that suggests ways students can apply lessons to their campus and community life. Finally, chapters in the new edition have major sections that apply the power of sociology to a wide range of current issues pertinent to students' lives as well as the world beyond.

**New chapter-opening vignettes.** This revision keeps the best of the popular chapter-opening vignettes and adds eight new ones. All vignettes add interest as students begin a chapter, and provide important lessons about the topic at hand.

**The latest statistical data.** Instructors count on this text for including the very latest statistical data. The second Canadian edition comes through again, making use of the latest data from the Internet as well as conventional bound publications of various government agencies and private organizations. The authors guarantee that the newest available statistics are used throughout the text—in many cases for 2000 and sometimes for 2001. In addition, the authors regularly review more than one dozen journals as well as a wide range of media publications. The result: readers will find several hundred new research citations as well as many familiar current events that elevate the interest of students.

**New topics.** The second Canadian edition of *Society: The Basics* is completely updated with new and expanded discussions in every chapter. Here is just a partial listing, by chapter. (All chapters end with the new Applications and Exercises feature, as well as Sites to See.)

- **Chapter 1 Sociology: Perspective, Theory, and Methods:** A new chapter opening contrasts the lives of a University of Victoria graduate and a former street youth who recently got her Grade 12 diploma; there are updates of suicide patterns in Canada and around the world, including a new figure on suicide rates in Canada; the discussion of social change and the emergence of sociology has been reorganized; there is a new Critical Thinking box on sports; the sociological methodology section has been heavily revised to contrast three approaches: scientific sociology, interpretive sociology, and critical sociology.

- **Chapter 2 Culture:** Many updated examples and illustrations are found throughout the chapter; there is a new subsection on conflicting values; Postindustrial Information Technology has been revised and updated; there is a new Controversy & Debate box on "the culture wars".

- **Chapter 3 Socialization**: This chapter includes an update on Canadian television-watching, and recent research on television and violence; there is new Canadian research on relentless teasing by peers and teenage suicide, including the case of Reena Virk; the section on class position has been expanded and updated with new Canadian research; there are updated statistics and research on aging and the elderly in Canada; there is a new Controversy & Debate box, "Are Canadians Free Within Society?"

- **Chapter 4 Social Interaction in Everyday Life**: This chapter for the first time covers Edward T. Hall's (1969) personal space index; there is now a greater emphasis on applications throughout, including a new Applying Sociology box, "Hide Those Lyin' Eyes: Can You Do It?"; there is a new Critical Thinking box on humorous headlines.

- **Chapter 5 Groups and Organizations**: A major reorganization of this chapter adds discussion of early scientific management and traces the evolution of organization toward a flatter, flexible, "intelligent" form; the chapter also contrasts the rise of intelligent organizations doing highly skilled postindustrial work with the countertrend toward low-skill service work often called "McJobs". In addition, there is expanded coverage of oligarchy, using the example of incumbents in the November 2000 Canadian elections; and a new Applying Sociology box on "spin".

- **Chapter 6 Deviance**: A new chapter opening on the wrongful conviction of David Milgaard points out weaknesses in the criminal justice system; the section on "Labelling Deviance" has been re-organized to present the theories of deviance more prominently; there are new sections on corporate crime and organized crime; the profile of the typical street criminal has been updated and expanded in the areas of age, gender, social class, and race; all Canadian and international crime statistics are updated; there are two new boxes.

- **Chapter 7 Sexuality**: This new chapter highlights the socially constructed character of human sexuality; the chapter takes a global view of sexuality, and also surveys a number of sexuality issues, from sexual orientation to sexual violence; as well, there are several new boxes. Canadian content includes the discussion of sexual attitudes in Canada and how they've changed since the 1960s; there is Canadian data on the sexual revolution, premarital sex among young people, the frequency of sexual activity and extramarital activity, teen pregnancy, sexual assault, and abortion. There are also discussions of the current legal situation in Canada regarding child pornography, and of prostitution in Canada.

- **Chapter 8 Social Stratification**: This chapter has a reorganized discussion of caste and class; recent changes in the British aristocracy are noted; statistics and figures on income and wealth disparity in Canada are thoroughly updated, including a new National Map on average income; there is a new Critical Thinking box on getting rich, new research and statistics on the global economy and the Canadian class structure, and updated statistics on schooling in Canada.

- **Chapter 9 Global Stratification**: A new opening recounts the story of boatloads of Chinese refugees who recently landed in British Columbia fleeing poverty in their homeland; a dramatic new Global Sociology box describes the culture of slavery in North Africa; there is a new Social Diversity box, "Modernization: New Challenges for Women"; and there are updates on global wealth and well-being.

- **Chapter 10 Gender Stratification**: The chapter opens with a pithy quotation from Nellie McClung on equal rights; the chapter includes statistical updates on women's pay, schooling, and work, including a new figure on how married men and women allocate their time; there is a new Global Map, " Power in Global Perspective"; new research on parental leaves is discussed.

- **Chapter 11 Race and Ethnicity**: This chapter contains new research on racism, sexism and immigration in our country; there are new two new figures on prejudice and discrimination and social disadvantage.

- **Chapter 12 The Economy and Politics**: There is a new chapter opening on the trend towards using temporary workers; find updated statistics on many aspects of the Canadian labor force; there is a new Social Diversity box on the changing workplace in Canada; we've added a new Global Map on service-sector employment in global perspective; the chapter includes an update on political freedoms around the world and updated coverage of the changing political spectrum, party identification, and voter apathy in Canada; there is an update on nuclear proliferation worldwide.

- **Chapter 13 Family and Religion**: The chapter opens with a new vignette on gay marriage in Canada; find updated statistics on ethnicity and race in Canadian families, divorce in Canada, violence against women in Canadian families, joint custody arrangements, cohabiting, and church attendance; find updated coverage of gay and lesbian couples in Canada; new research is cited on the role of the welfare state and men's involvement in child rearing; there is a new figure on religious attendance and statistical updates on all the trends regarding family and religious life.

- **Chapter 14 Education and Medicine**: Statistical updates are included for all measures of educational achievement and health; there is a new section on discipline and violence in schools; new research and statistics on family wealth and participation in post-secondary education and dropping out; in the Health section, a new Global Sociology box describes the free-fall in life expectancy among men following the collapse of the former Soviet Union; there is a new section on holistic health; the discussion of comparative health care systems has been updated; there are new figures on the incidence of tuberculosis among Canada's aboriginal peoples and AIDS transmission worldwide.

- **Chapter 15 Population, Urbanization, and Environment**: This chapter is an interesting combination of population, urbanization, and environment; a new chapter opening reports on urban sprawl in Vancouver; find the latest global population figures as well as new Canadian demographics on crude birth rates, death rates, infant mortality, population, life expectancy and fertility and population composition; there is an update on the development of urban regions and sprawl; throughout the chapter the focus is on the interplay of population, urbanization, and the physical environment.

- **Chapter 16 Social Change: Modern and Postmodern Societies**: A new chapter-opening vignette illustrates the extent of social change over the course of the twentieth century; expanded coverage of the theories of social movements includes a new discussion of culture theory; a new Applying Sociology box evaluates the changing quality of life in Canada.

## A WORD ABOUT LANGUAGE

This text's commitment to representing the social diversity of Canada and the world carries with it the responsibility to use language thoughtfully. For example, we prefer the term Aboriginal to the word Indian. Most tables and figures refer to "Visible Minorities" and "Aboriginals" separately because Statistics Canada employs these term in collecting statistical data about our population, and because that is the preference of many Aboriginals themselves.

Students should realize, however, that many individuals do not describe themselves using these terms. Although the term "Aboriginal" is commonly used in Canada, across Canada people of Aboriginal descent identify with a particular Aboriginal nation, whether it be the Métis Nation of Ontario or the Haida, or the Nisga'a of British Columbia.

The same holds true for visible minorities. Although this term is a useful shorthand in sociological analysis, most people think of themselves in terms of a specific country of origin (say, Japan, the Philippines, India, or Vietnam).

Throughout the text we have used the term "low-income" rather than "poor" (and "high-income" rather than "rich") for two reasons. First, while there are many consequences of poverty, the labelling of individuals, families, and nations as "poor" is primarily based on income, reflecting the primary, or direct, cause of poverty. So "low-income" is a more accurate description. Second, using the term low-income emphasizes the importance of thinking about the causes and consequences of poverty in an all-encompassing framework that includes individuals, families, and nations with high income.

## A WORD ABOUT WEB SITES

Because of the increasing importance of the Internet, each chapter of *Society: The Basics* ends with a listing of Sites to See. The goal is to provide sites that are current, informative, and, above all, relevant to the topic at hand.

However, students should be mindful of several potential problems. First, Web sites change all the time. Prior to publication, we make every effort to ensure that the sites listed meet our high standards. But readers may find that sites have changed substantially and some may have gone away entirely. Obviously, this problem is beyond our control.

Second, sites have been selected in order to provide different perspectives on various issues. The listing of a site does not imply that the author or publisher agrees with everything—or even anything—on the site. Indeed, we urge students to examine all sites critically.

Third, many of the Web sites listed in this text are popular. Because many people visit them, the sites may be slow in responding. Please be patient or, if a site is too busy, simply move on.

## SUPPLEMENTS

*Society: The Basics, Second Canadian Edition*, is the heart of a multimedia learning package that includes a wide range of proven instructional aids as well as several new ones. The supplements for this revision have been thoroughly updated, improved, and expanded.

### FOR THE INSTRUCTOR

**Data File.** This is the Instructor's Manual. It will be of interest even to those who have never used an instructor's manual before. The *Data File* provides detailed chapter outlines and discussion questions and additional information on the statistical profile of Canada and other nations, summaries of important developments and significant research and supplemental lecture material for every chapter of the text. The *Data File* is available as a Word file (downloadable from the Faculty Resources section of the Web site) as well as the traditional print version (ISBN: 013-0612952).

**Test Item File.** A revised test item file is available in both printed and computerized forms. The file contains 1600 items—averaging 100 per chapter—in multiple-choice, true-false, and essay formats. Questions are identified as simple "recall" items or more complex inferential issues, and the answers to all questions are page-referenced to the text. Pearson Education's Test Manager software is a test generator designed to allow the creation of personalized exams. It is available in Windows (ISBN: 013-0934348) and Macintosh formats (ISBN: 013-093433X) as well as a print version (ISBN: 013-0612960).

**CBC/Pearson Education Canada Video Library for *Sociology*.** Few will dispute that video is the most dynamic supplement you can use to enhance a class. The authors and editors of Pearson Education Canada have carefully selected videos on topics that complement *Sociology, Fourth Canadian Edition*, and can be used with *Society: The Basics* as well. In the Instructor's Manual, we have included notes on how to use this video in the classroom. An excellent video guide carefully and completely integrates the videos into your lecture. The guide has a synopsis of each video showing its

relation to the chapter and discussion questions to help students focus on how concepts and theories apply to real-life situations.

**PowerPoint™ Transparencies.** Created by text author Mikael Jansson, this PowerPoint™ slide set combines graphics and text in a colourful format to help you convey sociological principles in a new and exciting way. Created in PowerPoint™, an easy-to-use, widely available software program, this set contains over 200 slides keyed to each chapter in the text. They are easily downloadable from the password-protected Faculty Resources section of the *Companion Website™*.

### MEDIA SUPPLEMENTS

**Companion Website™.** In tandem with the text, students and professors can now take full advantage of the Internet to enrich their study of sociology. The *Society: The Basics Companion Website™* continues to lead the way in providing students with avenues for delving deeper into the topics covered in the text. Features of the *Companion Website™* include chapter objectives, study questions, and faculty resources, as well as links to interesting material and information from other sites on the Web that will reinforce and enhance the content of each chapter. Visit the site at **http://www. pearsoned.ca/macionis**, click on the cover of the second Canadian edition, and enter the access code. An innovative new feature of the *Companion Website™* is a research database—ContentSelect—developed by Prentice Hall and EBSCO, the world leader in online journal subscription management. With instant access to more than 100 sociological journals and leading popular magazines and newspapers, students have a twenty-four-hour-a-day window into the leading content in sociology from their own home computer.

**Online Learning Solutions.** Pearson Education Canada is committed to helping instructors offer courses over the Internet by developing relationships with the leading vendors—Blackboard and Web CT as well as our own course management system, Course Compass, powered by Blackboard. Through these relationships, we provide premium, book-specific content in the delivery method of your choice. Please contact your local Pearson representative to find out more about our solutions in this area.

### FOR THE STUDENT

**Study Guide.** This complete guide helps students to review and reflect on the material presented in *Society: The Basics, Second Canadian Edition*. Each of the sixteen chapters in the study guide provides an overview of the corresponding chapter in the student text, summarizes its major topics and concepts, offers applied exercises, and features end-of-chapter tests with solutions.

## IN APPRECIATION

The conventional practice of designating authors obscures the efforts of dozens of women and men that have resulted in *Society: The Basics, Second Canadian Edition*. The Canadian authors appreciate the vast amount of work that went into the U.S. version of this text by John Macionis and by the people at Prentice Hall. We also would like to thank the following friends and colleagues for helping out in the myriad of tasks directly involved in the writing of this new edition: Beverely Maclean-Alley (Victoria); Fran Rose (University of Victoria); Alan Hedley (University of Victoria); Lori Sugden (University of Victoria); Bill McCarthy (University of California, Davis); and Zheng Wu (University of Victoria).

We would like to thank the staff at Pearson Education Canada who worked on this text with us: David Stover, Editor-in-Chief, Softside Editorial, who got us on course and set the tone for the project; Jessica Mosher, Social Sciences Acquisitions Eeditor; John Polanszky, Associate Editor, Social Sciences; Developmental Editor Dawn du Quesnay; Production Editor Sherry Torchinsky, and copyeditor Allyson Latta.

It goes without saying that every colleague knows more about some topics covered in this book than the authors do. For that reason, we are grateful to the hundreds of faculty and students who have written to offer comments and suggestions. More formally, we are grateful to the following people who have reviewed some or all of this manuscript:

Brian Webb (Marianopolis College)
Edward Thompson (Waterloo)
Seema Ahluwalia (Kwantlen University College)
Francis Adu-Febiri (Camosun College)
Laura Pao-Mercier (Vanier College)
Barry Edginton (University of Winnipeg)
Bernie Belanger (Loyalist College)

We dedicate this book to our daughter, Annika, who at just 8 years old has shown tremendous understanding of her parents' need to work long hours finishing yet another chapter. We are unable to express in words the love we feel for you, Annika. Thanks so much for asking the two most important sociological questions: WHAT? and WHY? We hope that you will always listen to our attempts at answering your questions.

—Mikael Jansson and Cecilia Benoit

# ABOUT THE AUTHORS

## JOHN J. MACIONIS

John J. Macionis (pronounced ma-SHOW-nis) was born and raised in Philadelphia, Pennsylvania. He received his bachelor's degrees from Cornell University and his doctorate in sociology from the University of Pennsylvania. His publications are wide-ranging, focusing on community life in the United States, interpersonal intimacy in families, effective teaching, humour, and the importance of global education. He is the author of *Sociology*, the leading introductory textbook in the field, and coauthor of *Cities and Urban Life*. He and Nijole V. Benokraitis have edited *Seeing Ourselves: Classic, Contemporary, and Cross-Cultural Readings in Sociology*.

John Macionis is professor of sociology at Kenyon College. During a career of almost twenty-five years at Kenyon, he has chaired the Sociology Department, directed the college's multidisciplinary program in humane studies, and presided over the campus senate and the college's faculty. In 1998, The North Central Sociological Association named Macionis recipient of the Award for Distinguished Contribution to Teaching, citing his work with textbooks and his pioneering use of new technology in sociology.

Professor Macionis welcomes (and responds to) comments and suggestions about this book from faculty and students. Write to the Department of Sociology, Palme House, Kenyon College, Gambier, Ohio 43022, or direct e-mail to MACIONIS@KENYON.EDU.

## MIKAEL JANSSON

Mikael Jansson is Adjunct Assistant Professor in the Department of Sociology at the University of Victoria (British Columbia) and Professional Associate at the Population Studies Centre at the University of Western Ontario (London, Ontario). Mikael spent the first 16 years of his life living in six different communities in central Sweden before moving with his family to Canada in 1975. After spending his three high-school years in Montreal, Oakville (Ontario), and Edmonton, he finished his post-secondary education in Edmonton and London, Ontario, studying migration. Since graduating he has combined parenting, teaching (Introductory Sociology, Demography, Methods and Statistics) and research. His current research uses a combination of qualitative and quantitative approaches to understand the situation of marginalized youth. Mikael is the principal investigator of a multi-year evaluation project conducted with funding from the Crime Prevention Investment Fund at the National Crime Prevention Centre, Department of Justice, Canada.

## CECILIA BENOIT

Cecilia Benoit is a Professor in the Department of Sociology at the University of Victoria (British Columbia) and Associate Director of the Office of International Affairs. She has taught Introductory Sociology for over a decade, and receives high evaluations from her students because of her friendly approach, up-to-date knowledge, and international and gendered perspectives. Cecilia has published journal articles and book chapters on mothering in Canada and select other countries, comparative health and welfare systems, and midwives' caring work in cross-national perspective. She is author of *Midwives in Passage* (1991) and *Women, Work and Social Rights* (2000), coauthor of *Society: The Basics, Canadian Edition* (1999), and coeditor of *Professional Identities in Transition* (1999), *Birth By Design* (2001) and *Reconceiving Midwifery* (in press). She has previously served on the executive of one of the five national Centres of Women's Health, NNEWH (located at York University), and is currently a co-partner. Her most recent research projects have focused on non-urban women's access to maternity care, the health concerns of Aboriginal women in Vancouver's Downtown Eastside, and the working conditions and health status of sex workers in Victoria. She is co-principal investigator (with Mikael Jansson) of "Risky Business: Experiences of Children and Youth in the Sex Trade," one of the six target projects funded under the CAHR program, *Healthy Youth in a Healthy Society*.

The Benoit-Jansson family (or should that be the Jansson-Benoit family?) live in a small house close to the University of Victoria. Together with their daughter, Annika, they enjoy the lakes and forests on Vancouver Island, spending their leisure time fly-fishing in the spring, swimming in the summer, and gathering wild mushrooms in the fall (these being the only three seasons in Victoria).

## The Pearson Education Canada

# companion Website...

**Your Internet companion to the most exciting, state-of-the-art educational tools on the Web!**

The Pearson Education Canada Companion Website is easy to navigate and is organized to correspond to the chapters in this textbook. The Companion Website comprises these distinct, functional features:

## Customized Online Resources

## Online Interactive Study Guide

## Communication

## Table of Contents

Explore these areas in this Companion Website. Students and distance learners will discover resources for indepth study, research, and communication, empowering them in their quest for greater knowledge and maximizing their potential for success in the course.

# A NEW WAY TO DELIVER EDUCATIONAL CONTENT

## Course Management

Our Companion Websites provide instructors and students with the ability to access, exchange, and interact with material specially created for our individual textbooks.

- **Syllabus Manager** provides instructors with the option of creating online classes and constructing an online syllabus linked to specific modules in the Companion Website.

- **Grader** allows the student to take a test that is automatically marked by the program. The results of the test can be e-mailed to the instructor and then added to the student's record.

- **Help** includes an evaluation of the user's system and a tune-up area that makes updating browsers and plug-ins easier. This new feature will facilitate the use of our Companion Websites.

## Instructor Resources

This section features modules with additional teaching material organized by chapter for instructors. Downloadable PowerPoint Presentations, Electronic Transparencies, and an Instructor's Manual are just some of the materials that may be available in this section. Where appropriate, this section will be password protected. To get a password, simply contact your Pearson Education Canada representative or call Faculty Sales and Services at 1-800-850-5813.

## General Resources

This section contains information that is related to the entire book and that will be of interest to all users of the site. A Table of Contents and a Glossary are just two examples of the kind of information you may find in this section.

The General Resources section may also feature *Communication facilities* that provide a key element for distributed learning environments:

- **Message Board** – This module takes advantage of browser technology to provide the  users of each Companion Website with a national newsgroup to post and reply to relevant course topics.

- **Chat Room** – This module enables instructors to lead group activities in real time. Using our chat client, instructors can display website content while students participate in the discussion.

# Visit www.pearsoned.ca/macionis
## for great student resources

Pearson
Education
Canada

## Want some practice before an exam?

The Student Resources section contains the modules that form the core of the student learning experience in the Companion Website. The modules presented in this section may include the following:

- Learning Objectives
- Multiple-Choice Questions
- True/False Questions
- Essay Questions
- Internet Exercises
- Destinations
- Net Search

The question modules provide students with the ability to send answers to our grader and receive instant feedback on their progress through our Results Reporter. Coaching comments and references to the textbook may be available to ensure that students take advantage of all available resources to enhance their learning experience.

**Student Resources**

Chapter Overview

Multiple Choice

Key Terms Quiz

True / False

Critical Evaluation

Sociology Applied

Destinations

Controversy + Debate

Key Words

**Instructor Resources**

Syllabus Manager

**General Resources**

Welcome

Table of Contents

Glossary

Message Board

Live Chat

Feedback

Site Search

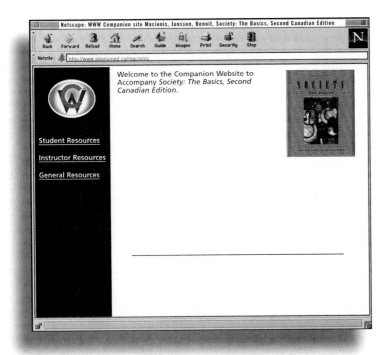

**Companion Websites are currently available for:**

- Macionis / Gerber: Sociology, Fourth Canadian Edition

**Note:** Companion Website content will vary slightly from site to site depending on discipline requirements.

The Companion Website for this text can be found at:
# www.pearsoned.ca/macionis

**PEARSON EDUCATION CANADA**

26 Prince Andrew Place
Toronto, Ontario M3C 2T8

**To order:**
Call: 1-800-567-3800
Fax: 1-800-263-7733

**For samples:**
Call: 1-800-850-5813
Fax: (416) 299-2539
E-mail:
phabinfo_pubcanada@pearsoned.com

# SOCIOLOGY:
# PERSPECTIVE, THEORY, AND METHOD

*O*n a warm spring day in 2000, two sets of friends and family gathered in the city of Victoria, B.C., to celebrate separate graduations. One ceremony was at a school you have probably heard of—the University of Victoria (UVic); the institution dates back to 1903 when Victoria College was founded in affiliation with McGill University and is today a comprehensive university that attracts many students from across Canada. The other ceremony was at a school you probably have not heard of—the GAP (Girls' Alternative Program), an all-girl high school.

 The two schools are close to each other in a physical sense, located just five or six blocks apart, northeast of downtown Victoria. But in a social sense, they are worlds apart.

 Sarah is a typical University of Victoria graduate: This bright, 20-year-old woman completed high school at the top of her class and was voted by her classmates as Most Likely to Succeed. At UVic, she continued to earn high grades, obtained a BA in Sociology, and then won a spot in a law school. After being called to the bar in 2001, she hopes to land a job at one of Canada's top law firms. Chances are, she will.

 Allison is typical of GAP graduates. Now 19, she dropped out of school during the seventh grade and lived for years on the streets, supporting herself within the street economy of panhandling, petty crime, and sex work. Three years ago, she got pregnant, and then through a public health nurse learned about GAP. Allison, now a mother of a happy and healthy baby, eventually completed her high school in the GAP program and later went on to a local college to earn her hair-styling certificate. ■

The sharp differences in Sarah's and Allison's stories catch our attention and lead us to wonder why people's lives can take such different courses. The answer is that our lives do not unfold according to sheer chance; nor do we decide for ourselves how to live, setting our biographies with what philosophers call "freewill." We do make many important decisions every day, of course, but we do so within a larger arena called "society"—a family, a school, a city, a nation, an entire world. The essential wisdom of sociology is that our social world guides our actions and life choices in much the same way that the seasons influence our clothing and activities.

## THE SOCIOLOGICAL PERSPECTIVE

**Sociology** is *the systematic study of human society.* At the heart of this discipline is a distinctive point of view called "the sociological perspective."

3

*We can easily grasp the power of society over the individual by imagining how different our lives would be had we been born in place of any of these children from, respectively, Bolivia, Sri Lanka, Ethiopia, Botswana, the People's Republic of China, and El Salvador.*

## SEEING THE GENERAL IN THE PARTICULAR

Peter Berger (1963) characterized the sociological perspective as *seeing the general in the particular*. That is, sociology helps us see *general* patterns in the behaviour of *particular* people. Although every individual is unique, society acts differently on various *categories* of people (say, children compared to adults, women versus men, the rich as opposed to the poor). We begin to think sociologically by realizing how the general categories into which we fall shape our particular life experiences.

This text explores the power of society to guide our actions, thoughts, and feelings. For instance, children differ from adults not just in biological maturity. The University of Victoria graduates mentioned in the chapter vignette, for example, come from more privileged social backgrounds than do the graduates of GAP. In general, the more privileged people's social background, the more confident and optimistic they

are about their own lives. And with good reason, as they are likely to have more opportunities, as well as the training and skills to take advantage of them.

## SEEING THE STRANGE IN THE FAMILIAR

At first, using the sociological perspective amounts to *seeing the strange in the familiar*. This does not mean that sociologists focus on the bizarre elements of society. Rather, looking at life sociologically requires giving up the familiar idea that human behaviour is simply a matter of what people *decide* to do, in favour of the initially strange notion that we are creatures of society.

For individualistic North Americans, learning to "see" how society affects us may take a bit of practice. Consider, for example, what seems to be the personal matter of deciding to change one's name, a practice common among celebrities. The Applying Sociology box on page 6 reveals a general pattern even in these particular choices.

*Whenever we come upon people whose habits differ from our own, we become more aware of social patterns. This is why travel is an excellent way to stimulate the sociological perspective. But even within Canada there is striking cultural diversity—some would even say "distinct societies"—that makes us conscious of our social surroundings.*

## SEEING INDIVIDUALITY IN SOCIAL CONTEXT

Perhaps the most compelling evidence of how social forces affect individual behaviour comes from the study of suicide. What choice could be more personal than that of taking one's own life? But Emile Durkheim (1858–1917), one of sociology's pioneers, showed that social forces are at work even in the act of self-destruction.

Examining official records in and around his native France, Durkheim found some categories of people were more likely than others to take their own lives. He found that men, Protestants, wealthy people, and the unmarried were groups that each had much higher suicide rates than did women, Catholics and Jews, the poor, and married people. Durkheim explained the differences in terms of *social integration*: categories of people with strong social ties had low suicide rates, whereas more individualistic people had high suicide rates.

In the male-dominated societies studied by Durkheim, men certainly had more freedom than women. But despite its advantages, freedom also contributes to social isolation and a higher suicide rate. Likewise, individualistic Protestants were more prone to suicide than traditional Catholics and Jews, whose rituals foster stronger social ties. The wealthy have more freedom than the poor but, once again, at the cost of a higher suicide rate. Finally, can you see why single people compared to married people are at greater risk?

A century later, Durkheim's analysis still holds true (Thorlindsson, Thorofleur & Bjarnason, 1998). Figure 1–1 on page 7 shows suicide rates for different categories of the Canadian population. In 1996, there were 13 recorded suicides for every 100 000 Canadians. Suicide is more common among males than among females across the life cycle. Men (20.8) are nearly four times more likely than women (5.6) to take their own lives. Further, among those in their early twenties, the rate for men (29.0) is six times that for women (5.0), and for those over 65 years, the male rate (25.6) is more than five times the female rate (4.5). Following Durkheim's logic, the higher suicide rate among men reflects their greater wealth, freedom, and lesser social integration. Variation in suicide rates also occurs across Canadian provinces and territories. Quebec (20), the Yukon (19.1), and the former Northwest Territories (34.4) are all outliers, recording suicide rates that are nearly three to five times the rate of Newfoundland (7). It is significant that Quebec and the Northwest Territories, with the lowest marriage rates in the country, have, along with the Yukon, experienced significant social change in recent times. They also have relatively mobile populations. Newfoundlanders, by contrast, are more likely to marry and move about much less than those in the other provinces (also see Chapter 15, p. 378, National Map 15–1, "Population, Urbanization, and Environment."

Some situations stimulate sociological insights for everyone. For example, social diversity prompts us to wonder why other people think and act differently than we do. But as we interact with people from social backgrounds that initially seem strange, we grasp the power of society to shape our lives and thus find ourselves easing into the role of sociologist.

By the same token, sociological thinking comes quickly to people whom our society tends to label as "different." Those who routinely experience *social marginality*—that is, being excluded as "outsiders"—quickly sense the power of society. People who self-identify as gays and lesbians, for example, are constantly reminded how sexuality shapes the way others view them. But

# What's in a Name?
## How Social Forces Affect Personal Choice

On July 4, 1918, twins were born to Abe and Becky Friedman in Sioux City, Iowa. They named the first to arrive Esther Pauline Friedman; her sister they called Pauline Esther Friedman. Today, these women are known to almost everyone in Canada, as well as south of the border, but by the new names they later adopted: Ann Landers and Abigail ("Dear Abby") Van Buren.

At first glance, a name change may seem to be simply a matter of personal preference. But take a closer look, from a sociological point of view, at the following list:

1. Thomas Mopother
2. Cherilyn Sarkisian
3. Cheryl Stoppelmoor
4. Robert Allen Zimmerman
5. John Mellencamp
6. Demetria Guynes
7. Paul Rubenfeld
8. George Kyriakou Panayiotou
9. Annie Mae Bullock
10. Patricia Andrejewski
11. Eldrick Woods
12. Jerome Silberman
13. Peggy Hyra
14. Karen Ziegler
15. Ramon Estevez
16. Henry John Deutschendorf, Jr.
17. Allen Stewart Konigsberg
18. Patsy McClenny
19. Jacob Cohen
20. David Kotkin
21. Lee Yuen Kam
22. Raquel Tejada
23. Nicholas Coppola
24. Sophia Scicoloni

Can you see the pattern in these changes? Historically, people of various national backgrounds have adopted *English-sounding* names. Why? Because our society has long accorded high social prestige to people of Anglo-Saxon background. In short, we see personal choices guided by social forces.

---

ANSWERS:
1. Tom Cruise, 2. Cher, 3. Cheryl Ladd, 4. Bob Dylan, 5. Johnny Cougar (early 1970s), John Cougar (1970s to 1980s), John Cougar Mellencamp (mid-1980s). 6. Demi Moore, 7. Pee Wee Herman, 8. George Michael, 9. Tina Turner, 10. Pat Benatar, 11. Tiger Woods, 12. Gene Wilder, 13. Meg Ryan, 14. Karen Black, 15. Martin Sheen, 16. John Denver, 17. Woody Allen, 18. Morgan Fairchild, 19. Rodney Dangerfield, 20. David Copperfield, 21. Bruce Lee, 22. Raquel Welch, 23. Nicolas Cage, 24. Sophia Loren.

---

because heterosexuals are the dominant majority in our society, they seldom are challenged to defend their particular sexual orientation. Finally, U.S. sociologist C. Wright Mills (1959) pointed out that periods of social crisis also spark sociological thinking. When, for example, the Great Depression of the 1930s threw one-third of the labour force out of work, unemployed workers could not help but see general social forces operating in their lives. Rather than claiming, "Something is wrong with me; I can't find a job," they were likely to say, "We're all out of work because the economy has collapsed!" Of course, just as change stimulates sociological thinking, so sociological thinking suggests possibilities for change. The 1930s was also a period of activism aimed at increasing the social security of the Canadian population.

## BENEFITS OF THE SOCIOLOGICAL PERSPECTIVE

Applying the sociological perspective to our daily lives benefits us in four ways:

1. **The sociological perspective helps us critically assess the truth of "common sense."** Ideas we take for granted are not always true. One good example, noted earlier, is the notion that we are free individuals personally responsible for our lives. If we think people decide their own fate, we may be quick to praise successful people as superior and consider people with more modest achievements personally deficient. A sociological approach, by contrast, encourages us to ask whether these beliefs are actually true and, to the extent that they are not, why they are so widely held.

2. **The sociological perspective helps us to see the opportunities and constraints in our lives.** Sociological thinking leads us to see that in the game of life, we have a say in how to play our cards, but it is society that deals us the hand. The more we understand the game, the better players we will be. Sociology helps us "size up" the world around us so we can pursue our goals more effectively.

3. **The sociological perspective empowers us to be active participants in our society.** The more we understand about how society operates, the more active citizens we become. For some, this may mean supporting society as it is; others, however, may attempt nothing less than changing

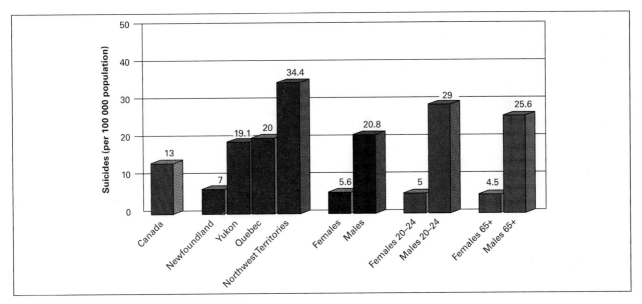

**FIGURE 1–1  Suicide Rates in Canada, Selected Categories, 1996**

Source: Federal, Provincial, and Territorial Advisory Committee on Population Health (1999).

the entire world in some way. Evaluating any aspect of social life—whatever your goal—requires you to identify social forces and assess their consequences.

4. **The sociological perspective helps us live in a diverse world.** Canadians represent a scant 0.5 percent of the world's population, and, as the remaining chapters of this book explain, much of the other 99.5 percent leads dramatically different lives from our own. Still, like people everywhere, we tend to view our way of life as "right," "natural," and "better." The sociological perspective prompts us to think critically about the strengths and weaknesses of all ways of life—including our own.

## APPLIED SOCIOLOGY

The benefits of sociology go well beyond our personal growth. Sociologists have helped shape public policy and law in countless ways, involving school desegregation and bussing, pornography, and social welfare. The work that Canadian researcher Robin Bagley (1984) did on sexual offences against children and youth had a real impact on public policy, leading among other things to the Canadian legislature's enactment in 1988 of section 212 of the *Criminal Code*, which prohibits attempts to purchase sex from persons under 18 years (Lowman, 1987).

Sociology is also good preparation for the working world. According to Statistics Canada, the Canadian Sociology and Anthropology Association, and the Canadian Association of University Teachers, sociology is sound training for jobs in fields as diverse as advertising, banking, criminal justice, education, government, health care, public relations, and research. Similar findings have also been reported elsewhere (Billson & Huber, 1993).

Most men and women who continue beyond a bachelor's degree to earn advanced training in sociology go on to careers in teaching and research. But an increasing number of professional sociologists work in all sorts of applied fields. Clinical sociologists, for example, work with troubled clients much the way clinical psychologists do. There is a basic difference, however: while psychologists focus on the individual, sociologists locate difficulties in a person's web of social relationships. Another type of applied sociology is evaluation research. In today's cost-conscious political climate, administrators must evaluate the effectiveness of virtually every program and policy. Sociologists—especially those with advanced research skills—are in high demand for this kind of work.

## THE IMPORTANCE OF A GLOBAL PERSPECTIVE

December 10, 1994—Fez, Morocco This medieval city—a web of narrow streets and alleyways, alive with the sounds of children at play, the silence of veiled women, and the steady gaze of men leading donkeys laden with goods—has changed little over the centuries. We

*One important reason to gain a global understanding is that, living in a high-income country, we can scarcely appreciate the suffering that goes on in much of the world. These flood victims in Mozambique are waiting for food. Indeed, throughout Africa, children have only a fifty-fifty chance to grow to adulthood.*

```
stand in northwest Africa in a strange
place that seems lost in time. Never
have we had such an adventure! Never
have we thought so much about home!
```

As new communications technology draws even the farthest reaches of the earth closer to each other, many academic disciplines take a **global perspective,** *the study of the larger world and our society's place in it.* What is the importance of a global perspective for sociology?

First, global awareness is a logical extension of the sociological perspective. Sociology shows us that our place in a society profoundly affects our life experiences. It stands to reason, then, that the position of this society in the larger world system affects everyone in Canada.

Global Map 1–1 shows the relative economic development of the world's countries. **High-income countries** are *industrialized nations in which most people enjoy relatively high incomes.*[1] High-income countries include Canada and the United States, the nations of Western Europe, Israel, Japan, New Zealand, and Australia. Taken together, these 50 nations generate most of the world's goods and services and control most of the planet's wealth. On average, individuals in these countries live well, not because they are smarter than anyone else, but because they had the good fortune to be born in an affluent region of the world.

The world's **middle-income countries** are *nations with limited industrialization in which most people have*

*moderate personal income.* Individuals living in any of roughly 90 nations—the countries of Eastern Europe, some of southern Africa, and almost all of Latin America—are as likely to live in villages as in cities, to walk or ride animals, bicycles, scooters, or tractors as they are to drive cars, and are likely to receive only a few years of schooling. Middle-income countries also have pronounced social inequality; while some people are extremely rich (the sheiks of oil-producing nations in the Middle East, for example), many more lack even safe housing and adequate nutrition.

Finally, almost half the world's people live in more than 60 **low-income countries**, *nations with little industrialization in which most people are poor.* As Global Map 1–1 shows, most of the poorest societies in the world are in Africa and Asia. Here again, a small number of people are rich, but the majority struggle to get by with unclean water, too little food, little or no sanitation, and, perhaps most serious of all, little chance to improve their lives.

Chapter 9 (Global Stratification) discusses the causes and consequences of global wealth and poverty. But every chapter highlights life in the world beyond our own borders for three reasons:

1.  **Societies the world over are increasingly interconnected.** People in Canada have long been more or less indifferent to the world around us. In recent decades, however, Canada and the rest of the world are becoming linked as never before. Electronic technology now transmits pictures, sounds, and written documents around the globe in seconds.

    One consequence of new technology, as later chapters will explain, is that people all over the world now share many tastes in music, clothing, and food. With their economic clout, high-income countries such as Canada influence other nations, whose people eagerly gobble up our hamburgers, dance to our music, and, more and more, speak the English language and use it in Internet communication.

    We are spreading our way of life around the world; but the larger world, too, has an impact on us. About 200 000 immigrants enter Canada each year, and we are quick to adopt many of their favourite sounds, tastes, and customs as our own, something that greatly enhances the cultural diversity of this country.

    Commerce across national borders has also created a global economy. Corporations make and market goods worldwide, just as global financial

---

[1]This text uses this terminology rather than the traditional but outdated terms "First World," "Second World," and "Third World." Chapter 9 (Global Stratification) provides a complete discussion of the issue.

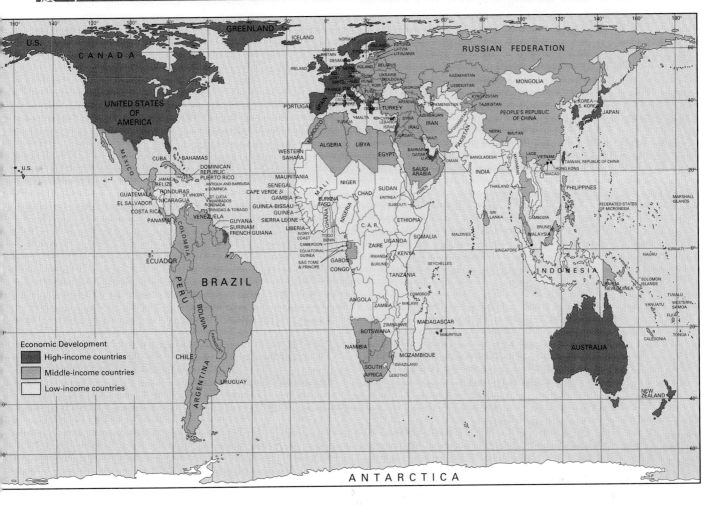

**GLOBAL MAP 1–1  Economic Development in Global Perspective***

In high-income countries—Canada, the United States, most of Western Europe, Israel, Australia, New Zealand, and Japan—industrial technology provides people with material plenty. Middle-income countries—found throughout Latin America and Eastern Europe—have limited industrial capacity and a standard of living that, while about average for the world as a whole, is far below that of most people in high-income countries. These nations have a significant share of poor people who barely scrape by with meager housing and diet. In the low-income countries of the world, poverty is severe and extensive. Although small numbers of elites live very well in these poorest nations, most people struggle to survive on a small fraction of the income common in Canada.

***Note**: High-income countries have per capita gross national product (GNP) of at least US$14 500. Many are far richer than this, however; the figure for Canada is US$23 725. Middle-income countries have a per capita GNP ranging from US$2500 to US$14 500. Low-income countries have a per capita GNP below US$2500. Figures used here reflect the United Nations "purchasing power parities" system. Rather than directly converting income figures into U.S. dollars, this calculation estimates the local purchasing power of each domestic currency.

Source: Prepared by the authors using data from The World Bank (2000).

centres linked by satellite now operate around the clock. Stock traders in Toronto follow the financial markets in Tokyo and Hong Kong, just as wheat farmers in Saskatchewan watch the price of grain in the former Soviet republic of Georgia.

2. **Many social problems that we face in Canada are far more serious elsewhere.** Poverty is a serious problem in this country, but, as Chapter 9 (Global Stratification) explains, poverty in Latin America, Africa, and Asia is both more widespread

and more severe. Similarly, although women have lower social standing than men do in Canada, inequality is generally much greater in the world's low-income countries.

3. **Thinking globally is a good way to learn more about ourselves.** We cannot walk the streets of a distant city without becoming keenly aware of what it means to live in Canada. Making these comparisons often leads to unexpected lessons. For instance, in Chapter 9 (Global Stratification), we visit a squatter settlement in Madras, India. There, despite a desperate lack of basic material goods, people thrive with the love and support of family members. Why, then, does poverty in Canada lead to isolation and anger? Are material goods—so crucial to our definition of a "rich" life—the best way to gauge human well-being?

In sum, in an increasingly interconnected world, we can understand ourselves only to the extent that we comprehend others (Macionis, 1993).

## THE ORIGINS OF SOCIOLOGY

Like the "choices" made by individuals, major historical events rarely just happen. So it was that the birth of sociology resulted from powerful and complex social forces.

Although humans have mused about society since the beginning of our history, sociology is among the youngest academic disciplines—far newer than history, physics, or economics. Only in 1838 did the French social thinker Auguste Comte (1798–1857) coin the term *sociology* to describe a new way of looking at the world.

### SCIENCE AND SOCIOLOGY

The nature of society fascinated the brilliant minds of the ancient world, including the Chinese philosopher K'ung Fu-tzu, or Confucius (551–479 B.C.E.), the Greek philosophers Plato (427–347 B.C.E.) and Aristotle (384–322 B.C.E.).[2] Later, the Roman emperor Marcus Aurelius (121–180), the medieval thinkers St. Thomas Aquinas (c. 1225–1274) and Christine de Pizan (c. 1363–1431), and the great English playwright William Shakespeare (1564–1616) took up the question.

---

[2] Throughout this text, the abbreviation B.C.E. designates "before the common era." This terminology is used in place of the traditional B.C. ("before Christ") in recognition of the religious pluralism of our society. Similarly, in place of the traditional A.D. (anno Domini, or "in the year of our Lord"), the abbreviation C.E. ("common era") is employed.

Yet these men and women were more interested in envisioning the ideal society than they were in analyzing society as it really was. In creating their new discipline, sociology's pioneers, including Auguste Comte and Emile Durkheim, certainly cared how society could be improved, but their major goal was to understand how society actually operates. Comte (1975; orig. 1851–1854) saw sociology as the product of a three-stage historical development. During the earliest *theological stage*, up to the end of the European Middle Ages, people took a religious view that society expressed God's will. With the Renaissance, this theological approach gradually gave way to a *metaphysical stage* in which people saw society as a natural rather than a supernatural phenomenon. The English philosopher Thomas Hobbes (1588–1679), for example, suggested that society reflected not the perfection of God so much as the failings of a selfish human nature.

What Comte called the *scientific stage* began with the work of early scientists such as the Polish astronomer Nicolaus Copernicus (1473–1543), the Italian astronomer and physicist Galileo (1564–1642), and the English physicist and mathematician Isaac Newton (1642–1727). Comte's contribution came in applying the scientific approach—first used to analyze the physical world—to the study of society.

Comte thus favoured **positivism**, *a way of understanding based on science*. As a positivist, Comte believed that society operates according to certain laws, just as the physical world operates according to laws of nature, such as gravity.

At the beginning of the 20th century, sociology took hold as an academic discipline in the United States (two decades earlier than in Canada), strongly influenced by Comte's ideas. And today, most sociologists still consider science a crucial element of sociology. But we now realize that human behaviour is far more complex than the movement of planets or the actions of other living things. We are creatures of imagination and spontaneity, so human behaviour can never be explained solely by the rigid "laws of society."

### SOCIAL CHANGE AND SOCIOLOGY

Striking transformations in 18th- and 19th-century Europe caused the social ground to tremble under people's feet. Understandably, they focussed their attention on society, leading to the rise of the new science of sociology.

**Industrial technology.** First came new scientific discoveries and technological advances—especially the harnessing of steam to power large machines—that produced a factory-based, industrial economy. Even at the beginning of the 18th century, most people in Europe still tilled fields near their village. Only a small number were engaged in home-based *manufacturing* (derived from Latin meaning "to make by hand") or what sociologists refer to as *cottage industries* (because the work was typically done in people's cottages). But by the middle of the 18th century, instead of labouring at home or in tightly knit groups, workers became part of a large, urban, and anonymous industrial labour force, toiling for strangers who owned the factories. This change in the system of production set off a rapid breakdown of traditions and social bonds that had guided small communities for centuries.

**The growth of cities.** Across Europe, factories drew people in need of work. Along with this "pull" came the "push" of what is known as the "enclosure movement." Landowners fenced off more and more land, turning farms into grazing land for sheep—the source of wool for the thriving textile mills. Without land, countless tenant farmers left the countryside in search of work in the new factories.

Cities grew to unprecedented size, and streets churned with strangers. Widespread social problems accompanied the new urbanization—including pollution, crime, and homelessness.

**Political change.** Economic development and the growth of cities brought new ways of thinking. In the writings of Thomas Hobbes (1588–1679), John Locke (1632–1704), and Adam Smith (1723–1790), we find less concern with people's moral obligations to God and political rulers and more focus on pursuing self-interest. Indeed, the key phrases in the new political climate were *individual liberty* and *individual rights*. Echoing the thoughts of Locke, our own Charter of Rights and Freedoms clearly spells out that each citizen has certain "fundamental freedoms," including "religion, belief, opinion, expression, peaceful assembly and association."

The political revolution in France that began in 1789 symbolized the Western world's break with political and social traditions. As the French social analyst Alexis de Tocqueville (1805–1859) declared after the French Revolution, the change in society amounted to "nothing short of the regeneration of the whole human race" (1955:13; orig. 1856). As the new industrial economy, enormous cities, and fresh political ideas combined to draw attention to society, sociology flowered in precisely those countries—France, Germany, and England—where changes were greatest.

Sociologists reacted differently to the new social order then, just as they respond differently to society today. Some, including Auguste Comte, feared that rapid change would overpower tradition and uproot long-established communities. Comte took a conservative turn, trying to shore up the family and traditional morality. Quite different were the ideas of German social critic Karl Marx (1818–1883), who

*Here we see Copernicus, the 16th-century astronomer, taking careful measurements of the world. Just as Copernicus challenged the common sense of his day, sociologists such as Auguste Comte later argued that society is neither fixed by God's will nor set by human nature. On the contrary, Comte claimed, society is a system we can study scientifically, and, based on what we learn, we can act intentionally to improve our lives.*

detested traditional society. But Marx also hated the way the new society concentrated its new wealth in the hands of a small elite, while the masses faced only hunger and misery. Thus Marx called for further change—albeit in a different direction.

Despite the differences between Comte and Marx, both believed that society rests on more than individual choice. The sociological perspective animates the work of each, revealing that people's lives reflect the broader society in which they live. This lesson, of course, remains as true today as it was a century ago.

## MARGINAL VOICES

Auguste Comte and Karl Marx stand among the giants of sociology. But in recent years, we have come to see the important contributions that others—pushed to the margins because of sex or race—have made.

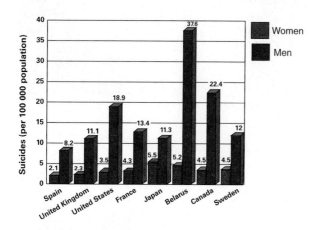

**FIGURE 1–2    Suicide Rates for Young\* Men and Women in Selected Countries, 1996–1998**

Canada's suicide rate is high compared with that of some other nations. Do these data support or contradict Durkheim's theory of suicide?

\*15 to 24 years old.

Source: World Health Organization [Online] May 29, 2001.

Harriet Martineau (1802–1876), born to a wealthy English family, first made her mark in 1853 by translating the writings of August Comte from French into English. Subsequently, she became a noted scholar in her own right, revealing the evils of slavery and arguing for laws to protect factory workers and to advance the standing of women.

In Canada, Nellie McClung (1873–1951) was a sociological pioneer who started school at 10 years of age and received a teaching certificate six years later. McClung was a supporter of suffrage for women, and a well-known advocate for the prohibition, factory laws for women, formal compulsory education, reform for Canadian prisons, and equal representation for women in the political realm. While an elected Liberal MLA in Alberta, she became a member of the Famous Five who, in 1927, petitioned the government of Canada to include women in the definition of "person" under the *British North America Act*. Their success in 1929 meant that women could subsequently be appointed to the Senate.

Another neglected pioneer, William Edward Burghardt Du Bois (1868–1963), made an important contribution to understanding race in the United States. Born to a poor Massachusetts family, Du Bois enrolled in Fisk University in Nashville, Tennessee, and then at Harvard University, where he eventually earned the first doctorate ever awarded by that university to a person

of colour. Like Martineau and McClung, Du Bois believed sociologists should try to solve contemporary problems. He therefore studied the black community (1899), spoke out against racial inequality, and served as a founding member of the National Association for the Advancement of Colored People (NAACP).

Widespread belief in the inferiority of women and African Americans in Canada and the United States kept Martineau, McClung, and Du Bois at the margins of sociology. Looking back with a sociological eye, we can see how the forces of society were at work in shaping even the history of sociology itself.

# SOCIOLOGICAL THEORY

Combining observations and abstract understanding brings us to another aspect of sociology: theory. A **theory** is *a statement of how and why specific facts are related*. To illustrate, recall Emile Durkheim's theory that categories of people with low social integration (men, Protestants, the wealthy, and the unmarried) are prone to suicide.

Like all scientists, sociologists conduct research to test and refine their theories. Figure 1–2, which displays the suicide rates for young men and women in selected countries, gives you a chance to do some theorizing of your own.

In building theory, sociologists face two basic questions. What issues should we study? How should we connect the facts? In answering these questions, sociologists look to one or more theoretical "roadmaps" or paradigms (Kuhn, 1970). A **theoretical paradigm** is *a basic image of society that guides thinking and research*. Three major paradigms in sociology are the structural-functional paradigm, the social-conflict paradigm, and the symbolic-interaction paradigm.

## THE STRUCTURAL-FUNCTIONAL PARADIGM

The **structural-functional paradigm** is based on *a theoretical framework that sees society as a complex system whose parts work together to promote solidarity and stability*. As its name suggests, this paradigm points to **social structure**, meaning *relatively stable patterns of social behaviour*. Social structure gives our lives shape in families, in the workplace, or in the college or university classroom. Second, this paradigm looks for any structure's **social functions**, or *consequences of the social pattern for the operation of society as a whole*. All social patterns—from a simple handshake to a complex religious ritual—function to reproduce society.

The structural-functional paradigm owes much to Auguste Comte, who pointed out the need for social integration during a time of rapid change. Emile Durkheim, who helped establish sociology in French

*People whose gender or race put them at the margins of their society also contributed to the development of society. Harriet Martineau (left), Nellie McClung (centre), and W.E.B. Du Bois (right) have only recently been recognized as important founders of the discipline.*

universities, also based his work on this approach. A third structural-functional pioneer was the English sociologist Herbert Spencer (1820–1903). Spencer compared society to the human body. Just as the structural parts of the human body—the skeleton, muscles, and various internal organs—function together to help the entire organism survive, social structures work together to preserve society. The structural-functional paradigm, then, leads sociologists to identify various structures of society and investigate their functions.

Contemporary U.S. sociologist Robert K. Merton expanded our understanding of social function by pointing out that any social structure probably has many functions, some more obvious than others. He called **manifest functions** the *consequences both recognized and intended by people in the society.* **Latent functions,** by contrast, are *consequences that are unintended and go largely unrecognized.* To illustrate, the obvious function of this country's system of higher education is to provide young people with the information and skills they need to perform jobs. Perhaps just as important, although less often acknowledged, is the college or university's function as a "marriage broker," bringing together young people of similar social backgrounds. Another latent function of higher education is keeping millions of people out of the labour market where, presumably, many of them would not find jobs.

But Merton also recognized that the effects of social structure are neither all good, nor, certainly, good for everybody. Thus, **social dysfunctions** are *any social pattern's undesirable consequences for the operation of society.* People usually disagree on what is beneficial and what is harmful. Moreover, what is functional for one category of people (say, factory owners or landlords) may well be dysfunctional for another category of people (say, factory workers or tenants).

**Critical evaluation.** The chief characteristic of the structural-functional paradigm is its vision of society as stable and orderly. The main goal of sociologists who use this paradigm, then, is to figure out what makes society "tick."

In the mid-1900s, most sociologists favoured the structural-functional paradigm. In recent decades, however, its influence has declined. By focussing attention on social stability and unity, critics point out, structural-functionalism ignores inequalities of social class, race, ethnicity, and gender, which can generate considerable tension and conflict. In general, focussing on stability at the expense of conflict makes this paradigm somewhat conservative. As a critical response to this approach, sociologists developed another theoretical orientation: the social-conflict paradigm.

## THE SOCIAL-CONFLICT PARADIGM

The **social-conflict paradigm** is *a framework for building theory that sees society as an arena of inequality that generates conflict and change.* Unlike the structural-functional emphasis on solidarity, this approach highlights inequality. Guided by this paradigm, sociologists investigate how factors such as race, ethnicity, gender, and age are linked to the unequal distribution of money, power, education, and social prestige. A conflict analysis rejects the idea that social structure promotes the operation of society as a whole, focussing instead on how any social pattern benefits some people while depriving others.

*The painting* Furnishings, *by Paul Marcus, presents the essential wisdom of social conflict theory. Society operates in a way that conveys wealth, power, and privilege to some at the expense of others. Take a look at the painting. What are most of the people doing? What do you make of the head hanging on the wall? The classical scene between the drapes? What categories of people does the artist suggest are disadvantaged?*

Source: ©Paul Marcus, *Furnishings*, oil painting on canvas, 64 in × 48 in. Studio SPM, Inc.

Sociologists using the social-conflict paradigm look at ongoing conflict between dominant and disadvantaged categories of people—the rich in relation to the poor, Anglo-Saxon in relation to Aboriginal, or men in relation to women. Typically, people on top strive to protect their privileges, while the disadvantaged try to gain more for themselves.

A conflict analysis of our educational system would explain how schooling perpetuates inequality by reproducing the class structure in every new generation. That is, secondary schools channel new students into either academic preparatory or vocational training programs. From a structural-functional point of view, such "tracking" benefits everyone by providing schooling that fits students' abilities. But conflict analysis counters that tracking often has less to do with talent than with social background, so that well-to-do students are placed in higher tracks while poor children end up in lower tracks. In this way, young people from privileged families get the best schooling, which serves as a springboard for high-income careers later on. The children of poor families, on the other hand, are not prepared for college or university, and, like their parents before them, typically enter low-paying jobs. In both cases, the social standing of one generation is passed on to another, with schools justifying the practice by linking it to individual merit (Bowles & Gintis, 1976; Oakes, 1982, 1985).

Many sociologists who use the social-conflict paradigm try not only to understand society, but to reduce inequality. This was the goal of Nellie McClung, who was guided by the social-conflict paradigm to raise the standing of women through her writing and political activity (Prentice et al., 1996:226). Likewise, Karl Marx championed the workers against those who owned the factories. In a well-known declaration (inscribed on his monument in London's Highgate Cemetery), Marx declared, "The philosophers have only interpreted the world, in various ways; the point, however, is to change it."

**Critical evaluation.** The social-conflict paradigm has gained a large following in recent decades, but, like other approaches, it has come in for its share of criticism. Because the paradigm focusses on inequality, it largely ignores how shared values and interdependence can unify members of a society. In addition, say critics, to the extent that this paradigm pursues political goals, it cannot claim scientific objectivity. This prompts supporters to counter that *all* social approaches have political consequences, albeit different ones.

A final criticism of the structural-functional and social-conflict paradigms is that they paint society in broad strokes—in terms of "family," "social class," "race," and so on. A third theoretical paradigm views society less in terms of generalizations and more in terms of everyday experiences.

## THE SYMBOLIC-INTERACTION PARADIGM

The structural-functional and social-conflict paradigms share a **macro-level orientation,** meaning *a concern with broad patterns that shape society as a whole.* Macro-level sociology takes in the big picture, rather like observing the city from a helicopter and seeing how highways help people move from place to place or how housing differs in rich and poor neighbourhoods. Sociology also has a **micro-level orientation,** *a focus on small-scale patterns of social interaction in specific settings.* Exploring urban life in this way occurs at street level, perhaps watching how children invent games on a school playground or how pedestrians respond to homeless people. The **symbolic-interaction paradigm,** then, is *a framework for building theory that sees society as the product of the everyday interactions of individuals.*

How does "society" result from the ongoing experiences of tens of millions of people? One answer,

## TABLE 1-1 The Three Major Theoretical Paradigms: A Summary

| Theoretical Paradigm | Orientation | Image of Society | Core Questions |
|---|---|---|---|
| Structural-functional | Macro-level | A system of interrelated parts that is relatively stable based on widespread consensus as to what is morally desirable; each part has functional consequences for the operation of society as a whole | How is society integrated? What are the major parts of society? How are these parts interrelated? What are the consequences of each one for the overall operation of society? |
| Social-conflict | Macro-level | A system characterized by social inequality; each part of society benefits some categories of people more than others; conflict-based social inequality promotes social change | How is society divided? What are the major patterns of social inequality? How do some categories of people attempt to protect their privileges? How do other categories of people challenge the status quo? |
| Symbolic-interaction | Micro-level | An ongoing process of social interaction in specific settings based on symbolic communications; individual perceptions of reality are variable and changing | How is society experienced? How do human beings interact to create, sustain, and change social patterns? How do individuals attempt to shape the reality perceived by others? How does individual behaviour change from one situation to another? |

detailed in Chapter 4 (Social Interaction in Everyday Life), is that society is nothing more than the reality people construct as they interact. That is, human beings are creatures who live in a world of symbols, attaching *meaning* to virtually everything. "Reality," therefore, is simply how we define our surroundings, our obligations toward others, even our own identities.

The symbolic-interaction paradigm has roots in the thinking of Max Weber (1864–1920), a German sociologist who emphasized understanding a setting from the point of view of people in that setting. Since Weber's time, sociologists have taken micro-sociology in a number of directions. Chapter 3 (Socialization: From Infancy to Old Age) discusses the ideas of George Herbert Mead (1863–1931), who explored how we create our personalities from social experience. Chapter 4 (Social Interaction in Everyday Life) presents the work of Erving Goffman (1922–1982), whose *dramaturgical analysis* describes how we resemble actors on a stage as we play out our various roles. Other contemporary sociologists, including George Homans and Peter Blau, have developed *social-exchange analysis*, the idea that interaction is guided by what each person stands to gain and lose from others (Molm, 1997; Mulford et al., 1998). In the ritual of courtship, for example, people seek mates who offer them at least as much—in terms of physical attractiveness, intelligence, and social background—as they give to the mate.

**Critical evaluation.** Without denying the existence of macro-level social structures such as "the family" and "social class," the symbolic-interaction paradigm reminds us that society basically amounts to *people interacting*. That is, micro-level sociology tries to convey how individuals actually experience society. But the flip side of the coin is that by emphasizing what is unique in each social scene, this approach risks overlooking the widespread effects of culture, as well as factors such as class, gender, and race.

Table 1–1 summarizes the distinctive features of the structural-functional paradigm, the social-conflict paradigm, and the symbolic-interaction paradigm. As you read the chapters in this book, keep in mind that each paradigm is helpful in answering particular kinds of questions. As the Critical Thinking box about sports on page 16 shows, the fullest understanding of society comes from using the sociological perspective with all three.

## SCIENTIFIC SOCIOLOGY

To test theories, sociologists conduct research. To investigate how and why we behave as we do, they rely on **science**, *a logical system that bases knowledge on direct, systematic observation*. Scientific knowledge is based on *empirical evidence*, meaning facts we verify with our senses.

Sociological research often challenges what we accept as "common sense." Here are three examples of widely held attitudes that are contradicted by scientific evidence:

1. **Differences in the social behaviour of women and men reflect "human nature."** Much of what we call "human nature" is constructed by the society in which we live. We know this because researchers have documented how definitions of *feminine* and *masculine* change over time and vary

# CRITICAL THINKING

## Sports: Playing the Theory Game

Who among us doesn't enjoy sports? Soccer moms and dads drive eager eight-year-olds to games, and teens play pickup basketball after school. Weekend television is filled with sporting events, and whole sections of our newspapers report the scores. What can we learn by applying sociology's three theoretical paradigms to this familiar element of life in Canada?

A structural-functional approach asks what sports do for our society as a whole. The manifest functions include recreation, physical conditioning, and a relatively harmless way to "let off steam." Sports have important latent functions as well, from fostering social relationships to creating countless jobs. Perhaps most important, though, sports encourage competition, which is central to this nation's way of life.

Sports also have dysfunctional consequences, of course. For example, universities intent on fielding winning teams sometimes recruit students for their athletic ability rather than their academic aptitude. This practice not only pulls down a school's academic standards, but also short-changes athletes who devote little time to academic work.

A social-conflict analysis might begin by pointing out how sports are linked to social inequality. Some sports—tennis, swimming, golf, and skiing—are expensive, so participation is largely limited to the well-to-do. Football, baseball, and basketball, however, are accessible to

people of all income levels. Thus, the games people play are not simply a matter of choice but also a reflection of people's social standing.

Moreover, men dominate sports. The first modern Olympic Games held in 1896, for example, excluded women from competition. In Canada, through most of the 20th century, even Little League teams barred girls from the playing field based on unfounded notions that girls lack the strength or the stamina to play sports or that they risk losing their femininity if they do. Both the Olympics and Little League are now open to females as well as males. But in the world of sports, women still take a back seat to men, particularly in sports that yield the greatest earnings and social prestige.

Although North American society long excluded blacks from professional sports, opportunities have expanded in recent decades. In 1947, Jackie Robinson broke through the "colour line" to become the first black player in major league baseball. In 1958, Canadian-born Willie O'Ree made headlines as the first black hockey player to be recruited into the National Hockey League. By 1997, African Americans (who make up 12 percent of the U.S. population) accounted for 15 percent of baseball players, 65 percent of National Football League (NFL) players, and 77 percent of National Basketball Association (NBA) players (Centre for the Study of Sport in Society, 2000).

One reason for the increasing share of blacks in professional sports is the fact that athletic performance—in terms of batting average or number of points scored per game—is objectively measured, regardless of any white prejudice. It is also true that some black people make a special effort to excel in athletics because they perceive more opportunity there than in other careers (Steele, 1990; Hoberman, 1997, 1998). In recent years, in fact, black athletes have earned higher salaries, on average, than white players.

But racial discrimination still taints professional sports in Canada and the United States. For one thing, race is linked to the *positions* athletes play on the field, a pattern called *stacking*. Figure 1–3 shows the results of a study of race in football. Notice that white players dominate in offence and also play the central positions on both sides of the line. More broadly, black athletes figure prominently in only five sports: basketball, football, baseball, boxing, and track. Across all professional sports, the vast majority of managers, head coaches, and team owners are still white (Gnida, 1995; Smith & Leonard, 1997).

Overall, who benefits most from professional sports? Although individual players may get sky-high salaries, and millions of fans love following their teams, the vast sums sports generate are controlled by a small number of people (predominantly white men). In other words, sports in Canada, as in the

from one society to another (see Chapter 10, Gender Stratification).

2. **Canada is a middle-class society in which most people are more or less equal.** As Chapter 8 (Social Stratification) explains, the richest 10 percent of our population controls more than half of the country's wealth, while almost 40 percent of the population has scarcely any wealth at all. If people are equal, then some are much "more equal" than others.

3. **People marry because they are in love.** Surprising as it may seem, research indicates that marriages in most societies have little to do with love. Chapter 13 (Family and Religion) explains why.

These examples confirm the old saying that "It's not what we don't know that gets us into trouble as much as things we *do* know that just aren't so."

United States, are bound up with inequalities based on gender, race, and wealth.

At a micro-level, a sporting event is a complex face-to-face interaction. In part, play is guided by assigned positions and, of course, by the rules of the game. But players are also spontaneous and unpredictable. The symbolic-interaction paradigm, then, sees sports less as a system than as an ongoing process. Furthermore, we expect each player to understand the game a little differently. Some thrive in a setting of stiff competition, while for others, love[3] of the game may be stronger than the need to win.

Team members also shape their particular realities according to the prejudices, jealousies, and ambitions they bring to the field. Moreover, the behaviour of any single player changes over time. A rookie in professional baseball, for example, typically feels self-conscious during the first few games in the big leagues but goes on to develop a level of comfort and sense of "fitting in" with the team. Coming to feel at home on the field was especially difficult for Jackie Robinson in 1947. At first, he

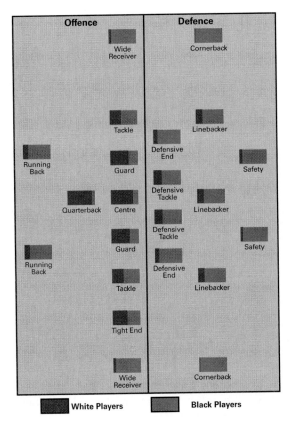

**FIGURE 1–3 Race and Sport: "Stacking" in Professional Football**

Source: Center for the Study of Sport in Society (2000).

was painfully aware that many white players and millions of white fans resented his presence. In time, however, his outstanding ability and his confident and cooperative manner won him the respect of the entire nation.

The three theoretical paradigms differ in their approaches to sports, but none is more correct than the others. Applied to any issue, each paradigm generates its own insights, so that to fully appreciate the power of the sociological perspective, you should become familiar with all three.

*What do you think?*

1. *What does it mean to describe both the structural-functionalist and social-conflict paradigms as "macro-level" approaches? How are they different from the symbolic-interaction paradigm, which is considered a "micro-level" approach?*

2. *Can you devise three additional questions about sports—one that could be answered using each of the three theoretical paradigms?*

3. *How might you apply these three paradigms to other social patterns, such as the workplace or family life?*

---

[3]The ancient Romans recognized this fact, evident in the Latin root of our word "amateur," literally, "lover," to mean someone who engages in an activity for the sheer love of it.

Scientific sociology is a useful way to assess many kinds of information.

## CONCEPTS, VARIABLES, AND MEASUREMENT

A basic element of science is the **concept**, *a mental construct that represents some aspect of the world in a simplified form.* Sociologists use concepts to label aspects of social life, including "family" and "the economy," and to categorize people in terms of their "gender," "race" or "social class."

A **variable** is *a concept whose value changes from case to case.* The familiar variable "price," for example, changes from item to item in a supermarket. Similarly, people use the concept "social class" to size up others as "upper class," "middle class," "working class," or "lower class."

The use of variables depends on **measurement**, *a procedure for determining the value of a variable in a specific case.* Some variables are easy to measure, as when a checkout clerk adds up the cost of our groceries. But measuring sociological variables can be far more difficult. For example, how would you measure a person's "social class"? You might be tempted to look at clothing, listen to patterns of speech, or note a home address. Or, trying to be more precise, you might ask about income, occupation, and education. Since there are many ways to measure almost anything, researchers must *operationalize* their variables—that is, they must specify exactly *what* they are measuring.

Sociologists also face the problem of dealing with a large number of people. How, for example, do you report income for thousands or even millions of individuals? Listing streams of numbers would carry little meaning and tell us nothing about the group as a whole. Therefore, sociologists employ *descriptive statistics* to state what is "average" for a large population. Most commonly used are the *mean* (the arithmetic average of all measures obtained by adding them up and dividing by the number of cases), the *median* (the middle score that divides a distribution in half), and the *mode* (the single score that appears most often).

**Reliability and validity.** Beyond carefully operationalizing variables, useful measurement must be reliable and valid. Reliability refers to consistency in measurement. For measurement to be reliable, in other words, the process must yield the same results when repeated. Even consistent results, however, may not be valid. Validity refers to measuring precisely what one intends to measure. Valid measurement means more than hitting the same spot on a target again and again—it means hitting the bull's-eye.

Say, for example, you want to know how religious people are. You might ask how often your respondents attend religious services. But is going to a church or temple really the same thing as being religious? Maybe not, since people take part in religious rituals for many reasons, not all of them religious; some devout believers, on the other hand, avoid organized religion altogether. Thus, even when a measure yields consistent results (making it reliable), it can still miss the real, intended target (and lack validity). In sum, sociological research depends on careful measurement, which is always a challenge to researchers.

## CORRELATION AND CAUSE

The real payoff in sociological research is determining how variables are related. **Correlation** means *a relationship by which two (or more) variables change together.* But sociologists want to know not just *how* variables change but *why*. The scientific ideal, then, is mapping out **cause and effect**, which means *a rela-tionship in which we know change in one variable causes change in another.* As we noted earlier, Emile Durkheim found that the degree of social integration (the cause) affected the suicide rate (the effect) among categories of people. Scientists refer to the causal factor as the *independent variable*, while calling the effect the *dependent variable*. Understanding cause and effect is valuable because it allows researchers to *predict* how one pattern of behaviour will produce another.

Just because two variables change together does not necessarily mean that they have a cause-and-effect relationship. Consider, for instance, that the marriage rate in Canada falls to its lowest point in January, exactly the same month that the national death rate peaks. This hardly means that people drop dead if they decide not to marry (or that they don't marry because they die). More likely, it is the dreary weather across much of the country during January (and perhaps also the post-holiday blahs) that causes both the low marriage rate and the high death rate.

When two variables change together but neither one causes the other, sociologists describe the relationship as a *spurious*, or false, correlation. A spurious correlation between two variables usually results from some third factor. For example, delinquency rates are high where young people live in crowded housing, but both of these factors result from being poor. To be sure of a real cause-and-effect relationship, we must show (1) that the two variables are correlated, (2) that the independent (or causal) variable precedes the dependent variable in time, and (3) that there is no evidence that the correlation is spurious because of some third variable.

## THE IDEAL OF OBJECTIVITY

Another goal of scientific study is *objectivity*, or personal neutrality, in conducting research. The ideal of objective inquiry is allowing the facts to speak for themselves rather than filtering them through the personal values and biases of the researcher. In reality, of course, achieving total neutrality is impossible for anyone. But carefully adhering to the logic of scientific research will maximize objectivity.

The German sociologist Max Weber expected people to choose *value-relevant* research topics. But once their work is underway, Weber cautioned, researchers need to be *value-free*. That is, we must be dedicated to finding truth *as it is* rather than *as we think it should be*. This difference, for Weber, sets science apart from politics. Researchers (unlike politicians) must try to stay open-minded and willing to accept whatever results come from their work, whether they like them or not.

Weber's argument still carries much weight in sociology, although most researchers concede that we can never be completely value-free or even aware of all our biases (Demerath, 1996). Moreover, sociologists are not representative of the population as a whole.

*Myths as well as scientific facts stand as an important part of human existence. In his painting,* Whence Do We Come?, *French artist Paul Gauguin (1848–1903) offers a mythic account of human origins. A myth (from Greek meaning "story") may or may not be factual in the literal sense, but it conveys some basic truth about the meaning and purpose of life. It is science, rather than art, that is powerless to address such questions of meaning.*

Most are white people who are highly educated and more politically liberal than the population as a whole (Wilson, 1979). Sociologists need to remember that they, too, are influenced by their social backgrounds.

## A SECOND FRAMEWORK: INTERPRETIVE SOCIOLOGY

All sociologists agree that studying social behaviour scientifically presents some real challenges. But some sociologists go further, suggesting that science as it is used to study the natural world misses a vital part of the social world: *meaning.*

Human beings do not simply act; we engage in *meaningful* action. Max Weber, the pioneer of this framework, argued that the proper focus of sociology, therefore, is *interpretation*—or understanding the meanings involved in everyday life. **Interpretive sociology**, therefore, is *the study of society focussing on the meanings people attach to their social world.*

Interpretive sociology differs from scientific or positivist sociology in three ways. First, scientific sociology focusses on action, what people do; interpretive sociology, by contrast, focusses on the meanings people attach to behaviour. Second, while scientific sociology sees an objective reality "out there," interpretive sociology sees reality constructed by people themselves in the course of their everyday lives. Third, while scientific sociology tends to favour *quantitative* data—that is, numerical measurements of social behaviour—interpretive sociology favours *qualitative* data—researchers' perceptions of how people understand their surroundings. In sum, the scientific approach is well suited for

research in a laboratory, where investigators stand back and take careful measurements. The interpretive approach is better suited for research in a natural setting, where investigators interact with people to learn how they make sense of their everyday lives.

Max Weber claimed the key to interpretive sociology lies in *Verstehen,* the German word for "understanding." It is the interpretive sociologist's job not just to observe *what* people do but to share in their world of meaning, coming to appreciate *why* they act as they do. Subjective thoughts and feelings—which science tends to dismiss as "bias"—now move to the centre of the researcher's attention (Berger & Kellner, 1981; Neuman, 1997).

## A THIRD FRAMEWORK: CRITICAL SOCIOLOGY

There is a third methodological approach in sociology. Like the interpretive approach, critical sociology developed in reaction to scientific research. This time, however, the problem is the scientific goal of objectivity.

Scientific sociology holds that reality is "out there" and that the researcher's task is to study and document this reality. But Karl Marx, who founded the critical approach, rejected the idea that society exists as a "natural" system with a fixed order. To assume this, he claimed, amounts to saying that society cannot be changed. Scientific sociology, then, ends up supporting the status quo.

**Critical sociology** is *the study of society focussing on the need for social change.* Rather than asking the scientific question "How does society work?" critical sociologists ask moral and political questions, especially

## TABLE 1–2  Three Methodological Approaches in Sociology

|  | Scientific | Interpretive | Critical |
|---|---|---|---|
| **What Is Reality?** | Society is an orderly system; reality is "out there." | Society is ongoing interaction; reality is socially constructed meanings. | Society is patterns of inequality; reality is that some dominate others. |
| **How Do We Conduct Research?** | Gather empirical data—ideally, quantitative; researcher tries to be an objective observer. | Develop a qualitative account of the subjective sense people make of their world; researcher is a participant. | Research is a strategy to bring about desired change; researcher is an activist. |
| **Corresponding Theoretical Paradigm** | Structural-functional paradigm | Symbolic-interaction paradigm | Social-conflict paradigm |

"Should society exist in its present form?" Their answer, typically, is that it should not. The point, said Marx (1972:109; orig. 1845), is not merely to study the world as it is but to *change* it. In making value judgments about how society should be improved, critical sociology rejects Weber's goal that researchers should be value-free. Similarly, Immanuel Wallerstein argues today that the role of sociologists should be ". . . to debate what might be a more substantively rational historical system than the one in which we are now living and which is coming to its term" (Wallerstein, 1998: 20).Sociologists using the critical approach seek to change not only society but the character of research itself. They consider their research participants as equals and encourage their involvement in deciding what to study and how to do the work. Often, researchers and research participants use their findings to provide a voice for less powerful people and advance the political goal of a more equal society (Nielsen, 1990; Stanley, 1990; Reinharz, 1992; Wolf, 1996; Hess, 1999). Scientific sociologists object to taking sides in this way, charging that critical sociology (whether feminist, Marxist, or another critical approach) is political and gives up any claim to objectivity. Critical sociologists respond that all research is political in that it either calls for change or it does not. Sociologists thus have no choice about their work being political, but they can choose *which* positions to support. Critical sociology, therefore, is an activist approach tying knowledge to action—seeking not just to understand the world but also to improve it. Generally speaking, scientific sociology tends to appeal to researchers with more conservative political views; critical sociology appeals to those with liberal and radical-left politics.

What about the link between methodological approaches and theory? In general, each of the three methodological approaches is related to one of the theoretical paradigms presented earlier in this chapter. The scientific approach corresponds to the structural-functional paradigm; the interpretive approach to the symbolic-interaction paradigm; and the critical approach to the social-conflict paradigm. Table 1–2 summarizes the differences among the three methodological approaches. Sociologists often favour one approach over another; however, most make use of all three (Gamson, 1999).

## RESEARCH AND GENDER

Research is also affected by **gender**, *the significance members of a society attach to being female or male.* Canadian sociologist Margrit Eichler (1988) identifies five ways in which gender can influence research:

1. **Androcentricity.** Androcentricity (*andro* is the Greek word for "male"; *centricity* refers to "being centred on") means acting as if only the actions of men are important, ignoring what women do. The parallel concept of *gynocentricity*—seeing the world from a female perspective—is a problem, too, but one that occurs less frequently in our male-dominated society.

2. **Overgeneralizing.** This problem occurs when sociologists use data obtained from men to support conclusions about all people. For example, a researcher might gather information from a handful of male public officials and draw conclusions about an entire community.

3. **Gender blindness.** Failing to consider gender at all is termed "gender blindness." A study of growing old in Canada that overlooks the fact that most elderly men live with spouses while elderly women generally live alone would be limited by gender blindness.

4. **Double standards.** Researchers must be careful not to judge men and women differently. For example, a family researcher who labels a couple "man and wife" implies the work of one sex is more significant than that of the other.

5. **Interference.** A fifth problem occurs when research participants react to the sex of the investigator in ways that interfere with the project. For instance, while conducting research in Sicily, Maureen Giovannini (1992) found many men reacted to her as a *woman* rather than as a *researcher*. Gender dynamics kept her from certain activities such as private conversations with men that were deemed inappropriate for single women.

There is nothing wrong with focussing research on one sex or the other. But all sociologists, as well as people who read their work, should be mindful of how gender can affect an investigation.

## RESEARCH ETHICS

Like all scientific investigators, sociologists must remember that their work can harm as well as help research participants and communities. For this reason, the Canadian Sociology and Anthropology Association (CSAA)—the major professional association for sociologists in Canada—has established formal guidelines for conducting research (1994).

Sociologists must strive to be both technically competent and fair-minded in their work. They must disclose their findings without omitting significant data, and they are ethically bound to share their work with other sociologists who may wish to try the study for themselves.

Sociologists must also strive to protect the rights and welfare of all individuals and groups affected by their work. First, the individuals and groups that are observed are entitled to privacy, confidentiality, and anonymity, including the option not to be studied at all. Second, sociologists must be mindful of the impact on any individuals and groups that are affected by the outcomes of the studies.

Whether social scientists need to inform people that they are the objects of study is a matter of continuing debate. No one objects to studying public behaviour (say, observing how people interact in a gambling casino) without announcing one's presence. But most sociologists agree that researchers should not target specific individuals for study without their permission, nor employ deception in their dealings with respondents. The CSAA guidelines state that "informed consent must be obtained when the risks of research are greater than the risks of everyday life."Another guideline concerns funding. Sociologists must include in their published results any sources of financial support. Furthermore, sociologists must avoid conflicts of interest (or even the appearance of such conflict) that may compromise the integrity of their work. For example, researchers must never accept funding from any organization that seeks to influence the research results for its own purposes.

Finally, there are global dimensions to research ethics. Before beginning work in another nation, investigators must become familiar enough with that society to understand what people *there* are likely to see as a violation of privacy or a source of personal danger. In a multicultural society, of course, the same rule applies to studying people whose background differs from one's own. The Social Diversity box offers tips about how outsiders can sensitively study minority populations.

## RESEARCH METHODS

A **research method** is *a systematic plan for conducting research.* Here we introduce four widely used methods of sociological investigation: experiments, surveys, participant observation, and use of existing sources. None is better or worse than any other. Rather, in the same way that a carpenter selects a particular tool for a particular task, researchers choose a method according to whom they wish to study and what they wish to learn.

### TESTING A HYPOTHESIS: THE EXPERIMENT

The **experiment** is *a research method used to investigate cause-and-effect relationships under highly controlled conditions.* Experiments test a specific *hypothesis*—that is, a statement of a possible relationship between two (or more) variables. A hypothesis is really an educated guess about how variables are linked. An experimenter gathers the evidence needed to accept or reject the hypothesis in three steps: (1) measuring the dependent variable (the effect), (2) exposing the dependent variable to the independent variable (the cause or treatment), and (3) measuring the dependent variable again to see if the predicted change took place. If the expected change took place, the experiment supports the hypothesis; if not, the hypothesis must be modified.

Successful experiments depend on carefully controlling all factors that might affect what is being measured. Control is easiest in a laboratory, an artificial setting specially constructed for this purpose. But experiments in an everyday location—"in the field," as sociologists say—have the advantage of letting researchers observe participants in their natural settings.

### ASKING QUESTIONS: THE SURVEY

A **survey** is *a research method in which respondents answer a series of statements or questions in a questionnaire or an interview.* The most widely used of all research strategies, the survey is well suited to studying what cannot be observed directly, such as political attitudes or religious beliefs.

A survey targets some *population*, such as unmarried mothers or adults living in rural counties of Manitoba. Sometimes every adult in the country is the

## SOCIAL DIVERSITY

# Conducting Research with Minorities

In a society as racially, ethnically, and religiously diverse as Canada, sociological investigators will inevitably confront people who differ from themselves. Learning—in advance—some of the distinctive traits of any category of people being studied can both facilitate the research and ensure that no hard feelings remain after the work is completed. Research with Aboriginals in Canada provides clues for conducting research in general. The success of the research process requires that investigators pay particular attention to a number of factors that might not be obvious:

*Researchers must always remain respectful of participants and mindful of their well-being. In part, this means investigators must become familiar—well ahead of time—with the cultural patterns of those they wish to study*

1. **Consider the impact of the investigators' characteristics.** Differences in culture and status have an impact on observations. For example, Aboriginal children are more likely to identify themselves as Aboriginals when interviewed by another Aboriginal than when interviewed by a non-Aboriginal. One way around this problem is to partner up with an Aboriginal co-researcher.

2. **Be careful with language.** Terms have different meanings in different cultures and even within cultures. For example, Cree is an Aboriginal

survey population, as in polls taken during national political campaigns. Of course, contacting a vast number of people is all but impossible, so researchers usually study a *sample*, a much smaller number of cases selected to represent the entire population. Surveys commonly provide very accurate estimates of national opinions based on samples of as few as 1500 people.

Beyond selecting respondents, the survey must have a specific plan for asking questions and recording answers. The most common way to do this is to give respondents a *questionnaire* with a series of written statements or questions. Often the researcher lets respondents choose possible responses to each item, similar to a multiple-choice examination. Sometimes, though, a researcher may want participants to respond freely, as a way of teasing out shades of opinion. Of course, this free-form approach requires the researcher later to make sense out of what can be a bewildering array of answers.

In an *interview*, a researcher personally asks participants a series of questions, thereby overcoming one problem typical of the questionnaire method: the failure of some respondents to return the questionnaire to the researcher. A further difference is that interviews afford participants considerable freedom to respond as they wish. Researchers often ask follow-up questions to clarify an answer or to probe a bit more deeply. When doing so, however, a researcher must avoid influencing the subject even in subtle ways, such as by raising an eyebrow as the subject offers an answer.

### IN THE FIELD: PARTICIPANT OBSERVATION

**Participant observation** is *a research method by which investigators systematically observe people while joining in their routine activities.* This strategy lets researchers study social life in a natural setting, from a motorcycle club to a religious seminary. Cultural anthropologists use participant observation to study other societies, calling this method "fieldwork."

Researchers may begin with few specific hypotheses, unsure of what the important questions will turn out to be. Compared to experiments and surveys, then, participant observation has few hard-and-fast rules. Flexibility can be an advantage, though, since investigators often must adapt to unexpected circumstances in an unfamiliar environment.

The goal is to gain entry to a setting without disturbing the routine behaviour of others. Participant observers must, therefore, take on a dual role. On the one hand, to gain an insider's viewpoint, they must become a participant in the setting—"hanging out" for months or even years, trying to act, think, and even feel the same way as the people they are observing. On the other hand, the researcher must remain an "observer," standing back from the action and applying the sociological perspective to social patterns that others take for granted.

Because the personal impressions of a researcher play such a central role, critics claim that participant observation lacks scientific rigour. Yet its personal

language in which terms for ownership are based on need and utility, whereas in English terms for ownership are largely based on individual control. The Cree language is highly inflected and words may be nonsensical in isolation. Terms such as "mine" must therefore be placed in context to make sense to a Cree respondent.

3. **Recognize that minority groups are heterogeneous.** *Aboriginal* is a term used by Statistics Canada to describe a category of individuals that belong to many different tribes and have different languages and dialects. In a study conducted in Alberta, among as few as eight Aboriginal women there were two different tribes and three different religions (not counting "no religion") repre-

sented. Many Aboriginals, in fact, identify themselves primarily as a member of a particular tribe or nation and not as a member of the census category "Aboriginal."

4. **Recognize differences in family life.** Generally speaking, Aboriginal cultures favour having many children. Aboriginal women are honoured as givers and creators of life. It is understandable, then, that Aboriginal women are reluctant to use birth control during sex with a steady partner, even if unprotected sex exposes them to HIV.

5. **Take time to build a relationship.** Many respondents are more concerned with the quality of the relationship with the researcher than with simply answering a series of

questions. Thus, the researcher who tries to rush through an interview in order to cover all questions may in the end not get a true (that is, a valid and reliable) response because he or she has not first established personal trust. This especially concerns personal and sensitive topics, such as custody of children.

In short, researchers must always remain respectful of research participants and mindful of their well-being. This means, in part, that investigators must become familiar—well ahead of time—with the cultural patterns of those they wish to study.

Sources: Annis (1986), Mill (1997), and Rudmin (1994).

approach is also a strength; where a high-profile team of sociologists administering a formal survey might disrupt a setting, a sensitive participant-observer can often gain considerable insight into people's natural behaviour.

## THE SECOND TIME AROUND: EXISTING SOURCES

Not all research requires new data collection. In many cases, sociologists save time and money by using existing sources, analyzing data collected by others. The most widely used data are gathered by government agencies such as Statistics Canada. Data about other nations in the world are found in various publications of the United Nations and the World Bank.

Sociologists with low budgets find drawing on available data appealing, and the data are often better than what they could hope to obtain on their own. However, data may not be available in the specific form a researcher wishes, and it may be difficult to know how accurate the data are. In his 19th-century study of suicide, described earlier, Emile Durkheim used official records. But Durkheim knew that some recorded suicides were really accidents, just as some true suicides were never recorded as such.

Characteristics of the four major methods of sociological investigation we have introduced are summarized in Table 1–3.

## PUTTING IT ALL TOGETHER: TEN STEPS IN SOCIOLOGICAL INVESTIGATION

The following 10 questions will guide you through a research project in sociology:

1. **What is your topic?** Curiosity—and use of the sociological perspective—will generate ideas for social research. Pick a topic you find important to study.

2. **What have others already learned?** Visit the library to learn what theories and methods others have applied to the topic. What problems did others have in studying your topic?

3. **What—exactly—are your questions?** Are you seeking to explore an unfamiliar setting? To describe some category of people? Or to investigate cause and effect among variables? Clearly state the goals of your research and operationalize—that is, define—all variables.

4. **What will you need to carry out research?** How much time and money are available to you? What special equipment or skills does the research require? Can you do all the work yourself?

5. **Are there ethical concerns?** Can the research harm anyone? How can you avoid injury? Will you promise participants anonymity? If so, how will you ensure that anonymity will be maintained?

## TABLE 1–3 Four Research Methods: A Summary

| Method | Application | Advantages | Limitations |
|---|---|---|---|
| **Experiment** | For explanatory research that specifies relationships among variables; generates quantitative data | Provides the greatest opportunity to specify cause-and-effect relationships; replication of research is relatively easy | Laboratory settings have an artificial quality; unless the research environment is carefully controlled, results may be biased |
| **Survey** | For gathering information about issues that cannot be directly observed, such as attitudes and values; useful for descriptive and explanatory research; generates quantitative or qualitative data | Sampling allows surveys of large populations using questionnaires; interviews provide in-depth responses | Questionnaires must be carefully prepared and may produce a low return rate; interviews are expensive and time consuming |
| **Participant observation** | For exploratory and descriptive study of people in a "natural" setting; generates qualitative data | Allows study of "natural" behaviour; usually inexpensive | Time consuming; replication of research is difficult; researcher must balance roles of participant and observer |
| **Secondary Analysis** | For exploratory, descriptive, or explanatory research whenever suitable data are available | Saves time and expense of data collection; makes historical research possible | Researcher has no control over possible biases in data; data may only partially fit current research needs |

6. **What method will you use?** Consider all major research strategies, as well as combinations of approaches. The best method depends on the kinds of questions you are asking as well as resources available to you.

7. **How will you record the data?** The research method you use guides your data collection. Be sure to record information accurately and in a way that will make sense later (it may be months before you actually write up the results of your work). Watch out for any bias that may creep into your work.

8. **What do the data tell you?** Determine what the data say about your initial questions. If your study involves a specific hypothesis, you should be able to confirm, reject, or modify it based on your findings. Keep in mind that there will be several ways to interpret your results, depending on the theoretical paradigm you apply. You should consider them all.

9. **What are your conclusions?** Prepare a final report indicating what you have learned. Also evaluate your own work. What problems arose during the research process? What questions were left unanswered?

10. **How can you share what you have learned?** Consider making a presentation to a class, or maybe even to a meeting of professional sociologists. The important point is to share what you have learned with others and to let them respond to your work.

To review many of the issues raised in this chapter, the Controversy & Debate box on page 25 examines how sociological generalizations differ from common stereotypes.

## SUMMARY

1. The sociological perspective shows that the general operation of society affects the experiences of particular people. In this way, sociology helps us better understand barriers and opportunities in our lives.

2. Early social thinkers focussed on what society *ought to be*; sociology—named by Auguste Comte in 1838—uses scientific methods to understand society *as it is*.

3. The rapid transformation of Europe during the 18th and 19th centuries triggered the development of sociology. The rise of an industrial economy, the explosive growth of cities, and the emergence of new political ideas combined to weaken tradition and make people more aware of their social world.

4. Theory is the process of linking facts to create meaning. Sociologists use theoretical paradigms to guide theory building.

5. The structural-functional paradigm is a framework for exploring how social structures work together to promote the overall operation of society.

6. The social-conflict paradigm highlights dimensions of social inequality that generate conflict and promote change.

# Is Sociology Nothing More than Stereotypes?

*"Children in public day care suffer from maternal deprivation."*

*"People in Canada? They're rich, they love to marry, and they love to divorce!"*

*"Everybody knows that a man cannot be a feminist!"*

Everyone—including sociologists—makes generalizations. But many beginning students of sociology may wonder how sociological generalizations differ from simple stereotypes.

All three statements above are examples of a **stereotype,** *exaggerated descriptions that applied to every person in a particular category.* First, rather than describing averages, each statement paints every individual in the category with the same brush; second, each ignores facts and distorts reality (even though many stereotypes do contain an element of truth); third, each sounds more like a put-down than a fair-minded assertion.

Good sociology, by contrast, involves generalizations, but with three conditions. *First, sociologists do not indiscriminately apply any generalization to individuals. Second, sociologists are careful that a generalization*

*squares with available facts. Third, sociologists offer generalizations fair-mindedly, with an interest in getting at the truth.*

Recall, first, that the sociological perspective reveals "the general in the particular"; therefore, a sociological insight is a generalization about some category of people. Consider, for example, the first statement above: that children in public day care suffer from maternal deprivation. This statement is inaccurate, since the evidence shows that children in well-organized and adequately funded day care are as socially adapted as children who spend their early years with their mother. The key to successful child development, then, is quality of care—not maternal attachment.

Second, sociologists shape their generalizations to available facts. A more factual version of the second statement above is that the Canadian population, by world standards, and on average, has a very high standard of living. It is also true that our marriage rate is one of the highest in the world. And although few people take pleasure in divorcing, so is our divorce rate.

Third, sociologists strive to be fair-minded and have a passion for truth.

The third statement above, that a man cannot be a feminist, is not good sociology for two reasons. First, it is simply not true (many men identify themselves as feminists and strive to enhance women's equality), and second, it also seems motivated by gender bias—in this instance, in the reverse of the usual direction.

Good sociology, then, stands apart from harmful stereotyping. That said, however, a sociology course is an excellent setting in which to talk about common stereotypes. The classroom encourages discussion, and offers the factual information that you need to help you decide if a particular belief is valid or just a stereotype.

*Continue the debate . . .*

1. *Do people in Canada have stereotypes of sociologists? What are they? Are they valid?*

2. *Do you think taking a sociology course dispels people's stereotypes? Does it generate new ones?*

3. *Can you identify a stereotype of your own that sociology challenges?*

---

7. In contrast to these macro-level approaches, the symbolic-interaction paradigm is a micro-level framework for studying how people in everyday interaction construct reality.

8. Sociological research uses the logic of science, based on empirical evidence that we confirm with our senses.

9. Measurement is the process of giving a value to a variable in a specific case. Sound measurement is both reliable and valid.

10. Science seeks to specify the relationships among variables. Ideally, researchers try to identify how one (independent) variable causes change in another (dependent) variable.

11. Although researchers select topics according to their personal interests, the scientific ideal of objectivity demands that they try to suspend personal values and biases as they conduct their research.

12. Interpretive sociology is a methodological approach that focusses on the meaning that people attach to behaviour. Reality is not "out there" (as scientific sociology claims) but is constructed by people in their everyday interactions.

13. Critical sociology is a methodological approach that uses research to bring about social change. It rejects the scientific principle of objectivity, claiming that all research has a scientific character.

14. Because their work can harm participants, professional sociologists must observe ethical guidelines in conducting research.

15. The logic of science is most clearly expressed in the experiment, which investigates cause-and-effect relationships between two (or more) variables under controlled, laboratory conditions.

16. A survey uses either a questionnaire or an interview to gather participants' responses to a series of questions.

17. Participant observation involves joining with people in a social setting for an extended period of time.

18. Often sociologists use existing sources rather than collecting their own data; doing so is attractive to researchers with limited research budgets.

19. Sociologists make generalizations about categories of people. Unlike stereotypes, these sociological statements (1) are not applied indiscriminately to all individuals, (2) are supported by research-based facts, and (3) are put forward in the fair-minded pursuit of truth.

## KEY CONCEPTS

**sociology** (p. 3) the systematic study of human society

**global perspective** (p. 8) the study of the larger world and our society's place in it

**high-income countries** (p. 8) industrial nations in which most people are relatively rich

**middle-income countries** (p. 8) nations with limited industrialization in which most people have moderate personal income

**low-income countries** (p. 8) nations with little industrialization in which most people are poor

**positivism** (p. 10) a way of understanding based on science

**theory** (p. 12) a statement of how and why specific facts are related

**theoretical paradigm** (p. 12) a set of fundamental assumptions that guides thinking and research

**structural-functional paradigm** (p. 12) a framework for building theory that sees society as a complex system whose parts work together to promote stability

**social structure** (p. 12) any relatively stable pattern of social behaviour

**social functions** (p. 12) the consequences of any social pattern for the operation of society as a whole

**manifest functions** (p. 13) the recognized and intended consequences of any social pattern

**latent functions** (p. 13) the unrecognized and unintended consequences of any social pattern

**social dysfunctions** (p. 13) the undesirable consequences of any social pattern for the operation of society

**social-conflict paradigm** (p. 13) a framework for building theory that sees society as an arena of inequality that generates conflict and change

**macro-level orientation** (p. 14) a concern with broad patterns that characterize society as a whole

**micro-level orientation** (p. 14) a concern with small-scale patterns of social interaction in specific settings

**symbolic-interaction paradigm** (p. 14) a framework for building theory that sees society as the product of the everyday interaction of individuals

**science** (p. 15) a logical system that bases knowledge on direct, systematic observation

**concept** (p. 17) an abstract idea that represents some aspect of the world, inevitably in a somewhat simplified form

**variable** (p. 17) a concept whose value changes from case to case

**measurement** (p. 18) the procedure for determining the value of a variable in a specific case

**reliability** (p. 18) consistency in measurement

**validity** (p. 18) the quality of measuring precisely what one intends to measure

**correlation** (p. 18) a relationship by which two (or more) variables change together

**cause and effect** (p. 18) a relationship in which we know that change in one (independent) variable causes change in another (dependent) variable

**interpretive sociology** (p. 19) the study of society that focusses on the meanings people attach to their social world

**critical sociology** (p. 19) the study of society that focusses on the need for social change

**gender** (p. 20) the significance that members of a society attach to being female or male

**research method** (p. 21) a systematic plan for conducting research

**experiment** (p. 21) a research method used to investigate cause-and-effect relationships under highly controlled conditions

**survey** (p. 21) a research method in which participants respond to a series of statements or questions in a questionnaire or an interview

**participant observation** (p. 22) a research method by which investigators systematically observe people while joining in their routine activities

**stereotype** (p. 25) an exaggerated description that one applies to all people in some category

## CRITICAL-THINKING QUESTIONS

1. In what ways does using the sociological perspective make us seem less in control of our lives? In what ways does it give us greater power over our surroundings?

2. Consider the following argument: Sociology would not have arisen if human behaviour were strictly predictable due to biological instincts (as is, say, the behaviour of ants); nor would sociology exist if human behaviour were utterly chaotic. Sociology thrives because humans are partly free and partly guided by social structure.

3. What factors explain why sociology developed where and when it did?

4. Guided by the discipline's three major theoretical paradigms, what kinds of questions might a sociologist ask about (a) television, (b) war, (c) humour, and (d) colleges and universities?

## APPLICATIONS AND EXERCISES

1. Spend several hours exploring your local community. Are there clear residential patterns? That is, do various neighbourhoods contain certain categories of people? As best you can, identify who lives where. What social forces explain such patterns?

2. Look ahead to Figure 13–3 on page xx, which shows the Canadian divorce rate over the past 30 years. What societal factors pushed the divorce rate up until the early 1980s, down in the mid-1980s, up in the late 1980s, and down again in the 1990s?

3. During a class, carefully observe the behaviour of the instructor and other students. What patterns do you see regarding how people use space? Regarding who speaks? Regarding what categories of people are there in the first place?

4. Say you were going to observe your sociology instructor to assess that individual's teaching skills. How would you operationalize the concept "good teaching"? What would you look for? Do you think students are always good judges of teaching?

5. Conduct a practice interview with a roommate or friend on the topic "What is the value of higher education?" Before the actual interview, prepare a list of specific questions or issues you think are relevant. Afterward, give some thought to why conducting a good interview is much harder than it may initially seem.

##  SITES TO SEE

**www.pearsoned.ca/macionis**

Pearson Education Canada and the authors provide a Web site that accompanies this text, offering outlines, review material, learning exercises, and practice tests for each chapter. At the main page, simply click on the cover of your book and follow the easy menus.

**www.TheSociologyPage.com
(or www.macionis.com)**

John Macionis maintains this Web site (use either address) where you will find information about sociology, as well as a Links Library that will connect you with dozens of other interesting sites.

**www.arts.ubc.ca/csaa/csaa.htm**

At the Canadian Sociology and Anthropology Association's Web site, read their Code of Professional Ethics to get a better idea of the ethical concerns surrounding sociological research.

**www.statcan.ca/start.html**

Data for Canada are available from Statistics Canada at this Web site.

CHAPTER

# 2

# CULTURE

*You should not eat soup from the dish, but put it neatly on your plate; if it is too hot, it is impolite to blow on each spoonful; you should wait until it has cooled. If you have the misfortune to burn your mouth, you should endure it patiently if you can, without showing it.*

*The Swiss sociologist Norbert Elias (1978) quotes an excerpt from Antoine de Courtin's* Nouveau traité de la civilité *(1672:127, 273) to illustrate the changing social graces that mark the modernization of Western Europe. Elias argues that culture is a process that changes throughout history. Social graces that are now considered "civilized" in western industrial societies were largely unknown in feudal Europe. Moreover, a glance back in time reveals manners and rules of etiquette that now seem associated with poverty and squalor rather than "civilization."*

*The excerpt goes on to note that*

*it is very impolite to touch anything greasy, a sauce or syrup, etc., with your fingers apart from the fact that it obliges you to commit two or three more improper acts. One is to wipe your hand frequently on your serviette and to soil it like a kitchen cloth, so that those who see you wipe your mouth with it feel nauseated. Another is to wipe your fingers on your bread, which again is very improper. The third is to lick them, which is the height of impropriety (quoted in Elias, 1978, pp. 92–3).*

*Why was it socially acceptable to touch greasy foods and wipe one's hands on bread during the Middle Ages, but no longer acceptable by the 17th century? How did this new "civility" regarding table manners and rules of etiquette develop? What societal factors shaped the "civilizing process"? Elias traces how the social behaviour and affective life of people in the Middle Ages slowly evolved over subsequent centuries as individuals learned feelings of shame and embarrassment associated with bodily functions, and began in general to display a more "delicate" nature.* ∎

The 6.2 billion people living on the earth are all members of a single biological species: Homo sapiens. Even so, differences among people within Canada, and more so around the world, can delight, puzzle, disturb, and sometimes overwhelm us.

Many differences in lifestyles are inconsequential. Newfoundlanders refer to the noon meal as "dinner," the evening meal as "supper," and a late-night snack as "lunch." At the other end of the country in British Columbia, people refer to the noon meal as "lunch," the evening meal as "dinner," and food eaten late at night as a "snack." To give another example, the Australians, British, and Japanese all drive on the left side of the road, while we drive on the right. Some cultural differences are quite charming, such as the practice of kissing—but there are differences. Most people in Canada kiss in public; the Chinese kiss only in private. The French kiss publicly twice (once on each cheek), while Belgians kiss three times (starting on either cheek). The New Zealand Maoris rub noses, while most Nigerians don't kiss at all. In a marriage ceremony, Canadian couples kiss, Koreans bow, and a Cambodian groom touches his nose to the bride's cheek. Cultural habits also vary *within* countries. For example, Canadian children of Anglo-Saxon heritage eagerly look forward to Halloween on every October 31st, while children of new Chinese immigrants to the country are at first confounded by this strange tradition of trick-or-treating. Why such weird costumes—ghosts, witches, goblins, mummies, and so forth? Why tricks if no treats?

Some cultural differences, however, are more profound. The world over, people have many or few offspring, honour or push aside the elderly, are peaceful or warlike, embrace different religious beliefs, and enjoy different kinds of art and music. In short, although we are the same creatures biologically, human beings have developed very different ideas about what is pleasant and repulsive, polite and rude, beautiful and ugly, right and wrong. This capacity for amazing diversity is expressed through culture.

## WHAT IS CULTURE?

**Culture** refers to *beliefs, values, behaviour, and material objects that constitute a people's way of life.* When studying culture, sociologists often distinguish between thoughts and things. *Nonmaterial culture* includes intangible human creations ranging from sympathy to animism; *material culture* refers to tangible creations of a society, everything from skyscrapers to patchwork quilts. The terms *culture* and *society* are obviously similar, but their precise meanings differ. Culture is a shared way of life or social heritage; **society** refers to *people interacting within a limited territory guided by their culture.* Neither society nor culture could exist without the other.

Culture not only shapes what we do, but also helps form our personalities—what we commonly, but inaccurately, describe as "human nature." The warlike Yanomamö of the Brazilian rain forest think aggressiveness is natural, while halfway around the world, the Semai of Malaysia live in peace and cooperation. The dominant cultures of Canada and Japan both stress achievement and hard work; but members of our society value individualism more than do the Japanese, who are more traditional and group-oriented. However, it is also the case that within Canada and Japan different cultural groups are more or less individualistic and group-oriented. Given the cultural differences within and across countries around the world

and people's tendency to view their own way of life as "natural," it is no wonder that travellers may experience **culture shock**, *personal disorientation that accompanies exposure to an unfamiliar way of life.* The Global Sociology box on page 32 presents one researcher's personal experience of cultural shock.

```
April 5, 2000—Hong Kong It is 5 p.m.,
offices are closing and the streets
are teeming with people on their way
somewhere else. I try to manoeuvre my
way through the crowd to get to my
appointment. It is no use; we are
packed together like sardines. I give
up, relax, and go with the flow of the
crowd. I notice that the people around
me do not appear to be disturbed in
the least by the snail pace and the
continuous brushing of shoulders
against their own. My thoughts carry
me back home to Victoria, B.C.
Afternoon rush hour is all but 20 min-
utes and bodies, even in "crowds,"
seldom touch. People certainly are
different from place to place.
```

No particular way of life is "natural" to humanity, even though most people around the world view their own behaviour that way. What is natural to our species is the capacity to *create culture.* Every other form of life—from mosquitoes to black bears—behaves in uniform, species-specific ways. To a world traveller, the enormous diversity of human life stands out in contrast to the behaviour of, say, wolves, which is the same everywhere. This uniformity follows from the fact that most living creatures are guided by *instincts*, biological programming over which animals have no control. A few animals—notably chimpanzees and related primates—have a limited capacity for culture, and researchers have observed them using tools and teaching simple skills to their offspring. But the creative power of humans far exceeds that of any other form of life. In short, *only humans rely on culture rather than instinct to ensure the survival of their kind* (Harris, 1987).

To understand how human culture came to be, we need to look back at the history of our species.

### CULTURE AND HUMAN INTELLIGENCE

In a universe that is 15 billion years old, our planet is a much younger 4.5 billion years of age (see the time lines inside the front cover of the text). Not for a billion years after the planet was formed did life appear. Several billion more years went by before dinosaurs

*Human beings around the globe create diverse wasy of life. Such differences begin with outward appearance: Contrast the women shown here from Brazil, Kenya, New Guinea, and Morocco, and the men from Canada, India, Peru, and New Guinea. Less obvious, but of even greater importance, are internal differences, since culture also shapes our goals in life, our sense of justice, and even our innermost personal feelings.*

ruled the earth, only to disappear. It was later, some 65 million years ago, that our history took a crucial turn—with the appearance of the creatures we call primates.

What sets primates apart is their intelligence: They have the largest brains relative to body size of all living creatures. About 12 million years ago, primates began to develop along two different lines, setting humans apart from the great apes, our closest relatives. But our common lineage is evident in traits that humans share even today with chimpanzees, gorillas, and orangutans: great sociability; affectionate and long-lasting bonds for child rearing and mutual protection; the ability to walk upright (normal in humans, but less

## Confronting the Yąnomamö: The Experience of Culture Shock

A small aluminum motorboat chugged steadily along the muddy Orinoco River, deep within South America's vast tropical rain forest. Anthropologist Napoleon Chagnon was nearing the end of a three-day journey to the home territory of the Yąnomamö, one of the most technologically simple societies on earth.

Some 12 000 Yąnomamö live in villages scattered along the border of Venezuela and Brazil. Their way of life could hardly be more different from our own. The Yąnomamö wear little clothing and live without electricity, cars, or other conveniences that most people in Canada take for granted. They use bows and arrows for hunting and warfare, as they have for centuries. Many of the Yąnomamö have had little contact with the outside world, so Chagnon would be as strange to them as they would be to him.

By 2:00 in the afternoon, Chagnon had almost reached his destination. The hot sun and humid air were unbearable. Chagnon's clothes were soaked with perspiration, and his face and hands swelled from the bites of gnats swarming around him. But he scarcely noticed, so preoccupied was he with the fact that in just a few moments he would be face to face with people unlike any he had ever known.

Chagnon's heart pounded as the boat slid onto the riverbank. Chagnon and his guide climbed from the boat and walked toward the Yąnomamö village, stooping as they pushed their way through the dense undergrowth. Chagnon describes what happened next.

> I looked up and gasped when I saw a dozen burly, naked, sweaty, hideous men staring at us down the shafts of their drawn arrows! Immense wads of green tobacco were stuck between their lower teeth and lips making them look even more hideous, and strands of

dark green slime dripped or hung from their nostrils—strands so long that they clung to their [chests] or drizzled down their chins.

> My next discovery was that there were a dozen or so vicious, underfed dogs snapping at my legs, circling me as if I were to be their next meal. I just stood there holding my notebook, helpless and pathetic. Then the stench of the decaying vegetation and filth hit me and I almost got sick. I was horrified. What kind of welcome was this for the person who came here to live with you and learn your way of life, to become friends with you? (1992:11–12)

Fortunately for Chagnon, the Yąnomamö villagers recognized his guide and lowered their weapons. Reassured that he would survive the afternoon, Chagnon still was shaken by his inability to make any sense of these people. And this was to be his home for a year and a half! He wondered why he had forsaken physics to study human culture in the first place.

Source: Chagnon (1992).

common among other primates); and hands that manipulate objects with great precision.

Fossil records show that 3 million years ago, our distant human ancestors grasped cultural fundamentals such as the use of fire, tools, and weapons, and were able to create simple shelters and fashion basic clothing. These Stone Age achievements may seem modest, but they mark the point at which our ancestors embarked on a distinct evolutionary course—making culture their primary strategy for survival.

Culture, then, is very recent and was a long time in the making. As it became a strategy for survival, our forebears descended from the trees into the tall grasses of central Africa. There, they learned the advantages of hunting in groups. As mental capacity expanded, our species emerged as *Homo sapiens*, Latin for "thinking person." Human became the only species that names itself, and the biological forces we call instincts gave way to a more efficient survival scheme: *Human beings developed the mental power to actively fashion the natural environment for themselves.* Ever since, humans have made and remade their worlds in countless ways, which explains the fascinating cultural diversity that is evident today within, as well as across, countries.

*People throughout the world communicate not just with spoken words but also with bodily gestures, which vary from culture to culture. To most Canadians, there is nothing unusual about the young woman shown in the left-hand photo. But to people living in Muslim societies—who typically use the left hand for bathroom hygiene—eating this way is disturbing, to say the least! Similarly, our familiar "thumbs up" gesture is likely to insult an Australian, who "reads" the message as "Up yours!" Finally, even the commonplace gesture we take to mean "Stop" or "No, thanks" can get you into trouble in many West African nations, where people take it to mean "You have five fathers" or, more simply, "You bastard!"*

## THE COMPONENTS OF CULTURE

Although cultures vary greatly, they all have common components, including language, values, and norms. We shall begin with the one that underlies all the others: symbols.

### SYMBOLS

Like all creatures, human beings sense the surrounding world, but unlike others, we also create a reality of *meaning*. Humans transform the elements of the world into **symbols**, *anything that carries a particular meaning recognized by people who share culture*. A high-five, a nod, a tattoo, a veil, a salute—all serve as symbols. We see the human capacity to create and manipulate symbols reflected, for example, in the different meanings associated with the simple act of winking the eye, which can convey, depending on the culture and the context, interest, understanding, or insult.

We are so dependent on our culture's symbols that we take them for granted. Often, however, we gain a heightened sense of the importance of a symbol when someone uses one in an unconventional way—say, when a young man cross-dresses at a party, or when nationalistic members of Parliament display Canadian flags at their seats. Entering an unfamiliar culture also reminds us of the power of symbols; culture shock is

really the inability to "read" meaning in new surroundings. Not understanding the symbols of a culture leaves a person feeling lost and isolated, unsure of how to act and sometimes frightened.

Culture shock is a two-way process. On the one hand, the traveller *experiences* culture shock when meeting people whose way of life is different. For example, North Americans who consider dogs beloved household pets might be put off by the Masai of eastern Africa, who ignore them and never feed them. The same travellers might be horrified to find that in parts of Indonesia and in the northern regions of the People's Republic of China, people roast dogs for dinner.

On the other hand, a traveller can *inflict* culture shock by acting in ways that offend others. A Canadian who asks for a cheeseburger in an Indian restaurant offends Hindus, who consider cows sacred and never to be eaten. Indeed, global travel provides endless opportunities for misunderstanding. When in an unfamiliar setting, we need to remember that even behaviour that seems innocent to us may spark offence among others whose symbolic system differs from our own. For example, the common "OK" gesture, by which Canadians signal approval, sends to the French the message "You're worth zero," while Germans take this gesture as a crude representation of "rectum." See the photos above for other examples.

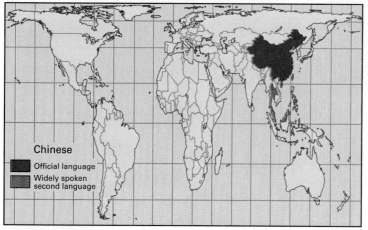

Chinese
- Official language
- Widely spoken second language

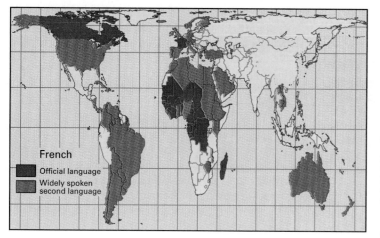

English
- Official language
- Widely spoken second language

French
- Official language
- Widely spoken second language

## GLOBAL MAP 2–1
### Language in Global Perspective

Chinese (including Mandarin, Cantonese, and dozens of other dialects) is the native tongue of one-fifth of the world's people, almost all of whom live in Asia. Although all Chinese people read and write with the same characters, they employ any of several dozen dialects. The "official" dialect, taught in schools throughout the People's Republic of China and the Republic of Taiwan, is Mandarin (the dialect of Beijing, China's historic capital city). Cantonese (the language of Canton, which differs in sound from Mandarin roughly the way French does from Spanish) is the second most common Chinese dialect.

English is the native tongue or official language in several world regions and has become the preferred second language in most of the world.

The largest concentration of French speakers is in France and in its former African colonies. French, of course, is also one of Canada's official languages, spoken mainly as a first language in Quebec and northern New Brunswick.

Source: *Peters Atlas of the World* (2000).

Symbolic meanings also vary within a single society. A Haida warrior mask, prized by a museum curator as an outstanding artifact, may represent to the Haida people an example of cultural loss, colonialism, and oppression. Similarly, the Canadian flag that for English speakers embodies national pride may symbolize ethnic oppression for some French-speaking people from Quebec. And the official broad-brimmed Stetson hat of the RCMP might have symbolized oppression for Sikhs until, in 1990, Baltej Singh Dhillon became the first Sikh RCMP officer to be allowed to wear a turban.

## LANGUAGE

The heart of a symbolic system is **language**, *a system of symbols that allows people to communicate with one another.* Humans have devised hundreds of alphabets, and many differing conventions for writing: Most people in North America and Europe write from left to right, while people in northern Africa and western Asia write right to left, and people in eastern Asia write from top to bottom. Global Map 2–1 shows where in the world one finds two of the three most widely spoken languages (Spanish being the third most common spoken language).

Language not only facilitates communication, but also ensures the continuity of culture. Language—spoken or written—is a cultural heritage in coded form, the key to **cultural transmission**, *the process by which one generation passes culture to the next.* Just as our bodies contain the genes of our ancestors, so our cultural heritage contains countless symbols of those who came before us. Language is the key that unlocks centuries of accumulated wisdom.

Language skills may link us to the past, but they also set free the human imagination. By connecting symbols in new ways, we can imagine an almost limitless range of future possibilities. Language sets apart human beings as the only creatures that are self-conscious, aware of our limitations and ultimate mortality, yet able to dream and hope for a future better than the present.

**The Sapir-Whorf thesis.** Do the Chinese, who think using one set of symbols, actually experience the world differently from Finns, who think mainly using Finnish and sometimes Swedish; or from Canadians, who think mainly using English or French? Some researchers say yes, since each language has its own distinct symbols that serve as the building blocks of the speaker's reality.

Edward Sapir and Benjamin Whorf claimed that languages are not merely different sets of labels for the same reality (Sapir, 1929, 1949; Whorf, 1956). Rather, each symbolic system is at least partly unique, with some words or expressions that have no precise counterpart

*Donning clothes displaying multiple reproductions of Canada's national flag, this spectator takes part in the Canada Day celebrations in Montreal.*

in another symbolic system. In addition, as multilingual people can attest, a single idea may "feel" different if spoken in Hindu rather than in Persian or Dutch (Falk, 1987). Formally, then, the **Sapir-Whorf thesis** holds that *people perceive the world only in terms of the symbols contained in their language.* The claim that the Inuit use numerous words for the single English term *snow* has been used to support the Sapir-Whorf thesis.

However, some critics maintain that Sapir-Whorf is not really a thesis at all, but rather an ideology or philosophical standpoint that is impossible to prove or disprove scientifically. While linguists who support Sapir-Whorf maintain that the Inuit do think of and describe snow differently than we do, and that colours have different meanings in different languages, other linguists argue just the opposite.

## VALUES AND BELIEFS

What accounts for the popularity of children's book and movie characters such as Barney, Franklin, the Berenstain Bears, and Mr. Dressup? Each teaches our children middle-class values such as hard work, competition, and respect for authority, which are all important for individual achievement in Canadian society. In applauding such characters, we are endorsing certain **values**, *culturally defined standards of desirability, goodness, and beauty that serve as broad guidelines for social living*. From the standpoint of culture, values are statements of what ought to be.

Values are broad principles that underlie **beliefs**, *specific statements that people hold to be true*. In other words, values are abstract standards of goodness, while beliefs are particular matters people hold to be true or false. For example, most Canadian adults would probably agree that their country should provide equal opportunities for all groups, including men and women. Yet in reality, only a small number of women actually makes it into politics in Canada (Inter-Parliamentary Union, 1997) and many of those who do so claim that politics remains an old boys' club (Angus Reid Group Inc., 1997d).

## CANADIAN VALUES

Because Canada is a country of Native peoples and immigrants, few values command the support of everyone. Even so, a number of dominant values have emerged. A recently commissioned report by the federal government, *Citizens' Forum on Canada's Future* (Report to the People and Government of Canada, 1991:35–45) identified the following seven important cultural values:

1. **Equality and fairness in a democratic society.** Canadians across the country express a belief in fairness for all citizens, including Aboriginal peoples, citizens of Quebec, and visible minorities.

2. **Consultation and dialogue.** As citizens, we should aim to settle our differences peacefully, through talking over our problems, learning about one another, and arriving at agreed-upon solutions to our problems.

3. **Importance of accommodation and tolerance.** Accommodating the traditions and customs of Canada's Aboriginal peoples and ethnic groups, including the French of Quebec, were central to this cultural value.

4. **Support for diversity.** Support for the country's many diversities—regional, ethnic, linguistic, cultural—is another central value that we share as a nation.

5. **Compassion and generosity.** People in Canada value the safety net provided by the welfare state—particularly its universal health care system and attractive social services, pension plans, openness toward refugees, and commitment to reduce regional disparities.

6. **Attachment to Canada's natural beauty.** Canada's wilderness is legendary, and Canadians believe that their governments should do more to protect the natural environment from pollution and other hazards of industrialization.

7. **Our world image: commitment to freedom, peace, and nonviolent change.** Canadians want to be seen from abroad as a free, peaceful, and nonviolent society, which, as a nation, plays an active role in international peacekeeping.

**Values: Sometimes in conflict.** Looking over the list above, we see that these dominant cultural values are often difficult to realize. For example, the federal government and national media tend to promote an image of Canada as "one" nation, bound together by shared values, traditions, and beliefs. Yet close attention to debates over "whose culture" is authentically Canadian indicates that there is little agreement on what constitutes a national culture in our country. To take another example, Canadians may express a belief in support for diversity, but at the same time demand the return of Chinese immigrants to their home country because they attempted to enter Canada "illegally." We may also verbally support tolerance and accommodation, yet oppose such values for particular groups. A recent example is Gay Pride Week, which was opposed by the mayors of a number of Canadian cities, including Fredericton, London, and Hamilton (Dull, 1997). Such conflicts in values inevitably cause strain, leading to awkward belief "balancing acts." In some cases we decide that one value is more important than another; in others, we may simply learn to live with inconsistencies.

## NORMS

Middle-class Canadians are reluctant to share with others the size of their paycheque, while people in China tend to share such "personal" information eagerly. Both patterns illustrate the operation of **norms**, *rules and expectations by which a society guides the behaviour of its members*. To take another example, gossip is legitimized by many cultures, but is condemned as rude and divisive, and against the norms, by other cultures.

Sociologist William Graham Sumner (1959; orig. 1906) coined the term **mores** (pronounced MORE-ays) to refer to *norms that are widely observed and have great moral significance*. Mores, or *taboos*, include, for example, our society's insistence that adults not engage in sexual relations with children.

People are more casual, however, about **folkways**, *less important norms that people apply with considerable individual discretion*. Examples include notions about appropriate greetings and proper dress. A woman who wears a low-cut dress while attending a formal dinner party may raise an eyebrow for violating folkways or "etiquette." By contrast, if she were to show up at the same dinner party wearing no dress at all, she would be violating cultural mores and inviting more serious sanctions!

Cultural norms, then, guide individual behaviour. Although we sometimes bristle when others pressure us to conform, we can all see that, in general, norms make our encounters with others more orderly and predictable.

As we learn cultural norms, we also gain the capacity to evaluate our own behaviour. Doing wrong (say, downloading a term paper from the Internet) can cause not only *shame*—the painful sense that others disapprove of our actions, but *guilt*—a negative judgment that we make of ourselves. Only cultural creatures can experience shame and guilt. This is what writer Mark Twain had in mind when he remarked that people "are the only animals that blush . . . or need to."

## "IDEAL" AND "REAL" CULTURE

Values and norms do not *describe* actual behaviour so much as they *prescribe* how members of a society should act. We learn to recognize some difference between *ideal culture*—expectations embodied in values and norms, and *real culture*—the patterns that actually occur in everyday life. When Canadian adults take marriage vows they promise each other sexual fidelity. However, in a recent poll, almost 22 percent of males and 14 percent of females reported having had an affair while married (Angus Reid Group Inc., 1997b). A number of prominent politicians from Canada and elsewhere have publicly endorsed sexual fidelity in marriage yet practised the opposite, just as some members of the Canadian clergy have taken vows of celibacy during their ordination yet later broken them. All the same, a culture's moral prodding is important, calling to mind the old saying "Do as I say, not as I do."

## TECHNOLOGY AND CULTURE

In addition to intangible elements such as values and norms, every culture includes a wide range of tangible (from Latin meaning "touchable") human creations called *artifacts*. The Chinese eat with chopsticks rather than knives and forks, the Japanese place mats on the floor rather than rugs, and many men and women in India prefer flowing robes to the tighter clothing common in most western countries. The material culture of a people can seem as strange to outsiders as their language, values, and norms.

A society's artifacts partly reflect underlying cultural values. The warlike Yąnomamö carefully craft their weapons and prize the poison tips on their arrows. By

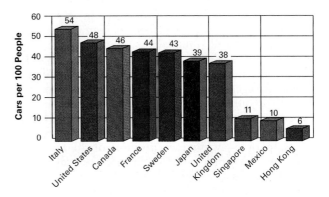

**FIGURE 2–1  Car Ownership in Global Perspective**
Source: The World Bank (2000).

contrast, as Figure 2–1 shows, Canadians embrace personal autonomy through their deep attachment to the automobile. We come in third, behind only the United States and Australia, in regard to car ownership per population.

Material culture, in addition to reflecting values, indicates a society's level of **technology**, *knowledge that people apply to the task of living in their surroundings*. The more complex a society's technology, the more its members are able to shape the world for themselves.

Gerhard and Jean Lenski and Patrick Nolan (1995) argue that a society's level of technology is crucial in determining what cultural ideas and artifacts emerge or are even possible. Thus, these researchers see *socio-cultural evolution*, or historical change in culture caused by new technology, as passing through four levels of development: hunting and gathering, horticulture and pastoralism, agriculture, and industry.[1]

## HUNTING AND GATHERING

The oldest and most basic way of life is **hunting and gathering**, *the use of simple tools to hunt animals and gather vegetation*. From the time of our earliest human ancestors 2 million years ago, until about 1800, most

---

[1]This account examines only the major types of societies described by the Lenskis; see Lenski, Nolan, & Lenski, 1995.

people in the world lived as hunters and gatherers. Today, however, this technology characterizes only a few societies, including some Kaska Dene Aboriginals of northwest Canada, the Pygmies of central Africa, the Bushmen of southwestern Africa, the Aborigines of Australia, and the Semai of Malaysia. In most cases, hunters and gatherers spend much of their time searching for game and edible plants. Their societies stay small—generally with several dozen people living in a family-like, nomadic group—moving on as they deplete an area's vegetation or pursue migratory animals.

Everyone helps to search for food, with the very young and the very old helping as they can. Women usually gather vegetation—the primary food source for these people—while men do most of the hunting. Despite having different roles, then, the two sexes have rough social parity (Leacock, 1978).

Hunters and gatherers have few formal leaders. They may recognize a man, or sometimes a woman, as a *shaman* who presides over spiritual concerns, but such a position is often temporary and provides no release from the daily responsibility to procure food.

Storms and droughts can easily wipe out their food supply, and they have few effective ways to respond to accident or the spread of disease. Not surprisingly, therefore, many children die in childhood; only half survive to the age of 20.

During this century, technologically complex societies have slowly closed in on the few remaining hunters and gatherers, reducing their available land and depleting game and vegetation, with the result that hunters and gatherers are fast vanishing from the earth. Fortunately, study of their way of life has already produced valuable information about humanity's sociocultural history and our fundamental ties to the natural environment.

## HORTICULTURE AND PASTORALISM

**Horticulture**, *the use of hand tools to raise crops*, first appeared some 10 000 years ago. The hoe and the digging stick (used to punch holes in the ground for seeds) appeared first in fertile regions of the Middle East and Southeast Asia, and by 6000 years ago such tools were in use from Western Europe to China. Central and South Americans, too, learned to cultivate plants, but rocky soil and mountainous terrain forced people such as the Yąnomamö to adopt this new technology while continuing to hunt and gather (Fisher, 1979; Chagnon, 1992).

In especially arid regions, societies turned not to raising crops but to **pastoralism**, *the domestication of animals*. Throughout the Americas, Africa, the Middle East, and Asia, many societies blend horticulture and pastoralism.

With the greater productivity that comes from domesticating plants and animals, these societies often expand to hundreds of members. While pastoral peoples remain nomadic, horticulturalists founded semi-permanent settlements, with the more advanced of them having permanent settlements. In such societies, the material surplus frees some people from food production to make crafts, engage in trade, or serve as full-time priests. Compared to hunters and gatherers, pastoral and advanced horticultural societies are more concerned with wealth possession (in regard to land, animals, weapons, and so on). Some families manage to acquire greater wealth than others, and end up operating as a ruling elite. Men are also likely to gain power over women in these societies since the bulk of the wealth ends up in male hands.

Having little control over nature, hunters and gatherers generally believe that spirits inhabit the world; all living things, human and non-human, are seen in a sacred context. Once people gain the power to raise plants and animals, however, they tend to conceive of a God (typically male) or creator of the world. The pastoral roots of Judaism and Christianity are evident in the term *pastor* for some members of the clergy and the common view of God as "shepherd," overseeing the well-being of all.

## AGRICULTURE

Five thousand years ago, further technological advances led to **agriculture**, *large-scale cultivation using plows harnessed to animals or more powerful energy sources*. Agrarian technology first appeared in the Middle East and gradually spread throughout the world. So important was the invention of the animal-drawn plow, the wheel, writing, numbers, and new metals, that historians call this era "the dawn of civilization" (Lenski, Nolan, & Lenski, 1995:175).

By turning the soil, plows allow land to be farmed for decades, so people can live in permanent settlements. Large food surpluses, transported on animal-powered wagons, let populations grow into the millions. Members of agrarian societies become ever more specialized in their work, leading to the invention of money as a form of common exchange to replace the earlier system of barter. While the development of agrarian technology expands human choices and fuels urban growth, it also makes social life more individualistic and impersonal.

Agriculture also brings about a dramatic increase in social inequality. While most people live as serfs or slaves, elites are freed from labour to cultivate a "refined" way of life based on the study of philosophy, art, and literature. At all levels of such a society, men gain pronounced power over women.

People with simple technology live much the same the world over, with minor differences due to variations

*Hunters and gatherers depend on nature to meet their basic needs. Pastoral peoples have a somewhat higher standard of living based on the ability to domesticate animals. Members of agrarian societies use animal power to plow and irrigate land, boosting their output even more. People in industrial societies are more productive still, utilizing powerful energy sources and huge machinery. Most recently, members of post-industrial societies manipulate symbols in the form of words, images, or music, often using computers.*

in climate. On the other hand, as the Lenskis explain, agrarian technology gives people enough control over the world that cultural diversity increases.

## INDUSTRY

Industrialization occurred as societies replaced the muscles of animals and humans with new forms of

# Virtual Culture: Is It Good for Us?

The Information Revolution promises that symbols—words, sounds, and images—will be generated and spread rapidly around the world. What are the implications of new information technology for human culture?

One important trend is that more and more of the cultural symbols that frame our lives will be *created*. In the past, sociologists have characterized culture as a way of life *transmitted* from generation to generation. In this traditional view, culture is an authentic heritage that belonged to our ancestors. But in the emerging cyber-society, more and more cultural symbols are new—intentionally generated by composers, writers, filmmakers, and others who work within the expanding information economy.

During the first half of this century, children tended to admire the heroes of written literature—animal characters, such as Peter Rabbit and Winnie-the-Pooh, or human-like creatures, such as Peter Pan or Alice-in-Wonderland. Today, young children are more and more preoccupied with *virtual culture*, elements that spring from the mind of a contemporary culture maker and that reach us through a screen: on television, in the movies, or through computer cyberspace. Today's "heroes" include the Swedish teddy bear

Björne, the Japanese Power Rangers, Barney the dinosaur, a continuous flow of Disney characters, and the ever-smiling fast-food clown Ronald McDonald. Certainly, at least some of these cultural icons embody cultural values that have shaped our past. But few of them have any historical existence, and almost all of them have come into being for the singular purpose of commercial gain.

As the Information Revolution proceeds, virtual culture is likely to take on increasing importance. Will virtual culture steadily erode our longstanding traditions? Will our children, for example, no longer be interested in written literature? And if so, how would such a development affect generations yet to come?

Source: Roland Johnson (1996), for the basic idea for this box. His Web site is personalwebs.myriad.net/Roland.

power. Formally, **industry** is *the production of goods using advanced sources of energy to drive large machinery*. The introduction of steam-power, starting in England about 1775, boosted productivity more than ever and transformed culture in the process.

While agrarian people work in or near the home, most people in industrial societies work in large factories, under the supervision of strangers. Thus, industrialization pushes aside the traditional cultural values that guided family-centred agrarian life for centuries.

Industry also made the world seem smaller. During the 19th century, railroads and steamships carried people across land and sea, faster and farther than ever before. This process continued during the 20th century, with the invention of the automobile, radio, and television.

Industrial technology raises living standards and extends lives. Schooling becomes the rule because industrial jobs demand more and more skills. Further, industrial societies steadily expand political rights and somewhat reduce economic inequality.

It is easy to see industrial societies as more "advanced" than those relying on simpler technology. After all, in industrial societies living standards rise and life expectancy increases significantly—to twice that of, say, the Yanomamö. Even so, industry intensifies individualism, which expands freedom but weakens human community. Then, too, industry has led people to abuse the natural environment—at our peril. And while advanced technology gives us work-saving machines and miraculous forms of medical treatment, it also contributes to unhealthy levels of stress and has created weapons capable of destroying, in a flash, everything that our species has achieved thus far.

## POST-INDUSTRIAL INFORMATION TECHNOLOGY

Going beyond the four categories discussed by the Lenskis, we see that many industrial societies, including Canada, have now entered a post-industrial stage of economic development based on new information technology. Production in industrial societies centres on factories that make *things*, while post-industrial production centres on computers and other electronic devices that create, process, store, and apply *ideas and information* (Bell, 1973).

The emergence of an information economy thus changes the skills that define a way of life. No longer are mechanical abilities the only key to success. People find that they must learn to work with symbols by speaking, writing, computing, and creating images and sounds in fields such as art, advertising, and entertainment. The overall effect of this transformation is that our society now has the capacity to generate symbolic culture on an unprecedented scale. The Critical Thinking box takes a closer look.

## CULTURAL DIVERSITY

Take a stroll down Yonge Street in Toronto or through Vancouver's Gastown, and it will soon become obvious to you that Canada is an extremely culturally diverse society. Heavy immigration over the past century-and-a-half has turned Canada into one of the most *multicultural* of all industrial countries. While in the past most immigrants to Canada came from Europe and the United States, today's immigrants come from various countries in Asia and Latin America. This immigration pattern is primarily responsible for the large proportion of Canadians who declare their cultural origin to be other than the predominant French or English (as shown in Figure 2–2). By contrast, Japan's historic isolation makes it the most *monocultural* of all industrial nations.

### HIGH CULTURE AND POPULAR CULTURE

Cultural diversity often involves social class. In fact, in everyday conversation we usually reserve the term *culture* for art forms such as literature, music, dance, and painting. We describe people who regularly go to the opera or the theatre as "cultured," because they presumably appreciate the "finer things in life."

We speak less generously of ordinary people, assuming that everyday culture is somehow less worthy. So we are tempted to judge the music of Beethoven as "more cultured" than the blues, couscous as better than corn bread, golfing as more polished than bowling, fly fishing as more refined than bait fishing, ballet as better

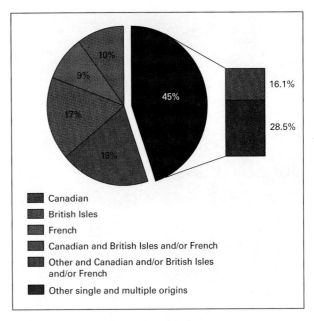

**FIGURE 2–2    Ethnicity, Canada, 1996**

Canadian multiculturalism is illustrated by the 45 percent of individuals that indicated an ethnic origin including something other than the predominant English, French, or Canadian. Note that the meaning of "Canadian" is unclear.

Source: Statistics Canada, *The Daily*, Tuesday, February 17, 1998.

than "ultimate" fighting, and the music of Ben Heppner superior to that of Céline Dion.

In short, many cultural patterns are readily accessible only to some members of a society (Hall & Neitz, 1993). Sociologists use the shorthand term **high culture**[2] to refer to *cultural patterns that distinguish a society's elite*, and **popular culture** to designate *cultural patterns widespread among a society's population*.

We should resist quick judgments about the merits of high culture over popular culture for two main reasons. First, neither elites nor ordinary people have uniform tastes and interests; people in both categories differ in numerous ways. Second, we may be praising high culture not because it is inherently better than popular culture, but simply because its supporters have more money, power, and prestige. For example, there is no difference between a violin and a fiddle; however, we name the instrument one way when it is used to produce a type of music typically enjoyed by a person of higher position, and the other way when it produces

---

[2]The term "high culture" is derived from the term "highbrow." A century ago, people influenced by phrenology—the bogus 19th-century theory that personality was affected by the shape of the human skull—praised the tastes of those they termed "highbrows" while dismissing the interests of others they derided as "lowbrows."

*Céline Dion and Ben Heppner are internationally renowned Canadian singers who have little in common except that both are Juno Award winners and Officers of the Order of Canada. How do we explain that Ben Heppner came before Céline Dion on the January 1, 2000* Maclean's *list of best performing artists of the century, even though Dion has sold millions more records than Heppner has and is probably known to hundreds of millions more people?*

music appreciated by people of lower social standing. Sociologists are uneasy, therefore, with distinctions between high and popular culture, preferring to use the term *culture* to refer to *all* elements of a society's way of life, including such things as styles of dress, speaking, eating, and other cultural habits of the rich and poor.

## SUBCULTURE

The term **subculture** refers to *cultural patterns that distinguish some segment of a society's population.* Young people who enjoy hip-hop music and fashion, Polish Canadians, Vancouver east side drug addicts, jazz musicians, Calgary cowboys, campus poets, computer "nerds," and West Coast wilderness campers—all display subcultural patterns.

It is easy, but often inaccurate, to slot people into subcultural categories, because almost everyone participates in many subcultures without necessarily closely identifying themselves with any of them. In some cases, however, commitment to a category, such as ethnicity and religion, can set people apart from one another—with tragic results. Consider the former nation of Yugoslavia in southeastern Europe. The recent civil war there was fuelled by astounding cultural diversity. This one small country made use of *two* alphabets, embraced *three* major religions, spoke *four* major languages, contained *five* major nationalities, was divided into *six* separate republics, and reflected the cultural influences of *seven* surrounding countries. The

cultural conflict that plunged this nation into civil war shows that subcultures are a source not only of pleasing variety but also of potential tension and outright violence (cf. Sekulic, Massey, & Hodson, 1994).

We in Canada have taught our children to view this country as a "mosaic" in which many nationalities make up the Canadian cultural identity. Despite some mixing over the decades, linguistic and cultural divisions remain powerful and persistent. Historically, we have viewed Canada as a "mosaic" in which many nationalities make up the Canadian cultural identity. But given our cultural diversity, how accurate is the "mosaic" image? For one thing, subcultures involve not just *difference* but *hierarchy*. Too often, what we view as "dominant" or "mainstream" culture is patterns favoured by powerful segments of the population, while what we view as "subculture" is, in fact, the patterns of disadvantage people. Hence, sociologist John Porter (1965) has characterized Canada as a "vertical mosaic," in which a privileged male elite consists overwhelmingly of people of British origin (Bell & Tepperman, 1979; Reitz, 1980). Some authors writing on the country's two dominant groups, English- and French-speaking, maintain that Canadians make up "two solitudes" (Rocher 1990), as is evident in the lack of formal and informal interaction among the French- and English-speaking intellectual elites within the Royal Society (Ogmundson & McLaughlin, 1994). Yet other researchers disagree that Canada is a closed society that has marginalized some groups at the expense of others.

For example, it has been shown that the political participation of foreign-born immigrants compares well with that of both their Canadian-born adult children and grandchildren, as well as with Charter Canadians, groups of first European settlers who have been given special rights and privileges (Chui, Curtis & Lambert, 1991). These varied insights have sparked a new approach to the study of culture—multiculturalism.

## MULTICULTURALISM

In recent years, Canada has been facing the challenge of **multiculturalism**, *an educational program recognizing the cultural diversity of Canada and promoting the equality of all cultural traditions.* This movement represents a sharp turning away from the past, when our society did not recognize the hierarchy of the cultural mosaic. Today, we debate spiritedly how to balance a celebration of cultural differences with our shared value of equality.

Multiculturalists point out that from the outset the European immigrants to the so-called New World (of course, "new" only to those who came from abroad) exploited the various Aboriginal cultures; some First Nations peoples were decimated, while others were severely reduced in numbers and marginalized on reserves (Dickason, 1992). After Canadian Confederation (1867), people of British origin gained the top political positions in the country, viewing those of other backgrounds (Aboriginal peoples, the French, southern Europeans, the Chinese, and so on) as being of "lower stock." As Porter (1965:62) states,

> After all, Canada was a British creation, though indifferently conceived by British statesmen of the day. In the first decades of Canada's existence, who would have doubted that the British were destined to an uninterrupted epoch of imperial splendour? Although the French participated in Confederation, Canada's political and economic leaders were British and were prepared to create a British North America. Born British subjects, they intended to die as such.

As a result of this hierarchy, Canadian historians have tended to focus on the descendants of the English and northern Europeans, describing historical events from their point of view. And historians have tended to push to the margins the perspectives and accomplishments of Aboriginals and people of African, Asian, and Latin American descent. Multiculturalists condemn this singular pattern as **Eurocentrism**, *the dominance of European (especially English) cultural patterns.* Molefi Kete Asante, a leading advocate of multiculturalism, argues that like "the 15th-century Europeans who could not cease believing that the earth was the centre of the universe, many today find it difficult to cease viewing European culture as the centre of the social universe" (1988:7).

Few Canadians would deny that our way of life has wide-ranging roots. But multiculturalism is controversial because it asks us to rethink norms and values that form the core of our culture. One currently contested issue surrounds language. In 1969, the *Official Languages Act* made both French and English the official languages of Canada—and the country officially became bilingual. However, as noted by the excerpt from the Citizens' Forum on Canada's Future, in the Social Diversity box, on page 44, many tensions remain over the actual implementation of Canada's language policy.

Another controversy centres on how our nation's schools should teach culture. Proponents defend multiculturalism, first, as a strategy to present a more accurate picture of Canada's *past.* Proposed educational reforms seek, for example, to tone down the simplistic praise commonly directed at Christopher Columbus and other European explorers, by acknowledging the tragic impact of the European conquest on the Aboriginal peoples of this hemisphere. Moreover, a multicultural approach recognizes the achievements of many women and men whose cultural backgrounds have, up to now, confined them to the sidelines of history.

Second, proponents claim, multiculturalism enables students to grasp our country's even more diverse *present.* A recent study on the population of Toronto revealed that 42 percent of Torontonians begin life speaking a language other than English. Of the 1.3 million people who were not born in Toronto, 25 percent are of Chinese origin, 25 percent are of South Asian origin, and 20 percent are black (Gee, 1998).

Third, proponents assert, multiculturalism can strengthen the academic achievement of Canada's Aboriginal and visible minority children, who may find little personal relevance in Eurocentric education (Ghosh, 1996). National Map 2–1 on page 45 takes a closer look at the languages used in households across Canada.

Fourth and finally, proponents see multiculturalism as needed preparation for living in a world in which nations are increasingly interdependent. Multiculturalism, in short, teaches global connectedness.

Although multiculturalism has found favour in recent years, it has provoked its share of criticism too. Most troubling to opponents of multiculturalism is its tendency to encourage divisiveness rather than unity, by encouraging people to identify only with their own category rather than with the nation as a whole. As critics see it, a multicultural approach moves Canada along the road that has led to social collapse in the former Yugoslavia and elsewhere.

Moreover, critics contend that multiculturalism erodes any claim of universal truth by evaluating ideas

# Language Rights in Canada: Unifying or Divisive?

Widely known as Bill 101, the Charter of the French Language in Quebec declares that French is the official language of the courts, civil administration, work and labour relations, commerce, business, and, to a large extent, education as well. This unique piece of legislation, designed to protect the language of the majority (French speakers) from the minority (non-French speakers), has proven to be a constant source of irritation between the two groups, most recently on three fronts: a) use of non-French store signs, including in Montreal's Chinatown; b) use of English on Internet sites based in the province; and c) rights of francophone parents to send their children to English schools.

Concerning the latter case, a Quebec Supreme Court judge recently ruled against a group of mainly francophone parents who wanted to send their children to English schools, thereby upholding the Charter of French Language. Some of the parents threaten to take the case, if necessary, all the way to the Supreme Court of Canada. The issue of a single declared language at the provincial level in the bilingual federation that is Canada is not likely to disappear overnight.

Source: Denis, 1990.

---

according to the race (and sex) of those who present them. Our common humanity, in other words, dissolves into an "Aboriginal experience," "Chinese experience," "European experience," and so on.

Finally, critics doubt that multiculturalism actually benefits minorities. On the one hand, multiculturalism seems to demand precisely the kind of ethnic and racial segregation that our nation has struggled for decades to end. On the other hand, an Aboriginal-centred or Afrocentric curriculum may well deny children important knowledge and skills by forcing them to study from a single point of view. Historian Arthur Schlesinger, Jr. (1991) puts the matter bluntly in regard to blacks: "If a Kleagle of the Ku Klux Klan wanted to use the schools to handicap black Americans, he could hardly come up with anything more effective than the 'Afrocentric' [the dominance of African cultural patterns] curriculum."

Is there any common ground in this debate? Virtually everyone agrees that we all need to gain greater appreciation of cultural diversity. But precisely where the balance is to be struck is likely to remain a divisive issue for some time to come (Davies & Guppy, 1998).

## COUNTERCULTURE

Cultural diversity also includes outright rejection of conventional ideas or behaviour. **Counterculture** refers to *cultural patterns that strongly oppose those widely accepted within a society.*

In many societies, counterculture springs from adolescence (Spates, 1976; Spates & Perkins, 1982). Most of us are familiar with the youth-oriented countercultures of the 1960s that rejected mainstream culture as overly competitive, self-centred, and materialistic. Instead, hippies (perhaps your parents or even your grandparents!) and other counterculturalists favoured a collective and cooperative lifestyle in which "being" took precedence over "doing," and the capacity for personal growth—or "expanded consciousness"—was prized over material possessions such as homes and cars. Such differences prompted some people to "drop out" of the larger society.

Countercultures are still flourishing. In the 1990s, the most significant counterculture involves militaristic bands of men and women, deeply suspicious of governments, many of whom have dropped out of the political system. Neo-Nazi skinheads are a recent example of a countercultural group made up largely of young white working-class males. Some members endorse a "far right" ideology of racial superiority, openly display Neo-Nazi insignia, and blame immigrants, among others, for their country's crises, such as high unemployment (Traynor, 1998:4).

## CULTURAL CHANGE

Perhaps the most basic human truth is that "All things shall pass." Even the dinosaurs, who thrived on this planet for 160 million years (see the time lines inside the front cover), exist today only as fossils. Will humanity survive for millions of years to come? No one knows. All we can say with certainty is that, given our reliance on culture, and for as long as we *do* survive, the human record will be one of continuous change.

Some things have changed only slightly: Today, as a generation ago, most men and women look forward to raising a family. Yet raising a family in the late 1990s is

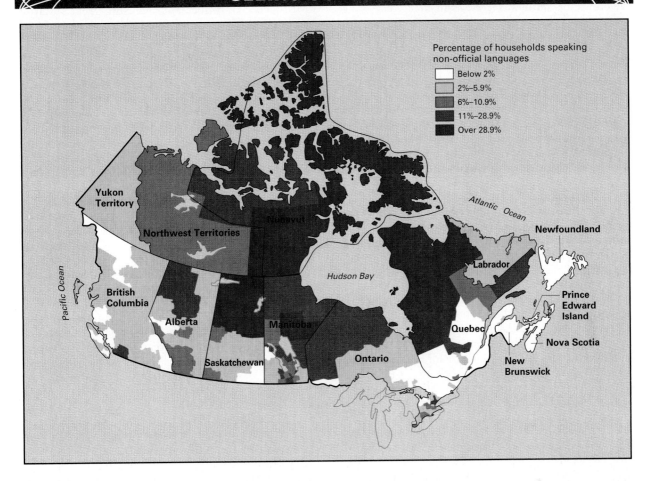

Percentage of households speaking
non-official languages

☐ Below 2%
☐ 2%–5.9%
☐ 6%–10.9%
☐ 11%–28.9%
☐ Over 28.9%

**NATIONAL MAP 2–1   Non-Official Home Languages across Canada, 1996**

The map shows that the percentage of households that use non-official languages at home varies greatly
across Canada. These households are concentrated in our largest urban centres and in northern Canada.
What explains this pattern? What other trends do you see?

Source: Based on Statistics Canada, Catalogue No. 95F0181XDB96001 (1998b).

an experience quite different from raising one in earlier times. The point is that change in one dimension of
a cultural system usually sparks changes in others. For
example, women's rising participation in the labour
force has paralleled changing family patterns, including first marriage at a later age, a rising divorce rate,
increased cohabitation, and a growing share of children
being raised in single-parent households (Balakrishnan
et al., 1993; Wu, 1999). Such connections illustrate the
principle of **cultural integration**, *the close relationship
among various elements of a cultural system.*

Of course, some parts of a cultural system change
more quickly than others. William Ogburn (1964)
observed that technology moves quickly, generating
new elements of material culture ("test-tube babies,"
for example) that outpace non-material culture (such
as ideas about parenthood). Ogburn called this inconsistency **cultural lag**, *the fact that some cultural elements
change more quickly than others, which may disrupt a cultural system.* In a culture with the capacity to allow one
woman to give birth to a child by using another
woman's egg, which has been fertilized in a laboratory

with the sperm of a total stranger, how are we to apply the traditional terms *motherhood* and *fatherhood*?

Cultural changes are set in motion in three ways. The first is *invention*, the process of creating new cultural elements such as the telephone (1876), the airplane (1903), and the aerosol spray can (1941).

*Discovery*, a second cause of change, involves recognizing and understanding something already in existence—from a distant star, to the foods of a foreign culture, to the athletic prowess of women. Many discoveries result from deliberate scientific research, but sometimes a stroke of luck yields an unexpected discovery, as when Marie Curie unintentionally left a "rock" on a piece of photographic paper in 1898 and discovered radium.

The third cause of cultural change is *diffusion*, the spread of objects or ideas from one cultural system to another. With new information technology sending words, sounds, and images around the world instantly, the level of cultural diffusion has never been greater than it is today.

Canadian society, for example, has contributed many significant cultural elements to the world, including the renowned classical music of pianist Glenn Gould and the popular novels of Margaret Atwood, who has been awarded the 2000 Booker Prize for her latest novel, *The Blind Assassin*. But diffusion works the other way as well, so that much of what Canadian citizens assume to be home-grown actually comes from other cultures—from our neighbour to the south and also from the other side of the Atlantic and even more distant Asia. Ralph Linton (1937) pointed out that most clothing and furniture, clocks, newspapers, money, and even most of the English language, are derived from other cultures.

## ETHNOCENTRISM AND CULTURAL RELATIVITY

We think of childhood as a time of innocence and freedom from adult burdens such as regular work. In less wealthy countries throughout the world, however, families depend on income earned by children. So what is right and natural to people in one society may puzzle or offend people elsewhere. Perhaps the Chinese philosopher Confucius had it right when he noted that "All people are the same; it's only their habits that are different."

Just about every imaginable social habit is subject to at least some variation around the world, and such differences cause travellers excitement and distress in about equal measure. The tradition in Japan is to name intersections rather than streets, a practice that confuses Canadians who do just the opposite; Egyptians move very close to others in conversation, irritating Canadians used to maintaining several feet of "personal space." Bathrooms (a term unknown almost anywhere

apart from Canada and the U.S.) throughout much of Morocco lack toilet paper, causing great agitation among westerners unaccustomed to using their left hand for bathroom hygiene.

Because a particular culture is the basis for everyone's reality, it is no wonder that people everywhere exhibit **ethnocentrism**, *the practice of judging another culture by the standards of one's own culture*. Some ethnocentrism is necessary if people are to be emotionally attached to a cultural system. But ethnocentrism also generates misunderstanding and conflict.

Take, for instance, the seemingly trivial matter of Canadians referring to China as the "Far East." Such a term, which has little meaning to the Chinese, is an ethnocentric expression for a region far east *of Europe*. The Chinese, too, ethnocentrically place themselves in the centre of their world, referring to their nation using a Chinese character that literally means "central state." The map shows ethnocentrism at work in a "down under" view of the Western Hemisphere.

The logical alternative to ethnocentrism is **cultural relativism**, *the practice of evaluating a culture by its own standards*. Cultural relativism doesn't come easily, since it requires us both to understand unfamiliar values and norms and to break the grasp of a culture we have known all our lives. But, as people of the world increasingly come into contact with one another, we have a growing need to understand the views of people in other societies.

Moreover, success in the emerging global economy depends on cultural sensitivity and sophistication. Consider the troubles several corporations had when they translated advertising slogans into Spanish. General Motors learned that sales of its Nova were hampered by a product whose name in Spanish means "no go." Coors' phrase "Turn It Loose" startled Spanish speakers who read the line to mean the beer would make you "Get the Runs." Eastern Airlines translated its slogan "We Earn Our Wings Daily" into "We Fly Daily to Heaven." And even a chicken restaurant slogan fell victim to poor marketing when the pitch "It Takes a Tough Man to Make a Tender Chicken," translated into Spanish as "It Takes a Sexually Aroused Man to Make a Chicken Affectionate" (Westerman, 1989; Helin, 1992).

But cultural relativity can also pose problems. Virtually every kind of behaviour is found somewhere in the world, yet does that mean that anything and everything is right just because *somebody* somewhere thinks so? Does the fact that some Indian and Moroccan families benefit from having their children work long hours justify the practice of child labour? Should we tolerate female circumcision?

Since we are all members of a single human species, surely there must be some standards of fair conduct for people everywhere. But which ones? And

**The View From "Down Under"**

North America should be "up" and South America "down," or so we think. But, because we live on a globe, such notions are conventions rather than absolutes. The reason that this map of the Western Hemisphere looks wrong to us is not that it is geographically inaccurate; it simply violates our ethnocentric assumption that Canada and the United States should be "above" the rest of the Americas.

Source: Jesse Levine, Laguna Sales, Palo Alto.

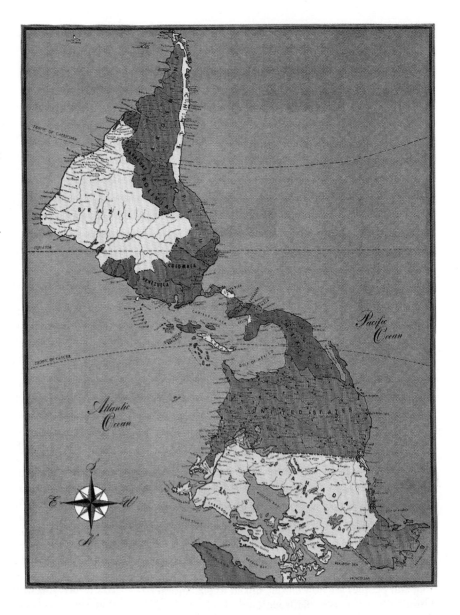

in trying to develop them, how can we avoid imposing our own standards of fair play on others? There are no simple answers. But when confronting an unfamiliar cultural practice, one should resist the impulse to make snap judgments, and instead take the time to grasp what the people in that culture think of the issue. We also need to remember that cultural contact is a two-way process by which we, too, can cause confusion and discomfort for others.

## A GLOBAL CULTURE?

New information technology also undermines local ways of life the world over in favour of western, media-driven culture. Walking the streets of Seoul (South

Korea), Kuala Lumpur (Malaysia), Madras (India), Cairo (Egypt), and Casablanca (Morocco), one readily spots jeans and other familiar forms of dress, hears well-known pop music, and observes advertising for many of the same products we use at home. Recall, too, from Global Map 2–1 (page 45) that English is rapidly emerging as the world's common language. Some scholars believe that we are witnessing the birth of a global culture (Fukuyama, 1992; Rifkin, 1995).

The world is still broken up into some 200 nation-states and thousands of different cultural systems. Yet societies of the world now have more contact with one another than ever before through the flow of information, goods, and people.

1. **Global communications: The flow of information.** Satellite-based communication now enables people throughout the world to experience the sights and sounds of events, often as they happen, and taking place thousands of miles away. Almost anywhere in today's world, no one is very far from a telephone, radio, television, facsimile (fax) machine, or personal computer.

2. **The global economy: The flow of goods.** The volume of international trade has never been greater. The emerging global economy has spurred cultural diffusion, introducing many of the same consumer goods (from automobiles to rock music to T-shirts) the world over. The 1993 North American Free Trade Agreement (NAFTA), designed to remove tariff barriers between Canada, the United States and Mexico, has lead among other things to the inclusion of the Spanish language labels (alongside the English and French) on many of our imported package materials.

3. **Global migration: The flow of people.** As people learn more about the world, they are increasingly likely to move to a place where they imagine life will be better. Transportation, too, is more efficient than ever before. As a result, most nations are home to a significant number of people born elsewhere; in 1996, for example, 42 percent of the population of Toronto, and 35 percent of the population of Vancouver, were immigrants (Statistics Canada, 1997a).

These global links have made the world's cultures more alike, at least in superficial respects. But there are three important limitations to the global culture thesis. First, the flow of information, goods, and people has been uneven throughout the world. Generally speaking, urban areas (centres of commerce, communication, and people) are now closely linked to one another, while rural villages remain isolated. Then, too, the greater economic and military power of high-income countries means that this small group of nations influences the rest of the world more than the other way around.

Second, the global culture thesis assumes that people everywhere can *afford* various new goods and services. As Chapter 8 (Global Stratification) explains, intense poverty in much of the world deprives many people of even the basic necessities for a safe and secure life (Hedley, 2000).

Third, although many cultural traits have now spread globally, not everyone attaches the same meanings to them. Do teenagers in Tokyo understand rap music the way their counterparts in Montreal or Vancouver do? Similarly, we mimic fashions from Asia, Africa, and Latin America with little understanding of

the lives of the people who first came up with them. In short, while the world's cultures seem more and more alike, profound differences remain (Featherstone, 1990; Hall & Neitz, 1993; Huntington, 1996; Eisenstadt, 1999).

## THEORETICAL ANALYSIS OF CULTURE

Culture is the key to understanding ourselves and the surrounding world. Sociologists, however, have the special task of understanding culture. To comprehend something as complex as culture requires several theoretical approaches, some of which are briefly discussed below.

### STRUCTURAL-FUNCTIONAL ANALYSIS

The structural-functional paradigm depicts culture as a relatively stable strategy for meeting human needs. This point of view borrows from the philosophical doctrine of *idealism* by asserting that values are the core of a culture (Parsons, 1966; Williams, 1970). A culture's values, in other words, give meaning to life and bind people together. Countless other cultural traits have various functions that support a way of life.

Take the Hutterites, for example, whose strongly religious communities in areas of Western Canada shun the notion of private property. An outsider may wonder at the Hutterite tradition of communal rather than private property, which includes even an individual's own clothing. From the Hutterite perspective, however, rejecting private property makes good sense because it helps maintain the Hutterites' collective identity and reinforce their core values (Curtis & Lambert, 1990:43). Of course, some Hutterite customs also have dysfunctional consequences. The subordinate role Hutterite women are assigned in relation to men may serve to keep families intact, but not necessarily without tension and conflict. The possible consequences are evident from the 1998 trial and subsequent conviction of a number of Hutterite males from a community in Alberta for sexual impropriety toward females.

Because cultures are strategies to meet human needs, we might expect to find many common patterns around the world. The term **cultural universals** refers to *traits that are part of every known culture*. After surveying hundreds of cultures, George Murdock (1945) identified dozens of traits common to them all. One cultural universal is the *family*, which functions everywhere to control sexual reproduction and to oversee the care and upbringing of children. Another example is *funeral rites*, since all human communities cope with death. Jokes, too, are ubiquitous, serving as a

*Following the structural-functional paradigm, what do you make of the Amish practice of "barn raising," by which everyone in a community joins together to build a family's new barn in a day? Why is such a ritual almost unknown today in rural areas outside Amish communities?*

relatively safe means of releasing social tensions, even though humour and interpretation differ significantly.

**Critical evaluation.** Structural-functional analysis has the strength of showing how culture operates to meet human needs. All cultures have much in common, but since there are many ways to meet almost any need, cultures around the world reveal striking diversity.

One limitation of structural-functional thinking is its tendency to highlight a society's dominant cultural patterns, directing less attention to cultural diversity and the tendency of a dominant culture to subjugate members of subcultures. Moreover, because this approach emphasizes cultural stability, it downplays the importance of change.

## SOCIAL-CONFLICT ANALYSIS

According to the social-conflict paradigm, a dominant culture often functions to the advantage of some more than others. Thus, culture operates as a dynamic arena in which social inequality fuels an ongoing power struggle.

Why does one set of values rather than another dominate a society? Many conflict theorists, especially Marxists, argue that culture is shaped by a society's system of economic production. "It is not the consciousness of men that determines their being," Marx asserted, "it is their social being that determines their consciousness" (Marx & Engels 1978:4; orig. 1859). Thus we see that the social-conflict paradigm draws on the philosophical doctrine of *materialism*, which holds that a society's system of material production

(such as our own industrial-capitalist economy) has a powerful effect on all dimensions of culture. Such a materialist approach contrasts with the idealist leanings of structural-functionalism.

Social-conflict analysis, then, suggests that our competitive and individualistic values reflect our capitalist economy. The culture of capitalism further teaches us to think that the rich and powerful have more talent and discipline than others, and therefore are deserving of their wealth and privileges. Viewing capitalism as somehow "natural" also discourages efforts to lessen economic disparity in western countries.

Social-conflict analysts claim that strains created by social inequality eventually transform cultural systems. The women's movement and the gay and lesbian movement exemplify the drive for change propelled by disadvantaged categories of people. Both, too, have encountered opposition from defenders of the status quo.

**Critical evaluation.** The strength of the social-conflict paradigm lies in its assertion that if cultural systems address human needs, they do so unequally. Simply put, the main "function" of many cultural elements is to maintain the dominance of some people over others. This inequity, in turn, promotes change.

However, the social-conflict paradigm falls short by stressing the divisiveness of culture while understating ways in which cultural patterns integrate members of a society. Thus, for a fuller understanding of culture, we should consider both social-conflict and structural-functional insights.

# Masculinity as Contest

By the time I was 10, the central fact in my life was the demand that I become a man. By then, the most important relationships by which I was taught to define myself were those I had with other boys. I already knew that I must see every encounter with another boy as a contest in which I must win or at least hold my own. . . . The same lesson continued [in school], after school, even in Sunday School. My par-

ents, relatives, teachers, the books I read, movies I saw, all taught me that my self-worth depended on my manliness, my willingness to stand up to the other boys. This usually didn't mean a physical fight, though the willingness to stand up and "fight like a man" always remained a final test. But the relationships between us usually had the character of an armed truce. Girls weren't part of this social world at all yet, just because they weren't

part of this contest. They didn't have to be bluffed, no credit was gained by cowing them, so they were more or less ignored. Sometimes when there were no grown-ups around we would let each other know that we liked each other, but most of the time we did as we were taught.

Source: Silverstein (1977).

## SOCIOBIOLOGY: WHERE BIOLOGY MEETS CULTURE

We know culture is a human creation, but does our biological existence influence how this process unfolds? A third theoretical paradigm, standing with one leg in biology and the other in sociology, is **sociobiology**, *a theoretical paradigm that studies ways in which biology affects how humans create culture.*

Sociobiology rests upon the theory of evolution proposed by Charles Darwin (1859) in his book *On the Origin of Species.* Darwin asserted that living organisms change over long periods of time as a result of *natural selection*, which is a matter of four simple principles. First, all living things live to reproduce themselves. Second, the blueprint for reproduction is in the genes, the basic units of life that carry traits of one generation into the next. Third, some random variation in genes allows each species to "try out" new life patterns in a particular environment. This variation enables some organisms to survive better than others do, and to pass on their advantageous genes to their offspring. Fourth and finally, over thousands of generations the genes that promote reproduction survive and become dominant. In this way, as biologists say, a species *adapts* to its environment, and dominant traits emerge as the "nature" of the organism.

Sociobiologists claim that the large number of cultural universals reflects the fact that all humans are members of a single biological species. It is our common biology that underlies, for example, the apparently universal male–female "double standard." As sex researcher Alfred Kinsey put it, "Among all

people everywhere in the world, the male is more likely than the female to desire sex with a variety of partners" (quoted in Barash, 1981:49). But why?

We all know that a child results from joining a woman's egg with a man's sperm. But the biological significance of a single sperm and a single egg differs dramatically. For a healthy man, sperm represents a "renewable resource" produced by the testes throughout his life. A man releases hundreds of millions of sperm in a single ejaculation—technically, enough to fertilize every woman in North America (Barash, 1981:47). A newborn female's ovaries, however, contain her entire lifetime allotment of immature eggs. A woman releases a single egg cell from the ovaries each month. So, while men are biologically capable of fathering thousands of offspring, women are able to bear a relatively small number of children.

Given this biological difference, the two sexes have distinctive strategies for reproduction. Men reproduce their genes most efficiently by being promiscuous—readily engaging in sex. But this scheme opposes the reproductive interests of women. Each of a woman's relatively few pregnancies demands that she carry the child, give birth, and provide care for some time afterward. Thus, efficient reproduction on the part of the woman depends on selecting a man whose qualities (beginning with the likelihood that he will simply stay around) will contribute to her child's survival and, later, to subsequent successful reproduction (Remoff, 1984).

The "double standard" certainly involves more than biology; it is also a product of the historical domination of women by men (Barry, 1983). But sociobiology suggests that this cultural pattern, like many others, has an underlying bio-logic. Simply put, the "double standard" exists around the world because women and men everywhere tend toward distinctive reproductive strategies.

**Critical evaluation.** Sociobiology has generated intriguing insights into the biological roots of some cultural patterns. But this perspective remains controversial for several reasons.

First, some critics fear that sociobiology may revive the biological arguments of a century ago that claimed the superiority of one race or sex. But defenders counter that sociobiology rejects the past pseudo-science of racial superiority. In fact, sociobiology unites all humanity because all people share a single evolutionary history. Sociobiology does assert that men and women differ biologically in some ways that culture may not overcome. But far from asserting that males are somehow more important than females, sociobiology emphasizes that both sexes are vital to human survival.

Second, say the critics, sociobiologists have little evidence to support their theories. Research to date suggests that biological forces do not *determine* human behaviour in any rigid sense. Rather, humans *learn* behaviour within a cultural system. The contribution of sociobiology, then, lies in explaining why some cultural patterns seem "easier to learn" than others (Barash, 1981).

## CULTURE AND HUMAN FREEDOM

Underlying the discussion throughout this chapter is an important question: To what extent are human beings, as cultural creatures, free? Does culture bind us to each other and to the past? Or does culture enhance our capacity for individual thought and independent choice?

Humans cannot live without culture. But living as symbolic creatures does have some drawbacks. We may be the only animals able to name ourselves, but living in a symbolic world also means that we are the only creatures who experience alienation. Then, too, culture is largely a matter of habit, which limits our choices and drives us to repeat troubling patterns, such as racial prejudice and sex discrimination, in each new generation. In addition, in this age of new information technology and virtual reality, we may wonder about the extent to which business-dominated media manipulate our culture in pursuit of profits.

Moreover, our insistence on competitive achievement urges us toward excellence, yet often at the cost of isolating us from one another. Material comforts comfort us in some ways but divert us from close relationships and spiritual strength.

For better and worse, human beings are cultural creatures, just as ants and bees are prisoners of their biology (Berger, 1967). But there is a crucial difference. Biological instincts create a ready-made world; culture, by contrast, forces us to *choose* as we make and remake a world for ourselves. No better evidence of this freedom exists than the cultural diversity of our own society and the even greater human diversity around the world.

Furthermore, culture is ever-changing as the result of human imagination. For this reason, members of our society hotly debate the future direction of our way of life. But, whatever one's politics, it is clear that the better we understand the workings of our culture, the better prepared we are to use the freedom it offers us.

## SUMMARY

1. Culture is a way of life shared by members of a society. Several species display limited capacity for culture, but only human beings rely on culture for survival.

2. As the human brain evolved, the first elements of culture appeared some 3 million years ago. The importance of culture steadily increased, replacing biological instincts as the foundation of human behaviour.

3. Culture relies on symbols. Language is the symbolic system by which one generation transmits culture to the next.

4. Values are culturally defined standards of what ought to be; beliefs are statements people who share a culture hold to be true. Norms, which guide human behaviour, are of two kinds: mores,

which have great moral significance, and folkways, which are everyday rules of politeness.

5. Culture is shaped by technology. We understand technological development in terms of stages of sociocultural evolution: hunting and gathering, horticulture and pastoralism, agriculture, industry, and the post-industrial Information Age.

6. High culture refers to patterns that distinguish a society's elites; popular culture includes patterns widespread in a society.

7. Canada stands among the most culturally diverse nations due to historically high levels of immigration. A subculture is a distinctive set of traits that characterizes a segment of society; counterculture refers to patterns strongly at odds with a conventional way of

life. Multiculturalism refers to efforts to enhance appreciation of cultural diversity.

8  Invention, discovery, and diffusion all generate cultural change. Cultural lag results when some parts of a cultural system change faster than others.

9. Ethnocentrism involves judging others using standards of one's own culture. By contrast, cultural relativism means evaluating another culture according to its particular standards.

10. Global cultural patterns result from the worldwide flow of goods, information, and people.

11. Structural-functional analysis views culture as a relatively stable system built on core values. Cultural traits function to maintain the overall system.

12  The social-conflict paradigm envisions culture as a dynamic arena of inequality and conflict. Cultural traits benefit some categories of people more than others.

13. Sociobiology studies how evolution shapes the human creation of culture.

14. The concept of cultural conflict refers to political debate ("culture wars") on the direction of cultural change in Canada.

15. Culture can constrain social possibilities; yet, as cultural creatures, we have the capacity to shape and reshape our world to meet our needs and pursue our dreams.

## KEY CONCEPTS

**culture** (p. 30) the beliefs, values, behaviour, and material objects that constitute a people's way of life

**society** (p. 30) people interacting in a limited territory guided by their culture

**culture shock** (p. 30) the personal disorientation accompanying exposure to an unfamiliar way of life

**symbol** (p. 33) anything that carries a particular meaning recognized by people who share a culture

**language** (p. 35) a system of symbols that allows people to communicate with one another

**cultural transmission** (p. 35) the process by which one generation passes culture on to the next

**Sapir-Whorf thesis** (p. 35) the assertion that people perceive the world only in terms of the symbols contained in their language

**values** (p. 36) culturally defined standards of desirability, goodness, and beauty that serve as broad guidelines for social living

**beliefs** (p. 36) specific statements people hold to be true

**norms** (p. 36) rules and expectations by which a society guides the behaviour of its members

**mores** (p. 36) norms that have great moral significance

**folkways** (p. 36) less important norms that people apply with considerable individual discretion

**technology** (p. 37) the knowledge that people apply to the practical tasks of living

**hunting and gathering** (p. 37) a way of life based on the use of simple tools to hunt animals and gather vegetation

**horticulture** (p. 38) a way of life based on the use of hand tools to raise crops

**pastoralism** (p. 38) a way of life based on the domestication of animals

**agriculture** (p. 38) large-scale cultivation using plows harnessed to animals or more powerful energy sources

**industry** (p. 40) the production of goods using advanced sources of energy to drive large machinery

**high culture** (p. 41) cultural patterns that distinguish a society's elite

**popular culture** (p. 41) cultural patterns widespread among a society's people

**subculture** (p. 42) cultural patterns that distinguish some segment of a society's population

**multiculturalism** (p. 43) an educational program recognizing the cultural diversity of Canada and promoting the equality of all cultural traditions

**Eurocentrism** (p. 43) the dominance of European (especially English) cultural patterns

**counterculture** (p. 44) cultural patterns that strongly oppose conventional culture

**cultural integration** (p. 45) the close relationship among various elements of a cultural system

**cultural lag** (p. 45) the fact some cultural elements change more quickly than others, which may disrupt a cultural system

**ethnocentrism** (p. 46) the practice of judging another culture by the standards of one's own culture

**cultural relativism** (p. 46) the practice of evaluating any culture by its own standards

**cultural universals** (p. 48) traits that are part of every known culture

**sociobiology** (p. 50) a theoretical paradigm that explains how biology affects how humans create culture

## CRITICAL-THINKING QUESTIONS

1. What is the cultural significance of a carefully manicured lawn in a highly mobile and largely anonymous society? What does a well-tended (or untended) front yard say about a person?

2. How does a schoolroom activity such as a "spelling bee" embody Canadian cultural values? What cultural values are expressed by children's stories such as *The Little Engine That Could*, and popular board games such as Snakes & Ladders, Monopoly, and Risk?

3. Why do members of every society tend to be ethnocentric? Point out at least one positive and negative function of ethnocentrism. Can you do the same with cultural relativism?

4. To what extent, in your opinion, is a global culture emerging? Do you regard the prospect of a global culture as positive or negative? Why?

## APPLICATIONS AND EXERCISES

1. Try to find someone on campus who has lived n another country. Ask for a chance to discuss how the culture of that society differs from the way of life here. Look for ways in which the other person sees Canadian culture differently from most people you know.

2. Make a list of words with the prefix "self" (self-service, self-esteem, self-image, self-destructive, and so on); there are hundreds of them. What does this fact suggest about our way of life?

3. Watch a Disney video such as *The Little Mermaid*, *Aladdin*, *Pocahontas*, or *Mulan*. All of these films share cultural themes, which is one reason for their popularity. According to these films, how should young people behave toward their parents? What makes these films especially "North American"?

4. An easy way to study popular culture is to pick up a number of super-hero comic books. Examine them to see what why some people are defined as heroes and others as villains. Does gender figure in this process? (cf. Hall & Lucal, 1999.)

##  SITES TO SEE

**www.pearsoned.ca/macionis**
Pearson Education Canada and the authors provide a Web site that accompanies this text, offering outlines, review material, learning exercises, and practice tests for each chapter. At the main page, simply click on the cover of your book and follow the easy menus.

**www.macionis.com
(or www.TheSociologyPage.com)**
Visit this Web site to view several short videos in which the author describes the excitement and challenges of travelling through other cultures.

**www.nationalgeographic.com**
The National Geographic Society offers information on world cultures, including search engines and a library of maps.

**www.gorilla.org**
What does a 204-kilogram (450-pound) gorilla say? Anything she wants! The Gorilla Foundation offers a look at the sign language used by a gorilla named Koko.

**linguistlist.org**
Visit this site fo find out more about the Sapir-Whorf debate.

# 3

# SOCIALIZATION:
# FROM INFANCY TO OLD AGE

Andrew Macara
*Footballers, Kos* 1993
Oil on canvas, 63.5 3 76.2 cm. Private Collection/The Bridgeman Art Library.

*On a cold winter day in 1938, a social worker investigating a possible case of child abuse at a Pennsylvania farmhouse discovered a five-year-old girl hidden in a second-floor storage room. The child, whose name was Anna, was wedged into an old chair with her arms tied above her head so that she couldn't move. She was wearing filthy garments, and her arms and legs were as thin as matchsticks (Davis, 1940:554).*

*Anna's situation can only be described as tragic. She was born in 1932 to an unmarried and mentally impaired woman of 26, who lived with her strict father. Enraged by his daughter's "illegitimate" motherhood, the grandfather did not even want the child in his house. For her first six months, Anna was shuttled among various welfare agencies. But when her mother was no longer able to pay for care, Anna returned to the home of her hostile grandfather.*

*To lessen the grandfather's anger, Anna's mother put the child in the storage room, giving her just enough milk to keep her alive. There she stayed—day after day, month after month, with almost no human contact—for five long years.*

*Learning of the discovery of Anna, sociologist Kingsley Davis (1940) immediately went to see the child. He found her with local authorities at a county home.*

*Davis was appalled by the emaciated girl, who could not laugh, speak, or even smile. Anna was completely unresponsive, as if alone in an empty world.* ■

## SOCIAL EXPERIENCE: THE KEY TO OUR HUMANITY

Here is a terrible case of a child deprived of social contact. Although physically alive, Anna hardly seemed human. Her plight reveals that without social experience, a child is incapable of thought, emotion, or meaningful action—more an *object* than a *person*.

Sociologists use the term **socialization** to refer to *the lifelong social experience by which individuals develop their human potential and learn culture.* Unlike other living species, whose behaviour is biologically set, humans need social experience to learn their culture and survive. Social experience is also the basis of **personality**, *a person's fairly consistent patterns of acting, thinking, and feeling.* We build a personality by internalizing—or taking in—our surroundings. But without social experience, as Anna's case shows, personality does not develop at all.

**55**

 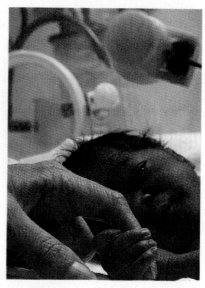 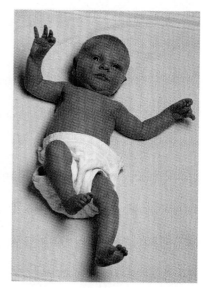

*Human infants display various reflexes—biologically based behaviour patterns that enhance survival. The sucking reflex, which actually begins before birth, enables the infant to obtain nourishment. The grasping reflex, triggered by placing a finger on the infant's palm and causing the hand to close, helps the infant to maintain contact with a parent, and later on to grasp objects. The Moro reflex, activated by startling the infant, prompts the infant to swing both arms outward and then bring them together across the chest. This action, which disappears after several months of life, probably developed among our evolutionary ancestors so that a falling infant could grasp the body hair of a parent.*

## HUMAN DEVELOPMENT: NATURE AND NURTURE

Helpless at birth, the human infant depends on others to provide nourishment and care. Anna's case makes these facts clear. A century ago, however, most people mistakenly believed that human behaviour was the product of biology.

Charles Darwin's groundbreaking studies of evolution, conducted in the mid-19th century and described in the last chapter, led most people to think that human behaviour was instinctive, simply the "nature" of our species. Such notions are still with us. People sometimes claim, for example, that our economic system reflects "instinctive human competitiveness," that some people are "born criminals," or that women are "naturally" emotional while men are "inherently" rational (Witkin-Lanoil, 1984).

People trying to understand cultural diversity also misunderstood Darwin's thinking. Centuries of world exploration had taught Western Europeans that people of other societies behaved quite differently. But Europeans linked these differences to biology rather than culture. It was a simple—although very damaging—leap to conclude that members of technologically simple societies were biologically less evolved and, thus, less human. One case in point is the view held by

Canada's former colonial powers— that Aboriginal peoples were "savages" and "barbarians" (Dickason, 1992). This ethnocentric view helped justify colonial practices: If Native peoples were not human in the same sense that the colonialists were, they could be exploited, even enslaved, without a second thought.

In this century, naturalistic explanations of human behaviour came under fire. Psychologist John B. Watson (1878–1958) devised a theory called *behaviourism*, which held that human behaviour is not instinctive but learned. Thus people the world over have the same claim to humanity, Watson insisted; people differ only in their cultural surroundings. Watson rejected the notion that human diversity reflects any evolutionary distinctions, asserting instead that human behaviour is shaped by people's environment. Watson, in short, rooted human behaviour in *nurture* rather than nature.

Today, social scientists are cautious about describing *any* human behaviour as instinctive. This does not mean that biology plays no part in human behaviour. Human life, after all, depends on the functioning of the human body. We also know that children often share biological traits (such as height, and hair and eye colour) with their parents and that heredity plays a part in intelligence, musical and artistic aptitude, and personality (such as how one reacts to frustration).

However, whether anyone *realizes* an inherited potential depends on the chance to develop it. In fact, unless children use their brains early in life, the brain itself does not fully develop (Plomin & Foch, 1980; Goldsmith, 1983; Begley, 1995).

Without denying the importance of nature, then, nurture matters more in shaping human behaviour. More precisely, as cultural creatures, *nurture is our nature*.

## SOCIAL ISOLATION

Of course, researchers must never isolate human beings in experiments. But, in the past, they did study the effects of social isolation on nonhuman primates.

**Research with monkeys.** Psychologists Harry and Margaret Harlow (1962) placed rhesus monkeys—whose behaviour is in some ways surprisingly similar to that of human beings—in various conditions of social isolation. They found that complete isolation (with adequate nutrition) for even six months seriously disturbed the monkeys' development. When returned to their group, these monkeys were passive, anxious, and fearful.

The Harlows then placed infant rhesus monkeys in cages with an artificial "mother" made of wire mesh, with a wooden head and a feeding tube "nipple." These monkeys, too, survived, but later were unable to interact with others.

But when they covered the artificial "mother" with soft terry cloth, the infant monkeys would cling to it. The Harlows concluded that the monkeys benefited from even this closeness, because the animals showed less developmental damage than earlier monkeys. The experiment confirmed how important it is that adults cradle infants affectionately.

Finally, the Harlows discovered that infant monkeys could recover from about three months of isolation. By about six months, however, isolation caused irreversible emotional and behavioural damage.

**Isolated children.** The rest of Anna's story squares with the Harlows' findings. After her discovery, Anna received extensive social contact and soon showed improvement. When Kingsley Davis (1940) revisited her after 10 days, he found her more alert and even smiling with obvious pleasure. Over the next year, Anna made slow but steady progress, showing more interest in other people and gradually learning to walk. After a year-and-a-half, she could feed herself and play with toys.

As the Harlows might have predicted, however, Anna's five years of social isolation had caused permanent damage. At age eight, her mental development was less than that of a two-year-old. Not until she was almost 10 did she begin to use words. Since Anna's mother was mentally challenged, perhaps Anna was

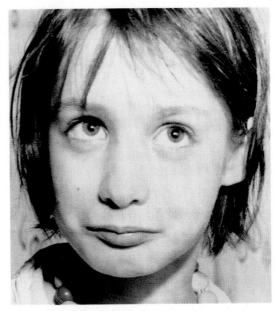

Like other children subjected to prolonged isolation, Genie never did develop a normal facility with language. Many researchers conclude that, unless a child learns language at an early age, this ability is permanently hindered. But others counter that children may well be intellectually damaged by such abuse. Thus, cases such as Genie do not settle "nature-nurture" debates about human development.

similarly so. Sadly, the riddle was never solved, because Anna died at age 10 of a blood disorder, possibly related to the years of abuse (Davis, 1940, 1947).

A second similar case involves another girl, found at about the same time as Anna and under much the same circumstances. After more than six years of virtual isolation, this girl—known as Isabelle—displayed the same lack of responsiveness as Anna. Unlike Anna, though, Isabelle benefited from a special learning program. Within a week, Isabelle was attempting to speak, and a year-and-a-half later, she knew some 2000 words. The researchers concluded that the intensive effort had propelled Isabelle through six years of normal development in only two years. By the time she was 14, Isabelle was attending sixth-grade classes; though damaged by her early ordeal, she was on her way to a somewhat normal life (Davis, 1947).

A more recent case of childhood isolation involves a California girl abused by her parents (Curtiss, 1977; Pines, 1981; Rymer, 1994). From about age two, Genie was tied to a potty chair in a dark garage. In 1970, when rescued at age 13, Genie weighed only 26 kilograms and had the mental development of a one-year-old. With intensive treatment, she became physically healthy, but her language ability remains that of a young child. Genie lives today in a home for developmentally challenged adults.

All evidence points to the crucial role of social experience in forming personality. Human beings can sometimes recover from abuse and isolation. But there is a point—precisely where is unclear from the small number of cases studied—at which isolation in infancy causes permanent developmental damage.

# UNDERSTANDING SOCIALIZATION

Socialization is a complex, lifelong process. The following sections highlight the work of important psychologists and sociologists who, in different ways, have made lasting contributions to our understanding of human development. We first present what psychologists have to say about human socialization.

## SIGMUND FREUD: THE ELEMENTS OF PERSONALITY

Sigmund Freud (1856–1939) lived in Vienna at a time when most Europeans considered human behaviour to be biologically fixed. Trained as a physician, Freud soon turned to the analysis of personality, and eventually developed the celebrated theory of psychoanalysis.

**Basic needs.** Freud claimed that biology plays a major part in human development, although not in terms of specific instincts the way it does in other species. He theorized that humans have two basic needs or drives. First is a need for bonding, which he termed the life instinct, or *eros* (from the Greek god of love). Second, we share an aggressive drive he called the death instinct, or *thanatos* (derived from Greek meaning "death"). To Freud, these opposing forces, operating at an unconscious level, generate deep inner tension.

**Freud's personality model.** Freud incorporated basic drives and the influence of society into a model of personality with three parts: id, ego, and superego. The **id** (Latin word for "it") represents *the human being's basic drives*, which are unconscious and demand immediate satisfaction. Rooted in biology, the id is present at birth, making a newborn a bundle of demands for attention, touching, and food. But society opposes the self-centred id, which is why one of the first words a child usually learns is "no."

To avoid frustration, a child must learn to approach the world realistically. This is done through the **ego** (Latin for "I"), which represents *a person's conscious efforts to balance innate pleasure-seeking drives with the demands of society*. The ego arises as we gain awareness of our distinct existence and face up to the fact that we cannot have everything we want.

In the human personality, **superego** (Latin meaning "above" or "beyond" the ego) is *the operation of culture within the individual*. The superego operates as our conscience, telling us *why* we cannot have everything we want. The superego begins to form as a child becomes aware of parental control, and matures as the child comes to understand that everyone's behaviour must take account of cultural norms.

Culture, in the form of superego, serves to *repress* selfish demands, forcing people to look beyond their own desires. Often the competing demands of self and society result in a compromise Freud called *sublimation*, which changes selfish drives into socially acceptable behaviour. Sexual urges, for example, may lead to common-law or legal marriage, just as aggression gives rise to competitive board games or team sports.

**Critical evaluation.** Freud's work sparked controversy in his own lifetime, since his society vigorously repressed sexuality, and few of Freud's contemporaries were prepared to acknowledge sex as a basic drive. More recent critics of Freud's work argue that his thinking depicts humanity strictly in male terms with a distorted view of women (Donovan & Littenberg, 1982), while other critics point to Freud's dismissal of the reality of incest (Russell, 1986). But Freud's ideas have unquestionably influenced virtually all who subsequently examined the human personality. Of special importance to sociology are his notions that we internalize social norms and that childhood experiences have lasting importance in the socialization process.

## JEAN PIAGET: COGNITIVE DEVELOPMENT

Swiss psychologist Jean Piaget (1896–1980) studied human *cognition*—how people think and understand. As Piaget watched his own three children grow, he wondered not only *what* they knew, but *how* they made sense of the world. Piaget went on to identify four stages of cognitive development.

**The sensorimotor stage.** Stage one is the **sensorimotor stage,** *the level of development in which individuals experience the world only through their senses.* For about the first two years of life, infants know the world only by touching, tasting, smelling, looking, and listening. "Knowing" to young children amounts to sensory experience.

**The preoperational stage.** At about age two, children enter the **preoperational stage,** *the level of development in which individuals first use language and other symbols.* Now children begin to think about the world mentally and begin to use their imagination. But "pre-op" children attach meanings only to specific experiences and objects. They can identify a special toy, for example, but they cannot describe what *kinds* of toys they like.

Lacking abstract concepts, a child cannot judge size, weight, or volume. In one of his best-known experiments, Piaget placed two identical glasses containing equal amounts of water on a table. He asked several five- and six-year-olds if the amount in each was the same. They nodded that it was. The children then watched Piaget take one of the glasses and pour its contents into a taller, narrower glass, raising the level of the water. He asked again if each glass held the same amount. The typical five- or six-year-old now insisted that the taller glass held more water. But by age seven, children were able to think more abstractly and realize that the amount of water stayed the same.

**The concrete operational stage.** Next comes the **concrete operational stage,** *the level of human development at which individuals first perceive causal connections in their surroundings.* Between ages 7 and 11, children focus on how and why things happen. In addition, children now attach more than one symbol to an event or object.

**The formal operational stage.** The last step in Piaget's model is the **formal operational stage,** *the level of human development at which individuals think abstractly and critically.* At about age 12, young people begin to reason abstractly, rather than thinking only of concrete situations. If, for example, you ask a child of seven "What would you like to be when you grow up?" you will get a concrete response such as "a teacher." But most teenagers can respond abstractly, saying, "I would like a job that helps others." This capacity for abstract thought also lets young people comprehend metaphors.

**Critical evaluation.** If Freud envisioned human beings as torn by the opposing forces of biology and society, Piaget saw the mind as active and creative so that children steadily gain the ability to shape their own social world. His contribution lies in showing that this capacity unfolds gradually as a result of both biological maturation and increasing social experience.

One limitation of Piaget's theory is that members of all cultures do not necessarily follow these stages according to the same time frame. For instance, living in a slowly changing society probably limits the capacity for abstract, critical thought. Finally, in our own society, a substantial proportion of adults—who encounter little creative thinking in their social circles—never reach the formal operational stage (Kohlberg & Gilligan, 1971).

## LAWRENCE KOHLBERG: MORAL DEVELOPMENT

Lawrence Kohlberg (1981) built on Piaget's work to study moral reasoning—that is, how individuals come to judge situations as right or wrong. Here, again, development occurs in stages.

*Which glass contains the most liquid?*

Young children who experience the world in terms of pain and pleasure (Piaget's sensorimotor stage) are at the *preconventional* level of moral development. At first, then, "rightness" amounts to "what feels good to me."

The *conventional* level, Kohlberg's second stage, appears by the teens (corresponding to Piaget's final, formal operational stage). At this point, young people shed some of their selfishness as they learn to define *right* and *wrong* in terms of what pleases parents and conforms to cultural norms.

In the final stage of moral development, the *postconventional* level, individuals move beyond their society's norms to consider abstract ethical principles. Now they think about liberty, freedom, or justice, perhaps arguing that what is lawful still may not be right.

**Critical evaluation.** Kohlberg's work resembles that of Piaget in that it casts moral development in identifiable stages. But here again, whether this model applies to people in all societies remains unclear. Furthermore, many people in Canada apparently do not reach the postconventional level of moral reasoning, although exactly why is still an open question.

The greatest limitation of Kohlberg's research, however, is that all his subjects were boys. Thus, Kohlberg committed a research error, as described in Chapter 1 (Sociology: Perspective, Theory, and Method), by generalizing the results of male subjects to all people. This provoked his student Carol Gilligan to further investigate how gender affects moral reasoning.

## CAROL GILLIGAN: THE GENDER FACTOR

Carol Gilligan (1982) set out to compare the moral development of girls and boys, and concluded that the

*In her more recent work, Carol Gilligan studied the social development of girls ranging in age from 6 to 18. She concluded that young girls have relatively high self-esteem, but they appear to lose this valuable resource as they move through adolescence. She links this loss to our culture's definition of women as cooperative and deferential to men. Note, too, that as girls move from elementary to secondary school, a greater share of the authority figures with whom they interact are men.*

two sexes use different standards of rightness. Males, she contends, have a *justice perspective*, relying on formal rules to define *right* and *wrong*. Girls, on the other hand, have a *care and responsibility perspective*, judging a situation with an eye toward personal relationships and loyalties. For example, as boys see it, stealing is wrong because it breaks the law. Girls, however, are more likely to wonder why someone would steal, and to be sympathetic toward someone who, for example, steals to feed a hungry child.

Kohlberg treats rule-based male reasoning as morally superior to the person-based female perspective. But Gilligan notes that impersonal rules have long governed men's lives in the workplace, whereas personal relationships are more relevant to women's lives as mothers and caregivers. Why, then, Gilligan asks, should we set up male patterns as the standards by which to judge everyone?

**Critical evaluation.** Gilligan's work sharpens our understanding of both human development and gender

issues in research. Yet, what accounts for the differences she documents between females and males? Is it nature or nurture? In Gilligan's view, cultural conditioning is at work. Recent cross-cultural research on women's caring work challenges Gilligan's psychological approach to gender socialization. There appears to be significant variation in the cultural shaping of women's caring work when viewed cross-nationally (Kahne & Giele, 1992; Leira, 1992; Baker, 1995; Benoit & Heitlinger, 1998).

## GEORGE HERBERT MEAD: THE SOCIAL SELF

In contrast to the psychological theories of human development outlined above, sociologist George Herbert Mead (1863–1931) developed a theory of *social behaviourism* to explain how social experience develops an individual's personality (1962; orig. 1934).

**The self.** Mead's central concept is the **self,** *that part of an individual's personality composed of self-awareness and self-image.* Mead's genius lay in seeing the self as the product of social experience.

First, said Mead, *the self develops only with social experience.* The self is not part of the body and does not exist at birth. Mead rejected the idea that personality is guided by biological drives (as Freud asserted) or even biological maturation (as Piaget claimed). For Mead, self develops only as the individual interacts with others. In the absence of interaction—as we see from isolated children—the body grows but no self emerges.

Second, Mead explained, *social experience is the exchange of symbols.* Only people use words, a wave of the hand, or a smile to create meaning. We can train a dog using reward and punishment, but the dog attaches no meaning to its actions. Human beings, by contrast, find meaning in action by imagining people's underlying intentions. Thus you can train a dog to go to the hallway and bring back an umbrella. But without understanding intention, if the dog cannot find the umbrella, it is incapable of the *human* response: to look for a raincoat instead.

Third, Mead continues, *to understand intention, you must imagine a situation from the other's point of view.* Symbols help us to imagine ourselves in another person's shoes and to see ourselves as that person does. This capacity lets us anticipate how others will respond to us even before we act. A simple toss of a ball, for example, requires us to step outside ourselves to imagine how the other will catch our throw. All symbolic interaction, then, involves seeing ourselves as others see us—a process Mead termed *taking the role of the other*.

**The looking-glass self.** In effect, others represent a mirror (which people used to call a "looking glass") in which we see ourselves. What we think of ourselves depends on what we think others think of us. In other words, if we think others see us as clever or clumsy, we will think of ourselves in the same way. Charles Horton Cooley (1864–1929) used the phrase **looking-glass self** to mean *a conception of self based on how we suppose others see us.*

**The I and the me.** Mead's fourth point is that *by taking the role of another, we become self-aware.* The self, then, has two parts. As subject, a self is active and spontaneous. Mead called the subjective side of the self the *I* (the subjective form of the personal pronoun). But the self is also an object, as we imagine ourselves as others see us. Mead called the objective side of the self the *me* (the objective form of the personal pronoun). All social experience has both components: We initiate action (the I phase of the self), and we continue the action based on how others respond to us (the me phase of the self).

**Stages of development.** The key to developing the self, in short, is learning to take the role of the other. With limited social experience, infants cannot do this; they respond to others only through *imitation.* That is, they mimic behaviour without understanding underlying intention, and thus have no self.

As children learn to use language and other symbols, the self emerges in the form of *play.* Play involves assuming roles modelled on important people—such as parents, guardians, or caregivers—who are sometimes termed *significant others.* Playing "mommy" or "daddy" (often putting themselves, literally, in the shoes of a parent) begins to teach children to imagine the world from a parent's point of view.

Gradually, children learn to take the roles of several others at once. This skill lets them move from simple play (say, throwing and catching a ball) involving one other person to *games* involving a web of roles and relationships (such as ice or field hockey) involving many others. By about age seven, most children have the social experience needed to engage in complicated group interchange.

Figure 3–1 on page 62 charts the progression from imitation to play to games. But a final stage in the development of self remains. Games involve dealing with many others in one situation, but social life demands that we see ourselves in terms of cultural norms as *anyone* else might. Mead used the term *generalized other* to refer to widespread cultural norms and values that we use as a reference in evaluating ourselves.

As life goes on, the self continues to change along with our social experiences. But no matter how much events change us, we remain creative beings. Thus, Mead concluded, we play a key role in our own socialization.

George Herbert Mead wrote: "No hard and fast line can be drawn between our own selves and the selves of others." The painting Manyness by Rimman Gerlovina and Valeriy Gerlovin conveys this important truth. Although we tend to think of ourselves as unique individuals, each person's characteristics develop in an ongoing process of interaction with others.

**Critical evaluation.** Mead's work explores the character of social experience itself. In symbolic interaction, Mead found the root of both self and society.

Some critics say Mead's view is completely social, allowing no biological element at all. In this, he stands apart from Freud (who identified general human drives) and Piaget (whose stages of development are tied to biological maturation).

Be careful not to confuse Mead's concepts of the I and the me with Freud's terms id and superego. Freud rooted the id in the biological organism, while Mead rejected any biological element of self (although he never clearly spelled out the origin of the I). Moreover, while the superego and id are locked in continual combat, the I and the me work cooperatively (Meltzer, 1978).

## AGENTS OF SOCIALIZATION

All of the thinkers we have discussed above point to childhood as the crucial time when personality takes shape. However, our personalities also change across the life course as we meet new challenges and interact with different *agents of socialization.* Below we discuss how four agents of socialization transmit culture to members of our society.

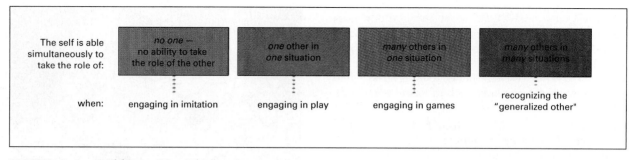

**FIGURE 3–1    Building on Social Experience**

George Herbert Mead described the development of the self as the process of gaining social experience. This is largely the matter of taking the role of the other with increasing sophistication.

## THE FAMILY

For most individuals, the family that they are born into has the greatest impact on socialization. Infants are totally dependent on others, and this responsibility typically falls on biological or adoptive parents and other family members. And at least until children begin school, their family has the job of teaching them skills, values, and beliefs.

Family learning is not all intentional. Children also learn from the kind of environment adults create. Whether children learn to see themselves as strong or weak, intelligent or dull, loved or simply tolerated, and whether they see the world as trustworthy or dangerous, largely depends on their surroundings. Children who find themselves unloved or, worse, abused by one or the other of their parents, or abandoned at an early age, may lack the basic tools needed to form and sustain social relationships. It is difficult to love if one has never known the experience oneself.

Another crucial family function is conferring a social position on children. That is, parents not only bring children into the physical world, but also place them in society in terms of class, religious and political beliefs, race, and ethnicity. In time, these elements of social identity become part of the child's self-concept. Of course, some aspects of social position may change later on but, as discussed throughout this book, social standing at birth affects us throughout our lives.

Why is class position important? Of course, affluent parents typically spend far more materially on their children than do parents of modest means. Moreover, Melvin Kohn (1977) found that middle-class parents tolerate a wide range of behaviour and show greater concern for the intentions and motivation that underlie their children's actions. Working-class parents, by contrast, stress behavioural conformity. But there is no conclusive evidence that poverty or affluence is directly related to the quality of parenting that children receive. Researcher shows that neither rich nor poor Canadians

have a monopoly on child-rearing skills. Rather, children with behaviour problems and low academic achievement come from different economic backgrounds, as do children who perform well socially and academically (Bertrand, McCain, Mustard, & Willms, 1999). Regardless of class background, Bernd Baldus and Verna Tribe (1992) argue that most children by grade six (age 11 years) use social inequality as a criterion to order the world around them. Further, grade six students have by this age learned to acquire cognitive and affective predispositions causing them to think that less economically advantaged persons are likely to be unsuccessful in life or engage in morally questionable behaviour.

Complicating matters still further, gender blends with class in the socialization process. Arlie Hochschild (1983:165) points out that young middle-class girls are taught to "manage their feelings." Girls are taught that they will depend on men for money in adult life. Therefore, displaying more emotion or feeling is a female way of repaying their debt, argues Hochschild, especially through emotional work "that affirms, enhances, and celebrates the well-being and status of others."

## THE SCHOOL

Schooling enlarges children's social world to include people with backgrounds different from their own. In the process, youngsters learn the importance that society attaches to gender and race. Studies document that children tend to cluster in play groups made up of one gender and race (Lever, 1978; Finkelstein & Haskins, 1983).

Schooling teaches children a wide range of knowledge and skills. But schools informally convey other lessons as well. The **hidden curriculum,** *subtle presentations of political or cultural ideas,* imparts important cultural values. Activities such as spelling bees and sports foster the value of competition, while cooperative games encourage the opposite. Children also receive countless informal lessons that their society's way of life is morally good.

School is most children's first experience with bureaucracy. The school day runs on impersonal rules and a strict time schedule. Of course, these are the traits of large organizations that will employ them later in life.

Finally, schools further socialize young people into culturally approved gender roles (Richer, 1979). Raphaela Best (1983) notes that at school, boys engage in more physical activities and spend more time outdoors, while girls tend to be more sedentary, often helping the teacher with various housekeeping chores, such as erasing the chalkboard, sharpening pencils, and so forth (Thorne, 1993).

Gender differences continue through post-secondary education. While gender decisions are changing, women still tend to major in the arts, humanities, or social sciences, while men gravitate toward economics, engineering and computer science, or the natural sciences. Moreover, even for women who enter the traditionally male-dominated professions, such as medicine and law, gender stratification persists both in regard to choice of specialty and income. In brief, women tend to cluster in specialties that are lower paying and more people-oriented (for example, pediatrics or family law), while male colleagues tend to be located in specialties above the "glass ceiling," such as surgery or corporate law (Riska & Wegar, 1993; Reskin & Padavic, 1994; Hagan & Kay, 1995).

## THE PEER GROUP

By the time they enter school, children have also discovered the **peer group**, *a group whose members have interests, social position, and age in common.* Unlike the family and the school, the peer group allows children to escape the direct supervision of adults. Among their peers, children learn how to form relationships on their own. Peer groups also offer the chance to discuss interests that adults may not share (such as clothes and popular music) or tolerate (such as drugs and sex).

In fact, a "generation gap" may separate the attitudes of parents and children. Especially in a rapidly changing society, peer groups often rival parents in influence. For example, the structure of the peer group has been shown as an important factor in trying to understand peer abuse—the abuse of children by children (Ambert, 1995). Relentless teasing by peers—girls as well as boys—can result in brutal beatings, and even murder (such as the 1997 case of 14-year-old Reena Virk of Victoria), or to suicide by the affected youth who is unable to withstand the taunting and other forms of abuse (Alphonso, 2000). The problem is that there is no single cause of bullying at our nation's schools. In

*Parents serve as their children's main role models, transmitting to them a variety of information, including what is and is not appropriate for their gender.*

addition, youth tend to condone bullying or even join in, rather than to speak out against it (Artz, 1998).

Even during adolescence, however, parental influence on children remains strong. While peers may guide short-term choices in dress and music, parents retain more sway over long-term aspirations. For example, one study concluded that parents had more influence than even best friends on young people's educational aspirations (Davies & Kandel, 1981).

Finally, any neighbourhood or school operates as a social mosaic composed of numerous peer groups. As Chapter 5 (Groups and Organizations) explains, members typically perceive their own peer groups in positive groups, then, contribute to socialization as individuals conform to one group while opposing others. In addition, people are often influenced by peer groups that they would like to join as much as by those to which they already belong. Such action represents what sociologists call **anticipatory socialization**, *social learning directed toward gaining a desired position.* In school, for example, young people may mimic the styles and slang of the group they hope will accept them. Or later in life, a young lawyer may conform to the attitudes and behaviour of her firms' partners in order to advance her career.

## THE MASS MEDIA

The **mass media** are *impersonal communications directed to a vast audience.* The term *media* is derived from Latin and means "middle." It indicates that the media serve to connect people. Mass media emerged as communications technology (first newspapers and then, later, radio and television, and increasingly the Internet) spread information on a mass scale.

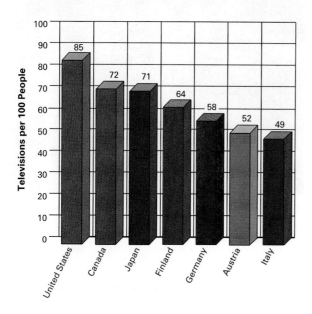

**Figure 3–2    Television Ownership in Global Perspective**

Source: The World Bank (2000).

In Canada, the mass media enormously affect our attitudes and behaviour, making the media central to socialization. Television, introduced in 1939, has rapidly become the dominant medium in North America in particular, although its impact can be felt increasingly around the globe. As Figure 3–2 indicates, the United States boasts a higher rate of television ownership than any other industrial country, with Canada not far behind. Put another way, by 1997 almost all (99 percent) Canadian households owned at least one colour television set and 52 percent of households owned two (Statistics Canada, 1997a).

Just how "glued to the television" are we? The latest statistics show that Canadian viewers watched television an average of 22.3 hours each week in the fall of 1998. Virtually everyone in Canada watches television, but not equally: Figure 3–3 identifies the amount of television viewing by gender and different regions of Canada. Women, French-speaking Quebecers and residents of the Atlantic provinces watched more television than other Canadians.

The British children's show *The Teletubbies* is capturing the attention of the youngest of Canadian infants, accompanied by product merchandising of the shapeless characters with TV screens in their stomachs and electronically generated monosyllabic vocabularies (O'Reilly & Saunders, 1998:A13). At the same time, Pokémon and Digimon compete for the attention of older kids. Canadian children watch television well before they learn to read, and the number of hours of viewing tends to increase with age, exceeding 30 hours per week for those ages 60 and over (Statistics Canada, 1999b).

Comedian Fred Allen once quipped that we call television a "medium" because it is rarely well done. For a variety of reasons, television (like other media) has provoked plenty of criticism. One issue involves alleged bias in television programming. Liberal critics maintain that television shows are conservative in that they rarely challenge the status quo (Gans, 1980; Parenti, 1986). For example, television has traditionally portrayed men in positions of power and women as mothers or subordinates (Cantor & Pingree, 1983; Ang, 1985; Brown, 1990). In addition, although racial and ethnic minorities watch more television than other people, until recently such minorities have been all but absent from programming. The Social Diversity box on page 66 offers an overview of the image of Canadian minorities in the media.

The number of people from minority groups that appear in the mass media has increased mainly because advertisers recognize the marketing advantages of appealing to these large segments of North American society (Wilson & Gutiérrez, 1985). In Canada, the wide popularity of such shows as *This Hour Has 22 Minutes* is a case in point, placing at centre stage representatives from Canada's poorest province to poke fun at our national quirks. On the other side of the debate, conservative critics argue that the television and film industries constitute a liberal "cultural elite," often portraying marginalized groups as "successful" only when they adopt a middle-class lifestyle and values.

A final issue concerns violence and the mass media. In 1996, the American Medical Association (AMA) objected to the violence in the mass media: An AMA survey (1996) found that three-fourths of U.S. adults have either walked out of a movie or turned off television because of too much violence. A more recent national study found that almost two-thirds of television shows contain violence, and that in most scenes characters show no remorse and are not punished (Wilson, 1998).

Like the U.S. television industry, the Canadian industry has moved to control television viewing of violent programming, especially by children. Both countries have adopted a rating system for programs. The Canadian Association of Broadcasters has a "violence code," which it uses to evaluate particular programs for violence content. The voluntary code bans the broadcast of shows containing gratuitous violence of any type, or that condone, encourage, or glamorize violence. As far as children are concerned, the code establishes a cut-off time of 9:00 p.m., prior to which violent programming aimed at adult viewers may not be broadcast.

But larger questions remain: Does viewing sexual or violent programming hurt people as much as critics say it does? More important, why do the mass media contain so much sex and violence in the first place?

In sum, television and other mass media have enriched our lives with entertaining and educational programming. The media also increase our exposure to diverse cultures and provoke discussion of current issues. At the same time, the power of the media—especially television and, more recently, the Internet—to shape how we think remains highly controversial. For example, is the North American phenomenon known as *copycat shooting* caused by the media? Some argue that the vivid portrayal of school shootings on TV, as well as rapid access to graphic details of such events via the Internet, causes other youth to commit parallel crimes.

This argument has recently been made about a shooting at a high school in Taber, a tranquil rural community 175 km southeast of Calgary. A 14-year-old male youth burst into Taber High and killed one student and seriously wounded another with a sawed-off .22-calibre rifle before he was captured and taken into custody. The Taber shooting follows a widely broadcasted shooting in the U.S. state of Colorado that occurred just a week before, when two teenage boys killed 12 classmates and a teacher before committing suicide. The Taber event is said to be a "copycat" of the incident south of the border. In both cases, the killers, who were unpopular with classmates, wore trench coats while committing their crimes.

## SOCIALIZATION AND THE LIFE COURSE

Although childhood has special importance to socialization, learning continues throughout our lives. An overview of the life course reveals that our society organizes human experience according to age—childhood, adolescence, adulthood, and, finally, old age.

### CHILDHOOD

In recent years, the Nike corporation, maker of popular athletic shoes, has come under fire. Their shoes are made in Taiwan and Indonesia, in many cases by children working in factories rather than going to school. In all, some 200 million of the world's children work full time, earning about 50 cents per hour (Gibbs, 1996). Global Map 3–1 on page 67 shows that child labour is most common in nations of Africa and Asia.

Criticism of Nike springs from the fact that most North Americans think of *childhood*—roughly the first 12 years of life—as a carefree time of learning and play.

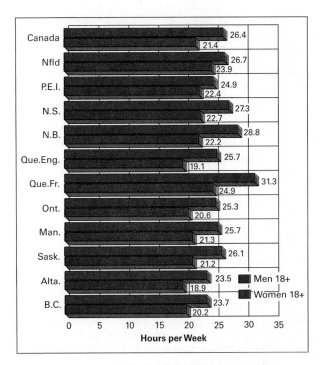

**FIGURE 3–3    Television Viewing by Gender—Canada and Provinces, 1998**

Source: Statistics Canada (2000b).

Yet childhood is a varying concept. Canadian sociologist Anthony Synnott shows how culture determines the image of children—varying from "little devils" or "little angels" to "little workers" or "a sacred trust" (Synnott, 1983). Historical time also shapes visions of childhood. Historian Philippe Ariès (1965) explains that in medieval Europe, as soon as children could survive without constant care, they were viewed as "little adults" and expected to fend for themselves. Adolescence as we know it did not exist as a stage in the life course. This meant that by age six or seven, poor children worked long and hard, just as adults did.

The notion of children toiling for long hours may be startling because our common sense suggests that youngsters are very different from adults—biologically immature and inexperienced. But much of this difference is rooted in society, not biology. Because high-income societies are more affluent, children can be freed from the burdens of work. In addition, societies with sophisticated technology extend childhood to allow time for young people to learn the complex skills required of adults. Thus we define children and adults in contrasting ways, with "irresponsible" children looked after by "responsible" adults (Benedict, 1938). From a global perspective, however, this pattern does not always hold true. The traits assigned to childhood—and even the recognition of this stage of life—are one variable dimension of culture.

# Minority Identity in Movies and Television

Visible minorities and Aboriginals are included more and more frequently in our popular media, including movies and television. But is this a reflection of a real change in societal understanding? Have the media given us genuine insight into what it is like to be a first-generation immigrant from China or India? Have minority actors really succeeded in changing the dominant group's image of race? And have minority producers succeeded in breaking through the formidable barriers of Eurocentrism to explore ethnic identities from a minority perspective?

Media observers note that we have indeed moved away from the savage and marginalized characters of yesterday's films to multifaceted representations in such popular Canadian TV shows as *The Beachcombers* and, more recently, *North of 60*. But is this a sign of more to come, or are the recent examples merely exceptions that detract from the overall criticism articulated by Thomas Builds-the-Fire in the movie *Smoke Signals*: "The only thing more pathetic than an Indian on TV is an Indian watching an Indian on TV."

Allan Smith (1996) argues that on the face of it, we are witnessing a revolutionary change in how most Canadians view minorities, particularly Aboriginals, in the media. A more open and multidimensional view of an increasingly assertive minority is emerging. Nevertheless, Smith maintains that "while European-descended groups may not be as resistant to seeing what is around them as they once were, they still remain some distance from a fully engaged [quoting Charles Taylor, 1992] 'politics of recognition.'"

After analyzing the evolving imaging of Aboriginals and minorities in Canadian and U.S. film and television, Smith notes that while their portrayal is not as simplistic as it has been in the past, it is nevertheless not clear that there have been fundamental changes. For one thing, minorities still have only limited access to the resources that media production requires, and distrib-

utors are still reluctant to carry authentic minority products to the larger market.

What, then, does the future hold? Not much change for the moment, says Smith, especially in a country such as Canada, where our need to define ourselves as one nation remains paramount (at least to the federal politicians), and where negotiation and adjustment are the main strategies for moving forward.

Yet perhaps not everyone will agree. Lorne Cardinal, who plays Big Bear's less-than-admirable son in the CBC miniseries *Big Bear* that aired in January 1999, maintains that the series is different from the typical cowboys-and-Indians dramas about "taming the West" and "civilizing the Natives." In most of these movies, according to Cardinal, the typical signal for him to appear on the scene is, "Okay, we're ready. Send out the Indians." Cardinal says that the opposite is the case with *Big Bear*: "On this set . . . they say, 'Send out the white guys'" (Dafoe, 1998: C1). At the same time, *North of 60* continues to be popular among Aboriginals, which is perhaps the surest gauge as to whether the media has succeeded in capturing minority points of view.

What do you think? Has the mass media improved its portrayal of minorities in Canada?

## ADOLESCENCE

As industrialization created childhood as a distinct stage of life, adolescence emerged as a buffer between childhood and adulthood. We generally link adolescence, or the teenage years, with emotional and social turmoil, as parents spar with young people who are trying to develop their own identities. Here again, we are tempted to attribute teenage turbulence to the biological changes of puberty. But this turmoil more correctly reflects cultural inconsistency. For example,

the mass media glorify sex and schools hand out condoms, even as parents urge restraint. Consider, too, that an 18-year-old male may face the adult duty of going to war, but he may lack the adult right to drink alcohol. In short, adolescence is a time of social contradictions: People are no longer children but neither are they adults.

Finally, like all stages of the life course, adolescence varies according to social background. Young people from working-class families commonly work part time while in high school and many, especially males, drop out altogether and move directly to the

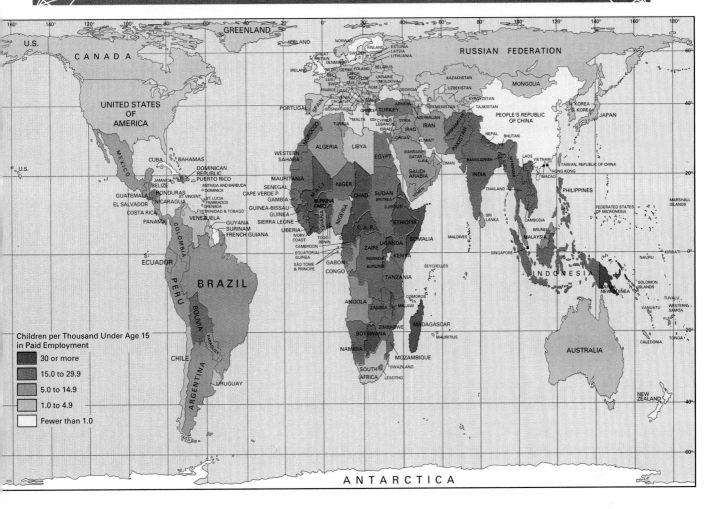

**GLOBAL MAP 3–1  Child Labour in Global Perspective**

Industrialization prolongs childhood and discourages children from engaging in work and other activities deemed suitable only for adults. Thus child labour is relatively uncommon in Canada and other high-income countries. In low-income countries of the world, however, children form a vital economic asset, and they typically begin working as soon as they are able to do so.

Source: *Peters Atlas of the World* (1990).

adult world of work and parenthood (Tanner, Krahn, & Hartnagel, 1995). Those from wealthier families, however, have privileged access to an "endless adolescence." They typically attend university, and perhaps even graduate school, until they are well into the late twenties or even thirties (Skolnick, 1996).

## ADULTHOOD

Adulthood, which begins between the late teens and early twenties depending on social background, is the

time of life when most accomplishments occur. Having completed their schooling, people embark on careers and raise families of their own. Personalities are now largely formed, although marked change in a person's environment—such as unemployment, divorce, or serious illness—may result in significant change to the self.

During early adulthood—until about age 40—young adults learn to manage for themselves a host of day-to-day responsibilities, often juggling conflicting priorities and demands on time from parents, partner, children, and work (Levinson et al., 1978). Women,

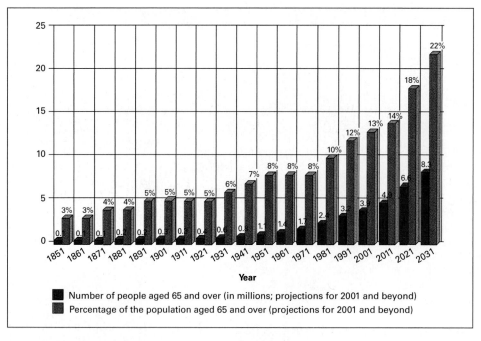

**FIGURE 3–4 The Greying of the Canadian Population**

Source: Statistics Canada (1994a).

especially, face the realization that "doing it all" can be extremely taxing: Our culture assigns them primary responsibility for child rearing and household chores, even if they work outside the home. Women in Canada find themselves occupied by an unending series of "family shifts" (Eichler, 1997) that result in little leisure and in chronic sleep deprivation. It should be noted, however, that access to public services such as quality child care (available, for example, in France and Sweden) has been shown to significantly reduce women's second shift of unpaid caring work in the home (Baker, 1995).

In middle adulthood—roughly between the ages of 40 and 60—people sense that their life circumstances are pretty well set. They also become more aware of the fragility of health, which the young typically take for granted. Women who have spent many years raising a family can find middle adulthood especially trying. Children grow up and require less attention, husbands become absorbed in their careers, leaving some women with spaces in their lives that are difficult to fill. Many women who divorce during middle adulthood also face serious financial problems (Weitzman, 1985, 1996). For all these reasons, an increasing number of women in middle adulthood return to school and seek new careers.

For everyone, growing older means facing physical decline, a prospect our culture makes more painful for

women. Because good looks are considered more important for women, wrinkles, added weight, and hair loss can be traumatic. Men, of course, have their own particular difficulties as they grow older. Some must admit that they are never going to reach their career goals. Others realize that the price of career success has been neglect of family or personal health (Farrell & Rosenberg, 1981; Wolf, 1990).

## OLD AGE

Old age comprises the later years of adulthood and the final stage of life, beginning about the mid-sixties. As Figure 3–4 shows, about one in nine members of our society is over the age of 65, so that there are now almost as many elderly as there are teenagers. By 2031, the proportion of the population aged 65 and over will have increased to almost one-quarter of the whole. The "oldest old"—people age 85 and over—are the fastest-growing segment of our population.

The "greying of Canada" will have consequences for everyone. More people will depend on our pension programs, health facilities will be increasingly burdened, and elderly people will be more prominent in all aspects of everyday life—although the impact may vary in different parts of Canada, as National Map 3–1 illustrates. Many middle-aged people (especially women) already think of themselves as a "sandwich

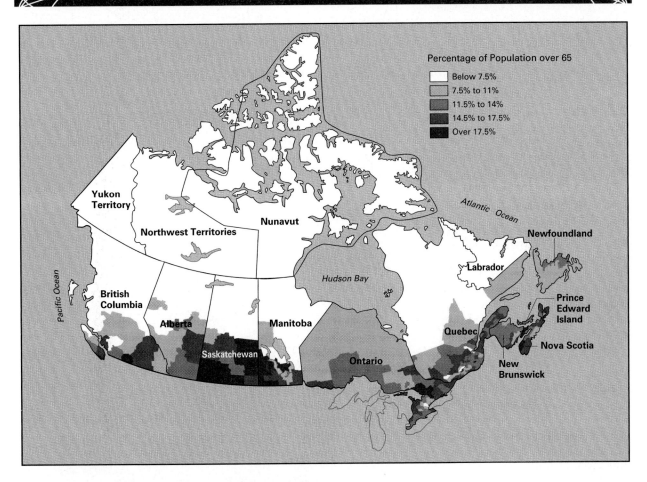

Percentage of Population over 65

Below 7.5%
7.5% to 11%
11.5% to 14%
14.5% to 17.5%
Over 17.5%

**NATIONAL MAP 3–1   Aging across Canada, 1996**

The aging of the population is largely a southern phenomenon. Even though we associate Victoria alone with the phrase "Newlyweds and Nearly Deads," the map shows that the concentration of those over age 65 is also high on the Prairies and north of Toronto. Which do you think primarily determines this pattern—social forces or individual choices?

Source: Based on Statistics Canada, 1998b.

generation," because they will spend as much time caring for dependent aging parents as they did for their dependent young children. The Critical Thinking box on page 70 provides a closer look.

The greying of the population of high-income nations has sparked the growth of the relatively new field of **gerontology** (from the Greek word *geron*, meaning "old person"), which is *the study of aging and the elderly*. Gerontologists study both the physical and social dimensions of growing old.

**Aging and biology.**   For most of our population, grey hair, wrinkles, and declining vitality begin in middle age. After about age 50, bones become more brittle so that injuries take longer to heal, and the risks of chronic illnesses (such as arthritis and diabetes) and life-threatening conditions (such as heart disease and cancer) rise steadily. Sensory abilities—taste, sight, touch, smell, and especially hearing—become less keen with age (Colloway & Dollevoet, 1977; Treas, 1995).

Even so, the bigger picture shows that most elderly people are not physically disabled. Only 1 in 10 reports trouble walking, and 1 in 20 requires the intensive care provided by a hospital or nursing home. No more than 1 percent of the elderly are bedridden. Overall, certainly, health declines with age. Nevertheless, for

# CRITICAL THINKING

# The Sandwich Generation:
# Who Should Care For Aging Parents?

Defining the sandwich generation as those between the ages of 25 and 54, with at least one child living at home and one surviving parent over age 64, a Statistics Canada study (2000m) investigated the characteristics of this group of people. According to the study, the sandwich generation comprises a relatively large group of people in some age groups, yet only a small proportion of the total population. Nearly one million—15 percent—of women in Canada in this age range care for children and provide care or assistance to a senior. By contrast, only 9 percent of males in this age range provide such care at both ends of the life cycle.

It is predicted that the number of Canadians with both children at home and parents over the age of 65 will continue to grow, at least until the baby boomers have retired (Statistics Canada, 1994b).

As the baby boomers stop working, their relatively low fertility may begin to haunt them—they have few children to assist them in old age.

So who should support the elderly? There are at least three possibilities: the elderly themselves, the elderly's adult children, and the government. Historically, the elderly have taken pri-

mary responsibility for their own welfare. Yet, this has often meant living in poverty, particularly for elderly females.

The duties of parents toward their young children are relatively clear compared with the obligations of children to aging parents. Many adult children simply do not have the resources—financial or emotional—to handle this often demanding caregiver role.

The greying of the Canadian population in the decades ahead means a rise

in the total social costs of supporting the elderly. With fewer adult children to meet this need, governments will be under increased pressure. Even though the sandwich generation is not a new phenomenon, the current regime of fiscal restraint will force us all to make some hard decisions.

Sources: Callahan (1987); Dumas (1994); Gelman (1985); Institute for Philosophy and Public Policy (1988); Statistics Canada (2000m); Stone, Cafferata, & Sangl (1987).

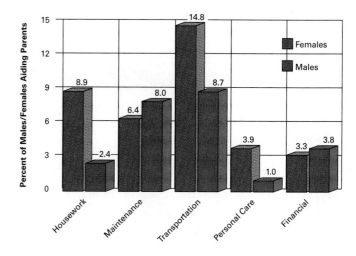

**FIGURE 3–5    Sandwich Generation—Aid to Parents, by Gender, Canada, 1990**

Source: Dumas (1994).

those over 65, only 5.4 percent of women living in a private household and 6.7 percent of male counterparts described their health as poor in 1997 (Statistics Canada, 2000m).

**Aging and Culture.** Culture shapes how we understand growing old. In low-income countries, old age gives people great influence and respect because they control the most land and have wisdom gained over a

lifetime (Sheehan, 1976; Hareven, 1982). A pre-industrial society, then, is usually a **gerontocracy**, *a form of social organization in which the elderly have the most wealth, power, and privileges.*

But industrialization lessens the social standing of the elderly. Older people typically live apart from their grown children, and rapid social change renders much of what seniors know obsolete, at least from the point of view of the young. A problem of industrial societies,

*The reality of growing old is as much a matter of culture as it is of biology. In the United States, being elderly is often synonymous with being inactive; yet, in Greece and other more traditional countries, old people commonly continue many familiar routines.*

therefore, is **ageism**, *prejudice and discrimination against the elderly.*

For all these reasons, growing old in Canada is a challenging experience. Earlier in life, growing older means entering new roles and taking on fresh responsibilities. The journey into old age, however, follows the opposite path: leaving behind roles that have provided social identity and prestige. Although retirement sometimes fits the common image of restful recreation after years of employment, it can also pull men and women out of familiar routines, so that they lose the self-worth derived from co-workers and sometimes suffer outright boredom.

Aging may mean living with diminished income. Financially, however, the Canadian elderly population as a whole is doing better than ever. The rate of poverty among the elderly, as measured by Statistics Canada's low-income cut-offs, has declined from about 34 percent in 1980, to 18.7 percent in 1997 (Statistics Canada, 2000m). Since 1994, in fact, poverty has been lower among the elderly than among those under 18. Put otherwise, a generation ago, old age carried the highest risk of poverty; today, childhood holds that unfortunate distinction (Ross et al., 2000).

Why the change? For one thing, better health helps today's older people earn more. In addition, pension programs are easing the financial burden on those who have retired.

Still, for most people in Canada, retirement leads to a significant decline in income. For many, home mortgages and children's university expenses are paid off; yet the expenses from some medical and dental care, household help, and home utilities typically rise. Many elderly people do not have sufficient savings or pension benefits to be self-supporting; for this reason, various pension programs, including the Canada Pension Plan, are their greatest source of income. Many retirees live with fixed incomes, so inflation tends to affect them more severely than it does younger working people. Women and visible minorities are especially likely to find that growing old means growing poorer (Statistics Canada, 2000m).

The shift in poverty away from the elderly and toward children may continue, given the increasing number—and political clout—of those ages 65 and older. A reasonable question, in light of this windfall for the elderly, is whether we should continue to favour the oldest members of our society and risk slighting the youngest—those who now suffer most from poverty. But Canadian researchers warn that we should be careful not to "oversell" population aging. While a definite challenge to policy makers, it is unlikely that the greying of the Canadian population will destroy the fabric of Canadian society or lead to other apocalyptic scenarios (Gee & Gutman, 2000).

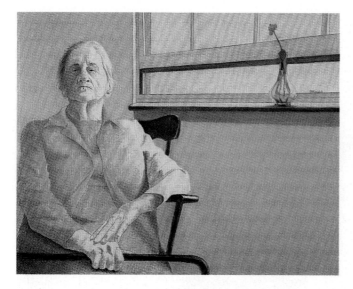

*Various categories of people experience the stages of the life course in distinctive ways. Most men, for example, pass through old age with the support of a partner. Women, who typically outlive men, endure much of their old age alone, a reality poignantly captured in G.G. Kopliak's painting Still Life.*

## SOCIALIZATION ACROSS THE LIFE COURSE: AN OVERVIEW

This brief examination of the life course leads to two general conclusions. First, although the essential traits of each stage of life—from infancy to old age—are linked to the biological process of aging, they are also socially constructed. For this reason, people in one society may experience a stage of life quite differently from those in another. Second, each phase of the life course presents characteristic problems and transitions that involve learning something new and, in many cases, unlearning what has become familiar.

Keep in mind, too, that the experience of growing older varies according to class, race, ethnicity, and gender. Thus, the general patterns we have described are all subject to modification as they apply to various categories of people.

Finally, people's life experiences also vary depending on when, in the history of a society, they were born. A **cohort** is *a category of people with a common characteristic, usually their age.* Age cohorts are likely to have been influenced by the same major events and thus display similar reactions to particular issues (Riley, Foner, & Waring, 1988). Most of today's university faculty, for example, grew up during an era of economic expansion that fuelled optimism about the future, an attitude that is far less characteristic of today's younger and recession-weary students. To take another example, in contrast to their grandmothers who tended to exit the workforce during their childbearing years, most young women in Canada today take for granted that they will have continuous careers spanning their adult lives.

## RESOCIALIZATION: TOTAL INSTITUTIONS

A final type of socialization involves people being confined—often against their will—in boot camps for young offenders, adult prisons, mental hospitals, and other total institutions, such as orphanages. This is the special world of a **total institution**, *a setting in which individuals are isolated from the rest of society and manipulated by an administrative staff.*

According to Erving Goffman (1961), total institutions have three distinctive characteristics. First, staff members supervise all spheres of daily life, including where residents (often called "inmates") eat, sleep, and work. Second, the environment of a total institution is highly standardized, with institutional food, uniforms, and one set of activities for everyone. Third, rules and schedules dictate when, where, and how inmates perform their daily routines.

The purpose of such regimentation is **resocialization**, *radically altering an inmate's personality through carefully controlling the environment.* Prisons and mental hospitals physically isolate inmates behind fences, barred windows, and locked doors, and control their access to the telephone, mail, and visitors. Cut off in this way, the institution is the inmate's entire world, making it easier for the staff to produce lasting change—or at least immediate compliance—in the inmate.

Resocialization is a two-part process. First, the staff breaks down a new inmate's existing identity using what Goffman (1961:14) describes as "abasements, degradations, humiliations, and profanations of self." For example, an inmate must surrender personal

*The penal system's requirement that new inmates suffer the indignity of having their heads shaved is more than a matter of hairstyle; such a degrading ritual is also the first stage in the process by which a total institution attempts to break down an individual's established social identity.*

possessions including clothing and grooming articles normally used to maintain a distinctive appearance. Instead, the staff provides standard-issue clothes so that everyone will look alike. The staff subjects new inmates to "mortifications of self," including searches, medical examinations, fingerprinting, and then assigns each a serial number. Once inside the walls, individuals also give up their privacy as guards routinely monitor their living quarters.

In the second part of the resocialization process, the staff tries to build a new self in the inmate through a system of rewards and punishments. Having a book to read, watching television, or accessing the Internet may seem trivial to the outsider, but in the rigid environment of the total institution, these simple priv-

ileges can be a powerful motivator to conform. In the end, the length of incarceration typically depends on how well the inmate cooperates with the staff.

Resocialization can bring about considerable change in an inmate, but total institutions affect people in different ways. While some inmates are considered "rehabilitated" or "recovered," others may change little, and still others may become hostile and bitter. Furthermore, over a long period of time, the rigidly controlled environment can leave some *institutionalized*, without the capacity for independent living.

But what of the rest of us? Does socialization crush our individuality or empower us? The Controversy & Debate box on page 74 takes a closer look at this vital question.

# Are Canadians Free within Society?

Throughout this chapter, we have stressed one key theme: Society through its agents (family, schools, peers, the mass media) shapes how we think, feel, and act. If this is so, then in what sense are we free?

Sociologists speak with many voices when addressing this question. One response is that individuals are *not* free of society—in fact, as social creatures, we never could be. But if we are condemned to live in a society with power over us, it is important to do what we can to make our home as just as possible. That is, we should work to lessen class differences and other barriers to opportunity for visible minorities and women. Another approach is that we *are* free because society can never dictate our dreams. Our history as a country—right from early settlement to the present—is one story after another of individuals pursuing personal goals in spite of great challenges. This argument says that individual efforts rather than progressive govern-ment social policies result in the greatest freedom for citizens.

We find both attitudes in George Herbert Mead's analysis of socialization. Mead recognized that society makes demands on us, sometimes setting itself before us as a barrier. But he also reminded us that human beings are spontaneous and creative, capable of continually acting back—individually and collectively—on society. Thus Mead noted the power of society while still affirming the human capacity to evaluate, criticize, and, ultimately, to choose and to change. A large number of children around the world are trapped into circumstances beyond their choosing, and often face lives of abuse and neglect. But some—though not all—manage to survive and sometimes flourish, emotionally, socially, and intellectually. In these more positive life histories, certain children with a deep inner drive and initiative also tend to be helped by significant others who are willing to lend economic and emotional support on a sustained basis. As Bonnie Leadbeater and Niobe Way (1996) note about inner-city adolescent girls, some are able to resist dominant stereotypes of them as sexually promiscuous, impoverished, and uneducated, create new positive identities for themselves, and take control of their lives.

In the end, we are both socialized into who we become as human beings and yet are also able to change the world around us. As anthropologist Margaret Mead once mused, "Do not make the mistake of thinking that concerned people cannot change the world; it's the only thing that ever has."

*Continue the debate...*

1. *Do you think our society affords more freedom to males than to females? Why or why not?*

2. *What about modern, industrial countries compared to traditional, agrarian nations: Are some of the world's people more free than others?*

3. *How does an understanding of sociology enhance personal freedom? Why?*

## SUMMARY

1. Socialization is the way individuals develop their humanity and particular identities. Through socialization, one generation transmits culture to the next.

2. A century ago, people thought most human behaviour was guided by biological instinct. Today, we recognize that human behaviour results mostly from nurture rather than nature.

3. The permanently damaging effects of social isolation reveal that social experience is essential to human development.

4. Sigmund Freud's model of human personality had three parts. The id expresses innate human needs or drives (the life and death instincts); the superego represents internalized cultural values and norms; the ego resolves competition between the demands of the id and restraints of the superego.

5. Jean Piaget believed that human development reflects both biological maturation and increasing social experience. He identified four stages of cognitive development: sensorimotor, preoperational, concrete operational, and formal operational.

6. Lawrence Kohlberg applied Piaget's approach to moral development. Individuals first judge rightness in preconventional terms, according to their individual needs. Next, conventional moral reasoning takes account of parents' attitudes and cultural norms. Finally, postconventional moral reasoning allows people to criticize society itself.

7. Carol Gilligan discovered that while males rely on abstract standards of rightness, females look at the effect of decisions on interpersonal relationships.

8. To George Herbert Mead, social experience generates the self, which Mead characterized as partly autonomous (the I) and partly guided by society (the me). Infants engage in imitation; children engage in play and games, and eventually recognize the "generalized other."

9. Charles Horton Cooley used the term "looking-glass self" to explain that we see ourselves as we imagine others see us.

10. Usually the first setting of socialization, the family is the greatest influence on a child's attitudes and behaviour.

11. Schools expose children to greater social diversity and introduce them to impersonal performance evaluations.

12. Peer groups free children from adult supervision and take on special significance during adolescence.

13. The mass media, especially television and more recently the Internet, also shape the socialization process. The average Canadian child now spends more time watching television than attending school or interacting with parents.

14. Each stage of the life course—from childhood to old age—is socially constructed in ways that vary from society to society.

15. Total institutions such as prisons, boot camps for young offenders, and mental hospitals try to resocialize inmates—that is, to radically change their personalities.

16. Socialization demonstrates the power of society to shape our thoughts, feelings, and actions. Yet, as humans, we have the ability to "act back," shaping both ourselves and our social world.

## KEY CONCEPTS

**socialization** (p. 55) the lifelong social experience by which individuals develop their human potential and learn culture

**personality** (p. 55) a person's fairly consistent patterns of acting, thinking, and feeling

**id** (p. 58) Freud's term for the human being's basic drives

**ego** (p. 58) Freud's term for a person's conscious attempts to balance the pleasure-seeking drives of the human organism and the demands of society

**superego** (p. 58) Freud's term for the presence of culture within the individual in the form of internalized values and norms

**sensorimotor stage** (p. 58) Piaget's term for the level of development in which individuals experience the world only through sensory contact

**preoperational stage** (p. 58) Piaget's term for the level of development in which individuals first use language and other symbols

**concrete operational stage** (p. 59) Piaget's term for the level of development in which individuals perceive causal connections in their surroundings

**formal operational stage** (p. 59) Piaget's term for the level of development in which individuals think abstractly and critically

**self** (p. 60) George Herbert Mead's term for that part of an individual's personality composed of self-awareness and self-image

**looking-glass self** (p. 61) Charles Horton Cooley's term referring to a conception of self based on how we suppose others see us

**hidden curriculum** (p. 62) Subtle presentations of political or cultural ideas

**peer group** (p. 63) a group whose members have interests, social position, and age in common

**anticipatory socialization** (p. 63) social learning directed toward gaining a desired position

**mass media** (p. 63) impersonal communications directed to a vast audience

**gerontology** (p. 69) the study of aging and the elderly

**gerontocracy** (p. 70) a form of social organization in which the elderly have the most wealth, power, and privileges

**ageism** (p. 71) prejudice and discrimination against the elderly

**cohort** (p. 72) a category of people with a common characteristic, usually their age

**total institution** (p. 72) a setting in which individuals are isolated from the rest of society and manipulated by an administrative staff

**resocialization** (p. 72) deliberate socialization intended to radically alter an individual's personality

## CRITICAL-THINKING QUESTIONS

1. What do cases of social isolation teach us about the importance of social experience to human beings?

2. State the two sides of the "nature–nurture" debate. In what sense are human nature and nurture not opposed to one another?

3. We have all seen young children place their hands in front of their faces and exclaim, "You can't see me!" They assume that if they cannot see you, you cannot see them. What does this behaviour suggest about a young child's ability to "take the role of the other"? Can a parent expect a young child to "see things from *my* point of view"?

4. Discuss the pros and cons of the statement "The media causes crime," in light of the recent copycat shootings in high schools in Canada and the United States.

## APPLICATIONS AND EXERCISES

1. Work with several members of your sociology class and gather some data by asking several classmates and friends to name traits they consider elements of "human nature." Then compare notes and discuss the extent to which these traits are the product of "nature" or "nurture."

2. Find a copy of the book or video *Lord of the Flies*, a tale by William Golding based on a Freudian model of personality. Jack (and his hunters) represent the power of the id; Piggy consistently opposes them as the superego; Ralph stands between the two as the ego, the voice of reason. Golding was inspired to write the book by participating in the bloody D-Day landing in France during the Second World War. Do you agree with his belief that violence is part of human nature?

3. Make a list of the personality traits you think characterize you. If you have the courage, ask several others who know you well what they think. Can you explain where these traits came from?

4. Watch several hours of prime time programming on network or cable television. Keep track of all the violence you see. Assign each program a "YIP rating," for the number of Years In Prison a person would serve for committing all the violent acts you witnessed (Fobes, 1996). On the basis of observing this small (and unrepresentative) sample of programs, what are your conclusions?

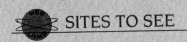 SITES TO SEE

**www.pearsoned.ca/macionis**

Pearson Education Canada and the authors provide a Web site that accompanies this text, offering outlines, review material, learning exercises, and practice tests for each chapter. At the main page, simply click on the cover of your book and follow the easy menus.

**www.macionis.com**
**(or www.TheSociologyPage.com)**

At the author's Web site, you can find brief biographies of George Herbert Mead and Charles Horton Cooley, as well as other sociologists.

**www.nypsa.org**

Learn more about Sigmund Freud and his work at the *FreudNet* site.

**www.piaget.org**

The Jean Piaget Society hosts this Web site, which presents the work of the celebrated social psychologist.

**www.nd.edu/~rbarger/kohlberg.html**

This Web site is dedicated to the ideas and research of Lawrence Kohlberg.

# SOCIAL INTERACTION IN EVERYDAY LIFE

*Harold and Sybil are on their way to another couple's home in an unfamiliar district of their city. They are now late because, for the past 20 minutes, they have travelled in circles looking for their destination. Harold, gripping the wheel ever tighter, is doing a slow burn. Sybil, sitting next to him, looks straight ahead, afraid to utter a word. Both realize that the evening is off to a bad start (Tannen, 1990:62).*

*There is more to this everyday situation than meets the eye. Harold and Sybil are lost in more ways than one, unable to understand why they grow enraged at their situation and at each other.*

*Consider the predicament from Harold's point of view. Like many men, Harold cannot tolerate getting lost. The longer he drives around, the more incompetent he feels. Sybil is seething, too, but for a different reason. She cannot figure out why Harold does not simply pull over and ask someone where the address is. If she were driving, she fumes to herself, they already would have arrived.*

*Why don't many men like to ask for directions? Because they value their independence, men are uncomfortable asking for help (and also reluctant to accept it). To ask someone for assistance is an admission of inadequacy and an acknowledgment that others know something they don't. If it takes Harold a few more minutes to find the address on his own, and secure his self-respect in the process, he thinks the bargain is a good one.*

*Yet it would be wrong to conclude that all men are like Howard. Though such easy generalizations are often made about men, part of the problem, says Gail Sheehy, is*

*that we don't understand "men's passages" very well. Sheehy (1998:52) argues that just as women desire autonomy and opportunities to gain independence, so too do men have a basic need for "intimacy—human closeness—that becomes more persistent as a man grows older." In sum, in day-to-day interaction with their partners, as well as with their children and significant others, men and women are continuously reconstructing themselves in multiple ways.* ■

The focus of this chapter is analyzing examples of interaction in everyday life. We begin by presenting many of the building blocks of common experience, and proceed to explore the almost magical way in which face-to-face interaction generates reality. The central concept throughout is **social interaction**, which may be defined as *the process by which people act and react in relation to others.* Social interaction is the key to creating the changing reality we perceive. And we interact according to particular social guidelines.

## SOCIAL STRUCTURE: A GUIDE TO EVERYDAY LIVING

Monday, September 8, 1998—Åbo, Finland
It is shortly before 8 a.m. when we
arrive at Folkhälsans Daghem (day care

79

*In any rigidly ranked setting, no interaction can proceed until people assess each other's social standing. Thus military personnel wear clear insignia to designate their level of authority. Don't we size up one another in much the same way in routine interactions—noting a person's rough age, quality of clothing, and manner—for clues about social position?*

centre) for the first time. We help our daughter discard her outside wear and change from sneakers to slippers at the space already labelled with her name. The other children are washing their hands—part of the arrival routine—and, eager to fit into her new environment, our daughter follows suit. Seated at two small square tables are a dozen or so children aged three to six, peacefully eating their breakfast with their non-parental caregivers. As Canadians, we used to attend to our daughter's dietary needs at day care ourselves—packed lunches and a snack. The communal arrangement seems very strange (and appealing) to us. We are all the more amazed to learn that Finnish law requires that all day care children be given a daily breakfast, hot lunch, and afternoon snack free of charge! When we pick our daughter up at the end of the day, we notice that she is the last one there at 4:30 p.m. Eager to fit in ourselves, we soon adjust our daily schedule and start to pick our daughter up around 4 p.m., as do the other parents.

Members of every society rely on social structure to make sense out of everyday situations. As one family's introduction to the child care system in Finland suggests, what is taken for granted in one society can seem "unfamiliar" and "strange" in another. So what, then, are the building blocks of our daily lives?

## STATUS

One building block of social organization is **status**, *a recognized social position that an individual occupies.* Sociologists do not use the term *status* in its everyday meaning of "prestige," as when a bank president has more "status" than a bank teller. Sociologically, however, both "president" and "teller" are higher statuses or positions within the bank organization.

Every status is part of our social identity and defines our relationship to others. In the college classroom, for example, professors and students have distinct, well-defined responsibilities. Of course, we each occupy many statuses at once. The term **status set** refers to *all the statuses a person holds at a particular time.* A teenage girl is a *daughter* to her parents, a *sister* to her brother, a *student* at her college, and a *goalie* to others on her hockey team. Status sets branch out in many directions, and also change over the life course. A child turns into a parent, a student becomes a lawyer, and people marry to become husbands and wives (sometimes becoming single again as a result of divorce or death). Joining an organization or finding a job enlarges our status set; retirement or withdrawing from activities makes it smaller. Over a lifetime, individuals gain and lose dozens of statuses.

### ASCRIBED AND ACHIEVED STATUS

Sociologists analyze statuses in terms of how people attain them. An **ascribed status** is *a social position a person receives at birth or assumes involuntarily later in life.* Examples of ascribed statuses are being a daughter, an Aboriginal, a teenager, or a widower. All ascribed statuses are matters about which people have little or no choice.

By contrast, an **achieved status** refers to *a social position that a person assumes voluntarily and that reflects personal ability and choice.* Achieved statuses include being an honours student, an Olympic athlete, a punk

*Role models teach us that any one person can truly make a difference for our world. In December 1955, the driver of a city bus in Montgomery, Alabama, asked Rosa Parks to give up her seat, as required by law, so a white man could sit down. She refused—and was arrested, fingerprinted, and later fined $14 for the offence. This courageous act prompted Birmingham's African-American population to boycott city buses, leading to the repeal of the bus segregation law.*

rocker, a born-again Christian, a computer programmer, or a drug dealer.

In practice, of course, most statuses involve a combination of ascription and achievement. That is, people's ascribed statuses influence the statuses they achieve. People who achieve the status of chief executive officer (CEO) of a national bank, for example, are likely to have been born into relatively privileged families and tend to be male. By the same token, many less desirable statuses, such as homeless person, drug addict, welfare recipient, or sex worker, are more easily "achieved" by people disadvantaged by ascription. Concerning the latter, Brock (1998:13) writes, "Prostitution is not so different from other jobs that women do in a social formation where race, class and gender, rather than individual choice and initiative, are the primary determinants of the kind of work one does."

## MASTER STATUS

Some statuses matter more than others. A **master status** is *a social position with exceptional importance for identity, often shaping a person's entire life.* In high-income societies, a person's occupation often functions as a master status because it indicates a great deal about his or her social background, education, and income. No doubt, this is why adults typically introduce themselves by stating their occupations along with their names. Similarly, being "an Eaton" or "a Bronfman" is enough by itself to push an individual into the Canadian limelight.

In a negative sense, life-threatening or contagious diseases also operate as a master status. Sometimes even lifelong friends avoid cancer patients or people with acquired immune deficiency syndrome (AIDS) simply because of the illness. Gender, too, often serves as a master status. For instance, women, whatever their

abilities, are in many societies viewed as creating chaos, or even as polluting the public realm, unless they are veiled and fully robed (Ertuk, 1991).

Finally, sometimes people's physical disabilities become their master status because they are perceived by others only in terms of their impairments. Many people tend to think of those with disabilities as child-like, asexual, or different in some fundamental sense (Orlansky & Heward, 1981; Cassidy et al., 1998).

## ROLE

A second component of social interaction is **role**, *behaviour expected of someone who holds a particular status.* Individuals *hold* a status and *perform* a role (Linton, 1937). Holding the status of student, for example, leads one to attend classes and complete assignments, and, more broadly, devote much of one's time to personal enrichment through academic study.

Both statuses and roles vary by culture. In Canada, the status "uncle" refers to a sibling of either one's mother or father; in Vietnam and Sweden, by contrast, specific terms designate uncles on each side of the family, and responsibilities differ accordingly. In every society, too, actual role performance varies according to an individual's unique personality, although high-income countries such as Canada permit more individual latitude than do traditional societies.

Because we occupy many statuses simultaneously—a status set—everyday life is a mix of multiple roles. Robert Merton (1968) introduced the term **role set** to identify *a number of roles attached to a single status.*

Figure 4–1 on page 82 depicts four statuses of one individual, each linked to a different role set. First, the woman occupies the status of "wife," with a "conjugal role" (as confidante and sexual partner) toward her

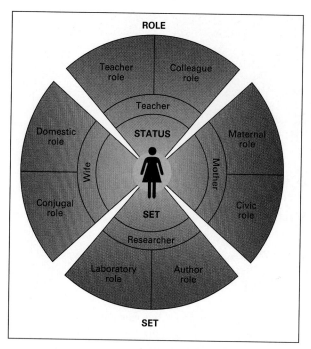

**FIGURE 4–1   Status Set and Role Set**

husband, with whom she would share a "domestic role" toward the household. Second, she also holds the status of "mother," with routine responsibilities for her children (the "maternal role") as well as obligations to their school and other organizations (the "civic role"). Third, as a professor, she interacts with students (the "teacher role") as well as her colleagues (the "colleague role"). Fourth, her work as a researcher (the "laboratory role") generates the data she uses in her publications (the "author role").

A global perspective reveals that the key roles people use to define their lives differ significantly from society to society. In low-income countries, for example, most people work in agriculture, and have few of the occupational choices enjoyed by members of high-income societies. Another dimension of difference is housework. As Global Map 4–1 shows, especially in low-income nations of the world, responsibility for housework falls heavily on women. By contrast, in the high-income country of Finland, where women currently make up 49 percent of the labour force, men are much more apt to share housework with their female partners.

## ROLE CONFLICT AND ROLE STRAIN

Canadians routinely juggle a host of responsibilities demanded by their various statuses and roles. As most mothers and fathers will testify, parenting as well as working outside the home taxes both physical and emotional strength. Sociologists thus recognize **role**

**conflict** as the *incompatibility among roles corresponding to two or more statuses.*

Even roles linked to a single status make competing demands on us. **Role strain** refers to *incompatibility among the roles corresponding to a single status.* A plant supervisor may enjoy being friendly with other workers. At the same time, however, the supervisor has production goals and must maintain the personal distance needed to evaluate employees. In short, performing the roles of even a single status can be something of a balancing act (Gigliotti & Huff, 1995).

One strategy for minimizing role conflict is "compartmentalizing" our lives so that we perform roles linked to one status at one time and place, and carry out those corresponding to another status elsewhere at another time. A familiar example of this scheme is heading home while leaving the job "at work" (Nippert-Eng, 1995), or, perhaps more relevant for Canadian women these days, leaving the family "home" while going to work (Hochschild, 1997).

## ROLE EXIT

After she herself left the life of a Catholic nun to become a university sociologist, Helen Rose Fuchs Ebaugh (1988) began to study *role exit*, the process by which people disengage from important social roles. Studying a range of "exes," including ex-nuns, ex-doctors, ex-husbands, and ex-alcoholics, Ebaugh identified elements common to the process of "becoming an ex."

According to Ebaugh, the process begins as people experience mounting doubts about their ability or willingness to perform a role. As they consider alternatives, they ultimately reach a turning point at which they decide to pursue a new life.

Even at this point, however, a past role may continue to influence their lives. "Exes" carry with them a self-image shaped by an earlier role, which can be a barrier to building a new sense of self. An ex-nun, for example, may hesitate to wear stylish clothing, have her hair coloured, or go out to a singles bar.

"Exes" must also rebuild relationships with people who may have known them in their "earlier life" and who may not realize just how new and unfamiliar their present role feels. And learning new social skills poses another challenge. For example, Ebaugh reports, nuns who begin dating after decades in the church are often startled to learn that sexual norms are now vastly different from those they knew as teenagers. However, other researchers who have tested the applicability of Ebaugh's role exit theory to stigmatized roles suggest the need for some modification. Brown (1996) points out, for example, that ex-criminals, rather than making a voluntary decision, may be pressured by external authorities to construct a new identity. Anderson and Bondi (1998) also note that the process of exiting a

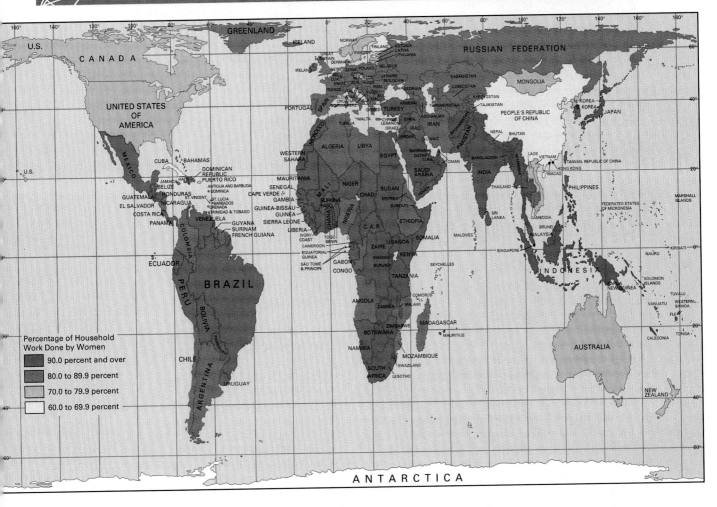

**GLOBAL MAP 4–1   Housework in Global Perspective**

Throughout the world, a major component of women's routines and identities involves housework. This is especially true in the poor societies of Latin America, Africa, and Asia, where women do not generally participate in the paid labour force. But our society, too, defines housework and child care as "feminine" activities, even though a majority of Canadian women work outside the home.

Source: *Peters Atlas of the World* (1990); updated by the authors.

drug-addict role is frequently characterized by relapse or lengthy vacillation between drug use and abstinence before a final exit is achieved, though other research shows that leaving drug addiction behind can sometimes be a more linear process (Biernacki, 1986).

## THE SOCIAL CONSTRUCTION OF REALITY

More than 50 years ago, the Italian playwright Luigi Pirandello created the character of Angelo Baldovino—

a brilliant man with a rather chequered past. In the play *The Pleasure of Honesty*, Baldovino enters the fashionable home of the Renni family and introduces himself in a most peculiar way:

> Inevitably we construct ourselves. Let me explain. I enter this house and immediately I become what I have to become, what I can become: I construct myself. That is, I present myself to you in a form suitable to the relationship I wish to achieve with you. And, of course, you do the same with me. . . . (1962:157–58).

*RCMP officers use pepper spray on unarmed student protesters during the APEC summit. Each side in this social interaction attempted to create its own version of reality.*

Baldovino's introduction suggests that while behaviour is guided by status and role, we also have considerable ability to shape what happens moment to moment. "Reality," in other words, is not as fixed as we may think.

The phrase **social construction of reality** describes *the process by which individuals creatively shape reality through social interaction*. This idea is the familiar foundation of the symbolic-interaction paradigm detailed in Chapter 1 (Sociology: Perspective, Theory, and Method). As Angelo Baldovino's remark suggests, quite a bit of "reality" remains unclear in everyone's mind, especially in unfamiliar situations. So we present ourselves in terms that suit the setting and our purposes—and as others do the same, reality emerges.

Social interaction thus amounts to negotiating reality. Most everyday situations involve at least some agreement about what is going on, although each of us has different interests and intentions.

In the fall of 1997, a group of students from University of British Columbia staged a protest at the Asia-Pacific Economic Cooperation (APEC) summit, during which some of them were arrested—a development that eventually led to the APEC inquiry in the fall of the next year. During this inquiry it became clear that there were two quite different visions of the APEC summit. The students, from their perspective, had planned a peaceful demonstration. They wanted to voice their strong beliefs that some of the leaders at the summit, in particular President Suharto of Indonesia, were perpetrators of human rights abuses and did not deserve the respect normally reserved for national leaders. In contrast, some powerful members of the Prime Minister's Office (PMO)—including Jean Chrétien

himself—were planning a high-level meeting of all the APEC member heads of state, including Suharto.

In between the student protesters and the PMO were the 4000 police and military personnel who were part of the $15-million security plan. Some of these security personnel, the inquiry showed, worried about the legality of ripping up protest signs and detaining peaceful protesters, while others followed the directions of the PMO without questioning them.

This situation reveals the drama—sometimes subtle, sometimes savage—by which human beings creatively build reality. But there are limits to how well even the most skillful personalities—as some of the student protesters apparently were—can orchestrate a situation. After all, the RCMP officers pepper-sprayed the students and arrested them for mischief, going so far as to jail some of them. For his part, the prime minister responded to the event with the joke (for which he later apologized) "For me, pepper, I put it on my plate" (O'Neil, 1997).

## THE THOMAS THEOREM

W.I. Thomas (1966:301; orig. 1931) captured the essence of such events in what is known as the **Thomas theorem**: *Situations that are defined as real become real in their consequences.*

Applied to social interaction, Thomas's insight means that reality is initially "indeterminate"; however, as it is fashioned it can become "solidified" in its effects. Although the APEC Alert protesters tried to define their protest as nonviolent, their anti-Suharto posters and bullhorn chants against the leader helped to confirm the PMO's fears. The PMO therefore defined the situation as violent and threatening, and, in reacting with force, actually made it so.

## ETHNOMETHODOLOGY

Rather than assume that reality is something "out there," the symbolic-interaction paradigm states that people create reality in everyday encounters. But how, exactly, do we define reality for ourselves? Answering this question is the objective of *ethnomethodology*, a specialized approach within the symbolic-interaction paradigm.

The term itself has two parts. The Greek *ethno* refers to people and how they understand their surroundings; "methodology" designates a set of methods or principles. Combining them makes **ethnomethodology**, *the study of the way people make sense of their everyday surroundings.*

Ethnomethodology is largely the creation of Harold Garfinkel (1967), who challenged the then dominant view of society as a broad, abstract "system." Garfinkel wanted to explore how we make sense of countless familiar situations. Our talk and behaviour, explained Garfinkel, rests on deeper assumptions about a world, that, typically, we take for granted.

Think, for a moment, about how much we assume about human behaviour in asking someone the simple question "How are you?" Upon being asked this question when arriving in Canada from Sweden, one of the authors of this text repeatedly gave an honest answer. He discovered later on that when Canadians ask this question, it is only out of politeness, and not because they are really interested in knowing one's true state.

Ethnomethodology, then, explores the process of making sense in social encounters. Garfinkel argues that the only way to discover how we make sense of events is to purposefully *break the rules*. By deliberately ignoring conventional norms and observing how people respond, we tease out how people build a reality. Thus, Garfinkel (1967) directed his students to refuse to "play the game" in a wide range of situations. Some students living with their parents started acting as if they were boarders rather than children; others entered stores and insisted on bargaining for items; others engaged people in simple games (like tic-tac-toe) only to ignore the rules; still others began conversations while slowly moving closer and closer to the other person.

The students then reported on people's reactions. Typically, the "victims" became annoyed, which suggests how important our everyday reality is to us. Trying to identify exactly *why* people were disturbed led students to consider the unspoken agreements that underlie family life, shopping, fair play, and the like.

Cultures frame reality in different ways. This man lay on the street in Bombay, India, for several hours, quietly dying. In Canada, such an event would probably have provoked someone to call for an ambulance. In a low-income country in which death on the streets is a fact of everyday life, however, many Indians responded not with alarm but with simple decency by placing flowers or incense on the man's body before continuing on their way. Are there east/west differences?

Some sociologists view ethnomethodology as less-than-serious research because it focusses on commonplace experiences and employs unusual—even bizarre—methods. Nevertheless, ethnomethodology heightens our awareness of the unnoticed patterns of everyday life.

## REALITY-BUILDING: CLASS AND CULTURE

People do not build everyday experience out of thin air. In part, how we act or what we see in our surroundings depends on our interests. Scanning the night sky, for example, lovers discover romance, while scientists view the same stars as hydrogen atoms fusing into helium. Social background also directs our perceptions, so that residents of, say, Hull, Quebec, experience the

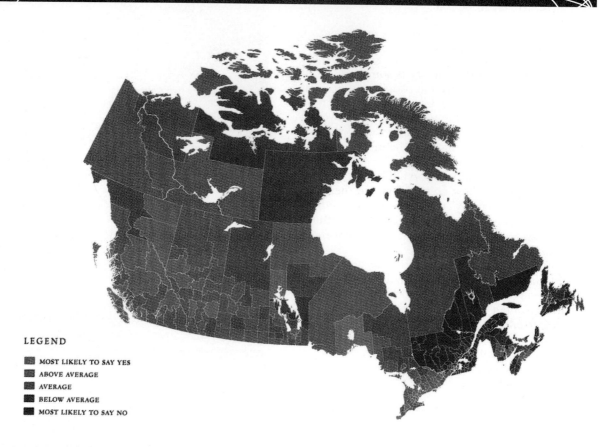

LEGEND

◻ MOST LIKELY TO SAY YES
◻ ABOVE AVERAGE
◻ AVERAGE
◼ BELOW AVERAGE
◼ MOST LIKELY TO SAY NO

**NATIONAL MAP 4–1   Do You Use Alternative Medicine?**

The use of alternative medicine cannot easily be explained if we only look at one important determinant. The map shows that there are probably significant differences in the usage by urban and rural residents. Don't you think that there might also be east–west differences? What about other possible causes: Aboriginal status and social class, for example?

Source: "Do you use alternative medicine?" *Saturday Night* (December 9, 2000).

world somewhat differently from most people living across the river in Ottawa, Ontario.

In truth, there are few common elements to the reality construction that goes on across Canada. Take alternative medicine, for example. As National Map 4–1 indicates, there is considerable variation in the use of alternative medicine across Canada.

In global perspective, reality construction is even more variable. Consider these everyday situations. People waiting for a bus in London typically "queue up" in a straight line; people in Winnipeg rarely are so orderly. The law forbids women in Saudi Arabia to drive cars, a constraint unheard of in Canada. Fear of crime in the big cities of the U.S. is considerably greater  than it is elsewhere—including London, Paris, Rome, Calcutta, Helsinki, and Hong Kong—and this sense of public danger shapes the daily realities of a

large number of U.S. citizens. Comparatively high private ownership of handguns, for example, illustrates how fear of strangers can prompt people to purchase a gun for protection. People build reality from the surrounding culture and find different meanings in specific gestures, so travellers sometimes find themselves building a most unexpected reality! Similarly, in a study of popular culture, JoEllen Shively (1992) screened "westerns" to two groups of males. Both categories claimed to enjoy the films, but for different reasons. White men interpreted the films as praising rugged people striking out for the West to impose their will on nature. Aboriginal men, by contrast, saw in the same films a celebration of land and nature apart from any human ambitions.

If people the world over construct different realities, what about human feelings? Are emotions much the same everywhere? Or are our deepest feelings a product of culture? Cross-cultural research, described in the Global Sociology box on page 88, indicates that emotions are rooted in biology and culture. If people from different societies inhabit different realities, which societies offer the greatest chances for happiness? People living in a high-income nation such as Canada have reason to feel fortunate. And, as Figure 4–2 indicates, global survey data suggest that members of our society are just behind the Swedes in feeling happy about life.

## DRAMATURGICAL ANALYSIS: THE PRESENTATION OF SELF

Erving Goffman (1922–1982) analyzed everyday behaviour by explaining how people are very much like actors performing on a stage. If we imagine ourselves as directors observing what goes on in the "theatre" of everyday life, we engage in what Goffman called **dramaturgical analysis**, *the investigation of social interaction in terms of theatrical performance.*

Dramaturgical analysis offers a fresh look at the concepts of status and role. A status is like a part in a play, and a role serves as a script, supplying dialogue and action for the characters. Goffman described each person's performance as the **presentation of self**, *an individual's efforts to create specific impressions in the minds of others.* This process, sometimes called *impression management*, has several distinctive elements (Goffman, 1959, 1967).

### PERFORMANCES

As we present ourselves in everyday situations, we convey information—consciously and unconsciously—to others. An individual's performance includes dress (costume), objects carried along (props), and tone of voice and gestures (manner). Setting, too, affects a performance. We may joke loudly on the sidewalk, for example, but assume a more reverent manner upon entering a synagogue or mosque. Equally important, individuals design settings, such as homes, offices, and corner pubs, to invoke desired reactions in others.

**An illustration: The doctor's office.** Consider how a physician's office conveys information to an audience of patients. Physicians enjoy considerable prestige and power in Canada, a fact evident to patients on entering the doctor's office. First, the physician is nowhere to be seen. Instead, in what Goffman describes as the "front region" of the setting, the patient encounters a receptionist who functions as a gatekeeper, deciding if and when the patient can see the physician. Who waits to see whom is, of course, a power game. A simple survey of the doctor's waiting room, with patients

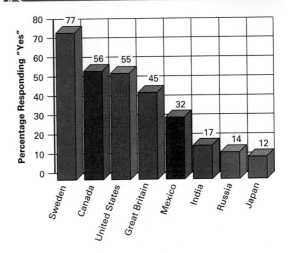

**FIGURE 4–2  Happiness: A Global Survey**

*Survey Question:* "We are interested in the way people are feeling these days. During the past few weeks, did you ever 'feel on top of the world,' feeling that life is wonderful?"

Source: World Values Survey (1994).

(often impatiently) waiting to gain entry to the inner sanctum, leaves little doubt that the physician controls events.

The physician's private office and examination room are the "back region" of the setting. Here the patient confronts a wide range of props, such as medical books and framed degrees, that reinforce the impression that the physician has the specialized knowledge necessary to call the shots. In the office, the physician usually remains seated behind a desk—the larger and grander the desk, the greater the statement of power—while the patient is provided with only a chair.

The physician's appearance and manner convey still more information. The usual costume of white lab coat may have the practical function of keeping clothes from becoming soiled, but its social function is to let others know at a glance the physician's status. A stethoscope around the neck or a black medical bag in hand serves the same purpose. A doctor's highly technical language—frequently mystifying to the patient—also emphasizes the hierarchy in the situation. Finally, patients use the title "Doctor," but they, in turn, are frequently addressed only by their first names, which also underscores the physician's dominant position. The overall message of a doctor's performance is clear: "I will help you, but you must allow me to take charge."

## GLOBAL SOCIOLOGY

# Emotions in Global Perspective: Do People Everywhere Feel the Same?

On the Stanley Park Seawall in Vancouver, a woman reacts angrily to the in-line skater who zooms past her. Her facial expression, accompanied by a few choice words, broadcasts a strong emotion that Canadians easily recognize. But would an observer from Nigeria, Nicaragua, or New Guinea be able to interpret her gestures? In other words, do people everywhere have similar feelings, and do they express them in the same way?

Paul Ekman (1980) and his colleagues studied emotional life in a number of countries—even among members of a small society in New Guinea. From this research, they concluded that people the world over share six basic emotions: anger, fear, disgust, happiness, surprise, and sadness. Moreover, people everywhere express these feelings using the same distinctive facial gestures. To Ekman, this commonality points to the fact that much of our emotional life is universal—rather than culturally variable—and that the

display of emotion is biologically rooted in our facial features, muscles, and central nervous system.

But Ekman notes three ways in which emotional life does differ in global perspective. First, *what triggers an emotion differs from one society to another.* Whether a particular situation is defined as an insult (causing anger), a loss (calling forth sadness), or a mystical event (provoking surprise) depends on culture. In other words, people in various societies might react quite differently to the same event.

Second, *people display emotions according to the norms of their culture.* Every society has its own rules about when, where, and to whom people may exhibit certain emotions. Members of our society, for example, typically express emotions more freely in the home among family members than in the workplace among colleagues. Similarly, we expect children to show emotion to parents, although parents are taught to guard their emotions in front of children.

Third, *societies differ in terms of how people cope with emotions.* Some cultures encourage the expression of feelings, while others belittle emotions and demand that people suppress them. Societies also display significant gender differences in this regard. Our culture tends to label emotional expression as feminine—expected of women but a sign of weakness among men (Lorber, 1994). In other societies, however, this sex typing of emotions is less pronounced or even reversed.

In sum, people everywhere experience the same basic emotions. But what sparks a particular emotion, how and where a person expresses it, and how people define emotions in general all vary as matters of culture. In global perspective, therefore, everyday life differs not only in terms of how people think and act, but how they infuse their lives with feeling.

Sources: Ekman (1980), Lutz & White (1986), and Lutz (1988).

---

### NONVERBAL COMMUNICATION

Novelist William Sansom describes the performance of a fictional Mr. Preedy—an English vacationer on a beach in Spain:

> He took care to avoid catching anyone's eye. First, he had to make it clear to those potential companions of his holiday that they were of no concern to him whatsoever. He stared through them, round them, over them—eyes lost in space. The beach might have been empty. If by chance a ball was thrown his way, he looked surprised; then let a smile of amusement light his face (Kindly Preedy), looked around dazed to see that there were people on the beach, tossed it back with a smile to himself and not a smile *at* the people. . . .
>
> . . . (He) then gathered together his beach-wrap and bag into a neat sand-resistant pile (Methodical and Sensible Preedy), rose slowly to stretch his huge frame

(Big-Cat Preedy), and tossed aside his sandals (Carefree Preedy, after all) (1956; cited in Goffman, 1959:4–5).

Without uttering a single word, Mr. Preedy offers a great deal of information about himself to anyone observing him. This illustrates the process of **nonverbal communication,** *communication using body movements, gestures, and facial expressions rather than speech.*

Many parts of the body can be used to generate *body language*—that is, to convey information to others. Facial expressions are the most significant form of body language. Smiling, for example, symbolizes pleasure, although we distinguish between the deliberate smile of Kindly Preedy on the beach, a spontaneous smile of joy at seeing a friend, a pained smile of embarrassment, and the full, unrestrained smile of self-satisfaction we often associate with the "cat who swallowed the canary."

Eye contact is another crucial element of nonverbal communication. Generally, we use eye contact to invite social interaction. Avoiding the eyes of another, by contrast, discourages communication. Someone across the room "catches our eye," sparking a conversation. Avoiding another's eyes, by contrast, discourages communication. Hands, too, speak for us. Common hand gestures within our culture convey, among other things, an insult, a request for a ride, an invitation for someone to join us, or a demand that others stop in their tracks. Gestures also supplement spoken words. Pointing in a menacing way at someone, for example, gives greater emphasis to a word of warning, as shrugging adds an air of indifference to the phrase "I don't know," and rapidly waving the arms lends urgency to the single word "Hurry!"

As any actor knows, it is very difficult to pull off a "perfect performance" in front of others. In everyday performances, unintended body language can contradict our planned meaning. A teenage boy explains why he is getting home so late, for example, but his mother doubts his words because he avoids looking her in the eye. The movie star on a television talk show claims that her recent flop at the box office is "no big deal," but the nervous swing of her leg suggests otherwise. Because nonverbal communication is hard to control, it provides clues to deception, in much the same way that a lie detector records telltale changes in breathing, pulse rate, perspiration, and blood pressure.

Detecting lies is difficult, because no bodily gesture directly indicates deceit the way, say, a smile indicates pleasure. Even so, because a performance involves so many expressions, few people can lie without allowing some piece of contradictory information to slip by, arousing the suspicions of a careful observer. Therefore, as discussed in the Applying Sociology box on page 90, the key to detecting deceit is to scan the whole performance with an eye for inconsistencies (Ekman, 1985).

## GENDER AND PERFORMANCES

Because women are socialized to be less assertive than men, they tend to be especially sensitive to nonverbal communication. In fact, gender is a central element in personal performances. Based on the work of Nancy Henley, Mykol Hamilton, and Barrie Thorne (1992), we can extend the conventional discussion of personal performances to spotlight the importance of gender.

**Demeanour.** Demeanour—general conduct or deportment—is a clue to social power. Simply put, powerful people enjoy more personal freedom in terms of how to act. Off-colour remarks, swearing, or removing shoes and putting feet up on the desk may be acceptable for the boss, but rarely for employees.

When we enter the presence of others, we "construct" ourselves and begin a "presentation of self" that has much in common with a dramatic performance. Such a presentation involves clothing (costume), other objects (props), certain typical behaviour (script), and it takes place in a particular setting (stage). No wonder the ancient Greeks, who understood the element of acting in everyday life, used the same word for person and mask.

Similarly, powerful people can interrupt others whenever they wish, while subordinates are expected to display deference through silence (Smith-Lovin & Brody, 1989; Henley, Hamilton, & Thorne, 1992).

For women, who generally occupy positions of low power, demeanour is a matter of particular concern. As Chapter 10 (Sex and Gender) explains, over 70 percent of women in Canada are employed in a small number of "feminine" occupations: teaching, nursing, health-related occupations, clerical service work, all of which are under the control of supervisors, in many cases males. Compared with men, then, women must carefully craft their personal performances on the surface and sometimes deep within themselves. Their jobs may require that they "manage their hearts" by conjuring up and displaying deep feelings of caring for those they serve (Hochschild, 1983).

**Use of space.** How much space does a personal performance require? Power plays a key role because using more space is a sign of personal importance. According to Henley, Hamilton, and Thorne (1992), men typically command more space than women, whether pacing back and forth before an audience or casually lounging on a beach. Why? Our culture traditionally has measured femininity by how *little* space women occupy (the standard of "daintiness") and masculinity by how *much* territory a man controls (the standard of "turf").

# Hide Those Lyin' Eyes: Can You Do It?

Poker players and police officers have long realized that a good liar has a real advantage. Deception is a familiar element of everyday interaction, if only because common politeness sometimes demands that we not say what we really think.

Can you tell when another person is trying to deceive you? Paul Ekman suggests paying close attention to four elements of a performance—words, voice, body language, and facial expression.

**Words.** Good liars mentally rehearse their lines, but they cannot always avoid a simple slip of the tongue—something they did not mean to say in quite that way. For example, a young man who is deceiving his parents by claiming that his roommate is a male friend rather than a female lover might mistakenly use the word "she" rather than "he" in conversation. The more complicated the deception, the more likely a performer is to make a revealing mistake.

**Voice.** Tone and patterns of speech contain clues to deception because they are hard to control. Especially when trying to hide a powerful emotion, a person cannot easily prevent the voice from trembling or breaking. Similarly, the individual may speak more quickly (suggesting anger) or slowly (indicating sadness). Nervous laughter, inappropriate pauses between words, or non-words such as "ah" and "um," also hint at discomfort.

**Body language.** A "leak" from body language may tip off an observer to deception as well. Subtle body movements, for example, give the impression of nervousness, as does sudden swallowing or rapid breathing. These are especially good clues to deception because few people can control them. Sometimes, not using the body in the expected way—as when a person's body fails to confirm words that suggest excitement—also suggests deception.

**Facial expressions.** Because facial expressions, too, are hard to control, they give away many phony performances. While a real smile usually has a relaxed expression and lots of "laugh lines" around the eyes, a phony smile seems forced and unnatural, with fewer wrinkles around the eyes.

Source: Based on Ekman (1985) and Golden (1999b).

The concept of **personal space** refers to *the surrounding area over which a person makes some claim to privacy.* In high-income countries such as Canada, people generally remain at least one metre apart, maintaining more personal space than people in, say, Egypt, who tend to stand closer to one another than Westerners are used to. Edward T. Hall (1969) discusses a personal space index that consists of four zones. *Intimate distance* is the private space of up to a half-metre from a person, and usually reserved, as least in Europe and North America, for close relations, such as lovers or parents and children. *Personal distance* (a half to a little more than one metre) is the typical space we allow for our colleagues and friends. *Social distance* (a little more than a metre to four metres) is the zone on the personal space index that is the norm for formal encounters, such as official meetings or face-to-face interviews. The final zone, *public distance*, is the space stretching beyond four metres and typically used during concerts, plays, and other forms of entertainment where there is a performer and audience.

**Staring, smiling, and touching.** Eye contact encourages interaction. In urban, industrial countries, women more than men work to sustain eye contact. But men have their own distinctive brand of eye contact: *staring.* When men stare at women, they are claiming social dominance and defining women as sexual objects.

Although frequently conveying pleasure, smiling is also a symbol of appeasement or submission. In a male-dominated world, say Henley, Hamilton, and Thorne, women smile more than men. In fact, many of the service jobs that women do require that they smile to please the customers.

Finally, mutual touching conveys intimacy and caring. Apart from in close relationships, however, touching is generally something men do to women (and rarely, in our culture, to other men). A male physician touches the shoulder of his female nurse as they examine a report, a young man touches the back of his female friend as he guides her across the street, or a male instructor touches young women as he teaches them to ski. In such examples the touching may evoke little response, but it amounts to a subtle ritual by which men claim dominance over women.

## IDEALIZATION

Complex motives underlie human behaviour. Even so, Goffman contends, we construct performances to *idealize* our intentions. That is, we try to convince

*To most Canadians, these expressions convey anger, fear, disgust, happiness, surprise, and sadness. But do people elsewhere in the world define them in the same way? Research suggests that all human beings experience the same basic emotions and display them to others in the same basic ways. But culture plays a part by specifying the situations that trigger one emotion or another.*

others (and perhaps ourselves) that our actions reflect ideal cultural standards rather than more selfish motives.

Idealization is easily illustrated by returning to the world of physicians and patients. In a hospital, physicians engage in a performance known as "making rounds." Entering a patient's room, the physician often stops at the foot of the bed and silently examines the chart. Afterward, physician and patient talk briefly. In ideal terms, this routine involves a physician making a personal visit to enquire about a patient's condition.

In reality, the picture is not so perfect. A physician may see dozens of patients a day and remember little about many of them, so reading the chart provides him or her a chance to recall the patient's name and medical problems. Revealing the impersonality of much medical care would undermine the cultural ideal of the physician as deeply concerned about the welfare of others.

Physicians, university professors, and other professionals typically idealize their motives for entering their chosen careers. They describe their work as "making a contribution to science," perhaps "serving the community," or even "answering a call from God." Rarely do people admit the less honourable, although common, motives of seeking the income, power, prestige, and leisure that these occupations provide (Abbott, 1988; Saks, 1998).

More generally, idealization is part of civility, since we all smile and make polite remarks to people we do not like. Such little lies ease our way through social interactions. Even when we suspect that others are putting on an act, we are unlikely to challenge their performance, for reasons that we shall explain next.

## EMBARRASSMENT AND TACT

The Marxist lecturing on the evils of capitalism nervously plays with the loose coins in his pocket; the visiting ambassador rises from the table to speak, unaware of the napkin that still hangs from her neck; the prime minister forgets himself and speaks in English to the French delegation. As carefully as individuals may craft

*Near the end of his life, Erving Goffman (1979) studied the place of gender in advertising—that is, how advertising portrays the relative social position of men and women. Look at this Pepsi ad from an earlier era: What messages does it convey about women and men? Do you think today's advertising is different in this regard?*

their performances, slip-ups of all kinds frequently occur. The result is *embarrassment* or discomfort following a spoiled performance. Goffman describes embarrassment simply as "losing face."

Embarrassment is an ever-present danger, first, because idealized performances typically contain some deception, and second, because most performances involve so many elements that a thoughtless moment can shatter the intended impression.

A curious fact is that an audience often overlooks flaws in a performance, allowing the actor to avoid embarrassment. If we do point out a misstep ("Excuse me, but do you know your fly is open?"), we do it discreetly and only to prevent the person experiencing some even greater loss of face. In Hans Christian Andersen's classic fable "The Emperor's New Clothes," the child who blurts out that the emperor is naked tells the truth, but is scolded for being rude. Often, too, members of an audience actually help the performer recover from a flawed performance.

*Tact* amounts to helping someone "save face." After hearing a supposed expert make embarrassingly inaccurate remarks, for example, people tactfully ignore the comment, as if it had never been said. Or mild laughter may indicate they wish to treat what was said as a joke. Or a listener may simply respond, "I'm sure you didn't mean that," noting the statement but not allowing it to destroy the actor's performance.

Why is tact so common? Because embarrassment provokes discomfort not simply for the actor but for *everyone*. Just as the entire audience feels uneasy when an actor forgets a line, people who observe awkward behaviour are reminded of how fragile their own performances often are. Socially constructed reality thus functions like a dam holding back a sea of chaos. Should one person's performance spring a leak, others tactfully help make repairs. Everyone, after all, lends a

hand in building reality, and no one wants it to be suddenly swept away.

In sum, Goffman's research shows that although behaviour is spontaneous in some respects, it is more patterned than we like to think. Almost 400 years ago, William Shakespeare captured this idea in memorable lines that still ring true:

> All the world's a stage,
> And all the men and women merely players.
> They have their exits and their entrances,
> And one man in his time plays many parts.
> (*As You Like It*, II)

## INTERACTION IN EVERYDAY LIFE: TWO APPLICATIONS

We have now examined the major elements of social interaction. The final sections of this chapter illustrate these lessons by focussing on two important dimensions of everyday life: language and humour.

### LANGUAGE: THE GENDER ISSUE

As Chapter 2 (Culture) explains, language is the thread that joins members of a society in the symbolic web that we call "culture." Language conveys not only surface message, but also deeper levels of meaning. One level involves gender. Language defines men and women differently in at least three ways—in terms of control, value, and attention.[1]

---

[1] The following sections draw primarily on Henley, Hamilton, & Thorne (1992). Additional material is drawn from Thorne, Kramarae, & Henley (1983), and MacKay (1983), and others as noted.

*Hand gestures vary widely from one culture to another. Yet people everywhere define a chuckle, grin, or smirk in response to someone's performance as an indication that the person does not take the performer seriously. Therefore, the world over, people who cannot restrain their mirth tactfully cover their faces.*

**Language and power.** A young man astride his new motorcycle rolls proudly up his friend's driveway and eagerly asks, "Isn't she a beauty?" On the surface, the question has little to do with gender. Yet why does the fellow use the pronoun "she" rather than "he" to refer to his prized possession?

The answer is that language helps men to establish control over their surroundings. That is, a man attaches a female pronoun to a motorcycle (car, boat, or other object) because it reflects *ownership*.

The interplay of power and language comes through clearly in how people are named. Traditionally in Canada, as well as in many other parts of the world, a woman takes the family name of the man she marries. While few today consider this an explicit statement of a man's ownership of a woman, many think it does reflect male dominance. For this reason, some Canadian women retain their own name after marriage and assign both family names to their children. Most likely, though, the children will want an explanation of why most of their classmates don't have hyphenated names.

**Language and value.** Language usually treats as masculine whatever has greater value, force, or significance. This pattern is deeply rooted in the English language. For instance, the positive adjective *virtuous*, meaning "morally worthy" or "excellent," is derived from the Latin word *vir* meaning "man." By contrast, the disparaging adjective *hysterical* comes from the Greek word *hyster*, meaning "uterus." Or take the word *seminal*, meaning "highly original" or "groundbreaking," derived from the word "semen" or "male seed." Feminist attempts to arrive at a substitute term *ovarian*, have not had the hoped-for impact on the English language (O'Brien, 1983).

In many more familiar ways, language also confers different value on the two sexes. Traditional masculine terms such as *king* or *lord* have retained their positive meaning, while some comparable terms, such as *queen*, *madam*, or *dame* have now assumed negative connotations. In short, language both mirrors social attitudes and helps to perpetuate them.

**Language and attention.** Language also shapes reality by directing attention to what is masculine. Consider the use of personal pronouns. In the English language, the plural pronoun *they* is gender-neutral, since it refers to both sexes. But the corresponding singular pronouns *he* and *she* convey gender. According to traditional grammatical practice, we use *he* (also, the possessive *his* and the objective *him*) to refer to *all people*. Thus, we assume that the masculine pronoun in the bit of wisdom "He who hesitates is lost" refers to women as well as men. But this practice also reflects the traditional cultural practice of neglecting the lives of women (MacKay, 1983).

The English language has no gender-neutral third-person singular pronoun. In recent years, however, the plural pronoun "they" has gained currency as a singular pronoun ("A person should do as they please"). This usage does violate grammatical rules. Yet, in an age of growing concern over gender-linked bias, some evolution of English (and other languages) seems likely. As well, gender-neutral nouns such as *chair* or *chairperson* and *salesperson* and *server* have become common substitutes for traditionally gender-specific terms.

Grammar aside, the mix of gender and language is likely to remain a source of miscommunication between women and men. In the Applying Sociology box on page 95, Harold and Sybil—whose misadventures while finding a friend's home opened this chapter—return to illustrate how the two sexes often seem to be speaking different languages.

*Why do we associate ownership with men and characterize what is owned as feminine? How easily can you imagine renaming this boat with the gender reversed?*

## HUMOUR: PLAYING WITH REALITY

Humour plays a vital part in everyday life. Comedians rank among our favourite entertainers, most newspapers contain cartoon pages, and even professors include humour in their performances: Did you hear the one about the two students who slept through their exam because they had been partying too late? They told their professor that they got a flat tire on their way back from visiting their parents in the nearby town. Both were delighted to accept the offer of their considerate professor to write a make-up exam the next day, and went home to study hard that evening. However, they were both a little confused when—seated in two different rooms—they noticed that their exam paper had only one question. Their feeling of confusion was replaced by another feeling when they read the question: "Which tire?"

As with many aspects of daily living, however, we largely take humour for granted. Many of the ideas developed in this chapter provide insights into the character of humour, as we shall now see.[2]

**The foundation of humour.** Humour is a product of reality construction; specifically, it stems from the contrast between two incongruous realities. Generally, one reality is *conventional*, corresponding to what people expect in a specific situation. The other reality is *unconventional*, representing some violation of cultural patterns. Humour, therefore, arises from contradiction, ambiguity, and "double meanings" generated by two differing definitions of a situation. Note how this principle works in one of Woody Allen's lines: "I'm not afraid to die; I just don't want to be there when it happens." Or take the old Czech folk saying: "All mushrooms are edible—but some only once." In these examples, the first thought represents a conventional notion; the second half, however, interjects an unconventional—even absurd—meaning that collides with what we are led to expect.

This same pattern holds true for virtually all humour. Rick Mercer's New Year's resolution to "not stop drinking altogether but to explore light beer as a lunchtime beverage" ends up being not much of a resolution after all. Note as well how this principle works in the newspaper headlines in the Critical Thinking box on page 96.

Of course, there are countless ways to mix realities and, thereby, generate humour. In some cases, contrasting realities emerge simply from reordering syllables, as in the case of the line from a country song "I'd rather have a bottle in front of me than a frontal lobotomy."

Of course, a joke can be built the other way around, so that the comic leads the audience to *expect* an unconventional answer, and then gives a very ordinary one. When a reporter asked the famous desperado Willy Sutton why he robbed banks, for example, he replied dryly, "Because that's where the money is." However a joke is constructed, the greater the opposition or incongruity between the two definitions of reality, the greater the potential for humour.

When telling jokes, the comedian can strengthen this opposition in various ways. One common technique used on the stage is to present the first, conventional remark in conversation with another actor, then turn toward the audience (or the camera) to deliver the second, unexpected line. In one of his films, Groucho Marx swaggers in front of a young woman and brags, "This morning I shot a lion in my pajamas." Then, dropping his voice and turning to the camera, he adds, "What the lion was doing in my pajamas, I'll *never* know . . ." Such "changing channels" underscores the incongruity of the two parts. Following the same logic, many stand-up comedians also "reset" the audience to

---

[2]The ideas contained in this discussion are those of Macionis (1987), except as otherwise noted. The general approach draws on work presented earlier in this chapter, especially on the ideas of Erving Goffman.

# Gender and Language: You Just Don't Understand!

Deborah Tannen, who has conducted extensive research on the linguistic differences that separate the sexes, claims that men tend to define most daily encounters as competitive situations; thus, getting lost is bad enough for a man, without asking for help and thereby letting someone else "one up" him. Men go to great lengths to avoid this. By contrast, because women have a generally subordinate position, they are socialized to ask for help. Sometimes, Tannen points out, women will ask for assistance even when they don't need it.

A similar gender-linked problem common to couples involves (what some men call) "nagging." Consider the following exchange (Adler, 1990: 74):

*Sybil:* "What's wrong, honey?"

*Harold:* "Nothing . . ."

*Sybil:* "Something is bothering you; I can tell."

*Harold:* "I told you nothing is bothering me. Leave me alone."

*Sybil:* "But I can see that something is wrong."

*Harold:* "OK. Just why do you think something is bothering me?"

*Sybil:* "Well, for one thing, you're bleeding all over your shirt."

*Harold* (now irritated): "It doesn't bother me."

*Sybil* (losing her temper): "WELL, IT SURE IS BOTHERING ME!"

*Harold:* "I'll go change my shirt."

The problem couples face in communicating is that what one partner intends by a comment is not always what the other hears in the words. To Sybil, her opening question is an effort at cooperative problem solving. She can see that something is wrong with Harold (who has carelessly cut himself while doing yard work) and she wants to help him. But Harold interprets her pointing out his problem as belittling, and tries to close off the discussion. Sybil, confident that Harold would respond to her in a more positive way if he just understood that she only wants to be helpful, repeats herself. This sets in motion a vicious cycle in which Harold, thinking his wife is trying to make him feel incapable of looking after himself, responds by digging in his heels. This, in turn, makes his wife all the more sure that there is a problem

that requires attention. And around it goes until somebody loses patience.

In the end, Harold gives in only to the extent that he agrees to change his shirt. But notice that he still refuses to discuss the original problem. Misunderstanding his wife's motives, Harold just wants Sybil to leave him alone. For her part, Sybil fails to understand Harold's view of the situation and walks away thinking that he is unnecessarily grouchy and insensitive.

Yet as noted in this chapter's opening vignette, some couples are casting off traditional gender roles and opening up new channels of communication that result in less distorted, more honest dialogue. More and more fathers say they want to nurture their children equally with their female partners, even if it means backing away from the corporate office or law firm to spend more quality time with their families. As Gail Sheehy (1998: 60) states, "[O]ne of the greatest benefits of entering midlife is that a man can take off the blinders of the young warrior . . . [and see that he] is a member of a community and a society that desperately need his contribution."

Sources: Adler (1990), Tannen (1990), and Sheehy (1998).

conventional expectations by interjecting "But, seriously, folks . . ." after one joke and before the next one.

To construct the strongest contrast in meaning, comedians pay careful attention to their performances—the precise words they use, as well as the timing of their delivery. A joke is "well told" if the comic creates the sharpest possible opposition between the realities. Since the key to humour lies in the opposition of realities, we can see why the climax of a joke is termed the "*punch* line."

**The dynamics of humour: "Getting it."** Someone who understands neither the expected nor the unexpected realities embedded in a joke may complain, "I don't get it." To "get" humour, members of an audience must understand the two realities involved well enough to appreciate their difference.

# CRITICAL THINKING

# Double Take:
# Real Headlines That Make People Laugh

Humour is generated by mixing together two opposing realities. Here are actual headlines from recent newspapers. Read each one and identify the conventional meaning intended by the writer as well as the unconventional interpretation that generates humour.

*What do you think?*

1. *For each headline, do you see the "expected" and "unexpected" meaning?*

2. *Which headlines are most funny? Why?*

3. *Can you think of other everyday examples of humour?*

Source: Thanks to Kay Fletcher.

| | | |
|---|---|---|
| Police Begin Campaign to Run Down Jaywalkers | Drunk Gets Nine Months in Violin Case | Survivor of Siamese Twins Joins Parents |
| Iraqi Head Seeks Arms | Stud Tires Out | Prostitutes Appeal to Pope |
| Panda Mating Fails: Veterinarian Takes Over | Soviet Virgin Lands Short of Goal Again | Teacher Strikes Idle Kids |
| Squad Helps Dog Bite Victim | Miners Refuse to Work After Death | Killer Sentenced to Die for Second Time in Ten Years |
| War Dims Hope for Peace | British Left Waffles on Falkland Islands | Stolen Painting Found by Tree |

But getting a joke can be challenging, because the comic may leave unstated some of the information listeners must grasp. The audience, in other words, must pay attention to the *stated* elements of the joke and fill in the missing pieces on their own. As a simple case, consider Mercer's comment on the NDP in Canada: "I wanted to work in a political campaign and went with them because, essentially, they'd take anyone." Here, "getting" the joke depends on realizing that the NDP has a relatively marginal status in Canada and is therefore not attractive to many volunteers.

Here is a more complex joke, found on the wall of a college rest room:

### Dyslexics of the world, untie!

To get this one, you must know, first, that people with dyslexia reverse letters; second, that the line is a play on Karl Marx's call to the world's workers to unite; and third, that "untie" as an anagram of "unite," as a disgruntled dyslexic person might write it.

Why would a comic ask an audience to make such an effort to understand a joke? Simply because our enjoyment of a joke is heightened by the pleasure of having completed the puzzle necessary to "get it." In addition, "getting" the joke confers a favoured insider status. We can also understand the frustration of *not* getting a joke: fear of being judged stupid coupled with a sense of being excluded from the pleasure shared by others. Not surprisingly, outsiders in such a situation sometimes fake "getting" the joke, or someone may tactfully explain a joke so a person doesn't feel left out.

But as the old saying goes, if a joke has to be explained, it isn't funny. Besides taking the edge off the language and timing on which the *punch* depends, an explanation removes the mental involvement and greatly reduces the listener's pleasure.

**The topics of humour.** People around the world smile and laugh, signifying humour as a universal human trait. But living in diverse cultures, the world's people differ in what they find funny—humour rarely travels well. Take the recent immigrant to Canada who says in rusty English to her Canadian dinner-party hosts, "Look at the little child over there. He is so nicely playing with [rather than by] himself." Everyone but the speaker laughs.

What is humorous to, say, the Japanese, may be lost on the Finns, Iraqis, or Canadians. To some degree, too, the social diversity of our own country means that people will find humour in different situations. People in Atlantic Canada and the Prairies have their own brands of humour, as do the French and English, 15- and 40-year-olds, investment bankers and construction workers. Aboriginal people and those from visible minority groups also make jokes that get back at people in more advantaged power positions.

But for everyone, humour deals with topics that lend themselves to double meanings or *controversy*. For example, the first jokes many of us learned as children concerned the cultural taboos associated with sex. The mere mention of "unmentionable acts" or even certain parts of the body can make children dissolve into laughter. Are there jokes that can break through the cultural barrier? Yes, but they must touch on universal human experiences, such as, say, turning against a friend: Two fellows are walking in the woods and come upon a huge bear. One guy leans over and tightens up the laces on his running shoes. "Jake," says the other, "what are you doing? You can't outrun this bear!" "I don't have to outrun the bear," responds Jake, "I just have to outrun you!"

The controversy inherent in humour often walks a fine line between what is funny and what is considered "sick." During the Middle Ages, the word *humours* (derived from the Latin *humidus*, meaning "moist") referred to a balance of bodily fluids that regulated a person's health. Researchers today document the power of humour to reduce stress and improve health, confirming the old saying "Laughter is the best medicine" (Robinson, 1983; Haig, 1988). At the extreme, however, people who always take conventional reality lightly risk being defined as deviant or even mentally ill (a common stereotype depicts insane people laughing uncontrollably, and we have long dubbed mental hospitals "funny farms").

Every social group considers certain topics too sensitive for humorous treatment. Of course, one *can* joke about such things, but doing so courts criticism for telling a "sick" joke (and, therefore, *being* sick). People's religious beliefs, tragic accidents, or appalling crimes are the stuff of "sick" jokes.

**The functions of humour.** Humour is found everywhere because it acts as a safety valve that vents potentially disruptive sentiments with little harm. Put another way, humour provides a way to discuss an opinion on a sensitive topic without being serious. Having said something controversial, a person can also use humour to diffuse the situation by simply stating, "I didn't mean anything by what I said—it was just a

*Because humour involves challenging established social conventions, comedians typically have been "outsiders" of some sort. Rick Mercer, originally from "The Rock" (Newfoundland), is among the many comics starring on radio and television who use their cultural roots to poke fun at themselves and their audiences. Mercer's recent six-episode TV series,* Made in Canada, *is another attempt at raw humour by the young comedian known for displaying the seamy side of Canadian life.*

joke!" Likewise, an audience may use humour as a form of tact, smiling, as if to say, "We could be angry at this, but we'll assume you were only kidding."

Similarly, people use humour to relieve tension in uncomfortable situations. One study of medical examinations found most patients begin to joke with doctors to ease their own nervousness (Baker et al., 1997).

**Humour and conflict.** If humour holds the potential to liberate those who laugh, it can also be used to oppress others. People who tell jokes about Aboriginals or Chinese Canadians, for example, may be voicing some measure of hostility toward these groups. Much the same can be said for jokes about feminists (Powell & Paton, 1988; Benokraitis & Feagin, 1995). Similarly, jokes at the expense of gay people reveal tensions surrounding sexual orientation in Canada. Humour is often a sign of real conflict in situations where one or both parties choose not to bring the conflict out into the open (Primeggia & Varacalli, 1990).

"Put-down" jokes make one category of people feel good at the expense of another. After analyzing jokes from many societies, Christie Davies (1990) confirmed that ethnic conflict is a driving force behind humour almost everywhere. The typical ethnic joke makes fun of some disadvantaged category of people, thereby making the jokester and the audience feel superior. In Canada, Newfoundlanders have long been the "butt" of jokes, as have the Irish in Scotland, the Scots in England, the Norwegians in Sweden (and vice versa), the Sikhs in India, the Hausas in Nigeria, the Tasmanians in Australia, and the Kurds in Iraq.

In turn, disadvantaged people, of course, also make fun of the powerful. Canadian women have long joked about Canadian men, just as French Canadians portray Anglos in humorous ways, and poor people poke fun at the rich. Throughout the world, people also target their leaders with humour, and officials in some countries take such jokes seriously enough to suppress them (Speier, 1998).

In sum, the significance of humour is much greater than we may think. Humour amounts to a means of mental escape from a conventional world that is never entirely to our liking (Flaherty, 1984, 1990; Yoels & Clair, 1995). As long as we maintain a sense of humour, we assert our freedom and are never prisoners of reality. By putting a smile on our faces, we change ourselves and the world just a little.

## SUMMARY

1. Social structure provides guidelines for behaviour, making everyday life understandable and predictable.

2. A major component of social structure is status. Within an entire status set, a master status has special importance for a person's identity.

3. Ascribed statuses are involuntary, whereas achieved statuses are earned. In practice, most statuses are both ascribed and achieved.

4. Role is the dynamic expression of a status. Incompatible roles corresponding to two or more statuses generate role conflict. Likewise, incompatible roles linked to a single status cause role strain.

5. The "social construction of reality" refers to the idea that we build the social world through our interactions with others.

6. The Thomas theorem states, "Situations defined as real become real in their consequences."

7. Ethnomethodology seeks to reveal the assumptions and understandings people have of their social world.

8. Dramaturgical analysis views everyday life as theatrical performances, noting how people try to create particular impressions in the minds of others.

9. Social power affects performances, which is one reason that men's behaviour typically differs from women's, working class people's differs from that of their upper-class counterparts, and visible minorities' differs from that of other Canadians.

10. Everyday behaviour carries the ever-present danger of embarrassment. People use tact to prevent others' performances from breaking down.

11. Language is vital to the process of socially constructing reality. In various ways, language defines women and men differently, generally to the advantage of men.

12. Humour stems from the difference between conventional and unconventional definitions of a situation. Because humour is an element of culture, people throughout the world find different situations funny.

## KEY CONCEPTS

**social interaction** (p. 79) the process by which people act and react in relation to others

**status** (p. 80) a recognized social position that an individual occupies

**status set** (p. 80) all the statuses a person holds at a particular time

**ascribed status** (p. 80) a social position that a person receives at birth or assumes involuntarily later in the life course

**achieved status** (p. 80) a social position that a person assumes voluntarily and that reflects a significant measure of personal ability and choice

**master status** (p. 81) a social position with exceptional importance for identity, often shaping a person's entire life

**role** (p. 81) normative patterns of behaviour for those holding a particular status

**role set** (p. 81) a number of roles attached to a single status

**role conflict** (p. 82) incompatibility among the roles corresponding to two or more statuses

**role strain** (p. 82) incompatibility among roles corresponding to a single status

**social construction of reality** (p. 84) the process by which individuals creatively build reality through social interaction

**Thomas theorem** (p. 84) the assertion that situations defined as real become real in their consequences

**ethnomethodology** (p. 85) the study of the way people make sense of their everyday surroundings

**dramaturgical analysis** (p. 87) the investigation of social interaction in terms of theatrical performance

**presentation of self** (p. 87) Goffman's term for the ways in which individuals, in various settings, try to create specific impressions in the minds of others

**nonverbal communication** (p. 88) communication using body movements, gestures, and facial expressions rather than speech

**personal space** (p. 90) the surrounding area over which a person makes some claim to privacy

## CRITICAL-THINKING QUESTIONS

1. Consider ways in which a physical disability can serve as a master status. What assumptions do people commonly make about someone with a physical disability such as cerebral palsy? What assumptions are made about the person's sexuality?

2. How do people on a first date present themselves to each other and, in the process, construct reality? What kind of information does each offer? Why do people in such a situation often begin with "small talk"?

3. George Jean Nathan once quipped, "I only drink to make other people interesting." What does this mean in terms of reality construction? Can you identify the elements of humour in this comment?

4. Here is a joke about sociologists: "Question—How many sociologists does it take to change a light bulb? Answer—None; there is nothing wrong with the light bulb; it's *the system* that needs to be changed!" What makes this joke funny? What sort of people are likely to "get it"? What kind of people probably won't? Why?

## APPLICATIONS AND EXERCISES

1. Write down as many of your own statuses as you can. Do you consider any statuses to be a master status? To what extent are each of your statuses ascribed or achieved?

2. During the next 24 hours, every time people ask, "How are you?" stop and actually give a full and truthful answer. What happens when you respond to a polite question in an unexpected way? (Watch people's body language and note what they say.) What does this experience suggest about everyday interactions?

3. This chapter illustrated Erving Goffman's ideas with a description of a physician's office. Investigate the offices of several professors in the same way. What furniture is there and how is it arranged? What "props" do professors use? How are the offices of physicians and professors different? Which are tidier? Why?

4. Spend an hour or two walking around the businesses of your town (or shops at a local mall). Observe the number of women and men in each business. Based on your observations, would you conclude that physical space is "gendered"?

##  SITES TO SEE

**www.pearsoned.ca/macionis**

Pearson Education Canada and the authors provide a Web site that accompanies this text, offering outlines, review material, learning exercises, and practice tests for each chapter. At the main page, simply click on the cover of your book and follow the easy menus.

**www.TheSociologyPlace.com (or www.macionis.com)**

The special Prentice Hall site contains a wide range of interesting materials and exercises that further develop your understanding of this chapter's discussions.

**www.ai.mit.edu/projects/kismet**

Is it possible to build a machine capable of human interaction? That is the goal of robotics engineers at the Massachusetts Institute of Technology. This Web site provides details and photographs: Look over their work and think about issues raised in this chapter. In what ways are machines able, and unable, to mimic human behaviour?

# CHAPTER

# 5

# GROUPS AND ORGANIZATIONS

*Back in 1948, people in Pasadena, California, paid little attention to the opening of a new restaurant. Yet this one small business—owned by brothers Maurice and Richard McDonald—would not only transform the restaurant industry, but also introduce a new business organizational model that would come to be copied by countless businesses of all kinds.*

*The McDonald brothers' basic concept—which we now call "fast food"—was to serve meals quickly and cheaply to a large number of people. The brothers trained employees to perform highly specialized jobs, so that one person grilled hamburgers, while others "dressed" them, made French fries, whipped up milk shakes, and presented the food to the customers in assembly-line fashion.*

*As the years went by, the McDonald brothers prospered, and they decided to move their single restaurant from Pasadena to San Bernardino. It was there, in 1954, that Ray Kroc, a travelling blender-and-mixer merchant, paid them a visit.*

*Kroc was fascinated by the efficiency of the brothers' system and saw the potential for a whole chain of fast-food restaurants. The three launched the plan as partners. Soon, however, Kroc bought out the McDonalds and went on to become one of the greatest business success stories of all time. Today, 23 000 McDonald's restaurants have served more than 150 billion hamburgers to people in Canada and 110 other countries around the world.* ■

McDonald's success is evidence of more than the popularity of hamburgers. The larger importance of McDonald's lies in the extent to which the principles that guide this company are coming to dominate social life around the globe (Ritzer, 1993, 1998).

We begin with an examination of *social groups*, the clusters of people with whom we interact in much of our daily lives. As we shall see, the scope of group life expanded greatly during the 20th century. Having evolved from a world of families, local neighbourhoods, and small businesses, our society now turns on the operation of huge businesses and other bureaucracies that sociologists describe as *formal organizations*. Understanding how this expanding scale of life came to be, and what it means for us as individuals, are this chapter's main objectives.

## SOCIAL GROUPS

Virtually everyone seeks a sense of belonging, which is the experience of group membership. A **social group** is *two or more people who identify and interact with one another.* Human beings come together in couples, families, circles of friends, churches, clubs, businesses, neighbourhoods, non-profit organizations, and large work bureaucracies. Whatever the form, groups contain people with shared experiences, loyalties, and interests. In short, while keeping their individuality, members of social groups also think of themselves as a special "we."

Not every collection of individuals forms a group. People with a status in common, such as "punk rocker,"

*A human beings, we live our lives as members of groups. Such groups may be large or small, temporary or long-lasting, and can be based on kinship, cultural heritage, or some shared interest.*

"civil servant," "East Asian," or "Nova Scotian," are not a group but, rather, a *category*. While they know others hold the same status, the vast majority are strangers to one another. Likewise, students sitting together in a large lecture hall interact to a very limited extent; thus, they are a loosely formed group that is better termed a *crowd*.

The right circumstances, however, could turn a crowd into a group. People riding on an elevator that stalls between floors become keenly aware of their common plight and turn to each other for help. Sometimes out of accidents and disasters, people form lasting relationships. The experience of carrying out a collective research project, to take another example, might well generate significant group interaction and identity among members of a first-year sociology class.

## PRIMARY AND SECONDARY GROUPS

Friends often greet one another with a smile and the simple phrase "Hi! How are you?" The response is usually "Just fine, thanks. How about you?" This answer, of course, is often more scripted than truthful. If you went into detail about how you really were doing, many listeners would feel so awkward that they would beat a hasty retreat.

Social groups fall into one of two types based on their members' degree of genuine personal concern toward one another. According to Charles Horton Cooley (1864–1929), a **primary group** is *a small social group whose members share personal and enduring relationships.* Joined by *primary relationships*, people spend a great deal of time together, engage in a wide range of activities, and feel that they know one another pretty well. In short, they display real concern for each other's welfare. The family is every society's most important primary group.

Cooley called personal and tightly integrated groups *primary*, because they are among the first groups we experience in life. In addition, family and friends have primary importance in the socialization process, shaping attitudes, behaviour, and social identity.

Members of primary groups help one another in many ways, but they generally think of their group as an end in itself rather than as a means to other ends. In other words, we prefer to think that kinship and friendship link people who "belong together." Moreover, members of a primary group tend to view each other as unique and irreplaceable. We usually do not care who cashes our cheque at the bank or drives the cross-town bus, but we are bound to kin and close friends by emotion and loyalty. This special tie is why young children have "separation anxiety" when first left with a baby-sitter; why brothers and sisters, though they do not always get along, may, out of a deep-rooted sense of family obligation, readily assist in any crisis.

In contrast to the primary group, the **secondary group** is *a large and impersonal social group whose members pursue a specific goal or activity.* In most respects, secondary groups have precisely the opposite characteristics of primary groups. *Secondary relationships* involve weak emotional ties and the members have little personal knowledge of one another. Many secondary groups are short term, beginning and ending for no particularly significant reason. Students in a first-year sociology course, for example, who may or may not see each other after the semester ends, exemplify the secondary group.

Secondary groups include many more people than do primary groups. For example, dozens or even hundreds of people may work together in the same company, yet most of them pay only passing attention to one another. Sometimes time transforms a group from secondary to primary, as with co-workers who share an office for many years. But generally, members of a secondary group do not think of themselves as "we."

Whereas members of primary groups display a *personal orientation*, people in secondary groups have a *goal orientation*. Secondary ties need not be hostile or cold, of course. Interaction among students, co-workers, and business associates is often quite pleasant, even if it is impersonal. But while primary-group members define each other according to *who* they are in terms of kinship or personal qualities, people in secondary groups look to one another for *what* they are—that is, what they can do for each other. In secondary groups, we tend to "keep score," mindful of what we give others and what we receive in return. This goal orientation means that secondary-group members usually remain formal and polite. The secondary relationship, therefore, is one in which we ask the question "How are you?" without expecting a truthful answer.

Table 5–1 summarizes the characteristics that distinguish primary and secondary groups. Keep in mind that these traits define two ideal types of groups; most real groups contain elements of both. But placing these concepts at opposite ends of a continuum helps us to describe and analyze group life.

Are some regions of Canada more primary in character than others? Many people think that small towns and rural areas emphasize primary relationships, while large cities are characterized by secondary ties. This generalization holds some truth, but some urban neighbourhoods—especially those populated by people of a single religious or ethnic category—are quite tightly knit (Li, 1998).

Finally, what about the world as a whole? In general, primary relationships predominate in low-income, pre-industrial societies in which people's lives centre on families and local villages. By contrast, secondary ties take precedence in high-income, industrial societies, in which people assume highly specialized social roles. Most people in Canada, especially in cities, routinely engage in impersonal, secondary contacts with virtual strangers—people about whom we know very little and whom we may never meet again (Wirth, 1938). The Internet may be changing this trend by helping Canadians to redefine their social interactions and even to start new relationships via the Web. Almost three in ten (28 percent) Canadian Internet users have made new friends online, and 39 percent of them have gone on to actually meet these "friends" face-to-face (Angus Reid Group Inc., 2000a).

## GROUP LEADERSHIP

How do groups operate? One important dimension of group dynamics is leadership. Though a small circle of

### TABLE 5–1 Primary Groups and Secondary Groups: A Summary

| | Primary ←→ Secondary<br>Group          Group | |
|---|---|---|
| | **Primary Group** | **Secondary Group** |
| **Quality of Relationships** | Personal orientation | Goal orientation |
| **Duration of Relationships** | Usually long term | Variable; often short term |
| **Breadth of Relationships** | Broad; usually involving many activities | Narrow; usually involving few activities |
| **Subjective Perception of Relationships** | As ends in themselves | As means to an end |
| **Typical Examples** | Families; circles of friends | Co-workers; political organizations |

friends may have no leader at all, most large, secondary groups place leaders in a formal chain of command.

**Instrumental and expressive leaders.** Groups typically benefit from two kinds of leadership. **Instrumental leadership** refers to *group leadership that emphasizes the completion of tasks.* Members look to instrumental leaders to "get things done." **Expressive leadership**, on the other hand, *focusses on collective well-being.* Expressive leaders take less of an interest in achieving the goals of a group than in raising group morale and minimizing tension and conflict among members.

Because they concentrate on performance, instrumental leaders usually have formal, secondary relationships with other members. These leaders give orders, and reward or punish members, according to the member's contribution to the group's efforts. Expressive leaders, however, cultivate more primary ties. They offer sympathy to a member going through a tough time, keep the group united, and lighten serious moments with humour. While successful instrumental leaders enjoy more *respect* from other members, expressive leaders generally receive more personal *affection*.

In the earliest types of societies, the same person combined both elements of leadership. In patriarchal societies, such as 19th- and early 20th-century Canada, conventional cultural norms bestowed instrumental leadership on men. As family "breadwinners" and "heads," men assumed primary responsibility for bringing in family income, made major decisions, and disciplined children, a responsibility that was strongly endorsed by the Canadian government of the time (Benoit, 2000a; Christie, 2000). Women were assigned an expressive leadership role, with the expectation that

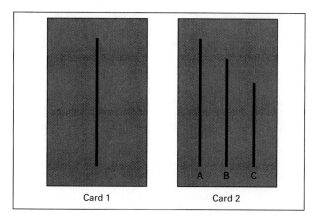

**FIGURE 5–1    Cards Used in Asch's Experiment in Group Conformity**

Source: Asch (1952).

they would lend family members emotional support and maintain peaceful family relationships.

Today, women are becoming involved in bread-winner roles, and men in family life. Yet if we consider the conventional division of leadership styles, it helps to explain why many children in earlier generations had greater respect for their fathers, but closer personal ties with their mothers (Parsons & Bales, 1955; Macionis, 1978).

Greater equality between men and women has blurred the gender-based distinction between instrumental and expressive leadership. In most group settings, women and men now can assume either type of role.

**Leadership styles.** Sociologists also characterize leadership in terms of its decision-making style. *Authoritarian leadership* focusses on instrumental concerns, takes personal charge of decision-making, and demands strict compliance from subordinates. Although this leadership style may win little affection from the group, people appreciate a fast-acting authoritarian leader in a crisis.

*Democratic leadership* is more expressive, making a point of including everyone in the decision-making process. Although less successful in a crisis, which leaves little time for discussion, democratic leaders generally draw on the ideas of all members to develop creative solutions to problems.

*Laissez-faire leadership* (a French phrase meaning roughly "to leave alone") allows the group to function more or less on its own. This style typically is the least effective in promoting group goals (White & Lippitt, 1953; Ridgeway, 1983).

## GROUP CONFORMITY

Groups influence the behaviour of their members, often promoting conformity. "Fitting in" provides a secure feeling of belonging, but, at the extreme, group pressure can be unpleasant and even dangerous. Moreover, even strangers can foster conformity, as experiments by Solomon Asch and Stanley Milgram showed.

**Asch's research.** Asch (1952) recruited students allegedly to study visual perception. Before the experiment began, he explained to all but one member of a small group that their real purpose was to put pressure on the remaining person. Placing six to eight students around a table, Asch showed them a "standard" line, as drawn on Card 1 in Figure 5–1, and asked them to match it to one of the three lines on Card 2.

Anyone with normal vision can see that the line marked *A* on Card 2 is the correct choice. Initially, as planned, everyone made the correct matches. But then Asch's accomplices began answering incorrectly, leaving the naive subject (seated at the table in order to answer next to last) bewildered and uncomfortable.

What happened? Asch found that one-third of all subjects chose to conform by answering incorrectly. Apparently, many of us are willing to compromise our own judgment to avoid the discomfort of being different, even from people we do not know.

**Milgram's research.** Stanley Milgram, a former student of Solomon Asch, conducted conformity experiments of his own. In Milgram's controversial study (Milgram, 1963, 1965; Miller, 1986), a researcher explained to male recruits that they would be taking part in a study of how punishment affects learning. One by one, he assigned them to the role of teacher and placed another individual—actually an accomplice of Milgram's—in a connecting room to pose as a learner.

The teacher watched the learner sit down in a contraption resembling an electric chair. As the teacher looked on, the researcher applied electrode paste to the learner's wrist, explaining that this would "prevent blisters and burns." The researcher then attached an electrode to the wrist and secured the leather straps, explaining that these would "prevent excessive movement while the learner was being shocked." Although the shocks would be painful, the researcher assured the teacher, they would cause "no permanent tissue damage."

The researcher then led the teacher back into the adjoining room, pointing out that the "electric chair" was connected to a "shock generator," actually a phony but realistic-looking piece of equipment with a label that read "Shock Generator, Type ZLB, Dyson Instrument Company, Waltham, Mass." On the front was a dial that supposedly regulated electric current, beginning with 15 volts (labelled "Slight Shock"), going up to 300 volts ("Intense Shock") and, finally, to 450 volts (marked "Danger: Severe Shock").

Seated in front of the "shock generator," the teacher was told to read aloud pairs of words. Then the teacher was to repeat the first word of each pair and wait for the learner to recall the second word. Whenever the learner failed to answer correctly, the teacher was instructed to apply an electric shock.

The researcher directed the teacher to begin at the lowest level (15 volts) and to increase the shock by another 15 volts every time the learner made a mistake. And so they did. At 75, 90, and 105 volts, the teacher heard moans from the learner; at 120 volts, shouts of pain; by 270 volts, screams; at 315 volts, pounding on the wall; after that, deadly silence. None of the 40 subjects assigned to the role of teacher during the initial research even questioned the procedure before reaching 300 volts, and 26 of the subjects—almost two-thirds—went all the way to 450 volts. Even Milgram was surprised at how readily people obeyed authority figures.

Milgram (1964) then modified his research to see if Solomon Asch had documented such a high degree of group conformity only because the task of matching lines was trivial. What if groups pressured people to administer electrical shocks?

This time, Milgram formed a group of three teachers, two of whom were his accomplices. Each of the teachers was to suggest a shock level when the learner made an error; the rule was that the group would then administer the lowest of the three suggestions. This arrangement gave the naive subject the power to deliver a lesser shock, regardless of what the others proposed.

The accomplices suggested increasing the shock level with each error, putting pressure on the subject to do the same. The subjects applied voltages three to four times higher than other subjects acting alone. Thus Milgram's research suggests that people are surprisingly likely to follow the directions not only of "legitimate authority figures," but also of groups of ordinary individuals, even when it means inflicting harm on another person.

**Janis's research.** Experts, too, cave in to group pressure, says Irving L. Janis (1972, 1989). Janis contends that a number of U.S. foreign-policy blunders in this century, including the failure to foresee the Japanese attack on Pearl Harbour and the ill-fated involvement in the Vietnam War, resulted from group conformity among high-ranking political leaders. A more recent

In many nonindustrial societies, young people of the same age participate in rituals that forge bonds among them and teach them a way of life. Here, young women in the African nation of Swaziland who are reaching adulthood perform a traditional reed dance.

example of group conformity among political leaders was discussed in the previous chapter—that is, the November 1998 incident in which RCMP officers in Vancouver pepper-sprayed unarmed student protesters during the Asia-Pacific Economic Cooperation summit.

Common sense tells us that group discussion improves decision-making. Janis counters that group members often seek consensus that closes off alternative points of view. Janis called this process **groupthink**, *the tendency of group members to conform, resulting in a narrow view of some issue.*

## REFERENCE GROUPS

How do we assess our own attitudes and behaviour? Frequently, we use a **reference group**, *a social group that serves as a point of reference in making evaluations and decisions.*

A young man who imagines his family's response to a woman he is dating is using his family as a refer-

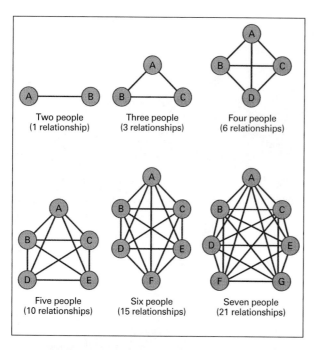

**FIGURE 5–2    Group Size and Relationships**

ence group. Similarly, a supervisor who tries to gauge her employees' reactions to a new vacation policy is using them as a standard of reference. As these examples suggest, reference groups can be primary or secondary. In either case, our need to conform means that others' attitudes greatly affect us.

We also use groups for reference even when we do *not* belong to them. Being well prepared for a job interview means showing up dressed the way people dress who work in that company. Conforming to groups we do not belong to is a strategy to win acceptance, and it illustrates the process of *anticipatory socialization* discussed in Chapter 3 (Socialization: From Infancy to Old Age).

**Stouffer's research.** Samuel A. Stouffer (1949) conducted a classic study of reference groups during the Second World War. Researchers asked soldiers to rate a competent soldier's chances of promotion in his branch of the army. One might guess that soldiers serving in outfits with high promotion rates would be optimistic about advancement. Yet Stouffer's research pointed to the opposite conclusion: Soldiers in army assignments with low promotion rates were actually more positive about their chances to move ahead.

The key to understanding Stouffer's results lies in the groups against which soldiers measured themselves. Those having assignments with lower promotion rates

looked around them and saw people making no more headway than they were. That is, although they had not been promoted, neither had many others, so they did not feel deprived.

Soldiers having assignments with a higher promotion rate, however, could easily think of people who had been promoted sooner or more often than they had. With such people in mind, even soldiers who had been promoted were likely to feel short-changed.

The point is that we do not make judgments about ourselves in isolation, nor do we compare ourselves with just anyone at random. Regardless of our situation in *absolute* terms, we form a subjective sense of our well-being by looking at ourselves *relative* to specific reference groups (Merton, 1968; Mirowsky, 1987).

## INGROUPS AND OUTGROUPS

Everyone favours some groups over others, whether due to political outlook, social prestige, or simply manner of dress. On the campus, for example, left-leaning student activists may look down on the Right to Life group whom they view as conservative; the anti-abortionists, in turn, may snub the computer "nerds" and "grinds" who work too hard. People in virtually every social setting develop such positive and negative evaluations.

Such judgments illustrate another key element of group dynamics: the opposition of ingroups and outgroups. An **ingroup** is *a social group commanding a member's esteem and loyalty*. An **outgroup**, by contrast, is *a social group toward which one feels competition or opposition*. Ingroups and outgroups are based on the idea that "we" have valued traits that "they" lack.

Tensions among groups sharpen their boundaries and give people a clearer social identity. However, members of ingroups generally hold overly positive views of themselves and unfairly negative views of various outgroups (Tajfel, 1982).

Power also shapes intergroup relations. A powerful ingroup can define others as a lower-status outgroup. In Canada, for example, the French and English have viewed people of Sikh and West Indian backgrounds as outgroups and subordinated them socially, politically, and economically. Internalizing these negative attitudes, minorities often struggle to overcome negative self-images. In this way, ingroups and outgroups foster loyalty but also generate conflict (Bobo & Hutchings, 1996; Allahar, 1998).

## GROUP SIZE

If you are the first person to arrive at a party, you are in a position to observe some fascinating group dynamics.

Until about six people enter the room, everyone generally shares a single conversation. But as more people arrive, the group soon divides into two or more clusters. Size plays a crucial role in how group members interact.

To understand why, note the mathematical number of relationships among two to seven people. As shown in Figure 5–2, two people form a single relationship; adding a third person results in three relationships; a fourth person yields six. Increasing the number of people one at a time, then, boosts the number of relationships much more rapidly because every new individual can interact with everyone already there. Thus, by the time seven people join one conversation, 21 "channels" connect them. With so many open channels, the group usually divides.

German sociologist Georg Simmel (1858–1918) explored the dynamics of the smallest social groups. Simmel (1950; orig. 1902) used the term **dyad** (from the Greek word for "pair") to designate *a social group with two members.*

Simmel explained that social interaction in a dyad is typically more intense than in larger groups, since neither member shares the other's attention with anyone else. In Canada, love affairs, marriages, and the closest friendships are dyadic.

But like a stool with only two legs, dyads are unstable. Both members of a dyad must work to keep the relationship going; if either withdraws, the group collapses. Because the stability of marriage is important to society, the marital dyad is supported with legal, economic, and often religious ties.

A **triad** is *a social group with three members.* A triad contains three relationships, each uniting two of the three people. A triad is more stable than a dyad because one member can act as a mediator if relations between the other two become strained. This bit of group dynamics explains why members of a dyad (say, a married couple) often seek out a third person (such as a counsellor) to air tensions between them.

On the other hand, two of the three can pair up to press their views on the third, or two may intensify their relationship, making the other feel left out. For example, when two of the three develop a romantic interest in each other, they discover the meaning of the old saying "Two's company, three's a crowd."

As groups grow beyond three people, they become more stable and capable of withstanding the loss of even several members. At the same time, increases in group size reduce the intense interaction possible in only the smallest groups. Larger groups are thus based less on personal attachments and more on formal rules and regulations. Such formality helps a group persist over time, though the group certainly is not immune to

*Throughout the world, the most intense social bonds join two people, such as these twin sisters. Even so, the dyad is also characteristically unstable, since withdrawal of either party causes the group to collapse.*

change. After all, the more members a group has, the more contact it has with the outside world, opening the door to new attitudes and behaviour (Carley, 1991).

## SOCIAL DIVERSITY: RACE, CLASS, AND GENDER

Race, ethnicity, class, and gender also affect group dynamics. Peter Blau (1977; Blau, Blum, & Schwarz, 1982; South & Messner, 1986) points out three ways in which social diversity influences intergroup contact:

1. **Large groups turn inward.** Blau explains that the larger a group, the more likely its members will concentrate on relationships among themselves. For example, say a school is trying to enhance social diversity by increasing the number of international students. These students may add a dimension of difference, but as their numbers rise they become more likely to form their own social group. Thus efforts to promote social diver-

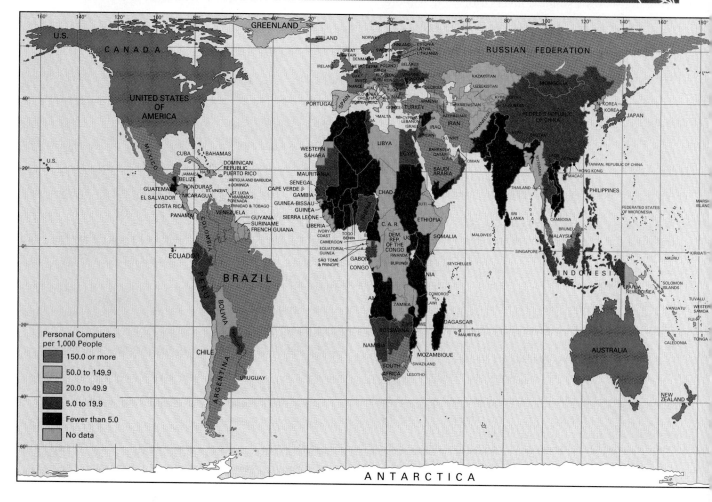

**GLOBAL MAP 5–1  High Technology in Global Perspective**

Countries with traditional cultures either cannot afford, ignore, or sometimes even resist technological innovation; nations with highly rationalized ways of life quickly embrace such changes. Personal computers, a central form of today's high technology, are numerous in high-income countries such as Canada. In low-income nations, by contrast, they are unknown to most people.

Source: The World Bank (1999).

sity may have the unintended effect of promoting separatism.

2. **Heterogeneous groups turn outward.** The more internally diverse a group is, the more likely it is to interact with outsiders. If you look at the various ethnic groups in your community, you are likely to find that ethnicities with a longer history in Canada are more heterogeneous and more likely to interact with others than are recent arrivals. Immigrants to Canada tend to settle in our major

cities. This is one reason that residents of Montreal and Vancouver have more intergroup contact than residents of small towns and outports, which comprise people of only one or a few types.

3. **Physical boundaries foster social boundaries.** To the extent that a social group is physically segregated from others (by having its own dorm or dining area, for example), its members are less likely to associate with other people. Military families in Canada and elsewhere serve as an example.

As Deborah Harrison and Lucie Laliberté (1994:21) point out, "[T]he military is a portable total institution that isolates its members from civilians . . . . As in the case of other total institutions, isolation from civilians facilitates control."

## NETWORKS

A **network** is *a web of weak social ties.* Think of a network as a "fuzzy" group containing people who come into occasional contact but lack a sense of boundaries and belonging. If we think of a group as a "circle of friends," then, we might think of a network as a "social web," one that expands outward, often reaching great distances and including a large number of people.

Some networks come close to being groups, as is the case with college friends who stay in touch by e-mail and telephone years after graduation. More commonly, however, a network includes people we *know of*—or who *know of us*—but with whom we interact rarely, if at all. As one woman with a reputation as a community organizer puts it, "I get calls at home, someone says, 'Are you Roseann Navarro? Somebody told me to call you. I have this problem . . .'" (Kaminer, 1984:94).

Networks may contain weak ties, but they can be a powerful resource. For immigrants seeking to become established in a new community, businesspeople seeking to expand their operations, or anyone looking for a job, *who you know* is often just as important as *what you know* (Luo, 1997; Hagan, 1998).

Networks are based on peoples' schools, clubs, neighbourhoods, political parties, and personal interests. Obviously, some networks are made up of people with considerably more wealth, power, and prestige than others, which is what the expression "well connected" means. An example might be members of the prestigious Royal Society of Canada. And some people have denser networks than others—that is, they are connected to more people—which makes for another type of power. Typically, the most extensive social networks are maintained by people who are young, well educated, and living in urban areas (Markovsky et al., 1993; Kadushin, 1995; O'Brien, Hassinger, & Dershem, 1996; Fernandez & Weinberg, 1997; Podolny & Baron, 1997; Wellman & Hampton, 1999). Barry Wellman (1999) goes further; rather than studying geographical communities, such as neighbourhoods, he studies social networks or ties that members use to gain resources, and calls these communities.

Gender, too, shapes networks. Although the networks of men and women are typically the same size, women count more relatives among their network contacts, while men include more co-workers in theirs. Women's networks, therefore, may not carry quite the

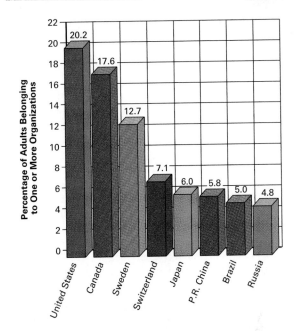

GLOBAL SNAPSHOT

**FIGURE 5-3  Membership in Cultural or Educational Organizations**

Source: World Values Survey (1994).

same clout as the "old boy" networks do. This seems to be the case in the "wired world," where men still tend to have the upper hand (Stewart Millar, 1998). Yet women are developing strategies to "crack the gender code." Further, as gender inequality lessens, research indicates that network differences will probably diminish (Moore, 1991, 1992; Wright, 1995).

Finally, new information technology has generated a global network, the Internet, which can potentially speed up communication among people with access to this new technology, wherever they might be located. Communication among the 5000-plus participants attending the 14th World Congress of Sociology, held in 1998 in Montreal, was primarily via the Internet—for registration, room bookings, payment of fees, and even downloading of receipts! The Global Sociology box on the next page takes a closer look at this 21st-century form of networking, while Global Map 5–1 shows access to computers around the world.

## FORMAL ORGANIZATIONS

A century ago, most Canadians lived in small groups of family, friends, and neighbours. Today, our lives

# The Internet: Welcome to Cyberspace!

Its origins could be right out of the 1960s cold war film *Dr. Strangelove*. Three decades ago, U.S. government officials and scientists were trying to imagine how to run the country after an atomic attack, which, they assumed, would wipe out in a flash all telephones and television. The brilliant solution they devised was a communication system with no central headquarters, no one in charge, and no main power switch—in short, an electronic web that would link the country in one vast network.

By 1985, the Internet was about to be born. Today, hundreds of thousands of government offices and schools, ranging from kindergarten to the most advanced research institution, are joined by the Internet and share in the cost of its operation. Add the individuals that connect

their home computers to the information superhighway using a telephone-line modem and a subscription to an Internet "gateway," and we arrive at estimates approaching 200 million users connected by the largest network in history.

Figure 5–4 shows that there is a great amount of variation among nations in the proportion of people accessing the Internet. There are easy-to-understand differences among nations based on wealth, but there are also differences among high-income nations.

What is available on the Internet? Popular "search engines" such as YAHOO! (**www.yahoo.ca**) list sites for just about any topic you can imagine—did you ever go "ego-surfing" by searching for your own name? The Internet also allows you to send e-mail: You can

start a cyber-romance, write to your textbook authors (macionis@kenyon.edu; cbenoit@uvic.ca; mjansson@island net. com), or even send a message to the prime minister of Canada (pm@pm.gc.ca). Through the Internet, you can join in discussion groups, visit museums for "virtual tours," locate data from government agencies (a good starting point is **www.statcan.ca**), explore sites of sociological interest though a virtual sociology library (**www.mcmaster.ca/ socscidocs/w3virtsoclib/index.htm**), or review for exams in this course (**www.pearsoned.ca/macionis**). With no formal rules for its use, the Internet's potential is limited only by our own imaginations.

Ironically, perhaps, it is precisely this freedom that disturbs some people.

---

revolve more and more around **formal organizations**, *large secondary groups that are organized to achieve their goals efficiently.* Formal organizations such as corporations and government offices differ from small primary groups in their impersonality and planned atmosphere.

When you think about it, organizing some 30 million people is a daunting feat involving countless jobs from collecting taxes to delivering the mail. To carry out most of these tasks, we rely upon large formal organizations that develop lives and cultures of their own so that, over the years and as members come and go, their operation can stay much the same.

## TYPES OF FORMAL ORGANIZATIONS

Amitai Etzioni (1975) identified three types of organizations distinguished by the reasons people participate. Just about everyone who works for income belongs to a *utilitarian organization.* Joining a utilitarian organization is usually a matter of individual choice, although, obviously, most people must join one or another such organization to make a living.

People join *normative organizations* not for income but to pursue some goal they think is morally worthwhile. Sometimes called *voluntary associations*, these

include community service groups (such as the Canadian International Development Agency [CIDA], the Lions Club, the Status of Women Canada, the Red Cross, or the whites-only organization Stormfront), political parties, and religious organizations. In global perspective, people in the United States, Canada, and Sweden are especially likely to be members of voluntary associations (Curtis, Grabb, & Baer, 1992). Figure 5–3 on page 109 provides a comparative glance at membership in cultural or educational organizations for selected countries.

*Coercive organizations* have an involuntary membership. That is, people are forced to join these organizations as a form of punishment (prisons) or treatment (psychiatric hospitals). Coercive organizations have special physical features, such as locked doors and barred windows, and are supervised by security personnel. They isolate people as "inmates" or "patients" for a period of time and sometimes radically alter those people's attitudes and behaviour (Goffman, 1961).

From differing points of view, a formal organization may fall into *all* of these categories. A mental hospital, for example, serves as a coercive organization for a patient, a utilitarian organization for

Critics claim that "electronic democracy" threatens our political system, parents fear that their children will access sexually explicit "adult sites," and purists bristle as the Internet becomes ever more flooded with advertising.

In its "anything goes" character, of course, the Internet is like the real world. Not surprisingly, then, a recent trend is that more and more users now employ passwords, fees, and other "gates" to create sub-networks limited to people like themselves. From one vast network is emerging a host of social groups. National governments, too, are beginning to enact legislation forcing search engines to block Web surfers from accessing certain featured information. Recently, for example, a French judge gave Yahoo! a three-month grace period to block users based in France from accessing pages on **auctions.yahoo.com**, where Nazi memorabilia is being auctioned off to the highest Internet bidder (*Times Colonist*, 2000).

Source: Based, in part, on Elmer-DeWitt (1993, 1994), Hafner (1994), O'Connor (1997), and Wellman & Gulia (1999).

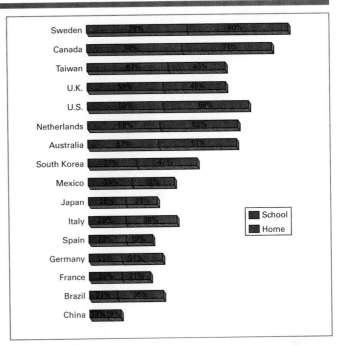

**Figure 5–4    Accessing the Internet**

**Note:** Percentage of students aged 12 to 24 who access the Internet at their school or home.

Source: Based on Data from Angus Reid Group (Foss, 2000)

a psychiatrist, and a normative organization for a part-time hospital volunteer.

## ORIGINS OF BUREAUCRACY

Formal organizations date back thousands of years. Elites who governed early empires relied on government officials to collect taxes, undertake military campaigns, and construct monumental structures, from the Great Wall of China to the pyramids of Egypt.

The efficiency of early organizations was limited, however, in two ways. First, they lacked the technology to travel over large distances, to communicate quickly, and to collect and store information. Second, pre-industrial societies usually had a traditional character. **Tradition**, according to German sociologist Max Weber, is *sentiments and beliefs about the world passed from generation to generation.* Tradition makes a society conservative, Weber explained, because it limits an organization's efficiency and ability to change.

By contrast, Weber characterized the modern world view as **rationality**, *deliberate, matter-of-fact calculation of the most efficient means to accomplish a particular task.* A rational world view pays little attention to the past and is open to change in whatever way seems likely to get the job done better or more quickly.

The rise of the "organizational society" rests on what Weber termed **rationalization**, *change from tradition to rationality as the dominant mode of human thought.* Modern society, he claimed, becomes "disenchanted" as sentimental ties give way to a rational focus on science, complex technology, and the organizational structure called *bureaucracy.*

## CHARACTERISTICS OF BUREAUCRACY

**Bureaucracy** is *an organizational model rationally designed to perform tasks efficiently.* Bureaucratic officials regularly enact and revise policy to increase efficiency. To appreciate the power and scope of bureaucratic organization, consider that any one of the millions of phones in Canada can connect you within seconds to any other phone in homes, businesses, automobiles, or even an oil rig located offshore on Canada's east coast. Such instant communication would have been beyond the imagination of people who lived in the ancient world.

Of course, the telephone system depends on technology such as electricity, fiber-optics, and computers. But the system could not exist without the

*Although formal organization is vital to modern, industrial societies, it is far from new. Twenty-five centuries ago, the Chinese philosopher and teacher K'ung Fu-Tzu (known to Westerners as Confucius) endorsed the idea that government offices should be filled by the most talented young men. This led to what was probably the world's first system of civil service examinations. Here, would-be bureaucrats compose essays to demonstrate their knowledge of Confucian texts.*

organizational capacity to keep track of every telephone call—recording which phone called which other phone, when, and for how long—and presenting all this information to the tens of millions of telephone users in the form of monthly bills.

What specific traits promote organizational efficiency? Max Weber (1978; orig. 1921) identified six key elements of the ideal bureaucratic organization:

1. **Specialization.** Our ancestors spent most of their time looking for food and finding shelter. Bureaucracy, by contrast, assigns individuals highly specialized duties.

2. **Hierarchy of offices.** Bureaucracies arrange personnel in a vertical ranking of offices. Each person is thus supervised by "higher-ups" in the organization while, in turn, supervising others in lower positions. Usually, with few people at the top and many at the bottom, bureaucratic organizations take the form of a pyramid.

3. **Rules and regulations.** Rationally enacted rules and regulations guide a bureaucracy's operation. Ideally, a bureaucracy seeks to operate in a completely predictable fashion.

4. **Technical competence.** Bureaucratic officials have the technical competence to carry out their duties. Bureaucracies typically recruit new members according to set criteria and, afterward, monitor their performance. Such impersonal evaluation contrasts with the ancient custom of favouring relatives—whatever their talents—over strangers.

5. **Impersonality.** Bureaucracy puts rules ahead of personal whim so that clients as well as workers are all treated uniformly. From this detached approach comes the notion of the "faceless bureaucrat."

6. **Formal, written communications.** Someone once said that the heart of bureaucracy is not people but paperwork. Rather than casual, face-to-face talk, bureaucracy relies on formal written memos and reports, which accumulate in vast files.

Bureaucratic organization promotes efficiency by carefully recruiting personnel and limiting the unpredictable effects of personal taste and opinion. Table 5–2 summarizes the differences between small social groups and large formal organizations.

## ORGANIZATIONAL ENVIRONMENT

No organization operates in a vacuum. How any organization performs depends not only on its own goals and policies but also on the **organizational environment**, *a range of factors outside the organization that affect its operation*. These factors include technology, economic and political systems, the available workforce, as well as other organizations.

Modern organizations are shaped by the *technology* of computers, telephone systems, and copiers. Computers give employees access to more information and people than ever before. At the same time, computer technology allows managers to monitor closely the activities of workers (Markoff, 1991).

*Economic and political trends* affect organizations. All organizations are helped or hindered by periodic economic growth or recession. Most industries also face competition from abroad as well as government regulation and changes in law—such as new environmental standards—at home.

*Population patterns*—such as the size and composition of the surrounding populace—also affect organizations. The average age, typical education, and social diversity of a local community determine the available workforce, and sometimes the market for an organization's products or services.

Fourth, *other organizations* also contribute to the organizational environment. To be competitive, a hospital in Canada must not only be responsive to budgetary constraints imposed by the provincial and federal governments and the rules and regulations of the regional health board, but also keep open clear lines of communication with provincial medical, nursing, and allied workers' professional associations and unions, keep abreast of the equipment and procedures available at nearby facilities, and be responsive to the needs and concerns of the local population served by the hospital (Armstrong & Armstrong, 1996).

## THE INFORMAL SIDE OF BUREAUCRACY

Weber's ideal bureaucracy deliberately regulates every activity. In actual organizations, however, human beings are creative (and stubborn) enough to resist bureaucratic blueprints. Informality may amount to simply cutting corners on the job, but it also can provide necessary flexibility (Scott, 1981).

In part, informality comes from the varying personalities of organizational leaders. Studies of large corporations document that the qualities and quirks of individuals—including personal charisma and interpersonal skills—greatly affect organizational outcomes (Halberstam, 1986).

Authoritarian, democratic, and laissez-faire types of leadership (described earlier in this chapter) reflect

### TABLE 5–2 Small Groups and Formal Organizations: A Comparison

| | Small Groups | Formal Organizations |
| --- | --- | --- |
| **Activities** | Members typically engage in many of the same activities | Members typically engage in distinct, highly specialized activities |
| **Hierarchy** | Often informal or nonexistent | Clearly defined, corresponding to offices |
| **Norms** | Informal application of general norms | Clearly defined rules and regulations |
| **Criteria for Membership** | Variable, often based on personal affection or kinship | Technical competence to carry out assigned tasks |
| **Relationships** | Variable; typically primary | Typically secondary, with selective primary ties |
| **Communications** | Typically casual and face-to-face | Typically formal and in writing |
| **Focus** | Person-oriented | Task-oriented |

individual personality as much as they do any organizational plan. Then, too, in the "real world" of organizations, leaders and their cronies sometimes seek to benefit personally through abuse of organizational power. Perhaps even more common, leaders take credit for the efforts of their subordinates. Many secretaries, for example, have far more authority and responsibility than their official job titles and salaries suggest.

Communication offers another example of organizational informality. Memos and other written documents are the formal way to spread information through the organization. Typically, however, people create informal networks or "grapevines" that spread information quickly, if not always accurately. Grapevines—using word-of-mouth and e-mail—are particularly important to rank-and-file workers because higher-ups often attempt to keep important information from them.

The spread of e-mail has "flattened" organizations somewhat, allowing even the lowest-ranking employee to bypass immediate superiors in order to communicate directly with the organization's leader or with all fellow employees at once. Some organizations consider such "open-channel" communication unwelcome, and therefore limit the use of e-mail. Leaders also may seek to protect themselves from a flood of messages each day. Microsoft Corporation (whose leader, Bill Gates,

*During the past 50 years in Canada, women have moved into management positions throughout the corporate world. While some men initially opposed women's presence in the executive office, it is now clear that women bring particular strengths to the job, including leadership flexibility and communication skills. Thus some analysts speak of women offering a "female advantage."*

has an "unlisted" address yet still receives hundreds of e-mail messages a day) has developed "screens" that allow messages from only approved people to reach a particular computer terminal (Gwynne & Dickerson, 1997).

Despite the highly regulated nature of bureaucracy, members of formal organizations still find ways to personalize their work and surroundings. Such efforts suggest that there are also some problems associated with bureaucracy.

## PROBLEMS OF BUREAUCRACY

We rely on bureaucracy to manage countless dimensions of everyday life, but many people are, at best, uneasy about large organizations. Bureaucracy can dehumanize as well as manipulate us, and some say it poses a threat to liberal democracies such as Canada.

**Bureaucratic alienation.** Max Weber touted bureaucracy as a model of productivity. Yet Weber was keenly aware of bureaucracy's potential to *dehumanize* the people it is supposed to serve. The same impersonality that fosters efficiency simultaneously keeps officials and clients from responding to each other's unique, personal needs. On the contrary, officials must treat each client impersonally as a standard "case."

Formal organizations create *alienation*, according to Max Weber, by reducing the human being to "a small cog in a ceaselessly moving mechanism" (1978:988; orig. 1921). Although formal organizations are designed to serve humanity, Weber feared that people might well end up serving formal organizations. The Applying Sociology box on page 116 provides the example of language used by the military to mask the horrors of war.

**Bureaucratic ritualism.** *Inefficiency*, the failure of a formal organization to carry out the work it exists to perform, is a familiar problem. Anyone who has ever tried to complain to Canada Post about a lost or damaged letter, to obtain a refund for a coupon attached to a purchased item, or to change an address at the university or college registrar's office knows that bureaucracies sometimes can be maddeningly unresponsive. According to one report, government agencies responsible for buying equipment for staff can take up to three years to process a request for a new computer. This ensures that by the time the computer arrives, it is already out of date (Gwynne & Dickerson, 1997).

The problem of inefficiency is captured in the concept of *red tape* (a term derived from the red tape used by 18-century English administrators to wrap official parcels and records; Shipley, 1985). To Robert Merton (1968), red tape amounts to a new twist on the already-familiar concept of group conformity. He coined the term **bureaucratic ritualism** to describe *a preoccupation with rules and regulations to the point of thwarting an organization's goals*.

**Bureaucratic inertia.** Though bureaucrats sometimes have little reason to work efficiently, they have every reason to protect their jobs. Thus, officials typically strive to keep their organization going, even when its goal has been realized. As Weber put it, "[O]nce fully established, bureaucracy is among the social structures which are hardest to destroy" (1978:987; orig. 1921).

**Bureaucratic inertia** refers to *the tendency of bureaucratic organizations to perpetuate themselves*. Formal organizations tend to take on a life of their own beyond their formal objectives. While, occasionally, a formal organization that meets its goals will simply disband, more commonly the organization stays in business by redefining its goals so it can continue to provide a livelihood for its members.

Consider the transitions that spy and military agencies have undergone since the "cold war" ended: The Canadian Security Intelligence Service (CSIS) now protect us from international terrorism and economic espionage rather than communists. Similarly, the North Atlantic Treaty Organization (NATO) now focusses on peace-keeping and humanitarian missions, and the organization includes the Czech Republic, Hungary, and Poland as member nations rather than the foes that NATO was originally created to defend against.

**Oligarchy.** Early in this century, Robert Michels (1876–1936) pointed out the link between bureaucracy and political **oligarchy,** *the rule of the many by the few* (1949; orig. 1911). According to what Michels called "the iron law of oligarchy," the pyramid shape of bureaucracy places a few leaders in charge of organizational resources.

Max Weber credited bureaucracy's strict hierarchy of responsibility with increasing organizational efficiency. By applying Weber's thesis to politics, however, Michels noted that hierarchy also undermines democracy. Moreover, political officials can—and often do—use their access to information and the media to promote their personal interests. Oligarchy, then, thrives in the hierarchical structure of bureaucracy, and can undermine people's confidence in their elected leaders (Tolson, 1995).

Many trade unions are also characterized by powerful leadership cliques that come to dominate the much larger rank-and-file membership. The Seafarers' International Union (SIU) provides a good example of such a trade union. Hal C. Banks, a U.S. convicted felon and union strong-arm, was recruited by the international union in 1949 to break up the communist-controlled unions that were blocking Canada's shipping industry. His aim was to replace them with a Canadian chapter of the SIU. Banks controlled the SIU leadership until 1962, when a small group of union members confronted him and his supporters. Eventually Banks was removed from power, and the union reorganized. Yet union oligarchy is not inevitable. Recently in Canada, for example, there has been a democratization movement from below in many unions, resulting in more members participating in important decisions (Krahn & Lowe, 1998:321).

Overall, however, bureaucracies tend to insulate top officials from the public, as in the case of the corporate president or public official who is "unavailable for comment" to the local press or the national leader who withholds documents from Parliament by claiming "executive privilege." Thus oligarchy thrives in the hierarchical structure of bureaucracy and reduces the accountability of leaders to the people (Tolson, 1995).

Political competition, term limits, and a system of checks and balances prevent the Canadian and other democratic governments from becoming out-and-out oligarchies. Even so, incumbents enjoy a significant advantage in Canadian politics. In the November 2000 Parliamentary elections, only two MPs running for reelection were defeated.

# THE EVOLUTION OF FORMAL ORGANIZATIONS

The problems of bureaucracy—especially the alienation it produces and its tendency toward oligarchy—

*According to Max Weber, bureaucracy is an organizational strategy that promotes efficiency. Impersonality, however, also fosters alienation among employees, who may become indifferent to the formal goals of the organization. The behaviour of this municipal employee in Bombay, India, would be understandable to members of formal organizations almost anywhere in the world.*

stem from two organizational traits: hierarchy and rigidity. To Weber, bureaucracy was a top-down system: Rules and regulations made at the top guide every facet of people's work down the chain of command. A century ago in North America, Weber's ideas took hold in an organizational model called "scientific management." We begin with a look at this model, and then describe three challenges over the course of the 20th century that gradually led to a new model—the "flexible organization."

## SCIENTIFIC MANAGEMENT

Frederick Winslow Taylor (1911) had a simple message: Most North American businesses were sadly inefficient. Most managers had little idea of how to increase their businesses' output and workers relied on the same tired skills of earlier generations. To increase efficiency, Taylor explained, business should apply the principles of science. **Scientific management** is *the application of scientific principles to the operation of a business or other large organization.*

Scientific management involves three steps. First, managers carefully observe the task performed by each worker, identifying all the operations involved and

## APPLYING SOCIOLOGY

# The "Spin" Game:
# Choosing Our Words Carefully

Military organizations, both in Canada and abroad, choose their words carefully to mask the horrors of war and make military action seem necessary and good. William Lutz (1996), an English professor, collected examples of language used by military officers in the 1991 Persian Gulf War. Read the following military terminology and the straight-talk translations. How do these terms put a "spin" on reality?

| Military Language | Everyday Meaning |
|---|---|
| Incontinent ordinance | Bombs or shells that miss their targets and hit civilians. |
| Area denial weapons | Cluster bombs that kill and destroy anything within a particular area |
| Coercive potential | The capacity of bombs and shells to kill and injure the enemy |
| Suppressing assets | Reducing the enemy's ability to fight by killing people and destroying equipment |
| Ballistically induced aperture | Bullet hole |
| Scenario dependent, post-crisis environment | Whether we win or lose |

measuring the time needed for each. Second, managers analyze their data, trying to discover ways for workers to perform each task more efficiently. Managers, for example, might decide to provide workers with different tools, or reposition various work operations within the factory. Third, management provides incentives for workers to do their jobs more efficiently. If a factory worker moves 20 tonnes of pig iron in one day, for example, management shows the worker how to do the job more efficiently, and then provides higher wages as the worker's productivity rises. Applying scientific principles in this way, Taylor concluded, companies become more profitable, workers earn higher wages, and, in the end, consumers end up paying lower prices. Auto pioneer Henry Ford, who was enthusiastic in his support of scientific management, put it this way: "Save 10 steps a day for each of 12 000 employees, and you will have saved 50 miles of wasted motion and misspent energy" (Allen & Hyman, 1999:209).

In the early 1900s, Ford and many other businesses followed Taylor's lead and improved their efficiency. As time went on, however, formal organizations faced three new challenges involving gender, rising competition from abroad, and changes in work itself. We look briefly at each in turn.

### THE FIRST CHALLENGE: GENDER

During the 1960s, critics pointed out that big businesses and other organizations were inefficient—and also unfair—in their hiring practices. Rather than hiring on the basis of competence, as Weber had proposed, they excluded women and other minorities. As a result, in the early 1960s, the vast majority of managers—just under 90 percent—were white men (Benoit, 2000a).

**Patterns of exclusion.** By 1987, 29 percent of managerial positions in Canada were held by women, and by 1999 the figure had risen to 35 percent. So even today, Canadian men still hold 65 percent of managerial jobs across the country. Further, women holding managerial positions tend to be clustered in lower-level managerial positions. In 1999, for example, women comprised only 29 percent of senior managers (Statistics Canada, 2000m:107).

*George Tooker's painting* Government Bureau *is a powerful statement about the human costs of bureaucracy. The artist depicts members of the public in monotonous similitude—reduced from human beings to mere "cases" to be disposed of as quickly as possible. Set apart from others by their positions, officials are "faceless bureaucrats" concerned more with numbers than with providing genuine assistance (notice that the artist places the fingers of the officials on calculators).*

Source: George Tooker, *Government Bureau*, 1956. Egg tempera on gesso panel, 19 5/8 Ñ 29 5/8 inches. The Metropolitan Museum of Art, George A. Hearn Fund, 1956 (56.78).

Rosabeth Moss Kanter (1977; Kanter & Stein, 1979) points out that excluding women from the workplace ignores the talents of more than half the population. Furthermore, underrepresented people in an organization often feel like socially isolated outgroups—uncomfortably visible, taken less seriously, and given fewer chances for promotion (Waldram, 1993).

"Opening up" an organization, Kanter claims, improves everyone's on-the-job performance by motivating employees to become "fast-trackers" who work harder and are more committed to the company. By contrast, an organization with many "dead-end" jobs turns workers into unproductive "zombies." An open organization also encourages leaders to seek out the input of everyone, which benefits the organization. It is officials in rigid organizations—those who have little reason themselves to be creative—who jealously guard their privileges and ride herd over their employees.

**The "female advantage."** Some organizational researchers argue that including more women brings special management skills that strengthen an organization. Deborah Tannen (1994) claims, for example, that women have a greater "information focus," and more readily ask questions in order to understand an issue. Men, on the other hand, have an "image focus" that makes them wonder how asking questions in a particular situation will affect their reputation.

In another study of female executives, Sally Helgesen (1990) found three additional gender-linked patterns. First, women place greater value on communication skills and share information more than men do. Second, women are more flexible leaders who typically give their employees greater autonomy. Third, compared to men, women tend to emphasize the interconnectedness of all organizational operations. Thus,

women bring a "female advantage" to companies striving to be more flexible and democratic.

In sum, one challenge to conventional bureaucracy is becoming more open and flexible in order to take advantage of everyone's experience, ideas, and creativity (Lowe, 2000). The result goes right to the bottom line: greater profits.

## THE SECOND CHALLENGE: THE JAPANESE ORGANIZATION

In 1980, the North American corporate world was shaken to discover that the most popular automobile model sold on the continent was not a Chevrolet, Ford, or Plymouth, but the Honda Accord, made in Japan. To people old enough to remember back to the 1950s, the words "made in Japan" generally meant a cheap, poorly made product. But times had changed. The success of the Japanese auto industry (and, soon after, companies making electronics, cameras, and other products) soon had analysts buzzing about the "Japanese organization." How else could so small a country challenge the North American economic powerhouse?

Japanese organizations reflect that nation's strong collective spirit. That is, while most members of our society prize rugged individualism, the Japanese value cooperation. In effect, then, formal organizations in Japan are like very large primary groups. William Ouchi (1981) highlights five differences between formal organizations in Japan and in North America:

1. **Hiring and advancement.** North American organizations hold out promotions and raises in salary as prizes to be won through individual competition. In Japanese organizations, however, companies hire new school graduates as a group, and everyone in

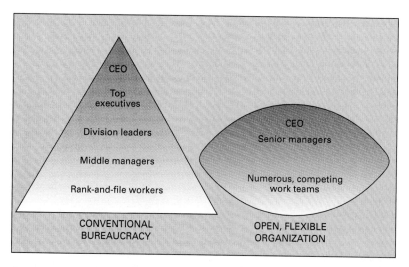

**FIGURE 5–5 Two Organizational Models**

The conventional model of bureaucratic organizations has a pyramid shape, with a clear chain of command. Directives flow from the top down, while reports of performance flow from the bottom up. Such organizations have extensive rules and regulations, and their workers have highly specialized jobs. More open and flexible organizations have a flatter shape, more like a football. With fewer levels in the hierarchy, responsibility for generating ideas and making decisions is shared throughout the organization. Many workers do their jobs in teams and have a broad knowledge of the entire organization's operation.

Source: Created by John Macionis.

that group receives the same salary and responsibilities. Only after several years is anyone likely to be singled out for special advancement.

2. **Lifetime security.** Employees in Canada and the United States expect to move from one company to another to advance their careers. North American companies are also prone to lay off employees during an economic setback. By contrast, most Japanese firms hire workers for life, fostering strong, mutual loyalties. If jobs become obsolete, Japanese companies avoid layoffs by retraining workers for new positions.

3. **Holistic involvement.** While we tend to see the home and the workplace as distinct spheres, Japanese companies play a much larger role in workers' lives. They provide home mortgages, sponsor recreational activities, and schedule social events. Such interaction beyond the workplace strengthens collective identity and offers the always respectful Japanese employees a venue in which to voice suggestions and criticisms informally.

4. **Broad-based training.** Workers in Canada and the U.S. are highly specialized, and many spend an entire career perfecting one set of skills. But a Japanese organization trains workers in all phases of its operation, again with the idea that employees will remain with the company for life.

5. **Collective decision making.** In most North American companies even today, key executives make the important decisions. Although Japanese leaders also take responsibility for their organization's performance, they involve workers in "quality circles" to discuss decisions that affect them. Japan's lower salary difference between executives and workers—about 10 percent of the difference typical in North America—also encourages a closer working relationship.

These characteristics give the Japanese a strong sense of organizational loyalty. Because their personal interests are tied to company interests, workers realize their ambitions through the organization. Japanese *groupism* is thus the cultural equivalent—and yet the opposite—of our society's emphasis on *individual* achievement.

On the other hand, it should be noted that the so-called Japanese Model is available only to workers belonging to the core labour market, typically a privileged male core of nationals (Kiely, 1998). "The cost of employing life-time workers means an incentive to subcontract all jobs not essential to the core. The other side of the Japanese job-for-life is a majority of low-paid, fragmented peripheral workers, facing an under-funded and inadequate welfare state" (Murray, 1989:46).

Further, given the recent downturn in the Japanese and some other Asian economies, the future of the core Japanese organizations remains uncertain. Does, then, the Japanese corporate model still warrant attention? Whatever the future of the model in the Japanese corporate world, there are nevertheless still important lessons to be learned, not the least of which is its people-focussed strategy, which involves valuing the people who work hard to make high-performance work systems achieve (Appelbaum & Batt, 1994; Lowe, 2000).

## THE THIRD CHALLENGE: THE CHANGING NATURE OF WORK

Beyond rising global competition, pressure to modify conventional organizations is also coming from changes in the nature of work itself. In recent decades, the Canadian economy has moved from industrial to post-industrial production. In other words, rather than working in factories using heavy machinery to make *things*, more people are using computers and other electronic technology to create or process *information*. Thus, a post-industrial society is characterized by information-based organizations.

Frederick Taylor developed his concept of scientific management at a time when jobs involved tasks that, while often backbreaking, were routine. Workers shovelled coal, poured liquid iron into moulds, attached body panels to automobiles on an assembly line, or shot hot rivets into steel girders to build skyscrapers. In addition, a large part of the Canadian labour force in Taylor's day was immigrants, most of whom had little schooling and many of whom knew little English. The routine nature of industrial jobs, coupled with the limited skills of the labour force, led Taylor to treat work as a series of fixed tasks, set down by management and followed by employees.

Many of today's information-age jobs are very different: The work of designers, artists, consultants, writers, editors, composers, programmers, business owners, and others now demands creativity and imagination. What does this mean for formal organizations? Here are several ways in which today's organizations differ from those of a century ago:

1. **Creative autonomy.** Organizations know that employees with information-age skills are a vital resource. Executives can set production goals, but cannot dictate how to accomplish tasks involving imagination and discovery. Thus, highly skilled workers have *creative autonomy*, which means they are subject to less day-to-day supervision as long as they generate good ideas in the long run.

2. **Competitive work teams.** Many organizations give several groups of employees the freedom to work on a problem, offering the greatest rewards to those who come up with the best solution. Competitive work teams—a strategy first used by Japanese and Swedish organizations—draw out the creative contributions of everyone and, at the same time, reduce the alienation often found in conventional organizations (Yeatts, 1991, 1994; Sandberg et al., 1992; Maddox, 1994).

3. **A flatter organization: From pyramid to football.** By spreading responsibility for creative

The "McDonaldization" of Canada has not only changed the way companies do business, but also sparked new collaborative efforts among diverse business sectors. At this Petro-Canada gas station in Toronto, customers can gas up, pay at the pump with a credit card, and then dash into the adjoining A & W Restaurant for fast food they ordered through a speaker at the pump.

problem solving throughout the workforce, organizations take on a flatter shape. That is, the pyramid shape of conventional bureaucracy is replaced by a new organizational form with fewer levels in the chain of command, as shown in Figure 5–5.

4. **Greater flexibility.** The typical industrial age organization was a rigid structure guided from the top. Such organizations may accomplish a good deal of work, but they are not especially creative or able to respond quickly to changes in their larger environment. The ideal model in the information age is a *flexible* organization, one that both generates new ideas and, in a rapidly changing global marketplace, adapts quickly.

As important as these changes are, bear in mind that many of today's jobs *do not* involve creative work at all. In reality, the post-industrial economy has created two, very different types of work: highly skilled, creative work and low-skill, service work. Work in the fast-food industry, for example, is routine and highly supervised, and thus has much more in common with the work of factory employees of a century ago than with the work of teams in information organizations. Therefore, at the same time that some organizations have taken on a flexible, flatter form, others continue to use the rigid chain of command, as we now explain.

## THE "McDONALDIZATION" OF SOCIETY [1]

As noted in the opening to this chapter, McDonald's has enjoyed enormous success, now operating some 30 000 restaurants in Canada and around the world. There are more than 850 "golden arches" in Japan, for example, and the world's largest McDonald's recently opened in China's capital city of Beijing.

October 9, 1994—Macau Here we are halfway around the world in the Portuguese colony of Macau—a little nub jutting from the Chinese coast. Few people speak English, and life on the streets seems a world apart from the urban rhythms of New York, Chicago, or Los Angeles. Then we turn the corner and stand face-to-face with (who else?) Ronald McDonald! After eating who-knows-what for many days, forgive us for giving in to the lure of the Big Mac. But the most amazing thing is that the food—the burger, fries, and drinks—looks, smells, and tastes exactly the same as it does back home, about 16 000 kilometres away!

McDonald's can be found almost everywhere these days. In North America, in fact, it is more than a restaurant—it has become a symbol of our way of life. People around the world associate McDonald's with North America. Even more important, the organizational principles that underlie McDonald's are coming to dominate our entire society. Our culture is becoming "McDonaldized," an awkward way of saying that many aspects of life are modelled on the famous restaurant chain. Parents buy toys at world-wide chain stores such as Toys 'Я' Us; we drive in to Jiffy Lube for a 10-minute oil change; face-to-face communication is sliding more and more toward voice-mail and e-mail; more vacations take the form of resort and tour packages; television presents news in the form of 10-second sound bites; college and university admission officers size up students they have never met by glancing at their GPA and SAT scores; and professors assign ghost-written textbooks[2] and evaluate students with tests mass-produced for them by publishing companies. The list goes on and on.

**Basic principles.** What do all these developments have in common? According to George Ritzer (1993), the "McDonaldization of society" involves four basic organizational principles:

1. **Efficiency.** Ray Kroc, the marketing genius behind McDonald's, set out with one goal: to serve a hamburger, French fries, and milk shake to a customer in 50 seconds or less. Today, one of the company's most popular items is the Egg McMuffin, an entire breakfast in a single sandwich. In the restaurant, customers bus their own trays or, better still, drive away from the pick-up window taking with them whatever mess they make!

   Efficiency is now a value virtually without critics in our society. We tend to think that anything done quickly is, for that reason alone, good.

2. **Calculability.** The first McDonald's operating manual, before Canada went metric, declared the weight of a regular raw hamburger to be 1.6 ounces, its size to be 3.875 inches across, and its fat content to be 19 percent. A slice of cheese weighs exactly half an ounce, and French fries are cut precisely 9/32 of an inch thick.

   Think about how many objects around the home, the workplace, or the campus are designed and mass-produced uniformly according to a standard plan. Not just our environment but our life experiences—from travelling the nation's highways to sitting at home viewing television—are now more deliberately planned than ever before.

3. **Uniformity and predictability.** An individual can walk into a McDonald's restaurant almost anywhere and buy the same sandwiches, drinks, and desserts prepared in precisely the same way.[3] Uniformity results from a highly rational system that specifies every action and leaves nothing to chance.

---

[1] Much of the material in this section is based on Ritzer (1993, 1998).

[2] Half a dozen popular sociology texts were not authored by the person or persons whose names appear on the cover. This book is not one of them.

[3] As McDonald's has "gone global," a few products have been added or modified according to local tastes. For example, in Uruguay, customers enjoy the McHuevo (hamburger with poached egg on top); Norwegians can buy McLaks (grilled salmon sandwiches); the Dutch favour the Groenteburger (vegetable burger); in Thailand, McDonald's serves Samurai pork burgers (pork burgers with teriyaki sauce); the Japanese can purchase Chicken Tatsuta Sandwich (chicken seasoned with soy and ginger); Filipinos eat McSpaghetti (spaghetti with tomato sauce and bits of hot dogs); in India, where Hindus eat no beef, McDonald's sells a vegetarian Maharaja Mac; and the Finns enjoy "rye" buns with their burgers (Sullivan, 1995).

4. **Control through automation.** The most unreliable element in the McDonald's system is human beings. People, after all, have good and bad days, sometimes let their minds wander, or decide to try something a different way. To minimize the unpredictable human element, McDonald's has automated its equipment to cook food at fixed temperatures for set lengths of time. Even the cash register at a McDonald's is keyed to pictures of the items, so that ringing up a customer's order is as simple as possible.

Similarly, automatic teller machines are replacing banks, highly automated bakeries produce bread with scarcely any human intervention, and chickens and eggs (or is it eggs and chickens?) emerge from automated hatcheries. In supermarkets, laser scanners are phasing out human checkers. Most of our shopping now occurs in malls, where everything from temperature and humidity to the kinds of stores and products are subject to continuous control and supervision (Idle & Cordell, 1994).

**Can rationality be irrational?** There can be no argument about the popularity or efficiency of McDonald's. But there is another side to the story.

Max Weber was alarmed at the increasing rationalization of the world, fearing that formal organizations would cage our imagination and crush the human spirit. As he saw it, rational systems were efficient but dehumanizing. McDonaldization bears him out. Each of the four principles just discussed limits human creativity, choice, and freedom. Echoing Weber, George Ritzer states that "the ultimate irrationality of McDonaldization is that people could lose control over the system and it would come to control us" (1993:145).

## THE FUTURE OF ORGANIZATIONS: OPPOSING TRENDS

Early in the 20th century, ever larger organizations arose in Canada, most taking on the bureaucratic form described by Max Weber. In many respects, these organizations resembled armies led by powerful generals who issued orders to their captains and lieutenants. Foot soldiers—working in the factories—did what they were told.

With the emergence of a post-industrial economy after mid-century, as well as with rising competition from abroad, many organizations evolved toward a flatter, more flexible model that prizes communication and creativity. Such "intelligent organizations" (Pinchot & Pinchot, 1993) have become more productive than ever. Just as important, for highly skilled people who enjoy "creative autonomy," these organizations create less of the alienation that so worried Max Weber.

But if the post-industrial economy created many highly skilled jobs, it created even more routine service jobs, as exemplified by McDonald's, where 1 in 8 North American adults has worked at some time (Ritzer, 1998). Work of this kind—which Ritzer terms "McJobs"—offers few of the benefits that today's highly skilled workers enjoy. On the contrary, the automated routines that define work in the fast-food industry, telemarketing, and similar fields are very much the same as Frederick Taylor described a century ago. The Critical Thinking box on page 121 asks, is efficiency always better? And efficiency for whom?

Moreover, the organizational "flexibility" that gives better-off workers more autonomy carries the ever-present threat of "downsizing" for rank-and-file employees (Sennett, 1998). That is, organizations facing global competition are eager to have creative employees, but they are just as eager to cut costs by eliminating as many routine jobs as possible. The net result is that some people are better off than ever, while others worry about holding their jobs and struggle to make ends meet—a trend that Chapter 8 (Social Stratification) explores in detail.

The complexity of organizational change, especially when we take into account the consumer, the worker, *and* management, cautions against asserting any "absolute truths" about formal organizations. And just as important, we must remain curious about the causes and consequences of changes in our future.

To end on a positive note, we should not assume that all large formal organizations easily fit the McDonaldization thesis. This is especially the case for non-profit organizations. Take, for example, Médecins Sans Frontières—Doctors Without Borders—a large formal international organization that annually sends more than 2000 volunteers to assist in some 80 nations. The non-profit organization received the 1999 Nobel Peace Prize for its humanitarian aid. How do the principle of "lean and mean" apply to this organization that sends highly qualified volunteers to provide medical care in countries that are often violent and dangerous?

# Is More Efficient and Convenient Always Better?

Some of you might have heard of a time, not so long ago, when the food store home-delivered called-in grocery orders, when we ordered our clothes through mail-order catalogues from Eaton's or Simpson-Sears, when attendants appeared to fill our empty gas tanks, when banks built their reputations on face-to-face services for customers, and when hospitals took pride in the bedside nursing care they provided for sick patients.

But those days are no longer. Today we hear about the amazing efficiency and enhanced personal convenience created by the "self-service revolution." Now we can go to "clerkless" stores, where the shopper, free from the clerk's gaze, has full personal control in picking and choosing items. The only human contact left is with the checkout clerk, whose task is to

scan—not to comment on or suggest additions to—one's purchases. Warehouse stores and super stores have replaced the mail-order catalogues, corner hardware stores, and family groceries. These new retailers promise that with only a skeleton staff, they offer convenience, hassle-free shopping, and a greater choice

of products at "rock bottom" prices. What more could we want!

As with most new developments, however, the movement from full-service to self-service is not all that it is made out to be. Who, we must ask, is this clerkless customer so much talked about by the marketing agencies? According to sociologist Nona Glaser (1993), most clerkless customers are women from lower- and middle-class backgrounds. When the cashier replaced the salesclerk, the modern customer became the do-it-yourself buyer. As Glaser (1993:103) sees it, contrary to being free and content with her new role, the clerkless customer has actually become the unpaid "other worker" at the end of the company's chain of command. This development is even more ironic given that service has declined

## SUMMARY

1. Social groups are building blocks of society that join members as well as perform various tasks.

2. Primary groups tend to be small and person-oriented; secondary groups are typically large and goal oriented.

3. Instrumental leadership is concerned with realizing a group's goals; expressive leadership focusses on members' morale and well-being.

4. Because group members often seek consensus, groups can pressure members toward conformity.

5. Individuals use reference groups—both ingroups and outgroups—to form attitudes and make evaluations.

6. Georg Simmel characterized the dyad as intense but unstable; a triad, he added, can easily dissolve into a dyad by excluding one member.

7. Peter Blau explored how group size, internal homogeneity, and physical segregation of groups all affect members' behaviour.

8. Social networks are relational webs that link people with little common identity and limited interaction. The Internet is a vast electronic network linking millions of people worldwide.

9. Formal organizations are large, secondary groups that try to perform complex tasks efficiently. They are classified as normative, coercive, or utilitarian, based on their members' reasons for joining.

at a time when women with families have entered the workforce and often require extra help.

Glaser argues that the much-admired "service society" is an illusion for most women with family responsibilities, unless they have the free time and disposable income to shop at specialty stores or top-of-the-line outlets. For their less fortunate sisters, however, "[h]igh productivity in manufacturing has freed them from producing goods in the household, but not from producing services for themselves and their families. It has given them more work to do in the stores from which they buy these energy-saving goods" (pp. 103–104).

Glaser observes that a similar development is now also affecting the organization of health care, especially nursing services. In the U.S., the corporate takeover of medicine is already well advanced. Yet there has been much talk of late in Canada, as well, about the apparently more humane (and efficient)

service that results from transferring people in hospitals, old-age homes, and mental institutions back to the community. Such transferring depends on "home-care support." But the question that seldom gets asked is this: What does "home care" mean in this instance (Benoit, 1998)? Who will care for the sick, the frail, and others unable to care for themselves, once they are no longer in formal institutions?

In Canada, there are at least three likely possibilities: 1) new immigrant and visible minority women working in people's homes for low wages; 2) community volunteers, who also tend to be women; 3) dutiful sisters and daughters, who Canadian sociologist Pat Armstrong (1994) sees as "the lowest, lowest cost care providers." In Canada, the evidence to date about the "work transfer" from nurses in public hospitals to other women in home care is only anecdotal. But the recent cutbacks in health funding in many

Canadian provinces mean that the changeover in nursing staff will increase pressure for family members to "help out"—either by doing (unpaid) shifts at the patient's hospital bedside or, better still, caring for the sick at home. For those with money to purchase private duty nurses, the situation may be disturbing but manageable. But those without disposable funds, mainly women—the ultimately flexible labour force— will take up the slack (sick patients) discarded by hospitals.

In sum, as Glaser (1993:219) puts it, the "post-industrial economy has not curtailed service work for the public. Instead, it has depended on the free labour of women as members of households." In brief, the enhanced efficiency and personal convenience of our service society may be good for businesses, hospitals, and perhaps a small group of privileged clients, but are unlikely to reduce the workload of most women.

10. Bureaucratic organization expands in modern societies to perform many complex tasks efficiently. Bureaucracy is based on specialization, hierarchy, rules and regulations, technical competence, impersonal interaction, and formal, written communications.

11. Technology, economic and political trends, population patterns, and other organizations all combine to form the environment in which a particular organization must operate.

12. Ideal bureaucracy promotes efficiency, but bureaucracy may generate alienation and oligarchy, and contributes to the erosion of personal privacy.

13. Frederick Taylor's "scientific management" shaped North American organizations a century ago. Since then, organizations have evolved toward a more open and flexible form, as they have

(1) included a larger share of women and other minorities; (2) responded to global competition, especially from Japan; and (3) shifted their focus from industrial to post-industrial, information production.

14. Reflecting the collective spirit of Japanese culture, formal organizations in Japan are based on personal ties more so than their North American counterparts.

15. The "McDonaldization of society" involves increasing automation and impersonality.

16. The future of organizations will likely involve opposing trends: toward more creative autonomy for highly skilled, information workers and toward supervision and discipline for less-skilled service workers.

# KEY CONCEPTS

**social group** (p. 101) two or more people who identify and interact with one another

**primary group** (p. 102) a small social group whose members share personal and enduring relationships

**secondary group** (p. 102) a large and impersonal social group whose members pursue a special interest or activity

**instrumental leadership** (p. 103) group leadership that emphasizes the completion of tasks

**expressive leadership** (p. 103) group leadership that emphasizes collective well-being

**groupthink** (p. 105) the tendency of group members to conform, resulting in a narrow view of some issue

**reference group** (p. 105) a social group that serves as a point of reference in making evaluations and decisions

**ingroup** (p. 106) an esteemed social group commanding a member's loyalty

**outgroup** (p. 106) a scorned social group toward which one feels competition or opposition

**dyad** (p. 107) a social group with two members

**triad** (p. 107) a social group with three members

**network** (p. 109) a web of weak social ties

**formal organization** (p. 110) a large secondary group that is organized to achieve specific goals

**tradition** (p. 111) sentiments and beliefs about the world that are passed from generation to generation

**rationality** (p. 111) deliberate, matter-of-fact calculation of the most efficient means to accomplish a particular task

**rationalization** (p. 111) Max Weber's term for the change from tradition to rationality as the dominant mode of human thought

**bureaucracy** (p. 111) an organizational model designed to perform tasks efficiently

**organizational environment** (p. 113) a range of factors outside the organization that affects it operation

**bureaucratic ritualism** (p. 114) a preoccupation with rules and regulations to the point of obstructing an organization's goals

**bureaucratic inertia** (p. 114) the tendency of bureaucratic organizations to perpetuate themselves

**oligarchy** (p. 115) the rule of the many by the few

**scientific management** (p. 115) Frederick Taylor's term for applying scientific principles to the operation of a business or other large organization

# CRITICAL-THINKING QUESTIONS

1. What are the key differences between primary and secondary groups? Identify examples of each in your own life.

2. According to Max Weber, what are the six characteristic traits of bureaucracy? In what ways do new, "flexible" organizations differ?

3. George Ritzer (1993:1), a critic of McDonaldization, suggests that fast-food restaurants carry the following label: *Sociologists warn us that habitual use of* *McDonald's systems are destructive to our physical and psychological well-being as well as to society as a whole.* Do you agree? Why or why not?

4. Have you ever worked in a front-line service job? If yes, discuss your experiences in this service position and comment on how close it was to your *ideal* job.

## APPLICATIONS AND EXERCISES

1. Visit a big public building with an elevator. Observe groups of people as they approach the elevator, and enter the elevator with them: Watch what happens next. What happens to the conversations? Where do people fix their eyes? Can you account for these patterns?

2. Make a list of ingroups and outgroups on your campus. What traits account for groups falling into each category? Ask several other people to see if they agree with your classifications.

3. Spend several hours observing customers at a fast-food restaurant. Think about ways in which not just employees but *customers* are trained to behave in certain ways. For example, customer norms include lining up to order and finding their own table. What other norms are at work?

4. Using available publications (and some assistance from an instructor), try to draw an "organizational pyramid" for your college or university, showing the key officials and how they supervise and report to each other.

5. Think of some examples of large formal organizations that are registered non-profits. Search out information on them in your university or college library or via the Internet, and share what you find with the class.

 SITES TO SEE

**www.pearsoned.ca/macionis**

Visit the Web site that accompanies this text to access various study materials and practice tests that will help review the material in this chapter.

**www.TheSociologyPage.com (or www.macionis.com)**

The special Prentice Hall site contains a wide range of interesting materials and exercises that further develop your understanding of this chapter's disscussions.

**www.saturnbp.com**

Visit Saturn's Web site to read about the car company's "flatter" organizational structure.

**www.msf.ca**

Visit the Canadian Web site of the non-profit organization *Médecins Sans Frontières*, and learn about its humanitarian efforts around the globe.

**groups.yahoo.com**

At this site, people build their own social groups for chat and exchanging personal information. Take a look and see what you think about "virtual groups."

*April, 1992—David Milgaard steps out of prison after spending 22 years in confinement for a crime he did not commit. When Gail Miller was brutally attacked and murdered in Saskatoon on January 31, 1969, Mr. Milgaard—who was then 16 years old—was partying with friends in an apartment a few blocks away. On the basis of circumstantial evidence and statements against him by his friends, he was sentenced to life in prison. However, David's mother, Joyce Milgaard, discovered that her son's friends had been pressured by police to make inaccurate statements, and also that the local police knew of a serial rapist operating at the time in Saskatoon. She did not let the matter rest. The Supreme Court of Canada eventually overturned Milgaard's conviction in 1992. Five years later he was fully vindicated, when DNA evidence proved beyond a doubt that he had not committed the fatal assault on Miller.* ■

There are many parallels among the stories of David Milgaard, Guy Paul Morin, and Thomas Sophonow—all Canadians who were released from prison after being wrongfully convicted. In these cases, brutal murders put pressure on local police to solve the crime. The result was that evidence pointing to suspects was overlooked, dismissed, or, in some cases, hidden by the police. Further, police obtained incriminating statements from witnesses by applying pressure to those who wanted to improve their own standing with the authorities. In each case, DNA evidence eventually was used to establish innocence.

This chapter explores the problem of violent crime and other offences, profiles offenders, and looks at the criminal justice system—a system that in some cases, such as those of Milgaard, Morin, and Sophonow, fails miserably. First, however, we tackle the broader issue of why societies develop standards of right and wrong in the first place. As we shall see, the law is simply one part of a complex system of social control: Society teaches us all to conform, at least most of the time, to countless rules. We begin our investigation by defining several basic concepts.

**127**

# WHAT IS DEVIANCE?

**Deviance** is *the recognized violation of cultural norms*. Norms guide virtually all human activities, so the concept of deviance is quite broad. One category of deviance is **crime**, *the violation of a society's formally enacted criminal law*. Even criminal deviance spans a wide range, from minor traffic violations to sexual assault to murder.

Not all deviance involves action or even choice. The very *existence* of some categories of people can be troublesome to others. To the young, elderly people may seem hopelessly "out of it"; and to some non-Aboriginals, the mere presence of an Aboriginal person may cause discomfort. Able-bodied people often view individuals with disabilities as an outgroup, just as affluent people may shun the poor for falling short of their standards.

Most familiar examples of nonconformity are negative cases of rule breaking, such as stealing from a convenience store, abusing a child, or driving while intoxicated. But we also define especially righteous people—students who volunteer too much in class or people who are overly enthusiastic about new computer technology—as deviant, even if we accord them a measure of respect (Huls, 1987). What those who perform deviant actions or hold deviant attitudes have in common is some element of *difference* that causes us to regard the person as an "outsider" (Becker, 1966).

All of us are subject to **social control**, *attempts by society to regulate people's thought and behaviour*. Often this process is informal, as when parents praise or scold their children or friends make fun of someone's musical taste. Cases of serious deviance, however, may provoke action by the **criminal justice system**, *a formal response by police, courts, and prison officials to alleged violations of the law*.

In sum, deviance is much more than a matter of individual choice or personal failing. *How* a society defines deviance, *who* is branded as "deviant," and *what* people decide to do about deviance are all issues of social organization. Only gradually, however, have people recognized this fact, as we shall now explain.

## THE BIOLOGICAL CONTEXT

Chapter 3 (Socialization: From Infancy to Old Age) explained that a century ago most people understood—or, more correctly, misunderstood—human behaviour as the result of biological instincts. Early interest in criminality thus focussed on biological causes. In 1876 Caesare Lombroso (1835–1909), an Italian physician who worked in prisons, proposed that criminals stand out physically, with low foreheads, prominent jaws and cheekbones, protruding ears, hairiness, and unusually long arms. Taken together, these characteristics made them look like humans' apelike ancestors.

But Lombroso's work was flawed, since the physical features he attributed to prisoners could be found throughout the entire population. We now know that no physical attributes, of the kind described by Lombroso, set off criminals from non-criminals (Goring, 1972; orig. 1913).

At mid-century, William Sheldon (Sheldon, Hartl, & McDermott, 1949) took a different tack, suggesting that body structure might predict criminality. He cross-checked hundreds of young men for body type and criminal history, and concluded that delinquency was most likely among boys with muscular, athletic builds. Sheldon Glueck and Eleanor Glueck (1950) confirmed Sheldon's conclusion, but cautioned that a powerful build does not necessarily *cause* or even predict criminality. Parents, they suggested, tend to be more distant from powerfully built sons, who, in turn, grow up to display less sensitivity toward others. Moreover, in a self-fulfilling prophecy, people who expect muscular boys to be bullies may act in ways that provoke the aggressive behaviour they expect.

Today, genetics research seeks possible links between biology and crime. Though no conclusive evidence connects criminality to any specific genetic trait, people's overall genetic composition, in combination with social influences, probably accounts for some tendency toward criminality. In other words, biological factors may have a real but modest effect on whether an individual becomes a criminal (Rowe, 1983; Rowe & Osgood, 1984; Wilson & Herrnstein, 1985; Jencks, 1987).

**Critical evaluation.** At best, biological theories offer a very limited explanation of crime. Recent sociobiological research—noting, for example, that violent crime is overwhelmingly male and that parents are more likely to abuse foster children than natural children—is promising, but we know too little about the links between genes and human behaviour to draw firm conclusions (Daly & Wilson, 1988).

Further, because a biological approach looks at the individual, it offers no insight as to how some kinds of behaviour come to be defined as deviant in the first place. Therefore, although there is much to learn about how human biology may affect behaviour, research currently places far greater emphasis on social influences (Gibbons & Krohn, 1986; Liska, 1991).

## PERSONALITY FACTORS

Like biological theories, psychological explanations of deviance focus on individual abnormality. Some personality traits are hereditary, but most psychologists think temperament is primarily shaped by social experience. Deviance, then, is viewed as the result of "unsuccessful" socialization.

Research by Walter Reckless and Simon Dinitz (1967) illustrates the psychological approach. Reckless and Dinitz began by asking teachers to categorize 12-year-old male students as either likely or unlikely to get into trouble with the law. They then interviewed both the boys and their mothers to assess each boy's self-concept and how he related to others. Analyzing their results, the researchers found that the "good boys" displayed a strong conscience (or superego, in Sigmund Freud's terminology), could handle frustration, and identified with cultural norms and values. The "bad boys," by contrast, had a weaker conscience, displayed little tolerance for frustration, and felt out of step with conventional culture.

As we might expect, the "good boys" went on to have fewer run-ins with the police than did the "bad boys." Since all the boys lived in areas where delinquency was widespread, the investigators attributed to the ones who stayed out of trouble a personality that reined in deviant impulses. Based on this conclusion, Reckless and Dinitz call their analysis *containment theory*.

**Critical evaluation.** Psychologists have shown that personality patterns bear some connection to deviance. However, the fact is, most serious crimes are committed by people whose psychological profiles are *normal*.

Overall, both biological and psychological research views deviance as an individual trait, without exploring how conceptions of right and wrong initially arise, why people define some rule breakers—but not others—as deviant, and what role power plays in shaping a society's system of social control. To explore these issues, we now turn to a sociological analysis of deviance.

## THE SOCIAL FOUNDATIONS OF DEVIANCE

Although we tend to view deviance as the free choice or personal failings of individuals, all behaviour—deviance as well as conformity—is shaped by society. Three *social* foundations of deviance are identified below and detailed later in this chapter:

1. **Deviance varies according to cultural norms.** No thought or action is inherently deviant; it becomes deviant only in relation to particular norms. In Saskatchewan, for example, it is illegal for businesses to offer both striptease and drinking; exotic dancing is fine, as is drinking, but the two must not occur together. Moreover, in some Canadian cities it is legal to play music on the sidewalk and to beg for money, while street musicians and panhandlers in other cities risk being fined or imprisoned.

   Around the world, deviance is even more diverse. Albania outlaws any public display of

*The kind of deviance people create reflects the moral values they embrace. The Berkeley campus of the University of California has long celebrated its open-minded tolerance of sexual diversity. Thus, in 1992, when Andrew Martinez decided to attend classes wearing virtually nothing, people were reluctant to accuse "The Naked Guy" of immoral conduct. However, in Berkeley's politically correct atmosphere, it was not long before school officials banned Martinez from campus—charging that his nudity constituted a form of sexual harassment.*

religious faith, such as "crossing" oneself; Cuba and Vietnam can prosecute citizens for meeting with foreigners; Singapore prohibits the sale of chewing gum and kissing in elevators; police in Iran can arrest a woman wearing makeup; and it is unlawful for Canadian companies to pay bribes to foreign officials, while such payments are tax-deductible in Germany.

2. **People become deviant as others define them that way.** Each of us violates cultural norms, occasionally to the extent of breaking the law. For example, most of us have at some time walked around talking to ourselves, or "borrowed" a pen from our workplace. Whether such activities are sufficient to define us as mentally ill or criminal depends on how others perceive, define, and respond to our behaviour.

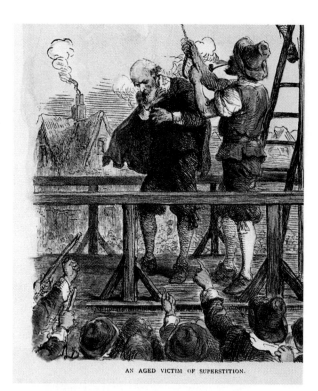

AN AGED VICTIM OF SUPERSTITION.

*Emile Durkheim's important insight is that no society can exist without deviance. Thus, after arriving in New England in the early 17th century, the very religious Puritans soon found themselves accusing some of their members of serious wrongdoing. The best known Puritan "crime wave" climaxed in the Salem witch trials of 1692, which led to two dozen executions of women and men thought to be doing the work of the devil.*

3.  **Both norms and the way people define situations involve social power.**   The law, declared Karl Marx, is the means by which powerful people protect their interests. A homeless person who stands on a street corner denouncing the government risks arrest for disturbing the peace; a political candidate during an election campaign does exactly the same thing and gets police protection. A women walking topless in a Canadian city—except in Ontario—is likely to be accused of "indecent exposure," while her bare-chested male companion merely risks not being served at McDonald's. In short, norms and their application are linked to social inequality.

## THE FUNCTIONS OF DEVIANCE: STRUCTURAL-FUNCTIONAL ANALYSIS

The key insight of the structural-functional paradigm is that deviance is a necessary element of social organization. This point was made a century ago by Emile Durkheim.

### DURKHEIM'S BASIC INSIGHT

In his pioneering study of deviance, Emile Durkheim (1964a, orig. 1895; 1964b, orig. 1893) made the surprising statement that there is nothing abnormal about deviance. In fact, it performs four essential functions:

1.  **Deviance affirms cultural values and norms.** As moral creatures, people must prefer some attitudes and behaviours to others. But any conception of virtue rests upon an opposing notion of vice: There can be no good without evil and no justice without crime. Deviance, then, is needed to define and sustain morality.

2.  **Responding to deviance clarifies moral boundaries.**   By defining some individuals as deviant, people draw a boundary between right and wrong. For example, a university marks the line between academic honesty and cheating by disciplining students who plagiarize.

3.  **Responding to deviance brings people together.**   People typically react to serious deviance with collective outrage. In doing so, Durkheim explained, they reaffirm the moral ties that bind them. For example, the shooting in Taber on April 28, 1999—only eight days after the Columbine High School tragedy in Colorado—was followed by feelings of anguish and outrage shared not just by the Alberta community but the entire nation.

4.  **Deviance encourages social change.**   Deviant people push a society's moral boundaries, suggesting alternatives to the status quo and encouraging change. Today's deviance, declared Durkheim, can become tomorrow's morality (1964a:71). For example, as discussed in Chapter 14, Robert Latimer forced our society to face the moral dilemma that underlies mercy killing.

### MERTON'S STRAIN THEORY

Some deviance may be necessary for a society to function, but Robert Merton (1938, 1968) argued that excessive deviance arises from particular social arrangements. Specifically, the extent and kind of deviance depends on whether a society provides the *means* (such as schooling and job opportunities) to achieve cultural *goals* (such as financial success).

Conformity, Merton begins, lies in pursuing conventional goals through approved means. Thus, the Canadian "success story" is someone who acquires wealth and prestige through talent, schooling, and hard work. But not everyone who desires conventional success has the opportunity to attain it. People raised in poverty, for example, may see little hope of becoming successful if they play by the rules. As a result, they may try to make money through crime—say, by dealing cocaine. Merton called this type of deviance *innovation*—using unconventional means (drug sales) to achieve a culturally approved goal (wealth). Figure 6–1 shows that innovation involves accepting the cultural goal (financial success) but rejecting the conventional means (hard work at a "straight" job).

According to Merton, the strain between our culture's emphasis on wealth and the limited opportunity to get rich gives rise, especially among the poor, to theft and selling illegal drugs or other forms of street crime. The inability to succeed by normative means may also prompt another type of deviance that Merton calls ritualism (see Figure 6–1). Lower-level bureaucrats, for example, may know they will achieve limited financial success, so they obsessively stick to the rules to feel, at least to themselves, respectable.

A third response to the inability to succeed is *retreatism*—rejecting both cultural goals and means so that one, in effect, "drops out." Some alcoholics, drug addicts, and street people are retreatists. The deviance of retreatists lies in unconventional living and, perhaps more seriously, in their apparent *willingness* to live that way.

The fourth response to failure is *rebellion*. Like retreatists, rebels reject both the cultural definition of success and the normative means of achieving it. Rebels—such as radical "survivalists"—go one step further by forming a counterculture and advocating alternatives to the existing social order.

## DEVIANT SUBCULTURES

Richard Cloward and Lloyd Ohlin (1966) extended Merton's theory, proposing that crime results not simply from limited legitimate (legal) opportunity but also from readily accessible illegitimate (illegal) opportunity. In short, deviance or conformity depends upon the *relative opportunity structure* that frames a person's life.

The life of Al Capone, a notorious gangster of the Prohibition era (which ran from 1920 to 1933), illustrates Cloward and Ohlin's theory. As a poor immigrant, Capone saw few legitimate ways to succeed, such as getting post-secondary education. Yet he did see illegitimate opportunity for success as a bootlegger. Where relative opportunity favours criminal activity, Cloward and Ohlin predict the development of *criminal subcultures*. Gangs, for example, may specialize in one or another type of crime, depending on available opportunities (Sheley et al., 1995).

But what happens when people are unable to find *any* opportunities, legal or illegal? Then delinquency

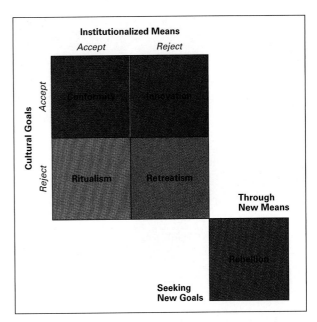

**FIGURE 6–1   Merton's Strain Theory of Deviance**
Source: Merton (1968).

may take the form of *conflict subcultures* (armed street gangs) where violence is ignited by frustration and a desire for respect. Alternatively, those who fail to achieve success, even through crime, may fall into *retreatist subcultures,* dropping out and abusing alcohol or other drugs.

Albert Cohen (1971) suggests that criminality is most common among lower-class youths because they have the least opportunity to achieve conventional success. Neglected by society, they seek self-respect by creating a delinquent subculture that "defines as meritorious the characteristics [these youths] *do* possess, the kinds of conduct of which they *are* capable" (1971:66). Being feared on the street, for example, may win few points with society as a whole, but it may satisfy a youth's desire to "be somebody" in the local neighbourhood.

Walter Miller (1970) adds that deviant subcultures are characterized by (1) *trouble*, arising from frequent conflict with teachers and police; (2) *toughness*, the value placed on physical size, strength, and agility, especially among males; (3) *smartness*, the ability to succeed on the streets, to out-smart or "con" others; (4) *a need for excitement*, the search for thrills, risk, or danger; (5) *a belief in fate*, a sense that people lack control over their own lives; and (6) *a desire for freedom*, often expressed as hostility toward all authority figures.

Finally, Elijah Anderson (1994) explains that in poor, urban neighbourhoods, most people manage to conform to conventional ("decent") values. Yet faced with the dangers of crime and violence, hostility from

*In the Kosovo region of Serbia, as in Canada, young people (especially males) cut off from legitimate opportunity may form deviant subcultures as a strategy to gain the prestige denied them by the larger society.*

police, and sometimes even neglect from their own parents, some young men adapt a "street code," which stresses their ability to take care of themselves. To survive on the street, a young man displays "nerve," a willingness to stand up to any threat. According to this code, Anderson explains, even a violent death is better than being "dissed" (disrespected) by others. Some manage to escape the dangers, but the risk of ending up in jail—or worse—is very high for these young men pushed to the margins of our society.

**Critical evaluation.** Durkheim made an important contribution by pointing out the functions of deviance. There is, however, evidence that a community does not always come together in reaction to crime; sometimes fear of crime drives people to withdraw from public life (Liska & Warner, 1991).

Merton's strain theory also has been criticized for explaining some kinds of deviance (theft, for example) better than others (crimes of passion or mental illness). Moreover, not everyone seeks success in conventional terms of wealth, as strain theory implies.

The general argument of Cloward and Ohlin, Cohen, and Miller—that deviance reflects the opportunity structure of society—has been confirmed by subsequent research (cf. Allan & Steffensmeier, 1989). However, these theories, too, fall short by assuming that everyone shares the same cultural standards for judging right and wrong. Moreover, we must be careful not to define deviance in terms that unfairly focus attention on poor people. If crime is defined to include stock fraud as well as street theft, then affluent people are just as likely to be defined as criminals. Finally, all structural-functional theories imply that everyone who breaks the rules will be labelled deviant. Becoming

deviant, however, is actually a highly complex process, as the next section explains.

# LABELLING DEVIANCE: THE SYMBOLIC-INTERACTION APPROACH

The symbolic-interaction paradigm explains how people define deviance in everyday situations. From this point of view, definitions of deviance and conformity are surprisingly flexible.

## LABELLING THEORY

The central contribution of symbolic-interaction analysis is **labelling theory,** *the assertion that deviance and conformity result not from what people do, but from how others respond to those actions.* Labelling theory stresses the relativity of deviance, meaning that people may define the same behaviour in any number of ways. Howard S. Becker claims that deviance is, therefore, nothing more than behaviour that people define as deviant (1966:9).

Consider these situations: A woman takes an article of clothing from a roommate; a married man at a convention in a distant city has sex with a prostitute; a premier gives a casino licence to a man who renovates the premier's home. We might define the first situation as carelessness, borrowing, or theft. The consequences of the second situation depend largely on whether the man's behaviour becomes known back home. In the third situation, is the official choosing the best proposal or paying off a personal debt? The social construction of reality is a highly variable process of detection, definition, and response.

## GLOBAL SOCIOLOGY

# Cockfighting:
# Cultural Ritual or Abuse of Animals?

You won't see it on television, but one of the world's most popular sports—from North America to Europe to Asia—is cockfighting. Legal in parts of the U.S., cockfighting is big business in Mexico, and is something of a national pastime in the Philippines. There, the local cock pit is as important as the hockey rink in Saskatchewan: Every village has one, and it draws a crowd on weekends and fiesta days.

On the surface, cockfights are about gambling. An afternoon or evening event might include 10 fights. A fight begins with the cock owners displaying their birds to one another, calling out for bets as to the stronger bird. Members of the audience weigh in with cash. Keeping track of the bets is the "cristo"—someone who stands, arms extended, taking money.

With the odds of winning set and the money on the table, the actual combat begins. Each rooster is outfitted with a small, sharp blade

strapped to the rear of the left leg. The cocks need little encouragement to fight, but the owners do a bit of strutting themselves, swinging their birds in front of each other before dropping them on lines drawn in the pit sand. Upon hitting the ground, the birds fly at one another, merging in a blur of legs and feathers.

Within minutes, one bird may collapse from exhaustion, the owner steps in to revive his cock, and the process is

repeated. Before long, however, a blade finds its mark. The victor, the bird who will live to fight another day, perches on the vanquished, which will not.

In many parts of the world, cockfighting is an important male ritual. Men raise their roosters for about two years, often at considerable expense, giving them the kind of care they offer to their sons. Then, through the ritual of the cockfight, men test their own claims to manhood, establish their own standing in the community pecking order, and pass on to their sons lessons about honour, competition, and masculinity.

Many outside observers are repulsed by the spectacle. But cockfighting is obviously deeply important to insiders. Should one condemn it as brutality or respect it as ceremony?

Source: Based on *The Economist* (1994), Harris (1994), and J. Macionis's research in the Philippines.

At a broader level, since "reality" depends on time and place, it is no surprise that one society's conformity may be another's deviance. The Global Sociology box describes cockfighting: Is this popular sport an important cultural ritual or a vicious abuse of animals?

## PRIMARY AND SECONDARY DEVIANCE

Edwin Lemert (1951, 1972) observed that some episodes of norm violation—say, skipping school or underage drinking—provoke slight reaction from others and have little effect on a person's self-concept. Lemert calls such passing episodes *primary deviance*.

But what happens if people take notice of someone's deviance and make something of it? If, for example, people begin to describe a young man as a "boozer" and evict him from their social circle, he may become embittered, drink even more, and seek the

company of those who approve of his behaviour. So the response to initial deviance can set in motion *secondary deviance*, by which an individual repeatedly violates a norm and begins to take on a deviant identity. The development of secondary deviance is one application of the Thomas theorem (see Chapter 4, Social Interaction in Everyday Life), which states that situations people define as real become real in their consequences.

## STIGMA

Secondary deviance marks the start of what Erving Goffman (1963) called a *deviant career*. As individuals acquire a stronger commitment to deviant behaviour, they typically acquire a **stigma**, *a powerfully negative label that radically changes a person's self-concept and social identity*. Stigma operates as a master status (see Chapter 4),

The world is full of people who are unusual in one way or another. This Indian man grew the fingernails on one hand for more than 30 years, just to do something that no one else had ever done. Should we define such behaviour as harmless eccentricity or as evidence of mental illness?

overpowering other dimensions of identity so that a person is discredited in the minds of others and, consequently, becomes socially isolated. Sometimes an entire community stigmatizes an individual through what Harold Garfinkel (1956) calls a *degradation ceremony*. A criminal prosecution is one example, operating much like a high school graduation in reverse: A person stands before the community to be labelled in a negative rather than a positive way.

Once people stigmatize an individual, they may engage in *retrospective labelling*, a reinterpretation of that individual's past in light of some present deviance (Scheff, 1984). For example, after discovering that a priest has sexually molested a child, others rethink his past, perhaps musing, "He always did want to be around young children." Retrospective labelling distorts a person's biography by being highly selective, a process that can deepen a deviant identity.

Similarly, people may engage in *projective labelling* of a stigmatized person. That is, people use a deviant identity to predict future action. Regarding the priest, people might say, "He's just going to keep at it until he gets caught." The more people think such a thing, of course, the greater the chance that it will come true.

## LABELLING AND MENTAL ILLNESS

Is a woman who believes that Jesus rides the bus to work with her every day seriously deluded or merely expressing her religious faith in a symbolic way? Is a homeless man who refuses to allow police to take him to a city shelter on a cold night mentally ill or simply trying to live independently?

Psychiatrist Thomas Szasz charges that people apply the label "insanity" to what is actually only "difference." Therefore, he concludes, we should abandon the notion of mental illness entirely (1961, 1970; 1994, 1995). Illness, Szasz continues, is physical and afflicts only the body; mental illness is, therefore, a myth. The world is full of people whose differences in thought or action may irritate others, but such differences are no grounds for defining someone as sick. Such labelling, Szasz claims, simply enforces conformity to the standards of people powerful enough to impose their will on others.

Many of Szasz's colleagues reject the notion that all mental illness is a fiction. But some hail his work for pointing out the danger of using medicine to promote conformity. Most of us, after all, experience periods of extreme stress or other mental instability from time to time. Such episodes, although upsetting, usually pass. If, however, others respond with labelling that forms the basis of a social stigma, the long-term result may be further deviance—a self-fulfilling prophecy (Scheff, 1984; Rosenfeld, 1997).

## THE MEDICALIZATION OF DEVIANCE

Labelling theory, particularly the ideas of Szasz and Goffman, helps explain an important shift in the way our society understands deviance. Over the past 50 years, the growing influence of psychiatry and medicine has led to the **medicalization of deviance**, *the transformation of moral and legal deviance into a medical condition.*

Medicalization amounts to swapping one set of labels for another. In moral terms, we evaluate people or their behaviour as "bad" or "good." However, the scientific objectivity of medicine passes no moral judgment, instead using clinical diagnoses such as "sick" or "well."

To illustrate, until the middle of this century, most people viewed alcoholics as morally weak people easily tempted by the pleasure of drink. Gradually, however, medical specialists redefined alcoholism so that most people now consider it a disease, rendering individuals who suffer from it "sick" rather than "bad." In the same way, obesity, drug addiction, child abuse, and other behaviours that used to be moral matters are

*Did Dorothy Joudrie get away with attempted murder? The Calgary Organization called the Families Against Crime Today Society believes so, although the court ruled that Joudrie was not criminally responsible for shooting and wounding her former husband six times in their Calgary home in January 1995. Ms. Joudrie received a conditional release in 1995 and was confined to a psychiatric hospital in Edmonton. In late 1996 she was released from the Alberta hospital, with orders from the review board to abstain from alcohol and to not attempt to contact her ex-husband or their two children.*

widely defined today as illnesses for which people need help rather than punishment.

Whether we define deviance as a moral or medical issue has three consequences. First, it affects *who responds* to deviance. An offence against common morality typically provokes a reaction from members of the community or the police. Applying medical labels, however, transfers the situation to the control of clinical specialists, including counsellors, psychiatrists, and physicians.

A second issue is *how people respond* to a deviant. A moral approach defines the deviant as an "offender" subject to punishment. Medically, however, "patients" need treatment (for their own good, of course). Therefore, while punishment is designed to fit the crime, treatment programs are tailored to the patient and may involve virtually any therapy that a specialist thinks might prevent future illness (von Hirsh, 1986.)

Third, and most important, the two labels differ on the issue of *the personal competence of the deviant person.* Morally speaking, whether we are right or wrong, we do take responsibility for our own behaviour. Once defined as sick, however, we are seen as unable to control (or, if "mentally ill," even understand) our actions. People who are incompetent are, in turn, subject to treatment, often against their will. For this reason alone, we should be cautious in defining deviance in medical terms.

## SUTHERLAND'S DIFFERENTIAL ASSOCIATION THEORY

Learning any social pattern—whether conventional or deviant—is a process that takes place in groups.

Therefore, according to Edwin Sutherland (1940), a person's tendency toward conformity or deviance depends upon the amount of contact with others who encourage—or reject—conventional behaviour. This is Sutherland's theory of *differential association*.

We can illustrate Sutherland's theory with a study of drug and alcohol use among young adults in the United States (Akers et al., 1979). Questionnaires completed by junior and senior high school students showed a close connection between the extent of alcohol and drug use and the degree to which peer groups encouraged such activity. The investigators concluded that young people embrace delinquent patterns to the degree that they are rewarded for defining deviance—rather than conformity—in positive terms.

## HIRSCHI'S CONTROL THEORY

Sociologist Travis Hirschi (1969, Gottfredson & Hirschi, 1995) developed a *control theory*, which states that social control depends on anticipating the consequences of one's behaviour. Hirschi assumes that everyone finds at least some deviance tempting. But most people are deterred by imagining the reactions of family or friends; others, by the thought of a ruined career. On the other hand, individuals who think that they have little to lose from deviance are likely to become rule-breakers.

Specifically, Hirschi links conformity to four types of social controls:

1. **Attachment.** Strong social attachments encourage conformity; weak relationships in the family,

peer group, and school leave people freer to engage in deviance.

2. **Commitment.** The greater a person's commitment to legitimate opportunity, the greater the advantages of conformity. By contrast, someone with little confidence in future success is freer to drift toward deviance.

3. **Involvement.** Extensive involvement in legitimate activities—such as holding a job, going to school, or playing sports—inhibits deviance. By contrast, people who simply "hang out" waiting for something to happen have time and energy for deviant activity.

4. **Belief.** Strong beliefs in conventional morality and respect for authority figures restrain tendencies toward deviance. By contrast, people with a weak conscience (and who are left supervised) are more vulnerable to temptation (Osgood et al., 1996).

Hirschi's analysis draws together a number of earlier ideas about the causes of deviant behaviour. Note that both a person's relative social privilege and strength of moral character are crucial in generating a stake in conformity to conventional norms (Wiatrowski, Griswold, & Roberts, 1981; Sampson & Laub, 1990; Free, 1992).

**Critical evaluation.** The various symbolic-interaction theories all see deviance as process. Labelling theory links deviance not to *action* but to the *reaction* of others. Thus some people are defined as deviant, while others who think or behave in the same way are not. The concepts of secondary deviance, deviant careers, and stigma demonstrate how being labelled a deviant can become a lasting self-concept.

Yet labelling theory has several limitations. First, because it takes a highly relative view of deviance, labelling theory ignores the fact that some kinds of behaviour—such as murder—are condemned virtually everywhere (Wellford, 1980). Labelling theory is thus most usefully applied to less serious deviance, such as sexual promiscuity or mental illness. Second, research on the consequences of deviant labelling is inconclusive (Smith & Gartin, 1989; Sherman & Smith, 1992). Does deviant labelling produce further deviance or discourage it? Third, not everyone resists being labelled as deviant; some people actually seek it out (Vold & Bernard, 1986). For example, people engage in civil disobedience leading to arrest in order to call attention to social injustice.

Both Sutherland's differential association theory and Hirschi's control theory have influenced sociology. But they provide little insight into why society's norms and laws define certain kinds of activities as deviant in the first place. This important question is addressed by social-conflict analysis, the focus of the next section.

## DEVIANCE AND INEQUALITY: SOCIAL-CONFLICT ANALYSIS

The social-conflict paradigm links deviance to social inequality. That is, *who* or *what* is labelled "deviant" depends on which categories of people hold power in a society.

### DEVIANCE AND POWER

Alexander Liazos (1972) points out that everyday conceptions of deviants—"nuts, sluts, and 'preverts'"—all share the trait of powerlessness. Bag ladies (not corporate polluters) and unemployed men on street corners (not arms dealers) carry the stigma of deviance.

Social-conflict theory explains this pattern in three ways. First, the norms—including laws—of any society generally reflect the interests of the rich and powerful. People who threaten the wealthy, either by taking their property or by advocating a more egalitarian society, are often defined as "common thieves" or "political radicals." Karl Marx, a major architect of the social-conflict approach, argued that the law (and all social institutions) supports the interests of the rich. Or, as Richard Quinney puts it, "Capitalist justice is by the capitalist class, for the capitalist class, and against the working class" (1977:3).

Second, even if their behaviour is called into question, the powerful have the resources to resist deviant labels. Government officials or corporate executives who might order or condone the dumping of hazardous wastes are rarely held personally accountable. Moreover, as the 1997 criminal trial of Calgary socialite Dorothy Joudrie made clear, even when charged with violent crimes, the rich have the resources to vigorously resist being labelled as criminal.

Third, the widespread belief that norms and laws are natural and good masks their political character. For this reason, we may condemn the *unequal application* of the law but give little thought to the charge that the *laws themselves* are inherently unfair (Quinney, 1977).

### DEVIANCE AND CAPITALISM

In the Marxist tradition, Steven Spitzer (1980) argues that deviant labels are applied to people who interfere with the operation of capitalism. First, because capitalism is based on private control of property, people who threaten the property of others—especially the poor who steal from the rich—are prime candidates for the deviant label. Conversely, the rich who exploit the poor are less likely to be labelled deviant. For example, landlords who charge poor tenants high rents and evict those who cannot pay are not considered a threat to anyone; they are simply "doing business."

Second, because capitalism depends on productive labour, people who cannot or will not work risk being labelled deviant. Many members of our society think people who are out of work—even if through no fault of their own—are somehow deviant.

Third, capitalism depends on respect for authority figures, so people who resist authority are labelled deviant. Examples are children who skip school or talk back to parents and teachers, and adults who do not cooperate with employers or police.

Fourth, anyone who directly challenges the capitalist status quo is likely to be defined as deviant. In this category are antiwar activists, radical environmentalists, and labour organizers.

On the other side of the coin, society positively labels whatever enhances the operation of capitalism. Winning athletes, for example, enjoy celebrity status because they make money and express the values of individual achievement and competition vital to capitalism. Additionally, Spitzer notes, we condemn using drugs of escape (marijuana, psychedelics, heroin, and crack) as deviant, but promote drugs that encourage adjustment to the status quo (alcohol and caffeine).

The capitalist system also strives to control people who don't fit in. The elderly, people with mental or physical disabilities, and Robert Merton's retreatists (including people addicted to alcohol or other drugs) represent a "costly yet relatively harmless burden" on society. Such people, claims Spitzer, are subject to control by social welfare agencies. But people who directly challenge the capitalist system, including the inner-city "underclass" and revolutionaries—Merton's innovators and rebels—are controlled by the criminal justice system or, in times of upheaval such as the FLQ crisis, military forces.

Note that both the social welfare and criminal justice systems blame individuals—not the system—for social problems. Welfare recipients are deemed unworthy freeloaders; poor people who vent rage at their plight are labelled rioters; anyone who actively challenges the government is branded a radical or a Communist; and those who attempt to gain illegally what they will never acquire legally are rounded up as common criminals.

## WHITE-COLLAR CRIME

It was a cool night in Jakarta, and the Shangri-La Hotel was all aglitter. Valentine's Day, 1997. Young couples swayed through the lobby. . . . A piano player sat at a full-size grand, playing Johnny Mathis tunes. . . . It was a bejewelled backdrop to the deal that went down that day, the forced one between Freeport-McMoRan's

*David Walsh died from a heart attack in 1998. He was never able to escape the scandal resulting from gaining more than $20 million from the sale of Bre-X stock before it became known that the stock was worthless. Nobody has been convicted of the fraud that led to Bre-X being valued at $6 billion by investors.*

Jim Bob Moffett and Bre-X's David Walsh, the one that was meant to settle the ownership of Busang. Busang. The mother of all gold mines. That's what was said. That's what was written. That's what I wrote (Wells, 1997).

CBC reporter Jennifer Wells was not the only one taken in by the Bre-X saga. At its peak, Bre-X Minerals Ltd. of Calgary controlled a gold mine of about 1500 tonnes, perhaps more. This is what the Bre-X CEO, David Walsh, publicly announced in February 1997. Canadians across the country rushed to "gamble on gold," buying out Bre-X shares. Less than a month later the bad news broke: Busang was in fact a terrible scam, perhaps the greatest fraud in the history of mining!

Bre-X's management activities exemplify **white-collar crime**, defined by Edwin Sutherland in 1940 as *crimes committed by people of high social position in the course of their occupations* (Sutherland & Cressey, 1978). As the Bre-X case suggests, white-collar crimes do not involve violence and rarely bring police with drawn guns to the scene. Rather, white-collar criminals use their powerful occupational offices to enrich themselves or others illegally, often causing significant public harm in the process (Hagan & Parker, 1985;

Vold & Bernard, 1986). For this reason, sociologists sometimes call white-collar offences *crime in the suites* as opposed to *crime in the streets*.

The most common white-collar crimes are bank embezzlement, business fraud, bribery, and antitrust violations. Certainly, some white-collar crime causes limited harm. But many white-collar crimes—such as the Bre-X scandal—attract a great deal of attention and cause great loss to the public (Weisburd et al., 1991). Pension plans were among the biggest losers when the value of Bre-X shares evaporated—the Ontario Teachers Pension Plan lost some $100 million; the *Caisse de dépôt et placement du Quebec*, $70 million; and the Ontario Municipal Employees Retirement Board, $45 million (Wells, 1997).

Sutherland (1940) explains that white-collar offences typically end up in a civil hearing rather than a criminal courtroom. *Civil law* regulates economic affairs between private parties, while *criminal law* defines every individual's moral responsibilities to society. In practice, then, a loser in a civil case pays for damage or injury, but is not labelled a criminal. Further, corporate officials are protected by the fact that most charges of white-collar crime target the organization rather than individuals.

In the rare cases that white-collar criminals are charged and convicted, the odds are that they will not go to jail. If they do go to jail—as did the former agent for NHL hockey players and founder of the NHL Players' Association, Alan Eagleson—chances are that they will apply for and receive parole at the earliest opportunity. In January 1998, Eagleson was fined $1 million and received an 18-month jail term, after being convicted on a number of charges, including skimming money from Canada Cup advertising, Labatt, Hockey Night in Canada, and the NHL Players' Association. Eagleson was released on parole just six months into his 18-month term.

## CORPORATE CRIME

Sometimes whole companies, rather than individuals, break the law. **Corporate crime** refers to *the illegal actions of a corporation or people acting on its behalf.*

Corporate crime ranges from knowingly selling faulty or dangerous products to deliberately polluting the environment (Benson & Cullen, 1998). As is the case with white-collar crime, most cases go unpunished and many are never a matter of public record. But the cost of corporate crime goes beyond dollars to human lives. For example, North American coal mining companies have hidden the dangers of bad air in the mines, so that hundreds of people die annually from "black lung" disease. The death toll from all job-related hazards known to companies probably reaches more

than 100 000 annually (Reiman, 1998; Carroll, 1999; J. Jones, 1999).

When corporations are accused of wrongdoing, however, they have the resources to fight back. In 1998, for example, the U.S. government charged software giant Microsoft with antitrust violations, accusing the company of knowingly establishing such control over a market that they could just about set their own prices. The corporation has vigorously defended itself, however, and the civil proceedings will continue for years (Nocera, 1999). Whatever the outcome, the company as a whole is on trial; individuals who lead the corporation are not subject to criminal prosecution.

## ORGANIZED CRIME

**Organized crime** is *a business supplying illegal goods or services.* Sometimes organized crime forces people to do business with them, as when a gang extorts money from shopkeepers for "protection." In most cases, however, organized crime involves selling illegal goods and services—including sex, drugs, or gambling—to a willing public.

Organized crime is flourishing in Canada. The scope of its operations garnered public attention in the fall of 2000 with the daylight shooting of Michel Augur, a Montreal journalist who has for many years written about the two motorcycle gangs The Rock Machine and Hell's Angels. During the late 1990s, some 150 people died as a result of fighting between these two rival gangs. At stake are the lucrative drug and sex trades (Canadian Press Newswire, October 21, 2000; Beltrame & Branswell 2000).

**Critical evaluation.** According to social-conflict theory, a capitalist society's inequality in wealth and power guides the creation and application of laws and other norms. The criminal justice and social welfare systems thus act as political agents, controlling categories of people who threaten the capitalist system.

Like other approaches to deviance, however, social-conflict theory has its critics. First, this approach implies that laws and other cultural norms are created directly by the rich and powerful. At the very least, this is an oversimplification, since laws also protect workers, consumers, and the environment, sometimes opposing the interests of the rich.

Second, social-conflict analysis implies that criminality springs up only to the extent that a society treats its members unequally. However, as Durkheim noted, deviance exists in all societies, whatever their economic system.

The sociological explanations for crime and other types of deviance that we have discussed are summarized in Table 6–1.

# DEVIANCE AND SOCIAL DIVERSITY

What we consider deviant reflects the relative power and privilege of different categories of people. The following sections offer two examples: how hate crimes are motivated by racial and ethnic hostility, and how gender is linked to deviance.

## HATE CRIMES

The term **hate crime** refers to *a criminal act against a person or a person's property by an offender motivated by racial or other bias.* A hate crime may express hostility toward someone based on race, religion, ancestry, sexual orientation, or physical disability.

Most people were stunned by the brutal killing of Nirmal Singh Gill—a Sikh temple caretaker—by five men active in white supremacist groups. Statistics collected by individual police departments in Toronto, Montreal, and Ottawa suggest that over half of the hate crimes in these three jurisdictions is directed toward specific racial groups. About 30 percent is aimed at religious groups and 10 percent at gays and lesbians (Roberts, 1995). People who contend with multiple stigmas, such as Jewish gay men, are especially likely to become victims of hate-motivated violence. The federal government does not collect data on hate crimes, and data collection varies across Canada. In addition, it is likely that many of these crimes go unreported. Nevertheless, it is estimated that there are more than 60 000 hate crimes committed every year in this country (Roberts, 1995).

## DEVIANCE AND GENDER

Virtually every society in the world applies more stringent normative controls to women than to men. Historically, our society has centred women's lives around the home. In Canada even today, women's opportunities in the workplace, in politics, and in the military are limited. Elsewhere in the world, the normative constraints on women are greater still. In Saudi Arabia, women cannot vote or legally operate motor vehicles; in Iran, women who expose their hair or wear makeup in public can be whipped.

Gender also figures into the theories about deviance noted earlier. Robert Merton's strain theory, for example, seems masculine in that it defines cultural goals in terms of financial success. Traditionally, at least, this goal has more to do with the lives of men, while women have been socialized to define success in terms of relationships, particularly marriage and motherhood (Leonard, 1982). A more woman-focussed theory might recognize the "strain" that results from

| TABLE 6–1 Sociological Explanations of Deviance: A Summary | |
|---|---|
| **Theoretical Paradigm** | **Major Contributions** |
| **Structural-functional analysis** | What is deviant may vary, but deviance is found in all societies; deviance and the social response it provokes sustain the moral foundation of society; deviance may also guide social change. |
| **Symbolic-interaction analysis** | Nothing is inherently deviant but may become defined as such through the response of others; the reactions of others are highly variable; labelling someone deviant may lead to the development of secondary deviance and deviant careers. |
| **Social-conflict analysis** | Laws and other norms reflect the interests of powerful members of society; those who threaten the status quo generally are defined as deviant; social injury caused by powerful people is less likely to be considered criminal than is social injury caused by people who have little social power. |

the cultural ideal of equality clashing with the reality of gender-based inequality.

In labelling theory, too, gender influences how we define deviance; people commonly use different standards to judge the behaviour of females as opposed to males. Further, because society puts men in positions of power over women, men often escape direct responsibility for actions that victimize women. In the past, at least, men who sexually harassed or assaulted women were only mildly labelled, if they were punished at all.

By contrast, women who are victimized may have to convince an unsympathetic audience that they are not to blame for their own sexual harassment. The ruling by the Ontario Court in favour of "Jane Doe," who sued the Metropolitan Toronto Police for negligence in their handling of a serial-rapist case, illustrates this point. Ms. Doe alleged that the police should have done more to warn women in her neighbourhood about the rapist. It took 12 years before the court finally ruled that Ms. Doe's rights under the Canadian Charter of Rights and Freedoms had been violated because the police failed to give her equal protection under the law. This example confirms what research tells us: Whether people define a situation as deviance—and, if so, whose deviance it is—depends on the sex of both the audience and the actors (King & Clayson, 1988).

Finally, in spite of its focus on social inequality, much social-conflict analysis does not address the issue of gender even as it is noted that disadvantaged women commit more crimes than advantaged women. If, as conflict theory suggests, economic disadvantage is a primary cause of crime, why do women (whose economic position is much worse than men's) commit far fewer crimes than men do? Some criminologists argue that as gender roles converge, so will the crime rates of men and women. There is some evidence in support of this argument when we look at the increase in property crime; however, the rate of violent crimes by females does not show signs of catching up to that by males.

## CRIME

Crime is the violation of criminal laws enacted by a country's central or branch governments. Technically, all crimes are composed of two distinct elements: an *act* (or, in some cases, the failure to do what the law requires) and *criminal intent* (in legal terminology *mens rea*, or "guilty mind"). Intent is a matter of degree, ranging from willful conduct to negligence. Someone who is negligent does not set out deliberately to hurt someone, but acts (or fails to act) in such a way that harm results. Prosecutors weigh the degree of intent, for example, in determining whether to charge someone with first-degree murder, second-degree murder, or negligent manslaughter. Alternatively, they may consider a killing justifiable, as in a case of self-defence.

### TYPES OF CRIME

The Canadian Centre for Justice Statistics provides summary reports on the basis of its Uniform Crime Reporting (UCR) survey. Statistics Canada originally designed the UCR survey with the agreement of, and help from, the Canadian Association of Chiefs of Police. Implemented in 1962, the aggregate UCR survey gathers crime statistics reported by police departments across the country. It is important to keep in mind (more on this point below) that these statistics are based only on "recorded crimes"—that is, crimes *reported* to the police in Canada—and not on all crimes that are actually committed.

**Crimes against the person** are *crimes that involve violence or the threat of violence against others*. Such "violent crimes" include murder and manslaughter (directly or indirectly causing the death of a human being), aggravated assault (wounding, maiming, disfiguring, or endangering a person), sexual assault (forcing a victim into sexual activity without voluntary agreement), and robbery (using violence or threats to overcome resistance to stealing).

**Crimes against property** involve *theft of goods belonging to others*. Property crimes include theft (unlawfully taking the property of another), break and enter (unlawfully entering a place to commit an offence), possession of stolen property (knowingly having property that was obtained unlawfully), and fraud (obtaining property, money, or a valuable security or service from the public or any person through deceit, falsehood, or other fraudulent means).

Third and fourth categories of Criminal Code offences—traffic and other—include **victimless crimes**, *violations of law in which there are no readily apparent victims*. Such crimes include illegal drug use (technically an offence against the *Narcotics Control Act*), prostitution, and gambling. The term "victimless crime" is misleading, however. How victimless is a crime when young people purchasing drugs may be embarking on a life of crime to support a drug habit? Or when a young pregnant woman, by smoking crack, permanently harms her baby? Or when a gambler falls so deeply into debt that he cannot make the mortgage payments on his house? Perhaps it is more correct to say that people who commit such crimes are themselves both offenders and victims.

Because public opinion about such activities varies considerably, the laws regulating victimless crimes differ from place to place. For example, prostitution—the exchange of money for sex—is not illegal in Canada. Nonetheless a person can be charged who "in a public place . . . communicates . . . for the purpose of engaging in prostitution . . . ." This law is often more heavily enforced when residents of a neighbourhood complain about prostitution (Statistics Canada, 1997g).

### CRIMINAL STATISTICS

Statistics gathered by police show crime rates rising from the early 1960s to 1991, but declining over the past decade. Even so, excluding traffic and drug incidents, police tallied 2.36 million Criminal Code offences in 1999 (Tremblay, 2000). Figure 6–2 shows the trends for various serious crimes.

Always read crime statistics with caution, however, since they include only crimes known to the police. Almost all homicides are reported, but other assaults—especially among acquaintances—often are not. Police records include even a smaller proportion of property crime, especially when the losses are small.

Researchers compare official crime statistics to data from *victimization surveys*, which ask a representative sample of people about their experience with crime. According to these surveys, the overall crime rate is about three times higher than official reports indicate (Besserer & Trainor, 2000).

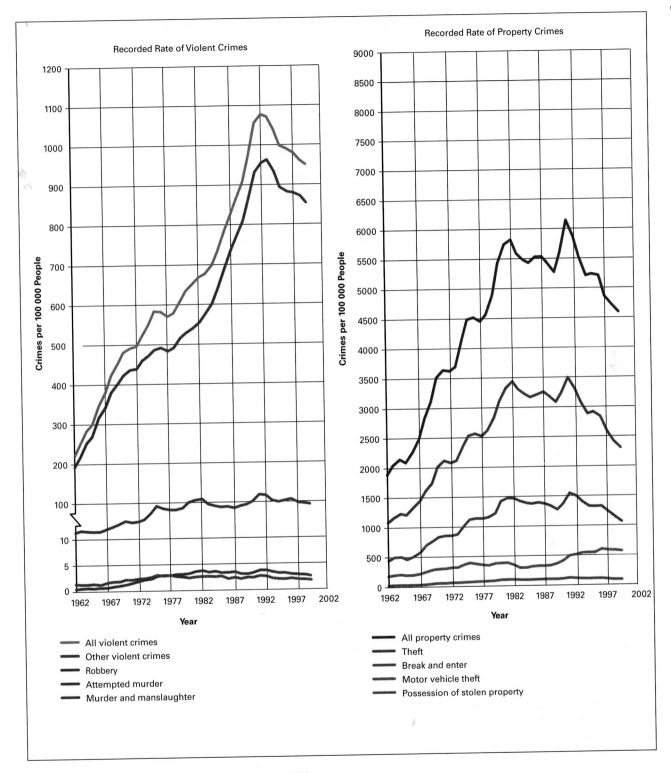

**FIGURE 6–2 Canadian Crime Rates, 1962–1999**

The graphs represent crime rates for various violent crimes and property crimes during recent decades. Most "Other violent crimes" are assaults.

Source: Calculated based on data in Statistics Canada, Catalogue No. 91-213-XPB (2000a), Cansim Series D9502-D9512, D31248.

*Do police look twice at young male Aboriginals when they are looking to solve a crime?*

## THE "STREET" CRIMINAL: A PROFILE

The typical street criminal can be characterized in the following manner. (This profile, it should be pointed out, is shaped by different **clearance rates**: *the rates at which police solve crime*. White-collar crimes have relatively low clearance rates compared with assault or property crimes, which police solve more successfully.)

**Age.** Crime rates rise sharply during adolescence, peak at ages 14 through 19, and then fall sharply again. While this age group represented just 8 percent of the Canadian population in 1999, it accounted for 33 percent of those accused of property crimes and 20 percent of those accused of violent crime (Cansim series C892268, C892319, and C892340). Those charged with violent crime are older (median age is 29) than those charged with property crime (where the median age is 23) (Tremblay, 2000).

**Gender.** Although each sex makes up roughly half of the population, police collared males in 78 percent of all property crime arrests in 1999. In other words, men are arrested more than three times as often as women for property crimes. In the case of violent crimes, the disparity is even greater for adults (18 and over): 86 percent of charges involved males compared to just 14 percent involving females (a six-to-one ratio).

Among youth (ages 12 to 17) the disparity is less pronounced: 75 percent of charges involved males (a three-to-one ratio). One reason for this disparity is that law enforcement officials are reluctant to define women as criminals. Even so, the difference in arrest rates for women and men, particularly among youth, has been narrowing, probably a reflection of increasing gender equality in our society.

Despite a decline during the late 1990s, the rate at which female youth were charged with violent crimes increased by 81 percent between 1989 and 1999, while the rate for male youth increased only 30 percent. Nevertheless, male youth are three times as likely to be charged with a violent crime (1254 per 100 000) compared to female youth (444 per 100 000) (Boritch, 1997; Tremblay, 2000). The higher rates for males is a pattern that holds true globally, with the greatest gender difference in crime rates occurring in societies that most limit the opportunities of women.

**Social class.** Police do not assess the social class of arrested persons, so no statistical data of the kind given above are available. But research has long indicated that criminality is more widespread among people of lower social position (Wolfgang, Figlio, & Sellin, 1972; Clinard & Abbott, 1973; Braithwaite, 1981; Thornberry & Farnsworth, 1982; Wolfgang, Thornberry, & Figlio, 1987).

Yet the connection between class and crime is more complicated than it appears on the surface. For one thing, many people look upon the poor as less worthy than the rich, whose wealth and power confer "respectability" (Tittle & Villemez, 1977; Tittle, Villemez, & Smith, 1978; Elias, 1986). While crime—especially violent crime—is a serious problem in the poorest inner-city neighbourhoods, most of these crimes are committed by a few hard-core offenders. The majority of poor people who live in these neighbourhoods have no criminal records at all (Wolfgang, Figlio, & Sellin, 1972; Elliott & Ageton, 1980; Harries, 1990).

Moreover, the connection between social standing and criminality depends on the kind of crime one is talking about (Braithwaite, 1981). If we expand our definition of crime beyond street offences to include white-collar crime, the "common criminal" suddenly looks much more affluent.

**Race and ethnicity.** In multicultural societies, such as Canada, both race and ethnicity are strongly correlated to crime rates, although the reasons are many and complex. Official U.S. statistics, for example, indicate that in 1999, 31.9 percent of arrests for property crimes and 40.2 percent of arrests for violent crimes involved black people, even though black people only made up 12.7 percent of the population (U.S. Federal Bureau of Investigation, 1999).

Firm conclusions about Canada are not as easy to come by because our police do not collect data on race and ethnicity. However, the available evidence points to the following two conclusions.

First, the situation is rather different with respect to visible ethnic minorities. In fact, they tend to be underrepresented in arrest data and prison populations. Second, Aboriginals and black people are two exceptions. Aboriginals are dramatically overrepresented in Canada's correctional facilities: In 1998–1999, Aboriginal persons made up 17 percent of admissions to custody, even though they make up only 2 percent of the Canadian population (Thomas, 2000). Similarly, research in the Metro Toronto area on self-declared "black," "white," and "Chinese" male residents shows that black males were almost twice as likely as white males to have been stopped by the police sometime in the previous two years—the percentage of black males who reported having been stopped *twice* (29 percent) is greater than the proportion of white males that were stopped *once* (25 percent) (The Commission on Systematic Racism in the Ontario Criminal Justice System, 1995; quoted in James, 1998).

What accounts for the disproportionate number of arrests among various ethnic groups? Two factors, as mentioned above, come into play. First, prejudice related to race prompts white police to arrest Aboriginal people more readily (Schissel, 1993). Second, Aboriginal status in Canada closely relates to social standing, which, as we have already explained, affects the likelihood of engaging in street crimes. Poor people living in the midst of affluence come to see society as unjust and thus are more likely to turn to crime (Blau & Blau, 1982; Anderson, 1994).

## CRIME IN GLOBAL PERSPECTIVE

By world standards, the crime rate in Canada is not high. This may seem surprising given the high crime rate characteristic of our neighbour to the south. For example, the homicide rate in the United States is five times that of Europe, the rape rate is seven times higher, and the rate of property crime is twice as high. The contrast is even greater with the nations of Asia, including India and Japan, where rates of violent and property crime are among the lowest in the world. The most significant difference between Canada and the U.S. is the homicide rate, which is much higher in the U.S., even though the Canadian rate is high compared with that of most countries in Northern Europe as Figure 6–3 shows.

Although recent crime trends are downward in Canada, the U.S. and in many other high-income countries, there were 16 914 murders in the United States in 1998, which amounts to one every half hour around the clock. In large cities such as

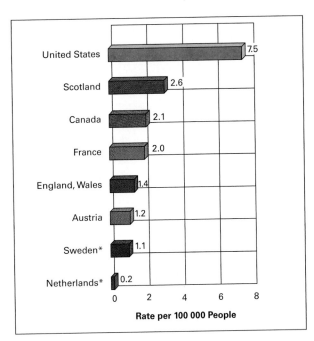

**FIGURE 6-3** **Homicide Rate for Selected Countries, 1995–1996**

*1995 data

Source: Besserer (1998).

New York, rarely does a day pass with no murder; in fact, more New Yorkers are hit with stray bullets than are deliberately gunned down in most large cities elsewhere in the world.

Elliott Currie (1985) suggests that the high crime rate in the U.S. stems from a cultural emphasis on individual economic success, frequently at the expense of strong families and neighbourhoods. The United States also has extraordinary cultural diversity, resulting from centuries of immigration. Moreover, economic inequality is higher in that country than in most other industrial societies. Thus, U.S. society's relatively weak social fabric, combined with considerable frustration among the have-nots, generates widespread criminal behaviour.

Proponents for gun registration in Canada point to another factor adding to violence in the United States—the extensive private ownership of guns. About two-thirds of murder victims in the U.S. die from shootings. Since the early 1990s, in Texas and several other southern states, shooting deaths have exceeded automobile-related fatalities. As Figure 6–4 on page 144 shows, the U.S. is the runaway leader in handgun deaths among industrial societies.

Surveys suggest that almost half of U.S. households have at least one gun (Gallup, 1993; Wright, 1995; NORC, 1999). Put differently, there are more guns than adults in the U.S., and one-third of these weapons are handguns that figure in violent crime. In large part, gun ownership reflects people's fear of

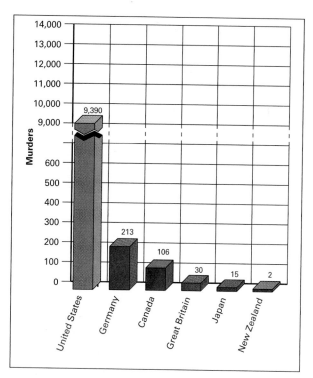

**FIGURE 6–4   Number of Murders by Handguns, 1996**

Source: Handgun Control, Inc. (2001).

crime; yet, ironically, easy availability of guns also makes crime more deadly.

But as critics of our gun registration point out, the registration of guns does not keep the weapons out of the hands of criminals, who almost always obtain guns illegally (Wright, 1995). Moreover, we should be cautious about assuming that gun control would be a magic "bullet," so to speak, in the war on crime. Elliott Currie (1985) notes, for example, that the number of Californians killed each year by knives alone exceeds the number of Canadians killed by weapons of all kinds. Most experts do agree, however, that stricter gun control laws would lower the level of deadly violence.

Crime rates are soaring in some of the largest cities of the world, such as Manila, Philippines, and São Paulo, Brazil, which have rapid population growth and millions of desperately poor people. Outside big cities, however, the traditional character of low-income societies and their strong family structure allow local communities to control crime informally (Clinard & Abbott, 1973; *Der Spiegel*, 1989).

International victimization surveys are another way to compare crime in different countries, although even with the best efforts, comparisons between countries is difficult because of cultural differences in the interpretation of questions and in the willingness of participants to disclose information to interviewers. Nevertheless, comparisons show that victimization generally is higher in low-income countries than in high-income countries. There are also differences, however, between high-income countries. One possible explanation for these differences in the victimization rate between different countries can be found in the differences in income inequality. Figure 6–5 (opposite) shows both the victimization rate and the Gini index (a measure of income inequality). Keeping in mind that both these measures are difficult to use to compare nations, it nevertheless appears that nations with less inequality have lower victimization rates.

Countries have different strategies for dealing with crime. The use of the death penalty provides a case in point. Global Map 6–1 on page 146 identifies countries that employ capital punishment in response to crime and those that do not. The global trend is toward abolition of the death penalty: Amnesty International (2000) reports that since 1980, more than 30 nations have ended this practice.

## THE CRIMINAL JUSTICE SYSTEM

December 10, 1994—Casablanca, Morocco Casablanca! An exciting mix of African, European, and Middle Eastern cultures. Returning from a stroll through the medina, the medieval section of this coastal, North African city, we confront lines of police along a boulevard, standing between us and our ship in the harbour. The police are providing security for many important leaders attending an Islamic conference at a nearby hotel. Are the streets closed? No one asks, but people stop short of an invisible line some 15 metres from the police officers. I play the brash North American and start across the street to enquire (in broken French) if we can pass by; but I stop cold as several officers draw a bead on me with their eyes. Their fingers nervously tap at the grips on their automatic weapons. This is no time to strike up a conversation.

The criminal justice system is a society's formal response to crime. In some of the world's countries, military police keep a tight rein on people's behaviour; in others including Canada, police have more limited powers and only respond to violations of the law. We shall briefly introduce the key elements of the criminal justice system: police, courts, and the punishment of convicted offenders.

## POLICE

The police generally serve as the point of contact between a population and the criminal justice system. In principle, the police maintain public order by enforcing the law. Of course, there is only so much 54 719 full-time police officers in Canada (in 1998) can do to monitor the activities of 30 million people. As a result, the police exercise considerable discretion over which situations warrant their attention and how to handle them.

How do police carry out their duties? In a study of police behaviour in five U.S. cities, Douglas Smith and Christy Visher (1981; Smith, 1987) concluded that because police must act swiftly, officers quickly size up situations in terms of six factors. First, the more serious police think the situation is, the more likely they are to make an arrest. Second, police take account of the victim's desire in deciding whether to make an arrest. Third, the odds of arrest go up the more uncooperative a suspect is. Fourth, police are more likely to take into custody someone they have arrested before, presumably because this suggests guilt. Fifth, the presence of bystanders increases the chances of arrest. According to Smith and Visher, the presence of observers prompts police to take stronger control of a situation, if only to move the encounter from the street (the suspect's turf) to the police department (where law officers have the edge). Sixth, all else being equal, police are more likely to arrest visible minorities than others, perceiving visible minorities as either more dangerous or more likely to be guilty.

## COURTS

After arrest, a court determines a suspect's guilt or innocence. In principle, our courts rely on an adversarial process involving attorneys—one representing the defendant and another the state—in the presence of a judge who monitors legal procedures.

In practice, however, many criminal cases are resolved prior to court appearance through **plea bargaining,** *a legal negotiation in which a prosecutor reduces a charge in exchange for a defendant's guilty plea.* For example, the state may offer a defendant charged with burglary a lesser charge of possessing burglary tools in exchange for a guilty plea.

Plea bargaining is widespread because it spares the system the time and expense of trials. A trial is usually unnecessary if there is little disagreement as to the facts

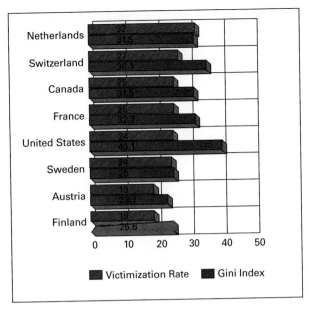

**FIGURE 6–5    Victimization and Inequality in Selected Countries, 1990s**

**Note:** Victimization is a measure of the percentage of respondents victimized over the previous 12 months. The Gini index ranges from 0 to 100, where a higher number indicates more inequality between high- and low-income earners in a population.

Source: Besserer (1998); World Bank (2000).

of the case. Moreover, since the number of cases entering the system doubled over the past decade, prosecutors could not possibly bring every case to trial. By selectively trying only a small proportion of the files, the courts channel their resources into the most important cases.

But plea bargaining pressures defendants (who are presumed innocent) to plead guilty. A person can exercise the right to a trial, but only at the risk of receiving a more severe sentence if found guilty. Furthermore, low-income defendants enter the process relying on a public defender—an attorney, often overworked and usually underpaid, who may devote little time even to a serious case (Novak, 1999). Overall, plea bargaining may be efficient but at the cost of undercutting the adversarial process as well as the rights of defendants.

## PUNISHMENT

When a person is brutally attacked and murdered—as in the case featured in the opening to this chapter—some people may wonder why, but almost everyone believes that *someone* should have to "pay" for the crime. Indeed, sometimes the desire to punish is so great that justice may not be served.

Such cases force us to ask *why* a society should punish its wrongdoers. Over many years, scholars have

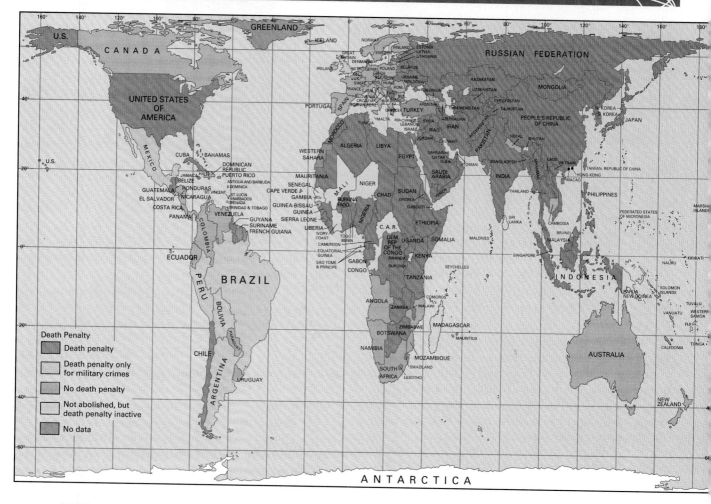

**GLOBAL MAP 6–1    Capital Punishment in Global Perspective**

The map identifies 91 countries and territories in which the law provides for the death penalty for ordinary crimes; in 14 more, the death penalty is reserved for exceptional crimes under military law or during times of war. The death penalty does not exist in 67 countries and territories; in 23 more, although the death penalty remains in law, no execution has taken place in more than a decade. Compare high-income and low-income nations: What general pattern do you see? In what way do the United States and Japan stand out?

Source: Amnesty International, "The Death Penalty: List of Abolitionist and Retentionist Countries," February 1999, www.amnesty.org/ailib/intcam/dp/abrelist.htm

pointed to four basic reasons to punish: retribution, deterrence, rehabilitation, and social protection.

**Retribution**. The oldest justification for punishment is to satisfy a society's need for **retribution**, *moral vengeance by which a society inflicts on an offender suffering comparable to that caused by the offence*. Retribution rests on a view of society as a system seeking a moral balance. When criminality upsets this balance, punishment enacted in comparable measure restores the moral order, as suggested by the biblical dictum "an eye for an eye."

During the Middle Ages, most people viewed crime as sin—an offence against God as well as society—that warranted a harsh response. Today, although critics point out that retribution does little to reform the offender, many people still consider vengeance reason enough for punishment.

**Deterrence.** A second justification for punishment is **deterrence**, *the use of punishment to discourage criminality.* Deterrence is based on the 18th-century Enlightenment idea that, as calculating and rational creatures, humans will not break the law if they think that the pains of the punishment outweigh the pleasures of the crime.

Deterrence emerged as a reform in response to the harsh punishments based on retribution. Why put someone to death for stealing, reformists reasoned, if theft can be discouraged by a prison sentence? As the concept of deterrence gained widespread acceptance, execution and physical mutilation of criminals in most industrial societies were replaced by milder forms of punishment, such as incarceration.

Punishment may deter crime in two ways. *Specific deterrence* convinces an individual offender that crime does not pay. Through *general deterrence*, punishing one person serves as an example to others.

**Rehabilitation.** The third justification for punishment, **rehabilitation**, involves *reforming the offender to preclude subsequent offences.* Rehabilitation arose along with the social sciences in the 19th century. Since then, sociologists have claimed that crime and other deviance spring from a social environment marked by poverty or lack of parental supervision. Logically, then, if offenders *learn* to be deviant, they can also *learn* to obey the rules; the key is controlling the environment. *Reformatories* or *houses of correction* served as a controlled environment structured to help offenders learn proper behaviour (recall the description of total institutions in Chapter 3, Socialization: From Infancy to Old Age).

Like deterrence, rehabilitation motivates the offender to conform. But rehabilitation emphasizes constructive improvement, while deterrence and retribution simply make the offender suffer. In addition, while retribution demands that the punishment fit the crime, rehabilitation tailors treatment to each offender. Thus, identical crimes would prompt similar acts of retribution but different rehabilitation programs.

**Social protection.** A final justification for punishment is **social protection**, or *rendering an offender incapable of committing further offences either temporarily through incarceration or permanently by execution.* The reason that there are more than 32 000 adults in Canadian prisons is partly a reflection of the widespread attitude that we should "get criminals off the streets." Remember that this number represents only about 20 percent of the total number under the supervision of the correctional system—almost 70 percent of the grand total are on probation and the remainder

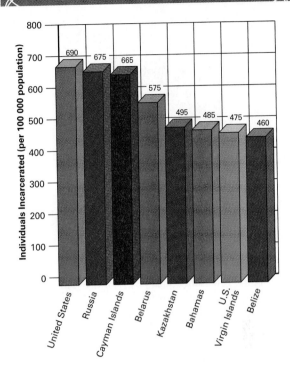

**FIGURE 6–6   Nations with the Highest Incarceration Rates, 2000**

Source: Walmsley (2000).

serve a conditional sentence or are on conditional release (Statistics Canada, 2000k).

Since the early 1990s, there has been a slight decrease in the number of admissions to Canadian jails (Thomas, 2000). This is in contrast to the situation in the U.S., where currently some 2 million people are incarcerated and another 4 million are on parole and probation. In response to tougher public attitudes and an increasing number of drug-related arrests, the U.S. prison population has tripled since 1980. As Figure 6–6 shows, the United States incarcerates a larger share of its population than do most other countries of the world.

**Critical evaluation.** Table 6–2 on page 148 summarizes these four justifications for punishment. Assessing the actual consequences of punishment, however, is no simple task.

The value of retribution lies in Durkheim's contention that punishing the deviant person increases society's moral awareness. For this reason, punishment was traditionally a public event.

Certainly, punishment deters some crime. Yet our society has a high rate of **criminal recidivism**, *subsequent offences by people previously convicted of crimes.*

*Incarceration severs whatever social ties inmates may have with the outside world, which, following Hirschi's control theory, leaves individuals prone to further crime upon their release.*

After being released, about half of those convicted of a Criminal Code offence are convicted of a new offence within three years, and some studies suggest that almost four out of five offenders are eventually convicted again (Burr et al., 2000; Hanson & Scott, 1995). In light of such patterns, we may well wonder about the extent to which punishment really deters crime. Then, too, only about one-third of all crimes are known to police, and of these, only about one in five results in an arrest. The old adage "crime doesn't pay" rings hollow when we consider that only a small percentage of offences are ever punished.

Prisons provide short-term societal protection by keeping offenders off the streets, but there are indications that they do little to reshape attitudes or behaviour in the long term (Carlson, 1976; Wright, 1994). Perhaps rehabilitation is an unrealistic expectation, since according to Sutherland's theory of differential association, locking up criminals together for years probably strengthens criminal attitudes and skills. Incarceration also severs whatever social ties inmates may have in the outside world, which, following Hirschi's control theory, leaves individuals prone to further crime upon their release.

Finally, inmates returning to the surrounding world contend with the stigma of being ex-convicts, often an obstacle to successful integration. One study of young offenders in Philadelphia found that boys who were sentenced to long prison terms—those likely to acquire a criminal stigma—went on to commit both more crimes and more serious ones (Wolfgang, Figlio, & Sellin, 1972). It is disconcerting, therefore, to learn that young Canadian offenders in many cases receive longer sentences than do adults for the same offence (Sanders, 2000).

Ultimately, we should never assume that the contemporary criminal justice system—the police, courts, and prisons—can eliminate crime. The Applying Sociology box (opposite) discusses the fact that the strategies of restorative justice and alternative sentencing are gaining ground in Canada and many other countries. But more is involved. As this chapter has explained, crime and other deviance results not just from the acts of "bad people," but from the way in which society itself operates.

| TABLE 6–2 | Four Justifications for Punishment: A Summary |
|---|---|
| **Retribution** | The oldest justification for punishment. Punishment is atonement for a moral wrong; in principle, punishment should be comparable in severity to the deviance itself. |
| **Deterrence** | An early modern approach. Deviance is considered social disruption, which society acts to control. People are viewed as rational and self-interested; deterrence works because the pains of punishment outweigh the pleasures of deviance. |
| **Rehabilitation** | A modern strategy linked to the development of social sciences. Deviance is viewed as the product of social problems (such as poverty) or personal problems (such as mental illness). Social conditions are improved; treatment is tailored to the offender's condition. |
| **Societal Protection** | A modern approach easier to implement than rehabilitation. If society is unable or unwilling to rehabilitate offenders or reform social conditions, people are protected by incarcerating or executing the offender. |

# Soft on Crime?

The rise of victims groups in Canada reminds us that each crime involves more than just a perpetrator that must be punished. With the exception of a few cases—for example, those of Milgaard, and Homolka and Bernardo—there has been little allowance for the victim and the victim's family to be active in the justice process. A renewed emphasis on *restorative justice* attempts to change our justice system, in part to facilitate such participation of victims. Kent Roach (2000, p. 256) defines restorative justice as a "circle model of justice"—one that typically involves all participants, in an informal setting without strict hierarchies, attempting to restore the equilibrium that was upset by the crime.

There is a surprising level of support from many groups for Alternative Measures in Canada. For some, the alternatives are promising because the focus on *retribution* and alternative measure strategies includes input from the victim, as well as compensation from the offender directly to the victim or community. For other supporters, the *rehabilitative* emphasis is attractive; in this nonadversarial system, an offender's admission of guilt is seen as a necessary start of the rehabilitation process. The offender's participation in determining the "punishment" is a further step in this direction. All supporters point to the high cost of keeping people in jail as evidence that we need to consider alternatives.

There is little evidence available, however, showing the deterrence value of these programs, although supporters argue that more effective strategies will deter at least some crime by reducing the recidivism rate.

Early evaluations of Aboriginal restorative justice programs across Canada found that less than half of the victims that participated in these programs declared them to be a positive experience and believed that the offender had been appropriately dealt with (LaPrairie, 1998). Unfortunately, without good comparative data, we do not know which alternative measures are better or worse from the victim's perspective. Yet, even while Canadians may believe that the sentencing in general is too lenient, they nevertheless support more spending on programs offering alternative measures and less spending on building new prisons (Doob, 2000).

Source: Doob (2000), LaPrairie (1998), Mckillop (1999), and Roach (2000).

## Alternative Measures Programs Across Canada

The current Canadian approach to restorative justice was legislated first for youth—the 1984 *Young Offender Act*—and more recently for adults in the 1996 *Sentencing Reform Act*. The approach is commonly referred to as Alternative Measures in Canada.

Here are some basic characteristics of this approach:

– Focus is on first-time and non-violent offenders
– There is sufficient evidence to lay charge under the Criminal Code or Young Offender Act
– Offender must admit guilt and be advised of right to legal counsel
– Offender must participate voluntarily
– Participation by the victim is encouraged but not required
– The offender signs a contract that defines the alternative measures

Typical alternative measures include the following:

– Apologies to the victim
– Financial compensation to the victim
– Charitable donations
– Personal services to the victim
– Participation in educational programs such as "john school"
– Community service

Once terms of contract are fulfilled, the case is closed and formal charges are dropped. Generally, the records of the offence and the alternative measures can be revisited if further offences are committed within two years following the closure of the file.

Source: Mackillop (1999).

## SUMMARY

1. Deviance refers to norm violations ranging from mild breaches of etiquette to serious violence.

2. Biological research, from Lombroso's 19th-century observations of convicts to recent genetic studies, has yet to offer much insight into the causes of deviance.

3. Psychological study links deviance to abnormal personality resulting from either biological or environmental causes. Psychological theories help explain some kinds of deviance.

4. Deviance has societal rather than individual roots because it (a) varies according to cultural norms, (b) is socially defined, and (c) reflects patterns of social power.

5. Using the structural-functional paradigm, Durkheim explained that deviance serves to affirm norms and values, clarify moral boundaries, promote social unity, and encourage social change.

6. The symbolic-interaction paradigm is the basis of labelling theory, which holds that deviance lies in people's reaction to a person's behaviour, not in the behaviour itself. When a person acquires the stigma of deviance, that stigma can lead to secondary deviance and a deviant career.

7. Based on Karl Marx's ideas, social-conflict theory holds that laws and other norms reflect the interests of powerful members of a society. White-collar crimes, for example, cause extensive social harm, but offenders are rarely branded criminals.

8. Official statistics indicate that arrest rates peak in late adolescence, then drop steadily with advancing age. Three-fourths of those arrested for property crimes and 83 percent of those arrested for violent crimes are males.

9. People of lower social position commit more street crime than do those with greater social privilege. When white-collar crimes are included among criminal offences, however, this disparity in criminal activity decreases.

10. Aboriginal and black people are arrested more often than whites in proportion to their respective populations. Other visible minorities have lower than average rates of arrest.

11. Police exercise considerable discretion in their work. Arrest is more likely if the offence is serious, bystanders are present, and the accused is a visible minority person.

12. Although ideally an adversarial system, Canadian courts predominantly resolve cases through plea bargaining. While efficient, this method puts less powerful people at a disadvantage.

13. Justifications of punishment include retribution, deterrence, rehabilitation, and social protection. Because its consequences are difficult to evaluate scientifically, punishment—like deviance itself—sparks considerable controversy.

## KEY CONCEPTS

**deviance** (p. 128) the recognized violation of cultural norms

**crime** (p. 128) the violation of norms formally enacted into criminal law

**social control** (p. 128) attempts by society to regulate the thought and behaviour of individuals

**criminal justice system** (p. 128) a formal response by police, courts, and prison officials to alleged crime

**labelling theory** (p. 132) the assertion that deviance and conformity result not so much from what people do, as from the response of others to those actions

**stigma** (p. 133) a powerfully negative label that radically changes a person's social identity and self-concept

**medicalization of deviance** (p. 134) the transformation of moral and legal deviance into a medical condition

**white-collar crime** (p. 137) crimes committed by people of high social position in the course of their occupations

**corporate crime** (p. 138) the illegal actions of a corporation or people acting on its behalf

**organized crime** (p. 138) a business supplying illegal goods or services

**hate crime** (p. 139) a criminal act against a person or a person's property by an offender motivated by racial or other bias

**crimes against the person** (violent crimes) (p. 140) crimes that involve violence or the threat of violence

**crimes against property** (property crimes) (p. 140) crimes that involve theft of goods belonging to others

**victimless crime** (p. 140) violation of law in which there is no readily apparent victim

**clearance rates** (p. 142) the rate at which police solve crime

**plea bargaining** (p. 145) a legal negotiation in which the prosecutor reduces a charge in exchange for a defendant's guilty plea

**retribution** (p. 146) inflicting suffering on an offender comparable to that caused by the offence

**deterrence** (p. 147) the use of punishment to discourage criminality

**rehabilitation** (p. 147) reforming the offender to preclude further offences

**social protection** (p. 147) rendering an offender incapable of further offences, either temporarily through incarceration or permanently by execution

**criminal recidivism** (p. 147) subsequent offences committed by people previously convicted of crimes

## CRITICAL-THINKING QUESTIONS

1. How does a sociological view of deviance differ from the common-sense notion that bad people do bad things?

2. List Durkheim's functions of deviance. From his point of view, can society ever be free from deviance? Why or why not?

3. An old saying is that "Sticks and stones can break my bones, but names can never hurt me." Explain how labelling theory contradicts this statement.

4. A recent study found that one in three black men in the U.S. between the ages of 20 and 29 is in jail, on probation, or on parole (Mauer, 2000). Based on the material in this chapter, what factors help explain this pattern?

## APPLICATIONS AND EXERCISES

1. Research computer crime. What new kinds of crime are emerging in the Information Age? Is computer technology also creating new ways of tracking down lawbreakers?

2. Rent a wheelchair (check with a local pharmacy or medical supply store), and try to use it as much as possible for a day or two. Not only will you gain a firsthand understanding of the accessibility issue, but you will discover that people respond to you in many new ways.

3. Watch an episode of the real-action police show *Cops*. Based on this program, how would you profile the people who commit crimes?

 ## SITES TO SEE

**www.pearsoned.ca/macionis**
Visit the interactive Web site that accompanies this text for many learning activities and additional Internet links to learn more about the topics included in this chapter.

**www.Nashville.Net/~police/risk**
Visit this site, run by the Nashville Police Department, that rates your chances of becoming a victim of a serious crime.

**www.civilrights.org/index_active.html**
The Leadership Conference on Civil Rights maintains this site dealing with hate crimes.

**www.aidwyc.org**
The Association in Defence of the Wrongfully Convicted maintains this Web site, which lists some of the criminal cases overturned in Canada.

**www.ncadp.org**
**www.uaa.alaska.edu/just/death/intl.html**
These two sites provide information on the death penalty. The first outlines the views of the National Coalition to Abolish the Death Penalty. The second puts the death penalty in global perspective.

**www.stop-the-hate.org**
A Web site dedicated to shaming hate groups on the Internet. The list includes Canada First Immigration Reform Committee (**www.freedom-site.org/cfirc/**) and Heritage Front Manitoba (**www.front14.org/comradejoe/Index1.html**). These groups give a new meaning to the nickname "The Great White North."

Andy Warhol, *Marilyn*, 1967. © 2001 Andy Warhol Foundation for the Visual Arts/Artists Rights Society (ARS), New York. Tate Gallery, London/Art Resource, NY.

*As the old saying goes, birds do it and so do the bees. So do frogs, chimps, and even the great elephants. Indeed, biologists tell us that the animal world contains countless, fascinating mating rituals. Take, for example, scorpions: The couple engages in a deadly dance, round and round, locked face-to-face with their mouths and claws. As the mating proceeds, the male repeatedly stings the female as she holds firm to him. In the end, however, it is the larger female that prevails. Once fertilized, she turns on her mate and, in a burst of strength and ferocity, devours him.*

*Nature offers many strange stories about animal mating. However, the most fascinating of all must be human beings. Humans—most people, at least—like to "do it," too. But as the only creatures who attach meaning to all behaviour, what humans do when it comes to sex varies quite a bit from culture to culture just as it does over time. Moreover, we are the only species whose members think about the purpose of sex, encourage some forms of sex while outlawing others, and, in an effort to learn more, even conduct research about our own sexuality.* ■

This chapter presents some of what we have learned about human sexuality. From a sociological point of view, the main question is how society shapes our sexuality.

# UNDERSTANDING SEXUALITY

How much of the day goes by without your giving any thought to sexuality? If you are like most people, the answer is "not very much." That is because sexuality is not just about "having sex." Sexuality is a theme found throughout society, apparent on campus, in the workplace, and especially in the mass media. In addition, the sex industry—including pornography and prostitution—is a multibillion dollar business in its own right. Then, too, sexuality is an important part of how we think about ourselves, as well as how we evaluate others. In truth, there are few areas of life in which sexuality does *not* play some part.

But in spite of its importance, few people understand sexuality. Through much of our colonial history, sex has been a cultural taboo to the extent that, at least in polite conversation, people do not talk about it. As a result, while sex can produce much pleasure, it also causes confusion, anxiety, and sometimes outright fear. Even scientists long considered sex off-limits for research. It was not until the middle of the last century that researchers turned attention to this pervasive dimension of social life. Since then, as this chapter reports, we have learned a great deal about human sexuality.

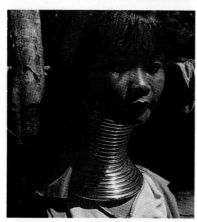

*We claim that beauty is in the eye of the beholder, which suggests the importance of culture in setting standards of attractiveness. All of the people pictured here—from Morocco, South Africa, Nigeria, Myanmar (Burma), Japan, Ecuador, and NorthAmerica—are beautiful to members of their own society. At the same time, sociobiologists point out that in every society on earth, people are attracted to youthfulness. The reason, as sociobiologists see it, is that attractiveness underlies our choices about reproduction, which is most readily accomplished in early adulthood.*

## SEX: A BIOLOGICAL ISSUE

**Sex** refers to *the biological distinction between females and males.* From a biological point of view, sex is the means by which humans reproduce. A female ovum and a male sperm, each containing 23 chromosomes (biological codes that guide physical development), combine to form a fertilized embryo. One of these chromosome pairs determines biological sex. The mother contributes an X chromosome and the father contributes either an X or a Y. A second X from the father produces a female (XX) embryo; a Y from the father produces a male (XY) embryo. Biological sex, then, is determined at conception. The initial human form (the ovum) is female. An embryo becomes male only if the sperm that fertilizes the ovum carries a Y chromosome.

Within weeks, the sex of an embryo starts to guide its development. If the embryo is male, testicular tissue starts to produce testosterone, a hormone that triggers the development of male genitals. If no testosterone is present, the embryo develops female genitals. While boys outnumber girls at birth, a higher death rate among males makes females a slight majority by the time people reach adulthood. Thus, females accounted for 50.4 percent of the total Canadian population in 1999 (Statistics Canada, 2000m).

## SEX AND THE BODY

Chapter 10 (Gender Stratification) defines *gender* as the personal traits and social meanings that members of a society attach to being female and male. Gender is, therefore, quite different from "sex," which is the biological differences that divide the human population into categories of female and male. Right from birth, the two sexes have different **primary sex characteristics**, namely, *the genitals, organs used for reproduction.* At puberty, individuals reach sexual maturity and additional sex differentiation takes place. At this point, individuals develop **secondary sex characteristics,** *bodily differences apart from the genitals that distinguish biologically mature females and males.* To allow for pregnancy, giving birth, and nurturing infants, mature females have wider hips, breasts, and soft fatty tissue that provides a reserve supply of nutrition for pregnancy and breast-feeding. Mature males, on the other hand, typically develop more muscle in the upper body, more extensive body hair, and deeper voices. Of course, these are general differences, since some males are smaller, and have less body hair and higher voices, than some females. As well, not all females are physically capable of conceiving.

**Intersexed people.** Sex is not always as clear-cut as we have just described. In rare cases, a hormone imbalance before birth produces an **intersexed person**, *a human being with some combination of female and male genitalia.* An *intersexed person* is the current term for what used to be called a "hermaphrodite," a word derived from Hermaphroditus (the offspring of the mythological Greek gods Hermes and Aphrodite) who embodied both sexes.

Because our culture is uneasy about sexual ambiguity, most parents respond to intersexuality in their infants with confusion and even dismay. In fact, in modern industrialized countries, including Canada and the U.S., intersexuality is usually dealt with shortly after birth. The choice of sex (usually female) is made by doctors and parents, and not the intersexed individuals themselves. But other cultures lead people to respond quite differently. The Pokot of eastern Africa, for example, pay little attention to what they consider a

*A transexual who goes by the name of Daniel Aranoff won a precedent-setting legal victory when he was granted permission to change the sex designation on his birth certificate from female to male.*

simple biological error; the Navaho look on intersexed people with awe, seeing in them the full potential of both the female and the male (Geertz, 1975).

**Transsexuals.** Some adults deliberately change their sex. **Transsexuals** are *people who feel they are one sex though biologically they are the other.* Tens of thousands of transsexuals in Canada and the United States have surgically changed their genitals because they feel "trapped in the wrong body" (Restak, 1979, cited in Offir, 1982:146; Gagne, Tewksbury, & McGaughey, 1997). Not all transsexuals undergo major genital surgery, however. Some "transgendered" people live with their sexual ambiguity, and choose not to change their genitals. This is especially the case with female-to-male transsexuals (FTM), for whom genital surgery techniques are less satisfactorily developed than for their male-to-female (MTF) counterparts (Mackie, 1985; Devor, 1997).

## SEX: A CULTURAL ISSUE

Sexuality has a biological foundation, which is possible though often difficult to change. Further, like all dimensions of human behaviour, sexuality is also very much a cultural issue. Biology is sufficient to explain the strange mating ritual of scorpions, described in the opening to this chapter, but humans have no similar biological program. Though there is a biological "sex drive" in the sense that people find sex pleasurable and may want to engage in sexual activity, our biology does not dictate any specific ways of being sexual any more than our desire to eat dictates any particular foods or table manners.

**Cultural variation.** Almost any sexual practice shows considerable variation from one society to another. In his pioneering study of sexuality in the United States, Alfred Kinsey (1948) found that most couples reported having intercourse in a single position—face-to-face, with the woman on the bottom and the man on top. Halfway around the world, in the South Seas, most couples *never* have sex in this way. In fact, when the people of the South Seas learned of our practice from missionaries, they poked fun at it as the strange "missionary position."

As noted in Chapter 2 (Culture), even the simple practice of displaying affection shows extensive cultural variation. While most people in Canada readily kiss in public, the Chinese kiss only in private. The French kiss publicly, often twice (once on each cheek), while Belgians go them one better, kissing three times (starting on either cheek). For their part, the Maoris of New Zealand rub noses, while most people in Nigeria don't kiss at all.

Modesty, too, is a culturally variable matter. If a women entering a bath is disturbed, what body parts does she cover? Helen Colton (1983) reports that an Islamic woman covers her face, a Laotian woman covers her breasts, a Samoan woman her navel, a Sumatran woman her knees, and that a European woman covers her breasts with one hand and her genital area with the other.

Around the world, some societies tend to restrict sexuality, while others are more permissive. In China, for example, norms closely regulate sexuality so that few people have sexual intercourse before they marry. In Canada, however—at least in recent decades—intercourse prior to marriage has become the norm, and people may choose to have sex even when there is no strong commitment to enter into either a common-law or legal marriage.

## THE INCEST TABOO

Are any cultural views of sex the same everywhere? The answer is yes. One cultural universal—an element found in every society the world over—is the **incest taboo,** *a norm forbidding sexual relations or marriage between certain relatives.* However, it is important to note that what gets defined as "close relatives" varies considerably across cultures. In Canada, the law and cultural mores prohibit close relatives (including brothers and sisters, parents and children) from having sex or marrying. Some societies (such as the North American Navajo) apply incest taboos to the mother and others on her "side" of the family. There are also societies (including ancient Peru and Egypt) on record that have approved brother–sister marriages among the nobility (Murdock, 1965). In past decades, it was not uncommon in many parts of Newfoundland for first cousins to marry each other.

Why does the incest taboo exist everywhere? Long before people were aware of the scientific explanation that reproduction between close relatives of any species risks offspring with mental or physical problems, they had an important social reason to observe an incest taboo. Controlling sexuality among close relatives seems a necessary element in the social organization of all human societies. For one thing, the incest taboo limits sexual competition in families by restricting sex to partners (ruling out, for example, sex between parent and child). Second, since family ties define people's rights and obligations toward each other, reproduction among close relatives would hopelessly confuse kinship (if a mother and son had a daughter, for example, what would the child's relationship be to the other two?) Third, by requiring people to "marry out," the incest taboo forges new social ties, enhances economic cooperation, and, ultimately, integrates the larger society as people look widely for partners to form new families (Lévi-Strauss, 1969).

The incest taboo has been an enduring sexual norm in Canada and elsewhere. But in this country, many sexual norms have changed over time. During the 20th century, as we now explain, our society experienced both a sexual revolution and, later, a sexual counterrevolution.

## SEXUAL ATTITUDES IN CANADA

What do Canadians think about sex? Cultural orientation toward sexuality dates back to early settlement. On the one hand, most of the Europeans who came to this continent held rigid notions that, ideally, sex was only for the purpose of reproduction within marriage. Early immigrants to Upper Canada (Ontario), for example, demanded conformity in both attitude and behaviour, and they imposed severe penalties for any misconduct—even if the sexual "misconduct" took place in the privacy of one's home (Errington, 1995).

Efforts to regulate sexuality continued well into the 20th century. Until 1969, for example, section 179 of the Criminal Code of Canada stated the following: "Everyone is guilty of an indictable offence and liable to two years' imprisonment who knowingly, without lawful excuse or justification, offers to sell, advertises, publishes an advertisement of or has for sale or disposal any medicine, drug or article intended or represented as a means of preventing conception or causing abortion" (quoted in McLaren & McLaren, 1986:19). Further, under subsection 159(1) of the Criminal Code, "every person who engages in an act of anal intercourse is guilty of an indictable offence and liable to imprisonment for a term not exceeding ten years or is guilty of an offence punishable on summary conviction."

It wasn't until 1969 that an exception clause was written into the law, stating that the subsection does not apply to acts that take place in private—defined as acts between two people present in a private space— between spouses, or between two consenting adults over the age of 18. And even today, the definition of *spouse* to include same-sex partners is still not recognized under federal law (Eichler, 1997).

But this is just one side of the story of sexuality in Canada. As Chapter 2 (Culture) explains, our culture is also individualistic, and many believe in giving people freedom to do pretty much as they wish, as long as they cause no direct harm to others. Such thinking—that what people do in the privacy of their own home is *their* own affair—makes sex a matter of individual freedom and personal choice. Canada's former prime minister, the late Pierre Elliott Trudeau, while still serving as the minister of justice, stated so in what is perhaps his most famous statement while in public office: "[T]he state has no business in the bedrooms of the nation."

So which is it? Is Canada a restrictive or permissive society when it comes to sexuality? The answer is that we are both. On the one hand, many Canadians still view sexual conduct as an important indicator of personal morality. On the other, sex is exploited and glorified everywhere in our culture and strongly promoted by the mass media—as if to say, "anything goes."

Within this general framework, we turn now to changes in sexual attitudes and behaviour over the course of the 20th century.

## THE SEXUAL REVOLUTION

During the past century, people witnessed profound changes in sexual attitudes and practices. The first indications of this change occurred in the 1920s, as millions from farms and small towns migrated to the rapidly growing cities. There, living apart from their families and meeting in the workplace, young men and women enjoyed considerable sexual freedom. Indeed, this is one reason the decade became known as the Roaring Twenties.

In the 1930s and 1940s, the Great Depression and the Second World War slowed the rate of change. But in the post-war period, after 1945, Alfred Kinsey set the stage for what later came to be known as the *sexual*

One sign of the growing openness about sexuality in North America after the Second World War was the 1953 publication of the first issue of Playboy. *Back then, it was conservatives who objected to the magazine on moral grounds; by the 1970s, many liberals also opposed such publications as demeaning to women.*

*revolution.* Kinsey and his colleagues published their first study of sexuality in 1948, and it raised eyebrows everywhere. It was not so much what Kinsey said about sexual behaviour that got people talking—although he did present some surprising results—but simply the fact that scientists were studying *sex* at all. At that time, after all, many people were uneasy talking about sex even privately at home.

But Kinsey's two books (1948 and 1953) became best sellers because they revealed that North Americans, on average, were far less conventional in sexual matters than most had thought. Thus, these books fostered a new openness toward sexuality, which helped propel the sexual revolution.

In the late 1960s, the sexual revolution truly came of age. Youth culture dominated public life and expressions like "if it feels good, do it" and "sex, drugs, and rock and roll" summed up a new freedom toward sexuality. Some people were turned off by the idea of "turning on," of course, but the baby boom generation born between 1945 and 1960 became the first cohort in

In March 2000, the supreme court choose not to hear the appeal by dominatrix Terri Jean Bedford of her 1998 conviction of running a common bawdy house in suburban Toronto. In June 2001 she opened a Bed and Breakfast in downtown Toronto which features role play in special dungeon theme rooms. According to her lawyer the establishment is legal as long as there is no incidental touching of the genitalia.

Canadian history to grow up with the idea that sex was part of everyone's life—married or not.

Technology, too, played a part in the sexual revolution. "The pill," introduced in 1960, not only prevented pregnancy, but made sex more convenient. Unlike a condom or diaphragm, which has to be used at the time of intercourse, the pill could be taken any time during the day. Now women as well as men could engage in sex without any special preparation.

According to the so-called "double standard," society allows (and even encourages) men to be sexually active ("boys will be boys"), while expecting women to remain chaste before marriage and faithful to their husbands afterward. The sexual revolution, then, had special significance for women because historically women were subject to greater sexual regulation than men. Survey data from the U.S support this conclusion. Among people born in the United States between 1933 and 1942 (that is, people in their mid-fifties to mid-sixties today), 56 percent of men but just 16 percent of women report having had two or more sexual partners by the time they were age 20. Compare this wide gap to the pattern among U.S. baby boomers born between 1953 and 1962 (people now in their forties), who came of age after the sexual revolution. In this category, 62 percent of men and 48 percent of women say they

had two or more sexual partners by age 20 (Laumann et al., 1994:198). Comparative Canadian data shown in Figure 7–1 indicate a similar trend. Canadian studies of post-secondary students show that between 1968 and 1988, there was a declining proportion of students that believed people should remain abstinent until marriage. The shift was especially remarkable among women; abstinence proponents decreased from 45 to 13 percent for Anglophone women and from 48 to 2 percent for Francophone women, compared to 28 to 13 percent for Anglophone males and 26 to 4.5 for Francophone males (Larson, Goltz, & Hobart 1994).

## THE SEXUAL COUNTERREVOLUTION

The sexual revolution made sex a topic of everyday discussion and sexual activity a matter of individual choice. But given that Canadian society has always had two minds about sex, the sexual revolution was also controversial. By 1980, the climate of sexual freedom that had marked the late 1960s and 1970s was criticized by some as evidence of our country's moral decline. Thus the *sexual counterrevolution* began.

Politically speaking, the sexual counterrevolution was a conservative call for a return to "family values," whereby sexual freedom was to be replaced by sexual responsibility. In practice, this meant moving sex back within marriage. Critics in both Canada and the United States objected not just to the idea of "free love," but also to trends such as cohabitation (living together) and having children out of wedlock. Others argued that sexual permissive practices among particular groups, including homosexuals, drug users, and prostitutes, had spread STDs and the deadly HIV/AIDS virus throughout the population. The media played a central role in the backlash against the sexual revolution, socially constructing as "deviant" particular groups whose lifestyles and sexual practices were associated with the spread of STDs (Brock, 1998).

Looking back, we can see that the sexual counterrevolution did not greatly change the idea that individuals should decide for themselves when and with whom to have a sexual relationship. What did happen, however, is that more people began choosing to limit their number of sexual partners or to abstain from sex entirely. In many cases, such decisions are made on moral grounds. For others, however, the decision to limit sexual activity reflects a fear of sexually transmitted diseases (STDs). As Chapter 14 (Education and Health and Medicine) explains, although rates of most infectious diseases fell after 1960, rates of STDs rose sharply. Moreover, the fact that some STDs (such as genital herpes) are incurable, and others (AIDS) are deadly, has given individuals good reason to consider carefully their sexual choices.

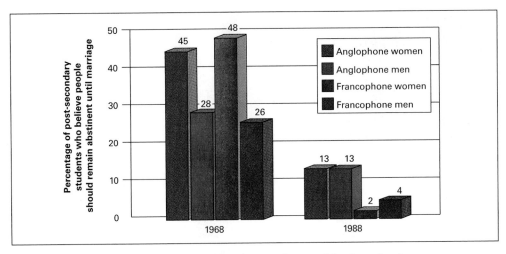

**FIGURE 7–1    The Sexual Revolution: Closing the Double Standard**
Source: Hobart (1990).

## PREMARITAL SEX

In light of the sexual revolution and the sexual counterrevolution, how much has sexual behaviour of
people in Canada and the United States really
changed? One interesting trend involves premarital
sex—that is, the likelihood that young people will have
sexual intercourse while they are teenagers or young
adults, before they marry.

The Kinsey studies (1948, 1953; see also Laumann
et al., 1994) reported that for people in the
United States born in the early 1900s, about 50 percent
of men but just 6 percent of women had premarital
sexual intercourse before age 19. Studies of baby
boomers born after the Second World War show a
slight increase in premarital intercourse among men,
but a large increase—to about one-third—among
women. The most recent studies, targeting men and
women born in the 1970s, shows that 76 percent of men
and 66 percent of women had premarital sexual intercourse by their senior year in high school (Laumann et
al., 1994:323–24). Similarly, Canadian studies show that
as high a proportion as 62 percent of teenage boys and
49 percent of teenage girls are sexually active (Nelson &
Robinson, 1999) Thus, although general public attitudes remain divided on premarital sex, this behaviour is
quite widely accepted among young people.

## SEX AMONG ADULTS

To hear the mass media tell it, Canadians are very
active sexually. But do popular images exaggerate
reality? According to a recent poll by the Angus Reid
Group Inc. (1998e), the frequency of sexual activity
varies widely in the Canadian population. In response
to the question "How many times a month do you have
sex?" the pattern breaks down like this: While on
average Canadians have sex 6.2 times per month, the
average is 7.5 times for Atlantic Canadians, 8.9 times
for adults between ages 18 and 34; 12 times for those
living with a partner; and 7.3 times for high-income
Canadians (defined as those with household incomes
over $55 000). In short, no single pattern accurately
describes sexual activity in Canada today.

We also know that sexual activity among Canadian
adults is lower today (64 percent) than it was in 1984
(75 percent). But precisely why Newfoundlanders, for
example, are deemed the "champions" in the nation's
bedrooms (77-percent sexual activity) and British
Columbians hold the unenviable position as the
country's "sexual slackers" (56 percent) remains a
mystery (Angus Reid Group Inc, 1998).

Moreover, despite the widespread image of
"swinging singles," it is actually those who are monogamous who report more sexual activity. Fixed relationships serve as a kind of "sex aid," while people who are
single and more likely to go out for their entertainment are, ironically, less likely to engage in sex (Angus
Reid Group Inc, 1998).

## EXTRAMARITAL SEX

What about couples having sex with someone other
than their partner—that is, what people commonly call
"adultery" (sociologists prefer more neutral-sounding
terms such as *affairs* or *extramarital sex*)? The research

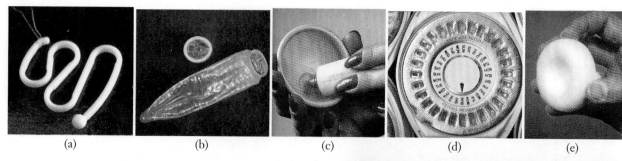

(a)  (b)  (c)  (d)  (e)

*Contraception has a long history, beginning with the intrauterine device or IUD (a) in ancient times (originally, stones were used); by 1500, men employed condoms (b), more to prevent disease than pregnancy; the early 1600s saw the invention of the diaphragm (c), later used with spermicidal jelly; the birth control pill (d) came on the scene in 1960; sponges (e) were first licensed in 1983; the Norplant skin implant (f) debuted in 1990, followed by the female condom (g) in 1993.*

(f)  (g)

shows that Canadians' attitudes toward the acceptability of extramarital affairs also vary. Table 7–1 shows that slightly more than half of Canadians surveyed stated that having an extramarital affair has become more acceptable in Canada today than it was a decade ago; one-quarter stated that it is less accepted today; just under 20 percent stated that there has been little or no change in the acceptability of having an affair over the past 10 years. Only 4 percent remained undecided on the issue (Angus Reid Group Inc., 1997b).

Further, while a substantial minority of Canadians still consider a person having sex with someone other than his or her partner to be "unacceptable" and while the norm of sexual fidelity remains a strong element among certain groups, this cultural belief often differs from real life. It probably comes as no surprise that extramarital sexual activity is more common than people say it should be. At the same time, extramarital sex is not as frequent as many believe. A recent study found that 80 percent of Canadians surveyed report that they have never had an affair, while nearly 20 percent of

Canadians report that they have had at least one affair, and 2 percent refused to answer the question. Reported affairs are highest among Atlantic Canadians (28 percent) and males (22 percent versus 14 percent for females) (Angus Reid Group Inc., 1997b).

## SEXUAL ORIENTATION

**Sexual orientation** refers to *a person's preference in terms of sexual partners: same sex, other sex, either sex, neither sex* (Lips, 1993). **Heterosexuality** (*hetero* is a Greek word meaning "the other of two") means sexual *attraction to someone of the other sex*. Heterosexism in Canadian society today is seen as the "norm," meaning that we have a prejudice in favour of sexual attraction between the genders. Yet in every society a significant share of people favour **homosexuality** (*homo* is the Greek word for "the same"), *sexual attraction to someone of the same sex*. In fact, among the ancient Greeks, upper-class men considered homosexuality the highest form of relationship, partly because they looked down on women as intellectually inferior. As men saw it, heterosexuality was necessary only so they could have children, and "real" men preferred other men as sexual partners (Kluckhohn, 1948; Ford & Beach, 1951; Greenberg, 1988).

When thinking sociologically about these categories, keep in mind that homosexuality and heterosexuality are not mutually exclusive. In short, people do not necessarily fall into one category or the other, but may have both sexual orientations to varying degrees. Figure 7–2 presents these two sexual orientations as a continuum, indicating that most people actually experience at least some degree of sexual attraction to people of both sexes.

**TABLE 7–1  Infidelity Then and Now, Canada, 1997**

*Survey Question:* "Now, thinking back 10 years ago, would you say that having an affair is more or less acceptable behaviour today than it was 10 years ago?"

| | |
|---|---|
| More acceptable | 51% |
| Same | 19% |
| Less acceptable | 26% |
| Don't know | 4% |

Source: Angus Reid Group Inc., 1997b.

The fact that sexual orientation is often not clear-cut points to the importance of a third category: **bisexuality**, which refers to *sexual attraction to people of both sexes*. Some bisexual people are equally attracted to males and females; many others, however, are attracted to one sex over the other in varying degrees. Finally, one additional sexual orientation is **asexuality**, which means *no sexual attraction to people of either sex*.

It is also important to note that sexual *attraction* is not the same thing as sexual *behaviour*. Many people, no doubt, have experienced some attraction to someone of the same sex, but fewer ever experience same-sex behaviour. This is in large part due to cultural constraints on our actions.

## WHAT GIVES US A SEXUAL ORIENTATION?

The question of *how* people come to have a sexual orientation in the first place is vigorously debated. But the arguments cluster into two general positions: first, that sexual orientation is a product of biology; second, that sexual orientation is a product of society.

### Sexual orientation: A product of biology.

This approach argues that sexual orientation is innate—that is, rooted in human biology. Arguing this position, Simon LeVay (1993) links sexual orientation to the structure of the human brain. LeVay studied the brains of both homosexual and heterosexual men, and found a small but important difference in the size of the hypothalamus, a part of the brain that regulates hormones. Such an anatomical difference, he claims, plays a part in shaping sexual orientation.

Genetics, too, may influence sexual orientation. One study of 44 pairs of brothers—all homosexual—found that 33 pairs had a distinctive genetic pattern involving the X chromosome. Moreover, the gay brothers had an unusually high number of gay male relatives—but only on their mother's side, the source of the X chromosome. Such evidence leads some researchers to think there may be a "gay gene" (Hamer & Copeland, 1994).

### Sexual orientation: A product of society.

This second view argues that people in any society construct a set of meanings that lets them make sense of sexuality. Understandings of sexuality, therefore, differ from place to place and over time. For example, Michel Foucault (1990) points out that there was no distinct category of people called "homosexuals" until a century ago, when scientists and, eventually, the public as a whole began labelling people that way. It was precisely at this time that "heterosexuality" became viewed as normal, thereby making homosexuality deviant (Warner, 1991). Throughout most of human history, in other words, some people no doubt had what we would call "homosexual experiences." But neither they nor others saw in this behaviour the basis for any

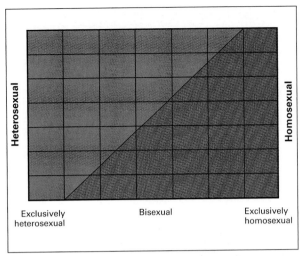

**FIGURE 7–2    The Sexual Orientation Continuum**

Source: Adapted from Kinsey et al. (1948).

special identity. Public "discontentment" regarding homosexuality is thus a very recent phenomenon (Weeks, 1985).

Anthropologists provide further evidence that sexual orientation is socially constructed. Studies show that various kinds of homosexuality exist in various societies. In Siberia, for example, the Chukchee Eskimo have a ritual practice by which one man dresses like a female and does a woman's work. The Sambia, who dwell in the Eastern Highlands of New Guinea, have a ritual in which young boys perform oral sex on older men in the belief that ingesting semen will enhance their masculinity (Herdt, 1993). Such diverse patterns seem to indicate that sexual orientation and sexual expression have much to do with society itself.

### Critical evaluation.

The best guess at present is that sexual orientation is derived from *both* society and biology (Gladue, Green, & Hellman, 1984; Weinrich, 1987; Troiden, 1988; Isay, 1989; Puterbaugh, 1990; Angier, 1992; Gelman, 1992). But we need to bear in mind that sexual orientation is not a matter of neat categories. That is, most people who think of themselves as homosexual have had some heterosexual experiences, just as many people who think of themselves as heterosexual have had some homosexual experiences. Thus, the task of explaining sexual orientation is extremely complex.

There is also a political issue here, with great importance for gay men and lesbians. To the extent that sexual orientation is seen as based in biology, homosexuality is not a matter of choice any more than, say, skin colour. If this is so, shouldn't gay men and lesbians expect the same legal protection from discrimination as women, Aboriginals, and visible minority Canadians (Herek, 1991)?

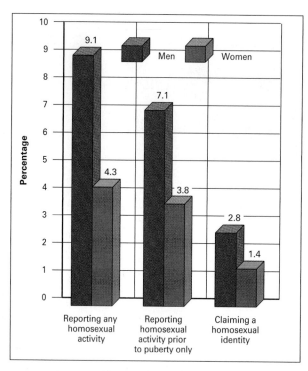

**FIGURE 7–3   Measuring Sexual Orientation: U.S. Survey Data**

Source: Adapted from Laumann et al. (1994).

## HOW MANY GAY PEOPLE?

What share of our population is gay? This is a hard question because, as we have explained, sexual orientation not a matter of neat categories. Moreover, people are not always willing to discuss sexuality with strangers or even family members. Pioneering sex researcher Alfred Kinsey (1948, 1953) estimated that about 4 percent of males and 2 percent of females have an exclusively same-sex orientation, although he thought that at least one-third of men and one-eighth of women have at least one homosexual experience leading to orgasm.

In light of the Kinsey studies, many U.S. social scientists put the gay share of the population at 10 percent. But a more recent survey of sexuality indicates that how one operationalizes "homosexuality" makes a big difference in the results (Laumann et al., 1994). As Figure 7–3 shows, about 9 percent of U.S. men and about 4 percent of women ages 18 to 59 reported homosexual activity *at some time* in their lives. The second set of numbers shows that a significant share of men (fewer women) have a homosexual experience during childhood but not after puberty. And 2.8 percent of men and 1.4 percent of women define themselves as partly or entirely homosexual. Though there are no comparable Canadian studies on the number of gay people, the results are likely to be about the same.

Finally, Kinsey treated sexual orientation as an "either–or" trait: To be more homosexual was, by definition, to be less heterosexual. But same-sex and other-sex attractions can operate independently. At one extreme, then, bisexual people feel strong attraction to people of both sexes; at the other, asexual people experience little sexual attraction to people of either sex.

In the survey noted above, less than 1 percent of adults described themselves as bisexual. But bisexual experiences appear to be fairly common (at least for a time) among younger people, especially on university campuses (Laumann et al., 1994; Leland, 1995). Many bisexuals, then, do not think of themselves as either gay or straight, and their behaviour reflects elements of both gay and straight living.

## THE GAY RIGHTS MOVEMENT

In the long term, the public attitude toward homosexuality is moving toward greater acceptance. In a recent Angus Reid national opinion poll (April 1998), for example, the majority in all provinces (64 percent of the population) agreed that "human rights legislation in Canada should protect gays and lesbians from discrimination based on their sexual orientation" (Angus Reid Group Inc., 1998b). This is an increase in support from a previous poll (May/June 1996), which found less public support on other gay rights issues. On the issue of same-sex spousal benefits, a majority (55 percent) of those polled said they believe that "the partners of homosexual employees should be entitled to the same spousal benefits as an employer provides to the partners of heterosexual employees," with 41 percent opposed. There was lower public support for legally recognizing same-sex marriages. When asked the question "[D]o you think homosexual couples who wish to marry should or should not qualify for legal recognition of the marriage?" 47 percent opposed and 49 percent supported the recognition.

On the third issue polled—gay and lesbian adoptions—public support was even lower, as indicated in Figure 7–4 on page 163. Fifty-two percent of the surveyed population opposed legal adoption of children by homosexual couples, compared with 42 percent who supported it. There were notable differences between the provinces, with Quebec and B.C. reporting a more liberal attitude on the issue (Angus Reid Group Inc., 1996d).

In large measure, this change came about through the gay rights movement that arose in the mid-20th century (Chauncey, 1994). At that time, most people did not discuss homosexuality, and it was common for companies (including the federal government and the armed forces) to fire anyone who was accused of being gay. Mental health professionals, too, took a hard line, describing homosexuals as "sick" and sometimes placing them in mental hospitals where, presumably, they might be cured.

In this climate of intolerance, most lesbians and gay men remained "in the closet"—closely guarding the secret of their sexual orientation. But the gay rights movement gained strength during the 1960s. One early milestone occurred in 1973, when the American Psychological Association declared that homosexuality was not an illness but simply "a form of sexual behaviour."

The gay rights movement also began using the term **homophobia**, which describes *the fear of close personal interaction with people thought to be gay, lesbian, or bisexual* (Weinberg, 1973).

Concepts such as homophobia (literally, "fear of sameness"), and more recently "heterosexism" and "heteronormativity," turn the tables on society. Instead of asking "What's wrong with gay people?" the question becomes "What's wrong with people who can't accept a different sexual orientation?" (Martindale, 1998; Warner, 1991).

## SEXUAL CONTROVERSIES

Sexuality lies at the heart of a number of controversies in Canada. Here we take a look at four issues: teen pregnancy, pornography, prostitution, and sexual violence.

### TEEN PREGNANCY

Being sexually active—especially having intercourse—clearly demands a high level of responsibility because pregnancy can result. Teenagers may be biologically mature, but many are not socially mature and may not appreciate all the consequences of their actions. An estimated 42 161 Canadian women between the ages of 15 to 19 became pregnant in 1997 (a portion gave birth; others had an abortion; and others experienced fetal loss via miscarriage or stillbirth). Teenage pregnancies are at a decade low in Canada; the teenage pregnancy rate was 42.7 pregnancies for every 1000 women ages 15 to 19 in 1997, the lowest in 10 years (Statistics Canada, 2000n).

Yet it needs to be pointed out that the rate has only dropped to where it was 13 years ago. Critics, including spokespersons from Planned Parenthood of Canada, blame the continuing high rate of unwanted teenage pregnancies in Canada on the lack of a national plan of action. Of the Canadian teens who become pregnant each year, most did not intend to do so. Pregnancy means not only that many young women (and sometimes young fathers-to-be) cannot finish school, but that they are at high risk for poverty. Figure 7–5 on page 164 shows that Canada's rate of teen pregnancy is moderately high compared to the levels in other high-income countries. The teen pregnancy rate ranges widely, from a low of 10 per 1000 adolescents aged 15 to 19 per year in Japan; 12 in the Netherlands;

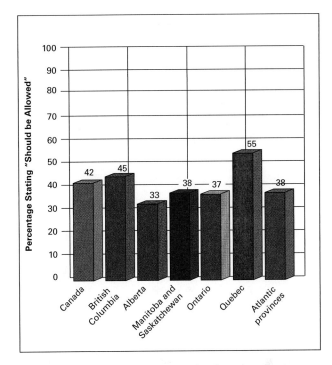

**FIGURE 7–4    Attitudes toward Adoptions by Gays and Lesbians, Canada, 1996**

*Survey Question:* "What do you think about the general issue of homosexual couples—either male or female—who what to adopt kids that are not the biological children of either of the partners in the relationship? In your opinion, assuming they meet the standards and requirements, should homosexual couples be legally allowed to adopt children?"

Source: Angus Reid Group Inc. (1996d).

24.9 in Sweden; 45.4 in Canada; and 83.6 in the U.S. The rate of the Russian Federation, at 102 per 1000 - adolescents, is more than double the Canadian rate.

Did the sexual revolution raise the level of teenage pregnancy? Surprisingly, perhaps, the answer is no. The rate in 1950 was actually higher than the rate today, but this is because people back then married at a younger age. Also, many pregnancies led to quick marriages. As a result, there were many pregnant teenagers, but most were married women. Today, by contrast, most teenagers who become pregnant are not married. Approximately half of these women have abortions; the other half keep their babies (Voydanoff & Donnelly, 1990; Holmes, 1996). Figure 7–6 on page 165 shows the teenage pregnancy rates and live births for females aged 15 to 19 in Canada in 1997.

Concern about Canada's moderately high rate of teenage pregnancy has led to sex education programs in schools. But such programs are controversial, as the Critical Thinking box on page 166 explains.

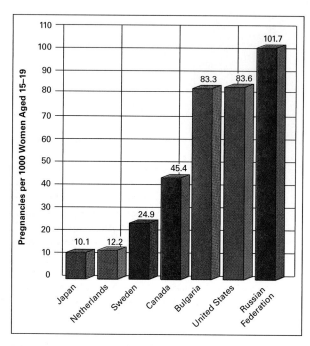

**FIGURE 7–5  Pregnancy Rate among Women 15–19 Years, Selected Countries, Most Recent Year Available**

**Note:** The most recent year is 1995, with the following exceptions: 1996—Bulgaria, Sweden, and the United States; 1992—the Netherlands.

Source: Singh & Darroch (2000).

## PORNOGRAPHY

In general terms, **pornography** refers to *sexually explicit material that causes sexual arousal*. But what—exactly—pornographic is, and what separates it from erotica have long been matters of heated debate. Some argue that pornography is associated with violence against women, while erotica is best seen as sexually explicit nonviolent material. But others argue that it is a matter of sexual politics as to what gets labelled pornography or erotica or escapes being labelled at all. Recognizing that people view the portrayal of sexuality differently, the Canadian Supreme Court gives local communities the power to decide for themselves what violates "community standards" of decency and lacks any redeeming social value. Child pornography is a very different matter, however. Section 163.1 of the Criminal Code states that "every person who possesses any child pornography is guilty of either a) an indictable offence and liable to imprisonment for a term not exceeding five years; or b) an offence punishable on summary conviction." Yet enforcement of even this law has proven to be difficult. In 1999 the B.C. Court of Appeal struck down subsection 4 of section 163.1 of the Criminal Code, which makes the possession of child pornography a criminal offence, because the subsection contravened the Charter of Rights and Freedoms. In January 2000, the

Supreme Court of Canada heard arguments in an appeal of the B.C. court decision. At the time of writing, Canadians are still waiting for a Supreme Court decision on this hotly debated issue.

Supreme Court decisions aside, pornography and erotica are popular in Canada: x-rated videos, "900" telephone numbers for sexual conversations, and a host of sexually explicit movies and magazines together constitute a multibillion dollar-a-year industry. One-third of Canadians report having taken out x-rated movies, and 20 percent of Canadians say that they read erotic literature or magazines (Angus Reid Group Inc., 1998e). The figure is rising as people buy more and more pornography from thousands of sites on the Web.

Yet pornography has its critics. Some claim pornography is a *power* issue because it endorses the cultural ideal of men as the legitimate controllers of both sexuality and women (MacKinnon, 1987). While it is difficult to document a scientific cause-and-effect relationship between what people view and how they act, research does support the idea that pornography makes men think of women as objects rather than as people (Malamuth & Donnerstein, 1984; Attorney General's Commission on Pornography, 1986). The public share a concern about pornography and violence, with many laypeople, as well as feminist researchers, holding the opinion that pornography encourages people to commit rape (Russell, 1998).

Though people everywhere object to sexual material they find offensive, many also value free speech and want to protect artistic expression. Nevertheless, pressure to restrict pornography is building from an unlikely coalition of conservatives (who oppose pornography on moral grounds), progressives (who condemn it for political reasons), and feminists (who argue that it justifies men's oppression of women by making females into sex objects to be viewed for men's pleasure).

## PROSTITUTION

**Prostitution** is *the selling of sexual services*. Often called "the world's oldest profession," prostitution has always been widespread, and about one in five adult men in the United States reports having paid for sex at some time (NORC, 1999:996). Comparative data for Canada are lacking, but one Canadian survey found that 4 percent of male respondents (n=989) admitted having paid for sexual favours one or more times (Peat Marwick, 1984). A more recent poll found that an even smaller number—2 percent—of Canadians has ever visited an erotic massage parlour, hired a sex worker, or used an escort service (Angus Reid Group Inc., 1998e). Even so, to the extent that people think of sex as an expression of interpersonal intimacy, they find the idea of sex for money disturbing. Even in this regard, however, there are no cross-cultural universals.

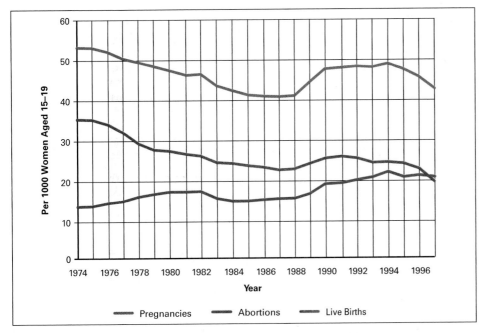

**FIGURE 7–6**   **Teenage Pregnancies, Abortions, and Live Births, Canada, 1974–1997**

Source: Statistics Canada. "Teenage Pregnancy." *Health Reports*. Vol. 12, No. 1 (Summer 2000): 9-20.
Ottawa: Health Statistics Division.

While prostitution is against the law everywhere in the United States (except for parts of Nevada), prostitution is actually not illegal in Canada. Rather, sex workers in Canada are arrested, prosecuted, and sometimes convicted not because they sell sex for money, but because they "communicate" in a public place for the purpose of engaging in prostitution (Shaver, 1993; Hackler, 1999). Meanwhile in Sweden, a recent law makes it legal for sex workers to sell sex but illegal for "johns" (customers) to purchase it (Boethus, 1999). Concerning the latter, the common belief in Canada is that sex workers (almost always depicted as female rather than male prostitutes) are more culpable and blameworthy than their customers. Regulatory strategies are much more likely to concentrate on women who sell sex rather than on their male customers, because of the assumption that most customers are "square johns who would not otherwise fall afoul with the law, while prostitutes are members of a criminal underclass whose lifestyle involves various types of law breaking" (Lowman, 1990:63–4). Consequently, as it is socially constructed and legally enforced, prostitution in Canada remains biased against women and in favour of men (Shaver, 1993; Boritch, 1997).

Around the world, prostitution is greatest in low-income countries where patriarchy is strong and traditional cultural norms limit women's ability to earn a living (Downe, 1998; Kempadoo & Doezema, 1998). Global Map 7–1 on page 167 shows where in the world prostitution is most widespread.

**Types of prostitution.** Though most prostitutes (many prefer the morally neutral term *sex workers*) are women, they fall into different categories. *Call girls* are elite sex workers, typically women who are young, attractive, well educated, and arrange their own "dates" with clients by telephone. The classified pages of any large city newspaper contain numerous ads for "escort services," through which women (and sometimes men) offer both companionship and sex for a fee.

A middle category of sex workers is located in "massage parlours" and brothels, which are under the control of managers. These sex workers have less choice about their clients, receive less money for their services, and get to keep only some of what they earn.

At the bottom of the sex-worker hierarchy are *streetwalkers*, women and men who "work the streets" of large cities. Many female streetwalkers are under the control of male pimps who take most of their earnings. Many streetwalkers fall victim to violence from pimps and clients (Gordon & Snyder, 1989). Canadian research shows that sex workers located in off-street "escort agencies" tend to enjoy safer, more stable, and more lucrative work conditions than do their counterparts working on the street (Lowman & Fraser, 1995; Brock, 1998; Lewis & Maticka-Tyndale, 1999).

Most, but not all, sex workers offer heterosexual services. But gay prostitutes, too, trade sex for money. Researchers report that many gay sex workers have suffered rejection by family and friends because of their sexual orientation (Weisberg, 1985; Boyer, 1989;

# Sex Education: Problem or Solution?

Most schools today have sex education programs that teach the basics of sexuality. Instructors explain to young people how their bodies grow and change, how reproduction occurs, and how to avoid pregnancy by using birth control or abstaining from sex.

Because nearly half of Canadian teenage boys and girls report having had sexual intercourse by grade 11 (Wadhera & Millar, 1996), "sex ed" programs seem to make sense. But critics point out that as the scope of sex education programs has expanded, the level of teenage sexual activity has actually gone *up*. This trend seems to suggest that sex education may not be discouraging sex among youngsters; on the contrary, learning more about sex may encourage young people to become sexually active sooner. Critics also say that it's parents who should be instructing their children about sex since, unlike teachers, parents can also teach their beliefs about what is right and wrong.

But supporters of sex education counter that there are many other influences apart from sex education that shape sexual activity among youth, not the least of which are peers and the media. Further, it is unrealistic to expect that in a culture that celebrates sexuality, children will not become sexually active. If this is the case, the sensible strategy is to ensure that they understand what they are doing and take reasonable precautions to protect themselves from unwanted pregnancy and sexually transmitted diseases— about half of women aged 15 to 19 who report having more than one sex partner in the past year also reported having sex without a condom at least once in the past year (Dryburgh, 2000).

*What do you think?*

1. *Schools can teach the facts about sexuality. But do you think they can address the emotional issues that often accompany sex? What about the moral issues? Why or why not?*

2. *What about parents? Are they doing their job as far as instructing children about sex? Ask members of your class how many received instruction in sexual matters from their parents.*

3. *Overall, do you think young people know too little about sexuality? Do you think they know too much? What specific changes would you suggest to address the problem of unwanted pregnancy among teens?*

Source: Gibbs (1993); Stodgill (1998); Wadhera & Millar (1996); Dryburgh (2000).

---

Kruks, 1991). Recent research on transgendered sex workers in the San Francisco Tenderloin area suggests that they face a similar situation of discrimination and rejection because of their sexual orientation (Weinberg, Shaver, & Williams, 2000).

**A victimless crime?** Prostitution is against the law in many countries, but many people consider it a victimless crime (see Chapter 8, Deviance). Thus, instead of enforcing prostitution laws all the time, police stage occasional crackdowns. Such a policy reflects a desire to control prostitution, with an underlying assumption that nothing will eliminate it.

In reality, is selling sex a victimless crime that hurts no one? Certainly, many people take this position, arguing that prostitution should be viewed as an occupation, as a way to make a living (Elias, Bullough, Elias, & Elders, 1998; Scambler & Scambler, 1997). For instance, because it is treated as a semi-illegal and illegitimate occupation in Canada, structural barriers prevent sex workers from being afforded the same benefits and rights as normal workers, such as sick leave, health insurance, social security, or worker's compensation (Shaver, 1993; Lowman & Fraser, 1995; Lewis & Maticka-Tyndale, 1999). Further, due to the absence of employment opportunities that

provide a livable wage for marginalized people, in particular working-class female single parents, the sex trade represents a viable choice from their perspective (Chapkis, 1997). But it is also true that prostitution subjects many women to abuse and outright violence, and plays a part in some countries in spreading sexually transmitted diseases, including AIDS. In addition, many poor women become trapped in a life of selling sex, especially in low-income nations. The Global Sociology box on page 168 offers a closer look at the flourishing sex-trade in Southeast Asia.

## SEXUAL VIOLENCE AND ABUSE

Ideally, sexual activity occurs within a loving relationship; but sex can sometimes be twisted by hate and violence. Sexual violence, which ranges from verbal abuse to rape and assault, is widespread in many countries around the world, including Canada.

**Sexual assault.** Although some people think sexual assault and rape is motivated solely by a desire for sex, they are actually expressions of power—violent acts that use sex to hurt, humiliate, or control another

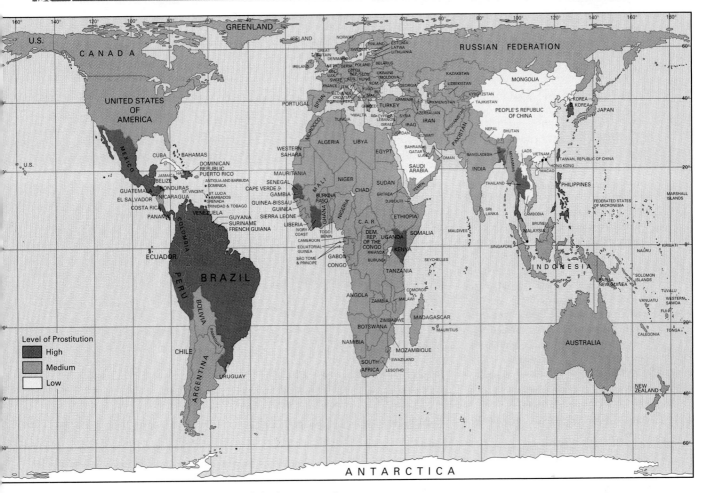

**GLOBAL MAP 7–1    Prostitution in Global Perspective**

Generally speaking, prostitution is widespread in societies of the world where women have low standing in relation to men. Officially, at least, the now-defunct socialist regimes in Eastern Europe and the former Soviet Union, as well as the People's Republic of China, boast of gender equality, including the elimination of "vice," such as prostitution, which oppresses women. By contrast, in much of Latin America, a region of pronounced patriarchy, prostitution is commonplace. In many Islamic societies patriarchy is also strong, but religion is a counterbalance so prostitution is limited. Western, industrial societies display a moderate amount of prostitution.

Source: *Peters Atlas of the World* (1990); updated by John Macionis.

person. According to the 1993 Violence Against Women Survey (Statistics Canada, 1993b), 40 percent of Canadian women have experienced at least one incident of sexual assault since the age of 16, and 2 million Canadian women ages 18 and over have been sexually assaulted by a stranger since turning 16. More recent data from the Canadian Centre for Justice Statistics indicates that 11 percent of female victims of crime in Canada in 1998 were victims of sexual assault, and 85 percent of the victims of sexual assault were

women (Statistics Canada, 2000m). Remember that these percentages reflect only the *reported* cases. The actual number of sexual assaults, therefore, is probably much higher (McCormick, 1994; U.S. Bureau of Justice Statistics, 1994).

*Sexual assault* is a comprehensive term referring to nonconsensual sexual activity ranging from sexual touching, kissing, and sexual intercourse, to sexual violence against a person's will. While men constitute 15 percent of sexual assault victims, women and

# Sexual Slavery: A Report from Thailand

Around the world, poverty forces many women and children into prostitution as their means of survival. Nowhere is this trend more evident that in Southeast Asia. Recent decades have witnessed an explosion of what amounts to sexual slavery, which exploits women and attracts men from high-income countries as "sex tourists."

Sex-tourism districts can be found in many large cities throughout Africa, Eastern Europe, and, especially, Southeast Asia. Bangkok, Thailand—called the sex-tourism capital of the world—receives tens of thousands of visitors from Japan, Western Europe, and North America each year. Thailand has some 2 million sex workers, with 10 percent of the female Thai population now working in the sex industry.

Almost all of these women are poor, and many come from rural regions where families struggle to survive. Some girls who see little future in a rural village make their own way to the

city, hoping to find work. With few skills and knowing little about the dangers they face, most fall under the control of pimps and end up working in brothels, soliciting in bars, or performing sex shows. In some cases, desperate parents sell their female infants to agents, who promise to see that the girls get work in the city. The agents take the girls, pay

*Young girls await customers in a Bangkok brothel.*

others to raise them, and then "harvest their crop" years later when the girls are old enough (sometimes as young as 12 or 13) to work the sex trade. In fact, prostitutes on average are getting younger and younger, because it is the younger girls who can earn the most money from sex tourists fearful of contracting sexually transmitted diseases.

Once working in the sex industry, the future for women is bleak. Pimps provide girls with clothes and housing, but at a cost that exceeds the girls' salaries. The result is a system of debt bondage that keeps these women virtual prisoners. To make matters worse, most sex-workers suffer from a host of diseases brought on by abuse and neglect. Worst of all, estimates suggest that about half are now infected with the virus that causes AIDS.

Source: Based, in part, on Santoli (1994) and Remy (1996).

children make up a disproportionate share. In 1998, more than half the female victims of sexual assault in Canada were under 18 years of age (Statistics Canada, 2000m).

**Date rape.** A common myth is that sexual assault usually involves strangers. In reality, however, most incidents of forced sexual activity involve people who know one another, and they usually take place in familiar surroundings—most often the home. For this reason, the term *date rape*, or "acquaintance rape," refers to forcible sexual violence against women by men they know.

Many victims of date rape do not report the crime. Some believe that because they know the offender, an attack could not have been rape. But the tide is turning, with more and more women speaking out. The Critical Thinking box on page 169 takes a closer look.

## THEORETICAL ANALYSIS OF SEXUALITY

We can better understanding human sexuality by using sociology's various theoretical paradigms. In the

following sections, we apply the three major paradigms in turn.

### STRUCTURAL-FUNCTIONAL ANALYSIS

The structural-functional approach highlights the contribution of any social pattern to the overall operation of society. Because sexuality is an important dimension of social life, society regulates sexual behaviour.

**The need to regulate sexuality.** From a biological point of view, sex allows our species to reproduce. But culture and social institutions regulate *with whom* and *when* people reproduce. For example, most societies condemn married people for having sex with someone other than their spouse. To do otherwise—to give the forces of sexual passion free reign—would threaten family life and, especially, the raising of children.

Another example, discussed earlier in this chapter, is the incest taboo. The fact that this norm exists everywhere shows clearly that no society is willing to permit completely free choice in sexual partners. Reproduction

# CRITICAL THINKING

# Date Rape: Exposing Dangerous Myths

On a June night in 1996, a 17-year-old woman was introduced to Private Andrew Anderson by a mutual acquaintance at a local bar near the Canadian Forces Base in Petawawa. After leaving the bar, Private Anderson and the woman shared a cab with friends back to the base, and he then offered to drive the woman home. But instead of taking her home, he persuaded her to go to the washroom, where they could talk privately. Once there, he started to unbutton her clothes. Her protests fell on deaf ears; he continued until he had raped her on the bathroom floor.

The case of this young woman is all too typical in Canada and many other high-income countries. Even today, in most incidences of sexual attack, a victim makes no report to police and no offender is arrested. The reason for this inaction is that many people have a misguided understanding of rape. Three inaccurate notions about rape are so common that they might be called "rape myths."

**Myth # 1: Rape involves strangers.**

A sexual assault brings to mind a strange man lurking in the shadows who suddenly springs on his victims. In truth, however, four out of five rapes are committed by offenders known to their victims. For this reason, people have begun to speak more realistically about *date rape*, or *acquaintance rape*.

**Myth # 2: Women provoke their attackers.**

Many people think a women who has been raped must have done *something* to make the man think she wanted to have sex. In the case described above, didn't the young woman willingly go into the washroom with the soldier? Self-doubt often paralyses victims. But sharing a drink or ride with a man—or even inviting him into her home—is not a woman's statement of consent to have sex.

**Myth # 3: Rape is simply sex.**

If there is no knife held to a woman's throat, or if she is not bound and gagged, what's the crime? The answer is that, under the law, forcing a woman to have sex without her consent is a *violent crime*. "Having sex" implies intimacy, caring, communication, and, most important of all, consent—none of which is present in rape. Beyond the brutality of being physically violated, date rape also undermines a victim's sense of trust. Psychological scars are especially serious among the half of rape victims who are under 18 years of age, many of whom are attacked by their own fathers or stepfathers (Greenfield, 1996; Eshleman & Wilson, 1998). The ancient

*Is a person who drinks alcohol to excess capable of making a responsible decision about having sex? What role does alcohol play in date rape on the campus?*

Babylonians stoned married women who fell victim to rape, convinced that the women had committed adultery. Ideas about rape have changed little over thousands of years, which helps to explain why, even today, only about 1 in 20 rapes results in an offender being sent to jail.

Nowhere has date rape been more of an issue than on the campus. The collegiate environment brings students together in casual settings and encourages trust. At the same time, many young people have much to learn about relationships and about themselves. So while college life promotes communication, it also invites sexual violence. A survey of 1853 university women across 44 Canadian campuses in 1993 showed that 28.8 percent had been sexually abused in the previous year (Boritch, 1997:215).

To counter the problem, colleges and universities have been facing—and debunking—myths about rape. In addition, attention has centred on the large role of alcohol in campus life and the effect of cultural patterns that define sex as a sport. To address the serious societal problem of date rape, everyone needs to understand two simple truths: Forcing sex without a woman's consent is rape, and when a woman says "no," she means just that.

*What do you think?*

1. *Why, in your opinion, are myths about rape so widespread?*

2. *What programs or policies exist on your campus to address sexual assault?*

3. *What else needs to be done?*

Source: Gibbs (1991a, 1991b); Gilbert (1992), and Boritch (1997).

---

by family members other than married partners would break down the system of kinship and hopelessly confuse human relationships.

Historically, the social control of sexuality was strong, mostly because sex commonly led to childbirth.

We see this in the traditional distinction between "legitimate" reproduction (within marriage) and "illegitimate" reproduction (out of wedlock). But once a society can effectively control births, its norms become more permissive. This occurred in Canada, where, over

*Europeans developed the concept of virginity during the Middle Ages with the rise of feudal estates. With property and titles to pass on, males needed to be certain of their heirs, and thus desired to marry a woman who had never had sex to ensure she was not pregnant with another man's child. The loss of virginity became a significant life-course event for women, a fact captured in Jean-Baptiste Greuze's painting,* The Broken Jug *(1773).*

the course of the 20th century, sex moved beyond its basic reproductive function and became a form of intimacy and even recreation (Giddens, 1992).

**Latent functions: The case of prostitution.**   It is easy to see that prostitution is harmful because it spreads disease and exploits women and children. But are there latent functions that help explain why prostitution is everywhere despite society's attempts to limit it? Definitely, explains Kingsley Davis (1971): prostitution performs several useful functions. Prostitution is one way to meet the sexual needs of a large number of people who do not have ready access to sex, including soldiers, travellers, and people who have trouble establishing relationships. Moreover, adds Davis, the availability of sex without commitment may even help to stabilize some loveless marriages that might otherwise collapse.

**Critical evaluation.**  The structural-functional paradigm helps us appreciate the way in which sexuality plays an

important part in how society is organized. The incest taboo and other cultural norms also suggest that society has always paid attention to who has sex with whom, and, especially, who reproduces with whom.

At the same time, this approach pays little attention to the great diversity of sexual ideas and practices found within every society, and seems to justify male dominance in sexual matters. Moreover, sexual patterns change over time, just as they differ in remarkable ways around the world. To appreciate the varied and changeable character of sexuality, we turn to the symbolic-interaction paradigm.

## SYMBOLIC-INTERACTION ANALYSIS

The symbolic-interaction paradigm highlights how as people interact, they construct everyday reality. As Chapter 4 (Social Interaction in Everyday Life) explains, the process of reality construction is highly variable, so that one group's or society's views of sexuality may well differ from another's. In the same way, how people understand sexuality can and does change over time.

**The social construction of sexuality.**  Almost all social patterns involving sexuality have seen considerable change over the course of the 20th century. One good illustration is the changing importance of virginity. A century ago, our society's norm—for women, at least—was virginity before marriage. This norm was strong because there was no effective birth control, and virginity was the only assurance a man had that his bride-to-be was not carrying another man's child. Today, however, we have gone a long way toward separating sex from reproduction, and the virginity norm has weakened.

Another example of our society's construction of sexuality involves young people. A century ago, childhood was a time of innocence in sexual matters. In recent decades, however, the thinking has changed. Though few people condone sexual activity among children, most people believe children should be educated about sex so that they can make intelligent choices about their own behaviour as they grow older.

**Global comparisons.**  The broader our view, the more variation we see in the meanings people attach to sexuality. In global perspective, differences can be striking, indeed. Anthropologists report that some cultures are far more accepting of childhood sexuality than are people in Canada. Studying the Melanesian people of southeast New Guinea, anthropologist Ruth Benedict (1938) concluded that adults paid little attention when young children engaged in sexual experimentation with one another. Parents in Melanesia shrugged off such activity because, before puberty, sex cannot lead to reproduction.

**Critical evaluation.** The strength of the symbolic-interaction paradigm lies in revealing the constructed character of familiar social patterns. Understanding that people "construct" sexuality, we can better appreciate the variety of sexual practices found over history and around the world.

One limitation of this approach, however, is that not everything is so variable. Throughout our own history—and around the world—men are more likely to see women in sexual terms than vice versa. If this pattern is widespread, some broader social structure must be at work, as we shall see in the next section.

## SOCIAL-CONFLICT ANALYSIS

The social-conflict paradigm highlights dimensions of inequality. This approach, therefore, shows how sexuality both reflects patterns of social inequality and helps create them.

**Sexuality: Reflecting social inequality.** Recall our discussion of prostitution, a practice that is either illegal or criminalized in many countries. Even so, enforcement is uneven at best, especially when it comes to who is and is not likely to be arrested. As noted above, although two parties are involved, the record shows that police are far more likely to arrest (less powerful) female sex workers than (more powerful) male clients (Boritch, 1997). Similarly, of all women engaged in the sex trade, it is streetwalkers—predominantly working-class women with the least income and those from an Aboriginal or a visible minority background—who face the highest risk of arrest (Brock, 1998; Lowman & Fraser, 1995; COYOTE, 2000). Then, too, we might wonder if so many women would be involved in prostitution at all if they had economic opportunities equal to those of men.

**Sexuality: Creating social inequality.** Social-conflict theorists—especially feminists—point to sexuality as being at the root of inequality between women and men. How can this be? Defining women in sexual terms amounts to devaluing them from full human beings into objects of men's interest and attention. Is it any wonder that the word *pornography* comes from the Greek word *porne*, meaning a "man's sexual slave"?

If men define women in sexual terms, it is easy to see why many people consider pornography—almost all of which is consumed by males—a power issue. Since pornography typically depicts women seeking to please men, it supports the idea that men have power over women.

Some radical critics doubt that this element of power can ever be removed from heterosexual relations (Dworkin, 1987). While most social-conflict theorists do not reject heterosexuality, they do agree that sexuality tends to degrade women in patriarchal societies. They

*Prostitution involves two people, but far more female prostitutes than male "Johns" face arrest for this crime. Moreover, of all categories of prostitutes, low-income street walkers are at the highest risk of arrest, disease, and violence.*

point out that our culture often depicts sexuality in terms of sport (men "scoring" with women) and also violence ("slamming," "banging," and "hitting on," for example, are verbs used for both fighting and sex).

**Queer theory.** Finally, social-conflict theory has taken aim not only at men dominating women, but also at heterosexuals dominating homosexuals. In recent years, just as many lesbians and gay men have come out in search of public acceptance, so some sociologists have tried to add a gay voice to their discipline. The term **queer theory** refers to *a growing body of knowledge that challenges the heterosexual bias in society.*

Queer theory begins with the assertion that our society is characterized by **heterosexism,** *a view stigmatizing anyone who is not heterosexual as "queer."* Our heterosexual culture victimizes a wide range of people, including gay men, lesbians, bisexuals, transsexuals, and even asexual people. Further, although most people agree that bias against women (sexism) and people of colour (racism) is wrong, heterosexism is widely tolerated and sometimes well within the law.

Heterosexism also exists at a more subtle level in our everyday understanding of the world. When we describe something as "sexy," for example, don't we really mean attractive to *heterosexuals*?

# CONTROVERSY & DEBATE

## The Abortion Controversy

A black van pulls up in front of the storefront in a busy section of the city. Two women get out of the front seat and cautiously scan the sidewalk. After a moment, one nods to the other, and they open the rear door to let a third young woman out of the van. Standing to the right and left of their charge, the two quickly whisk her inside the building.

Is this a description of two RCMP officers escorting a convict to a police station? It might be. But it is actually an account of two clinic workers escorting a young woman who has decided to have an abortion. Why should they be so cautious? Anyone who has read the papers in recent years knows about the heated confrontations taking place at abortion clinics across Canada and the United States. In fact, some opponents have even targeted and killed several doctors who perform abortions. Overall, abortion is probably the most hotly contested issue in North America today.

Abortion has not always been so controversial. During the colonial era, midwives and other healers performed abortions with little community opposition and with full approval of the law. But controversy arose in the course of the 19th century, not just in Canada but throughout the western world (Prentice et al., 1996). Middle-class reformists worried that the Anglo-Saxon population

was facing "race suicide," not just because of abortions, but also, as noted earlier in the chapter, due to the use of other forms of birth control (McLaren & McLaren, 1986). Ultimately the federal government passed legislation—in force until 1969—that made abortion illegal.

Such laws did not end abortion, but they greatly reduced the number. In addition, these laws drove abortion underground, so that many women—especially those who were poor—had little choice but to seek help from unlicensed "back alley" abortionists, sometimes with tragic results. In British Columbia alone, abortion-related mortalities were responsible for 20 percent of all maternal deaths between 1946 and 1968 (McLaren & McLaren, 1986:52–53).

In light of these and other developments, opposition to Canada's abortion law rose throughout the 1960s, until, in 1969, the federal government amended the provisions of the Criminal Code dealing with contraception and abortion. Yet the criminality surrounding abortions still remained, since the amendment permitted abortion only when performed by a doctor in an accredited hospital under specified conditions. Dr. Henry Morgentaler defied the law by offering abortion services to women in private clinics in a number of Canadian cities

(Morton, 1993). The Charter of Rights and Freedoms finally provided the opportunity for the Supreme Court in 1988 to strike down as unconstitutional the federal law on abortion. A new abortion bill—C-43—making abortion illegal unless a doctor certified that the woman's life was in danger, was passed by the House of Commons but was narrowly defeated in the Senate. The result: abortion was left to the provinces to regulate under their own health policies. Since then, the abortion rate has risen, partly due to the increase in the number of out-of-hospital abortion clinics now operating in many provinces. In 1995, the total abortion rate (procedures in both hospitals and freestanding clinics) was 28 per 100 live births (Statistics Canada, 2000m).

Even so, the abortion controversy continues. On one side of the issue are people who describe themselves as "pro-choice," supporting a woman's right to choose abortion. On the other side are those who call themselves "pro-life," opposing abortion as morally wrong. These people would like to see the re-criminalization of abortions across the country.

How strong is the support for each side of the abortion controversy? A recent Gallup Poll (Edwards & Mazzuca, 1999) asked a sample of Canadians the question "Do you think

---

**Critical evaluation.** By applying the social-conflict paradigm, we see how sexuality is both a cause and effect of inequality. In particular, this paradigm helps us understand men's power over women and heterosexual people's domination of homosexual people.

At the same time, this approach overlooks the fact that sexuality is not a power issue for everyone: Many couples enjoy a vital sexual relationship that deepens their commitment to one another. In addition, the social-conflict paradigm pays little attention to strides our society has made toward reducing inequality. Men today, in public, at least, are less likely to describe

women as sex objects than they were a few decades ago; moreover, our rising public concern about sexual harassment (see Chapter 10, Gender Stratification) has had some effect in reducing sexuality in the workplace. Likewise, there is ample evidence that the gay rights movement has secured greater opportunities and social acceptance for gay people.

We bring this chapter to a close with a look at what is perhaps the most divisive sexuality issue of all: **abortion,** *the deliberate termination of a pregnancy.* The issue cuts to the heart of just about everyone's sense of justice, as described in the Controversy & Debate box.

that abortion should be legal under any circumstance, legal only under certain circumstances, or illegal in all circumstances?" In response, 28 percent said yes to abortion being legal in all circumstances. As in 1998, 55 percent expressed the opinion that abortion should be available only in certain circumstances, such as when a women's health is in danger or she has a very low income. Up slightly from 1998, 15 percent of those polled would ban abortions in all circumstances, and 3 percent had no opinion on the abortion issue.

A closer look, however, shows that particular circumstances make a big difference in how people see this issue. Figure 7–7 shows that an increasingly large majority of Canadian adults favour legal abortion if a pregnancy seriously threatens a woman's health (96 percent), if she became pregnant as a result of rape or incest (88 percent), or if a fetus is very likely to have a serious defect (75 percent). The bottom line is this: Between one-quarter and one-third of Canadians support access to abortion under *any* circumstances, but about 85 percent support access to abortion under *some* circumstances.

Many pro-life people feel strongly that abortion is nothing more than killing unborn children. To them, people never have the right to end innocent life in this way. But pro-choice people are no less committed to their position. As they see it, the abortion debate is really about the standing of women in society.

Why? Because, they believe, women must have control over their own sexuality. If pregnancy dictates the course of women's lives, women will never be able to compete with men on equal terms, whether on campus or in the workplace. Thus, the pro-life position concludes, women must have access to legal, safe abortion as a necessary condition to full participation in society.

*Continue the debate . . .*

1. *The more conservative pro-life people see abortion as a moral issue, while more liberal pro-choice people see abortion as a power issue. Can you see a parallel to how conservatives and liberals view the issue of pornography?*

2. *Surveys show that men and women have almost the same opinions about abortion. Does this surprise you? Why?*

3. *Why do you think the abortion controversy is often so bitter? Why has our nation been unable to find a middle ground on which all can agree?*

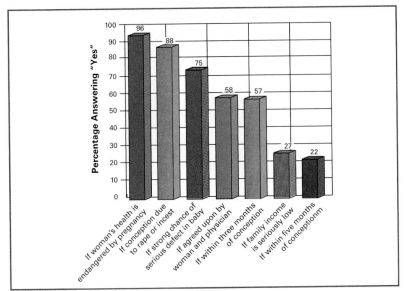

**FIGURE 7–7 Acceptable Circumstances for Abortion—Trend in the 1990s**
Source: Gallup Poll 1999 data.

Source: Based, in part, on Luker (1984), Tannahill (1992), and various news reports.

## SUMMARY

1. Canadian culture has long defined sex as a taboo topic. The Kinsey studies (1948 and 1953) were among the first publications by social scientists on human sexuality.

2. Sex refers to the biological distinction between females and males, which is determined at conception as a male sperm joins a female ovum.

3. Males and females are distinguished not only by their genitals (primary sex characteristics), but also by bodily development as they mature (secondary sex characteristics). Hermaphrodites have some combination of both male and female genitalia. Transsexuals are people who feel they are one sex, although biologically they are the other.

4. For most species, sex is rigidly directed by biology; for human beings, sex is a matter of cultural definition as well as personal choice. Patterns of kissing, modesty, and beauty all vary around the world, revealing the cultural foundation of sexual practices.

5. Though in the early part of the 20th century Canadian society held rigid attitudes toward sexuality, over time these attitudes have become more permissive.

6. The sexual revolution, which came of age in the 1960s and 1970s, brought a far greater openness in matters of sexuality. Research shows that changes in sexuality were greater for women than for men. By 1980, a sexual counterrevolution was taking form, condemning permissiveness and urging a return to more conservative "family values."

7. The share of people in Canada who have premarital sexual intercourse increased over the course of the 20th century. As many as two-thirds of teenage boys and nearly half of teenage girls are sexually active by their senior year in high school.

8. The level of sexual activity varies within the population of Canadian adults: on average Canadians have sex about six times per month, but the average is higher for three groups: Atlantic Canadians, young adults, and those living with a partner.

9. Although extramarital sex is widely condemned, about 20 percent of Canadians report being sexually unfaithful to their spouses at some time. Men report being unfaithful more often than women.

10. Sexual orientation refers to people's preference in terms of sexual partners. Four major orientations are heterosexuality, homosexuality, bisexuality, and asexuality. Sexual orientation is caused by some combination of biological and cultural factors.

11. The share of the population that is homosexual depends on how researchers define *homosexuality*. More men and women report having some homosexual experience than report having a homosexual identity.

12. The gay rights movement has worked to gain greater acceptance for gay people. Largely due to this movement, the share of the Canadian population condemning homosexuality as morally wrong has steadily decreased over recent decades. The vast majority of Canadians believe that human rights legislation should protect gays and lesbians from discrimination.

13. More than 40 000 Canadian women between the ages of 15 and 19 became pregnant in 1997. The rate of teenage pregnancy has dropped since 1950, prior to which many teens were marrying and having children. Today, however, most pregnant teens are not married, and also are at high risk of poverty, especially when the pregnancy forces them to drop out of school.

14. With no universal definition of *pornography*, the law allows local communities to set standards of decency. Conservatives condemn pornography as immoral; liberals, by contrast, condemn it as demeaning to women.

15. Prostitution, the selling of sexual services, is not illegal in Canada; however, sex workers can be arrested, prosecuted, and convicted because they "communicate" in a public place for the purpose of engaging in prostitution. Although many people think of prostitution as a victimless crime, others argue that it victimizes women and spreads sexually transmitted diseases.

16. Nearly half of Canadian women have experienced at least one incident of sexual assault or rape since the age of 16, and 2 million Canadian women ages 18 and over have been sexually assaulted by a stranger since turning 16. The actual number is perhaps several times greater since many sexual assaults are never reported to the police. Although many people think of rape as a sexual act, rape is really a violent expression of power. Most sexual assaults involve people who know one another.

17. Structural-functional theory highlights society's need to regulate sexual activity. A universal norm in this regard is the incest taboo that keeps kinship relations clear.

18. The symbolic-interaction paradigm points up how people attach various meanings to sexuality. Thus, societies differ from one another in terms of sexual attitudes and practices; similarly, sexual patterns change within any one society over time.

19. Social-conflict theory links sexuality to inequality. From this point of view, men dominate women, in part by devaluing females as sexual objects.

## KEY CONCEPTS

**sex** (p. 154) the biological distinction between females and males

**primary sex characteristics** (p. 155) the genitals, organs used for reproduction

**secondary sex characteristics** (p. 155) bodily development, apart from the genitals, that distinguishes biologically mature females and males

**intersexed person** (p. 155) a human being with some combination of female and male genitalia

**transsexuals** (p. 155) people who feel they are one sex even though biologically they are the other

**incest taboo** (p. 156) cultural norms that forbid sex or marriage between certain relatives

**sexual orientation** (p. 160) a person's preference in terms of sexual partners: same sex, other sex, either sex, neither sex

**heterosexuality** (p. 160) sexual attraction to someone of the other sex

**homosexuality** (p. 160) sexual attraction to someone of the same sex

**bisexuality** (p. 161) sexual orientation in which someone is sexually attracted to people of both sexes

**asexuality** (p. 161) sexual attraction to people of either sex

**homophobia** (p. 163) the fear of close personal interaction with people thought to be gay, lesbian, or bisexual

**pornography** (p. 164) sexually explicit material that causes sexual arousal

**prostitution** (p. 164) the selling of sexual services

**queer theory** (p. 171) a growing body of knowledge that challenges an allegedly heterosexual bias in sociology

**heterosexism** (p. 171) a view stigmatizing anyone who is not heterosexual as "queer"

**abortion** (p. 172) the deliberate termination of a pregnancy

## CRITICAL-THINKING QUESTIONS

1. What do sociologists mean by the *sexual revolution*? What did the sexual revolution change? Can you suggest some of the reasons that these changes occurred?

2. What is sexual orientation? Why is this characteristic difficult for researchers to measure?

3. Do you think laws should regulate the portrayal of sex in books, films, or on the Internet? Why or why not?

4. Overall, do you think sexuality plays too great a role in the mass media and other dimensions of everyday life? Why or why not?

## APPLICATIONS AND EXERCISES

1. The most complete study of sexual patterns in North America to date is *The Social Organization of Sexuality: Sexual Practices in the United States*, by Edward Laumann and colleagues. You can find this book in your campus or community library. Get a copy and browse through some of the chapters most interesting to you.

2. Contact your school's student services office, and ask what information there is about the extent of sexual violence on your campus. Do people report such crimes? What policies and procedures does your school have to respond to sexual violence?

3. The enforcement of Canada's prositution law is quite different across Canada. Some communities, for example, no longer charge sex trade workers. Do some research to determine how this law is enforced in your community.

 ## SITES TO SEE

**www.pearsoned.ca/macionis**
Visit the Companion Web site for this text to find additional links and access a host of other learning features including a chat room to share your ideas and opinions.

**www.agi-dc.org**
Visit the Web site for research on public policy and family planning.

**www.teenpregnancy.org**
Visit the Web site for teen pregnancy, an organization formed to guide teens toward responsible sexual behaviour. What are the key parts of this organization's program? How effective would you imagine it is? Why?

**www.ippf.org**
Visit this site of the International Planned Parenthood Federation, which is the largest voluntary organization in the field of sexual and reproductive health, representing more than 180 countries around the world.

**www.qrd.org**
This Web site, the Queer Resource Directory, looks at a wide range of issues—including family, religion, education, and health—from a "queer theory" perspective. Visit this site to see in what ways various social institutions can be considered "heterosexist." Do you agree? Why?

**www.gay.com**
This is a search engine for all sorts of information on issues involving homosexuality.

**seescape.homestead.com/frontseescape.html**
This Web site is a super resource for women working to support women and girls as they leave prostitution. It also has links to issues of concern regarding women and mental health.

**www.dmoz.org/Society/Transgendered**
Search this Web site for information on a variety of sex-related topics, including ones on people who are intersexed, transsexed, transgendered, or genderqueer.

# SOCIAL STRATIFICATION

*On April 10, 1912, the ocean liner* Titanic *slipped away from the docks of Southampton, England, on its maiden voyage across the North Atlantic to New York. A proud symbol of the new industrial age, the towering ship carried 2300 passengers, some enjoying more luxury than most travellers even today could imagine. Poor people, however, crowded the lower decks, journeying to what they hoped would be a better life on the other side of the Atlantic.*

*Two days out, the crew received reports of icebergs in the area—but paid little notice. Then, near midnight, as the ship steamed swiftly westward, a stunned lookout reported a massive shape rising out of the dark ocean directly ahead. Moments later, the* Titanic *collided with a huge iceberg, as tall as the ship itself, that split open its side as if the grand vessel were just a giant tin can.*

*Seawater flooded into the lower levels, pulling the ship down by the bow. Within 25 minutes of impact, people were rushing for the lifeboats. By 2:00 a.m., the bow was completely submerged and the stern rose high above the water. Clinging to the deck, quietly observed by those in lifeboats, hundreds of helpless passengers solemnly passed their final minutes before the ship disappeared into the frigid waters (Lord, 1976).* ■

The tragic loss of more than 1600 lives made news around the world. Looking back on this terrible event with a sociological eye, however, we see that some categories of passengers had much better odds of survival than others. In an age of conventional gallantry, women and children boarded the lifeboats first, so that 80 percent of the casualties were men. Class, too, was at work. More than 60 percent of those holding first-class tickets were saved because they were on the upper decks, where warnings were sounded first and lifeboats were accessible. Only 36 percent of the second-class passengers survived, and of the third-class passengers on the lower decks, only 24 percent escaped drowning. On board the *Titanic*, class turned out to mean more

**177**

The personal experience of poverty is captured in Sebastiao Salgado's haunting photograph, which stands as a universal portrait of human suffering. The essential sociological insight is that however strongly individuals feel the effects of social standing, it is largely a consequence of the way in which a society (or a world of societies) structures opportunity and reward. To the core of our being, then, we are all the products of social stratification.

than the quality of accommodations: Class was a matter of life or death.

The fate of those aboard the *Titanic* dramatically illustrates how social inequality affects the way people live—and sometimes whether they live at all. This chapter explores the important concept of social stratification and surveys social inequality in Canada.

## WHAT IS SOCIAL STRATIFICATION?

Every society is marked by inequality, with some people having more money, schooling, health, and power than others. **Social stratification** refers to *a system by which a society ranks categories of people in a hierarchy*. Social stratification involves four basic principles:

1. **Social stratification is a trait of an entire society, not simply a reflection of individual differences.** Many of us tend to think of social standing in terms of personal talent and effort, often exaggerating the extent to which we control our own destinies. Did a higher percentage of the first-class passengers on the *Titanic* survive because they were better swimmers than second- and third-class passengers? Hardly. They fared better because of their privileged position on the ship. Similarly, children born into wealthy families are more likely than children born into poverty to enjoy good health, do well in school, succeed in a career, and live a long life. Neither the rich nor poor are

responsible for creating social stratification, yet this system shapes the lives of us all.

2. **Social stratification persists over generations.** To see that stratification is a trait of societies rather than individuals, we have only to look at how inequality persists from generation to generation as parents pass their social position on to their children.

   Especially in industrial societies, some individuals do experience **social mobility**, *change in one's position in a social hierarchy*. For most people, however, social standing remains much the same over a lifetime.

3. **Social stratification is universal but variable.** Social stratification is found everywhere. Yet *what* is unequal and *how* unequal it is varies from one society to another. In some societies inequality is mostly a matter of prestige, while in others, wealth or power is the key dimension of difference. Moreover, some societies display more inequality than others.

4. **Social stratification involves not just inequality but beliefs.** Any system of inequality not only gives some people more than others, but also defines these arrangements as fair. Just as *what* is unequal differs from one society to another, so does the explanation of *why* people should be unequal.

## CASTE AND CLASS SYSTEMS

Sociologists distinguish between "closed" systems that allow for little change in social position and "open" systems that permit some social mobility (Tumin, 1985).

### THE CASTE SYSTEM

A **caste system** amounts to *social stratification based on ascription*. A pure caste system is "closed" because birth alone determines one's destiny, with little or no social mobility based on individual effort. In caste systems, people are ranked in rigid categories, where they live out their lives.

**An illustration: India.** Many of the world's societies—most of them agrarian—approximate caste systems. One example is India, or at least India's traditional villages, where most of the people still live. The Indian system identifies four major castes (or *varna*, a Sanskrit word that means "colour"): Brahmin, Kshatriya, Vaishya, and Shudra. On the local level, however, each of these is composed of hundreds of subcaste (or *jati*) groups.

In India, the traditional caste system still guides people's choice of work, especially in rural areas. Below the four basic castes are the Harijans, people defined as "outcasts" or "untouchables." These people perform jobs, such as turning leather into shoes, defined as unclean for others of higher social position.

From birth, caste position determines the shape of people's lives. First, families in each caste perform one type of work. Some work (like farming) is open to all, but castes are known for the work that their members do (as priests, barbers, leather workers, sweepers, and so on).

Second, a caste system demands that people marry others of the same ranking. If people married outside their castes, what rank would their children hold? Sociologists call this pattern *endogamous* marriage ("endo" stems from the Greek word meaning "within"). According to tradition, Indian parents select their children's marriage partners, often before the children reach their teens.

Third, caste systems shape people's beliefs. Indian culture is built on the Hindu tradition that accepting one's parents' choice of spouse, as well as one's life work, is a moral duty.

Fourth, caste guides everyday life by keeping people in the company of "their own kind." Norms enforce this practice, stating that a ritually "pure" person of higher-caste position is "polluted" by contact with someone of lower standing.

Caste systems are typical of agrarian societies because agriculture and similar work demands a lifelong routine of hard work; by instilling a sense of duty to perform the same work as one's parents, a caste system ensures that people have a sense of duty and discipline. Thus, caste hangs on in rural India more than half a century after being formally outlawed. People living in cities where commerce, industry, and finance are located tend to have far more choice about their work and marriage partners.

Another country dominated by caste is South Africa, although the racial system of *apartheid* is now in decline. The Global Sociology box on page 180 takes a closer look.

## THE CLASS SYSTEM

Farming, by its nature, demands the lifelong discipline created by caste systems. But a modern economy depends on developing people's talents, giving rise to a **class system**, *social stratification based on both birth and individual achievement.*

Class systems are more "open," so that individuals who gain schooling and skills may be socially mobile in relation to their parents and siblings. Such mobility, in turn, blurs class distinctions so that even blood relatives may have different social standings. Categorizing people according to their colour, gender, or social background comes to be seen as wrong in modern societies, as all people acquire political rights and, in principle, equal standing before the law. Moreover, work is no longer fixed at birth, but involves some personal choice. Greater individuality also translates into more freedom in selecting a marital partner.

**Meritocracy.** Compared to agrarian societies where caste is the rule, industrial societies move toward **meritocracy**, *a system in which social position is based entirely on personal merit.* Because industrial societies need to develop a broad range of abilities (beyond farming), stratification is based not only on the accident of birth, but also on "merit"—that is, what job one does and how well one does it. To advance meritocracy, industrial societies expand equality of opportunity, although people still expect inequality of outcomes.

In a pure meritocracy, social position would depend entirely on a person's ability and effort. Such a system would have ongoing social mobility, blurring social categories as individuals continuously move up or down in the system depending on their latest performance.

Caste societies define *merit* (from Latin, meaning "worthy of praise") as dutifully performing whatever

# Race as Caste: A Report from South Africa

At the southern tip of the African continent lies South Africa, about the size of Quebec, with a population of about 45 million in 2000. Long inhabited by people of African descent, the region attracted Dutch traders and farmers in the mid-17th century. Early in the 19th century, a second wave of British colonization pushed the Dutch inland. By the early 1900s, the British had taken over the country, proclaiming it the Union of South Africa. In 1961, the Republic of South Africa declared its independence.

But freedom was a reality only for the white minority. To ensure their control over the black majority, whites relied on a policy of *apartheid*, or racial separation. Apartheid, formalized as law in 1948, denied blacks citizenship, ownership of land, and any voice in the government. As a subordinate caste, blacks received little schooling and performed menial, low-paying jobs. Even middle-class white people had at least one black household servant.

The white minority defended apartheid by claiming that blacks threatened white cultural traditions, and, more simply, were inferior beings. But resistance to apartheid rose steadily, prompting whites to resort to brutal military repression to maintain their power.

Steady resistance—primarily from younger blacks impatient for political

and economic opportunity—gradually forced change. Adding to the internal pressure was criticism from other countries, including Canada and the United States. By the mid-1980s, the tide began to turn as South Africa granted some rights to people of mixed race and Asian ancestry. Then came the right for all people to form labour unions, to enter various occupations once restricted to whites, and to own property. Officials also repealed laws that separated the races in public places, such as beaches and hospitals.

The pace of change increased in 1990 with Nelson Mandela's release from prison. In 1994, the first national election open to all races named Mandela

president, ending centuries of white minority rule.

Despite this dramatic political change, social position in South Africa is still based on race. Even with the right to own property, about one-third of black South Africans have no work, and the majority remain dirt poor. The worst off are the 7 million *ukuhleleleka*, which means "marginal people" in the Xhosa language. Soweto-by-the-Sea may sound like a summer getaway, but it is home to thousands of people crammed into shacks made from packing cases, corrugated metal, cardboard, and other discarded materials. There is no electricity for lights or refrigeration. Without plumbing, people use buckets to haul sewage; women line up to take a turn at a single water tap that serves more than 1000 people. Any job is hard to come by, and those who do find work are lucky to earn $200 a month.

South Africa's new president, Thabo Mbeki, elected in 1999, leads a nation still twisted by centuries of racial caste. Tourism is up and holds out promise of an economic boom in years to come. But the country can only shed its past by providing real opportunity to all its people.

Sources: Fredrickson (1981), Wren (1991), Hawthorne (1999), and Mabry & Masland (1999).

job comes with a person's birth. Caste systems waste human potential, of course, but they are very orderly. And herein lies the answer to an important question: Why do modern, industrial societies keep some element of caste—such as letting wealth pass from generation to generation—rather than becoming complete meritocracies? Simply because a pure meritocracy erodes families and other social groupings. Economic performance is not *everything*, after all. Would we want to evaluate our family members solely

on their jobs? Probably not. Therefore, class systems in industrial societies move toward meritocracy to promote productivity and efficiency, but retain some caste elements to maintain order and social cohesion.

**Status consistency. Status consistency** refers to *the degree of consistency in a person's social standing across various dimensions of inequality.* A caste system has little social mobility and high status consistency, so that the typical person has the same relative standing with regard to wealth, power, and prestige. The greater mobility of class systems, however, produces less status consistency. In Canada, then, a college or university professor with an advanced degree might enjoy high social prestige but earn a moderate income. Because of lower status consistency in high-income countries, *classes* are less well defined than *castes*.

**An illustration: The United Kingdom.** The mix of meritocracy and caste in class systems is well illustrated by the United Kingdom (composed of England, Wales, Scotland, and Northern Ireland), a high-income country with a long agrarian history.

In the Middle Ages, England had a caste-like system of three *estates*. The *first estate* was a hereditary nobility composed of 5 percent of the population that controlled most of the land—the chief form of wealth (Laslett, 1984). Most nobles had no occupation at all since they deemed engaging in trade or doing other work for income beneath them. Well tended by servants, nobles used their leisure time to develop refined tastes in art, music, and literature.

To prevent vast landholdings from being divided by heirs, the law of *primogeniture* (from Latin, meaning "first born") stated that all landholdings pass to a man's eldest son or other male relation. Younger sons therefore had to find other means of support. Some entered the clergy—the *second estate*—where spiritual power was supported by the church's extensive landholdings. Other men of high birth became military officers, lawyers, or took up other professions considered honourable for gentlemen. In an age when no woman could inherit her father's property and few women had the chance to earn a living on their own, a noble daughter depended for her security on marrying well. A convent or a nunnery was her only other option.

Below the nobility and the clergy, the vast majority of men and women formed the *third estate*, or commoners. Most commoners were serfs working land owned by nobles. Unlike nobles or clergy, most commoners had little formal schooling and were illiterate.

As the Industrial Revolution expanded England's economy beginning in the mid-18th century, some commoners living in cities made enough money to challenge the nobility. More emphasis on meritocracy, the growing importance of money, and the expansion of schooling and legal rights eventually blurred social rankings and gave rise to a class system.

Perhaps it is a sign of the times that these days traditional titles are put up for sale by nobles who simply need the money. In 1996, for example, the title "Lord of Wimbledon" was put on the block by Earl Spencer—Princess Diana's brother—to raise the $300 000 he needed to redo the plumbing in one of his large homes (McKee, 1996).

Yet the legacy of England's feudal past remains evident today. A small cluster of families still enjoys

*Older people have fared comparatively well in Canada in recent decades, in large part because of increased governmental support. The trend has been in the opposite direction in eastern Europe where the support system for seniors has been drastically reduced. Scenes like this one—a Moscow woman begging for money—have become all too common.*

considerable inherited wealth, which confers the highest prestige, admission to elite universities, and political influence. A traditional monarch stands as the United Kingdom's head of state, and Parliament's House of Lords comprises "peers," most of noble birth. Even so, actual control of government resides in the House of Commons, where the prime minister and other ministers typically reach their positions through achievement—winning an election—rather than ascription.

Further down, roughly one-fourth of the British people fall into the "middle class." Some earn comfortable incomes from professions and business, and are among the 10 to 15 percent of Britons who own stocks and bonds. Below the middle class, perhaps half of all Britons consider themselves "working class," earning modest incomes through manual work. The remaining one-fourth of the British people make up the lower class, the poor who lack steady work. They are concentrated in the nation's northern and western regions, which are plagued by the closing of mines and factories.

Today's British class system mixes caste elements and meritocracy, producing a highly stratified society with opportunity to move upward or downward. One legacy of the historical estate system, however, is that social mobility occurs less frequently in the United Kingdom than in Canada and the United States (Kerckhoff, Campbell, & Winfield-Laird, 1985). The difference in mobility between the U.K. and the two North American countries is reflected in the importance attached to accent. Distinctive patterns of speech develop when people are set off from one another over many generations. Whereas people in Canada treat accent as a clue to where one lives (there is little mistaking an East Coast Canadian accent from a Southern Ontario one), Britons use accent as a mark of social class (elites speak the "King's English," while most people speak like "commoners"). So different are these two accents that the British seem to be, as the saying goes, a single people divided by a common language.

## CLASSLESS SOCIETIES?

Nowhere in the world do we find a society without social inequality. Yet some nations have claimed that they are classless.

**An illustration: The former Soviet Union.** The Union of Soviet Socialist Republics (USSR), a major military superpower since the middle of the 20th century, was born out of revolution in 1917. The Russian Revolution ended the feudal estate system ruled by a hereditary nobility, and transferred most farms, factories, and other productive property from private ownership to state control. Following the lead of Karl Marx—who believed that private ownership of property was the basis for social classes—Soviet leaders boasted of becoming a classless society.

Yet high government officials, or *apparatchiks*, ranked highest in the social order, followed by intellectuals and other professionals, manual workers, and, at the lowest level, rural peasantry. The fact that these rankings had very different living standards shows that the former Soviet Union never really did become classless.

In 1985, Mikhail Gorbachev came to power with a new economic program, known as *perestroika*, meaning "restructuring." Gorbachev saw that while the Soviet system had reduced economic inequality, everyone was relatively poor and living standards lagged far behind other industrial nations. Gorbachev tried to generate economic expansion by reducing inefficient centralized control of the economy.

Gorbachev's reforms turned into one of the most dramatic social movements in history. People throughout Eastern Europe toppled their socialist governments, and, in 1991, the Soviet Union itself collapsed. People blamed their poverty as well as their lack of basic freedoms on a repressive ruling class of Communist party officials. In the Soviet Union, for example, just 6 percent of the population formed the Communist party, which ran the whole country.

The Soviet story shows that social inequality involves more than economic resources. Soviet society may not have had the extremes of wealth and poverty found in Great Britain, Japan, the United States, and Canada. But an elite class existed all the same—one based on power rather than wealth.

What about social mobility in so-called classless societies? During the 20th century, there was as much upward social mobility in the Soviet Union as in Great Britain or Canada. Rapidly expanding industry and government drew many poor rural peasants into factories and offices. This trend illustrates what sociologists call **structural social mobility,** *a shift in the social position of a large number of people due to changes in society itself.*

December 20, 1998—Tallinn, Estonia
Tallinn is located only 90 minutes across the Baltic Sea from Helsinki, Finland. Yet the visual contrast between the two capital cities—apart from the common winter snow—is so great that we wonder if we have not docked in a distant land. As we walk the cobblestone streets of the Medieval part of the city with our tour guide—a retired school teacher whose pension is so low that she is forced to supplement her income by entertaining visitors such as ourselves—we marvel at the Christmas decorations in the numerous shops and restaurants. The snow starts to fall while we are enjoying a nice meal in a warmly lit restaurant off the main square. It is nearly 11 p.m. before we make our way back to our hotel, and on our way we notice that work crews are starting to shovel the snow away from the square. We are surprised to notice a woman who appears to be well into her seventies working beside a man a decade or two younger. They are both bundled up in large overcoats to help fend off the bitter cold while they sweep. . . . We see firsthand what happens when the pensions that people have worked 40 or more years to earn are suddenly eliminated. Independence, it seems, has not resulted in material wealth for all of Tallinn's population.

Estonia, partly due to financial aid from neighbouring Finland and Sweden, has gradually begun to revitalize its economy and social institutions. By contrast, structural social mobility in the Russian Federation turned downward in the 1990s. In fact, between 1990 and 1998, the average life span for Soviet men declined by eight years, and for women, two years. Many factors are involved, including Russia's poor health care system, but the Russian people clearly are suffering from a turbulent period of economic change

(Róna-Tas, 1994; Specter, 1997; Bohlen, 1998; Gerber & Hout, 1998).

Estonia, and indeed all of Russia's neighbours in the region, are in close watch, fearing that unless the Russian economy improves, tension in the Baltic region will escalate further. Figure 8–1 indicates that the gulf between rich and poor in Russia is wider than in Canada and most other high-income countries, but narrower than in some other countries, such as Brazil and Panama.

## IDEOLOGY: THE POWER BEHIND STRATIFICATION

Noting the extent of social inequality around the world, we might wonder how societies persist without sharing resources more equally. The British estate system lasted for centuries, and for two thousand years people in India accepted the idea that they should be privileged or poor due to the accident of birth.

A major reason that social hierarchies endure is **ideology**, *cultural beliefs that justify social stratification.* Any beliefs—for example, the idea that the rich are smart while the poor are lazy—are ideological to the extent that they define the wealthy as worthy and suggest that poor people deserve their plight.

The ancient Greek philosopher Plato (427–347 B.C.E.) defined justice as agreement about who should have what. Every culture, Plato explained, considers some type of inequality "fair." Karl Marx, too, understood this fact, although he was far more critical of inequality than was Plato. Marx took capitalist societies to task for defending wealth and power in the hands of a few as "a law of the marketplace." Capitalist law, Marx continued, defines the right to own property and ensures that money stays within the same families from one generation to the next. In short, Marx concluded, culture and institutions combine to shore up a society's elite, which is why established hierarchies last so long.

Ideology changes along with a society's economy and technology. Because agrarian societies depend on the routine labour of their people, they develop caste systems that make performing the duties of one's "station" a moral responsibility. With the emergence of industrial capitalism, an ideology of meritocracy arises, defining wealth and power as prizes to be won by those who perform the best. This change means that the poor, objects of charity under feudalism, are scorned as personally undeserving under industrial capitalism. This harsh view is linked with the work of Herbert Spencer, as explained in the Applying Sociology box on page 185.

History shows how difficult it is to change social stratification. However, challenges to the status quo always arise. Traditional notions about "a woman's

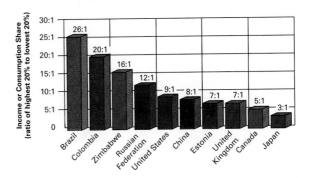

**FIGURE 8–1   Economic Inequality in Selected Countries, 1990s**

Source: World Bank (2001).

place," for example, are losing their power to deprive women of economic opportunity. The continuing struggle for racial equality in South Africa also exemplifies widespread rejection of the ideology of apartheid.

## THE FUNCTIONS OF SOCIAL STRATIFICATION

Why does social stratification exist? According to the structural-functional paradigm, social stratification plays a vital part in the operation of society. This argument was presented some 50 years ago by Kingsley Davis and Wilbert Moore (1945).

### THE DAVIS-MOORE THESIS

The **Davis-Moore thesis** states that *social stratification has beneficial consequences for the operation of a society.* How else, ask Davis and Moore, can we explain the fact that some form of social stratification has been found in every known society?

Davis and Moore note that industrial societies have hundreds of occupational positions of varying importance. Certain jobs—say, washing windows, collecting garbage, or answering a telephone—are fairly easy and can be performed by almost anyone. Other jobs—such as designing new generations of computers—are quite difficult and demand the scarce talents of people with extensive (and expensive) training.

Therefore, Davis and Moore explain, the greater the functional importance of a position, the more rewards a society attaches to it. This strategy promotes

Medieval Europe accepted rigid social differences as part of a divine plan for the world. This 15th-century painting by the Limbourg brothers shows peasants toiling in the fields, while nobles, who are not to be seen, reside in the castle well-attended by servants.

Source: *September: Harvesting Grapes*, by the Limbourg Brothers. *Très riches heures du duc de Berry* (early 15th century). Victoria and Albert Museum, London, UK. The Bridgeman Art Library.

productivity and efficiency, since rewarding important work with income, prestige, power, or leisure encourages people to do these things, and to work better, longer, and harder. In short, unequal rewards—which is what social stratification is—benefits society as a whole.

Davis and Moore concede that any society can be egalitarian, but only to the extent that people are willing to let *anyone* perform *any* job. Equality also demands that someone who does a job poorly be rewarded on a par with someone who performs well. Such a system clearly offers little incentive for people to try their best and thereby reduces a society's productive efficiency.

The Davis-Moore thesis suggests why *some* form of stratification exists everywhere; it does not state precisely what rewards a society should give to any occupational position or how unequal the rewards should be. Davis and Moore merely point out that positions which a society considers crucial must yield sufficient rewards to draw talent away from less important work.

**Critical evaluation.** Although the Davis-Moore thesis is an important contribution, Melvin Tumin (1953) wonders, first, how we assess how important any occupation really is. Perhaps the high rewards our society gives to, say, physicians partly results from deliberate efforts by medical schools to limit the supply of physicians and thereby increase the demand for their services. Moreover, do rewards actually reflect the contribution one makes to society? With income approaching $150 million per year, television personality Oprah Winfrey earns more in one day than the prime minister of Canada earns in a year. Would anyone argue that hosting a talk show is more important than leading the country? And does multi-millionaire pop singer Céline Dion contribute that much more to Canadian society than, for example, a pediatric nurse or an early childhood educator, both of whom earn a minuscule amount compared to Dion?

Second, Tumin claims that Davis and Moore ignore how the caste elements of social stratification can *prevent* the development of individual talent. Born to inequality, rich children may develop their abilities, something many gifted poor children can never do.

Third, by suggesting that social stratification benefits all of society, the Davis-Moore thesis ignores how social inequality promotes conflict and even outright revolution. This criticism leads to the social-conflict paradigm, which provides a very different explanation for social hierarchy.

## STRATIFICATION AND CONFLICT

Social-conflict analysis argues that, rather than benefiting society as a whole, stratification provides some people with advantages over others. This analysis draws heavily on the ideas of Karl Marx, with contributions from Max Weber.

### KARL MARX: CLASS CONFLICT

As Marx saw it, the Industrial Revolution promised humanity a society free from want. Yet the capitalist economy had done little to improve the lives of most people. Marx devoted his life to explaining a glaring contradiction: how, in a society so rich, so many could be so poor.

# Is Getting Rich "The Survival of the Fittest"?

"The survival of the fittest"—we have all heard these words used to describe society as a competitive jungle. The phrase was coined by one of sociology's pioneers, Herbert Spencer (1820–1903), whose ideas about social inequality are still widespread today.

Spencer, who lived in England, eagerly followed the work of the natural scientist Charles Darwin (1809–1882). Darwin's theory of biological evolution held that a species changes physically over many generations as it adapts to the natural environment. Spencer, however, distorted Darwin's theory, applying it to the operation of society. Society became the "jungle," with the "fittest" people rising to wealth and the deficient gradually sinking into miserable poverty.

It is no surprise that Spencer's views were popular among the rising industrialists at that time. John D. Rockefeller (1839–1937), who made a vast fortune building the oil industry, recited Spencer's "social gospel" to young children in Sunday School. As Rockefeller saw it, the growth of giant corporations—and the astounding wealth of their owners—was merely the "survival of the fittest," a basic fact of nature. Neither Spencer nor Rockefeller had much sympathy for the poor, seeing poverty as evidence of people not measuring up in a competitive world. Spencer opposed social welfare programs on the basis that they allegedly penalized society's "best" people (through taxes) and rewarded its "worst" members (through welfare benefits).

Today's sociologists are quick to point out that society is far from a meritocracy, as Spencer contended. From private schools to private health care, parental wealth has a great impact on the probability of children achieving wealth and longevity. Moreover, it is not the case that companies or individuals who generate lots of money necessarily benefit society. Yet, Spencer's view that people get more or less what they deserve in life remains part of our individualistic culture.

In Marx's view, social stratification is rooted in people's relationships to the means of production. Individuals either (1) own productive property or (2) labour for others. In feudal Europe, the nobility and the church owned the productive land; the peasants toiled as farmers. Under industrial capitalism, the nobility was replaced by **capitalists** (sometimes termed the *bourgeoisie*, a French word meaning "of the town"), *people who own and operate factories and other businesses in pursuit of profits.* Serfs became the **proletariat**, *people who sell their productive labour for wages.* Capitalists and proletariat have opposing interests and are separated by a vast gulf of wealth and power, making class conflict inevitable.

Marx's analysis reflects the capitalism he observed in the 19th century, when industry had raised some to great wealth while most made do with low wages. During this era, wealthy capitalists such as Andrew Carnegie, J.P. Morgan, and John Jacob Astor (one of the few rich passengers to drown on the *Titanic*) lived in fabulous mansions filled with priceless art and staffed by dozens of servants. Even by today's standards, their incomes were staggering. Carnegie, for example, earned more than $20 million in 1900 (more than $100 million in today's dollars)—when the average worker's wages totalled perhaps $500 a year (Baltzell, 1964; Pessen, 1990).

In time, Marx believed, the working majority would overthrow the capitalists once and for all. Capitalism would bring about its own downfall, Marx reasoned, by making workers poorer and poorer, and giving them little control over the workplace or what they made. Under capitalism, work produces only **alienation**, *the experience of powerlessness in social life.*

Marx imagined, as a replacement for capitalism, a *socialist* system to meet the needs of all, rather than just the few. Thus, Marx looked to the future with hope: "The proletarians have nothing to lose but their chains. They have a world to win" (Marx & Engels 1972:362; orig. 1848).

**Critical evaluation.** There is no doubt that Marx has had enormous influence on sociological thinking. But seen as a revolutionary—calling for the overthrow of capitalist society—Marx is also highly controversial.

One of the strongest criticisms of the Marxist approach is that it ignores a central idea of the Davis-Moore thesis: that motivating people to do their work well requires a system of unequal rewards. Marx separated reward from performance; his egalitarian ideal was based on the principle "to each according to need, from each according to ability" (Marx & Engels, 1972:388). But severing rewards from performance may be precisely what caused the low productivity of

*In his painting* Work, *U.S. artist Ford Maddox Brown (1821–1893) suggests that the early capitalist era sharply divided society in the manner that Marx described. Today, more than a century since Brown lived, do you think class differences in Canada and the United States have increased or decreased? Why?*

the former Soviet Union and other socialist economies around the world. Even so, defenders respond by asking why we assume humanity is inherently selfish rather than social. That is, individual rewards are not the only way to motivate people to perform their social roles (Clark, 1991; Fiske, 1991).

A second problem is that the revolutionary change Marx predicted has failed to happen, at least in advanced capitalist societies. The next section takes a closer look at this issue.

## WHY NO MARXIST REVOLUTION?

Despite Marx's prediction, capitalism is still thriving. Why have industrial workers not overthrown capitalism? Ralf Dahrendorf (1959) proposed four reasons:

1. **The fragmentation of the capitalist class.** Today, tens of millions of stockholders rather than single families own most large companies. Moreover, day-to-day corporate operations is in the hands of a large managerial class, whose members may or may not be major stockholders. With stock so widely held—by 2000, more than 50 percent of the Canadian population was "in the market"—more and more people have a direct stake in the capitalist system (Agus Reid Group Inc., 1998a).

2. **A higher standard of living.** As Chapter 12 (Economics and Politics) explains, a century ago most Canadian workers were in factories or on farms performing **blue-collar occupations,** *lower-prestige work that involves mostly manual labour.* Today, most workers hold **white-collar occupations,** *higher-prestige work that involves mostly mental activity.* These jobs are in sales, management, and other service fields. Most of today's white-collar

workers do not think of themselves as an "industrial proletariat." Just as important, the average income in Canada has risen multifold over the course of this century, even allowing for inflation—and the work week is shorter to boot. As a result, most workers see themselves as better off than their parents and grandparents, a case of structural mobility that helps people accept the status quo (Edwards, 1979; Gagliani, 1981; Wright & Martin, 1987).

3. **More worker organization.** Employees have organizational clout that they lacked a century ago. Workers have the right to form labour unions that, backed by threats of work slowdowns and strikes, make demands of management. In other words, worker–management disputes are settled without threatening the capitalist system.

4. **More extensive legal protections.** During this century, new laws made the workplace safer, and employment insurance, disability protection, and pension funds now provide workers with greater financial security.

**A counterpoint.** These developments suggest that our society has smoothed many of capitalism's rough edges. Yet many claim that Marx's analysis of capitalism is still largely valid (Miliband, 1969; Edwards, 1979; Giddens, 1982; Domhoff, 1983; Stephens, 1986). First, wealth remains highly concentrated, with much of the privately controlled corporate stock in the hands of a small proportion of our population. Second, many of today's white-collar jobs offer no more income, security, or satisfaction than factory work did a century ago (Reid, 1996; Lowe, 2000). Third, many benefits enjoyed by today's workers came about through the class conflict Marx described, and workers still struggle

## TABLE 8-1 Two Explanations of Social Stratification: A Summary

| Structural-Functional Paradigm | Social-Conflict Paradigm |
|---|---|
| Social stratification keeps society operating. Linking greater rewards to more important social positions benefits society as a whole. | Social stratification is the result of social conflict. Differences in social resources serve the interests of some and harm others. |
| Social stratification matches talents and abilities to appropriate occupational positions. | Social stratification ensures that much talent and ability in society will not be developed at all. |
| Social stratification is both useful and inevitable. | Social stratification is useful only to some people; it is not inevitable. |
| The values and beliefs that legitimize social inequality are widely shared throughout society. | Values and beliefs tend to be ideological; they reflect the interests of the more powerful members of society. |
| Because systems of social stratification are useful to society as a whole and are supported by cultural values and beliefs, they are usually stable over time. | Because systems of social stratification reflect the interests of only part of society, they are unlikely to remain stable over time. |

Source: Adapted, in part, from Arthur L. Stinchcombe, "Some Empirical Consequences of the Davis-Moore Theory of Stratification," *American Sociological Review*, Vol. 28, No. 5 (October 1963):808.

to hold on to what they have. Fourth, while workers have gained legal protections, the law has not helped ordinary people use the legal system as effectively as the rich use it. Therefore, social-conflict theorists conclude, the absence of a socialist revolution in countries such as Canada or the United States does not negate Marx's analysis of capitalism.

Table 8–1 summarizes the two contrasting explanations of social stratification.

## MAX WEBER: CLASS, STATUS, AND POWER

Max Weber agreed with Karl Marx that social stratification causes social conflict, but he saw Marx's two-class model as simplistic. Instead, he thought social stratification resulted from the interplay of three distinct kinds of inequality.

The first dimension is economic inequality—the issue so vital to Marx—which Weber termed *class* position. Weber did not think of "classes" as well-defined categories but as a continuum ranging from high to low. Weber's second dimension is *status*, or social prestige, and the third is *power*.

**The socioeconomic status hierarchy.** Marx viewed prestige and power as simple reflections of economic position, and did not treat them as distinct dimensions of inequality. But Weber noted that status consistency in modern societies is often quite low: a local official, say, might wield considerable power yet have little wealth or social prestige.

Weber's contribution, then, is painting stratification in industrial societies as a multidimensional ranking rather than a hierarchy of clearly defined classes. In line with Weber's thinking, sociologists use the term **socioeconomic status (SES)** to refer to *a composite social ranking based on various dimensions of inequality.*

**Inequality in history.** Weber observed that each of his three dimensions of social inequality stands out at a different time in the evolution of human societies. Status or social prestige is the main dimension of difference in agrarian societies, taking the form of honour. Members of these societies gain prestige by conforming to cultural norms corresponding to their rank.

Industrialization and the development of capitalism level traditional rankings based on birth but generate striking financial inequality. Thus, Weber argued, the crucial difference among industrial people is the economic dimension of class.

Over time, industrial societies witness growth of a bureaucratic state. Bigger government, and the spread of all kinds of other organizations, makes power more important in the stratification system. Especially in socialist societies, because government regulates many aspects of life, high-ranking officials become the new ruling elite.

This historical analysis points to a final difference between Weber and Marx. Marx thought societies could eliminate social stratification by abolishing private ownership of productive property. Weber doubted that overthrowing capitalism would significantly diminish social stratification. It might lessen economic disparity, he reasoned, but socialism would increase inequality by expanding government and concentrating power in the hands of a political elite. The uprisings against entrenched bureaucracies in Eastern Europe and the former Soviet Union support Weber's position.

**Critical evaluation.** Weber's multidimensional view of social stratification has enormously influenced sociologists. But critics (particularly those who favour Marx's ideas) argue that although social class boundaries may have blurred, all industrial nations still show enduring patterns of social inequality. This is the case even in the mixed economies of the Nordic countries

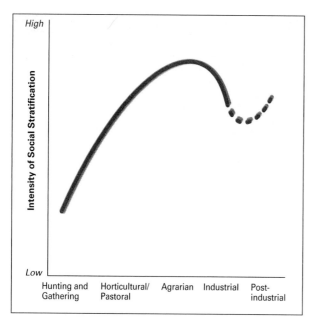

**FIGURE 8–2** **Social Stratification and Technological Development: The Kuznets Curve**

The Kuznets Curve shows that greater technological sophistication is generally accompanied by more pronounced social stratification. The trend reverses itself, however, as industrial societies gradually become more egalitarian. Rigid caste-like distinctions are relaxed in favour of greater opportunity and equality under the law. Political rights are more widely extended, and there is even some leveling of economic differences. The Kuznets Curve may also be usefully applied to the relative social standing of the two sexes. The emergence of post-industrial society may signal greater social inequality, as the broken line indicates.

Source: Created by John Macionis, based on Kuznets (1955).

of Europe, where the social safety net is much more extensive than in North America (Abrahamson, 1999). Moreover, as we shall see presently, economic inequality has recently increased in Canada (a trend that has also taken place in the U.S.). Thus, while some people favour Weber's multidimensional hierarchy, others think Marx's view of the rich versus the poor is closer to the mark.

## STRATIFICATION AND TECHNOLOGY: A GLOBAL PERSPECTIVE

We can weave together a number of observations made in this chapter by considering the relationship between a society's technology and its type of social stratification. This analysis draws on Gerhard Lenski and Jean Lenski's model of sociocultural evolution discussed in Chapter 2 (Culture).

With simple technology, hunters and gatherers produce only what is necessary for day-to-day living. Some people may produce more than others, but the group's survival depends on all sharing what they have. Thus, no categories of people emerge as better off than others.

But as technological advances generate a surplus, social inequality increases. In horticultural and pastoral societies, a small elite controls most of the surplus. Larger-scale agriculture is more productive still, and thus striking inequality—as great as at any time in history—places the nobility in an almost godlike position over the masses.

Industrialization turns the tide, nudging inequality downward. Prompted by the need to develop people's talents, meritocracy takes hold and erodes the power of traditional elites. Industrial productivity also raises the living standards of the historically poor majority. Specialized work demands schooling for all, sharply reducing illiteracy. A literate population, in turn, presses for a greater voice in political decision making, reducing social inequality and lessening male domination of women.

Over time, even wealth becomes somewhat less concentrated (countering the trend predicted by Marx). For example, when we look at the wealthiest country in the world, we notice that the share of wealth controlled by the richest 1 percent of U.S. families, which peaked at 36 percent just before the stock market crash in 1929, fell to 30 percent by 1990 (Williamson & Lindert, 1980; Beeghley, 1989; *1991 Green Book*). Such trends help explain why Marxist revolutions occurred in *agrarian* societies—such as Russia (1917), Cuba (1959), and Nicaragua (1979)—where social inequality is most pronounced, rather than in *industrial* societies, as Marx predicted.

In human history, then, technological advancement first increases but then moderates the intensity of social stratification. Greater inequality is functional for agrarian societies, but industrial societies benefit from a less unequal system. This historical pattern, recognized by Nobel Prize–winning economist Simon Kuznets (1955, 1966), is illustrated by the Kuznets Curve shown in Figure 8–2.

Patterns of global inequality square with the Kuznets Curve. Global Map 8–1 shows that industrial nations have somewhat less income inequality than do predominantly agrarian countries (such as those in Latin America and Africa). Of course, income disparity reflects not just technology, but also political and economic priorities. Countries that have had socialist economies (including the People's Republic of China) display relatively less income inequality, albeit with a rather low standard of living. They also have pronounced inequality on non-economic dimensions such as political power.

And what of the future? Notice that in Figure 8–2 we extend the trend described by Kuznets to the post-

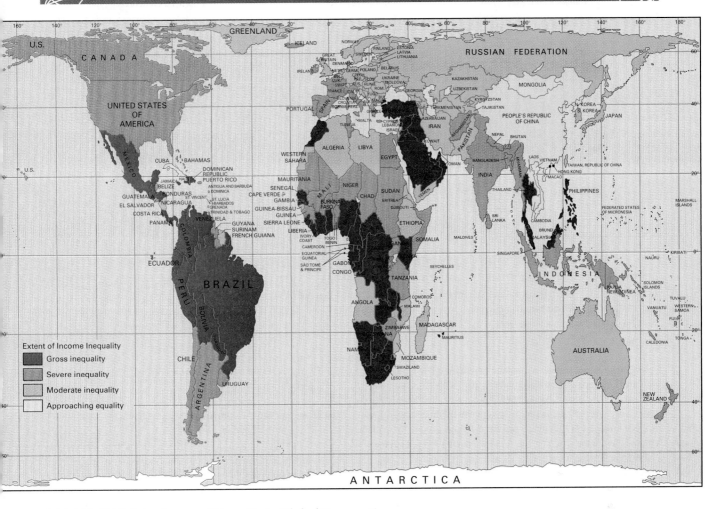

**GLOBAL MAP 8–1   Income Disparity in Global Perspective**

Societies throughout the world differ in the rigidity and intensity of social stratification, as well as in overall standard of living. This map highlights income inequality. Generally speaking, countries that have had centralized, socialist economies (including the People's Republic of China, the former Soviet Union, and Cuba) display the least income inequality, although their standard of living has been relatively low. Post-industrial societies with predominantly capitalist economies, including Canada and most of Western Europe, have higher overall living standards, accompanied by severe income disparity. The low-income countries of Latin America and Africa (including Mexico, Brazil, and Zaire) exhibit the most pronounced inequality of income.

Source: *Peters Atlas of the World* (1990); updates by the authors from United Nations Development Programme (1999).

industrial era (the broken line) to show social inequality increasing once again. That is, as the Information Revolution moves ahead, we are experiencing some economic polarization suggesting that the long-term trend may differ from what Kuznets observed half a century ago (Nielsen & Alderson, 1997).

## INEQUALITY IN CANADA

Canada stands apart from most European nations in never having had a titled aristocracy. Even though we have never known a caste system that rigidly ranks categories of people, our racial history shows that there is a strong relationship between race and social class.

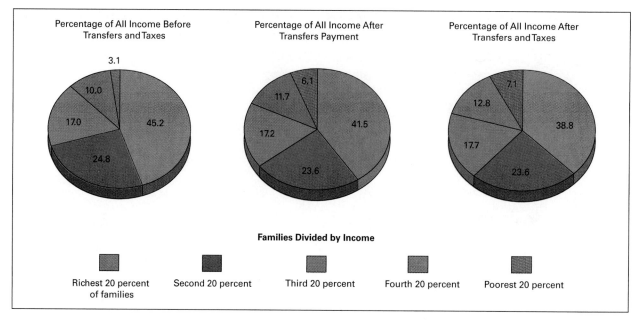

Percentage of All Income Before
Transfers and Taxes

3.1
10.0
17.0
24.8
45.2

Percentage of All Income After
Transfers Payment

6.1
11.7
17.2
23.6
41.5

Percentage of All Income After
Transfers and Taxes

7.1
12.8
17.7
23.6
38.8

**Families Divided by Income**

Richest 20 percent of families | Second 20 percent | Third 20 percent | Fourth 20 percent | Poorest 20 percent

**FIGURE 8–3    Distribution of Income Before and After Transfer Payments and Taxes, Canada, 1998.**

Source: Statistics Canada, (2000o).

Canadian society is highly stratified. Not only do the rich have most of the money, but also they receive the most schooling, enjoy the best health, and consume the lion's share of goods and services. Such privilege contrasts sharply with the poverty of tens of thousands of women and men who worry about paying next month's rent and getting food on the table. Many Canadians think that we live in a "middle-class society," but is this really the case?

## INCOME, WEALTH, AND POWER

One important dimension of economic inequality involves **market income**, *wages or salary from work, and earnings from investments and private pensions*. Statistics Canada reports that the average market income for all families in 1998 was $55 224, up 4.7 percent from the previous year after adjusting for inflation (Statistics Canada, 2000o). The first part of Figure 8–3 shows the distribution of market income among all families in the country in 1998. The second and third part of Figure 8–3 illustrates the Canadian family income after transfer payments—federal and provincial payments to families and individuals—and taxes. Despite the important equalizing effect of taxes and transfer payments, large differences remain between Canadian families earning the most and those earning the least. Even after taxes and transfer payments, the richest 20 percent of families (with an average total income of $96 175) received 38.8 percent of all income, while the bottom 20 percent

(with an average total income of $17 662) received only 7.1 percent.

Table 8–2 takes a closer look at the 1996 census data on income distribution after transfer payments. The highest-paid 5 percent of Canadian families earned more than $122 145 in 1995, while the lowest-paid 5 percent earned less than $8815. In short, while a small number of people have very high incomes, the majority make do with far less.

Income is only one component of a person's or family's **wealth**, *the total value of money and other assets, minus outstanding debts*. Wealth—including stocks, bonds, and real estate—is distributed even less equally than market income. The richest 20 percent of Canadian families own roughly four-fifths of the country's entire wealth. High up in this privileged category are the wealthiest 10 percent of families—the "very rich," who control over half of all property.

When financial assets are balanced against debts, the lowest-ranking 30 percent of families have virtually no wealth at all. The poorest 10 percent of families have a negative wealth—that is, they actually live in debt.

In Canada, wealth is an important source of power. Therefore, the small proportion of families that controls most of the wealth also has the ability to shape the agenda of the entire society. As explained in Chapter 12 (Economics and Politics), some sociologists argue that such concentrated wealth undermines democracy because the political system ends up serving the interests of the "super-rich" families.

## OCCUPATIONAL PRESTIGE

Beyond generating income, work is also an important source of prestige. We commonly evaluate each other according to the kind of work we do, respecting those who do what we consider important work while looking down on others with less prestigious jobs.

Sociologists monitor the relative social prestige of various occupations (Counts, 1925; Hodge, Treiman, & Rossi, 1966; NORC, 1999). Table 8–3 on page 192 shows that people accord high prestige to occupations—such as physicians, lawyers, professors, and engineers—that require extensive training and generate high income. By contrast, less prestigious work—as a waitress or janitor, for example—requires less ability and schooling, and also pays less. Occupational prestige rankings are much the same in all industrial societies (Ma, 1987; Lin & Xie, 1988).

In any society, high-prestige occupations go to privileged categories of people. In Table 8–3, for example, the highest-ranking occupations are dominated by men. Quite a bit farther down the list we find Registered Nurse, a category dominated by women. Similarly, going up from the bottom, notice how many low-prestige jobs are commonly performed by people from visible minority groups.

## SCHOOLING

Industrial societies expand schooling, but some people receive much more than others. In 1999, while almost three out of four Canadians over 25 had completed high school, only about 47 percent were university or college graduates (Statistics Canada, 2000j).

Schooling affects both occupation and income, since most (but not all) of the better-paying, white-collar occupations shown in Table 8–3 (192) require a university or college degree or other advanced study. By contrast, most blue-collar jobs, which bring lower income and social prestige, require less schooling.

## ANCESTRY, RACE, ETHNICITY, AND GENDER

A class system rewards individual talent and effort. But nothing affects social standing as much as does birth into a particular family. Ancestry has a strong bearing on future schooling, occupation, and income. Research suggests that at least half of the richest individuals in the U.S.—those with hundreds of millions of dollars in wealth—derived their fortunes mostly from inheritance (Thurow, 1987; Queenan, 1989). The situation is much the same in Canada (Porter, 1965; Clement, 1975; Olsen, 1980; Brym & Fox, 1989). By the same token, inherited poverty just as surely shapes the future of others.

| TABLE 8-2 Canadian Census Family Income, 1995 | |
|---|---|
| Highest paid... | Annually earns at least |
| 5% | 122 145 |
| 10 | 98 655 |
| 20 | 77 910 |
| 30 | 65 460 |
| 40 | 55 685 |
| 50 | 46 951 |
| 60 | 39 015 |
| 70 | 31 115 |
| 80 | 23 190 |
| 90 | 15 135 |
| 95% | $8 815 |

Source: 50th percentile from Statistics Canada, Catalogue No. 93F0029XDB96007 (1998q); other figures estimated based on data from Statistics Canada, Catalogue No. 93F0029XDB96007 (1998q).

Race and ethnicity, too, are closely linked to social position in Canada. While the average 1995 employment income was $26 474, visible minorities earned an average $22 498 (about 15 percent less), while Aboriginal people earned $17 382, or 34 percent below the national average. The larger proportion of young and part-time workers among visible minorities and Aboriginals accounts for much of this income disparity. In addition, the varying levels of education of these three populations make a difference: visible minorities tend to have a higher level of education than other Canadians, but Aboriginals are disadvantaged in this respect. Nevertheless, even after discounting the difference in age and work patterns, visible minorities earn 4 percent less than other Canadians, despite their higher education level. The average Aboriginal income, on the other hand, is about 14 percent below the national average, even after removing the impact of a younger age structure, different work patterns, and lower education (Statistics Canada, 1998i).

Of course, both men and women are found in families at every social level. Yet, on average, women claim less income, wealth, and occupational prestige than men. Even more important, households headed by women are much more likely to be poor than those headed by men. Chapter 10 (Gender Stratification) fully examines the link between gender and social stratification.

## TABLE 8–3  International Occupational Prestige Score for Selected Occupations

| Occupation | Score | Occupation | Score |
|---|---|---|---|
| Physician | 77.9 | Garage mechanic | 42.9 |
| University professor | 77.6 | Mechanic, repairman | 42.8 |
| Lawyer, trial lawyer | 70.6 | Shopkeeper | 42.4 |
| Head of large firm | 70.4 | Printer | 42.3 |
| Engineer, civil engineer | 70.3 | Typist, stenographer | 41.6 |
| Banker | 67.0 | Police officer | 39.8 |
| Airline pilot | 66.5 | Tailor | 39.5 |
| High school teacher | 64.2 | Foreperson | 39.3 |
| Pharmacist | 64.1 | Soldier | 38.7 |
| Armed forces officer | 63.2 | Carpenter | 37.2 |
| Member of the clergy | 59.7 | Mason | 34.1 |
| Artist | 57.2 | Plumber | 33.9 |
| Teacher, primary teacher | 57.0 | Sales clerk | 33.6 |
| Journalist | 54.9 | Mail carrier | 32.8 |
| Accountant | 54.6 | Driver, truck driver | 32.6 |
| Civil servant, minor | 53.6 | Bus, tram driver | 32.4 |
| Nurse | 53.6 | Miner | 31.5 |
| Building contractor | 53.4 | Barber | 30.4 |
| Actor, actress | 51.5 | Shoemaker, repairer | 28.1 |
| Bookkeeper | 49.0 | Waiter | 23.2 |
| Travelling salesperson | 46.9 | Farm hand | 22.9 |
| Farmer | 46.8 | Street vendor, peddler | 21.9 |
| Electrician | 44.5 | Janitor | 21.0 |
| Insurance Agent | 44.5 | Servant | 17.2 |
| Office clerk | 43.3 | Street sweeper | 13.4 |

Source: Treiman (1977).

## SOCIAL CLASSES IN CANADA

As we have explained, rankings in a rigid caste system are obvious to all. Defining the social categories in a more fluid class system, however, is not so easy. Followers of Karl Marx see two major social classes—capitalists and proletariat; other sociologists, however, find six classes (Warner & Lunt, 1941) or even seven (Coleman & Rainwater, 1978). Still others side with Max Weber, believing that people form not clear-cut classes, but a multidimensional status hierarchy.

Defining classes in Canada is difficult, in part due to the relatively low status-consistency. Especially toward the middle of the hierarchy, people's social position on one dimension may contradict their standing on another. A government official, for example, may have the power to administer a multimillion-dollar budget, yet earn a modest personal salary. Similarly, many members of the clergy enjoy ample prestige but only moderate power and low pay. Or consider a lucky day-trader in the stock market who wins no special respect but makes a lot of money.

Finally, the social mobility characteristic of class systems—again, most pronounced near the middle—means that social position may change during a person's lifetime, further blurring class boundaries. With these problems in mind, we can describe four general rankings: the upper class, the middle class, the working class, and the lower class.

### THE UPPER CLASS

Families in the upper class—5 percent of the Canadian population—have annual earnings of at least $120 000, and many earn 10 times that much. As a general rule, the more a family's income comes from inherited wealth in the form of stocks and bonds, real estate, and other investments, the stronger a family's claim to being upper class.

In 1996, the *Financial Post* profiled the richest 50 people or families in Canada, estimating their combined wealth at $39 billion, or about 1 percent of the total national wealth. These richest people had a *minimum* net worth of $145 million and included more than eight billionaires (Hamilton, 1996). In 2000, *Forbes* listed 15 Canadian billionaires (up from 5 in 1996), with a combined fortune of $US 46.2 billion (*Forbes*, 2000). Canadian media giant Kenneth Thompson has assets valued at $US 16.1 billion himself, making him the richest person in Canada and the tenth richest in the world. The upper class are Karl Marx's "capitalists"—those who own most of the means of production and, thus, most of the nation's private wealth. Many upper-class people work as top executives in large corporations and as senior government officials. Historically, though less so today, the upper class has comprised white Anglo-Saxon Protestants (WASPs) (Porter, 1965; Clement, 1975).

**Upper-uppers.** The *upper-upper class*, sometimes called "bluebloods" or simply "society," includes less than 1 percent of the Canadian population. Membership is almost always the result of birth, as suggested by the old quip that the easiest way to become an "upper-upper" is to be born one. Most of these families possess enormous wealth that is primarily inherited. For this reason, members of the upper-upper class are said to have *old money*.

Set apart by their wealth, members of the upper-upper class live in exclusive neighbourhoods such as Westmount in Montreal, Forest Hill in Toronto, or the Uplands in Victoria. Their children typically attend private secondary schools with others of similar background and complete their formal education at high-prestige colleges and universities. In the historical pattern of European aristocrats, they study liberal arts rather than vocational skills. Women of the upper-upper class often do volunteer work for charitable organizations. While helping the larger community, these activities also build networks that broaden this elite's power (Ostrander, 1980, 1984).

**Lower-uppers.** Most upper-class people actually fall into the *lower-upper class*. To most of us, the 3 to 4 percent of the Canadian population in this category seem every bit as privileged as the upper-upper class. The major difference is that lower-uppers are the "working rich"; earnings rather than inherited wealth are the primary source of their income. While so-called "new-rich" families generally live in expensive neighbourhoods, most do not gain entry into the clubs and associations of "old-money" families.

## THE MIDDLE CLASS

Including 40 to 45 percent of the Canadian population, the large middle class has a tremendous influence on our culture. Television and movies usually show middle-class people, and most commercial advertising is directed at these average consumers. The middle class contains far more ethnic and racial diversity than does the upper class.

**Upper-middles.** The top third of this category is termed the *upper-middle class*, based on their above-average income in the range of $75 000 to $120 000 a year. Such income allows upper-middle-class families to accumulate considerable property—a comfortable house in a fairly expensive area, several automobiles, and investments. Most upper-middle-class children receive university educations, and postgraduate degrees are common. Many go on to high-prestige occupations as physicians, engineers, lawyers, accountants, or business executives. Lacking the power of the richest people to influence national or international events, upper-middles often play an important role in local political affairs.

**Average-middles.** The rest of the middle class falls close to the centre of the Canadian class structure. *Average middles* typically work in less prestigious white-collar occupations as bank tellers, middle managers, or sales clerks, or in highly skilled blue-collar jobs such as electrical work and carpentry. Household income falls between $45 000 and $75 000 a year, which is roughly the national average.

Middle-class people generally accumulate a small amount of wealth over the course of their working lives, mostly in the form of a house and a retirement account. Most middle-class men and women are likely to be high school graduates, and many send their children to seek post-secondary education at a college or university, but usually close to home to save on cost of accommodation.

## THE WORKING CLASS

About one-third of the population is working class (sometimes called the "lower-middle class"). In Marxist terms, the working class forms the core of the industrial proletariat. Their blue-collar occupations generally yield a family income of between $20 000 and $45 000 a year, somewhat below the national average, and they have little or no wealth. Working-class families thus are vulnerable to financial problems caused by unemployment or illness.

Many working-class jobs provide little personal satisfaction—requiring discipline but rarely imagination—and subject workers to continual supervision. These jobs also offer fewer benefits such as dental insurance and pension plans. About half of working-class families own their homes, usually in lower-cost neighbourhoods. College or university is a goal that only about one-third of working-class children realize.

*Life expectancy is closely related to social-class position. In cities around the world, poor people—especially young males—who struggle to get by have a strikingly high rate of death and injury from illness, accident, and violence. Some individuals caught up in poverty engage in perilous behaviour because they have little reason to think the future will be brighter than the present.*

## THE LOWER CLASS

The remaining 20 percent of our population forms the lower class. Low income makes their lives unstable and insecure. According to the National Council of Welfare, more than 4.9 million people in Canada lived in poverty in 1998 (National Council of Welfare, 2000). Many belong to the so-called "working poor." They are just slightly better off than unemployed people, holding low-prestige jobs that provide little satisfaction and minimal income. Barely half manage to complete high school, and fewer than one in three ever reach college or university.

Society segregates the lower class, especially when the poor are racial or ethnic minorities. Only some lower-class families own their own home, typically in the least desirable neighbourhoods. Although poor neighbourhoods are found in our inner cities, lower-class families also live in rural areas.

## THE DIFFERENCE CLASS MAKES

September 2, 1995—Hull, Quebec My bike leans right, leaving the trail for the rest station that offers a stretch and a drink of water. Here I encounter Linda, a 30-something woman having trouble with her inline skates. Eye contact and a perplexed look are a call for help, so I walk over to see what I

might offer. Several of her boot buckles require adjustment. Close up, she doesn't look well. "Are you okay?" I ask gently. "Very tired," Linda responds, and goes on to explain why. Now divorced, she cannot pay off her debts with one low-income job, an 11 a.m.–7 p.m. shift as a computer clerk at a bank in town. Catching five or so hours of sleep after work, she then drives across the bridge to Ottawa, where she sits at another computer, processing catalogue orders from 2 a.m. until 10 a.m That leaves just enough time to drive back to Hull, shower and change her clothes, and start all over again at the bank . . .

## HEALTH

Health is closely related to social standing. Children born into poor families are more likely to die—from disease, neglect, accidents, or violence—during their first year of life than are children born into privileged families. Among adults, people with the lowest incomes were five times more likely than those from the highest income groups to describe their health as only fair or poor. Moreover, richer Canadians live, on average, longer because they eat more nutritious foods, live in safer and less stressful environments, and are much more likely to have dental care (Federal, Provincial and Territorial Advisory Committee on Population Health, 1999).

## VALUES AND ATTITUDES

Some cultural values, too, vary from class to class. The "old rich" have an unusually strong sense of family history, since their position is based on wealth passed down from generation to generation (Baltzell, 1979). With their birthright privileges, upper-uppers also favour understated manners and tastes, while many "new-rich" people practise *conspicuous consumption*, using homes, cars, and even airplanes as *status symbols* that make a statement about their social position.

Affluent people with greater education, financial security, and understanding of "political correctness" are also more openly tolerant of controversial behaviour such as homosexuality. Working-class people, who grow up in an atmosphere of greater supervision and discipline and are less likely to attend college or university, tend to be less tolerant (Kohn, 1977; NORC, 1999). Political affiliations flow along class lines. By and large, more privileged people support the Alliance, Progressive Conservative, or Liberal party, while less advantaged people favour the NDP. But issue by issue, the pattern is more complex. A desire to protect wealth prompts well-off people to take a more conservative approach to *economic* issues, favouring, for example, lower taxes. But on *social* matters, such as abortion and gay rights, highly educated, more affluent people are more liberal. People of lower social standing, on the other hand, tend to be economic liberals, favouring government social programs, but to support a more conservative social agenda (Angus Reid Group Inc. 1996e, 1998b).

## FAMILY AND GENDER

Finally, social class also shapes family life. Generally, lower-class families are somewhat larger than middle-class families, due to earlier marriage and less use of birth control. In addition, working-class parents encourage children to conform to conventional norms and to respect authority figures. Parents of higher social standing transmit a different "cultural capital" to their children, teaching them to more freely express their individuality and imagination (Kohn, 1977; McLeod, 1995).

Of course, the more money a family has, the better the parents can develop their children's talents and abilities. According to some calculations, the cost of raising a child in Canada to age 18 is more than $150 000 (Scott, 1996). Given the large amount of money involved, it stands to reason that only those families with the highest incomes can afford to pay for such luxuries as private schools. Privilege, then, tends to beget privilege, as family life reproduces the class structure in each generation.

Class also shapes our world of relationships. Elizabeth Bott (1971) found that most working-class couples divide their responsibilities according to gender; middle-class couples, by contrast, are more egalitarian, sharing more activities and expressing greater intimacy. More recently, Karen Walker (1995) discovered that working-class friendships typically provide material assistance; middle-class friendships, however, are likely to involve shared interests and leisure pursuits.

## SOCIAL MOBILITY

Ours is a dynamic society marked by significant social movement. Earning a college or university degree, landing a higher-paying job, or marrying someone who earns a high income contributes to *upward social mobility*, while dropping out of school, losing a job, or getting divorced (especially for women) may signal *downward social mobility*.

Over the long term, though, social mobility is not so much a matter of individual changes as changes in

*When these children living in poverty grow up, they will be five times more likely than adults from the highest income groups to describe their health as only fair or poor.*

society itself. During the first half of this century, for example, industrialization expanded the Canadian economy, pushing up living standards. Even without being very good swimmers, so to speak, people rode a rising tide of prosperity. More recently, *structural social mobility* in a downward direction has dealt many people economic setbacks.

Sociologists distinguish between shorter- and longer-term changes in social position. **Intragenerational social mobility** refers to *a change in social position occurring during a person's lifetime*. **Intergenerational social mobility**, *upward or downward social mobility of children in relation to their parents*, is important because it reveals long-term changes in society that affect almost everyone.

## MYTH VERSUS REALITY

In few societies do people think about getting ahead as much as they do in Canada and the United States. "Moving up" has historically been seen as central to North American culture. But is there as much social mobility as we like to think?

Studies of intergenerational mobility (almost all of which, unfortunately, have focussed exclusively on

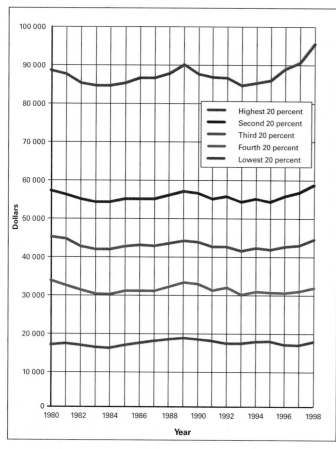

**FIGURE 8–4    Average Income, Canadian Families, 1980–1998**

Source: Statistics Canada, (2000o).

growth of white-collar work over the course of this century have boosted living standards.

3. **Within a single generation, social mobility is usually minimal.** Most young families increase their income over time (Duncan, 1998). Yet very few people move "from rags to riches." While sharp rises or falls in individual fortunes may attract public attention, most social mobility involves limited movement *within* one class level rather than striking moves *between* classes.

4. **Social mobility since the 1970s has been uneven.** Real income (that is, adjusted for inflation) rose during the 20th century, until the 1970s when it hit a plateau. During the 1980s, real income remained stagnant for many people, rising again by the end of the 1990s. But these general trends mask the experiences of different categories of people, as the next section explains.

## MOBILITY BY INCOME LEVEL

In Figure 8–4, we see how Canadian families at different income levels fared between 1980 and 1998 (in 1998 dollars). Well-to-do families (the highest 20 percent, but not necessarily the same families over the entire period) saw their incomes jump from an average $88 765 in 1980 to $96 175 in 1998. By contrast, the lowest-income 20 percent saw their income increase by $255, from $17 407 in 1980 to $17 662 in 1998. People in the second lowest and middle quintiles actually lost ground over these two decades by 5.3 and 2.7 percent respectively (Statistics Canada, 2000o).

A comparison of the change in income level over these two decades reveals an interesting pattern. In both decades, average income decreased in the first half and increased in the second half. However, the change in income of these five income groups was different over these two decades. In both decades, the initial decline was particularly steep for the lower income groups. During the recovery, on the other hand, the lower income groups also recovered more quickly in the 1980s, whereas the recovery in the latter part of the 1990s left the lower half of income earners behind. By 1998, the average income of the highest income group was almost 10 percent higher than in 1980, whereas the lowest income group was still almost 3 percent below their 1990 income level. If this trend continues, it will be echoing that of the U.S., where the highest income earners experienced a sharp increase in after-tax earnings since 1980 of 44 percent, while those at the lowest income levels had on average a lower income in 1998 than in 1980 (Macionis, 2001).

National Map 8–1 shows that average income differs significantly between Canada's census districts.

men), show that almost 40 percent of the sons of blue-collar workers attained white-collar jobs and about 30 percent of sons born into white-collar families ended up doing blue-collar work. *Horizontal social mobility*—changing occupation at one class level—is even more common, so that overall about 80 percent of sons showed some type of social mobility in relation to their fathers (Blau & Duncan, 1967; Featherman & Hauser, 1978; Hout, 1998).

Research points to four general conclusions about social mobility in Canada and the United States:

1. **Social mobility, at least among men, has been fairly high.** The widespread notion that Canada and the United States have a lot of social mobility is true. Mobility is what we would expect in an industrial class system.

2. **The long-term trend in social mobility has been upward.** Industrialization, which greatly expanded the North American economies, and the

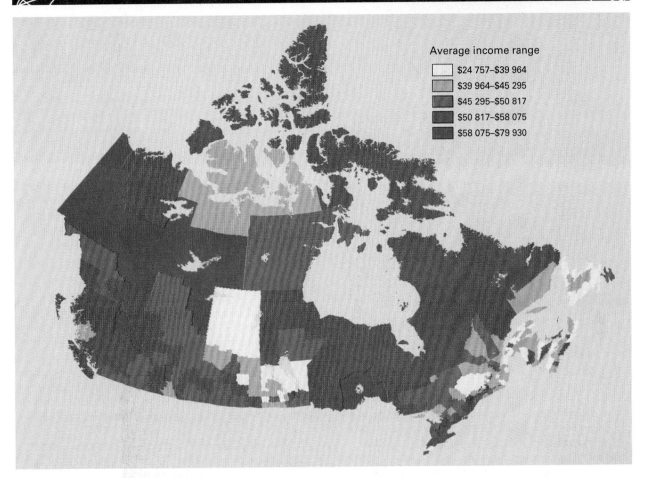

**NATIONAL MAP 8–1   Average Income across Canada, 1995 (by census district)**

This map shows the average per family income by census district based on the 1996 census. The richest and poorest areas are not spread randomly across Canada. Looking at the map, what patterns do you see in the distribution of income across Canada? Do these patterns support our assertion linking affluence to urban living and poverty to rural places?

Source: Statistics Canada, (1998b).

## MOBILITY BY GENDER

Historically, women have had less chance for upward mobility than men, since most working women hold clerical jobs (such as secretary) and service positions (such as waitress) that offer few promotions. In addition, when marriages end in divorce (as almost a third do), women commonly experience downward social mobility, since they may lose not only income but a host of benefits, including retirement contributions, dental care, and insurance coverage (Weitzman, 1996; Eichler, 1997; Benoit, 2000a).

Over time, however, the earnings gap between women and men has been narrowing. Canadian women working full time in 1967 earned 58.4 percent

as much as men working full time; by 1997, women earned just under 73 percent as much. Unfortunately, much of this change was due to a *stagnation* in men's earnings through the 1980s, while the income of women increased (Statistics Canada, 2000m).

## THE GLOBAL ECONOMY AND THE CANADIAN CLASS STRUCTURE

Underlying shifts in the Canadian class structure is global economic change. Much of the industrial production that gave Canadian workers high-paying jobs a generation ago has moved overseas. With less industry at home, Canada now serves as a vast market for

*Faced with little opportunity to improve their lives, many young people fall into despair and numb themselves with drugs. Substance abuse is at crisis levels among the Innu children of Davis Inlet.*

industrial goods such as cars, stereos, cameras, and computers produced in Japan, South Korea, and elsewhere.

High-paying jobs in manufacturing, held by 31 percent of Canadian workers in 1951, support 20 percent of workers today (Krahn & Lowe, 1998). In their place, the economy offers "service work," which often pays far less. Thus, traditionally high-paying corporations such as the auto-manufacturers now employ fewer people, while McDonald's continues to expand—and fast-food clerks make only a fraction of what steel workers earn.

The global reorganization of work is not bad news for everyone. On the contrary, the global economy is driving upward social mobility for educated people who specialize in law, finance, marketing, and computer technology. Moreover, global economic expansion helped push up the North American stock market almost ten-fold between 1980 and 2000, reaping huge profits for families with money to invest.

But the same trend has hurt many average workers, some of whom have seen their factory jobs relocate overseas. Moreover, many companies have downsized—cutting the ranks of their workforce—to become competitive in world markets. As a result, although 61.3 percent of two-partner families in 1997 had two partners earning incomes—a notable increase from 32.7 percent in 1967—many families are work-

ing harder simply to hold on to what they have (Lowe, 2000; Statistics Canada, 2000o).

## POVERTY IN CANADA

Social stratification creates both "haves" and "have-nots." All systems of social inequality, therefore, generate poverty—or at least **relative poverty,** *the deprivation of some people in relation to those who have more.* A more serious but preventable problem is **absolute poverty**, *a deprivation of resources that is life-threatening.*

As Chapter 9 (Global Stratification) explains, about 800 million human beings around the world—one in seven—are at risk of absolute poverty. Even in affluent Canada, families go hungry, live in inadequate housing, and suffer poor health because of wrenching poverty.

### THE EXTENT OF POVERTY

The closest measure to a poverty line that we have in Canada is the Low Income Cut-Off level (LICO) calculated by Statistics Canada. According to this measure, a family has an income below the LICO if it spends more than 64 percent of its after-tax income (or 55 percent of its pre-tax income) on the necessities of food, clothing, and shelter, including corrections for different family sizes and the cost of living in particular communities. For example, in 1998, a family of four living in a large urban area (more than 500 000 people) with an after-tax income below $27 890 lived below the LICO. Similarly, this same family would have to earn a before-tax income above $33 063 in order to be living above the LICO (Statistics Canada, 2000o).

The choice of poverty measure between before- and after-tax income is an important one because it has a dramatic impact on the estimated level of poverty. Traditionally, Canadians have looked at before-tax income, and using this measure Statistics Canada estimated that 16.9 percent of Canadians lived below the LICO in 1998. This is the measure used by the National Council of Welfare in the estimate of the number of Canadians living in poverty. However, a strong case can be made for analyzing after-tax income because of Canada's progressive taxation system, under which those with a higher income pay a greater proportion of their income to taxes. Using after-tax income, Statistics Canada estimates that about 12.2 percent of Canadians lived below the LICO in 1998.

While thinking about the best way to measure poverty, we should remember that families with incomes below the LICO would on average need an additional $6638 in order to rise above the LICO. What this means is that, on average, four-person families in large urban areas that earn less than the LICO earn just a little more than $21 000 per year after taxes.

The remainder of the chapter will use the traditional pre-tax measure of income.

## WHO ARE THE POOR?

Although there is no single profile of poor people, poverty is pronounced among certain categories of our population. Where these categories overlap, the problem is especially serious.

**Age.** A generation ago, the elderly were at greatest risk for poverty, but no longer. From 34 percent in 1980, the poverty rate for seniors over the age of 65 plummeted to 18.7 percent in 1997, or 662 000 elderly poor. The poverty rate of the elderly has fallen due to better retirement programs from private employers and government. Still, with the number of older people increasing, about 13 percent of the poor are elderly people.

Today, the burden of poverty falls most heavily on children. In 1997, 19.8 percent of people under age eighteen (1.4 million children) were poor. Tallied another way, more than 4 in 10 of the Canadian poor are children under age eighteen (Statistics Canada, 1999c).

**Race and ethnicity.** The poverty rates for visible minorities and Aboriginals are much higher than the national average. The 1995 poverty rate of both groups was around twice the national average—36 percent among visible minorities and more than 44 percent among Aboriginals.[1] The situation is particularly dismal for Aboriginal children—three out of five of them live below the poverty line. Among Aboriginal youth ages 6 to 14, about one in every two is poor; this contrasts with the national average of about one in five for this age group (Statistics Canada, 1998i).

**Gender and family patterns.** Of all poor people, 55 percent are female and 45 percent are male. This disparity reflects the fact that women who head households bear the brunt of poverty. Of all female lone-parent families, 53 percent earn less than the LICO. The comparative figure for males is 23 percent.

The term **feminization of poverty** describes *the trend by which women are overrepresented among the poor.* Analyzing differences between males and females, we notice that unattached females have higher poverty rates than do unattached males and that the difference is largest among seniors—39.4 percent of unattached females were poor compared to 28.9 percent of unattached male seniors. Once women have fallen into

poverty they also tend to remain poor for a longer period of time than men do. Among those over age 65 who were poor in 1998, 14 percent of the women had been poor for at least six years, whereas only 3.3 percent of the men had been poor for that long (Statistics Canada, 2000o).

**Urban and rural poverty.** The highest concentration of poverty is in Canada's largest cities: 40 percent of the total number of people living below the poverty line in 1995 lived in Toronto, Montreal, or Vancouver (at the time, 33 percent of Canada's population lived in these three cities). Nevertheless, many poor people do live in rural areas. National Map 8–2 on page 200 provides a picture of the proportion of people in different areas of Canada that live below the poverty line.

## EXPLAINING POVERTY

For one of the richest nations on earth to contain millions of poor people raises serious questions. It is true, as some analysts remind us, that most poor people in Canada are far better off than the poor in other countries—for example, health care and education is publicly funded here. Nevertheless, poverty harms the overall health of millions of people in this country.

What are the causes of poverty? One approach holds that *the poor are primarily responsible for their own poverty.* Throughout our history, people in Canada have valued self-reliance, convinced that social standing is mostly a matter of individual talent and effort. This view sees society offering plenty of opportunity to anyone able and willing to take advantage of it. From this point of view, the poor are those who cannot or will not work—women and men with fewer skills, less schooling, and little motivation.

In a study of Latin American cities, the anthropologist Oscar Lewis (1961) concluded that the poor become trapped in a *culture of poverty,* a lower-class subculture that can destroy people's ambition to improve their lives. Socialized in poor families, children become resigned to their plight, producing a self-perpetuating cycle of poverty.

An alternative position, argued by William Julius Wilson (1996a, b), holds that *society is primarily responsible for poverty.* Wilson points to the loss of jobs in our inner cities as the primary cause of poverty, claiming there simply is not enough work to support families. Thus, Wilson sees any apparent lack of trying on the part of the poor as a *result of little opportunity* rather than a *cause of poverty.* From this point of view, Oscar Lewis's analysis amounts to "blaming the victims" for their own suffering (Ryan, 1976). To combat poverty, Wilson argues the government should fund jobs that move people from welfare to work, and provide affordable child care for low-income mothers and fathers.

---

[1] For technical reasons the calculations of the poverty rate among Aboriginals exclude those living on reserves and those living in the Yukon Territory, Northwest Territories and Nunavut. If the calculations included the population living on reserves, the poverty rate would likely be even higher, since the income of Aboriginals is generally higher among those living outside reserves.

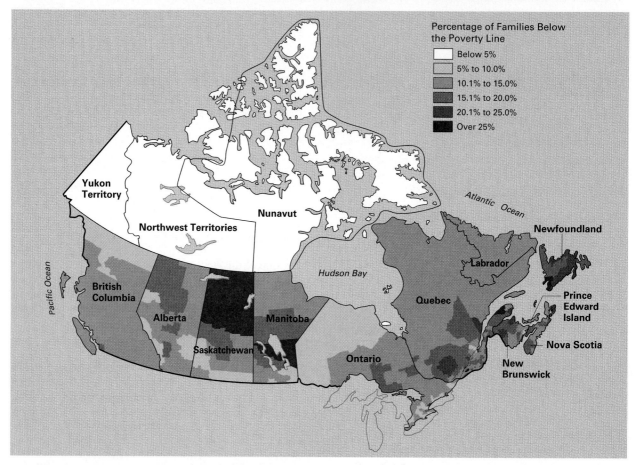

**NATIONAL MAP 8–2    Percentage of Families Below the Poverty Line, Canada, 1995**

This map shows that some rural areas have the lowest rates of poverty in Canada. But the highest rates of poverty can also be found in rural areas. Why is that?

Note: Data missing from the Yukon Territory, Northwest Territories, and Nunavut.

Source: Statistics Canada, (1998b).

**Critical evaluation.** As Figure 8–5 on page 201 shows, the Canadian public is evenly divided over whether government or people themselves are primarily to blame for poverty (World Values Survey, 1994), and both sides have evidence to support their positions. Government statistics show that at least 27 percent of the non-elderly families below the LICO in 1998 did not have any member that received an income or wage during that year (Statistics Canada, 2000o). Such a fact seems to support the "blame the poor" position, since a major cause of poverty is *not holding a job*.

But the *reasons* that people do not work are more in step with the "blame society" position. Middle-class women may be able to combine working and child

rearing, but this is much harder for poor women who cannot afford child care, and few employers provide child-care programs for their employees. Moreover, as William Julius Wilson explains, many people are idle not because they are avoiding work, but because there are not enough jobs. In short, most poor people in Canada find few opportunities and alternatives (Popkin, 1990; Schiller, 1994; Edin & Lein, 1996; Wilson, 1996a; Pease & Martin, 1997).

But not all poor people are jobless, and the *working poor* command the sympathy and support of people on both sides of the poverty debate. In 1998, 20 percent of the non-elderly families with the lowest incomes had two or more wage earners, and an additional 34 per-

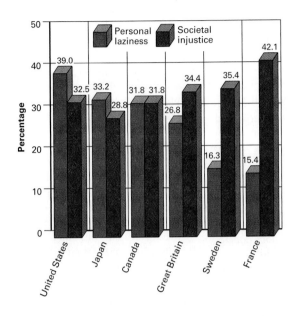

*Even two full-time workers earning minimum wage in Canada cannot keep a family of four above the poverty line in an urban area of more than 500 000 residents.*

**FIGURE 8–5    Assessing the Causes of Poverty**

*Survey Question:* "Why are there people in this country who live in need?" Percentages reflect respondents' identification of either "personal laziness" or "societal injustice" as the primary cause of poverty.

Note: Percentages for each country do not add up to 100 because the figure omits less frequently identified causes of poverty.

Source: World Values Survey (1994).

cent had one wage or income recipient (Statistics Canada, 2000o). From another angle, almost 4 percent of all married and common-law couples had a total family income below the poverty line even though both partners were earners. It is clear that most poor families remained poor *despite* employment. A key cause for "working poverty" is that even two full-time workers earning minimum wages—in 2001, ranging from $5.50 per hour in Newfoundland to $7.60 in British Columbia—cannot keep a family of four above the poverty line in an urban area with a population of more than 500 000.

To sum up, individual ability and personal initiative do play a part in shaping everyone's social position. However, the weight of sociological evidence points toward society—not individual character traits—as the primary source of poverty. Society must be at fault because the poor are *categories* of people—female heads of families, Aboriginal people, people isolated from the

larger society in inner-city neighbourhoods—who face special barriers and limited opportunities.

## HOMELESSNESS

Many low-income people in Canada cannot afford even basic housing. There is no precise count of homeless people, but experts estimate that in 1996 there were 20 000 homeless in Montreal and about the same number of street youth in Toronto (Hagan & McCarthy, 1997; Corelli, 1996).

The familiar stereotypes of homeless people—men sleeping in doorways and women carrying everything they own in shopping bags—have recently been undermined by the reality of the "new homeless": some thrown out of work because of plant closings, others forced out of apartments by rising rents, and still others who cannot meet mortgage or rent payments as a result of their low wages. Today, no stereotype paints a complete picture of the homeless.

But virtually all homeless people have one thing in common: poverty. For that reason, the approaches already used in explaining poverty also apply to homelessness. One side of the debate places responsibility on personal traits of the homeless themselves. One-third of homeless people are substance abusers, and one-fourth are mentally ill. Perhaps we should not be surprised that a fraction of 1 percent of our population, for one reason or another, is unable to cope with

# The Bell Curve Debate:
# Are Rich People Really Smarter?

It is rare that the publication of a new book in the social sciences captures the attention of the public. But *The Bell Curve: Intelligence and Class Structure in American Life*, by Richard J. Herrnstein and Charles Murray, did that and more, igniting a firestorm of controversy over why pronounced social stratification divides our society and, just as important, what should be done about it.

*The Bell Curve* is a lengthy book (800 pages) that addresses many important issues and resists simple summarization. But its basic thesis is captured in the following propositions:

1. Something we can describe as "general intelligence" exists; people who have more of it tend to be more successful in their careers than those who have less.

2. At least half the variation in human intelligence (Herrnstein and Murray use figures of 60 and 70 percent) is

transmitted genetically from one generation to another; the remaining variability is due to environmental factors.

3. Over the course of this century—and especially since the Information Revolution—intelligence has become more necessary to the performance of our society's top occupational positions.

4. Simultaneously, the best North American colleges and universities have shifted their admissions policies away from favouring children of inherited wealth to admitting young people who perform best on standardized tests.

5. As a result of these changes in the workplace and higher education, our society is now coming to be dominated by a "cognitive elite," who are, on average, not only better trained than most people but actually more intelligent.

6. Because more intelligent people are socially segregated on the college or university campus and in the workplace, it is no surprise that they tend to pair up, marry, and have intelligent children, perpetuating the "cognitive elite."

7. Near the bottom of the social ladder, a similar process is at work: Increasingly, poor people are individuals with lower intelligence, who live segregated from others and who tend to pass along their modest abilities to their children.

Resting on the validity of the seven assertions presented above, Herrnstein and Murray then offer, as an eighth point, a basic approach to public policy:

8. To the extent that membership in the affluent elite or the impoverished underclass is rooted in intelligence and determined mostly by genetic

our complex and highly competitive society (Bassuk, 1984; Whitman, 1989).

On the other side of the debate, advocates assert that homelessness results from societal factors, including a lack of low-income housing, unemployment, and the increasing number of low-income jobs (Hagan & McCarthy, 1997; Kozol, 1988; Schutt, 1989; Bohannan, 1991). Supporters of this position point out that one-third of all homeless people are entire families, and that children are the fastest-growing subcategory among the homeless.

No one disputes that a large proportion of homeless people are personally impaired to some degree, although it is difficult to untangle how much is cause and how much effect. But structural changes in the Canadian economy, the closing down of mental institutions in recent decades, limited government support

for lower-income people—all have certainly contributed to homelessness.

## CLASS, WELFARE, POLITICS, AND VALUES

We have now presented many facts about social inequality. In the end, however, what we think about wealth and poverty depends not just on facts but also on our politics and values. As we might expect, the idea that social standing reflects personal merit is popular among well-off people—an issue highlighted in the Controversy & Debate box. The opposing idea that society should spread wealth more equally finds favour among those with few advantages (NORC, 1999).

In comparative perspective, Figure 8–5 on page 201 shows that people in Canada are more likely than people in many other industrial countries to

inheritance, programs to assist underprivileged people (from school lunches to equity policies) will have little practical benefit.

Most social scientists joined *The Bell Curve*'s critics. In response to the book's thesis, they first questioned exactly what one means by "intelligence," doubting that anyone's innate abilities can ever be separated from the effects of socialization. Of course rich children perform better on intelligence tests, they explained: These people have had all the advantages! Some critics dismiss the concept of "intelligence" outright as a product of phony science. Others take a more moderate road, claiming that we should not think of "intelligence" as the sole cause of achievement, since recent research indicates that mental abilities and life experiences are interactive, each affecting the other.

Second, while most researchers who study intelligence agree that genetics does play some part in transmitting intelligence, the consensus is that at most 25 to 40 percent is inherited—roughly half what Herrnstein and

Murray contend. Therefore, critics conclude, *The Bell Curve* wrongly misleads readers into thinking that social stratification is both natural and inevitable. In its assumptions and conclusions, moreover, *The Bell Curve* amounts to little more than a rehash of the social Darwinism popular a century ago, which heralded the success of industrial tycoons as merely "the survival of the fittest."

Perhaps, as one commentator suggested, the more society seems like a jungle, the more people think of stratification as a matter of blood rather than upbringing. But despite its flaws and exaggerations, *The Bell Curve*'s success raises many issues we cannot easily ignore. Can our democratic society tolerate the "dangerous knowledge" that elites (including not only rich people but our political leaders) are at least somewhat more intelligent than the rest of us? What of *The Bell Curve*'s description—which few challenge—that elites in such countries as Canada and the U.S. are increasingly insulating themselves from social problems, including

crime, homelessness, and poverty? Acknowledging that such problems have become worse in recent years, how do we resist the easy explanation that poor people themselves are hobbled by limited ability? And, perhaps most basically, what should be done to ensure that all people have the opportunity to develop their abilities as fully as possible?

*Continue the debate . . .*

1. *Do you agree that "general intelligence" exists? Why or why not?*

2. *Overall, do you think that people of higher social position are more intelligent than those of low social status? If you think intelligence differs by social standing, which factor is cause and which is effect? How do you know?*

3. *Do you think sociologists should study controversial issues such as differences in human intelligence? Why or why not?*

Sources: Herrnstein & Murray (1994), Jacoby, Russell, & Glauberman (1995), and Taylor (1995).

blame individuals rather than society for poverty. Our cultural emphasis on individual responsibility encourages us to see successful people as personally worthy and the poor as personally lacking. Such attitudes go a long way to explain why our society spends much more than other industrial nations on education (to promote opportunity) but much less on public assistance programs or child-care services (which directly support the poor).

Most members of our society accept a high level of income disparity, and many hold a harsh view of the

poor. Moreover, to the extent that we define poor people as undeserving, we perceive public assistance programs at best as a waste of money, and at worst as a threat to personal initiative.

Finally, the drama of social stratification extends far beyond Canada's borders. The most striking social disparities are found not by looking inside one country but by comparing living standards in various parts of the world. In Chapter 9, we broaden our focus by investigating global stratification.

# SUMMARY

1. Social stratification refers to categories of people ranked in a hierarchy. Caste systems, common in agrarian societies, are based on ascription and permit little or no social mobility. Class systems, with an element of meritocracy, are found in industrial societies and allow social mobility based on individual achievement.

2. The Davis-Moore thesis states that social stratification is universal because it is useful to a society. In class systems, unequal rewards attract the most able people to the most important jobs.

3. For Karl Marx, conflict in industrial societies places the capitalists, who own the means of production and seek profits, in opposition to the proletariat, who provide labour in exchange for wages.

4. Max Weber identified three distinct dimensions of social stratification: economic class, social status or prestige, and power. Together, these form a multidimensional hierarchy of socioeconomic standing (SES).

5. Gerhard and Jean Lenski explained that historically, advancing technology tends to increase social inequality. Some reversal of this trend occurs in industrial societies, as represented by the Kuznets Curve; even so, the new post-industrial society shows an increase in economic inequality.

6. The upper class (5 percent of the population) includes this country's richest and most powerful individuals. Members of the upper-upper class, or the "old-rich," typically inherit great wealth; those in the lower-upper class, or "new rich," depend on earned income.

7. The middle class (40 to 45 percent) enjoys reasonable financial security, but only some of these people (the upper-middle class) have significant wealth. With below-average incomes, members of the working class or lower-middle class (33 percent) typically perform blue-collar work, and only one-third of their children acquire post-secondary education.

8. About one-fifth of the Canadian population belongs to the lower class. Aboriginal people and women are disproportionately represented in the lower class.

9. Social mobility is common in Canada, as it is in other industrial societies; typically, however, there are only small changes from one generation to the next.

10. The growing global economy has increased the wealth of rich families in Canada, but stalled or even lowered the standard of living of low-income families.

11. The government classifies 5 million people as having incomes below the Low Income Cut-off (LICO) level, often referred to as the "poverty line." Young people and women—particularly in a single-parent family—face the highest probability of being poor.

12. The "culture of poverty" thesis suggests that poverty is caused by shortcomings in the poor themselves. An alternative approach claims that poverty is caused by a society's unequal distribution of income and wealth.

13. The Canadian cultural emphasis on individual responsibility helps explain why public assistance for the poor is controversial.

# KEY CONCEPTS

**social stratification** (p. 178) a system by which a society ranks categories of people in a hierarchy

**social mobility** (p. 178) a change of position in a stratification system

**caste system** (p. 178) social stratification based on ascription

**class system** (p. 179) social stratification based on both birth and individual achievement

**meritocracy** (p. 179) social stratification based on personal merit

**status consistency** (p. 180) the degree of consistency in a person's social standing across various dimensions of inequality

**structural social mobility** (p. 182) a shift in the social position of a large number of people due to changes in society itself

**ideology** (p. 183) cultural beliefs that justify social stratification

**Davis-Moore thesis** (p. 183) the assertion that social stratification is universal because it benefits the operation of a society

**capitalist** (p. 185) one who owns a factory or other productive enterprise in pursuit of profits

**proletariat** (p. 185) people who sell their productive labour

**alienation** (p. 185) the experience of powerlessness in social life

**blue-collar occupation** (p. 186) lower-prestige work that involves mostly manual labour

**white-collar occupation** (p. 186) higher-prestige work that involves mostly mental activity

**socioeconomic status** (p. 187) a composite social ranking based on various dimensions of inequality

**market income** (p. 190) wages or salary from work, earnings from investments and private pensions

**wealth** (p. 190) the total value of money and other assets, minus outstanding debts

**intragenerational social mobility** (p. 195) a change in social position occurring during a person's lifetime

**intergenerational social mobility** (p. 195) the social standing of children in relation to their parents

**relative poverty** (p. 198) the deprivation of some people in relation to others who have more

**absolute poverty** (p. 198) a deprivation of resources that is life-threatening

**feminization of poverty** (p. 199) the trend by which women are overrepresented among the poor

## CRITICAL-THINKING QUESTIONS

1. How is social stratification a creation of society rather than simply an expression of individual differences?

2. How do caste and class systems differ? What do they have in common?

3. Would you be in favour of class-based affirmative action? That is, should Canadian society give people born to lower-class families an edge in university and college admissions and in company hiring? Why or why not?

4. Our society is always ready to assist the "worthy" poor, including elderly people whom we do not expect to fend for themselves. At the same time, we are less generous toward the "unworthy poor," able-bodied people who, we think, could take care of themselves but do not. If this is so, why has Canadian society not done more to reduce poverty among children, who surely fall into the "worthy" category?

## APPLICATIONS AND EXERCISES

1. Sit down with parents, grandparents, or other relatives and try to assess the social position of your family over the past three generations. Has social mobility taken place? Why or why not?

2. Develop several simple questions that, taken together, would let you measure someone's social class position. The trick is to decide exactly what you think "social class" really means. Then try your questions on several adults, refining the questions as you proceed.

3. Visit the social services office that oversees financial assistance to people with low incomes in your community. See what you can learn about the effect of the recent welfare reforms.

 ## SITES TO SEE

**www.pearsoned.ca/macionis**
Visit the Web site that accompanies this text to review material in this chapter, take practice tests, and find additional Internet links.

**ccsd.ca**
**www.cfc-efc.ca**
Here are two Web sites that are worth a visit to learn more about poverty in Canada. The first is operated by the Canadian Council on Social Development, and the second by Child & Family Canada. Both sites offer many documents and statistics on poverty.

**www.ncwcnbes.net**
This site operated by the National Council of Welfare includes the annual Poverty Profile that uses Statistics Canada data to illustrate poverty in Canada.

**www.napo-onap.ca**
The National Anti-Poverty Organization is an advocacy group for Canada's poor. This site includes a list of myths related to poverty in Canada.

# GLOBAL STRATIFICATION

*August 11, 1999. After many days on the open ocean, 150 men, women, and children drop off a ship into the cold Pacific and wade to shore at Gilbert Bay in the Queen Charlotte Islands. They come from Fujian province in China with dreams of getting rich in North America. But first they must work off the cost of the trip—more than $50 000 per person. With limited language and formal skills, they are forced to accept jobs paying less than minimum wage. The result: many work 34 hours each week just to pay the interest on their loan.*

*At least four more boats came to Canada in 1999 carrying about 600 Fujians who claimed refugee status in Canada. By December 2000, 272 had been returned to China, 67 remained in custody, 191 had been released while waiting for their refugee hearing—and 149 of those released had disappeared (Mooney & Xue, 2000).* ■

The fact is that billions of people in the world who work hard every day are miserably poor. As this chapter explains, while poverty is a reality in Canada, this problem is both more severe and more widespread in the low-income countries of the world.

## GLOBAL STRATIFICATION: AN OVERVIEW

Chapter 8 (Social Stratification) described social inequality in Canada. In global perspective, however, social stratification is far more pronounced. Recall that the 40 percent of the Canadian population with the lowest incomes earns just 20 percent of the national income (see Figure 8–3 on page 190). The 40 percent of the global population living in low-income countries, however, receives just 11 percent of world income. At the other extreme, the 40 percent of the Canadian population with the highest incomes earns just over 60 percent of our national income; the 15 percent of the global population living in high-income countries earns almost as large a share of the global income (56 percent). Because global income is so concentrated, even people in Canada with an income below Statistics Canada's Low Income Cut-Off measure live far better than the majority of the earth's people. Figure 9–1, on page 208 shows the extent of poverty in some of the world's middle- and low-income countries. The average person living in a high-income nation such as Canada is quite well-off by world standards. At the top of the pyramid, the wealth of the world's three richest *individuals* roughly equals the annual economic output of the world's 48 poorest *countries* (Annan, 1998).

### A WORD ABOUT TERMINOLOGY

A familiar model for describing the global stratification that developed after the Second World War labelled the rich, industrial countries the "First World," the less industrialized, socialist countries the "Second World," and the non-industrialized, poor countries the "Third World." But the Three Worlds label was a product of cold war politics by which the capitalist West (the First World) faced off against the socialist East (the Second World), while other nations (the Third World) remained more or less on the sidelines. The sweeping changes in Eastern Europe and the collapse of the former Soviet Union means that a distinctive Second World no longer exists.

**Percentage of Global Income**

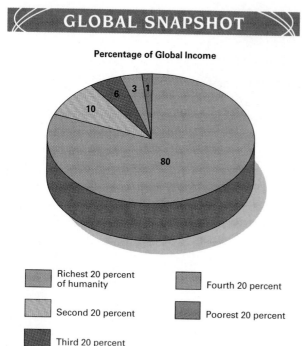

Richest 20 percent of humanity

Second 20 percent

Third 20 percent

Fourth 20 percent

Poorest 20 percent

**FIGURE 9–1    Percentage Living on Less than $2 per day, Selected Countries, 1990s**

**Note:** Less than 1 percent of the Canadian population is estimated to live on less than $2 a day.

Source: World Bank (2001).

A second problem is that the Three Worlds model lumped together more than 100 countries as the Third World. In reality, some relatively better-off nations of the Third World (such as Chile in South America) have 20 times the per-person productivity seen in the poorest countries of the world (including Ethiopia in Eastern Africa).

These facts call for a modestly revised system of classification. Here, we define *high-income countries* as the richest 55 nations with the highest overall standard of living. Next, the world's 90 *middle-income countries* are somewhat poorer, with economic development more or less typical for the world as a whole. Finally, the remaining 60 *low-income countries* have the lowest productivity and the most severe and extensive poverty.

This new model has two advantages over the older Three Worlds system. First, it focusses on economic development rather than whether societies are capitalist or socialist. Second, it gives a better picture of the relative economic development of various countries because it does not lump together all less-industrialized nations into a single Third World.

Still, classifying more than 200 nations on earth into any three categories ignores many striking differences. These nations have rich and varied histories, speak different languages, and take pride in their distinctive cultures.

Keep in mind, too, that every country on earth is also internally stratified. Thus, the extent of global inequality is actually greater than national comparisons suggest, since the most well-off people in high-income countries (such as Canada) live worlds apart from the poorest people in low-income countries (such as Haiti, Sudan, and India).

## HIGH-INCOME COUNTRIES

In nations where the Industrial Revolution first took place more than two centuries ago, productivity increased one hundred-fold. To understand the power of industrialization, consider that the small European nation of The Netherlands is more productive than the vast continent of Africa south of the Sahara Desert; likewise, tiny Belgium outproduces all of India.

A look back at Global Map 1–1 on page 9 identifies the 55 high-income countries of the world. They include the Canada and United States, most of the nations of Western Europe, Japan, Singapore, and Hong Kong (now part of the People's Republic of China), Australia, and New Zealand.

Taken together, countries with the most developed economies cover roughly 25 percent of the earth's land area—including parts of five continents—and lie mostly in the Northern Hemisphere. In 2000, the population of these nations was around 900 million, or 15 percent of the world's people. About three-fourths of the people in high-income countries live in or near cities.

Significant cultural differences exist among high-income countries—the nations of Europe, for example, recognize more than 30 official languages. But these societies share an industrial capacity that generates, on average, a rich material life for their people. Per capita income ranges from about US$14 500 annually (in Greece and Slovenia) to more than US$25 000 annually (in the United States, Switzerland, and Singapore)—Canada's per capita income figure was US$23 725.[1] In fact, people in high-income countries enjoy more than half the world's total income.

[1] High-income countries have per capita annual income of at least US$14 500. Low-income countries have per capita annual income of US$2500 or less. All data reflect the United Nations' concept of "purchasing power parities" (PPP), which avoids distortion caused by exchange rates when converting all currencies to U.S. dollars. Instead, the data represent the local purchasing power of each nation's currency.

*Japan represents the world's high-income countries, in which industrial technology and economic expansion have produced material prosperity. The presence of market forces is evident in this view of downtown Tokyo (above, left). The Russian Federation represents the middle-income countries of the world. Industrial development has been slower in the former Soviet Union, as socialist economies have performed sluggishly. Residents of Moscow, for example, chafe at having to wait in long lines for their daily needs (above, right). The hope is that the introduction of a market system will raise living standards, although it probably also will increase economic disparity. Bangladesh (right) represents the low-income countries of the world. As the photograph suggests, these nations have limited economic development and rapidly increasing populations. The result is widespread poverty.*

## MIDDLE-INCOME COUNTRIES

*Middle-income countries* have per capita income ranging from US$2500 to US$14 500, roughly the median for the world's *nations* (but above that for the world's *people* since more people live in low-income countries than in high-income countries). Industrialization is limited and exists mostly in cities. About half of the people still live in rural areas and work in agriculture (World Bank, 2001). Especially in the countryside, schooling, health care, adequate housing, and even safe water are hard to come by.

Looking back at Global Map 1–1 (page 9) about 90 of the world's nations fall into the middle-income category. At the high end are the Czech Republic and Hungary. At the low end are Guyana, Albania, Ecuador and China.

One cluster of middle-income countries includes the former Soviet Union and the nations of Eastern Europe (in the past, known as the Second World). These countries had mostly socialist economies until popular revolts between 1989 and 1991 swept aside their governments. Since then, these nations have

begun to introduce market systems, but, so far, the results have been uneven. Some (including the Czech Republic) have improving economies, while in others (including Russia) the living standards have actually fallen.

A second category of less-developed countries is the oil-producing nations of the Middle East (or, less ethnocentrically, Western Asia). These nations—including Saudi Arabia, Oman, and Iran—are very rich, but their wealth is so concentrated that most people do not benefit and remain poor.

The third, and largest, category of middle-income nations includes Argentina and Brazil in South America, as well as Algeria and Botswana in Africa. Although South Africa's white minority lives as well as people in the United States, it, too, is a middle-income nation because its majority black population has far less income.

Taken together, middle-income countries span roughly 50 percent of the earth's land area and include about 2.7 billion people, or almost half of humanity. Some countries (like El Salvador) are far more crowded than others (like Russia), but compared to high-income countries, these societies are densely populated.

*By and large, rich nations such as the United States wrestle with the problem of relative poverty, meaning that poor people get by with less than we think they should have. In poor countries such as Ethiopia, absolute poverty means that people lack what they need to survive. What kind of diet, medical care, and access to clean water do you think families like this one have?*

## LOW-INCOME COUNTRIES

Low-income countries, where most people are very poor, are largely agrarian societies with some industry. Most of these 60 nations, identified in Global Map 1–1 on page 9, are found in Central and East Africa as well as Asia. Low-income countries cover 25 percent of the planet's land area but are home to 40 percent of its people. Population density is, therefore, generally high, although greater in Asian countries (such as Bangladesh and India) than in Central African nations (such as Chad and the Democratic Republic of Congo).

In low-income countries, about 30 percent of the people live in cities; most inhabit villages and farm as their ancestors have done for centuries. In fact, half the world's people are peasants, who, by and large, follow cultural traditions. Without industrial technology, peasants are not very productive, one reason that many endure severe poverty. Hunger, disease, and unsafe housing frame the lives of the world's poorest people.

People living in affluent nations such as Canada find it hard to grasp the scope of want in much of the world. From time to time, televised pictures of famine in very poor countries such as Ethiopia and Bangladesh give us a shocking glimpse of the poverty that makes every day a life-and-death struggle. Behind these images lie cultural, historical, and economic forces that we shall explore in the remainder of this chapter.

## GLOBAL WEALTH AND POVERTY

*November, 1999.* Long Quang lives in a small dilapidated trailer in the Holland Marsh area north of Toronto, with her mother, her husband, and their 15-month-old son. Their home is surrounded by five other trailers and two outhouses for the dozen men who harvest carrots from sunup to sundown six days a week for $500. Being the cook for the camp residents, she does not mind the squalor that surrounds her so much as the boredom of her life in the marsh. Nevertheless, she is glad to be in Canada with her husband.

Quang lives a mere 60 kilometres from Toronto, where Ah-Xiu has achieved what many of the Fujians are hoping for. Since entering Canada 10 years ago, she has now become a Canadian citizen and is the owner of a small clothing factory that employs up to 10 workers—many of them recent refugees from Fujian province. She spent many years to work off the $50 000 she owed the smugglers who brought her to Canada, but now she earns about that amount every year from her small factory—far more than the average annual income of about $2000 that she would earn in her native province (based on Fennell & Xue, 2000).

Low-income nations are home to some rich and many poor people. For most, incomes of only several hundred dollars a year mean the burden of poverty is far greater among them than among the poor of Canada. This does not mean that poverty here is a minor problem. In so rich a country, too little food, substandard housing, and limited access to health care for millions of people—almost half of them children—amounts to a national tragedy. Yet poverty in poor counties is both *more severe* and *more extensive* than in Canada.

## THE SEVERITY OF POVERTY

*Poverty in poor countries is more severe than it is in rich countries.* The data in Table 9–1 show why. The first column of figures gives gross national product (GNP) for countries at each level of economic development.[2] A large, industrial nation such as the United States had a 1999 GNP of more than $8 trillion; Canada's GNP was about $726 billion. Comparing GNP figures shows that the world's high-come nations produce goods and services worth thousands of times the value of the production in the poorest countries.

The second column of figures in Table 9–1 indicates per capita GNP in terms of what the United Nations (1995) calls "purchasing power parities"—what people can buy using their income in the local economy. The per capita GNP for high-income countries such as Canada, Switzerland, and the United States is very high—on average over US$20 000. For middle-income countries, such as Malaysia and Poland, the figures are much lower—about US$5000 on average. In the world's low-income countries, per capita annual income is typically less than US$2000, and in many cases just a few hundred dollars. In Ethiopia or Sierra Leone, for example, a typical person labours all year to make what the average worker in Canada earns in less than a week.

The last column of Table 9–1 provides a measure of quality of life in the various nations. This index, calculated by the United Nations, combines income, education (extent of adult literacy and average years of schooling), and longevity (how long people typically live). Index values are decimals that fall between hypothetical extremes of 1 (highest) and zero (lowest). By this calculation, Canadians enjoy the highest quality of life (.935), with residents of the United States close behind (.929). At the other extreme, people in the African nations of Ethiopia and Sierra Leone have the lowest quality of life (.309 and .252, respectively).

A key reason that quality of life differs so much around the world is that economic productivity is lowest in precisely the regions of the globe where population growth is highest. Figure 9–2 on page 212 shows the division of global population and global income for countries at each level of economic development. High-income countries are by far the most advantaged, with 56 percent of global income supporting just 15 percent of humanity. In middle-income nations, 44 percent of the world's people earn 34 percent of global income. This leaves 40 percent of the planet's population with just 11 percent of global income. In short, for every dollar received by individuals in a low-income country, someone in a high-income nation takes home $14.

**Relative versus absolute poverty.** The distinction between relative and absolute poverty, made in the last chapter, has an important application to global

---

[2] Gross national product refers to all the goods and services produced by a nation's economy in a given year, plus income from abroad, minus income sent abroad.

| TABLE 9–1 Wealth and Well-Being in Global Perspective, 1998–1999* | | | |
|---|---|---|---|
| Country | Gross National Product (US$ billion) | GNP per Capita (US$) | Human Development Index |
| **High-income countries** | | | |
| Canada | 726 | 23 725 | 0.935 |
| United States | 8350 | 30 600 | 0.929 |
| Australia | 426 | 22 448 | 0.929 |
| Sweden | 184 | 20 824 | 0.926 |
| Japan | 3043 | 24 041 | 0.924 |
| United Kingdom | 1234 | 20 883 | 0.918 |
| France | 1294 | 21 897 | 0.917 |
| Switzerland | 196 | 27 486 | 0.915 |
| **Middle-income countries** | | | |
| **Eastern Europe** | | | |
| Czech Republic | 126 | 12 289 | 0.843 |
| Hungary | 106 | 10 479 | 0.817 |
| Poland | 306 | 7894 | 0.814 |
| Russian Federation | 929 | 6339 | 0.771 |
| **Latin America** | | | |
| Argentina | 414 | 11 324 | 0.837 |
| Mexico | 752 | 7719 | 0.784 |
| Brazil | 1062 | 6317 | 0.747 |
| **Eastern Asia** | | | |
| Malaysia | 181 | 7963 | 0.772 |
| Thailand | 345 | 5599 | 0.745 |
| China, People's Republic | 4112 | 3291 | 0.706 |
| **Western Asia** | | | |
| Lebanon | 18 | 4129 | 0.735 |
| Turkey | 394 | 6126 | 0.732 |
| **Africa** | | | |
| Algeria | 142 | 4753 | 0.683 |
| Botswana | 10 | 6032 | 0.593 |
| **Low-income Countries** | | | |
| **Latin America** | | | |
| Honduras | 14 | 2254 | 0.653 |
| Haiti | 11 | 1407 | 0.440 |
| **Asia** | | | |
| India | 2144 | 2149 | 0.563 |
| **Africa** | | | |
| Chad | 6 | 816 | 0.367 |
| Ethiopia | 38 | 599 | 0.309 |
| Sierra Leone | 2 | 414 | 0.252 |

\* These data are based on "purchasing power parity" calculations that avoid currency distortion by showing the local purchasing power of each domestic currency.

Source: Income data from World Bank (2001), human development data from United Nations Development Programme (2000).

inequality. People living in high-income countries generally focus on the *relative poverty*, meaning that some people lack resources that others take for granted. Relative poverty, by definition, cuts across every society, whether rich or poor.

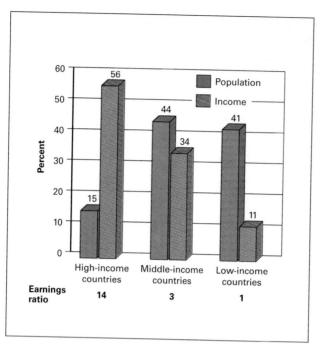

**FIGURE 9–2    The Relative Share of Global Income (PPP) and Population by Income Level, 1999**

Source: Based on data in World Bank (2001).

More important in a global perspective, however, is *absolute poverty*, a lack of resources that is life threatening. Human beings in absolute poverty lack the nutrition necessary for health and long-term survival. To be sure, some absolute poverty exists in Canada. But such immediately life-threatening poverty strikes only a small proportion of the Canadian population; in low-income countries, by contrast, one-third or more of the people are in desperate need.

Since absolute poverty is deadly, one global indicator of this problem is the median age at death. Global Map 9–1 identifies the age by which half of all people born in a nation die. In high-income countries, most people die after the age of 75; in low-income nations, half of all deaths occur among children under the age of 10.

## THE EXTENT OF POVERTY

*Poverty in poor countries is more extensive than it is in rich nations such as Canada.* Chapter 8 (Social Stratification) indicated Statistics Canada declares that about 16.4 percent of the population lives below the Low Income Cut-off level in 1998. In low-income countries, however, most people live no better than the poor in Canada, and many are far worse off. As Global Map 9–1 shows, the high death rates among children indicate that absolute poverty is greatest there, where half the population is malnourished. In the world as a whole, at any given time, 15 percent of the people (about 1 billion) suffer from chronic hunger, which leaves them less able to work and puts them at highrisk for disease (Kates, 1996; United Nations Development Programme, 1999).

The typical adult in a high-income nation, such as Canada, consumes about 3500 calories a day, too much for optimal health. The typical adult in a low-income country not only does more physical labour but consumes just 2000 calories a day. The result is undernourishment: too little food or not enough of the right kinds of food.

In the 10 minutes it takes to read through this section of the chapter, about 300 people in the world who are sick and weakened from hunger will die. This amounts to about 40 000 people a day, or 15 million people each year. Clearly, easing world hunger is one of the most serious responsibilities facing humanity today.

## POVERTY AND CHILDREN

Death comes early in low-income societies, where families lack adequate food, safe water, secure housing, and access to health care. Organizations combating child poverty estimate that at least 100 million city children in low-income countries beg, steal, sell sex, or work for drug gangs to provide income for their families. Such a life almost always means dropping out of school and places children at high risk for disease and violence. Many girls, with little or no access to medical assistance, become pregnant—a case of children who cannot support themselves being forced to have still more children.

Perhaps 100 million of the world's children leave their families altogether, sleeping and living on the streets as best they can. Perhaps half of all street children are found in Latin America (One World, 1998). Some 10 000 homeless children roam throughout Mexico City (Ross, 1996). In Brazil, millions of street children live in makeshift huts, under bridges, or in alleyways. In Rio de Janeiro, known to many in Canada as Brazil's seaside resort, police try to keep the number of street children in check; at times, death squads sweep through a neighbourhood in a bloody ritual of "urban cleansing." Several hundred street children are murdered in that city each year (Larmer, 1992; U.S. House of Representatives, 1992).

## POVERTY AND WOMEN

In high-income societies, the work women do is typically unrecognized, undervalued, and underpaid. In poor societies, even more so. Workers in the sweatshops found in poor countries are mostly women.

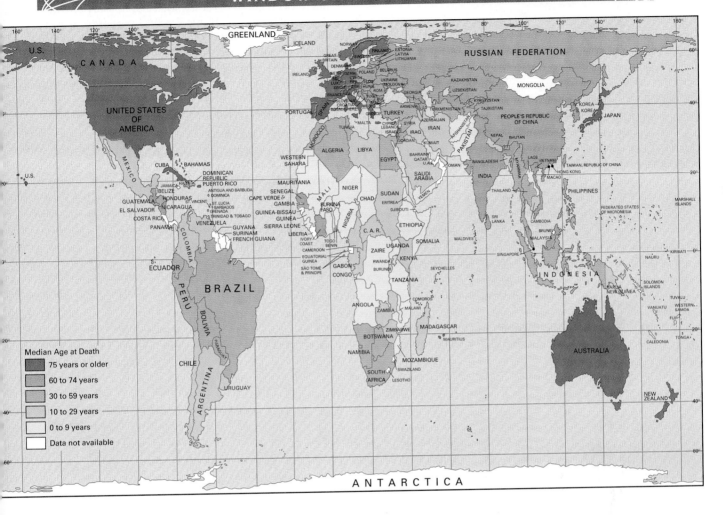

**GLOBAL MAP 9–1   Median Age at Death in Global Perspective**

This map identifies the age below which half of all deaths occur in any year. In the high-income countries of the world, including Canada, it is the elderly who face death—that is, people ages 75 or older. In middle-income countries, including most of Latin America, most people die years or even decades earlier. In low-income countries, especially in Africa and parts of Asia, even children die prematurely, half of them never reaching their tenth birthdays.

Sources: The World Bank (1993); map projection from *Peters Atlas of the World* (1990).

Families in low-income societies depend on women's wages. At the same time, tradition bars many women from attending school, and gives them primary responsibility for child rearing and maintaining the household. The United Nations estimates that in low-income countries, men own 90 percent of the land, a far greater gender disparity in wealth than is found in high-income nations. Thus, about 70 percent of the world's 1 billion people living near absolute poverty are women (Hymowitz, 1995).

Women in low-income countries have limited access to birth control (which raises the birth rate) and they typically give birth without the assistance of any trained health personnel. Figure 9–3 on page 214 draws a stark contrast between high- and low-income countries in this regard.

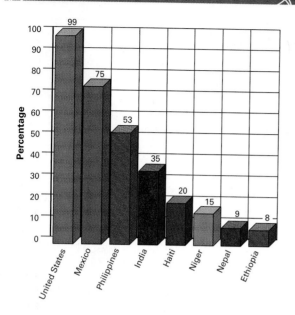

**FIGURE 9–3   Percentage of Births Attended by Trained Health Personnel**

Source: The World Bank (2000).

## SLAVERY

Low-income societies are vulnerable to many problems: hunger, illiteracy, warfare, and slavery. The British Empire banned slavery in 1833; the United States followed suit in 1865. But according to Anti-Slavery International (ASI), as many as 400 million men, women, and children (almost 7 percent of humanity) live today in conditions that amount to slavery (Janus, 1996).

ASI distinguishes four types of slavery. First is *chattel slavery*, in which one person owns another. The number of chattel slaves is difficult to estimate because this practice is against the law almost everywhere. But the buying and selling of slaves still takes place in many countries in Asia, the Middle East, and especially Africa. The Global Sociology box (opposite) describes the reality of one slave's life in the African nation of Mauritania.

A second, more common form of bondage is *child slavery*, in which desperately poor families let their children take to the streets to do what they can to survive. Perhaps 100 million children—many in low- and middle-income countries of Latin America—fall into this category.

Third, *debt bondage* refers to the practice by which employers hold workers by paying them too little to cover their debts. In this case, workers do receive a wage, but not enough to cover the food and housing provided by an employer. Thus, for practical purposes, they are enslaved. The stories of some illegal immigrants to Canada from China are one example of debt bondage.

Fourth, *servile forms of marriage* may also amount to slavery. In India, Thailand, and some African nations, families marry off women against their will. Many end up as slaves, performing work for their husband's family; some are forced into prostitution.

In 1948, the United Nations issued a Universal Declaration of Human Rights, which states, "No one shall be held in slavery or servitude; slavery and the slave trade shall be prohibited in all their forms." Unfortunately, more than 50 years later, the social evil persists.

## CORRELATES OF GLOBAL POVERTY

What accounts for severe and extensive poverty throughout much of the world? The rest of this chapter weaves together explanations from the following facts about low-income societies:

1. **Technology.**   About one-third of people in low-income countries farm the land using human muscle or beasts of burden. Since this energy falls far short of the force of steam, oil, or nuclear power, there is little use of complex machinery.

2. **Population growth.**   As Chapter 22 (Population, Urbanization, and the Environment) explains, low-income countries have the world's highest birth rates. Despite the death toll from poverty, the populations of some countries in Africa, for example, double every 25 years. In these countries, half the people are teenagers or younger. With such numbers entering their childbearing years, the result is a wave of population growth. In recent years, for example, the population of Uganda swelled by 3.0 percent annually, so that even with economic development, living standards have fallen.

3. **Cultural patterns.**   Low-income societies are usually traditional. Adhering to long-established ways of life, people resist innovations—even those that promise a richer material life. The Global Sociology box on page 217 explains why traditional people in India respond to their poverty differently than do poor people in Canada.

4. **Social stratification.**   Low-income societies distribute their wealth very unequally. Chapter 8 (Social Stratification) explained that social inequality is more pronounced in agrarian societies than in industrial societies. In Brazil, for example, half of all farmland is owned by just 1 percent of landowners (Bergamo & Camarotti, 1996).

# GLOBAL SOCIOLOGY

## "God Made Me to Be a Slave"

Fatma Mint Mamadou is a young woman living in north Africa's Islamic Republic of Mauritania. Asked her age, she pauses and smiles. She has no idea when she was born. Nor can she read or write. What she knows is tending camels, herding sheep, hauling bags of water, sweeping, and serving tea to her owners. This young woman is one of perhaps 90 000 slaves in Mauritania.

In the central region of this nation, if one has dark brown skin, it almost always means one is a slave to an Arab owner. Fatma has always accepted her situation; she has known nothing else. She explains in a matter-of-fact voice that she is a slave as was her mother before her. And her grandmother before that. "Just as God created a camel to be a camel"— she shrugs — "he created me to be a slave."

Fatma, her mother, and her brothers and sisters live together in a squatter settlement on the edge of Nauakchott, Mauritania's capital

city. Their home is a two-by-three–metre hut that they built from wood scraps and other building material taken from construction sites. The roof is nothing more than a piece of cloth; there is no plumbing; there is not even any furniture. The nearest water comes from a well that's one kilometre down the road.

*Human slavery continues to exist in the 21st century*

In this region, slavery began 500 years ago, about the time Columbus sailed west toward the New World. Then, Arab and Berber tribes moved across the region spreading Islam and raiding local villages, making slaves of the people. So it has been for dozens of generations since. In 1905, the French colonial rulers of Mauritania banned slavery, and after the nation gained independence in 1961, the new government reaffirmed the ban. But such proclamations have done little to change strong traditions. Indeed, people like Fatma have no idea what "freedom to choose" means.

The next question is more personal: "Are you and other girls ever raped?" Again, Fatma hesitates. With no hint of emotion, she responds, "Of course, in the night the men come to breed us. Is that what you mean by rape?"

Source: Based on Burkett (1997).

---

5. **Gender inequality.** Extreme gender inequality in low-income societies means women lack opportunities and typically have many children. An expanding population, in turn, slows economic development. Thus, many analysts conclude, raising living standards in much of the world depends on improving the social standing of women.

6. **Global power relationships.** A final cause of global poverty lies in the relationships among the nations of the world. Historically, wealth flowed from poor societies to rich nations through **colonialism,** *the process by which some nations enrich themselves through political and economic control of other nations.* The countries of Western Europe colonized much of Latin America and Africa beginning roughly 500 years ago. Such global exploitation of resources allowed some nations to develop economically at the expense of others.

Although 130 former colonies gained their independence during the 20th century, exploitation continues through **neocolonialism** (*neo* is a Greek word for "new"), *a new form of global power relationship that involves not direct political control but economic exploitation by multinational corporations.* **Multinational corporations** are *huge businesses that operate in many countries.* Corporate leaders can impose their will on countries where they do business to create favourable economic conditions, just as colonizers did in the past.

## GLOBAL STRATIFICATION: THEORETICAL ANALYSIS

There are two major explanations for the unequal distribution of the world's wealth and power—*modernization theory* and *dependency theory.* Each theory suggests a different path toward relieving the suffering of hungry people in much of the world.

Brazil's Rio de Janeiro is known the world over as a spectacular resort city. The other side of Rio is poverty, which forces thousands of children and young people to live on the streets. These young people are vulnerable to hunger, disease, and violence. Here, a 17-year-old victim of a gunning lies dead in the streets of the Lapa district near the centre of Rio.

## MODERNIZATION THEORY

**Modernization theory** is *a model of economic and social development that explains global inequality in terms of technological and cultural differences among societies.* Modernization theory emerged in the 1950s, a time when Canadian society was fascinated with new technology. To counter the growing influence of the Soviet Union in much of the world, European and North American policy makers drafted foreign policies that were pro-market, and these policies have been with us ever since. [3]

**Historical perspective.** Modernization theorists point out that as recently as several centuries ago, the entire world was poor. Because poverty has been the norm throughout human history, it is, in fact, *affluence* that demands an explanation.

Affluence came within reach of a growing share of people in Western Europe during the late Middle Ages, as the scope of world exploration and trade expanded. Soon, the Industrial Revolution was under way, transforming first Western Europe and later North America. Industrial technology coupled with the spirit of capitalism created new wealth on an unprecedented scale. At the outset, this new wealth benefited only a few. But industrial technology was so productive that gradually the living standard of even the poorest people began to improve. The spectre of absolute poverty, which had cast a menacing shadow over humanity for its entire history, was finally being routed.

During this century, the standard of living in high-income countries, where the Industrial Revolution began, has jumped at least fourfold. Many middle-income nations in Asia and Latin America are now industrializing, and they, too, are becoming richer. But those low-income countries where many people remain in agriculture have changed little.

**The importance of culture.** Why didn't the Industrial Revolution sweep away poverty the world over? Modernization theory points out that not every society has been eager to seek out new technology. Doing so requires a cultural environment that emphasizes the benefits of materialism and innovation.

Modernization theory identifies *tradition* as the greatest barrier to economic development. In societies with strong family systems and a reverence for the past, "cultural inertia" discourages people from adopting new technologies that would raise their living standards. Even today, many people, from the North American Amish to the Islamic people of Iran to the Semai of Malaysia, oppose technological advances as a threat to their family relationships, customs, and religious beliefs.

Max Weber (1958; orig. 1904–5) found that, at the end of the Middle Ages, Western Europe was quite another story: a cultural environment that favoured change. As explained in Chapter 13 (Family and Religion), the Protestant Reformation had reshaped traditional Catholicism to generate a progress-oriented way of life. Wealth—regarded with suspicion by the Catholic church—became a sign of personal virtue, and the growing importance of individualism steadily replaced the traditional emphasis on kinship and community. Taken together, these new cultural patterns nurtured the Industrial Revolution, which propelled one segment of humanity from poverty to prosperity.

---

[3] The following discussion of modernization theory draws primarily on Rostow (1960, 1978), Bauer (1981), and Berger (1986); see also Firebaugh (1996) and Firebaugh & Sandu (1998).

# A Different Kind of Poverty:
# A Report from India

Most North Americans know that India is one of the poorest nations on earth. A vast country with per capita gross domestic product (GNP) of only US$2149 per year (see Table 9–1 on page 211), India is home to one-third of all the world's hungry people.

But most North Americans do not readily understand the reality of poverty in India. Most of the country's 1 billion people live in conditions far worse than those our society labels "poor." A traveller's first experience of Indian life can be shocking. Madras, one of India's largest cities with 7 million inhabitants, seems chaotic to the outsider, with streets choked by motorbikes and trucks, carts pulled by oxen, and waves of people. Along the roadway, vendors sit on burlap cloth and hawk fruits, vegetables, and cooked food, while people nearby work, talk, bathe, and sleep.

Madras is dotted by more than 1000 shanty settlements, where half a million people from rural villages have come in search of a better life. Shantytowns are clusters of huts built with branches, leaves, and pieces of discarded cardboard and tin. These dwellings offer little privacy, and lack

refrigeration, running water, and bathrooms. The visitor from Canada may feel uneasy in such an area, since the poorest sections of our inner cities seethe with frustration and sometimes explode with violence.

India's people, however, understand poverty differently than we do. No restless young men hang out at the corner, no drug dealers work the streets, and there is little danger of violence. In Canada, poverty often means anger and

*Low-income societies may be poor, but strong traditions and vital families place most people in a network of social support. Thus people endure poverty with the help of their kin, which contrasts to the often isolating poverty in Canada.*

isolation; in India, even shantytowns are organized around strong families—children, parents, and often grandparents—who offer a smile and a welcome to a stranger.

For traditional people in India, life is shaped by *dharma*, the Hindu concept of duty and destiny that teaches people to accept their fate, whatever it may be. Mother Teresa, who worked among the poorest of India's people, goes to the heart of the cultural differences: "Americans have angry poverty," she explains. "In India, there is worse poverty, but it is a happy poverty."

Perhaps we should not describe anyone who clings to the edge of survival as happy. But in India, the strength and support of families and communities, a sense that existence has a purpose, and a worldview that encourages each person to accept whatever life offers—these things ease the poverty. As a result, a visitor may well come away from a first encounter with Indian poverty in confusion: "How can people be so poor, and yet apparently content, active, and *joyful*?"

Source: Based on one of the authors' research in Madras, India, November 1988.

**Rostow's stages of modernization.** Modernization theory holds that the door to affluence is open to all. Indeed, as technological advances diffuse around the world, all low-income societies are gradually industrializing. According to W.W. Rostow (1960, 1978), modernization occurs in four stages:

1. **Traditional stage.** Socialized to venerate the past, people in traditional societies cannot easily imagine how life can be very different. Therefore, they build their lives around families and local communities, and follow well-worn paths that allow for little individual freedom or change. Life is often spiritually rich, but lacking in material abundance.

A century ago, much of the world was in this initial stage of economic development. Nations such as Bangladesh, Niger, and Somalia are still at the traditional stage and remain impoverished.

2. **Take-off stage.** As a society shakes off the grip of tradition, people start to use their talents and imagination, sparking economic growth. A market emerges as people produce goods not just for their own consumption but in order to trade with others for profit. Greater individualism, a willingness to take risks, and a desire for material goods also take hold, often at the expense of family ties and time-honoured norms and values.

*In high-income nations such as the United States and Canada, most parents expect their children to enjoy years of childhood, largely free from the responsibilities of adult life. This is not the case in the low-income nations across Latin America, Africa, and Asia. Poor families depend on whatever income their children can earn, and many children as young as six years of age work full days weaving or performing other manual labour. Child labour lies behind the low prices of many products imported for sale in this country.*

Great Britain reached take-off by about 1800, the United States by 1820, and Canada by about the time of Confederation in 1867 (Krahn & Lowe, 1998). Thailand, a middle-income country in Eastern Asia, is now within this stage. Such development typically is speeded by progressive influences from high-income nations, including foreign aid, the availability of advanced technology and investment capital, and opportunities for schooling abroad.

3. **Drive to technological maturity.** As this stage begins, "growth" is a widely accepted concept that fuels a society's pursuit of higher living standards. A diversified economy drives a population eager to enjoy the benefits of industrial technology. At the same time, however, people begin to realize (and sometimes lament) that industrialization is eroding traditional family and local community life. Great Britain entered this stage by about 1840, the United States by 1860, and Canada at the turn of the 20th century. Today, Mexico, the U.S. territory of Puerto Rico, and South Korea are among the nations driving to technological maturity.

Societies in stage three have greatly reduced absolute poverty. Cities swell with people who leave rural villages in search of economic opportunity; occupational specialization makes relationships less personal, and heightened individualism generates social movements demanding greater political rights. Societies approaching technological maturity also provide basic schooling to all their people, and advanced training for some. The newly educated consider tradition "backward," opening the door to further change. The social position of women steadily becomes more equal to that of

men. Even so, in the short term, the process of development may subject women to unexpected problems, as the Social Diversity box explains.

4. **High mass consumption.** Economic development driven by industrial technology steadily raises living standards, as mass production stimulates mass consumption. Simply put, people soon learn to "need" the expanding array of goods that their society produces.

Britain and the United States entered this stage of development by 1900, soon followed by Canada and other high-income nations. Now entering this level of economic development are two former British colonies that are now prosperous small societies of East Asia: Hong Kong (now part of the People's Republic of China) and Singapore (independent since 1965).

**The role of rich nations.** Modernization theory claims that high-income countries play four important roles in global economic development.

1. **Helping control population.** Since population growth is greatest in the low-income countries, rising population can overtake economic advances. High-income nations can help limit population growth by exporting birth control technology and promoting its use. Once economic development is under way, birth rates should decline as they have in high-income nations, because children are no longer an economic asset.

2. **Increasing food production.** High-income nations can export "high-tech" farming methods to poor nations, raising agricultural yields. Such techniques—collectively referred to as the Green

# Modernization: New Challenges for Women

Around the world, gender inequality is greatest where people are poorest. Economic development, then, depends on giving women opportunities to attend school and to work outside the home, which reduce birth rates and, in the process, weaken traditional male domination.

But modernization also poses dangers for women. Investigating the lives of women in a poor, rural district of Bangladesh, Sultana Alam (1985) reports several hazards.

First, as economic opportunity draws men from rural areas to cities in search of work, women and children must fend for themselves. Some men sell their land and simply abandon their wives, who are left with nothing but their children.

Second, the eroding strength of the family and neighbourhood leaves women who are deserted in this way with little assistance. The same holds true for women who become single through divorce or the death of a spouse. In the past, Alam reports, kin or neighbours readily took in a Bangladeshi woman who found herself alone. Today, as Bangladesh seeks to advance economically, the number of households headed by women is increasing, and most are poor. Rather than enhancing women's autonomy, Alam argues, a new spirit of individualism has lowered the social standing of women.

Third, economic development—as well as the growing influence of Western movies and mass media—undermine women's traditional roles as wives, sisters, and mothers, defining them instead as objects of sexual attention. A new cultural emphasis on sexuality now encourages men in low-income countries to abandon their aging spouses for younger, more physically attractive partners. The same emphasis contributes to the world's rising tide of prostitution.

Thus modernization does not affect men and women in the same ways. In the long run, the evidence suggests, modernization does give the sexes more equal standing. In the short run, however, women may endure setbacks as they face new challenges virtually unknown in traditional societies.

Sources: Based on Alam (1985) and Mink (1989).

---

Revolution—include using new hybrid seeds, modern irrigation methods, chemical fertilizers, and pesticides for insect control.

3. **Introducing industrial technology.** High-income nations can accelerate economic growth in low-income societies by introducing machinery and information technology, which raise productivity. Industrialization also transforms work from farming to skilled industrial and service jobs.

4. **Providing foreign aid.** Investment capital from high-income nations can boost the prospects of low-income societies striving to reach Rostow's "take-off" stage. Foreign aid can help raise agricultural productivity—for example, helping low-income countries use more fertilizer and irrigation. In addition, financial and technical assistance to build power plants and factories improves industrial output.

**Critical evaluation.** Modernization theory has many influential supporters among social scientists (Parsons, 1966; W. Moore, 1977, 1979; Bauer, 1981; Berger, 1986; Firebaugh & Beck, 1994; Firebaugh, 1996; Firebaugh & Sandu, 1998). Moreover, for decades it has shaped the foreign policy of Canada and other high-income nations. Proponents point to rapid economic development in Asia—including South Korea, Taiwan, Singapore, and Hong Kong—as proof that the affluence created in Western Europe and North America is within reach of all countries.

But modernization theory comes under fire from socialist countries (and also from left-leaning analysts in the West) as a thinly veiled defence of capitalism. Its most serious flaw, according to critics, is that modernization simply has not occurred in many low-income countries. The United Nations recently reported that living standards in a number of nations, including Haiti and Nicaragua in Latin America, and Sudan, Ghana, and Rwanda in Africa, are actually lower than they were in 1960 (United Nations Development Programme, 1996).

A second criticism lodged against modernization theory is that it fails to recognize how high-income nations, which benefit from the status quo, often block paths to development for low-income countries. Centuries ago, critics charge, high-income countries industrialized from a position of global *strength*; can we expect low-income countries today to do so from a position of global *weakness?*

Third, critics continue, modernization theory treats high- and low-income societies as worlds individually, ignoring how international relations have affected all nations. To begin with, it was colonization that boosted the fortunes of Europe. This economic windfall has left countries in Latin America and Asia reeling to this day.

Fourth, critics contend that modernization theory holds up the world's most-developed countries as the standard for judging the rest of humanity, thus revealing an ethnocentric bias. We need to remember that our Western conception of "progress" has caused us to degrade the physical environment throughout the world and to rush headlong into a competitive, materialistic way of life.

Fifth, and finally, modernization theory draws criticism for suggesting that the causes of global poverty lie almost entirely in the low-income societies themselves. Critics see this analysis as little more than "blaming the victims" for their own plight. Instead, they argue, an analysis of global inequality should focus as much on the behaviour of *high-income* nations as on that of low-income nations (Wiarda, 1987).

Such concerns reflect a second major approach to understanding global inequality: dependency theory.

## DEPENDENCY THEORY

**Dependency theory** is *a model of economic and social development that explains global inequality in terms of the historical exploitation of poor societies by rich ones.* This analysis places primary responsibility for global poverty at the feet of high-income nations. It holds that high-income countries have systematically impoverished low-income countries, making low-income nations dependent on high-income ones. This destructive process extends back for centuries and persists today.

**Historical perspective.** Everyone agrees that before the Industrial Revolution, there was little affluence in the world. Dependency theory asserts, however, that people living in low-income countries were actually better off economically in the past than their descendants are now. André Gunder Frank (1975), a noted proponent of this theory, argues that the colonial process that helped develop high-income nations also *underdeveloped* poor societies.

Dependency theory is based on the idea that the economic positions of the high- and low-income nations of the world are linked and cannot be understood in isolation from one another. Low-income nations are not simply lagging behind high-income ones on the "path of progress"; rather, the prosperity of the high-income countries came largely at the expense of low- and middle-income nations. In short, then, some nations became rich only because other nations became poor. Both are products of the onset of global commerce that began five centuries ago.

**The importance of colonialism.** Late in the 15th century, Europeans began surveying the Americas to the west, Africa to the south, and Asia to the east, in order to establish colonies. They were so successful in their efforts that a century ago, Great Britain controlled about one-fourth of the world's land, boasting that "the sun never sets on the British Empire."

Meanwhile, Europeans and Africans engaged in a brutal form of human exploitation—the slave trade—from about 1500 until 1850. But even as the world was rejecting slavery, Europeans took control of Africa itself, as Figure 9–4 shows. European powers dominated most of the continent until the early 1960s.

Formal colonialism has almost disappeared from the world. However, according to dependency theory, political liberation has not meant economic autonomy. Far from it: The economic relationship between poor and rich nations still perpetuates the colonial pattern of domination. This neocolonialism is the essence of the capitalist world economy.

**Wallerstein's capitalist world economy.** Immanuel Wallerstein (1974, 1979, 1983, 1984) explains global stratification using a model of the "capitalist world economy." Wallerstein's term *world economy* suggests that the prosperity or poverty of any country is the product of a global economic system. He traces the roots of the global economy to the onset of colonization some 500 years ago, when Europeans began gathering wealth from the rest of the world. Since the global economy is based in high-income countries, it is capitalist in character.[4]

Wallerstein calls the high-income nations the *core* of the world economy. Colonialism enriched this core by funnelling raw materials from around the world to Western Europe, where they fuelled the Industrial Revolution. Today, multinational corporations operate profitably worldwide, channelling wealth to North America, Western Europe, Australia, and Japan.

---

[4] While based on Wallerstein's ideas, this section also reflects the work of Frank (1980, 1981), Delacroix & Ragin (1981), Bergesen (1983), Dixon & Boswell (1996), and Kentor, (1998).

Low-income countries, on the other hand, represent the *periphery* of the world economy. Drawn into the world economy by colonial exploitation, poor nations continue to support rich ones by providing inexpensive labour and a vast market for industrial products. The remaining countries are considered the *semiperiphery* of the world economy. They include middle-income countries such as Mexico and South Africa that have closer ties to the global economic core.

According to Wallerstein, the world economy benefits high-income societies (by generating profits) and harms the rest of the world (by perpetuating poverty). The world economy thus makes low-income nations dependent on high-income ones. This dependency involves the following three factors:

1. **Narrow, export-oriented economies.** Low-income nations produce only a few crops for export to high-income countries. Examples include coffee and fruits from Latin American nations, oil from Nigeria, hardwoods from the Philippines, and palm oil from Malaysia.

   Today's multinational corporations purchase raw materials cheaply in low-income societies and transport them to core nations, where factories process them for profitable sale. Thus, low-income nations develop few industries of their own.

2. **Lack of industrial capacity.** Without an industrial base, low-income societies face a double bind: They depend on high-income nations to buy their inexpensive raw materials, *and* look to high-income nations to sell them whatever expensive manufactured goods they can afford. In a classic example of this dependency, British colonialists encouraged the people of India to raise cotton, but prevented them from weaving their own cloth. Instead, the British shipped Indian cotton to English textile mills in Birmingham and Manchester, manufactured the cloth, and shipped finished goods back for profitable sale in India.

   Dependency theorists claim that the Green Revolution—widely praised by modernization theorists—works the same way. Low-income countries sell cheap raw materials to high-income nations, and then try to buy expensive fertilizers, pesticides, and mechanical equipment in return. Typically, high-income countries profit from this exchange more than do low-income nations.

3. **Foreign debt.** Unequal trade patterns have plunged low-income countries into debt to industrialized nations. Collectively, the low- and middle-income nations of the world owe more than $2.5 trillion, including hundreds of billions of dollars owed to Canada and the United States.

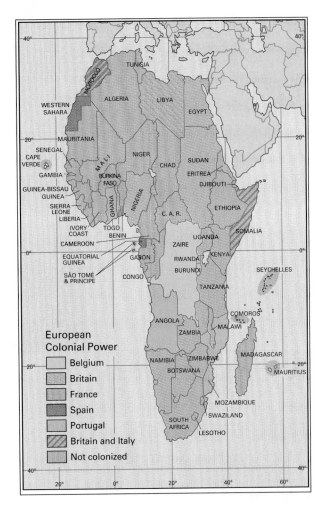

**FIGURE 9–4   Africa's Colonial History**

Such staggering debt paralyzes a country with high unemployment and rampant inflation. Canada is one of the leaders among nations that are trying to develop plans to forgive at least the interest on these loans (Walton & Ragin, 1990; The World Bank, 2000, Scoffield, 2000).

**The role of high-income nations.**   Nowhere is the difference between modernization theory and dependency theory drawn more sharply than in the role each assigns to high-income nations. Modernization theory maintains that high-income societies *produce wealth* through capital investment and technological innovation. Accordingly, as low-income nations adopt pro-growth policies and more productive technology, they, too, will prosper. By contrast, dependency theory views global inequality in terms of how countries *distribute wealth*, arguing that high-income nations have *over*developed themselves as they have *under*developed the rest of the world.

*Was the arrival of the Europeans in the Western Hemisphere a tale of brave explorers or greedy conquerors? The painting* Colonial Domination, *a mural by Mexican artist Diego Rivera, clearly presents the artist's point of view.*

Source: Diego Rivera, *Colonial Domination*. The Granger Collection.© Banco de Mexico, Diego Rivera Museums Trust.

Dependency theorists dismiss the idea that strategies by high-income countries to control population and boost agricultural and industrial output will help raise living standards in low-income countries. Instead, they contend, such programs actually benefit high-income nations, and the ruling elites, not the poor majority, in low-income countries (Lappé, Collins, & Kinley, 1981).

Hunger activists Frances Moore Lappé and Joseph Collins (1986) maintain that the capitalist culture of high-income countries encourages people to think of poverty as somehow inevitable. Following this line of reasoning, poverty results from "natural" processes, including having too many children, and natural disasters such as droughts. But global poverty is far from inevitable; it results from deliberate policies. Lappé and Collins point out that the world already produces enough food to allow every person on the planet to grow quite fat. Moreover, India and most of Africa actually *export* food, even though many of their own people go hungry.

According to Lappé and Collins, the contradiction of poverty amid plenty stems from the high-income nation policy of producing food for profit, not people. That is, corporations in high-income nations cooperate with elites in low-income countries to grow and export profitable crops such as coffee, which means using land that could otherwise produce staples such as beans and corn for local families. Governments of low-income countries support the practice of "growing for export" because they need food profits to repay massive for-eign debt. At the core of this vicious cycle, according to Lappé and Collins, is the capitalist corporate structure of the global economy.

**Critical evaluation.** The main idea behind dependency theory is that no nation develops (or fails to develop) in isolation, because the global economy shapes the destiny of all nations. Citing Latin America and other low-income regions of the world, dependency theorists claim that development simply cannot proceed under the constraints currently imposed by high-income countries. Rather, they call for radical reform of the entire world economy so that it operates in the interests of the majority of people.

Critics, however, charge that dependency theory wrongly treats wealth as a zero-sum commodity, as if no one gets richer without someone else getting poorer. Not so, critics continue, since corporations, small business owners, and farmers can and do create new wealth through their drive and imaginative use of new technology. After all, they point out, the entire world's wealth has swelled sixfold since 1950.

Second, critics continue, dependency theory is wrong in blaming high-income nations for global poverty, because many of the world's poorest countries (like Ethiopia) have had little contact with high-income nations. On the contrary, a long history of trade with high-income countries has dramatically improved the economies of nations that include Sri Lanka, Singapore, and Hong Kong (all former British colonies), as well as South Korea and Japan. In short, say the critics, most evidence shows that foreign investment by high-income nations fosters economic growth, as modernization theory claims, not economic decline, as dependency theorists assert (Vogel, 1991; Firebaugh, 1992).

Third, critics contend that dependency theory is simplistic for pointing the finger at a single factor—world capitalism—as the cause of global inequality (Worsley, 1990). Dependency theory thereby casts low-income societies as passive victims and ignores factors inside these countries that contribute to their economic plight. Sociologists have long recognized the vital role of culture in shaping people's willingness to embrace or resist change. Iran's brand of fundamentalist Islam, for example, has deliberately discouraged economic ties with other countries. Capitalist societies, then, need hardly accept the blame for Iran's economic stagnation.

Nor can high-income societies be saddled with responsibility for the reckless behaviour of foreign leaders whose corruption and militaristic campaigns impoverish their countries (examples include the regimes of Ferdinand Marcos in the Philippines, François Duvalier in Haiti, Manuel Noriega in Panama, Mobutu Sese Seko in Zaire, and Saddam Hussein in Iraq). Some leaders even use food supplies as a weapon in internal political struggles, leaving the masses starving, as in the African nations of Ethiopia, Sudan, and Somalia. Other regimes throughout the world have done little to improve the status of women or to control population growth.

Fourth, critics chide dependency theorists for downplaying the economic dependency fostered by the former Soviet Union. The Soviet army seized control of most of Eastern Europe during the Second World War, and then politically and economically dominated these countries. Many see the uprisings between 1989 and 1991 as a wholesale rejection of the Soviet Union's socialist colonial system.

Fifth, critics fault this approach for offering only vague solutions to global poverty. Most dependency theorists urge low-income nations to end all contact with high-income countries, and some call for nationalizing foreign-owned industries. In other words, dependency theory amounts to a thinly disguised call for some sort of world socialism. In light of the difficulties socialist societies have had in meeting the needs of their own people, critics ask, should we really expect such a system to rescue the entire world from poverty?

## LOOKING AHEAD: GLOBAL STRATIFICATION

Among the most important trends of recent decades is the development of a global economy. Rising production and sales abroad have brought record profits to many corporations and their stockholders. At the same

Hong Kong—until 1998 a British colony—falls within the "semiperiphery" category in Wallerstein's model of the world economy. Although some districts of this city are centres for international business and playgrounds for the rich, other areas—such as this squatter settlement in the foreground—contain thousands of poor people.

time, the global economy has cut factory jobs in this country, hurting many average workers. Since signing the Free Trade Agreement (FTA) in 1989 with the U.S. and the expanded North American Free Trade Agreement (NAFTA) in 1994, which also included Mexico, many manufactring industries in Canada either closed shop or set up in countries where labour and material were cheaper. On the other hand, NAFTA has expanded jobs in the service sector, which currectly dominates the Canadian economy.

In short, the global reorganization of work is not bad news for everyone here at home and abroad. On the contrary, the global economy has pushed the stock market up fivefold between 1980 and 1996, reaping substantial profits for investors. But this trend has hurt many "average" workers whose factories are now overseas. Moreover, many companies "downsizing" to become competitive in world markets have also eliminated some white-collar jobs while creating new ones in service and the high-tech industry.

As this chapter has noted, however, social inequality is far more striking in global context. The

## TABLE 9–2 Modernization Theory and Dependency Theory: A Summary

| | Modernization Theory | Dependency Theory |
|---|---|---|
| **Historical Pattern** | The entire world was poor several centuries ago; the Industrial Revolution brought affluence to high-income countries; as industrialization gradually transforms low-income countries, all nations are likely to become more equal and alike. | Global parity was disrupted by colonialism, which made some countries rich while simultaneously making other countries poor; barring radical change in the world capitalist system, high-income countries will grow richer and low-income countries will become poorer. |
| **Primary Causes of Global Poverty** | Characteristics of low-income countries cause their poverty, including lack of industrial technology, traditional cultural patterns that discourage innovation, and rapid population growth. | Global economic relations—historical colonialism and the operation of multinational corporations—have enriched high-income countries while placing low-income countries in a state of economic dependency. |
| **Role of high-income nations** | High-income countries can and do assist low-income countries through programs of population control, technology transfers that increase food production and stimulate industrial development, and investment capital in the form of foreign aid. | High-income countries have concentrated global resources, conferring advantages on themselves while generating massive foreign debt in low-income countries; high-income countries impede the economic development of low-income countries. |

concentration of wealth among high-income countries, coupled with the grinding poverty typical of low-income nations, may well be the biggest problem facing humanity in the 21st century.

Finding answers to questions about global poverty, therefore, takes on some urgency. Both modernization theory and dependency theory have their merits and their limitations. Table 9–2 summarizes important arguments of each approach.

In searching for truth, we must consider empirical evidence. According to a recent survey of the world conducted by the United Nations (1996), people in about one-third of the world's countries are living far better than they have in the past. These nations—identified in Global Map 9–2—include most of the high-income countries but also dozens of low- and middle-income countries, especially in Asia. These prospering nations stand as evidence that the market forces endorsed by modernization theory can raise living standards.

In another one-third of the world's countries, however, living standards were actually lower in 1996 than they were in 1980. A rising wave of poverty, especially in the nations of sub-Saharan Africa, supports the dependency theory assertion that current economic arrangements are leaving hundreds of millions of people behind.

The picture now emerging from this evidence calls into question both modernization and dependency theories, and each camp is revising its view of proper "paths to development." On the one hand, few societies seeking economic growth now favour a market economy completely free of government control, which challenges orthodox modernization theory and its free-market approach to development. On the other hand, recent upheavals in the former Soviet Union and Eastern Europe demonstrate that a global evaluation

of socialism is currently under way. Since these uprisings follow decades of poor economic performance and political repression, many low-income societies are reluctant to consider a government-controlled path to development. Because dependency theory has historically supported socialist economic systems, changes in world socialism will generate new thinking here as well.

Perhaps the basic problem for everyone to face is hunger. As the Controversy & Debate box on page 226 explains, many analysts wonder if we have the determination to rid the planet of hunger before it overtakes the world.

Although the world's future is uncertain, we have learned a great deal about global stratification. One major insight, offered by modernization theory, is that poverty is partly a *problem of technology*. A higher standard of living for a surging world population depends on raising agricultural and industrial productivity. A second insight, derived from dependency theory, is that global inequality is also a *political issue*. Even with higher productivity, the human community must address crucial questions concerning how resources are distributed—both within societies and around the globe.

Note, too, that while economic development increases living standards, it also places greater strains on the natural environment. Imagine, for example, if the 1 billion people in India were suddenly to become middle class, with automobiles spewing hydrocarbons into the atmosphere and refrigerators drawing all available electricity.

Finally, the vast gulf that separates the world's richest and poorest people puts everyone at greater risk of war, as the most impoverished people act to challenge the social arrangements that threaten their very existence. In the long run, we can achieve peace on this planet only by ensuring that all people live with dignity and security.

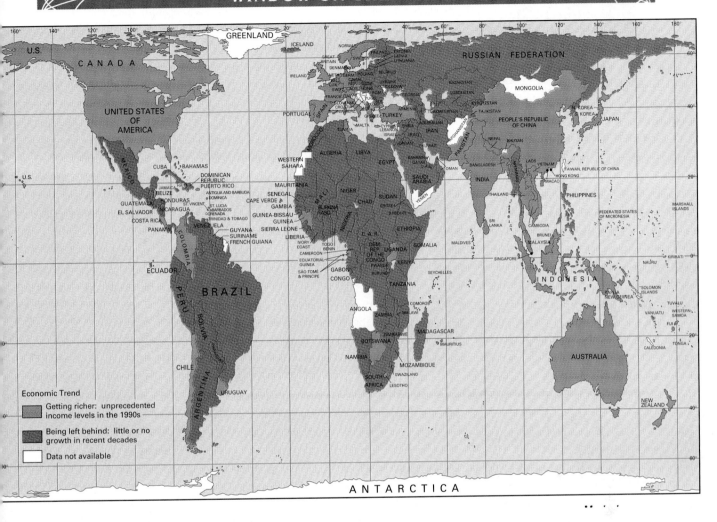

**Economic Trend**

- Getting richer: unprecedented income levels in the 1990s
- Being left behind: little or no growth in recent decades
- Data not available

**GLOBAL MAP 9–2    Prosperity and Stagnation in Global Perspective**

In about 60 nations of the world, people are enjoying a higher standard of living than ever before. These prospering countries include some high-income nations (such as Canada) and some low- and middle-income nations (especially in Asia). For most countries, however, living standards have remained steady or even slipped in recent decades. Especially in Eastern Europe and the Middle East, since the 1980s, some nations have experienced economic setbacks. And in sub-Saharan Africa, some nations are no better off than they were in 1960. The overall pattern is economic polarization, with an increasing gap between high- and low-income nations.

Source: United Nations Development Programme (1996); updated by John Macionis.

## CONTROVERSY & DEBATE

# Will the World Starve?

The animals' feet leave their prints on the desert's face.

Hunger is so real, so very real,

that it can make you walk around a barren tree looking for nourishment.

Not once,

Not twice,

Not thrice . . .

These lines, by Indian poet Amit Jayaram, describe the appalling hunger found in Rajasthan, in northwest India. As this chapter has explained, however, hunger casts its menacing shadow not only over regions of much of Africa, but also parts of Latin America, Asia, and even

North America. Throughout the world, hundreds of millions of adults do not eat enough food to enable them to work. Most tragically, some 10 million children die each year because of hunger. As we begin the 21st century, what are the prospects for

ending the wretched misery of daily hunger?

Pessimists point out that the population of low-income countries is currently increasing by 70 million people annually—equivalent to adding another Egypt to the world every year. Low-income countries can scarcely feed the people they have now; how will they ever feed *twice* as many people a generation in the future?

In addition, hunger forces poor people to exploit the earth's resources by using short-term strategies for food production, which leads to long-term disaster. For example, farmers are cutting rain forests in order to increase their farmland. But without the protective canopy of trees, it is only a matter of time before much of this land turns to desert. Taken together,

## SUMMARY

1. In the world as a whole, social stratification is more pronounced than in Canada. About 15 percent of the world's people live in industrialized, high-income countries such as Canada, and receives 55 percent of all income. Another 45 percent of humanity lives in middle-income countries with limited industrialization and receives about 35 percent of all income. Forty percent of the world's population lives in low-income countries with limited industrialization and earns only 11 percent of global income.

2. While relative poverty is found everywhere, low-income societies grapple with widespread, absolute poverty. Worldwide, the lives of some 1 billion people are at risk due to poor nutrition. About 15 million people, most of them children, die annually from various causes because they lack adequate nourishment.

3. Nearly everywhere in the world, women are more likely than men to be poor. Gender bias against women is greatest in low-income, agrarian societies.

4. The poverty found in much of the world is a complex problem reflecting limited industrial technology, rapid population growth, traditional cultural patterns, internal social stratification, male domination, and global power relationships.

5. Modernization theory maintains that successful development hinges on breaking out of traditional cultural patterns to acquire advanced technology.

6. Modernization theorist W.W. Rostow identifies four stages of development: traditional, take-off, drive to technological maturity, and high mass consumption.

rising populations and short-sighted policies raise the spectre of unprecedented hunger, human misery, and political calamity.

There are also some grounds for optimism, however. Thanks to the Green Revolution, food production the world over is up sharply over the past 50 years, well outpacing the growth in population. Taking a broader view, the world's economic productivity has risen steadily, so that the average person on the planet has more income now to purchase food and other necessities than ever before. This growth has increased daily calorie intake as well as life expectancy, access to safe water, and adult literacy, while around the world infant mortality is half of what it was in 1960.

So what are the prospects for eradicating world hunger? Overall, we see less hunger in both high-income and low-income countries, and in a smaller *share* of the world's people now than back in 1960. But as global population increases, with 90 percent of children born in middle- and low-income countries, the *number* of lives at risk is as great today as ever before. Thus, many low-income countries have made solid gains, but many more are stagnating or even losing ground.

The best-case region of the world is Eastern Asia, where incomes controlled for inflation have tripled over the past generation. Optimists in the global hunger debate point to Asia for evidence that low-income countries can and do raise living standards and reduce hunger. The worst-case region of the world is sub-Saharan Africa, where living standards have fallen over the past decade. It is here that high technology is least evident and birth rates are highest. Pessimists typically look to Africa when they argue that low-income countries are losing ground in the struggle to feed their people.

Television brings home the tragedy of hunger when news cameras focus on starving people in places like Ethiopia and Somalia. But hunger—and the early death from illness—is the plight of millions all year round. The world has the technical means to feed everyone; the question is, do we have the moral determination?

*Continue the debate . . .*

1. *In your opinion, what are the primary causes of global hunger?*

2. *Do you place more responsibility for solving this problem on low-income countries or high-income ones? Why?*

3. *Do you consider yourself an "optimist" or a "pessimist" about the problem of global hunger? Why?*

Sources: United Nations Development Programme (1994, 1995, 1996, 1997, 1998, 1999).

7. Arguing that high-income societies hold the keys to creating wealth, modernization theory claims that high-income nations can assist low-income nations by providing (a) population control programs, (b) agricultural technology such as hybrid seeds and fertilizers to increase food production, (c) industrial technology including machinery and information technology, and (d) foreign aid to help pay for power plants and factories.

8. Critics of modernization theory say that high-income nations do not spread economic development around the world. Further, they claim, low-income nations cannot follow the path to development taken by high-income nations centuries ago.

9. Dependency theory claims global wealth and poverty are the historical products of the capitalist world economy, first because of colonialism, and more recently because of the operation of multinational corporations.

10. Immanuel Wallerstein views the high-income countries as the advantaged "core" of the capitalist world economy, middle-income nations as the "semiperiphery," and low-income societies as the global "periphery."

11. Three key factors—export-oriented economies, a lack of industrial capacity, and foreign debt—perpetuate low-income countries' dependency on high-income nations.

12. Critics of dependency theory argue that this approach overlooks the sixfold increase in the world's wealth since 1950. Furthermore, the world's poorest societies are not those with the strongest ties to high-income countries.

13. Both modernization and dependency approaches offer useful insights into the development of global inequality. Some evidence supports each view. Less controversial is the urgent need to address the various problems caused by worldwide poverty.

## KEY CONCEPTS

**colonialism** (p. 215) the process by which some nations enrich themselves through political and economic control of other nations

**neocolonialism** (p. 215) a new form of global power relationships that involves not direct political control but economic exploitation by multinational corporations

**multinational corporation** (p. 215) a large business that operates in many countries

**modernization theory** (p. 216) a model of economic and social development that explains global inequality in terms of technological and cultural differences among societies

**dependency theory** (p. 220) a model of economic development that explains global inequality in terms of the historical exploitation of low-income societies by high-income ones

## CRITICAL-THINKING QUESTIONS

1. Based on what you have read here and elsewhere, what is your prediction about the extent of global hunger 50 years from now? Will the problem be more or less serious? Why?

2. What is the difference between relative and absolute poverty? Use these two concepts to describe social stratification in Canada and around the world.

3. Why do many analysts argue that economic development in low-income countries depends on raising the social standing of women?

4. State the basic tenets of modernization theory and dependency theory. Spell out several criticisms of each approach.

## APPLICATIONS AND EXERCISES

1. Keep a log book of mass media advertising, mentioning low-income countries (selling, say, coffee from Colombia or exotic vacations to a Caribbean island). What image of life in low-income countries does the advertising present? In light of this chapter, do you think this image is accurate?

2. Thousands of students from abroad study in Canadian schools. See if you can identify a woman and a man on your campus raised in a low-income country. Approach them, explain your interest in global stratification, and ask if they are willing to share what life is like back home. You may be able to learn quite a bit from them.

3. By comparing the Global Maps in this text, identify social traits associated with the world's richest and poorest nations. Try to use both modernization theory and dependency theory to build theoretical explanations of the patterns you find.

# SITES TO SEE

**www.pearsoned.ca/macionis**

Visit the Web site that accompanies this text to use the electronic study guide, which contains outlines, summaries, practice tests, a chat room, and many additional Internet links.

**members.aol.com/casmasalc**

This is the Web site for the Coalition Against Slavery in Mauritania and Sudan. This site provides information about the problem of slavery as well as links to similar organizations.

**www.oneworld.net**

This site highlights a variety of issues and controversies relating to global stratification.

**www.fh.org**
**www.worldconcern.org**
**www.worldvision.org**
**www.care.org**

Here are the sites for various organizations active in the struggle to reduce global inequality. The first is operated by Food for the Hungry International; the second takes you to the home page for World Concern; the third organization is World Vision; the fourth is CARE. Visit them all and watch for differences in the focus and strategies of the various organizations.

**www.census.gov/ipc/wwwidbnew.html**
**www.prb.org/index.html**

These two sites—operated by the U.S. Bureau of the Census and the Population Reference Bureau—offer a statistical profile of world nations.

**www.fao.org/FOCUS/E/SOFI00/sofi001-e.htm**

Read a United Nations report titled *The State of Food Insecurity in the World 2000*, which surveys the extent of poverty in low-, middle-, and high-income countries.

**www.worldbank.org/poverty/data/index.htm**

This site, operated by the World Bank, provides data and analysis of global poverty. Through this site you can also access electronic versions of the *World Development Report* (www.worldbank.org/wdr/index.htm).

**www.globalexchange.org/education/speakers/CarmencitaAbad.html**

Read about a woman who spent six years working at a sweatshop in Saipan producing clothing sold by The Gap in the United States.

**www.un.org/rights/50/decla.htm**

More than 50 years ago, the United Nations published the Universal Declaration of Human Rights. What does this document say about social inequality in the world?

**www.undp.org/hdro**

The United Nations Development Programme publishes the annual *Human Development Report*. Compare the most recent one to the data presented in this chapter. Do you notice any dramatic changes?

# GENDER STRATIFICATION

*We went to the Manitoba Legislature asking for plain, common justice, an old-fashioned square deal, and in reply to that we got hat-lifting. I felt that when a man offers hat-lifting when we ask for justice we should tell him to keep his hat right on. I will go further and say that we should tell him not only to keep his hat on but to pull it right down over his face.* ■

So wrote Nellie McClung in her book, *In These Times,* which tells the story of her struggle to gain equal rights for women in the public realm. Born in Ontario in 1873, McClung migrated west as a child with her family, first settling in Manitoba and later, as an adult, moving to Alberta and British Columbia. By the time she was 40, she had given birth to five children and had become a well-known public speaker for women's rights. Back then, in much of Canada, women could not own property or keep their wages if they were married; they could not draft a will; they were barred from filing lawsuits in a court, including seeking custody of their own children; they could not attend university; and they legally could be beaten by their husbands as long as the stick used was no wider than a thumb (the origin of today's phrase "the rule of thumb").

Nor could women express their disapproval of such conditions. In this "land of the free," many more decades would pass before all Canadian women gained the right to vote. At that time, most people considered such a proposal absurd and outrageous. Toronto journalist Goldwin Smith argued that giving women the right to vote would lead to "national emasculation." . Smith also protested the right for women to enter universities (Prentice et al., 1996:221).

Much has changed in the 125 years since McClung's birth. Many of the proposals she and other early feminists made are now accepted as a matter of basic fairness. But as this chapter explains, women and men still lead different lives in Canada and elsewhere in the world, and in most respects men still dominate. This chapter explores the importance of gender, and explains how gender, like class position, is a major dimension of social stratification.

## GENDER AND INEQUALITY

Chapter 7 (Sexuality) explained that biological differences divide the human population into categories of female and male. **Gender** refers to *the personal traits and social meanings that members of a society attach to being female and male.* Gender, then, is a dimension of social organization, shaping how we interact with others and even how we think about ourselves. Even more important, gender involves *hierarchy,* placing men and women in different positions in terms of power, wealth, and other resources. This is why sociologists speak of

*Sex is a biological distinction that develops prior to birth. Gender is the meaning that society attaches to being female or male. Gender differences are a matter of power, as what is masculine typically has social priority over what is feminine. The importance of gender is not evident among infants, of course, but the ways in which we think of boys and girls set in motion patterns that will continue for a lifetime.*

**gender stratification**, *the unequal distribution of wealth, power, and privilege between men and women.* Gender, in short, affects the opportunities and constraints each one of us faces throughout our lives (Ferree & Hall, 1996; Riley, 1997), though the opportunities and constraints available to men and women also vary across countries (Boje & Leira, 2000).

## MALE–FEMALE DIFFERENCES

Many people think there is something "natural" about gender, since, after all, biological factors make one sex different from the other. But we must be careful not to think of social differences in biological terms. Back in the 19th century, for example, women were denied the vote because many people assumed that women "naturally" lacked sufficient intelligence and political interest. Such attitudes had nothing to do with biology; rather, they reflected the *cultural conventions* of that time and place.

Figure 10–1 presents another example: a history of athletic performances in running marathons. Back in 1925, most people would have doubted that the best female runners could ever finish a marathon in anywhere near the time that men could. Today, as the figure shows, the best women routinely post better times than the fastest men of decades past, and the performance gap between the sexes has narrowed greatly. Here, again, most of the differences between men and women turn out to be socially created.

True, there are differences in physical ability between the sexes. On average, males are 10 percent taller, 20 percent heavier, and 30 percent stronger, especially in their upper bodies (Ehrenreich, 1999). On the other hand, women outperform men in the ultimate game of life itself: While life expectancy for men is 75.7 years, women can expect to live 81.4 years (Statistics Canada, 1999d).

In adolescence, males show greater mathematical ability, while adolescent females excel in verbal skills, a difference that reflects both biology and the socialization process (Maccoby & Jacklin, 1974; Baker et al., 1980; Lengermann & Wallace, 1985). However, research points to no overall differences in intelligence between males and females.

Biologically, then, men and women differ in limited ways, with neither one naturally superior. But culture can define the two sexes differently, as the global study of gender shows.

**The Israeli kibbutzim.** In Israel, collective Jewish settlements are called *kibbutzim*. The kibbutz (the singular form) is important for gender research because gender equality is one of its goals, with men and women sharing in both work and decision making.

Members of kibbutzim consider gender irrelevant to most of everyday life. Both men and women take care of children, cook, clean, repair buildings, and make day-to-day decisions. Girls and boys are raised in the same way, and from the first weeks of life children live together in dormitories. Women and men in the kibbutzim have achieved a remarkable degree of (although not complete) social equality. Thus, kibbutzim are evidence of the wide latitude that cultures have in defining what is feminine and what is masculine.

**Margaret Mead's research.** Anthropologist Margaret Mead carried out groundbreaking research on gender. To the extent that gender reflects the biological facts of sex, she reasoned, people everywhere should define "feminine" and "masculine" in the same way; if gender is cultural, these conceptions should vary.

Mead studied three societies in New Guinea (1963; orig. 1935). In the mountainous home of the Arapesh, Mead observed men and women with remarkably similar attitudes and behaviour. Both sexes, she reported, were cooperative and sensitive to others—in short, what our culture would label "feminine."

Moving south, Mead studied the Mundugumor, whose headhunting and cannibalism stood in striking contrast to the gentle ways of the Arapesh. Both sexes were typically selfish and aggressive, traits we define as more "masculine."

Finally, travelling west to the Tchambuli, Mead discovered a culture that, like our own, defined females and males differently. But, Mead reported, the Tchambuli *reversed* many of our notions of gender: Females were dominant and rational, while males were submissive, emotional, and nurturing toward children. Based on her observations, Mead concluded that culture is the key to gender, since what one society defines as masculine, another may see as feminine.

Some critics consider Mead's findings "too neat," as if she saw in these societies just the patterns she was looking for. Deborah Gewertz (1981) challenged Mead's "reversal hypothesis," claiming that Tchambuli males are really more aggressive and Tchambuli females more submissive. Gewertz explains that Mead visited the Tchambuli (who actually call themselves the *Chambri*) during the 1930s, after they had lost much of their property in tribal wars, and observed men rebuilding their homes. Men working in the home, she claims, was a temporary role for Chambri men.

**George Murdock's research.** In a broader study of more than 200 pre-industrial societies, George Murdock (1937) found some global agreement on which tasks are feminine and which ones masculine. Hunting and warfare, Murdock observed, generally fall to men, while home-centred tasks such as cooking and child care tend to be women's work. With their simple technology, pre-industrial societies apparently assign roles reflecting men's and women's physical attributes. With greater size and strength, men hunt game and protect the group; because women bear children, they assume domestic duties.

But beyond this general pattern, Murdock found significant variation. Consider agriculture: Women did the farming in about the same number of societies as did men; in most societies, the two sexes divided this work. When it came to many other tasks—from building shelters to tattooing the body—Murdock found societies of the world were as likely to turn to one sex as the other.

**In sum: Gender and culture.** Global comparisons show that, by and large, societies vary widely in defining tasks as either feminine or masculine. With indus-

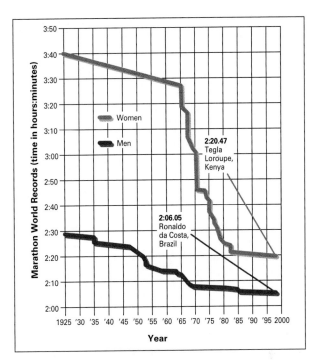

**FIGURE 10–1  Men's and Women's Athletic Performance**

Do men naturally outperform women in athletic competition? The answer is not obvious. Early in this century, men outdistanced women by many kilometres in marathon races. But as opportunities for women in athletics increased, women have been closing the performance gap. Less than 15 minutes separate the current world marathon records for women and for men (both set in 1998).

trialization, moreover, the importance of muscle power declines further, reducing gender differences (Lenski, Nolan, & Lenski, 1995). Thus gender is simply too variable simply to be an expression of biology. Instead, as with many other elements of culture, what it means to be female and male is mostly a creation of society.

## PATRIARCHY AND SEXISM

Although conceptions of gender vary, everywhere in the world we find some degree of **patriarchy** (literally, "the rule of fathers"), *a form of social organization in which males dominate females*. Despite mythical tales of societies run by female "Amazons," **matriarchy**, *a form of social organization in which females dominate males* has never been documented in human history (Gough, 1971; Harris, 1977; Lengermann & Wallace, 1985).

But while some degree of patriarchy may be universal, Global Map 10–1 shows great variation in

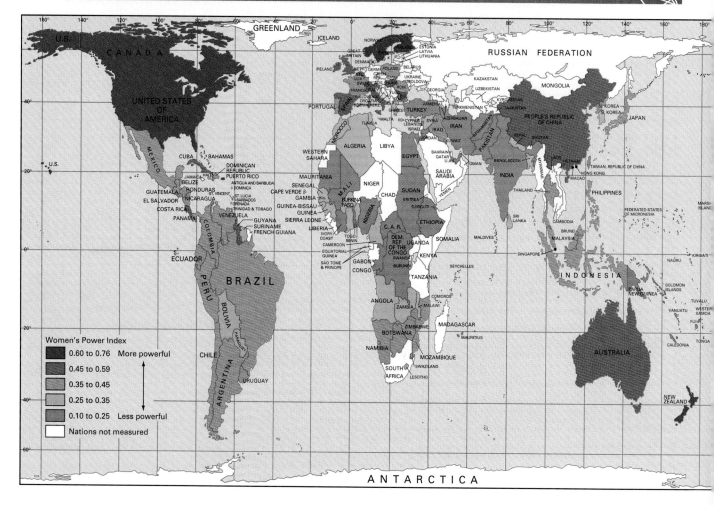

**GLOBAL MAP 10–1   Women's Power in Global Perspective**

A recent United Nations study ranked 116 nations on a scale of 0 (women have no power) to 1 (women have as much power as men). In general, women fare better in rich nations than in poor. Yet some countries stand out: Nordic societies lead the world in promoting women's power.

Source: *The Christian Science Monitor* (1995). Reprinted with permission of *The Christian Science Monitor*. All rights reserved.

the relative power and privilege of women around the world. According to the United Nations, three Nordic countries—Norway, Sweden, and Finland—afford women the highest social standing; by contrast, in the Asian nations of Pakistan and Afghanistan and the East African nation of Djibouti, women have the lowest social standing compared to men (United Nations, 1995).

   **Sexism,** *the belief that one sex is innately superior to the other,* is the ideological basis of patriarchy. Sexism is not just a matter of individual attitudes, it is built into the institutions of our society. *Institutional sexism*

pervades the economy: women are highly concentrated in lower-paying jobs, for example. Similarly, the legal system has long excused violence against women, especially on the part of boyfriends, husbands, and fathers (Landers, 1990; Johnson, 1996; Boritch, 1997; Duffy, 1998).

**The costs of sexism.**   Sexism stunts the talents and limits the ambitions of women, who are half the population. And though men benefit in some respects from sexism, their privilege comes at a high price. Masculinity in our culture calls for men to engage in many high-risk behaviours, including using tobacco and alcohol, playing dangerous sports, and even driving recklessly, so that motor-vehicle accidents are the leading cause of death among young males. Moreover, as Marilyn French (1985) argues, patriarchy compels men to relentlessly seek control—not only of women, but of themselves and their world. Thus, masculinity is linked not only to accidents but to suicide, violence, and stress-related diseases. The Type A personality—marked by chronic impatience, driving ambition, competitiveness, and free-floating hostility—is a recipe for heart disease and almost perfectly matches the behaviour our culture considers masculine (Ehrenreich, 1983).

Finally, insofar as men seek control over others, they lose opportunities for intimacy and trust. As one researcher put it, competition is supposed to separate "the men from the boys." In practice, however, it separates men from men and everyone else (Raphael, 1988).

**Is patriarchy inevitable?**   In pre-industrial societies, women have little control over pregnancy and childbirth, which limits the scope of their lives. Similarly, men's greater height and physical strength are valued resources. But industrialization—including birth ontrol technology—gives people choices about how to live. In societies like our own, then, biological differences offer little justification for patriarchy.

But legitimate or not, male dominance remains in Canada and elsewhere. Does this mean that patriarchy is inevitable? Some sociologists claim that biological factors "wire" the sexes with different motivations and behaviours—especially more aggressiveness in males—making patriarchy difficult, perhaps even impossible, to eliminate (Goldberg 1974, 1987; Rossi, 1985; Popenoe, 1993b). Most sociologists, however, believe that gender is a social construct that *can* be changed. Just because no society has yet eliminated male dominance does not mean that we must stay prisoners of the past.

To understand the persistence of male dominance, we need to examine how gender is rooted and reproduced in society, a process that begins in childhood and continues throughout our lives.

## GENDER AND SOCIALIZATION

From birth right up until death, gender has a hand in shaping human feelings, thoughts, and actions. Children quickly learn that their society defines females and males as different kinds of people; by about age three, they begin to apply gender standards to themselves.

Table 10–1 present traits that people in Canada and the United States traditionally link to "feminine" and "masculine" behaviour. Such opposition exists even though research shows that most young people do not

### TABLE 10–1 Traditional Notions of Gender Identity

| Feminine Traits | Masculine Traits |
| --- | --- |
| Submissive | Dominant |
| Dependent | Independent |
| Unintelligent and incapable | Intelligent and competent |
| Emotional | Rational |
| Receptive | Assertive |
| Intuitive | Analytical |
| Weak | Strong |
| Timid | Brave |
| Content | Ambitious |
| Passive | Active |
| Cooperative | Competitive |
| Sensitive | Insensitive |
| Sex object | Sexually aggressive |
| Attractive because of physical appearance | Attractive because of achievement |

develop consistently feminine or masculine personalities (L.C. Bernard, 1980; Bem, 1993).

Just as gender affects how we think of ourselves, so it teaches us to *act* in normative ways. **Gender roles** (or sex roles) are *attitudes and activities that a society links to each sex.* Insofar as our culture defines males as ambitious and competitive, we expect them to play team sports and aspire to positions of leadership. To the extent that we define females as deferential and emotional, we expect them to be supportive helpers and to be quick to cry.

## GENDER AND THE FAMILY

The first question people usually ask about a newborn—"Is it a boy or a girl?"—looms large because the answer involves not just gender but the likely direction of a child's entire life.

In fact, gender is at work even before a child is born, since parents generally hope to have a boy rather than a girl. Soon after birth, family members usher infants into the "pink world" of girls or the "blue world" of boys (Bernard, 1981). Parents even send gender messages in the way they handle daughters and sons. One researcher at a British university presented an infant dressed as either a boy or a girl to a number of women; her subjects handled the "female" child tenderly, with frequent hugs and caresses, while treating the "male" child more aggressively, often lifting him up high in the air or bouncing him on the knee (Bonner, 1984). The lesson is clear: The female world revolves around passivity and emotion, while the male world places a premium on independence and action.

*In every society, people assume certain jobs, patterns of behaviour, and ways of dressing are "naturally" feminine while others are just as obviously masculine. But in global perspective, we see remarkable variety in such social definitions. These men, Wodaabe pastoral nomads who live in the African nation of Niger, are proud to engage in a display of beauty most people in our society would consider feminine.*

## GENDER AND THE PEER GROUP

About the time they enter school, children move outside the family, making friends with others their own age. Peer groups teach additional lessons about gender.

After spending a year watching children at play, Janet Lever (1978) concluded that boys favour team sports with complex rules and clear objectives such as scoring a run or a touchdown. Such games nearly always involve winners and losers, reinforcing masculine traits of aggression and control.

Girls, on the other hand, play team sports. But, Lever explains, girls also play hopscotch or jump rope, or simply talk, sing, or dance. These activities have few rules, and rarely is "victory" the ultimate goal. Instead of teaching girls to be competitive, Lever explains, female peer groups promote interpersonal skills of communication and cooperation—presumably the basis for girls' future roles as wives and mothers.

Lever's observations recall Carol Gilligan's (1982) gender-based theory of moral reasoning. Boys, Gilligan contends, reason according to abstract principles. For them, "rightness" amounts to "playing by the rules." Girls, by contrast, consider morality a matter of responsibility to others. Thus, the games we play have serious implications for our later lives. Yet, as indicated by the recent murder of a teenage girl in Victoria by her female classmates, violent play among female adolescents in Canada is on the rise. Although still much rarer than among males, such incidents suggest that

gender polarity may be breaking down, with some girls, at least, less willing to place concern for others above their own self-interest.

## GENDER AND SCHOOLING

In high school, more girls than boys learn secretarial skills and take vocational classes such as cosmetology and food services. Classes in woodworking and auto mechanics, conversely, attract mostly young men.

In college and university, the pattern continues, with men disproportionately represented in mathematics and the sciences—including physics, chemistry, and engineering. Women cluster in the humanities (such as English), the fine arts (painting, music, dance, and drama), and the social sciences (including anthropology and sociology). New areas of study are also likely to be gender-typed. Computer science, for example, enrolls mostly men, while courses in gender studies tend to enroll more women.

## GENDER AND THE MASS MEDIA

Since television first captured the public imagination in the 1950s, white males have held centre stage; racial and ethnic minorities were all but absent from television until the early 1970s. Even when both sexes appear on camera, men generally play the brilliant detectives, fearless explorers, and skilled surgeons. Women, by contrast, play the less capable and unnecessary characters, except for the sexual interest they add to the story.

Historically, ads have presented women in the home, cheerfully using cleaning products, serving food, trying out appliances, and modelling clothes. Men, on the other hand, predominate in ads for cars, travel, banking services, industrial companies, and alcoholic beverages. The authoritative "voiceover"—the faceless voice that describes a product in television and radio advertising—is almost always male (Courtney & Whipple, 1983; Davis, 1993).

Advertising also perpetuates what Naomi Wolf called the "beauty myth." The Global Sociology box takes a closer look at how this myth affects women.

# GENDER AND SOCIAL STRATIFICATION

Gender is about more than how people think and act. It is also about social hierarchy. The reality of gender stratification can be seen, first, in the world of work.

## WORKING MEN AND WOMEN

In 1891, just 11.4 percent of females in Canada were engaged in paid employment. In 1999, 55 percent of

# Pretty Is as Pretty Does: The Beauty Myth

The Duchess of Windsor once quipped, "A woman cannot be too rich or too thin." The first half of her observation might apply to men as well, but certainly not the second. After all, most ads placed by the multibillion-dollar-a-year cosmetics and diet industries target women.

According to Naomi Wolf (1990), certain cultural patterns create a "beauty myth" that is damaging to women. The beauty myth arises, first, because society teaches women to measure themselves in terms of physical appearance (Backman & Adams, 1991). Yet, the standards of beauty (such as the *Playboy* centrefold or the 45-kilogram fashion model) are unattainable for most women.

The way society teaches women to prize relationships with men, whom they presumably attract with their beauty, also contributes to the beauty myth. Striving for beauty not only drives women to be extremely disciplined, but also forces them to be highly attuned and responsive to men. Beauty-minded women, in short, try to please men and avoid challenging male power.

The beauty myth affects males, as well: Men should want to possess beautiful women. Thus, our ideas about beauty reduce women to objects and motivate men to possess women as if they were dolls rather than human beings.

Wolf stresses that the beauty myth is not so much about appearance as about behaviour. It should not be surprising, therefore, that the beauty myth surfaced in our culture during the 1890s, the 1920s, and the 1980s—all decades of heightened debate about the social standing of women. A recent survey indicates that the 1990s may not be any different in this respect. When asked what they would most like to change in their lives, 50 percent of middle-aged women and nearly all teenage women said they wanted to lose weight and keep it off (Kilbourne, 1995).

Source: Based on Wolf (1990); Kilbourne, (1995).

women ages 15 and over worked for income, and just under three-fourths of working women did so full time (Statistics Canada, 2000m). The traditional view that earning an income is a "man's role" no longer holds true, as Figure 10–2 on page 238 shows.

Factors that changed the Canadian labour force include the decline of farming, the growth of cities, a shrinking family size, and a rising divorce rate. Thus, Canada and other industrial societies today consider women working for income to be the rule rather than the exception. In fact, 61 percent of Canadian married and common-law couples now depend on two incomes. Women represent almost half the workforce in Canada; as Global Map 10–2 on page 239 shows, this is not the case in many of the low-income countries of the world.

In the past, many women in the labour force were childless. In 1999, 61 percent of women with children under age 3 worked for income, as did 66 percent whose youngest child was aged 3 to 5, and 69 percent of women with children under age 16 living at home (Statistics Canada, 2000m). National Map 10–1 on page 240 indicates the variation by census division in the labour force participation of women with children under age 6.

**Gender and occupations.** While the shares of women and men in the labour force have been converging, to a large extent the work they do remains different. Statistics Canada (2000m) reports that nearly half of working women have one of just two job types. Clerical and administrative support work draws 24.7 percent of working women, most of whom are secretaries or other office workers. These are often called "pink-collar" jobs because three-quarters are filled by women. Another 31.6 percent of employed women are in sales and service work. Most of these jobs are in clothing and food-service industries, child care and health care.

Table 10–2 on page 241 shows the occupations with the highest concentrations of women. Overall, although more women now work for pay, they remain segregated in the labour force in jobs at the middle and low end of the pay scale, usually supervised by men, and with limited opportunity for advancement (Charles, 1992; Krahn & Lowe, 1998; Benoit, 2000a; Statistics Canada, 2000m).

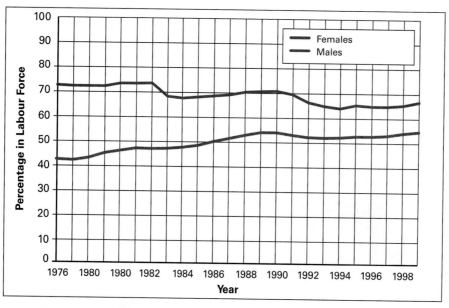

**FIGURE 10–2    Men and Women Over Age 15 in Canadian Labour Force,
1976–1999**

Source: Statistics Canada (2000m).

Men dominate in certain job categories, such as the building trades; virtually all brick and stone masons, structural metal workers, and heavy-equipment mechanics are men. Likewise, the majority of engineers, physicians, judges and lawyers, and corporate managers are men. At the top of the business world, men dominate senior management jobs, with just 12 percent of women holding corporate officer positions at Canada's 560 largest companies in 1999. The number of women holding "clout" jobs (CEOs, chairs, presidents, and so on) is even smaller. Just 3.4 percent of these positions were held by women in the country's 560 largest companies in 1999 (Catalyst, 2000).

Gender stratification in the workplace is easy to see: Female nurses tend to assist male physicians, female secretaries serve male executives, and female flight attendants tend to be under the command of male airline pilots. Moreover, in any field, the greater a job's income and prestige, the more likely it is to be held by a man. For example, in 1997–98, women made up 63 percent of all elementary and secondary school teachers, but only 40 percent of college instructors, and just 26.2 percent of tenured faculty in universities (Statistics Canada, 2000h).

But one challenge to male domination in the workplace comes from women who are entrepreneurs. Canadian women now make up more than 35 percent of self-employed workers—a 9-percent increase from a decade ago. Although 70 percent of these businesses are one-person operations, women have shown they can make opportunities for themselves outside large, male-dominated companies (Gardner, 1995; Statistics Canada, 2000m).

## HOUSEWORK: WOMEN'S "SECOND SHIFT"

Global Map 4–1 on page 83 shows that housework—maintaining the home and caring for children—is the province of women throughout the world. In Canada, housework has always embodied a cultural contradiction: We claim it is essential for family life, but housework carries little prestige or reward (Luxton, 1980).

Despite women's rapid entry into the labour force, the amount of housework performed by women has declined, but the *share* women do has declined only slightly. Figure 10–3 on page 242 shows that in 1998, a woman employed full-time who is living with a partner and at least one child under age 19 puts in an average of 4.9 hours of unpaid work per day. Her male partner puts in an average 3.3 hours of unpaid work per day, or one-and-a-half hours less than his female counterpart.

In sum, men support the idea of women entering the paid labour force, and most count on the money that the women earn. But many, although not all, men still resist taking on a more equal share of household duties (Luxton, 1980; Komarovsky, 1973; Cowan, 1992; Robinson & Spitze, 1992; Lennon & Rosenfeld, 1994; Heath & Bourne, 1995; Harpster & Monk-Turner, 1998: Lynn & Todoroff, 1998; McFarlane, Beaujot & Haddad, 2000).

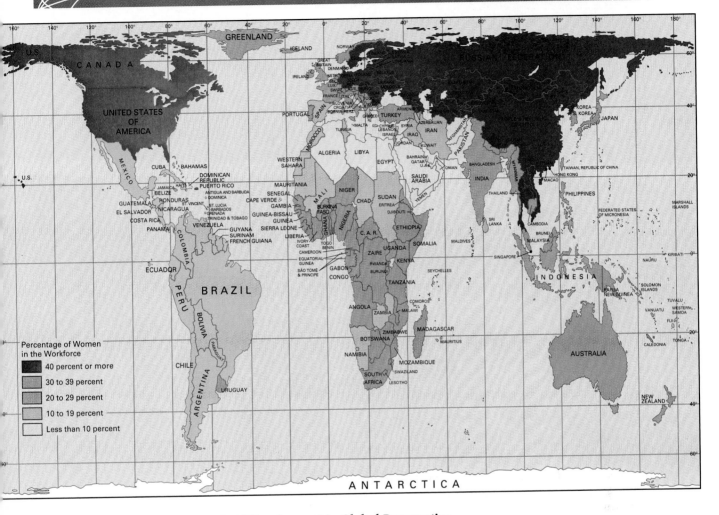

## GLOBAL MAP 10–2   Women's Paid Employment in Global Perspective

In 1994, women made up 45 percent of the labour force in Canada—a substantial increase over the last generation. Throughout the industrialized world, nearly one-half of the labour force is made up of women. In low-income societies, however, women work even harder than they do in this country, but they are less likely to be paid for their efforts. In Latin America, for example, women represent one-third of the paid labour force; in Islamic societies of northern Africa and the Middle East, the figure is significantly lower.

Source: *Peters Atlas of the World* (1990).

## GENDER, INCOME, AND WEALTH

In 1997, the average earnings for women working full time year-round were just under $30 915, while men working full time earned an average of $42 626. This means that for every dollar earned by men, women earned 72.5 cents.

While women's incomes vary by occupational status and age, it is noteworthy that their average earnings are below those of men in all occupational groupings and every age category (Statistics Canada, 2000m).

The main reason women earn less is the *kind* of work they do: largely clerical, sales, and service jobs. In effect, jobs and gender interact: People still perceive jobs with less clout as "women's work," just as people devalue work simply because it is performed by women (Armstrong, 1994; Krahn & Lowe, 1998; Looker & Thiessen, 1999; Benoit, 2000a; England, 1992; Bellas, 1994; Huffman, Velasco, & Bielby, 1996).

In recent decades, proponents of gender equality proposed a policy of "comparable worth." That is,

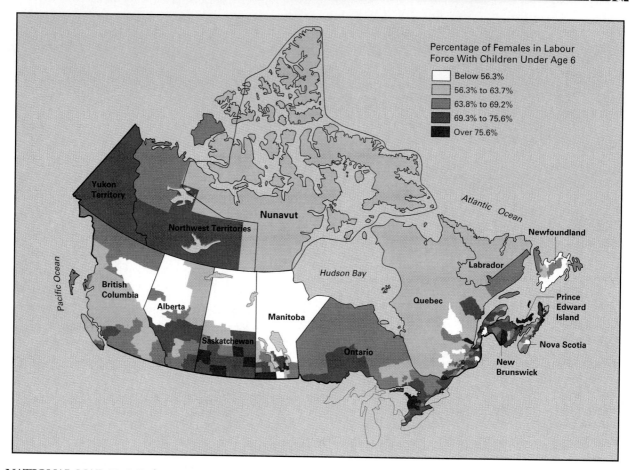

**NATIONAL MAP 10–1  Labour Force Participation for Females over Age 15 Years with Children under Age 6 Years, Canada, 1996**

The map shows that most women with children under age six are in the labour force. There are only a few areas where fewer than 50 percent participate in the labour force. Why do you think the labour force participation rate for these women is so high, even outside the largest urban areas?

Source: Calculated based on data in Statistics Canada Catalogue No. 95F0181XDB96001 (1998b).

people should be paid not according to the historical double standard but according to the worth of what they actually do. Several nations, including Canada, Great Britain, and Australia, have adopted comparable worth policies, but in the United States, at least, these have found limited acceptance. The dedication to the pay-equity principle was tested in the summer of 1998 when the Canadian Human Rights Tribunal found that female federal workers were owed an estimated $5 billion. The federal government found itself torn between supporting the pay-equity principle and dealing with the cost of doing so (Greenspoon, 1998). Finally, on October 29, 1999, the Public Service Alliance of Canada and the federal government came to an agree-

ment to implement the 1998 Canadian Human Rights Tribunal decision.

A second cause of this gender-based income disparity has to do with the family. Both men and women have children, of course, but our culture defines parenting as more of a women's responsibility than a man's. Being pregnancy and raising small children keep many younger women out of the labour force altogether, at a time when their male peers are making significant occupational gains. When female workers return to the labour force, they have less job seniority than their male counterparts (Fuchs, 1986; Stier, 1996; Waldfogel, 1997). Variation does exist across industrial nations, however. Countries with

**TABLE 10–2  Number of Average Earnings for Full Year, Full-time Workers in the 10 Highest-Paying and 10 Lowest-Paying Occupations, by Gender, Canada, 1995**

| Selected Occupational Categories | Number of Workers | | Average Earnings ($) | | Number of Workers per 10 000 | | Women's Income as a Percentage of Men's |
|---|---|---|---|---|---|---|---|
| | Men | Women | Men | Women | Men | Women | |
| All occupations | 4 514 850 | 2 998 940 | 42 488 | 30 130 | | | 71 |
| Total—10 highest-paying occupations | 158 795 | 38 940 | 99 605 | 64 716 | 352 | 130 | 65 |
| Judges | 1 360 | 405 | 128 791 | 117 707 | 3 | 1 | 91 |
| Specialist physicians | 9 345 | 3 220 | 137 019 | 86 086 | 21 | 11 | 63 |
| General practitioners and family physicians | 16 055 | 5 615 | 116 750 | 81 512 | 36 | 19 | 70 |
| Dentists | 6 995 | 1 535 | 109 187 | 71 587 | 15 | 5 | 66 |
| Senior managers—goods production, utilities, transportation and construction | 32 625 | 2 880 | 102 971 | 58 463 | 72 | 10 | 57 |
| Senior managers—financial, communications carriers, and other business services | 19 190 | 3 860 | 104 715 | 71 270 | 43 | 13 | 68 |
| Lawyers and Quebec notaries | 32 305 | 12 080 | 89 353 | 60 930 | 72 | 40 | 68 |
| Senior managers—trade, broadcasting, and other services | 24 610 | 4 060 | 84 237 | 48 651 | 55 | 14 | 58 |
| Primary production managers (except agriculture) | 6 670 | 405 | 78 421 | 48 479 | 15 | 1 | 62 |
| Securities agents, investment dealers, and traders | 9 640 | 4 880 | 90 391 | 47 323 | 21 | 16 | 52 |
| Total—10 lowest-paying occupations | 49 810 | 181 105 | 18 640 | 15 146 | 110 | 604 | 81 |
| Sewing machine operators | 2 490 | 27 750 | 20 664 | 17 340 | 6 | 93 | 84 |
| Cashiers | 9 025 | 47 110 | 20 557 | 16 977 | 20 | 157 | 83 |
| Ironing, pressing, and finishing occupations | 990 | 2 375 | 19 297 | 16 499 | 2 | 8 | 86 |
| Artisans and craftspersons | 2 840 | 3 040 | 20 555 | 13 565 | 6 | 10 | 66 |
| Bartenders | 7 080 | 8 495 | 18 899 | 14 940 | 16 | 28 | 79 |
| Harvesting labourers | 525 | 605 | 18 683 | 14 465 | 1 | 2 | 77 |
| Service station attendants | 8 630 | 2 175 | 16 520 | 14 947 | 19 | 7 | 90 |
| Food service counter attendants and food preparers | 5 550 | 16 680 | 17 912 | 14 681 | 12 | 56 | 82 |
| Food and beverage servers | 11 940 | 38 250 | 18 192 | 13 861 | 26 | 128 | 76 |
| Babysitters, nannies, and parents' helpers | 740 | 34 625 | 15 106 | 12 662 | 2 | 115 | 84 |

Source: Statistics Canada, *The Daily*, Tuesday, May 12 (1998i), and author calculations.

"women-friendly" parental leaves and benefits and publicly funded child-care programs lessen the cost of childbearing for female workers (Leira, 2000; Benoit, 2000b). Canada's newly extended year-long parental and maternity leave policy moves the country closer to the Nordic norm of at least one year of paid leave for new parents with their newborns.

Moreover, women who choose to have children may be reluctant or unable to maintain fast-paced jobs that tie up their evenings and weekends. To avoid role strain, they may take jobs that offer a shorter commuting distance, more flexible hours, and employer child-care services. Women pursuing both a career and a family are torn between their dual responsibilities in ways that men are not. Consider this: At age 40, among those in executive positions, 90 percent of men—but only 35 percent of women—have at least one child (F. Schwartz, 1989).

The two factors noted so far—type of work and family responsibilities—account for about two-thirds of the earnings disparity between women and men. A third factor—discrimination against women—accounts for most of the remainder (Pear, 1987; Fuller & Schoenberger, 1991).

Because discrimination is illegal, it is practised in subtle ways (Benokraitis & Feagin, 1995). Corporate women often encounter a *glass ceiling*, a barrier that is invisible because it is denied by company officials, but that effectively prevents women from rising above middle management.

For all these reasons, then, women earn less than men in all major occupational categories. As shown in Table 10–3 on page 243 this disparity varies from job to job, but in only four of the major job classifications do women earn more than 75 percent as much as men.

Finally, perhaps because women typically outlive men, many people think that women own most of the country's wealth. None of the individuals identified in *Forbes* 2000 magazine as the richest people in the world was a Canadian women, while, as noted in Chapter 8

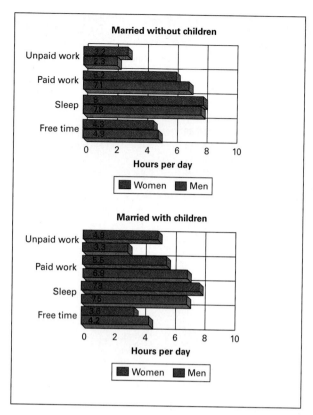

**Married without children**

| | |
|---|---|
| Unpaid work | Women: 3.2, Men: 2.3 |
| Paid work | Women: 6.2, Men: 7.1 |
| Sleep | Women: 8, Men: 7.8 |
| Free time | Women: 4.3, Men: 4.8 |

Hours per day

■ Women   ■ Men

**Married with children**

| | |
|---|---|
| Unpaid work | Women: 4.9, Men: 3.3 |
| Paid work | Women: 5.5, Men: 6.9 |
| Sleep | Women: 7.8, Men: 7.6 |
| Free time | Women: 3.6, Men: 4.2 |

Hours per day

■ Women   ■ Men

**FIGURE 10–3   Time Allocation of Married Men and Women Aged 25–44 Employed Full Time, 1998.**

Source: Statistics Canada (2000m).

(Social Stratification), 15 Canadian men made the billionaire list (Forbes.com, 2000).

## GENDER AND EDUCATION

In the past, our society thought schooling was irrelevant for women because their lives revolved around the home. But times have changed. By 1994, women earned a majority (58 percent) of all university bachelor's degrees and first professional degrees (Statistics Canada, 1997e); in 1997, that proportion had risen slightly to 59 percent (Statistics Canada, 2000h).

College and university doors have opened to women, and differences in men's and women's majors are becoming smaller. In 1972–73, for example, women made up just 3 percent of students in engineering and applied sciences. In 1997–98, the percentage had increased to 22 percent. Women's enrollment in mathematics and physical sciences increased from 19 to 29 percent in this time period (Statistics Canada, 2000h).

In the mid-1990s, for the first time, women were earning half of postgraduate degrees, often a springboard to high-prestige jobs. For all areas of study in 1997, women earned 51 percent of master's degrees and 36 percent of all doctorates.

Men continue to dominate some professional fields, however. In 1997, 60 percent of doctoral candidates in agricultural and biological sciences were male, as were 77 percent of those in mathematics and physical sciences, and 84 percent of those in engineering and applied sciences (Statistics Canada, 2000m). Our society still defines high-paying professions (and the drive and competitiveness needed to succeed in them) as masculine; this fact helps explain why just as many women as men begin most pre-professional graduate programs, but women are less likely to complete their degrees (Fiorentine, 1987; Fiorentine & Cole, 1992). Even so, the proportion of women in all these professions is steadily rising.

## GENDER AND POLITICS

A century ago, virtually no women held elected office in any industrial country, including Canada. In fact, women were legally barred from voting in national elections until 1918 in our country, and it was not until more than a decade later that they were permitted to sit in the Canadian Senate (Prentice et al., 1996). Canada is no exception in this regard. Women in most countries were legally barred from voting in national elections until the early decades of this century. By 2000, this picture of gender exclusion in the political life of industrial countries had changed, but not as much as one might imagine. Table 10–4 on page 244 shows that there have been significant gains for women in the Nordic countries, limited progress in most other industrial nations, and even fewer gains for counterparts in many low-income countries.

According to the Geneva-based Inter-Parliamentary Union, in a study of 179 parliaments around the world, women held 13.8 percent of all seats in 2000—a decrease from 1988 when women held 14.6 percent of seats. Only in the Nordic countries do women hold more than a third of parliamentary seats, with Sweden topping the list and Denmark, Finland, and Norway following close behind.

Nevertheless, a small number of Canadian female politicians have achieved national prominence, as in the cases of Kim Campbell who, in 1993, served as Canada's first female prime minister, and Alexa McDonough, recently reelected as leader of the national New Democratic Party. Nevertheless, in 2001, our provincial premiers and territorial leaders, as well as our prime minister, make up a completely male cast!

**TABLE 10-3  Average Earnings of Men and Women in Different Occupations, Full-Time, Full-year Workers, Canada, 1997**

| Selected Occupational Categories | Women | Men | Earnings Ratio |
|---|---|---|---|
| Managerial/administrative | 37 092 | 56 640 | 65.5 |
| Professionals | | | |
| Natural sciences | 41 221 | 49 962 | 82.5 |
| Social sciences/religion | 37 280 | 55 767 | 66.8 |
| Teaching | 40 888 | 50 305 | 81.3 |
| Medicine/health | 35 407 | 62 354 | 56.8 |
| Artistic/recreational | 29 324 | 41 251 | 71.1 |
| Clerical | 28 151 | 34 863 | 80.7 |
| Sales | 28 843 | 39 475 | 73.1 |
| Service | 21 516 | 33 225 | 64.8 |
| Agriculture | 18 366 | 25 126 | 73.1 |
| Processing | 26 886 | 40 655 | 66.1 |
| Product assembly/fabrication/repair | 24 384 | 38 111 | 64 |
| Transport equipment operation | 30 253 | 38 396 | 78.8 |
| Material handling | 22 810 | 35 821 | 63.7 |
| **Total** | **30 915** | **42 626** | **72.5** |

**Note:** Earnings ratio represents women's earnings as a percentage of men's earnings.

Source: Statistics Canada (2000m).

## ARE WOMEN A MINORITY?

A **minority**[1] is *any category of people, characterized by physical or cultural difference, that a society sets apart as subordinates.* Given the clear economic disadvantage of being a woman in our society, it seems reasonable to say that Canadian women are a minority.

Even so, most white women do *not* think of themselves this way (Hacker, 1951; Lengermann, Madoo & Wallace, 1985). This is partly because, unlike racial minorities and ethnic minorities, white women are well represented at all levels of the class structure, including the very top.

Bear in mind, however, that at every class level, women typically have less income, wealth, education, and power than men. In fact, patriarchy makes women dependent for much of their social standing on men—first their fathers and later their husbands (Eichler, 1997).

## MINORITY WOMEN

If women are defined as a minority, what about minority women? Are they doubly handicapped? Generally speaking, the answer is yes, as we can show with some

income comparisons. Looking first at race and ethnicity, Aboriginal women have, on average, very low income compared to non-Aboriginal women in Canada. The average income in 1996 from all sources (including employment income, investments, transfer payments) for Aboriginal women ages 15 and over was $13 300, more than $6000 less than that of non-Aboriginal females and $5000 less than that of Aboriginal males. Visible minority women also have relatively low average incomes. In 1995, their average income from all sources was $16 600, slightly higher than that of Aboriginal women but less than that of other women in Canada ($19 500) (Statistics Canada, 2000m).

These data confirm that although gender has a powerful effect on our lives, it never operates alone. Class position, race and ethnicity, and gender form a multilayered system of disadvantage for some and privilege for others (Arat-Koc, 1989; Ng, 1993; Ginsburg & Tsing, 1990; St. Jean & Feagin, 1998).

## VIOLENCE AGAINST WOMEN

The phrase "rule of thumb" entered our language about 150 years ago when common decency of the day demanded that a man should not beat his wife with a stick thicker than his thumb. Even today, a great deal of "manly" violence is directed against women. A 1993

---

[1] We use the term "minority" instead of "minority group" because, as explained in Chapter 5 (Groups and Organizations), a minority is a category, not a group.

| TABLE 10–4 | Women in National Parliaments, Lower or Single House, as of December 15, 2000, Selected Countries | | | |
|---|---|---|---|---|
| Rank | Country | Seats | Women | Percentage of Women |
| 1 | Sweden | 349 | 149 | 42.7 |
| 2 | Denmark | 179 | 67 | 37.4 |
| 3 | Finland | 200 | 73 | 36.5 |
| 4 | Norway | 165 | 60 | 36.4 |
| 5 | Netherlands | 150 | 54 | 36.0 |
| 7 | Germany | 669 | 207 | 30.9 |
| 9 | Mozambique | 250 | 75 | 30.0 |
| 10 | South Africa | 399 | 119 | 29.8 |
| 12 | Cuba | 601 | 166 | 27.6 |
| 15 | Argentina | 257 | 68 | 26.5 |
| 18 | Rwanda | 70 | 18 | 25.7 |
| 19 | Namibia | 72 | 18 | 25.0 |
| 20 | Seychelles | 34 | 8 | 23.5 |
| 22(tie) | Australia | 148 | 34 | 23.0 |
| 22(tie) | Switzerland | 200 | 46 | 23.0 |
| 24 | Monaco | 18 | 4 | 22.2 |
| 25 | China | 2984 | 650 | 21.8 |
| 29 | Canada | 301 | 60 | 19.9 |
| 30 | Costa Rica | 57 | 11 | 19.3 |
| 31 | Guyana | 65 | 12 | 18.5 |
| 32 | United Kingdom | 659 | 121 | 18.4 |
| 49(tie) | Jamaica | 60 | 8 | 13.3 |
| 49(tie) | Saint Kitts and Nevis | 15 | 2 | 13.3 |
| 49(tie) | San Marino | 60 | 8 | 13.3 |
| 49(tie) | United States | 435 | 58 | 13.3 |
| 59 | Colombia | 161 | 19 | 11.8 |
| 66 | France | 577 | 63 | 10.9 |
| 71 | Mongolia | 76 | 8 | 10.5 |
| 77 | Nicaragua | 93 | 9 | 9.7 |
| 87 | India | 544 | 49 | 9.0 |
| 91 | Greece | 300 | 26 | 8.7 |
| 101(tie) | Ethiopia | 546 | 42 | 7.7 |
| 101(tie) | Russian Federation | 441 | 34 | 7.7 |
| 117(tie) | Brazil | 513 | 29 | 5.7 |
| 117(tie) | Mauritius | 70 | 4 | 5.7 |
| 150(tie) | Kuwait | 65 | 0 | 0.0 |
| 150(tie) | United Arab Emirates | 40 | 0 | 0.0 |

Note: Updated by authors.

Source: Inter-Parliamentary Union (2001).

Statistics Canada study found that 54 percent of Canadian women reported having experienced at least one instance of unwanted sexual attention (Statistics Canada, 1993b). While men also can be victims of sexual assault, 85 percent of all victims in 1998 were female, indicating a strong association between gender and this type of violent activity (Statistics Canada, 2000m).

Most gender-linked violence occurs where men and women interact most—in the home. Richard Gelles (cited in Roesch, 1984) argues that except for the police and the military, the family is the most violent organization. Both sexes suffer from family violence, although by and large, women sustain more serious injuries than do men (Straus & Gelles, 1986; Schwartz, 1987; Shupe, Stacey, & Hazlewood, 1987; Gelles & Cornell, 1990; Smolowe, 1994).

Violence toward women also occurs in casual relationships. As noted in Chapter 7 (Sexuality), most rapes involve not strangers but men known, and often trusted, by the victim. Dianne Herman (2001) argues that the extent of sexual abuse shows that some tendency toward sexual violence is built into our way of life. All forms of violence against women—from the wolf whistles that intimidate women on city streets to a pinch in a crowded subway to physical assaults that occur at home—express what she calls a "rape culture" of men trying to dominate women. In fact, sexual violence is fundamentally about *power*, not sex, and therefore should be understood as a dimension of gender stratification.

**Sexual harassment.** The term **sexual harassment** refers to *comments, gestures, or physical contact of a sexual nature that are deliberate, repeated, and unwelcome.* During the 1990s, sexual harassment became an issue of national importance that rewrote the rules for workplace interaction.

Most (but not all) victims of sexual harassment are women. This is because, first, our culture encourages men to be sexually assertive and to perceive women in sexual terms. As a result, social interaction in the workplace, on campus, and elsewhere can readily take on sexual overtones. Second, most individuals in positions of power—including business executives, physicians, bureau chiefs, assembly line supervisors, professors, and military officers—are men who oversee the work of women.

Sexual harassment is sometimes blatant and direct: A supervisor may solicit sexual favours from an employee coupled with threat of reprisals if the advances are refused. Courts have declared such *quid pro quo* sexual harassment (the Latin phrase means "one thing in return for another") to be a violation of civil rights.

More often, however, the problem of unwelcome sexual attention is a matter of subtle behaviour—sexual teasing, off-colour jokes, pin-ups displayed in the workplace—that may not even be *intended* to harass anyone. But, using the *effect* standard favoured by many feminists, such actions add up to creating a *hostile environment* (Cohen, 1991; Paul, 1991). Incidents of this kind are far more complex because they involve very different perceptions of the same behaviour. For example, a man may think that complimenting a co-worker on her appearance is simply a friendly gesture; she, on the other hand, may feel his behaviour hinders her job performance (Crocker & Kalemba, 1999).

*Many private companies and public organizations have adopted policies to discourage forms of behaviour that might create a "hostile or intimidating environment." In practice, such policies seek to remove sexuality from the workplace so employees can do their jobs while steering clear of traditional notions about female and male relationships. The hope is that sexual harassment policies will develop a comfortable, informal atmosphere in which people can interact freely and easily.*

**Pornography.** A precise definition of *pornography* has long eluded scholars and lawmakers. Unable to set specific standards that distinguish what is pornographic from what is not, the Supreme Court allows the provinces, territories, and smaller jurisdictions to decide for themselves what violates "community standards" of decency and lacks any redeeming social value.

Definitions aside, pornography (loosely defined) is extremely popular in Canada: X-rated videos, 900 telephone numbers for sexual conversation, and a host of sexually explicit movies and magazines constitute a multimillion-dollar-a-year industry (Cheney, 2000).

Traditionally, society has cast pornography as a *moral* issue. A more recent view focusses on pornography as demeaning to women. That is, pornography is really a *power* issue because it implies that men should control both sexuality and women. In other words, pornography is one foundation of male dominance because it dehumanizes women as the playthings of men. Worth noting, in this context, is that the term *pornography* is derived from the Greek word *porne*, meaning a harlot who acts as a man's sexual slave.

Another way pornography involves male power, according to many analysts, is by promoting violence against women. Depicting women as merely the playthings of men amounts to defining women as weak and undeserving of respect. Men show contempt for women defined in this way by striking out against them. Surveys show that about half of adults believe pornography encourages people to commit rape (NORC, 1999:237).

Like sexual harassment, pornography raises complex and conflicting concerns. While everyone objects to offensive material, many also endorse rights of free speech and artistic expression. Nevertheless, pressure to restrict pornography has increased in recent years, both from conservative people who oppose pornography on moral grounds and liberal people who oppose it as demeaning and threatening to women.

# THEORETICAL ANALYSIS OF GENDER

Each of sociology's major theoretical paradigms addresses the significance of gender in social organization.

## STRUCTURAL-FUNCTIONAL ANALYSIS

The structural-functional paradigm views society as a complex system of many separate but integrated parts. From this point of view, gender serves as a means to organize social life.

As Chapter 2 (Culture) explained, the earliest hunting and gathering societies had little power over the forces of biology. Lacking effective birth control, women were frequently pregnant, and the responsibilities of child care kept them close to home. At the same time, men's greater strength made them better suited for warfare and hunting game. Over the centuries, this gender-based division of labour became institutionalized and largely taken for granted (Lengermann, Madoo & Wallace, 1985).

Industrial technology, however, opens up a vastly greater range of cultural possibilities. Human muscle power is no longer the main energy source, and so the physical strength of men becomes less significant. In addition, the ability to control reproduction gives women greater choice in shaping their lives. Modern societies relax traditional gender roles because such rules waste an enormous amount of human talent; yet change comes slowly because gender is deeply embedded in culture.

*Are the traditional gender roles depicted in this photo normally complementary or do they cause tension and conflict?*

**Talcott Parsons: Gender and complementarity.** As Talcott Parsons (1942, 1951, 1954) observed, gender helps integrate society—at least in its traditional form. Gender forms a *complementary* set of roles that link women and men into family units for carrying out various important tasks. Women take primary responsibility for managing the household and raising children. Men connect the family to the larger world as they participate in the labour force.

Parsons further argued that distinctive socialization teaches the two sexes their appropriate gender identity and skills needed for adult life. Thus society teaches boys—who are presumably destined for the labour force—to be rational, self-assured, and competitive. This complex of traits Parsons termed *instrumental*. To prepare girls for child rearing, socialization stresses *expressive* qualities, such as emotional responsiveness and sensitivity to others.

Society, explains Parsons, encourages gender conformity by instilling in men and women a fear that straying too far from accepted standards of masculinity or femininity courts rejection by the opposite sex. In simple terms, women learn to view non-masculine men as sexually unattractive, while men learn to shun unfeminine women.

**Critical evaluation.** Structural-functionalism puts forward a theory of complementarity by which gender integrates society both structurally (in terms of what people do) and morally (in terms of what they believe). Influential at mid-century, this approach has lost much of its standing today.

First, functionalism assumes a singular vision of society that is not shared by everyone. For example, many women have traditionally worked outside the home because of economic necessity, a fact not reflected in Parsons's conventional, middle-class view

of social life. Second, Parsons's analysis ignores personal strains and social costs of rigid gender roles (Giele, 1988). Third, to those who seek sexual equality, what Parsons describes as gender "complementarity" amounts to little more than male domination.

## SOCIAL-CONFLICT ANALYSIS

From a social-conflict point of view, gender involves differences not just in behaviour but in power. Consider the striking parallel between the ways ideas about gender have benefited men and the way oppression of racial and ethnic minorities has benefited whites (Hacker, 1951, 1974; Collins, 1971; Lengermann & Wallace, 1985; Eichler, 1997; Smith, 1987). That is, conventional ideas about gender promote not cohesion but division and tension, with men seeking to protect their privileges as women challenge the status quo.

As earlier chapters noted, the social-conflict paradigm draws heavily on the ideas of Karl Marx. Yet Marx was a product of his time insofar as his writings focussed almost exclusively on men. His friend and collaborator Friedrich Engels, however, did develop a theory of gender stratification (1902; orig. 1884).

**Friedrich Engels: Gender and class.** Looking back through history, Engels saw that in hunting and gathering societies the activities of women and men, while different, had the same importance. A successful hunt brought men great prestige, but the vegetation gathered by women provided most of a group's food supply. As technological advances led to a productive surplus, however, social equality and communal sharing gave way to private property and, ultimately, a class hierarchy. At this point, men gained pronounced power over women. With surplus wealth to pass on to heirs, upper-class men wanted to be sure of their paternity, which led them to control the sexuality of women. The desire to control property, then, prompted the creation of monogamous marriage and the family. Women were taught to remain virgins until marriage, to remain faithful to their husbands thereafter, and to build their lives around bearing and raising one man's children.

Furthermore, said Engels, capitalism intensifies this male domination. For one thing, capitalism creates more wealth, which confers greater power on men as owners of property and as primary wage earners. Second, an expanding capitalist economy depends on turning people—especially women—into consumers who seek personal fulfillment through buying and using products. Third, to free men to work in factories, society assigns women the task of maintaining the home. The double exploitation of capitalism, as Engels saw it, lies in paying low wages for male labour and no wages for female work (Eisenstein, 1979; Barry, 1983; Jagger, 1983; Vogel, 1983).

**Critical evaluation.**   Social-conflict analysis of gender highlights how society places the two sexes in unequal positions of wealth, power, and privilege. It is decidedly critical of conventional ideas about gender, claiming society would be better off if we minimized or even eliminated this dimension of social structure.

But social-conflict analysis, too, has its critics. One problem is that this approach sees conventional families—defended by traditionalists as morally positive—as a social evil. Second, from a more practical point of view, social-conflict analysis minimizes the extent to which women and men live together cooperatively, and often happily, in families. A third problem with this approach lies in its assertion that capitalism is the root of gender stratification. In fact, agrarian societies are typically more patriarchal than industrial-capitalist societies, and former socialist nations—including the People's Republic of China and the Soviet Union prior to its break up—were strongly patriarchal (Moore, 1992; Rosendahl, 1997).

# FEMINISM

**Feminism** is *the advocacy of social equality for men and women, in opposition to patriarchy and sexism.* The "first wave" of the feminist movement in Canada began in the mid-19th century as women sought to gain equal property rights, as well as voting rights. The latter was finally achieved at the federal level in 1918. Achieving the right to vote in provincial elections for all Canadian women took another 22 years—that's when the province of Quebec extended the right to women under its jurisdiction. But other disadvantages persisted, and a "second wave" of feminism arose in the 1960s.

Nellie McClung, Alice Jamieson, and Emily Murphy were three of Canada's earliest suffragists. McClung's story was mentioned in the chapter opening. Jamieson was one of the country's first magistrates. Murphy was an Alberta worker and reformer.

## BASIC FEMINIST IDEAS

Feminism views the personal experiences of women and men through the lens of gender. How we think of ourselves (gender identity), how we act (gender roles), and our sex's social standing (gender stratification) are all rooted in the operation of society.

Although people who consider themselves feminists disagree about many things, most support five general principles:

1. **The importance of change.**   Feminist thinking is decidedly political; it relates ideas to action. It is also critical of the status quo, advocating change toward social equality for women and men (Smith, 1987; Smith, 1999).

2. **Expanding human choice.**   Feminists argue that cultural conceptions of gender divide the full range of human qualities into two opposing and limiting spheres: the female world of emotion and cooperation, and the male world of rationality and competition. As an alternative, feminists propose a "reintegration of humanity," by which *all* individuals develop *all* human traits (Eichler, 1997).

3. **Eliminating gender stratification.**   Feminism opposes laws and cultural norms that limit the education, income, and job opportunities of women.

4. **Ending sexual violence.**   Today's women's movement seeks to eliminate sexual violence. Feminists argue that patriarchy distorts the relationships between women and men, encouraging violence against women in the form of rape,

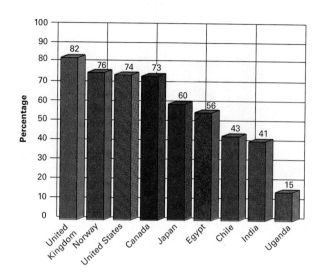

**FIGURE 10–4  Use of Contraception by Women of Childbearing Age**

Source: United Nations Development Programme (2000).

domestic abuse, sexual harassment, and pornography (Millet, 1970; J. Bernard, 1973; Dworkin, 1987).

5. **Promoting sexual freedom.**  Finally, feminism advocates women's control over their sexuality and reproduction. Feminists advocate the free availability of birth control information. As Figure 10–4 shows, contraceptives are much less available in most of the world than in Canada. Most feminists also support a woman's right to choose whether to bear children or to terminate a pregnancy, rather than allowing men—as male partners, physicians, and legislators—to control their reproduction. Many feminists also support gay people's efforts to overcome prejudice and discrimination in a predominantly heterosexual culture (Deckard, 1979; Barry, 1983; Jagger, 1983).

## TYPES OF FEMINISM

Though feminists agree on the goal of more gender equality, there are three strategies for change: liberal feminism, socialist feminism, and radical feminism (Barry, 1983; Jagger, 1983; Stacey, 1983; Vogel, 1983).

*Liberal feminism* is rooted in classic liberal thinking that individuals should be free to develop their own talents and pursue their own interests. Liberal feminism accepts the basic organization of our society, but seeks to expand the rights and opportunities of women, in part laid down in Canada's Charter of Rights and Freedoms.

Liberal feminists endorse reproductive freedom for all women. They respect the family as a social institution but seek changes, including more widely available maternity and paternity leave and child care for parents who wish to work.

*Socialist feminism* evolved from the ideas of Karl Marx and Friedrich Engels, in part as a critical response to Marx's inattention to gender. From this point of view, capitalism increases patriarchy by concentrating wealth and power in the hands of a small number of men. Socialist feminists do not think that the reforms sought by liberal feminism go far enough. The bourgeois family fostered by capitalism must change if we are to replace "domestic slavery" with some collective means of carrying out housework and child care. Moreover, replacing the traditional family can come about only through a socialist revolution that creates a state-centred economy to meet the needs of all.

*Radical feminism*, too, finds liberal feminism inadequate. Moreover, radical feminists do not believe that even a socialist revolution would end patriarchy. Instead, to attain gender equality, society must eliminate gender itself. One possible way to achieve this goal is to use new reproductive technology (see Chapter 13, Family and Religion) to separate women's bodies from the process of childbearing. With an end to motherhood, radical feminists reason, society could leave behind the entire family system, liberating women, men, and children from the tyranny of family, gender, and sex itself (Dworkin, 1987). Thus, radical feminism envisions an egalitarian and gender-free society—a revolution much more radical than that sought by Marx.

## OPPOSITION TO FEMINISM

Feminism provokes criticism and resistance from all men and women who hold conventional ideas about gender. Some men oppose sexual equality for the same reason that many white people have historically opposed social equality for ethnic and racial minorities: They do not want to give up their privileges. Other men and women, including those who are neither rich nor powerful, distrust a social movement (especially its more radical forms) that attacks the traditional family and rejects patterns that have guided male–female relations for centuries.

Further, for some men, feminism threatens the basis of their status and self-respect: their masculinity. Men who have been socialized to value strength and dominance may feel uneasy about feminist ideals of men as gentle and warm (Doyle, 1983). Similarly, women who have built their lives around husbands and children may see feminism as disparaging the social roles that give meaning to their lives (Marshall, 1985).

Resistance to feminism also comes from academic circles. Some sociologists charge that feminism ignores a growing body of evidence that men and women do think and act in somewhat different ways, which may make gender equality impossible. Furthermore, say critics, feminism, with its drive to enhance women's presence in the workplace, belittles the crucial and unique contribution women make to the development of children, especially in the first years of a child's life (Baydar & Brooks-Gunn, 1991; Popenoe, 1993).

Finally, there is the question of *how* women should go about improving their social standing. A large majority of Canadian adults think that women should have equal rights, but many also believe that women should advance individually, according to their training and abilities. In sum, most opposition to feminism is directed against its socialist and radical forms, while support for liberal feminism is widespread. Moreover, we are seeing an unmistakable trend toward gender equality, with more and more Canadian women participating in the labour force and an increasing number of male partners sharing responsibilities in the home. While gender equality in family and working life is more apparent in dual-career marriages of professional men and women (Hertz, 1986), pro-feminist men argue that their gender can be taught that both masculine and feminine identities are changing and that many of the choices open to them conflict with archaic masculine values (Morra & Smith, 1998).

*Dorothy Smith is perhaps the foremost feminist sociologist in Canada today. She has authored numerous books and articles that draw upon a variety of theoretical points of view (Marxism, ethnomethodology, postmodernism, and so on) to develop a critical sociology of women in society that at the same time aims to change women's subordinate position.*

## LOOKING AHEAD: GENDER IN THE TWENTY-FIRST CENTURY

At best, predictions about the future are informed speculation. Just as economists disagree about the probable inflation rate a year from now, so sociologists offer only general observations about the probable future of gender and society.

To begin with, change so far has been remarkable. A century ago, women occupied a position of striking subordination. Husbands controlled property in marriage, and laws barred women from most jobs, from holding political office, and from voting. Although women remain socially disadvantaged, the movement toward equality has surged ahead. Two-thirds of people entering the workforce during the 1990s were women, and today's economy *depends* on the earnings of women.

Many factors have contributed to this transformation. Perhaps most important, industrialization as well as the more recent Information Revolution have shifted the nature of work from physically demanding tasks that favoured male strength to jobs that require thought and imagination. Today, women and men are on an even footing. In addition, since we control reproduction, women's lives are less constrained by unwanted pregnancies.

Many women and men have also deliberately pursued social equality. Sexual harassment complaints are now are taken much more seriously in the workplace. And as more women assume positions of power in the corporate and political worlds, social change in the new century may be as great as what we have already witnessed.

Gender is an important part of personal identity and family life. It is deeply woven into the moral fabric of our society. Therefore, efforts to change our ideas will continue to provoke opposition, as the Controversy & Debate box on page 251 illustrates. On balance, however, we are seeing movement toward a society in which women and men enjoy equal rights and opportunities.

*As a general rule, patriarchy is strongest in nations with traditional cultures and less economic development. Here, we see a husband dragging his wife through the streets of Dhaka, Bangladesh, reportedly because she did not do the cooking on time. While violence against women in North America may not be so public, here as well it remains a serious problem linked to women's subordination.*

## SUMMARY

1. Gender refers to the meaning a culture attaches to being female or male. Because society gives more power and other resources to men than to women, gender is an important dimension of social stratification.

2. Although some degree of patriarchy exists everywhere, gender varies throughout history and across cultures.

3. Through the socialization process, people incorporate gender into their personalities (gender identity) as well as their actions (gender roles). The major agents of socialization—family, peer groups, schools, and the mass media—reinforce cultural definitions of what is feminine and masculine.

4. Gender stratification shapes the workplace. Although most women are now in the paid labour force, most hold clerical, sales, or service jobs. Unpaid housework remains a task performed mostly by women, whether or not they hold jobs outside the home.

5. On average, women earn just under 73 percent as much as men. This disparity stems from differences in jobs and family responsibilities, as well as from discrimination.

6. Women now earn a slight majority of all bachelor's and master's degrees. Men still earn a majority of doctorate degrees.

7. The number of women in politics has increased sharply in recent decades. Still, the vast majority of elected officials, especially at the national level, are men.

8. Because women have a distinctive identity and are disadvantaged, they are a minority, although most do not think of themselves that way. Minority women encounter greater social disadvantages than do white women.

9. Violence against women is a widespread problem in Canada. Our society is also grappling with issues of sexual harassment and pornography.

10. Structural-functional analysis suggests that in preindustrial societies, distinct roles for females and males reflect biological differences between the sexes. In industrial societies, marked gender inequality becomes dysfunctional and gradually decreases. Talcott Parsons claimed that complementary gender roles promote the social integration of families and society as a whole.

## CONTROVERSY & DEBATE

# A Closer Look: Are Men *Really* So Privileged?

Anti-male discrimination has become far greater in scope, in degree, and in damage than any which may exist against women.

— *Men's rights advocate Richard F. Doyle*

It is men, this chapter argues, who dominate society. Men enjoy higher earnings, control more wealth, exercise more power, do less housework, and get more respect than women do. But Doyle's assertion above states an important counterpoint advanced by the "men's rights movement"—that the male world is not nearly as privileged as some people think.

If men are so privileged in our society, why do they turn to crime more often than women? Moreover, the criminal justice system does not give men any special privileges. Probably most people would not be surprised to learn that police are reluctant to arrest a woman, especially if she has children. This fact helps explain why 80 percent of arrests for serious crime put the handcuffs on a male. Neither do men get a break from the courts, since in 1997–98 males made up 91 percent of adults in provincial and territorial prisons and 95 percent of those in federal penitentiaries (Statistics Canada, 2000m).

Culture is not always generous to men, either. Our way of life praises as "real men" males who work, live, and play hard, and who drink, smoke, and speed on the highways. Given this view of maleness, is it any wonder that men are twice as likely as women to suffer serious assault, three times more likely to fall victim to homicide, and four times more likely to commit suicide? In light of these statistics, how do we explain our society's attention to violence against *women*? Perhaps, critics suggest, we are in the grip of a cultural double standard: We accept harm that comes to males while showing sympathy for the far fewer cases of violence against women. It is this same double standard, the argument continues, that moves women and children out of harm's way and expects men to "go down with the ship" or die defending their country on the battlefield.

Child custody is another sore point from the perspective of many men. Despite decades of consciousness-raising in pursuit of gender fairness, and clear evidence that men earn more than women, courts across Canada routinely award primary care of children to mothers. To make matters worse, men separated from their children by the courts are often stigmatized as "runaway fathers" or "dead-beat dads."

Finally, male advocates point out that affirmative action laws now cover the majority of the population, but notably exclude white males. Therefore, in today's affirmative action climate, women have the inside track to university (where they now outnumber men) as well as the workforce (where businesses know they will be called to account for hiring practices).

Even nature seems to plot against men as, on average, women live six years longer. The controversial question is this: When society plays favourites, who is favoured?

*Continue the debate . . .*

1. *Do you think the criminal justice system favours women over men? Or do men simply get what they deserve? Why, in your opinion, are so many more men than women in prison?*

2. *On your campus, do male organizations (such as fraternities and athletic teams) enjoy special privileges? What about women's organizations?*

3. *On balance, do you agree or disagree with the "men's rights perspective"? What specific points do you find convincing or wrong? Why?*

Sources: Based on Doyle (1980), Scanlon (1992), Rosenfeld (1998), and Kleinfeld (1999).

---

11. Social-conflict analysis views gender as a dimension of social inequality and conflict. Friedrich Engels tied gender stratification to the development of private property.

12. Feminism endorses the social equality of the sexes and opposes patriarchy and sexism. Feminism also seeks to eliminate violence against women and give women control over their sexuality and reproduction.

13. There are three variants of feminist thinking. Liberal feminism seeks equal opportunity for both sexes within current social arrangements; socialist feminism advocates abolishing private property as the means to social equality; radical feminism seeks to create a gender-free society.

## KEY CONCEPTS

**gender** (p. 231) the personal traits and social meanings that members of a society attach to being female and male

**gender stratification** (p. 232) the unequal distribution of wealth, power, and privilege between women and men

**patriarchy** (p. 233) a form of social organization in which males dominate females

**matriarchy** (p. 233) a form of social organization in which females dominate males

**sexism** (p. 234) the belief that one sex is innately superior to the other

**gender roles** (sex roles) (p. 235) attitudes and activities that a society links to males and females

**minority** (p. 243) any category of people, distinguished by physical or cultural difference, that a society sets apart and subordinates

**sexual harassment** (p. 244) comments, gestures, or physical contact of a sexual nature that are deliberate, repeated, and unwelcome

**feminism** (p. 247) the advocacy of social equality for women and men, in opposition to patriarchy and sexism

## CRITICAL-THINKING QUESTIONS

1. How do we know that the different and unequal social standing of women and men is not natural and inevitable?

2. What techniques do the mass media use to "sell" conventional ideas about gender to women and men?

3. Why is gender a dimension of social stratification? How does gender overlap with inequality based on class, race, and ethnicity?

4. What are the key assertions of feminism? How do liberal, socialist, and radical feminism differ from one another?

5. A number of European nations, including Great Britain, Norway, Denmark, and Finland, require that at least 25 percent of candidates for national offices be women. Should Canada do likewise?

## APPLICATIONS AND EXERCISES

1. Take a walk through the business area of your local community. Which businesses are frequented almost entirely by women? By men? By both men and women? Try to explain the patterns you find.

2. Watch several hours of children's television programming on a Saturday morning. Notice the advertising, which mostly sells toys and breakfast cereal. Keep track of what share of toys are "gendered," that is, aimed at one sex or the other. What traits do you associate with toys intended for boys and those intended for girls?

3. Do some research on the history of women's issues in your province. When was the first woman sent to Parliament? What laws have existed restricting the work women could do? Are there any such laws today? What share of political officials today is women?

 SITES TO SEE

**www.pearsoned.ca/macionis**
Pearson Education Canada and the authors provide a Web site that accompanies this text, provided outlines, review material, learning exercises, and practice tests for each chapter. At the main page, simple click on the cover of your book and follow the easy menus.

**www.psac.com**
Visit the Public Service Alliance of Canada's Web site and learn about pay equity issues.

**www.swc-cfc.gc.ca**
Visit the Web site for the Status of Women Canada to discover the goals and strategies of this organization.

**www.cwhn.ca**
Another informative site is run by the Canadian Women's Health Network. Identify the issues this organization finds most important.

**www.wwwomen.com**
This site provides a search engine to locate all sorts of information concerning women.

**www.educationindex.com/women**
This site provides numerous and widely varied links to sites concerned with women's issues.

**www.womenspace.ca**
The Women's space Web site discusses ways of using the Net for women's activism.

**www.catalystwomen.org**
This site includes research and information on the social standing of Canadian and U.S. women in business.

**www.feminist.com/resources/links/links_men.html**
This informative site lists a number of pro-feminist men's groups.

# 11

# RACE AND ETHNICITY

*Colonial attitudes and practices, enshrined in official legislation, took a huge toll on Canada's Aboriginal peoples. The infamous* Indian Act *of 1874 legally authorized federal government jurisdiction over Aboriginal communities across the country. Among other things, the* Indian Act *institutionalized a residential school system. Federally appointed education authorities removed—by physical force, if parents objected—Aboriginal children of both genders from their families and communities, relocating them in distant residential schools where a foreign language, religion, and culture were imposed.*

*Aboriginal youth who "successfully" completed the school program later faced a different set of concerns; they often found their newly acquired "foreign" knowledge wanting. They had not learned how to forge intimate relationships with others, including their elders, or how to parent effectively. The knowledge they acquired from the white Christian teachers left them caught between two worlds; they found it difficult to accept the teachings of their elders and yet felt isolated from mainstream society. In brief, the proud and "educated" Aboriginal was left "hanging in the middle of the two cultures and he is not a white man and he is not an Indian. [The missionary teachers] washed away practically everything an Indian needed to help himself, to think the way a human person should in order to survive" (Sluman & Goodwill, quoted in Dickason, 1992:336).*

*Much is changing for Canada's Aboriginal people today. The federal government has started to return political control to the Aboriginal people, allowing them to* decide *what educational system and other social institutions are best for their children. And the United Church has formally apologized for the sexual abuse of Aboriginal children in the residential system. Yet deep scars remain. In many pockets of the country, former religious teachers are only now being brought to justice for the physical and sexual abuse they inflicted on generations of Aboriginal children, who continue to be treated in many respects as second-class citizens in a country that prides itself on its tolerance and concern for others (Benoit & Carroll, 1995).*

*Around the world, the pattern of inequality and conflict based on colour and culture is even more striking. Since the fall of the former Soviet Union, Ukrainians, Moldavians, Azerbaijanis, and a host of other ethnic peoples in Eastern Europe have struggled to recover their cultural identity. In the Middle East, Arabs and Jews are trying to overcome deep-rooted tensions, as are Northern Ireland's Protestants and Catholics. In dozens of the world's nations, colour and culture often flare into violent confrontation.* ■

An irony of the human condition is that colour and culture—the source of great pride—also cause people to degrade themselves with hatred and violence. This chapter examines the meaning of race and ethnicity, explains how these social constructs have shaped our history, and suggests why they continue to play such a central part—for better or worse—in the world today.

*The range of biological variation in human beings is far greater than any system of racial classification allows. This fact is made obvious by trying to place all of the people pictured here into simple racial categories.*

## THE SOCIAL MEANING OF RACE AND ETHNICITY

People frequently confuse the terms *race* and *ethnicity*. For this reason, we begin with important definitions.

### RACE

A **race** is *a socially constructed category composed of people who share biologically transmitted traits that members of a society consider important*. People classify each other racially based on physical characteristics such as skin colour, facial features, hair texture, and body shape.

Racial diversity appeared among our human ancestors as the result of living in different regions of the world. In regions of intense heat, for example, people developed darker skin (from the natural pigment melanin) as protection from the sun; in moderate climates, people developed lighter skin. Such traits are—literally—only skin deep, because *every* human being the world over is a member of one biological species.

The striking variety of racial traits found today is also the product of migration, so that genetic characteristics once common to a single place are now found in many lands. Especially pronounced is the racial mix in the Middle East (that is, Western Asia), which was

historically a "crossroads" of migration. Greater racial uniformity, by contrast, characterizes more isolated peoples such as the island-dwelling Japanese. But every population has some genetic mixture, and increasing contact among the world's people ensures even more racial blending in the future.

Although racial categories point to some biological elements, race is a socially constructed concept. This means that racial categories only come into being because a society considers some physical traits important. Around the world, societies show considerable variation in this regard: Typically, people in Canada attach more meaning to skin colour than, say, do people in Brazil.

**Racial types.** Race came into being as a social category as 19th-century biologists tried to organize the world's physical diversity by constructing three racial types. They called people with light skin and fine hair *Caucasoid*; people with dark skin and coarse hair, *Negroid*; and people with yellow or brown skin and distinctive folds on the eyelids, *Mongoloid*.

Sociologists consider such terms misleading at best, and harmful at worst (Satzewich, 1998). For one thing, no society contains biologically "pure" people. The skin colour of people we might call "Caucasoid" (or "Indo-European," "Caucasian," or, more commonly, "white") ranges from very light (typical in Scandinavia) to very dark (in southern India). The same variation exists among so-called "Negroids" (Africans, or, more commonly, "black" people) and "Mongoloids" (that is, "Asians"). In fact, many "white" people (say, in southern India) actually have darker skin than many "black" people (like the Negroid aborigines of Australia).

The population of Canada, too, is quite mixed. Over many generations and throughout the Americas, the genetic traits of Negroid Africans, Caucasoid Europeans, and Mongoloid Native Americans (whose ancestors came from Asia) have intermingled. Many "black" people, therefore, have a significant Caucasoid ancestry, many "white" people have some Negroid genes, and many "Aboriginals" have either or sometimes both. In short, whatever people may think, race is no black-and-white issue.

Why, then, do people construct these racial categories in the first place? The reason is that such categories allow societies to rank people in a racial hierarchy, claiming some are inherently "better" than others, although no sound scientific evidence supports such beliefs (Reitz & Breton, 1994). But because so much is at stake, societies may construct racial categories in ways that seem extreme. Through much of the 20th century, for example, many southern U.S. states labelled as "coloured" anyone with as little as 1/32 African ancestry (that is, one African-American great-great-great-grandparent). Today, U.S. law allows parents to declare the race of a child as they may wish. Even so, most people in the United States are still very sensitive to people's racial background. Meanwhile, biologically speaking, race has less and less meaning in most countries, as they become increasingly diverse and intermixed. Take the example of golf superstar Tiger Woods, who describes his own "race" as Cablinasian, meaning a Caucasian-black-Indian-Asian. Woods's father was part black (half-black, one-quarter American Indian, one-quarter white) and his mother was mixed Asian (half-Thai and half-Chinese). As Woods told Oprah Winfrey, "I am just who I am . . . whoever you see in front of you" (Kamiya, 1997).

## ETHNICITY

**Ethnicity** is *a shared cultural heritage.* People define themselves—or others—as members of an *ethnic category* based on having common ancestors, language, and religion that confer a distinctive social identity. Canada is a multiethnic society in which English and French are the "official languages," yet many people speak other languages at home, including Mandarin, Cantonese, Hindu, Thai, Italian, German, Spanish, or Swedish. Similarly, while Catholicism has the largest number of followers, many Canadians identify

| Ethnic Group | Total Reponses | Percentage of Population Declaring Being Only | Percentage of Population Declaring as One of Several |
|---|---|---|---|
| Canadian | 8 806 275 | 18.7 | 12.2 |
| English | 6 832 095 | 7.2 | 16.8 |
| French | 5 597 845 | 9.3 | 10.3 |
| Scottish | 4 260 840 | 2.3 | 12.7 |
| Irish | 3 767 610 | 1.8 | 11.4 |
| German | 2 757 140 | 2.5 | 7.1 |
| Italian | 1 207 475 | 2.6 | 1.7 |
| Ukrainian | 1 026 475 | 1.2 | 2.4 |
| Chinese | 921 585 | 2.8 | 0.4 |
| Dutch (Netherlands) | 916 215 | 1.1 | 2.1 |
| North American Indian | 867 225 | 1.4 | 1.7 |
| Polish | 786 735 | 0.9 | 1.8 |
| East Indian | 548 080 | 1.5 | 0.4 |
| Jewish | 351 705 | 0.7 | 0.5 |
| Norwegian | 346 310 | 0.2 | 1.0 |
| Welsh | 338 905 | 0.1 | 1.1 |
| Portuguese | 335 110 | 0.9 | 0.3 |
| Swedish | 278 975 | 0.1 | 0.9 |
| Russian | 272 335 | 0.2 | 0.8 |
| Hungarian (Magyar) | 250 525 | 0.3 | 0.5 |
| Filipino | 242 880 | 0.7 | 0.2 |
| Métis | 220 740 | 0.2 | 0.6 |
| American | 211 790 | 0.1 | 0.7 |
| Spanish | 204 360 | 0.3 | 0.5 |
| Greek | 203 345 | 0.5 | 0.2 |
| Jamaican | 188 770 | 0.5 | 0.2 |
| Danish | 163 125 | 0.1 | 0.4 |
| Austrian | 140 520 | 0.1 | 0.4 |
| Vietnamese | 136 810 | 0.4 | 0.1 |
| Lebanese | 131 385 | 0.3 | 0.2 |
| Belgian | 123 595 | 0.1 | 0.3 |
| Finnish | 108 720 | 0.1 | 0.3 |
| Romanian | 107 150 | 0.1 | 0.2 |
| Swiss | 104 240 | 0.1 | 0.3 |
| Croatian | 84 495 | 0.2 | 0.1 |
| Haitian | 83 680 | 0.3 | 0.0 |
| Québécois | 80 400 | 0.2 | 0.1 |
| Japanese | 77 130 | 0.2 | 0.1 |
| Czech | 71 915 | 0.1 | 0.2 |
| Icelandic | 70 685 | 0.0 | 0.2 |
| Korean | 66 655 | 0.2 | 0.0 |
| Iranian | 64 405 | 0.2 | 0.0 |
| Acadian | 57 425 | 0.1 | 0.1 |
| West Indian | 54 475 | 0.1 | 0.1 |
| Inuit | 49 845 | 0.1 | 0.1 |
| Punjabi | 49 840 | 0.1 | 0.1 |
| Black | 47 340 | 0.1 | 0.1 |
| **Total Responses** | **45 271 885** | **18 303 565** | **26 968 265** |
| **Total Population** | **28 528 125** | **64.2** | **35.8** |

Source: Statistics Canada, The Nation: 1996 Census of Canada, Electronic data file. Statistics Canada Catalogue No. 93F0029XDB96005, Table n05_1205.ivt. (1998q).

*Racial and ethnic stereotypes are deeply embedded in our culture and language. Many people speak of someone "gypping" another, without realizing that this word insults European gypsies, a category of people long pushed to the margins of European society. What about terms such as "Dutch treat," "French kiss," and "Indian giver"?*

dominant majority, in other words, minorities are set apart and subordinated. The scope of the term *minority* has expanded in recent years beyond race and ethnicity also to encompass, as discussed in Chapter 10 (Gender Stratification), Canadian women as a minority.

The 1996 census was the first in which "Canadian" was included in the examples accompanying the question on ethnicity. While 18.7 percent of the population stated "Canadian" as their only ethnic origin, another 12.2 percent included it in among up to six permissible ethnic origins. Table 11–1 also illustrates the ethnic diversity of Canada. If we disregard the first category, "Canadian," and focus on the segment of the population that stated only one ethnic background, the lengthy list covers only 42.4 percent of the Canadian population in 1996. In addition to the 145 specific ethnic backgrounds listed, there are 16 other ethnic categories that list those "not included elsewhere" (n.i.e.), down to the smallest of these—"Pacific Islander, n.i.e." (this category includes 100 people). Nevertheless, the numerical dominance of first, the British, and second, the French, is evident, given that these two ethnic groups alone make up more than 20 percent of all Canadians who claim only one ethnic background.

Minorities have two major characteristics. First, they share a *distinct identity*. Because societies attach importance to race, and these physical traits are virtually impossible for a person to change, most minority men and women are keenly aware of their physical appearance. The significance of ethnicity (which people *can* change) is more variable. Throughout Canadian history, some people (such as the Irish and the Dutch) have downplayed their historic ethnicity, while others (including many Orthodox Jews and Hutterites) have maintained distinctive cultural traditions and even formed their own neighbourhoods and communities.

A second characteristic of minorities is *subordination*. As the remainder of this chapter shows, many of Canada's minorities typically have lower income, lower occupational prestige, and limited schooling. This applies to women in Canada as a whole, and also to Canada's official government subcategory of visible minorities, which include blacks, South Asians (referred to as "Indo-Pakistanis" in 1986), Chinese, Koreans, Japanese, Southeast Asians, Filipinos, West Asians, Arabs, Latin Americans, and Pacific Islanders. This means that class, race, and ethnicity, as well as gender, are overlapping and reinforcing dimensions of social stratification.

Of course, not all members of any minority category are disadvantaged. Some Aboriginals, for example, are quite wealthy; other Aboriginals are celebrated artistic leaders. But even the greatest success rarely allows individuals to transcend their minority standing (Benjamin, 1991). That is, race or ethnicity often serve as a *master status* (described in Chapter 4,

themselves as Protestants, while many others of Greek, Ukrainian, and Russian descent are affiliated with the Eastern Orthodox Church. About 1 percent of the Canadian population claim Judaism as their faith, and others have a Muslim religious heritage. Table 11–1 on the previous page presents the broad sweep of ethnic diversity in Canada, as recorded by the 1996 census.

People can fairly easily modify their ethnicity: immigrants may discard their cultural traditions over time or, like many people of Aboriginal descent recently, try to revive their heritage (Dickason, 1992; Nagel, 1994; Spencer, 1994).

Finally, ethnicity involves a great deal of variability, for most people identify more than one ethnic background. In Canada, for example, one-third of the population declare themselves to belong to more than one ethnic category.

## MINORITIES

A racial or ethnic minority is a socially constructed category of people, distinguished by physical or cultural traits, that is disadvantaged. Distinct from the

*Star Trek has been a television favourite for more than 30 years. Compare the cast of the original show, which first aired in 1966, to the crew of the most recent* Star Trek: Voyager. *What does the difference in casting suggest about our society's changing view of racial and ethnic minorities?*

Social Interaction in Everyday Life) that overshadows personal accomplishments.

Finally, minorities are usually—but not always—a small proportion of a society's population. For example, black South Africans are disadvantaged even though they are a numerical majority in their country. In Canada, women represent slightly more than half the population, but are still struggling for the opportunities and privileges enjoyed by men.

## PREJUDICE AND STEREOTYPES

November 19, 1995—Jerusalem, Israel
We are driving along the outskirts of this historic city—a holy place to Jews, Christians, and Muslims—when Razi, our taxi driver, spots a small group of Ethiopians at a street corner. "Those people over there," he begins, "they are different. They don't drive cars. They don't want to improve themselves. Even when our country offers them schooling, they don't take it." He shakes his head and pronounces the Ethiopians "socially incorrigible."

**Prejudice** is *a rigid and irrational generalization about an entire category of people.* Prejudice is irrational insofar as it involves inflexible attitudes supported by little or no direct evidence. Prejudice may target people of a particular social class, sex, sexual orientation, age, political affiliation, race, or ethnicity.

Prejudices are *prejudgments* that can be positive or negative. Our positive prejudices exaggerate the virtues of people like ourselves, while our negative prejudices condemn those who differ from us. Negative prejudice runs along a continuum from mild aversion to outright hostility. Because such attitudes are embedded in culture, everyone has at least some measure of prejudice.

Prejudice often takes the form of stereotypes (*stereo* is derived from Greek meaning "hard" or "solid"), which are biased characterizations of some category of people. Many white people hold stereotypical views of minorities. But minorities, too, use stereotypes, sometimes of whites and sometimes of other minorities, including themselves. Some Koreans, for example, portray African Americans as dishonest. Some blacks, in turn, express the same attitude toward Jewish people (Smith, 1996).

## RACISM

A powerful and destructive form of prejudice, **racism** refers to *the belief that one racial category is innately superior or inferior to another.* Racism has pervaded world history. The ancient Greeks, the peoples of India, and the Chinese—despite their many notable achievements—were all quick to consider people unlike themselves as inferior.

Racism has also been widespread in the United States, where, for centuries, ideas about racial inferiority supported slavery. Today, overt racism in the

# Does Race Affect Intelligence?

Are Asians smarter than white people? Is the typical white person more intelligent than the average black person? Throughout the histories of Canada and the United States, we have painted one category of people as intellectually more gifted than another. Moreover, people have used such thinking to justify the privileges of the allegedly superior category and even to bar supposedly inferior people from entering our countries.

Scientists know that the distribution of the intelligence of individuals forms a "bell curve," as shown in the figure at the right. By convention, average performance is defined as an IQ score of 100. (Technically, an IQ score is mental age as measured by a test divided by age in years with the result multiplied by one hundred; thus, an eight-year-old who performs like a ten-year-old has an IQ of

$10/8=1.2 \times 100=120$. As discussed below, some scholars argue that IQ tests are poor measures of intelligence because they ask questions that are geared toward middle-class white culture).

In a controversial study of intelligence and social inequality, Richard Herrnstein and Charles Murray (1994) claimed that overwhelming evidence shows race to be related to measures of intelligence. More specifically, they said the average intelligence quotient (IQ) of people with European ancestry is 100, the average for people of East Asian, 103; and the average for people of African descent, 90. A University of Western Ontario psychology professor, Philippe Rushton, makes a similar claim in developing his "race hierarchy" scale, which has the Chinese at the apex of the racial hierarchy, white people in the middle, and blacks at the bottom (Rushton & Bogaert, 1987).

Of course, assertions of this kind are explosive because they fly in the face of our democratic and egalitarian sentiments, which say that no racial type is inherently "better" than another. Such assertions have led some critics to charge that intelligence tests are not valid, and even that the concept of intelligence has little real meaning.

Most social scientists acknowledge that IQ tests do measure something important that we think of as "intelligence," and they agree that some *individuals* vary in intellectual aptitude. But they reject the notion that any *category* of people, on average, is smarter than any other. Research does show that categories of people display small differences in measured intelligence. The crucial question is *why*.

Thomas Sowell explains that most of the documented differences in intelligence

---

U.S. has subsided to some extent because the more egalitarian culture urges an evaluation of people, in Dr. Martin Luther King Jr.'s words, "not by the colour of their skin but by the content of their character." Canadian historical records also contain racism: We should not forget that Canada has a long history of oppression. The practice of slavery is recorded among many of the fishing communities of the Pacific Northwest coast predating European contact (Donald, 1997). Racism was also practised in British North America prior to Canadian Confederation, and officially ended only in 1834 (Brand, 1992; Ponting, 1994; Prentice et al., 1996). More recently, evidence has been found of the interplay between racism, sexism, and immigration in our country (Ng, 1993; Ng & Das Gupta, 1993; Iacovetta, 1995).

Further, racism—in thought and deed—remains a serious social problem everywhere as people still contend that some social categories of people are "better" than others (Henry et al., 1995). Indeed, some people wonder if members of one race are smarter than those of another. As the Applying Sociology box explains, however, measures of intelligence are affected by environment rather than biology.

## THEORIES OF PREJUDICE

What are the origins of prejudice? Social scientists provide various answers to this vexing question, focussing on frustration, personality, culture, and social conflict.

**Scapegoat theory.** *Scapegoat theory* holds that prejudice springs from frustration among people who are themselves disadvantaged (Dollard, 1939). Take the case of a white woman unhappy with the low wages she earns at a textile factory. Directing hostility at the powerful people who employ her carries obvious risk; therefore, she may blame her low pay on the presence of minority co-workers. Her prejudice does not improve her situation, but it serves as a relatively safe way to vent anger, and it may give her the comforting sense that at least she is superior to someone.

A **scapegoat**, then, is *a person or category of people, typically with little power, whom others unfairly blame for their troubles*. Because minorities are "safe targets," they are often scapegoats.

**Authoritarian personality theory.** According to T.W. Adorno (1950), extreme prejudice is a personality

are not due to biology but to environment. In some skillful sociological detective work, Sowell traced IQ scores for various racial and ethnic categories throughout this century. He found that, on average, immigrants to North America from European nations such as Poland, Lithuania, Italy, and Greece, as well as Asian countries including China and Japan, scored 10 to 15 points below the U.S. average. But today, people in these same categories have IQ scores that are average or above average. Among Italian Americans, for example, average IQ jumped almost 10 points in 50 years; among Polish and Chinese Americans, the jump was almost 20 points.

Because genetic changes occur over thousands of years and most people in the various categories married others like themselves, biological factors cannot explain such a rapid rise in IQ scores. The only plausible explanation is cultural. The descendants of early immigrants improved their intellectual performance as their living conditions improved and their opportunities for schooling increased.

Sowell found a similar pattern applies to African Americans. Historically, the average IQ score of African Americans living in the northern part of North America is about 10 points higher than the average score of those living farther south. In addition, among the

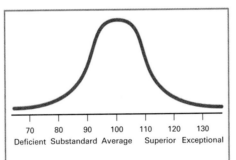

70    80    90    100    110    120    130
Deficient Substandard Average    Superior Exceptional

descendants of African Americans who migrated from the South to the North after 1940, IQ scores went up just as they did with descendants of earlier immigrants. Thus, if environmental factors are the same for various categories of people, racial IQ differences largely disappear.

What these test score differences do tell us, Sowell continues, is that *cultural patterns* matter. Asians who score high on tests are no smarter than other people, but they have been raised to value learning and pursue excellence. For their part, African Americans are no less intelligent than anyone else, but they carry a legacy of disadvantage that can undermine self-confidence and discourage achievement.

Sources: Herrnstein & Murray (1994); Rushton & Bogaert (1987); Sowell (1994, 1995).

trait in certain individuals. This conclusion is supported by research showing that people who display strong prejudice toward one minority are usually intolerant of all minorities. These *authoritarian personalities* rigidly conform to conventional cultural values; see moral issues as clear-cut matters of right and wrong; and look upon society as naturally competitive, with "better" people (like themselves) inevitably dominating those who are weaker.

Adorno also found that people tolerant toward one minority are likely to be accepting of all. They tend to be more flexible in their moral judgments and treat all people as equals.

Adorno thought that people with little education and those raised by cold and demanding parents tend to develop authoritarian personalities. Filled with anger and anxiety as children, they grow into hostile and aggressive adults, seeking scapegoats whom they consider inferior.

**Cultural theory.** A third theory contends that while extreme prejudice is found in certain people, some prejudice is found in everyone because it is embedded in culture. Emory Bogardus (1968) studied the effects of culturally rooted prejudices for more than 40 years. He developed the concept of *social distance* to gauge how close or distant people feel toward various racial and ethnic categories. Bogardus found that people from the United States feel closest to individuals with English, Canadian, and Scottish backgrounds, even welcoming marriage with them. Attitudes are less favourable toward the French, Germans, Swedes, and Dutch, and most negative toward people of Asian and African descent.

According to Bogardus, prejudice is so widespread that we cannot explain it as merely a trait of a handful of people with authoritarian personalities, as Adorno suggests. Rather, Bogardus believed everyone in North American society expresses some bigotry because we live in a "culture of prejudice" that has taught us to view certain categories of people as inferior to others. As shown in the Social Diversity box on page 262, a substantial minority of Canadians are prejudiced toward others least like themselves, and to some extent this continues to be the case today (Reitz & Breton, 1994).

**Conflict theory.** A fourth explanation is that powerful people use prejudice to justify oppressing others. The consequence of white employers looking down on Chinese immigrants in Vancouver, for example, is that

# SOCIAL DIVERSITY

# Racism in Canada: Numbers and Places in the News

The following information collected from surveys and newspaper and magazine articles reveals a pattern of racism in Canada.

## In the Past

- In 1907, 50 percent of Vancouver's population attended the Asiatic Exclusion League parade, where the signs "Keep Canada White" and "Stop the Yellow Peril" were present.
- In 1922, the Victoria, B.C. school board segregated Asian-Canadian students.
- Until 1949, Canadian-born Chinese were not allowed to vote.[1]

## More Recently

- In 1996, 49 percent of Canada's population felt that "Current immigration numbers are too high."[2]
- In 1996, Canadians responded to the statement "Non-whites should not be allowed to immigrate to Canada" as follows: Scores are on a scale of 1 (strongly agree) to 5 (strongly disagree). The lower the score, the greater the intolerance.[3]

| | |
|---|---|
| Vancouver | 4.67 |
| Prairies | 4.64 |
| Ontario (except Toronto) | 4.61 |
| B.C. (except Vancouver) | 4.43 |
| Atlantic Canada | 4.38 |
| Montreal | 4.42 |
| Quebec (except Montreal) | 4.33 |
| Toronto | 4.09 |
| Canada | 4.47 |

- In 1998, Sikh temple caretaker Nirmal Singh Gill, age 65, was beaten to death in B.C. The five men accused of the murder were active in white power groups.[4]

## "Visible Minorities": What Canadians Believe

- Percentage of white Toronto respondents who, in 1996:[5]

  Believed that visible minorities had made an important contribution to Canada: 85

  Disagreed with the statement: Visible minorities are not prepared to work hard: 79

  Believed that it should be against the law to treat visible minorities differently from others: 81

  Believed that visible minorities often bring discrimination on themselves: 67

  Believed that visible minorities are often better treated than other Canadians: 58

- Percentage of "minority" Toronto respondents who, in 1996:[6]

  Did not believe that visible minorities are often better treated than other Canadians: 74

## A Canadian Symbol: The Royal Canadian Mounted Police (RCMP)[7]

- Percentage of white male Royal Canadian Mounted Police (RCMP) who, in 1996:

  Agreed that it is more difficult for white males to get into the RCMP

than for women, Aboriginals, or people from other minorities: 96

  Felt that female, Aboriginal, and minority members "see discrimination where it does not exist": 50

  Agreed that "Aboriginal members respect RCMP tradition as much as anyone": 48

- Percentage of white male Mounties who, in 1996:

  Agreed that "visible minority" members respect RCMP tradition as much as anyone": 38

- Percentage of "minority" Mounties who agreed with the above statement: 80

- Percentage of Aboriginal Mounties who agreed with the above statement: 59

## Canadian Racists: Who Are They?[8]

- The largest concentration of right-wing racists in Canada is in Toronto.
- The second-largest concentration of right-wing racists in Canada is in B.C.'s lower mainland.
- The average age of a Canadian racist is 18 to 20 years old.

Notes:
1 Hume (1995).
2 Gardner (1997).
3 Miller (1997).
4 Wood (1998).
5 Borovoy (1996).
6 Desmond (1996).
7 Mofina (1996).
8 McDonald (1995).

well-off people can pay the immigrants low wages for hard work. Similarly, all elites benefit when prejudice divides workers along racial and ethnic lines and discourages them from working together to advance their common interests (Geschwender, 1978; Olzak, 1989).

Another conflict-based argument, advanced by Shelby Steele (1990), is that minorities themselves cultivate a climate of *race consciousness* in order to win greater power and privileges. Because of their historic disadvantage, minorities claim that they are now victims entitled to special consideration based on their race. While this argument may yield short-term gains, Steele cautions that such thinking may spark a backlash from whites or others who oppose "special treatment" for anyone on the basis of race or ethnicity.

## DISCRIMINATION

Closely related to prejudice is **discrimination**, *treating various categories of people unequally*. While prejudice refers to attitudes, discrimination is a matter of action. Like prejudice, discrimination can be either positive (providing special advantages) or negative (creating obstacles). Discrimination also ranges from subtle to blatant.

Prejudice and discrimination often occur together: A prejudiced personnel manager, for example, may refuse to hire minorities. Robert Merton (1976) describes such a person as an *active bigot*, as shown in Figure 11–1a. But prejudice and discrimination may not occur together, as in the case of the prejudiced personnel manager who, out of fear of lawsuits, *does* hire minorities. Merton calls this person a *timid bigot*. People who are generally tolerant of minorities yet discriminate when it is to their advantage to do so are *fair-weather liberals*. Finally, Merton's *all-weather liberal* is free of both prejudice and discrimination.

## INSTITUTIONAL PREJUDICE AND DISCRIMINATION

We typically think of prejudice and discrimination as the hateful ideas or actions of specific people. But 30 years ago, Stokely Carmichael and Charles Hamilton (1967) pointed out that far greater harm results from **institutional prejudice and discrimination**, which refers to *bias inherent in the operation of society's institutions*, including schools, hospitals, the police, and the workplace (Satzewich, 1998:39–41).

Canada has its own forms of institutional discrimination, as shown by the above-mentioned *Indian Act* and its harsh rules toward Aboriginal people (Jamieson, 1986; Ponting & Kiely, 1997). The Act specifically discriminated against Aboriginal women. If a Status Indian woman married a non-Status Indian man, she lost her legal status and was denied rights and benefits under the *Indian Act*. This meant that many women and children of subsequent generations were culturally alienated from their traditional communities. According to Jeffries (1992:92–3),

> The government's treatment of women under the *Indian Act* was particularly devastating and tantamount to cultural genocide, because women were responsible for maintaining culture. If a woman chose to marry a non-Indian man, she was removed from government's list of registered Indians . . . Upon marriage, the woman could no longer live in the community in which she was born, nor could she participate in any matters respecting

**FIGURE 11–1 Patterns of Prejudice and Discrimination**

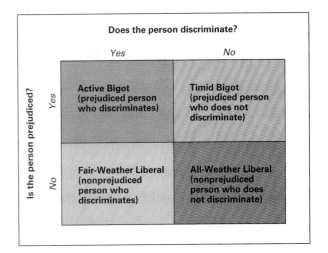

**(a) Prejudice and Discrimination: Various Combinations**

Source: Merton (1976).

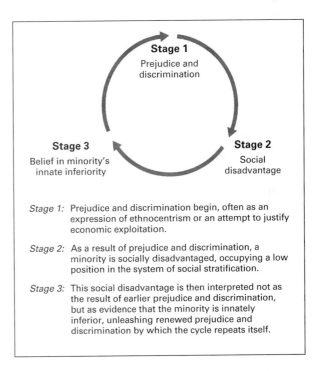

*Stage 1:* Prejudice and discrimination begin, often as an expression of ethnocentrism or an attempt to justify economic exploitation.

*Stage 2:* As a result of prejudice and discrimination, a minority is socially disadvantaged, occupying a low position in the system of social stratification.

*Stage 3:* This social disadvantage is then interpreted not as the result of earlier prejudice and discrimination, but as evidence that the minority is innately inferior, unleashing renewed prejudice and discrimination by which the cycle repeats itself.

**(b) The Vicious Circle**

Prejudice and discrimination can form a vicious circle, perpetuating themselves.

the community. The final insult was upon death: neither she nor any of her children could be buried in a family plot on band land.

*Most Canadian cities today have distinct ethnic enclaves. Some people see this as a positive trend, arguing that it validates the uniqueness of ethnic cultures. Others argue the opposite, viewing ethnic enclaves as indicative of the ghettoization of marginalized groups in our society.*

With the passage of Bill C-31 in 1985, this patriarchal principle was finally revoked. Yet Aboriginal women's access to land and housing remains problematic to this day (Benoit & Carroll, 1995). Since provincial divorce laws do not hold on reserves, Aboriginal women are at risk of losing all common property after separation or divorce. In fact, this holds true even with the proposed new federal bill to transfer control of reserve land to band councils. The new bill would allow band councils to distribute leases and licences, and to establish property-management plans to be voted on by community members and approved by the federal Department of Indian Affairs (Anderssen, 1998:A3). Pending divorce, however, Aboriginal women still would be left without legal means to claim equal access to family property.

### PREJUDICE AND DISCRIMINATION: THE VICIOUS CIRCLE

Prejudice and discrimination reinforce each other. The Thomas Theorem, discussed in Chapter 4 (Social Interaction in Everyday Life), offers a simple explanation of this fact: *Situations that are defined as real become real in their consequences* (1966:301; orig. 1931).

As W.I. Thomas recognized, stereotypes become real to people who believe them, sometimes even to those victimized by them. Prejudice on the part of white people toward African Americans, for example, does not produce *innate* inferiority but it can produce *social* inferiority, pushing minorities into low-paying jobs. Then, if white people interpret social disadvantage as evidence that minorities do not measure up to their standards, they unleash a new round of prejudice and discrimination, giving rise to a vicious circle whereby

each perpetuates the other, as shown in Figure 11–1b on page 263.

## MAJORITY AND MINORITY: PATTERNS OF INTERACTION

Social scientists describe interaction between majority and minority members of a society in terms of four models: pluralism, assimilation, segregation, and genocide.

### PLURALISM

**Pluralism** is *a state in which people of all races and ethnicities, while distinct, have social parity*. In other words, people who differ in appearance or social heritage all share resources more or less equally.

Canada is pluralistic to the extent that all people have equal standing under the law. Moreover, our cities contain countless "ethnic villages" where people proudly display the traditions of their immigrant ancestors. These include Chinatowns found in Victoria, Vancouver, and Toronto; the Jewish area around Avenue du Parc in Montreal; and the Portuguese neighbourhoods around Dundas Street West in Toronto.

But Canada is not really pluralistic—for three reasons. First, while many people appreciate their cultural heritage, only a small proportion want to live with only their "own kind." Second, our tolerance for social diversity is limited. One reaction to the growing proportion of minorities in Canada, for example, is the rise of white supremacist groups in many Canadian cities. Third, as we shall see later in this chapter, it is simply a fact that people of various colours and cultures have unequal social standing.

## ASSIMILATION

Sociologists use the term **assimilation** to describe *the process by which minorities gradually adopt patterns of the dominant category.* Assimilation involves changing styles of dress, values, religion, language, and friends. Many people traditionally have viewed Canada as a "mosaic" in which disparate cultural groups join together to create a tolerant and peaceful multicultural society. Rather than everyone joining as equals in some new cultural pattern, however, minorities typically adopt the traits of the dominant culture established by the earliest settlers. Why? As an avenue to upward social mobility and to escape the prejudice and discrimination directed against more visible foreigners (Newman, 1973). But multiculturalists find fault with the assimilationist model because it tends to paint minorities as "the problem" and define them (rather than elites) as the ones who need to do all the changing.

As a cultural process, assimilation involves changes in ethnicity but not in race. For example, many descendants of Japanese and Chinese immigrants have abandoned their traditions but retain their racial identity. However, distinctive racial traits do diminish over generations as a result of **miscegenation**, *the biological process of interbreeding among racial categories.* Resistance to such biological mixing remains very strong in countries such as South Africa and the United States. In Canada, too, research on biological mixing suggests that we have some way to go before racial identity is a non-issue for Canadians when choosing marriage partners and potential co-parents of their children (Driedger, 1996; Reitz & Breton, 1994).

## SEGREGATION

**Segregation** is *the physical and social separation of categories of people.* Sometimes minorities, especially religious orders such as the Hutterites and Mennonites of Western Canada, voluntarily segregate themselves. Usually, however, majorities segregate minorities by excluding them. Table 11–2 illustrates that people in Canada are more likely to feel comfortable with immigrants from certain ethnic groups. Neighbourhoods, schools, occupations, hospitals, and even cemeteries can be segregated. While pluralism fosters distinctiveness without disadvantage, segregation enforces separation to the detriment of a minority.

South Africa's system of apartheid (described in Chapter 7, Social Stratification) illustrates racial segregation that has been both rigid and pervasive. Apartheid was created by the white European minority it served, and historically was enforced through the use of brutal power (Frederickson, 1981). South Africa is now in the process of dismantling apartheid, but, as yet, the country's basic racial structure has changed

**TABLE 11–2  Comfort around Recent Immigrants, by Ethnicity of Immigrant, Canada, 1991**

|  | Percentage Very Comfortable |
|---|---|
| British | 83 |
| Italians | 77 |
| French | 74 |
| Jews | 74 |
| Ukrainians | 73 |
| Germans | 72 |
| Portuguese | 70 |
| Chinese | 69 |
| West Indian Blacks | 61 |
| Arabs | 52 |
| Muslims | 50 |
| Indo-Pakistanis | 48 |
| Sikhs | 43 |

**Note:** Question was "How comfortable would you feel being around recent immigrants?" On a seven-point scale, 1 meant not comfortable and 7 meant very comfortable. Responses of 6 and 7 were interpreted as meaning "very comfortable."

Source: Angus Reid Group, Inc., (1991).

little; it remains essentially two different societies that touch only when blacks provide services for whites.

Racial segregation also has a long history in Canada, as mentioned above, starting with the segregation of Aboriginal peoples on reserves. Apart from the internment of Japanese Canadians during the Second World War (Kogawa, 1981; Omatsu, 1992), *de jure* (Latin meaning "by law") discrimination in Canada has been relatively rare, in contrast, for example, with the United States. However, de facto ("in fact") segregation continues to this day.

Research by Balakrishnan and Hou (1995) has documented the concentration of different groups in Canada's urban centres. The authors found that visible minorities and Jews tend to live in specific areas of a city rather than being dispersed throughout. This contrasts with the British, Germans, and French, who are relatively evenly distributed (the British in Montreal are an exception to this general pattern).

Balakrishnan and Hou also documented the changing nature of residential segregation. First, even though the composition of the immigration stream to Canada has changed in recent decades—a larger proportion of today's immigrants are from Asia—the authors found that the distribution of Asians in urban areas is not changing. Balakrishnan and Hou attributed this to the fact that the selective nature of immigration policy has led to immigrants being highly skilled and therefore not

On December 7, 1941, Japan attacked Pearl Harbor and Hong Kong. Just weeks later, the Canadian federal government, under the War Measures Act, demanded the evacuation of all Japanese Canadians residing within about 160 kilometres of the Pacific Coast. Although apparently relocated for reasons of national security, no Japanese Canadian was ever charged with disloyalty to the country. In all, 20 000 men, women, and children of Japanese descent were forced to leave their homes for camps in the interior of British Columbia and farms in Alberta and Manitoba.

Source: William Lyon Mackenzie King Collection/National Archives of Canada/C-24452.

colonized vast empires. Some native people fell victim to calculated killing—for example, the Beothuk—but most succumbed to "European" diseases, to which they had no natural defences (Dickason, 1992; Matthiessen, 1984; Sale, 1990).

Genocide also occurred in the 20th century. Unimaginable horror befell European Jews in the 1930s and 1940s during Adolf Hitler's reign of terror, known as the Holocaust. The Nazis murdered more than 6 million Jewish men, women, and children. The Soviet dictator Josef Stalin murdered on an even greater scale, killing some 30 million real and imagined enemies during his violent rule. Between 1975 and 1980, Pol Pot's Communist regime in Cambodia butchered all "capitalists," which included anyone able to speak a Western language. In all, some 2 million people (one-fourth of the population) perished in the Cambodian "killing fields" (Shawcross, 1979).

Tragically, genocide continues. Recent examples include Hutus killing Tutsis in the African nation of Rwanda and Serbs killing Bosnians in the Balkans of Eastern Europe.

These four patterns of minority-majority contact have all been played out in Canada. While many people proudly point to patterns of pluralism and assimilation, it is also important to recognize the degree to which Canadian society has been built on segregation (of black Canadians in Eastern Canada and Japanese Canadians in British Columbia) and genocide (of Aboriginal Canadians). The remainder of this chapter examines how these four patterns have shaped the past and present social standing of major racial and ethnic categories in Canada.

## RACE AND ETHNICITY IN CANADA

Like all people who have nothing, I lived on dreams. I burned my way through stone walls to get to America.

Nu, I got to America.

Ten hours I pushed a machine in a shirtwaist factory, when I was yet lucky to get work.

And always my head was drying up with saving and pinching and worrying to send home a little from the little I earned.

Where are my dreams that were so real to me in the old country?

These words by Jewish immigrant Anzia Yezierska (quoted in Frager, 1992:10) capture the dreams and subsequent disappointments of many European immigrants who made the difficult journey across the Atlantic to find work in the emerging cities of the New World—including "Little York" (Toronto) in

choosing to live in the traditional low-income areas of our cities. Second, the authors pointed out, a certain amount of residential segregation comes from families and individuals choosing to live together rather than being forced into ethnic ghettos. The Jewish population is a case in point. Even though this population is above average in income and education—factors that historically imply freedom of choice—Jews are also among the most segregated ethnic groups in Canada.

### GENOCIDE

**Genocide** is *the systematic killing of one category of people by another.* Although this deadly form of racism and ethnocentrism violates nearly every recognized moral standard, it has occurred time and again in human history.

Genocide figured prominently in contact between Europeans and the original inhabitants of the Americas, from the 16th century on, as the Spanish, Portuguese, English, French, and Dutch forcefully

*More than six millions Jews were killed during the Holocaust in the 1930s and 1940s. Here, survivors of Bergen-Belsen walk along the main street of the camp past a pile of victims' shoes.*

Upper Canada and "Ville-Marie" (Montreal) in Lower Canada. As the following history of Canada's racial and ethnic minorities reveals, our nation's golden door has opened more widely for some than for others.

## CANADA'S ABORIGINAL PEOPLES

Some 30 000 years before Columbus "discovered" the Americas, migrating peoples crossed a land bridge from Asia to North America where the Bering Strait (off the coast of Alaska) lies today. Gradually, they made their way throughout North and South America.

When the first Europeans arrived late in the 15th century, Native Americans numbered in the millions. But by the beginning of this century, after relentless subjugation and even acts of genocide, the "vanishing Americans" numbered a mere 250 000 (Dobyns, 1966; Tyler, 1973).

It was Christopher Columbus (1446–1506) who first referred to Native Americans as "Indians"; when he landed in the Bahama Islands in the Caribbean, he mistakenly thought he had reached India. Columbus found the indigenous people to be passive and peaceful, a stark contrast with the more materialistic and competitive Europeans (Matthiessen, 1984; Sale, 1990). Even as Europeans seized the land of Native Americans, they demeaned their victims as thieves and murderers to justify their actions (Unruh, 1979; Josephy, 1982).

At the beginning of the 18th century there were about 10 Aboriginal people for every European settler in Canada; by 1881 there were about 40 Europeans for every Aboriginal person (Jaffe, 1992). This was not primarily because of a natural increase of European immigrants, however. Traders and later settlers to New France and British North America (later renamed Upper and Lower Canada) brought with them not only trade items, but also racist attitudes toward the non-Christian "savages" who resided in the New World. The Europeans were even prepared to use their superior military power to subdue any Aboriginal peoples unwilling to be colonized.

Europeans also brought with them deadly diseases. Smallpox and other epidemic diseases (including measles, influenza, tuberculosis) had killed many Europeans in the previous centuries. However, for the Aboriginal peoples of the New World, these contagions were "virgin soil epidemics," ravaging hitherto unexposed populations without any built-up immunity to soften the impact (Cohen, 1989). These "diseases of civilization," along with the ill effects of adulterated whisky, reduced the Aboriginal population of British Columbia, for example, by nearly two-thirds before the end of the 1800s (Jaffe, 1992). So marginalized were Canada's Aboriginal peoples that they were not entitled to vote alongside non-Aboriginal Canadian citizens until 1960.

Today, Aboriginal peoples in Canada comprise a diverse and growing population. About 1.1 million persons claimed some Aboriginal ancestry in the 1996 census, up from 1 million in 1991 (Statistics Canada, 1998c). Within this large population, just under 800 000 had adopted an Aboriginal identity—that is, they considered themselves Aboriginal persons. Of these, the majority identified themselves as "North American Indians," a minority declared themselves to be "Métis," and a smaller number reported "Inuit" ancestry. Table 11–3 on page 268 shows the geographic distribution of Canada's Aboriginal peoples.

Despite their growing number, Aboriginal peoples in Canada continue to earn far below the median average income for Canadians. Aboriginal peoples also are more likely to live in single-parent families, and they record higher rates of unemployment and have lower

*There has recently been a resurgence in Aboriginals' pride in their heritage. Do you think that this resurgence is because of, or despite, being a minority group?*

| TABLE 11–3 Aboriginal Population, Canada 1996 | | | |
|---|---|---|---|
| | Total Aboriginal Population | Aboriginal Population as % of Total Population | Geographic Distribution of Aboriginal Population |
| Canada | 799 010 | 2.6 | 100.0 |
| Newfoundland | 14 205 | 2.6 | 1.8 |
| Prince Edward Island | 950 | 0.7 | 0.1 |
| Nova Scotia | 12 380 | 1.4 | 1.5 |
| New Brunswick | 10 250 | 1.4 | 1.3 |
| Quebec | 71 415 | 1.0 | 8.9 |
| Ontario | 141 525 | 1.3 | 17.7 |
| Manitoba | 128 685 | 11.7 | 16.1 |
| Saskatchewan | 111 245 | 11.4 | 13.9 |
| Alberta | 122 840 | 4.6 | 15.4 |
| British Columbia | 139 655 | 3.8 | 17.5 |
| Yukon Territory | 6 175 | 20.1 | 0.8 |
| Northwest Territories | 39 690 | 61.9 | 5.0 |

Source: Statistics Canada, *The Daily*, Tuesday, January 13 (1998c).

rates of school attendance. Their health status is also bleak when compared with that of the country's non-Aboriginal population. Aboriginal peoples have higher tuberculosis and suicide rates, and much shorter life expectancies, than their non-Aboriginal counterparts (Statistics Canada, 1995b).

Like other racial and ethnic minorities in Canada, Aboriginal peoples have recently reasserted pride in their cultural heritage. Some are finally resolving negotiations over territorial lands. Yet, as discussed in the Controversy and Debate box on page 270, not all Canadians are comfortable with special rights for Aboriginal groups, such as the Nisga'a of British Columbia.

## BRITISH CANADIANS

British Canadians—sometimes referred to as White Anglo-Saxon Protestants (WASPs)—were not the first people to inhabit Canada, but they came to dominate this nation once European settlement began. Most British Canadians are of English descent, but this category also includes Scots, Welsh, and Irish. Excluding the 5.3 million people who reported "Canadian" as their single ethnic ancestry in the 1996 census, 4.9 million, or 17 percent of the national population, claimed British ancestry only (Statistics Canada, 1998e).

Historically, British immigrants were highly skilled and motivated by what we now call the "Protestant work ethic." Because of their number and power, British Canadians (with the possible exception of the Irish Catholics) were not subject to the prejudice and discrimination experienced by other categories of immigrants. The historical dominance of British Canadians has been so great that, as noted earlier, others have sought to become more like them.

And the British cultural legacy still stands: English remained, until recent decades, Canada's only official language, and it still dominates the country's media and electronic communication systems. The Canadian legal and political systems, too, reflect their British origins.

## FRENCH CANADIANS

The French explorers arrived in Canada in the 16th century, initially involving themselves in fishing and fur trading. Eventually more French immigrated in search of a better life in "New France." By 1760, there were about 70 000 inhabitants of the colony, with approximately the same number of women as men (Prentice et al., 1996:37). When Acadia (now Nova Scotia) passed from French to British hands in 1713, men and women from that region were either deported to France or resettled in the northeastern regions of what was then "British North America." In the aftermath of the Seven Years' War (1756–1763),

Canada fell under British colonial rule. Though the French retained some control over their own language, religion, and legal institutions, English Canada gained control over economic, political, and social matters.

To some extent, this remains the case even today. The historical legacy of the "two solitudes"—French and English—joined in an uneasy political union resulted in the so-called Quiet Revolution of the 1960s in Quebec. At its most intense, the Quiet Revolution involved the use of radical terrorism as a political weapon against the English (Rocher, 1990). And though the province has undergone substantial change in subsequent decades, in many respects French Quebec and English Canada can still be said to be "two nations warring in the bosom of the same state" (Guindon, 1990:30).

In the 1996 census, about 2.7 million people, or 9 percent of the national population, identified themselves as having French-only ancestry; 19 000 people identified themselves as Acadian; and another 12 000 stated that they were both French and Acadian. Unlike the economy of earlier times when English merchants and traders were in control, the Quebec economy today is mainly under the control of francophone entrepreneurs. Politics has also changed significantly. Two French political parties control the majority of seats in the province, with the Parti Québécois holding power in the Quebec Legislature (the National Assembly) and a new separatist party—the Bloc Québécois—leading the separatist cause at the federal level. The razor-thin defeat of the separatists in the Quebec referendum of 1995 (by a mere 1 percent of the vote) opened the eyes of other Canadians to the very real possibility of the break-up of the country.

On the other hand, many English-speaking Canadian parents have, in the past few decades, enrolled their children in French immersion school programs, and the civil service has become increasingly staffed with Francophones. Yet many issues remain unresolved regarding the future of Quebec, or indeed, of French Canadians in Canada. These issues include Quebec's recent law that "French-only" signs be prominently displayed on public and commercial establishments, the requirement that new immigrants to the province educate their children in French, and the insistence that the lands claimed by the Aboriginal peoples of the province's north be included in the territory proposed for a sovereign Quebec.

## CANADA'S OTHER IMMIGRANTS

As previously noted, Canada is a country of founding peoples, but also of immigrants. Four distinct historical eras can be distinguished when investigating international migration to the country (Gee, 1990). As mentioned above, the French were the original immigrants to the part of the New World that was later to be called

*The Quebec language law—Bill 101—was upheld in April 2000, when the Quebec superior court ruled that French had to be the predominant language on commercial signs. A spray can quickly changes the familiar stop sign into a political message.*

"Canada." The French immigrants eventually established the colony of New France between 1608 and 1760. During the 19th century, a new wave of immigrants came, mainly from Britain, in two population flows: a) the United Empire Loyalists came from the American colonies, fleeing the American Independence movement; and b) immigrants came directly from the British Isles. Smaller numbers of other Europeans also immigrated to Canada during this time, including Germans, Scandinavians, and Eastern Europeans.

The last decades of the 19th century and the early 20th century saw the arrival of the largest wave of immigrants to the country up to that point. Their numbers ranged from 3.7 to 4.6 million (Kalbach & McVey, 1979). Among them were 15 000 Chinese who were permitted to come to Canada as a cheap source of labour for the construction of the transcontinental railroad. Between 1886 and 1923, Canada barred all Asians from settling permanently in the country and imposed a "head tax" on all Chinese wishing to emigrate. The initial head tax was $50, later $100, and finally, in 1904, $500, a very large sum indeed at the time. The head tax on Chinese immigrants was not lifted until 1947. Everyone seemed to line up against the Chinese, as captured in a popular phrase of the time that a person "didn't have a Chinaman's chance" (Sung, 1967).

## CONTROVERSY & DEBATE

# Should Certain Groups in Canada Enjoy Special Rights?

July 23, 1998, marked the conclusion to treaty negotiations among the federal government, the provincia government of British Columbia, and the Nisga'a people of the Nass Valley in northwestern B.C. The box shows the highlights of the treaty that involve sums estimated to reach $448 million. Among the gains for the Nisga'a is the right to elect their own government, with authority to make laws in several key provincial jurisdictions, including those regarding land use, culture, and employment.

Such "special rights" accompanying the groundbreaking treaty (which, it is worth noting, had been pursued by the Nisga'a people for six generations), ignited a heated debate in the province, as well as across the country. People

questioned whether any group—Aboriginal or otherwise—should have legal rights that are different from those of other Canadian citizens. Some critics of the deal argued that it entrenches inequality in Canadian society and called for a province-wide referendum to let the public decide whether the treaty should become law. Others, sympathetic to the Nisga'a people's historical struggle, welcomed the agreement as a compromise that was finally acceptable to the Nisga'a. Such a compromise, argued proponents, would allow the Nisga'a to get on with tackling the high unemployment and other problems affecting their people. Supporters pointed out as well that the Nisga'a had given up other (similarly special) rights they previously held under the *Indian Act*.

### Highlights of Nisga'a Treaty

**Land.** The Nisga'a receive 1930 square kilometres of Crown land and title to 62 square kilometres of land currently designated as Indian reserves. Nisga'a lands do not include private property held by non-natives or agricultural leases. Provincial laws continue to apply to several parcels of land owned by non-natives, which will be surrounded by Nisga'a lands.

**Self-government.** Elections for a central Nisga'a government and four village governments must be held no later than six months after the treaty comes into force. Only Nisga'a can vote for the Nisga'a government, which will adopt a constitution recognizing the rights and freedoms of its citizens.

The head tax and generally racist attitude of many Canadians toward the Chinese created domestic hardship, because in Canada (and similarly in the U.S.) Chinese men outnumbered Chinese women (Hsu, 1971; Lai, 1980; Prentice et al., 1996). For the relatively few Chinese women who managed to enter the country, the situation was far from friendly. Below, a female of Chinese background recalls her life in Nanaimo, British Columbia, in the early decades of this century:

> When I went to school in Nanaimo in the 1920s we had to go to a segregated school. In those days there was still segregation for the "Others." We had to go to a special school because we were not white . . . We had to walk past the better schools, which were only for the white people or westerners, to go to this "ward" school that housed all the Indians, the ethnic people, or "Others" (quoted in Yee, 1992:235–6).

With the relaxation of Canadian immigration laws after 1947, and the more open immigration polices of recent decades, Chinese immigrants to Canada have received a warmer, if not wholehearted, welcome.

The Chinese were not the only immigrants to enter the country during the early part of the 20th century, however. Many immigrants came from the United

States, some from Britain and other parts of Europe, and others from as far away as India.

The last wave of immigrants to Canada arrived in the post-Second World War period—more than 5 million of them—many from middle- and low-income countries around the globe. Canada does not have a quota system in place regarding how many immigrants may enter the country annually. The current regulations emphasize "economic immigration"—that is, the preferred immigrants ideally possess the particular skills and disposable capital to establish themselves economically after migration.

The 1996 census showed that almost 5 million people in Canada—that is, 17 percent of the population—were born outside Canada. The top three birthplaces named in 1996 were the United Kingdom, Italy, and the United States. Together these three origins accounted for 25 percent of all immigrants. The composition of the immigration stream is changing substantially. Among immigrants who have arrived since 1961, there are only two European origins that make the top-10 list—Poland in sixth position and the United Kingdom in tenth. With the exception of the U.S. (ninth position) the remaining top-10 positions are all of Asian origin (Statistics Canada, 1997c). In fact, over half of the immigrant population since 1970, and three-

The Nisga'a government can make laws on Nisga'a citizenship, language, culture, property, public order, safety, employment, traffic, family, and health services, child to provide policing, and correctional and court services.

Non-Nisga'a Canadians can participate in elected bodies that directly affect them by making representations and seeking elections to public agencies such as the health board. Local laws affecting everything from traffic to garbage collection will apply to non-Nisga'a within Nisga'a lands, but most laws will apply only to Nisga'a citizens.

Nisga'a continue to be Aboriginal peoples under the Constitution and are entitled to the same rights as other Canadian citizens. The Charter of Rights and Freedoms and all federal and provincial laws continue to apply to Nisga'a people. However, Nisga'a people will no longer be exempt from sales and income taxes.

**Resources.** Ownership of all forests within Nisga'a lands, and all mineral, oil, and other subsurface resources, will be transferred to the Nisga'a, who can set conditions for their use. Current forest licences will remain in effect for five years. Nisga'a management standards must meet or exceed provincial standards.

Public access to Nisga'a lands for hunting, fishing, and recreation will be provided, although the Nisga'a government may make laws regulating public access for public safety or environmental reasons.

Nisga'a people will be guaranteed 26 percent of the Nass River allowable catch for salmon, and will be allowed to sell their salmon. Any federal commercial or recreational ban on fishing will also apply to the Nisga'a.

Key geographic features will be renamed with Nisga'a names and important cultural sites will be designated as heritage sites. The treaty states that it is the final settlement of Nisga'a Aboriginal rights.

*Continue the debate . . .*

1. *What is your interpretation of the Nisga'a treaty? Is it right that the treaty bestows special rights on a group of people?*

2. *Should other Aboriginal groups in Canada also be able to claim "special legal rights" to the land and resources of their forebears? Why or why not?*

3. *How can sociology play a part in understanding this and other debates over Aboriginal land claims?*

Source: Excerpt from Matas & McInnes (1998).

quarters since the 1990s, are members of a visible minority group. It is to this category that we now turn.

## VISIBLE MINORITIES

The *Canadian Employment Equity Act* defines visible minorities as "persons, other than Aboriginal peoples, who are non-Caucasian in race or non-white in colour." As shown in Table 11–4 on page 272, based on this definition the following ethnic groups are designated as visible minorities in Canada: Chinese, South Asians, blacks, Arabs and West Asians, Filipinos, Southeast Asians, Latin Americans, Japanese, Koreans, and Pacific Islanders. These visible minorities comprise about 3.2 million people, representing 11.2 percent of the total population. According to the 1996 census, one in three visible minority persons was born in Canada. As with the Chinese immigrants who came a century earlier, Canada's visible minorities tend to live in the larger metropolitan areas (94 percent), with three-quarters of visible minorities residing in just two provinces—Ontario and British Columbia.

It is clear that the total integration of visible minorities into Canadian society is not complete since visible minorities are more likely to hold university degrees yet have lower average incomes than other Canadians. As indicated in Table 11–5 on page 272, and as we discussed in detail in the Chapter 10 (Gender Stratification), gender is another kind of minority status that deepens our understanding of the Canadian mosaic.

## LOOKING AHEAD: RACE AND ETHNICITY

Canada is a land of Aboriginal peoples and immigrants. This combination of peoples has generated striking cultural diversity, as well as tales of success, hope, and struggle, told in hundreds of tongues. As shown in National Map 11–1 on page 273, Canada's cultural mosaic is reflected in the concentration of visible minorities throughout particular areas of the country.

For immigrants who came to this country during the second wave of immigration that peaked about 1910, the next generations brought gradual economic gains and at least some cultural assimilation. The government also granted basic freedoms that earlier had been denied, including citizenship and the right to vote and hold public office.

A third wave of immigration began after the Second World War, and swelled as immigration laws

*Asian immigrants are more likely than any other category of people migrating to North America to be small-scale entrepreneurs. Although families may earn above-average incomes operating businesses such as this grocery store, they typically rely on the labour of many people for long hours.*

were relaxed in the 1960s. Since 1990, more than 200 000 people have come to Canada each year, twice the number that arrived during the Great Immigration a century ago (although newcomers now enter a country with a much larger population). Most contemporary immigrants come not from Europe but from middle- and low-income countries.

Many new arrivals face much the same prejudice and discrimination that was directed toward the country's Aboriginal peoples, as well as toward earlier generations of immigrants. Indeed, recent years have witnessed rising hostility toward foreigners (sometimes called *xenophobia*, with Greek roots meaning "fear of what is strange"). This is especially the case in the United States, where, in 1994, California voters passed Proposition 187, which mandates a cut-off in social services (including schooling) to illegal immigrants. The

rise of neo-Nazi groups in Canada, and indeed across many high-income countries, suggests that the U.S. is not alone in its fears of foreigners. The recent media coverage of the "Blackshirts" in Russia, who wear swastikas and express hatred of all Jews, indicates similar developments in middle-income countries as well (Meek, 1998).

Even so, like Canada's Aboriginal peoples, who are enjoying a cultural revival, many new immigrants now try to join Canadian society while maintaining their traditional cultures. Some have also built racial and ethnic enclaves to keep their ethnic traditions and celebrations alive for the next generation. Others have been more open to joining the Canadian mainstream, adhering to the traditional hope of their predecessors—that racial and ethnic diversity, while a dimension of difference, will not be viewed as a badge of inferiority.

### TABLE 11–4 Visible Minority Population by Group, Canada, 1996

| | Individuals | Percentage |
|---|---|---|
| **Total visible minority population** | 3 197 480 | 100.0 |
| Chinese | 860 150 | 26.9 |
| South Asian | 670 585 | 21.0 |
| Black | 573 860 | 17.9 |
| Arab/West Asian | 244 665 | 7.7 |
| Filipino | 234 200 | 7.3 |
| Latin American | 176 975 | 5.5 |
| Southeast Asian | 172 765 | 5.4 |
| Japanese | 68 135 | 2.1 |
| Korean | 64 835 | 2.0 |
| Visible minority, n.i.e.[1] | 69 745 | 2.2 |
| Multiple visible minority[2] | 61 570 | 1.9 |

[1] Includes Pacific Islanders and other visible minority groups (n.i.e. = not included elsewhere).

[2] Includes respondents who reported more than one visible minority group.

Source: Statistics Canada, *The Daily*, Tuesday, February 17 (1998e).

### TABLE 11–5 Average Incomes for People in Visible Minorities and Other People, by Gender, Canada, 1990

| Persons Aged | Visible Minorities | | Other Persons | |
|---|---|---|---|---|
| | Women | Men | Women | Men |
| 15–24 | $17 039 | $18 437 | $17 268 | $20 674 |
| 25–44 | $25 036 | $33 786 | $27 147 | $38 572 |
| 45–54 | $26 787 | $40 840 | $27 819 | $45 867 |
| 55–64 | $23 570 | $37 040 | $24 580 | $41 519 |
| Total aged 15–64 | $24 712 | $34 597 | $26 160 | $39 245 |
| 65 and over | $16 664 | $26 755 | $14 632 | $29 630 |
| Total aged 15 and over | $24 650 | $34 495 | $26 037 | $39 081 |

**Note:** Includes only those employed on a full-year, full-time basis.

Source: Statistics Canada, *Women in Canada: A Statistical Report* (1995).

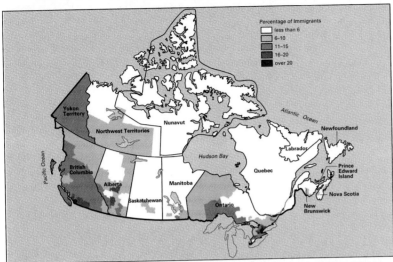

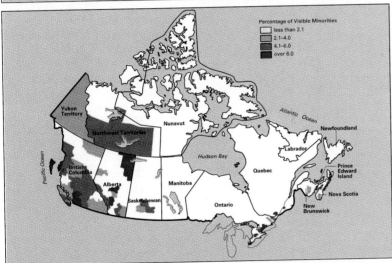

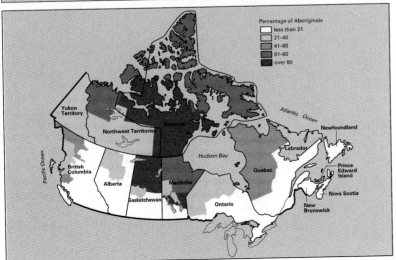

**NATIONAL MAP 11–1**

**The Percentage of Immigrants, Visible Minorities, and Aboriginals by Census Division, Canada, 1996**

These maps show that the largest cities have the greatest concentration of immigrants and visible minorities. The heaviest concentration of Aboriginals, on the other hand, is farther away from the large cities in southern Canada. What do you think helped determine these patterns? Can you identify any other patterns? Do you think these patterns will change in the coming decades?

Source: Calculations based on data in Statistics Canada, Catalogue No. 95F0181XDB96001 (1998b).

# SUMMARY

1. Races are socially constructed categories by which societies set apart people with various physical traits. Although a century ago scientists identified three broad categories—Caucasoids, Negroids, and Mongoloids—there are, in fact, no pure races.

2. Ethnicity is based not on biology but on shared cultural heritage.

3. Minorities—including people of certain races and ethnicities—are categories of people society sets apart, making them both distinct and disadvantaged.

4. Prejudice is a rigid and biased generalization about a category of people. Racism, a destructive type of prejudice, asserts that one race is innately superior or inferior to another.

5. Discrimination is a pattern of action by which a person treats various categories of people unequally.

6. Pluralism means that racial and ethnic categories, although distinct, have equal social standing. Assimilation is a process by which minorities gradually adopt the patterns of the dominant culture. Segregation is the physical and social separation of categories of people. Genocide is the extermination of a category of people.

7. Native Americans—the earliest human inhabitants of the Americas—have endured genocide, segregation, and forced assimilation. Native Americans in Canada are usually referred to as "Aboriginal peoples" and include Native Indians, Métis, and Inuit. Today, Aboriginal peoples have social standing well below the national average.

8. The British WASPs predominated among the original European settlers of Canada, and many continue to enjoy high social standing today.

9. The French group includes both French-only ancestry and Acadians. Though the French were the first to colonize Canada, they subsequently fell under the control of British Canadians. Many French Canadians still express the desire to establish their own separate nation.

10. Canada is a country of Aboriginal peoples, the descendants of two colonial powers and a diversity of other immigrants. Chinese and Japanese immigrants historically have suffered both racial and ethnic discrimination.

11. Chinese and Japanese immigrants in Canada are categorized as "visible minorities," that is, persons, other than Aboriginal peoples, who are non-Caucasian in race or non-white. Based on this definition, the following ethnic groups are designated as visible minorities in Canada: Chinese and South Asians, blacks, Arabs and West Asians, Filipinos, Southeast Asians, Latin Americans, Japanese, Koreans, and Pacific Islanders.

12. The Canadian vertical mosaic also includes immigrants of other European ancestries: Germans, Scandinavians, and East Europeans.

13. Immigration has increased in recent years. No longer primarily from Europe, most immigrants now arrive from Latin America and Asia.

# KEY CONCEPTS

**race** (p. 256) a socially constructed category composed of men and women who share biologically transmitted traits that members of a society deem socially significant

**ethnicity** (p. 257) a shared cultural heritage

**prejudice** (p. 259) a rigid and irrational generalization about an entire category of people

**racism** (p. 259) the belief that one racial category is innately superior or inferior to another

**scapegoat** (p. 260) a person or category of people, typically with little power, whom others unfairly blame for thier troubles.

**discrimination** (p. 263) treating various categories of people unequally

**institutional prejudice and discrimination** (p. 263) bias inherent in the operation of society's institutions

**pluralism** (p. 264) a state in which people of all races and ethnicities are distinct but have social parity

**assimilation** (p. 265) the process by which minorities gradually adopt patterns of the dominant category

**miscegenation** (p. 265) biological reproduction by partners of different racial categories

**segregation** (p. 265) the physical and social separation of categories of people

**genocide** (p. 266) the systematic killing of one category of people by another

# CRITICAL-THINKING QUESTIONS

1. Differentiate between race and ethnicity. Do you think all non-white people should be considered minorities, even if they have above-average incomes? Why or why not?

2. In what ways do prejudice and discrimination reinforce each other?

3. What does the growing popularity of Latin music by performers such as Gloria and Emilio Estéfan and Ricky Martin suggest about ethnicity in Canada?

4. Do you think Canadian society is becoming more or less colour-blind? Is colour-blindness a goal worth striving for? Why or why not?

# APPLICATIONS AND EXERCISES

1. Does your college or university take account of race and ethnicity in its admissions policies? Ask to speak with an admissions officer, and see what you can learn about your school's policies and the reasons for them. Ask, too, if there is a "legacy" policy that favours children of parents who attended the school.

2. Give several of your friends or family members a quick quiz, asking them what share of the Canadian population is French or English (see Table 11–1 on page 257). Many people overestimate the share of these ethnic groups in the Canadian population. What do your results indicate?

3. It is quite likely that many people in your class are immigrants. Consider the behaviour of your colleagues. Are there bigger differences between immigrants and non-immigrants than between those born in Canada?

#  SITES TO SEE

**www.pearsoned.ca/macionis**

Visit the Web site that accompanies this text for a complete study guide that helps you review material in this chapter, for additional Internet links, and to share your ideas and opinions in the chat room.

**www.inac.gc.ca/ch/rcap**

Check this Web site for information on the *Report of the Royal Commission on Aboriginal Peoples of Canada.*

**www.interlog.com/~ccma/About.htm**

This Web site is the location of the Canadian Centre on Minority Affairs, a non-governmental organization aimed at improving the quality of life for present and future generations of black and Caribbean Canadians.

**www.bnaibrith.ca/nfindex.htm**

Visit this site for information on Jewish efforts to combat anti-Semitism, bigotry, and racism in Canada and abroad.

**www.ccnc.ca**

The Chinese Canadian National Council aims to promote the rights of Chinese Canadians and to encourage their participation throughout society.

# ECONOMICS AND POLITICS

*S*ome years back, you could spot the office temps in a minute. Around the office, they were the ones with the unfamiliar faces and the questions about where everything was. Just about the time they figured everything out, off they went to another company to begin the process all over again.

But in the 1980s, things began to change. Big companies were merging and laying off lots of workers—a process executives called "restructuring" and "downsiz-

ing." Cautious about adding full-time employees until economic trends became clearer, companies began meeting their needs by hiring more and more temporary and part-time workers. By the 1990s, the number of part-time workers soared from 1.2 million in 1976 to 2.7 million in 1999. Why? Companies discovered that using lots of temps and part-time workers lowered wages and salaries, reduced the costs of benefits (since many part-time workers do not receive benefits), and gave businesses the option to let *people go at any time (Eisenberg, 1999; Marshall 2000; Lowe, 2000).*

*The university and college campuses, too, are now awash with temporary instructors. By one count, more than half of first-year classes at 14 Canadian universities are taught by faculty that have temporary contracts (Maclean's, 2000:78).*

*Whether in business or academia, some part-time workers are happy to keep their options open. But more than 700 000 part-time workers would prefer to have a full-time job. Across the country, the "nomads" of the labour force are seeking a return to the old idea that just as companies expect loyalty from employees, companies in return should offer some security.* ■

This chapter explores the economy and the closely related institution of politics. As the chapter-opening story suggests, the economy does not always operate to everyone's advantage. Indeed, sociologists debate how both the economy and the political system ought to work and whose interests they ought to serve.

Economics and politics are each a major **social institution**, *an organized sphere of social life, or societal subsystem, designed to meet human needs.* The two chapters that follow consider other social institutions: Chapter 13 focusses on the family and religion, and Chapter 14 highlights education, and health and medicine. The discussions show how all these social institutions have changed over the course of history, how they operate today, and what important controversies will shape them tomorrow.

# THE ECONOMY: HISTORICAL OVERVIEW

The **economy** is *the social institution that organizes a society's production, distribution, and consumption of goods and services.* As an institution, the economy operates—for better or worse—in a more-or-less predictable manner. *Goods* are commodities ranging from necessities (such as food, clothing, and shelter) to luxury items (such as automobiles, swimming pools, and yachts). *Services* refer to activities that benefit others (including the work of priests, child care workers, professors, and parole officers).

## THE AGRICULTURAL REVOLUTION

As Chapter 2 (Culture) explained, the earliest societies were hunters and gatherers living off the land. In such societies, there was no distinct economy: producing and consuming were all part of family life.

Agriculture, which produced 20 times as much food as did hunting and gathering, developed some 5000 years ago as people began to harness animals to plows. The resulting surplus meant that not everyone had to produce food, so many people took on specialized work: making tools, raising animals, and building dwellings. Soon towns sprang up, linked by networks of traders (Jacobs, 1970). These four factors—agricultural technology, specialized work, permanent settlements, and trade—made the economy a social institution.

## THE INDUSTRIAL REVOLUTION

By the middle of the 18th century, a second technological revolution began, first in England and then in North America. Industrialization brought even greater change than agriculture had, in five ways:

1. **New sources of energy.** Throughout history, "energy" had meant the muscle power of people or animals. Then, in 1765, the English inventor James Watt introduced the steam engine. A hundred times more powerful than muscle power, early steam engines soon drove heavy machinery.

2. **The centralization of work in factories.** Steam-powered machinery moved work from homes to factories—centralized workplaces housing the machines.

3. **Manufacturing and mass production.** Before the Industrial Revolution, most people grew or gathered raw materials (such as grain, wood, or wool). In an industrial economy, people working in factories turned raw materials into finished products (such as furniture and clothing).

4. **Specialization.** Historically, artisans at home made products from beginning to end. In the factory, a labourer repeated a single task over and over, making only a small contribution to the finished product.

5. **Wage labour.** Instead of working for themselves in a household, factory workers became wage earners who sold their labour to strangers that often cared less for them than for the machines.

The Industrial Revolution raised living standards as countless new products filled an expanding economy. However, the benefits of industrial technology were shared unequally, especially at the beginning. Some factory owners made vast fortunes, while the majority of workers lived close to poverty. Children, too, toiled in factories or deep in coal mines for pennies a day. With time, though, workers formed labour unions to collectively represent their interests to factory owners. During the 20th century, new laws banned child labour, set minimum wage levels, improved workplace safety, and extended schooling and political rights to a larger segment of the population (Krahn & Lowe, 1998).

## THE INFORMATION REVOLUTION AND THE POST-INDUSTRIAL SOCIETY

By about 1950, the nature of production was changing once again. Canada was creating a **post-industrial economy**, *a productive system based on service work and high technology.* Automated machinery (and, more recently, robotics) reduced the role of human labour in production while simultaneously expanding the ranks of clerical workers and managers. Service industries—such as public relations, health care, advertising, banking, and sales—employ most working people in this country. The post-industrial era, then, is marked by a shift from industrial work to service work.

Driving this economic change is a third technological breakthrough: the computer. Just as factories did two centuries ago, the Information Revolution has introduced new kinds of products and new forms of communication, and has changed the character of work. In general, we see three changes:

1. **Tangible products to ideas.** The industrial era was defined by the production of goods; in the post-industrial era, work involves manipulating symbols. Computer programmers, writers, financial analysts, advertising executives, architects, editors, and all sorts of consultants make up the labour force of the information age.

2. **Mechanical skills to literacy skills.** The Industrial Revolution required mechanical skills, but the Information Revolution requires literacy skills—speaking and writing well and, of course, using computers. People able to communicate effectively enjoy new opportunities; people without these skills face declining prospects.

3. **Factories to almost anywhere.** Industrial technology drew workers to factories that were near power sources, but computer technology allows workers to be almost anywhere. Laptop computers, cell phones, and portable facsimile (fax) machines can turn the home, car, or even an airplane into a "virtual office." In short, new information technology blurs the line between work and home life.

## SECTORS OF THE ECONOMY

The three revolutions just described reflect a shifting balance among the three sectors of the economy. The **primary sector** is *the part of the economy that draws raw materials from the natural environment.* The primary sector—agriculture, livestock raising, fishing, forestry, and mining—is largest in low-income, pre-industrial nations. Figure 12–1 on page 280 shows that 23 percent of the economic output of low-income countries is in the primary sector, compared to 9 percent in

Canada is now a "post-industrial" society: Industry involves just 22 percent of the labor force, while the service sector involves 74 percent of workers. How does this transformation change the nature as well as the location of work?

middle-income nations and just 2 percent in high-income countries such as Canada.

The **secondary sector** is *the part of the economy that transforms raw materials into manufactured goods.* This sector grows as societies industrialize, and includes refining petroleum and turning metals into tools and automobiles.

The **tertiary sector** is *the part of the economy that involves services rather than goods.* Accounting for just 38 percent of economic output in low-income countries, the tertiary sector grows with industrialization, and dominates the economies of high-income, post-industrial nations. Today, about three out of every four workers in the Canadian labour force does service work, including secretarial and clerical jobs and positions in food service, sales, law, health care, advertising, and teaching (Statistics Canada, 1998f).

## THE GLOBAL ECONOMY

New information technology is drawing nations of the world closer together, creating a **global economy**, *expanding economic activity with little regard for national borders.* The development of a global economy has four main consequences. First, we see a global division of labour so that different regions of the world specialize in one sector of economic activity. As Global Map 12–1 on page 281 shows, agriculture occupies more than half of the workforce in the world's poorest countries. Global Map 12–2 (page 281) indicates that service-sector work dominates the economies of the world's middle- and high-income nations of the world. High-income nations—including Canada—now specialize in service-sector activity.

Second, an increasing number of products pass through more than one nation. Look no further than your morning coffee, which may well have been grown

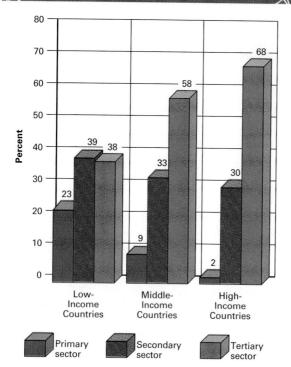

**FIGURE 12–1    The Size of Economic Sectors by Income Level of Country**

Source: Author estimates based on United Nations Development Programme (2000) and The World Bank (2000).

# ECONOMIC SYSTEMS: PATHS TO JUSTICE

October 20, 1995—Saigon, Vietnam
Sailing up the narrow Saigon River is an unsettling experience for anyone who came of age during the 1960s. We need to remember that Vietnam is a country not a war, and that 20 years have passed since the last U.S. helicopter lifted off from the rooftop of the U.S. Embassy, ending that country's presence here.

Saigon is on the brink of becoming a boom town. Neon signs bathe the city's waterfront in colour; hotels, bankrolled by Western corporations, push skyward from a dozen construction sites; taxi meters record fares in dollars, not Vietnamese dong; VISA and American Express stickers decorate the doors of fashionable shops that cater to tourists from around the globe, including Canada, Japan, France, and the United States. (The U.S. embargo on visiting Vietnam was lifted in 1994.)

There is heavy irony here: After decades of fighting, the loss of millions of lives on both sides, and the victory of Communist forces, the Vietnamese are doing an about-face and turning toward capitalism.

Every society's economy makes a statement about justice, since it determines who gets what. Two general economic models are capitalism and socialism. No nation has an economy that is completely one or the other; capitalism and socialism represent two ends of a spectrum along which actual economies can be located. We will look at each type in turn.

## CAPITALISM

**Capitalism** refers to *an economic system in which natural resources and the means of producing goods and services are privately owned.* An ideal capitalist economy would have three distinctive features:

1. **Private ownership of property.**   In a capitalist economy, individuals can own almost anything. The more capitalist an economy is, the more private ownership there is of wealth-producing property such as factories, real estate, and natural resources.

in Colombia, and transported to Vancouver on a freighter registered in Liberia, made in Japan using steel from Korea, and fuelled by oil from Venezuela.

A third consequence of the global economy is that national governments no longer control the economic activity that takes place within their borders. In fact, governments cannot even regulate the value of their national currencies, since dollars, pounds sterling, yen, and other currencies are traded around the clock in the financial centres of Tokyo, London, New York, and Toronto. Global markets are the result of satellite communications that link the world's cities.

The fourth consequence of the global economy is that a small number of businesses, operating internationally, now control a vast share of the world's economic activity. According to one estimate, the 600 largest multinational companies account for half the world's entire economic output (Kidron & Segal, 1991).

The planet is still divided into over 200 politically distinct nations. But increasing international economic activity makes "nationhood" less significant than it was even a decade ago.

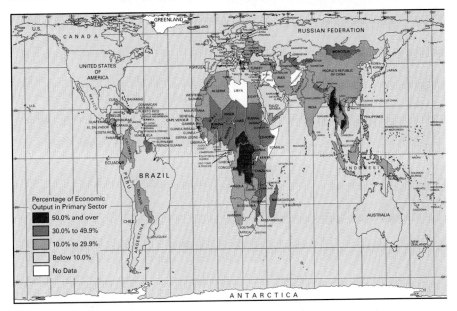

**GLOBAL MAP 12–1**
**Agricultural Employment in Global Perspective**

The primary sector of the economy is largest in societies that are least developed. Thus, in the poor countries of Africa and Asia, up to half of all workers are farmers. This picture is altogether different in the world's high-income countries—including Canada, the United States, Great Britain, and Australia—each of which has 2 percent of its workforce in agriculture.

Percentage of Economic Output in Primary Sector
- 50.0% and over
- 30.0% to 49.9%
- 10.0% to 29.9%
- Below 10.0%
- No Data

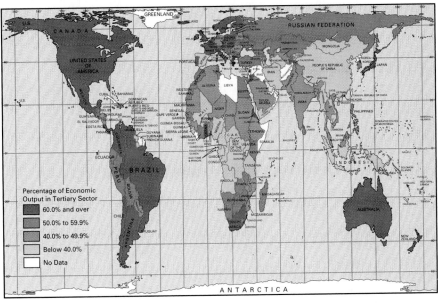

**GLOBAL MAP 12–2**
**Service-Sector Employment in Global Perspective**

The tertiary sector of the economy becomes ever larger as a nation's income level rises. In Canada, the United States, the countries of Western Europe, Australia, and Japan, about two-thirds of the labour force performs service work.

Source: Estimated by John Macionis, using data from United Nations Development Programme (2000) and The World Bank (2000); map projection from *Peters Atlas of the World* (1990).

Percentage of Economic Output in Tertiary Sector
- 60.0% and over
- 50.0% to 59.9%
- 40.0% to 49.9%
- Below 40.0%
- No Data

2. **Pursuit of personal profit.** A capitalist society promotes profit and wealth. The "profit motive" is considered the natural way of "doing business."

3. **Competition and consumer choice.** A purely capitalist economy is a free-market system with no government interference (sometimes called a *laissez-faire* economy, from the French meaning "to leave alone"). The Scottish economist Adam Smith (1723–1790) held that a freely competitive economy regulates itself by the "invisible hand" of the law of supply and demand (1937; 1776).

Consumers guide a market economy, Smith continued, by selecting goods and services offering the greatest value. As producers compete for the customer's business, they provide the highest-quality goods at the lowest prices. In Smith's time-honoured phrase, from narrow self-interest comes "the greatest good for the greatest number of people." Government control of an

*Capitalism still thrives in Hong Kong (left), evident in streets choked with advertising and shoppers. Socialism is more the rule in China's capital of Beijing (right), a city dominated by government buildings rather than a downtown business district.*

economy, on the other hand, distorts market forces, reduces producer motivation, diminishes quality, and shortchanges consumers.

"Justice," in a capitalist context, amounts to market freedom to produce, buy, and invest according to individual self-interest. The worth of products and labour is determined by the dynamic process of supply and demand. Replacing much of the workforce with lower-paid temporary workers, as described in the opening of this chapter, is "just" if it is profitable to the company's owners.

Canada is a capitalist nation because the vast majority of businesses are privately owned. Even so, government plays an extensive role in economic affairs. Government itself owns in part or completely a number of productive organizations, including almost all of this country's schools, roads, parks, and museums, Canada Post, Petro-Canada, VIA Rail, and the Canadian military. In addition, governments use taxation and other forms of regulation to influence what companies produce, to control the quality and cost of merchandise, to regulate what businesses import and export, and to motivate consumers to conserve natural resources.

Further, government sets minimum wage levels and enforces workplace safety standards, regulates corporate mergers, provides farm price supports, and gives income in the form of employment insurance, public pensions, social assistance, student loans, child tax credits, and subsidies for child and elder care, to a majority of people in Canada. Municipal, provincial, territorial, and federal governments together are the nation's biggest employer, with 16 percent of the labour force

on their payrolls in 1998 (Statistics Canada 1998l, Statistics Canada 1998m).

## SOCIALISM

**Socialism** is *an economic system in which natural resources and the means of producing goods and services are collectively owned.* In its ideal form, a socialist economy would oppose each of the three characteristics of capitalism just described:

1.  **Collective ownership of property.** A socialist economy limits rights to private property, especially property used to generate income. Government controls such property and makes housing and other goods available to all, not just the people with the most money.

2.  **Pursuit of collective goals.** The individualistic pursuit of profit is at odds with the collective orientation of socialism. What capitalism celebrates as the "entrepreneurial spirit," socialism condemns as "greed;" individuals are urged to work for the common good of all.

3.  **Government control of the economy.** Socialism rejects capitalism's laissez-faire approach in favour of a *centrally controlled* or *command* economy operated by government. Thus commercial advertising does not play a large role in socialist economies.

"Justice" in a socialist context is not competing to accumulate wealth, but working to meet everyone's needs in a more-or-less equal manner. From a socialist point of view, a capitalist practice such as cutting back on workers' wages and benefits to boost company earnings—as described in the opening to this chapter—puts profits before people and thus is an injustice.

The People's Republic of China and some two dozen nations in Asia, Africa, and Latin America have socialist economies, with almost all wealth-generating property under state control (McColm et al., 1991). The extent of world socialism has declined in recent years as countries in Eastern Europe and the former Soviet Union have geared their economies toward a market system.

## WELFARE CAPITALISM AND STATE CAPITALISM

Some nations in Western Europe—including Sweden and Italy—have a market-based economy but also offer broad social welfare programs. Analysts call this "third way" **welfare capitalism**, *an economic and political system that combines a mostly market-based economy with extensive social-welfare programs.*

Under welfare capitalism, the government owns some of the largest industries and services, such as transportation, the mass media, and health care. In Sweden and Italy, about 12 percent of economic production is "nationalized," or state controlled. That leaves most industry in private hands, although subject to extensive government regulation. High taxation (aimed especially at the rich) funds a wide range of social welfare programs, including universal health care and child care (Olsen, 1996).

Yet another alternative is **state capitalism**, *an economic and political system in which companies are privately owned but cooperate closely with the government.* State capitalism is the rule in the nations along the Pacific Rim. Japan, South Korea, and Singapore, for example, are all capitalist countries, but their governments work in partnership with large companies, supplying financial assistance and controlling foreign imports to help their businesses compete in world markets (Gerlach, 1992).

## RELATIVE ADVANTAGES OF CAPITALISM AND SOCIALISM

In practice, which economic system works best? Comparing economic models is difficult because all countries mix capitalism and socialism to varying degrees. Moreover, nations differ in cultural attitudes toward work, natural resources, technological development, and patterns of trade (Gregory & Stuart, 1985). Despite such complicating factors, some crude comparisons are revealing.

**Economic productivity.**  One key dimension of economic performance is productivity. A commonly used measure of output is Gross Domestic Product (GDP), the total value of all goods and services produced annually. "Per capita" (per person) GDP allows us to compare the economic performance of nations of different population sizes.

While the output of mostly capitalist countries at the end of the 1980s varied somewhat, the average of figures for Canada, the United States, and the nations of Western Europe yields a per capita GDP of about $13 500. The comparable figure for the former Soviet Union and the nations of Eastern Europe is about $5000. This means that the capitalist countries outproduced the socialist nations by a ratio of 2.7 to 1 (United Nations Development Programme, 1990).

**Economic equality.**  How resources are distributed within the population is another important measure. A comparative study in the mid-1970s looked at income ratios based on the earnings of the richest 5 percent of the population and the poorest 5 percent (Wiles, 1977). The result was that societies with mostly capitalist economies had an income ratio of about 10 to 1; the figure for socialist countries was 5 to 1. In other words, *capitalist economies support a higher overall standard of living but with greater income disparity.* Or, put otherwise, *socialist economies create more economic equality but with a lower overall living standard.*

**Personal freedom.**  One additional consideration in evaluating capitalism and socialism is the personal freedom each system affords its people. Capitalism emphasizes *freedom to* pursue one's self-interest. Capitalism, after all, depends on the freedom of producers and consumers to interact with little interference from the state. On the other hand, socialism emphasizes *freedom from* basic want. Equality is the goal, which requires state intervention in the economy, which in turn limits personal choices for citizens.

No system has yet been able to offer both political freedom and economic equality. In capitalist Canada, our political system offers many personal freedoms, but are they worth as much to a poor person as to a rich one? On the other side of the coin, China has more economic equality, but its people cannot freely express themselves or easily move inside and outside its borders.

## CHANGES IN SOCIALIST COUNTRIES

In 1989 and 1990, the nations of Eastern Europe, which had been seized by the former Soviet Union at the end of the Second World War, shook off their socialist regimes. These nations—including the German Democratic Republic, the Czech Republic, Slovakia, Hungary, Romania, and Bulgaria—are moving toward market systems after decades of state-controlled economies. In 1992, the Soviet Union itself formally dissolved, and has since introduced some free-market principles.

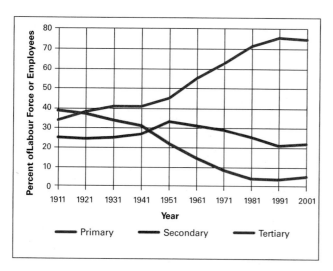

**FIGURE 12–2    The Changing Pattern of Work in Canada, 1911–2000**

Source: Estimated based on data in Bowlby (2001), Leacy (1999), and Cansim Tables D137024-D137028, D137032, D137051, D137052, D137056, D137059-D137061, D137067.

There were many reasons for these sweeping changes. First, the mostly socialist economies under-produced relative to their capitalist counterparts. They were successful in achieving economic equality, but living standards were low compared to those of Western Europe. Second, Soviet socialism was heavy-handed, rigidly controlling the media and restricting individual freedoms. In short, socialism did away with *economic* elites, as Karl Marx predicted. But, as Max Weber foresaw, socialism increased the clout of *political* elites.

So far, the market reforms in Eastern Europe are proceeding unevenly. Some nations (Czech Republic, Slovakia, Poland, and the Baltic states of Latvia, Estonia, and Lithuania) are faring pretty well. But other countries (Romania, Bulgaria, and the Russian Federation) are buffeted by price increases and falling living standards. Officials hope that expanding pro-duction eventually will result in a turnaround. There is already evidence, though, that a rising standard of living will be accompanied by increasing economic inequality (Pohl, 1996; Buraway, 1997; Specter, 1997a).

## WORK IN THE POST-INDUSTRIAL ECONOMY

Economic change is occurring not just in the socialist world, but also in Canada. In 1999, the Canadian gov-ernment reports, approximately 14.5 million people were in the labour force, representing two-thirds of those aged 16 and over (Marshall, 2000). A larger share of men (66.8 percent) than women (54.6 percent) had

income-producing jobs, although the gap is closing (Statistics Canada, 2000m). Among men, 64.6 percent of those of visible minority background are in the labour force, compared to 48 percent of Aboriginal men and 74.1 percent of other Canadian men. Among women, 53 percent of those from visible minority groups are employed, compared to 41 percent of Aboriginal women and 63.3 percent of other women (Statistics Canada, 2000m).

### THE CHANGING WORKPLACE

In 1911, about 40 percent of Canadian workers had jobs in the primary sector. In 2000, just 4 percent were in this part of the economy. Figure 12–2 illustrates the shrinking role of the primary sector in the Canadian economy.

Similarly, a century ago, industrialization swelled the ranks of workers in the manufacturing sector. By the mid-1900s, however, a white-collar revolution was gaining momentum. More than 90 percent of new jobs in 2000 were in the service sector, and 75 percent of the labour force performed service work.

As Chapter 8 (Social Stratification) explained, much service work—including sales, clerical positions, and work in hospitals and restaurants—yields little of the income and prestige of white-collar professions and, at the same time, offers fewer rewards than fac-tory work. In sum, many jobs in this post-industrial era provide only a modest standard of living.

### LABOUR UNIONS

The changing economy has seen a change in *labour unions*, organizations that seek to improve wages and working conditions. Canadian union membership increased rapidly after 1935 to more than one-third of non-farm workers by 1950. It then fell slightly during the 1960s, but increased during the 1970s to return to the 1950 level, where it has remained.

In 1999, the unionized rate for the total employed workforce in Canada was 32 percent (Marshall, 2000). In Japan, about 33 percent of workers belong to unions; across Europe, about 40 percent belong; in the Nordic countries, the share is 80 percent (Western, 1993, 1995). Yet, overall there has been a decline in union rates across high-income countries, though not to the extent seen in the United States, where only about 14 percent of non-farm workers are unionized.

The global decline in unions follows the shrink-ing industrial sector of the economy. In addition, newer service jobs are less likely to be unionized. But, as some analysts see it, decreased job security may well make unions more popular in years to come. Nevertheless, unions will have to adapt to the new global economy. Union members in Canada and the United States, used

*Teaching is one of the most personally rewarding occupations anyone can have. But do all teachers have equal claim to being professionals? Primary school teachers (such as the teacher on the left) usually teach a curriculum controlled by the school and provincial officials. University and college teachers (such as the man on the right) typically have far more autonomy in deciding what, how, when, and where they teach. What factors account for this difference?*

to seeing foreign workers as "the enemy," will have to build new international alliances (Mabry, 1992; Church, 1994).

## PROFESSIONS

All kinds of work today are called *professional*—we hear of professional tennis players, professional house cleaners, and even professional exterminators. As distinct from an *amateur* (from Latin for "lover," meaning one who acts out of love for the activity itself), a professional does some task for a living. But what exactly is a *profession*?

A **profession** is *a prestigious, white-collar occupation that requires extensive formal education*. Those performing this kind of work make a profession—or public declaration—of willingness to abide by certain principles. Professions include the ministry, medicine, law, academia, and, more recently, architecture, accountancy, and social work. Occupations are professional to the extent that they demonstrate the following four characteristics (W. Goode, 1960; Ritzer & Walczak, 1990):

1. **Theoretical knowledge.** Professionals have theoretical knowledge of their field rather than mere technical training. Anyone can learn first-aid skills, for example, but physicians have a theoretical understanding of human health.

2. **Self-regulating practice.** The typical professional is self-employed—"in practice," rather than working for a company. Professionals oversee their own work and observe a code of ethics.

3. **Authority over clients.** Based on extensive training, professionals advise clients and expect those clients to follow their directions.

4. **Community orientation rather than self-interest.** The traditional "professing" of duty states an intention to serve the community rather than merely to seek income.

Many new occupations in the post-industrial economy seek to *professionalize* their services (MacDonald, 1995). Claiming professional standing usually begins by renaming the work to imply special, theoretical knowledge, and distances the field from its previously less-distinguished reputation. Stock room workers, for example, become "inventory supply managers," and exterminators are reborn as "insect control specialists."

Interested parties may also form a professional association to formally attest to their skills. The organization licenses people who perform the work and writes a code of ethics emphasizing the occupation's role in the community. To win public acceptance, a professional association may also establish schools or other training facilities and perhaps start a professional journal (Abbott, 1988). Not all occupations try to claim professional status. Some *paraprofessionals*, including paralegals and medical technicians, possess specialized skills but lack the extensive theoretical education required of full professionals.

*Jose Clemente Orozco's painting* The Unemployed *is a powerful statement of the personal collapse and private despair that afflict men and women who are not employed. How does a sociological perspective help us to understand being out of work as more than a personal problem?*

Source: Jose Clemente Orozco, *The Unemployed.* © Christie's Images.
© Estate of Jose Clemente Orozco/Licensed by VAGA, New York, N.Y.

## SELF-EMPLOYMENT

*Self-employment*—earning a living without working for a large organization—was once common in Canada. While in 1800 the vast majority of workers were self-employed, in 1999 just 17 percent of workers were self-employed, down slightly from 18 percent in 1997 (Marshall, 2000). In 1999, 12.9 percent of female workers were self-employed, compared to 20 percent of men (Statistics Canada, 2000m).

Lawyers, physicians, and other professionals are well represented among the ranks of the self-employed. In addition, the number of people using the Internet to run a small business is growing. But most self-employed workers are farmers, small business owners, plumbers, child minders, carpenters, freelance writers and editors, artists, and long-distance truck drivers. Overall, the self-employed are more likely to have blue-collar than white-collar jobs.

Finally, a notable trend is that self-employment has grown faster for Canadian women than men during the past two decades (Benoit, 2000). As a result, women accounted for 35 percent of this nation's small businesses in 1999, up from 31 percent in 1990 and 26 percent in 1976 (Statistics Canada, 2000m).

## UNEMPLOYMENT

Every society has some unemployment. Few young people entering the labour force find a job right away; workers may temporarily leave their jobs to seek new work or have children; some may be on strike; others suffer from long-term illnesses; and still others are illiterate or without the skills to perform useful work.

But unemployment is also caused by the economy itself. Jobs disappear as occupations become obsolete, businesses close in the face of foreign competition or economic recession, and companies "downsize" to become more profitable. Since 1980, the largest Canadian businesses and different levels of government have eliminated thousands of jobs in manufacturing and the public service.

At the end of 2000, 1.089 million people over the age of 16 were unemployed—about 6.8 percent of the civilian labour force (down from 8.5 percent in 1998). As National Map 12-1 shows, some regions of Canada, including parts of Newfoundland and Labrador and Quebec, have high unemployment that, in some cases, reaches more than twice the national rate (Statistics Canada, 2001a).

Figure 12–3 on page 288 shows that the 1996 unemployment rate among visible minority men between 15 and 64 years of age (13.2 percent) was substantially higher than that among other men in Canada (9.9 percent) and that of Aboriginal men (27.4 percent) is almost three times that of other Canadian men. In 1996, the unemployment rate for visible minority women (15.3) was lower than that of Aboriginal women (21.6) but higher than the unemployment rate of other females (9.4).

## WORKPLACE DIVERSITY: RACE AND GENDER

Traditionally, white men have been the mainstay of the Canadian labour force. As explained in Chapter 11 (Race and Ethnicity), however, our country's proportion of minorities is rapidly rising. Between 1986 and 2001, the proportion of visible minorities in Canada's population is estimated to have increased from 6.3 percent to 17.7 percent (Samuel, 1992). The Social Diversity box on page 289 takes a closer look at how increasing social diversity will affect the workplace.

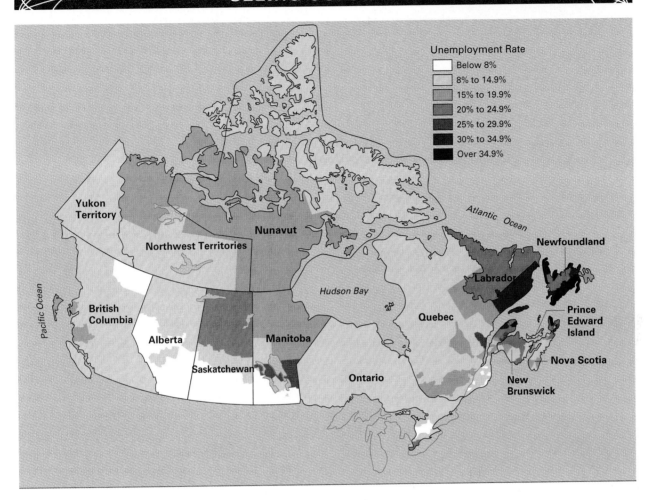

**Unemployment Rate**

| | |
|---|---|
| | Below 8% |
| | 8% to 14.9% |
| | 15% to 19.9% |
| | 20% to 24.9% |
| | 25% to 29.9% |
| | 30% to 34.9% |
| | Over 34.9% |

**NATIONAL MAP 12–1   Unemployment Rates across Canada**

The 1996 census reported an unemployment rate of 10.1 percent for all of Canada. Newfoundland had the highest unemployment rate of all provinces, at 25.1 percent, although some areas in the province exceed even that figure. The depiction of the unemployment rate on this map makes us think of the structural causes and consequences of unemployment. Do you usually consider structural or personal factors when you try to understand the unemployment that exists where you live?

Source:  Statistics Canada, 1996 Census.

## NEW INFORMATION TECHNOLOGY AND WORK

Another workplace issue of this new century is the central role of computers and new information technology. The Information Revolution is changing what people do in some basic ways (Zuboff, 1982; Rule & Brantley, 1992; Vallas & Beck, 1996):

1. **Computers are "de-skilling" labour.**   Just as industrial machines replaced the master crafts-workers of an earlier era, so computers now threaten the skills of managers. More business operations are based not on executive decisions but on computer modelling. In other words, a machine decides whether to place an order, re-supply a client, or approve a loan application.

CHAPTER 12  Economics and Politics   **287**

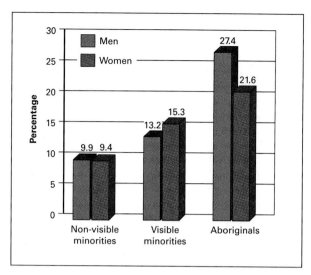

**FIGURE 12–3    Unemployment Among Visible Minority and Aboriginal Men and Women**

Source: Based on Statistics Canada, (2000m).

2. **Computers are making work more abstract.** Most industrial workers have a hands-on relationship with their product. Post-industrial workers manipulate symbols in pursuit of abstract goals, such as making a company more profitable or making software more user-friendly.

3. **Computers limit workplace interaction.** As workers spend more time at computer terminals, they become isolated from one another.

4. **Computers increase the employer's control of workers.** Computers allow supervisors to check output continuously, whether the employee works at a keyboard or an assembly line.

Such changes remind us that technology is not socially neutral. Computers alter not only the way we work, but also the balance of power between employer and employees. Understandably, then, people may welcome some aspects of the Information Revolution but oppose others.

## CORPORATIONS

At the core of today's capitalist economy is the **corporation,** *an organization with a legal existence, including rights and liabilities, apart from those of its members.* Incorporating makes an organization a legal entity unto itself, able to enter into contracts and own property. Incorporating also protects the wealth of owners from lawsuits arising from business debts or harm to consumers, and may lower taxes on profits.

## ECONOMIC CONCENTRATION

Most of Canada's corporations are small—more than 200 000 Canadians are self-employed and operate one or more corporations without any employees (Statistics Canada, 1998p). The largest corporations, however, dominate our nation's economy. In 1997, there were 11 corporations with revenues exceeding $10 billion. The largest Canadian corporation in terms of sales is General Motors, which had over $34 billion in revenue in 1997 (*Financial Post 500 Magazine,* 1998).

## CORPORATE LINKAGES

Economic concentration creates *conglomerates,* giant corporations composed of many smaller corporations. Conglomerates form as corporations enter new markets, spin off new companies, or merge with other companies. For example, RJR-Nabisco is a conglomerate that sells not only cigarettes but dozens of familiar household products. While Canada's conglomerates make up only 1 percent of all businesses in the country, they generate more than one-third of all business income and employ about one-quarter of the workforce (Statistics Canada, 2000e).

Yet another corporate linkage is the *interlocking directorate,* a social network of people who serve as directors of many corporations (Herman, 1981; Scott & Griff, 1985; Weidenbaum, 1995; Kono et al., 1998). These boardroom connections provide corporations with access to valuable information about one another's products and marketing strategies. Beth Mintz and Michael Schwartz (1981) found that General Motors is linked through board members to 700 other companies. Such linkages do not necessarily oppose the public interest, but they may encourage illegal activity such as price fixing, and they certainly concentrate wealth and power.

## CORPORATIONS: ARE THEY COMPETITIVE?

According to the capitalist model, businesses operate independently in a competitive market. But large corporations have extensive linkages, which means that they do not operate independently. Second, a small number of corporations dominate many large markets. Large corporations are not, therefore, truly competitive.

Law forbids a large company from establishing a **monopoly,** *domination of a market by a single producer,* because a monopoly could simply dictate prices. But a common practice is **oligopoly,** *domination of a market by a few producers.* Oligopoly results from the vast investment needed to enter a new market such as the auto industry. Moreover, true competition means risk, which big business tries to avoid.

# Diversity in the New Century:
# Changes in the Workplace

An upward trend in the Canadian visible minority population is changing the workplace. The number of visible minorities employed in Canada is projected to increase from 6.3 percent in 1986 to 17.7 percent in 2001. The line graph shows that over a similar period, the number and proportion of women employed has markedly increased, while a significantly lower proportion of men are employed than was the case 25 years ago.

The overall result? Within a decade, white men will represent a minority of all workers, and that figure will continue to drop. Therefore, companies that welcome social diversity will tap the largest talent pool and enjoy a competitive advantage.

Welcoming social diversity means, first, recruiting talented workers of both sexes as well as all colours and cultural backgrounds. But developing the potential of all employees requires meeting the special needs of women and other minorities, which may not be the same as those of white men. For example, in the new century corporations will be pressed to provide child care at the workplace.

Second, businesses need to develop effective ways to defuse tension that arises from social differences. They will have to work harder at treating workers equally and respectfully. No corporate culture can tolerate racial or sexual harassment.

Third, companies will have to rethink current promotion practices. As noted in Chapter 10 (Gender Stratification), men dominate senior management jobs in the business world, with just 12 percent of women holding corporate officer positions at Canada's 560 largest companies in 1999 and only 3.4 percent holding CEO or equivalent positions (Catalyst, 2000). Visible minorities and Aboriginals are even less likely to occupy managerial jobs, especially at the top levels (Statistics Canada, 2000m).

In sum, "glass ceilings" that limit the advancement of skilled workers not only discourage effort but deprive companies of their largest source of talent—women and other minorities.

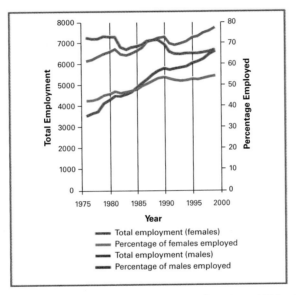

**Men and Women Employed, Canada, 1976–1999**
Source: Statistics Canada, (2000m).

Sources: Samuel, (1992); Statistics Canada, (1995); Statistics Canada, (2000m); Catalyst (2000).

## CORPORATIONS AND THE GLOBAL ECONOMY

Corporations have grown so large that they now account for most of the world's economic output. The biggest corporations are based in the United States, Japan, and Western Europe, but they consider the entire world one huge marketplace.

Low-income nations attract the attention of global corporations because most of the world's people and resources are found within their borders. In addition, as shown in Figure 12–4 on page 291, labour costs there are far lower. A manufacturing worker in Mexico labours for a month to earn roughly what a German worker earns in a single day.

The impact of multinationals on low-income countries is controversial, as Chapter 9 (Global Stratification) explains. On one side of the argument, modernization theorists claim that multinationals unleash the great productivity of capitalism to raise living standards in poor nations. Specifically, corporations offer poor nations tax revenues, capital investment, new jobs, and advanced technology, which together accelerate economic growth (Rostow, 1978; Madsen, 1980; Berger, 1986; Firebaugh & Beck, 1994).

Dependency theorists, on the other hand, respond that multinationals intensify global inequality. Multinationals, they contend, actually create few jobs because they block the development of local industries and push poor countries to make goods for export

*Although the Information Revolution is centred in high-income countries such as Canada, the effects of high technology are becoming evident even in low-income nations. Do you think the expansion of information technology will change the lives of rural people such as these peasants in Vietnam? If so, how?*

rather than food and other products for local consumption. From this standpoint, multinationals make poor nations poorer and increasingly dependent on rich nations (Vaughan, 1978; Wallerstein, 1979; Delacroix & Ragin, 1981; Bergesen, 1983; Walton & Ragin, 1990).

## LOOKING AHEAD: THE ECONOMY OF THE TWENTY-FIRST CENTURY

Social institutions are a society's way of meeting people's needs. But, as we have seen, the Canadian economy only partly succeeds in this respect. Although highly productive, our economy provides for some much better than for others. Moreover, as we begin the 21st century, the Information Revolution continues to change our economy. First, the share of the Canadian labour force engaged in manufacturing is now a small portion of what it was in 1960; service work—especially computer-related jobs—has grown significantly in the past 40 years. For industrial workers, then, the post-industrial economy has brought unemployment and declining wages. Our society must face up to the challenge of providing thousands of men and women with the language and computer skills needed in the new economy.

A second transformation that will mark the new century is the expansion of the global economy. Two centuries ago, the ups and downs of a local economy reflected events and trends in a single town. One century ago, communities across the country became economically linked so that one town's prosperity depended on producing goods demanded by people elsewhere in the country. Today, it makes less sense to speak of a national economy, since what people in a Saskatchewan farm town produce and consume may

be affected more by what happens in the wheat-growing region of Russia than by events in their own provincial capital. In short, Canadian workers are not only creating new products and services, but working in response to factors and forces that are distant and unseen.

Finally, analysts around the world are rethinking conventional economic models. The global economy shows that socialism is less productive than capitalism, one important reason for the recent collapse of socialist regimes in Eastern Europe and the former Soviet Union. But capitalism, too, is changing and now operates with significant government regulation, partly to address the economic inequality generated by market systems.

What are the long-term effects of these changes? Two conclusions seem inescapable. First, the economic future of Canada and other nations will be played out in a global arena. The new post-industrial economy in Canada is, after all, inseparable from the increasing industrial production of other nations. Second, we must address the pressing challenge of global inequality and population increase (Firebaugh, 1999). Whether the world economy reduces or deepens the disparity between rich and poor societies may end up steering our planet toward peace or war.

## POLITICS: HISTORICAL OVERVIEW

Closely related to economics is **politics** (or "the polity"), *the social institution that distributes power, sets a society's agenda, and makes decisions.* Early in this century, Max Weber (1978; orig. 1921) defined **power** as *the ability to achieve desired ends despite opposition.*

Brute force is the most basic form of power. But no society that derives power *only* from sheer force lasts for long, and life in such a society would be a nightmare of terror. On the contrary, social organization depends on creating agreement about goals and how to attain them. This brings us to the concept of **authority**, *power that people perceive as legitimate rather than coercive.*

A society's source of authority depends, in turn, on its economy. According to Max Weber, pre-industrial societies rely on *traditional authority*, power legitimized through respect for long-established cultural patterns. Woven into a society's collective memory, traditional authority may seem almost sacred. Chinese emperors in antiquity were legitimized by tradition, as were the nobles in medieval Europe.

But traditional authority declines as societies industrialize. Royal families still exist in 10 European nations, for example, but their democratic cultures have shifted power to commoners elected to office. Thus, Weber said, the expansion of rational bureaucracy provides a distinctly modern path to authority. *Rational-legal authority* (sometimes called *bureaucratic authority*), said Weber, is power legitimized by rationally enacted law.

Just as traditional authority is tied to family, rational-legal authority flows from offices in governments. In other words, while a traditional monarch passes on the heirs, a modern prime minister or president takes and gives up power according to law.

Weber described one additional type of authority that has surfaced throughout history. *Charismatic authority* is power legitimized by the extraordinary personal abilities—charisma—of a leader. Unlike its traditional and rational-legal counterparts, charismatic authority depends less on a person's ancestry or office than on his or her individual personality. Followers see in charismatic leaders some special—perhaps even divine—power. Examples of charismatic leaders include Jesus of Nazareth, Nazi Germany's Adolph Hitler, and the liberator of India, Mahatma Gandhi. All charismatic leaders share a goal of transforming society, which makes them highly controversial (and explains why many charismatics do not die of old age).

Because charismatic authority flows from a single individual, the leader's death creates a crisis. The survival of a charismatic movement, Max Weber explained, requires the **routinization of charisma**, *the transformation of charismatic authority into some combination of traditional and bureaucratic authority.* After the death of Jesus, for example, followers institutionalized his teachings in a church built on tradition and bureaucracy—one that flourishes today, 2000 years later.

## GLOBAL POLITICAL SYSTEMS

The world's political systems differ in countless ways. Generally, however, they fall into four categories: monarchy, democracy, authoritarianism, and totalitarianism.

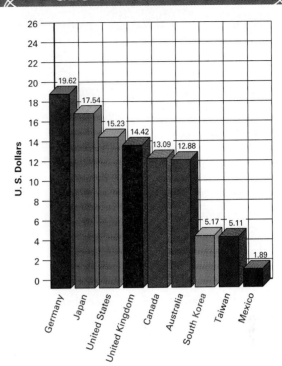

**GLOBAL SNAPSHOT**

**FIGURE 12–4   Average Hourly Wages for Workers in Manufacturing, U.S. Dollars, 1998**

Source: Calculations by John Macionis based on U.S. Department of Labor (2001).

## MONARCHY

**Monarchy** (with Latin and Greek roots meaning "one ruler") is *a type of political system in which a single family rules from generation to generation.* Monarchy is commonly found in agrarian societies; the Bible, for example, tells of great kings such as David and Solomon. In the world today, 28 nations have royal families[1]; most trace their ancestry back for centuries. In Weber's analysis, then, monarchy is legitimized by tradition.

During the Middle Ages, *absolute monarchs* throughout much of the world claimed a virtual monopoly of power based on divine right. In some nations—including Kuwait, Saudi Arabia, and Brunei—

[1] In Europe, Sweden, Norway, Denmark, Great Britain, The Netherlands, Liechtenstein, Luxembourg, Belgium, Spain, and Monaco; in the Middle East, Jordan, Saudi Arabia, Oman, and Qatar, Bahrain, and Kuwait; in Africa, Lesotho, Swaziland, and Morocco; in Asia, Brunei, Samoa, Tonga, Thailand, Malaysia, Cambodia, Nepal, Bhutan, and Japan.

*In 1998, just 28 of the world's nations were political monarchies where single families pass power from generation to generation. The African nation of Swaziland recently celebrated the coronation of a young king.*

monarchs still exercise virtually absolute control over their people.

With industrialization, however, monarchs gradually pass from the scene in favour of elected officials. All the European societies where royal families remain are *constitutional monarchies*, in that their monarchs are little more than symbolic heads of state; actual governing is the responsibility of elected officials, led by a prime minister and guided by a constitution. In these countries, nobility formally reign, but elected officials actually rule.

## DEMOCRACY

The historical trend in the world has favoured **democracy**, *a political system giving power to the people as a whole*. More correctly, a system of *representative democracy* puts authority in the hands of leaders that from time to time stand for election.

Most high-income countries in the world claim to be democratic (including those who still have royal families). Industrialization and democracy go together because both require a literate populace. Moreover, the traditional legitimation of power in a monarchy gives way, with industrialization, to rational-legal authority. Thus, democracy and rational-legal authority are linked, just as are monarchy and traditional authority.

But high-income countries such as Canada are not truly democratic for two reasons. First, there is the problem of bureaucracy. The number of people

employed at the various levels of government in Canada (federal, provincial, territorial, and municipal) is nearly 1 million strong. The vast majority of government officials are never elected by anyone and are not directly accountable to the people (Scaff, 1981; Edwards, 1985; Etzioni-Halevy, 1985).

The second problem involves economic inequality, since rich people have far more political clout than poor people. One reason why U.S. president George W. Bush got off to such a fast start in the 2000 presidential campaign was that being a rich man with many rich friends, he was able to raise more than $50 million in a short time. Though many of Canada's elected leaders do not come from wealthy families, some have substantial personal wealth (including our former prime minister, Pierre Elliot Trudeau). Moreover, Canadian politicians are privileged by their education, with two-thirds of them having some background in law.

Still, democratic nations provide many rights and freedoms. Global Map 12–3 shows one organization's assessment of the extent of political freedom around the world. According to Freedom House, an organization that tracks political trends, by 1999, 88 of the world's nations (containing 40 percent of the global population) were "free," with considerable respect for civil liberties. This represents a strong gain for democracy: just 58 nations were free a decade earlier (Freedom House, 1999).

## AUTHORITARIANISM

Not all governments try to involve their people in politics. **Authoritarianism** refers to *a political system that denies popular participation in government*. An authoritarian government is both indifferent to people's needs and offers them no voice in selecting leaders. The absolute monarchies in Saudi Arabia and Kuwait are authoritarian, as are the military juntas in Iraq and Ethiopia.

## TOTALITARIANISM

October 22, 1994—near Saigon, Vietnam Six of our students have been arrested, allegedly for talking to Vietnamese students and also taking pictures at the university. The Vietnamese Minister of Education has cancelled the reception tonight, claiming that our students meeting with their students threatens Vietnam's security.

The most intensely controlled political form is **totalitarianism**, *a highly centralized political system that extensively regulates people's lives*. Totalitarian systems

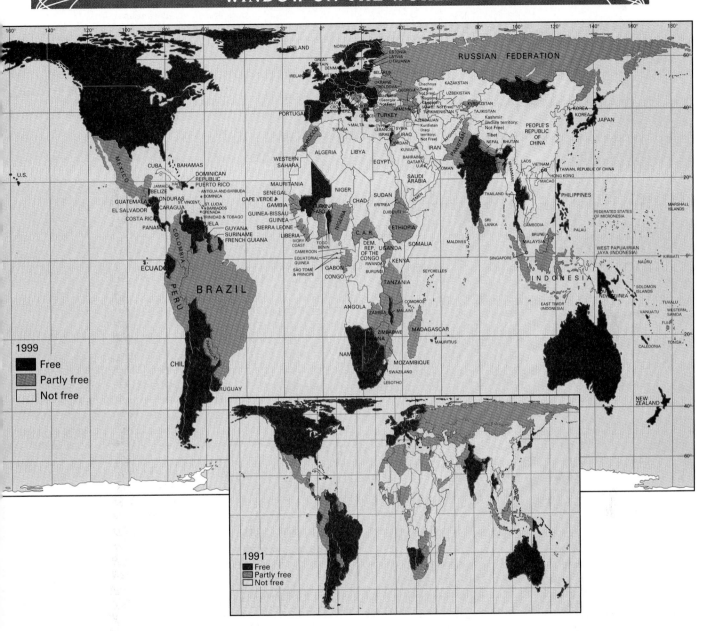

**GLOBAL MAP 12–3    Political Freedom in Global Perspective**

In 1999, 88 of the world's nations, containing 40 percent of all people, were politically "free"—that is, they offered their citizens extensive political rights and civil liberties. Another 53 countries, which included 27 percent of the world's people, were "partly free," with limited rights and liberties. The remaining 50 nations, home to 34 percent of humanity, fall into the category of "not free." In these countries, government sharply restricts individual initiative. Between 1980 and 1999, democracy made significant gains, largely in Latin America and Eastern Europe. India (containing nearly 1 billion people) returned to the "free" category in 1999.

Source: Freedom House (1999).

*Throughout our nation's history, company leaders have been able to enlist the help of the state to defend their interests. In 1941, workers at Mine Mill in Kirkland Lake organized a strike when the company refused to allow them to vote on whether to join the union. The government provided a police escort for workers who wanted to cross the picket line.*

emerged during the 20th century, as governments gained the ability to rigidly regulate a population. The Vietnamese government closely monitors the activities not just of visitors but of all its citizens. Similarly, the government of North Korea uses surveillance equipment and powerful computers to collect and store information and thereby control the entire population.

Some totalitarian governments claim to represent the will of the people, but most seek to bend people to the will of the government. Such governments are *total* concentrations of power, allowing no organized opposition. Denying people the right to assemble and controlling access to information, these governments create an atmosphere of isolation and fear. In the former Soviet Union, for example, most citizens could not own telephone directories, copying equipment, fax machines, or even accurate city maps.

Socialization in totalitarian societies is highly political, seeking not just obedience but commitment to the system. In North Korea, one of the most totalitarian states in the world, pictures of leaders and political messages are everywhere, reminding citizens that they owe total allegiance to the state. Government-controlled schools and mass media present only official versions of events.

Totalitarian governments have spanned the political spectrum from fascist (including former Nazi Germany) to communist (such as North Korea). In some totalitarian states, businesses are privately owned (as in Nazi Germany and, more recently, Chile); in others, businesses are government owned (as in North Korea, Cuba, and the former Soviet Union). In all cases, however, one party claims total control of the society and permits no opposition.

## A GLOBAL POLITICAL SYSTEM?

We have already noted the emergence of a global economy. Is there a parallel development of a global political system? On one level, the answer is no. Although most of today's economic activity is international, the world remains divided into nation-states just as it has for centuries. The United Nations (founded in 1945) was a small step toward global government, but to date its political role in world affairs has been limited.

On another level, however, politics has become a global process. For some analysts, multinational - corporations represent a new political order since they have enormous power to shape events throughout the world. In other words, politics is dissolving into business, as corporations grow larger than governments.

Then, too, the Information Revolution has moved national politics onto the world stage. Electronic mail over the Internet, cellular phones, satellite transmission systems, and fax machines mean that few countries can conduct their political affairs in complete isolation and privacy. Finally, several thousand *non-governmental organizations (NGOs)* seek to advance global issues, such as human rights (Amnesty International) and protection of the environment (Greenpeace). In the new century, NGOs will almost certainly play a key role in expanding the global political culture (Boli & Thomas, 1997).

In sum, just as individual nations cannot fully manage their own economies without considering other countries, governments cannot fully control the political events that occur within their borders.

# POLITICS IN CANADA

In contrast to the United States's revolutionary break with Great Britain, Canada's political independence came about through a peaceful transition from monarchial rule to democratic decision making. Our nation's political development reflects its distinctive history, capitalist economy, and cultural heritage.

## CANADIAN CULTURE AND THE RISE OF THE WELFARE STATE

Our cultural emphasis on individualism is reflected in the *Canadian Human Rights Act* and the Canadian Charter of Rights and Freedoms, both of which make explicit that all individuals have an equal right to make the lives for themselves that they are able to and wish to achieve. In order to make the best life for themselves, some people in Canada—and many more in the United States, no doubt—share the sentiment of 19th-century philosopher and poet Ralph Waldo Emerson: "The government that governs best is the government that governs least." Yet many other Canadians view the government in a more positive light, agreeing to pay higher taxes to support quality public services.

What is clear is that our government has grown into a vast and complex **welfare state,** *a range of government agencies and programs that provide benefits to the population.* Government benefits begin even before birth (through prenatal nutrition programs, and coverage of physicians' fees and hospital stays) and continue into old age (through public pensions). Some programs are especially important to the poor, who are not well served by our capitalist economic system; nevertheless, students, farmers, homeowners, small business operators, veterans, performing artists, and even giant corporations also get various subsidies and supports. In fact, virtually all Canadian adults look to the government to fund their health care services as well as public education programs for their children, and a majority of us also look to government for at least part of our income (Caplow et al., 1982; Devine, 1985; Myles, 1996; Bartlett & Steele, 1998; Benoit, 2000).

Today's welfare state is the result of a gradual increase in the size and scope of government. At the time of Confederation in 1867, in most communities the presence of the federal government amounted to little more than a flag. Since then, the federal budget has steadily risen, reaching $162 billion in 2000–2001.

As much as government has expanded in this country, the Canadian welfare state, though larger than that of our neighbour to the south, is still smaller than in many other industrial nations. Figure 12–5 shows that government is larger in most of Europe, and especially in Scandinavian countries such as Denmark and Sweden.

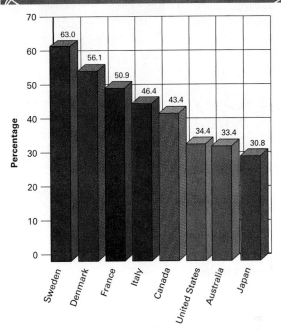

**FIGURE 12–5   The Size of Government: Tax Revenues as Share of Gross Domestic Product, 1996**

Source: U.S. Census Bureau (1998).

## THE POLITICAL SPECTRUM

Who supports the welfare state? Who would want to see it grow? Who might want to see it cut way back? Such questions tap attitudes that form the *political spectrum,* which ranges from the extremely liberal on the left to the extremely conservative on the right.

One cluster of attitudes concerns *economic issues.* Supporters of the New Democratic Party (NDP) call for extensive government regulation of the economy in order to reduce disparities in income. Progressive Conservative and Canadian Alliance party members want to limit the hand of government in the economy and allow market forces freer rein, while Liberal Party supporters attempt to strike a balance between public and private responsibility for the individual well-being of citizens.

*Social issues* are moral questions ranging from abortion and the death penalty to gay rights and treatment of minorities. NDP members endorse equal rights and opportunities for all categories of people, view abortion as a matter of individual choice, and oppose the death penalty because it has been unfairly applied to minorities. The "family values" agenda of Alliance members, and to a lesser extent the Conservatives, supports traditional gender roles and opposes gay

*The federal party leaders share a lighter moment. Alexa McDonough (NDP) shakes hands with the leaders of the other political parties. With the exception of the brief tenure of Conservative leader, Kim Campbell, the NDP stands out from the other official Canadian parties in that it has supported a woman leader for an extended period of time.*

families, affirmative action, and other "special programs" for minorities. Alliance and Conservative supporters tend to condemn abortion as morally wrong and many support the death penalty. Again, Liberal members tend to adopt a middle ground on most social issues, focussing on extending choice rather than favouring a single solution.

Until a few decades ago, there were two major political parties in Canada: the Progressive Conservatives ("Tories") and Liberals ("Grits"). A third party, the New Democrat Party, usually, but not always, campaigned for political office along the lines described above. But Canada's political spectrum has changed recently, with a number of newer political parties competing for the public's attention and, ultimately, their votes. These include the highly conservative Canadian Alliance Party (formerly the Reform Party), almost exclusively based in Western Canada; and the provincial Parti Québécois and federal Bloc Québécois, French parties based in Quebec. Both continuity and change in the political power matrix were observable in the 2000 federal election. Jean Chrétien's Liberals were returned to power once again—the third time in row—with an even greater majority of seats (172) than before the 2000 election. The second largest number of seats (66) was won by the Canadian Alliance, which, though advantaged by becoming the official opposition, failed to make a significant breakthrough east of Saskatchewan. The Bloc Québécois (38 seats) lost support to the Liberal Party. Meanwhile, the once-powerful Progressive Conservatives (12 seats) just managed to retain official party status, as did the New Democrats (13 seats).

## PARTY IDENTIFICATION

Because many people hold mixed political attitudes—with liberal views on some issues and conservative stands on others—party identification in Canada tends to be weak. Figure 12–6 shows the results of national surveys of party identification among Canadian adults between the federal elections in October 1993 and November 2000. During this time the Liberals enjoyed popular support that dropped below 40 percent only during the 1997 and 2000 elections, while only the Alliance managed to achieve popular support above 20 percent (Angus Reid Group Inc, 1995, 1996b, 1997c, 1998c, 2000b).

Although more than eight in every ten people polled preferred one party over another, most were not strongly committed to their party of choice. But most individuals do not hold views entirely consistent with either party of preference. With wealth to protect, well-to-do people generally hold conservative views on economic issues. Yet their extensive schooling and secure social standing encourage them to adopt liberal attitudes on many social issues. Individuals of low social position exhibit the opposite pattern, tending toward social democratic views on economic policy and embracing a socially conservative agenda (Nunn, Crocket, & Williams, 1978; Erikson, Luttbeg, & Tedin, 1980; Syzmanski, 1983; Humphries, 1984; McBroom & Reed, 1990).

## SPECIAL-INTEREST GROUPS

In the wake of events such as school shootings across North America, public support for gun control has been rising. In 1995, the Canadian government passed Bill C-68, which radically changed firearms legislation. The keystone of the law is universal firearms registration, requiring gun owners across the country to register their guns by January 1, 2001. The Canadian Association of Police Chiefs has been a strong supporter of the legislation, arguing that it will improve police safety across the country. Yet members of the

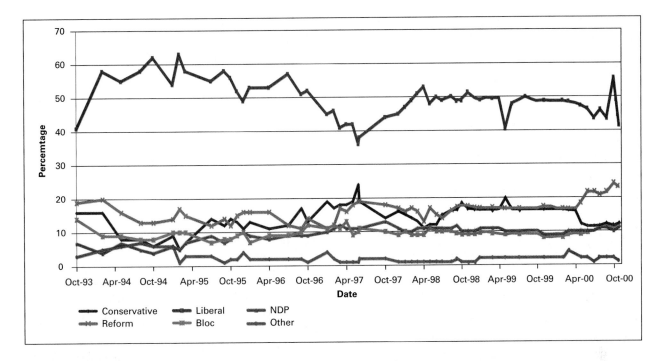

**FIGURE 12–6  Political Party Popular Support, Canada 1993–2000**

**Note:** October 1993, June 1997, and November 27, 2000 are based on election results.

Source: Angus Reid Group Inc. (1995, 1996b, 1997c, 1998c, 2000b).

National Firearms Association and its supporters have steadily worked in opposition to the legislation.

Groups for and against the "gun lobby" are examples of *special-interest groups*, people with an interest in some economic or social issue. Special-interest groups, which include associations of senior citizens, farmers, fireworks producers, and environmentalists, flourish in nations such as Canada, where loyalty to political parties tends to be low. Many special-interest groups employ *lobbyists* to work on their behalf.

## VOTER APATHY

It is a disturbing fact of political life that many Canadians are indifferent about voting. In fact, Canadian citizens are less likely to vote today than they were a century ago. In the 2000 federal election, only 63 percent of eligible voters showed up at the polls—the lowest turnout since 1896, and a lower turnout generally than in almost all other industrialized nations except for the U.S.

Who is and is not likely to vote? Canadian woman are less likely to cast a ballot than are men. Seniors are more likely to vote than are young people. White people are more likely to vote than are visible minorities, and Aboriginals are the least likely of all to vote.

Generally speaking, people with a bigger stake in society—homeowners, parents with children at home, people with good jobs and extensive schooling—are most likely to vote. Income matters, too: People with incomes in the top 20 percent are much more likely to vote than are people with incomes in the bottom 20 percent (Bennett, 1991; Hackey, 1992; Lewis, McCracken, & Hunt, 1994; DeLuca, 1998; Fetto, 1999).

Some non-voting, of course, is to be expected. At any given time, many people are sick or disabled; many more are away from home, having made no arrangement to submit an absentee ballot. Others forget to reregister after moving to a new neighbourhood. Moreover, registering and voting depend on the ability to read and write, which discourages Canadian adults who have limited literacy skills. Recent electoral reforms made it possible for homeless people to vote in the 2000 federal election, a privilege that was previously denied them because they had no fixed address.

Conservatives suggest that apathy amounts to *indifference* to politics because most people are, by and large, content with their lives. Liberals, and especially political radicals, counter that apathy reflects *alienation* from politics: People are so deeply dissatisfied with society that they doubt elections will make any real difference.

# THEORETICAL ANALYSIS OF POLITICS

Sociologists have long debated the distribution of power among different groups in Canada. Power is one of the most difficult topics to study because decision making is complex and takes place behind closed doors. Moreover, theories about power are hard to separate from the theorists' political leanings. Nevertheless, three competing models of power in Canada have emerged.

## THE PLURALIST MODEL: THE PEOPLE RULE

The **pluralist model,** closely allied with structural-functional theory, is *an analysis of politics that sees power as dispersed among many competing interest groups.* Pluralists claim, first, that politics is an arena of negotiation. With limited resources, no organization can expect to achieve all of its goals. Organizations, therefore, operate as *veto groups,* realizing some objectives but mostly keeping opponents from achieving all of their ends. The political process, then, relies heavily on forging alliances and compromises among numerous interest groups so that policies gain wide support. In short, pluralists see power as widely dispersed throughout society, with all people having at least some voice in the political system (Dahl, 1961, 1982; Rothman & Black, 1998).

## THE POWER-ELITE MODEL: A FEW PEOPLE RULE

The **power-elite model,** based on social-conflict theory, is *an analysis of politics that sees power as concentrated among the rich.* The term *power elite* was coined by C. Wright Mills (1956), a social-conflict theorist who argued that the upper class holds most of society's wealth, prestige, and power.

Mills claimed that members of the power elite head up the three major sectors of Canadian society: the economy, government, and the military. Elites in this privileged category move easily from one sector to another, Mills continued, consolidating power as they go. Wallace Clement (1975) argues this point about the Canadian elite, concluding that the corporate elite controls both the economy and the mass media, and also has a major influence over politics. The Canadian corporate media giants Kenneth Thomson, Ted Rogers, Israel (Izzy) Asper, André Chagnon, and Conrad Black are cases in point.

Power-elite theorists challenge the claim that countries such as Canada and the United States are democracies; they say the concentration of wealth and power is simply too great for the average person's voice to be heard. They reject the pluralist idea that various centres of power serve as checks and balances on one another. According to the power-elite model, those at the top encounter no real opposition.

## THE MARXIST MODEL: BIAS IN THE SYSTEM ITSELF

A third approach to understanding Canadian politics is the **Marxist political-economy model,** *an analysis that explains politics in terms of the operation of a society's economic system.* Like the power-elite model, the Marxist approach is a social-conflict model that rejects the idea that Canada is a political democracy. But while the power-elite model focusses on the disproportionate wealth and power of certain individuals, the Marxist model looks to the bias rooted in this nation's institutions, especially its economy. Karl Marx believed that a society's economic system (capitalist or socialist) shapes its political system. Power elites, therefore, do not simply appear on the scene; they are creations of capitalism itself.

From this point of view, reforming the political system—say, by limiting the amount of money that rich people can contribute to political candidates—is unlikely to bring about true democracy. The problem does not lie in the *people* who exercise great power or the *people* who don't vote; the problem is the *system* itself—what Marxists term the "political economy of capitalism." In other words, as long as Canada has a predominantly capitalist economy, just as the majority of people are exploited in the workplace, so will they be shut out of politics.

**Critical evaluation.** Which of the three different models of the Canadian political system is correct? Over the years, research has provided support for each, suggesting a case can be made for all three. In the end, of course, how one thinks our political system ought to work is as much a matter of political values as scientific fact.

Research by Nelson Polsby (1959) supports the pluralist model. Polsby studied the politics of New Haven, Connecticut, in the U.S., where he found that key decisions involving urban renewal, selection of political candidates, and the running of the city's schools were each made by different groups. Polsby concluded that no one group—not even the New Haven upper class—rules all the others.

Supporting the power-elite position, Robert and Helen Lynd (1937) studied Muncie, Indiana (which they called "Middletown," to suggest it was a typical city), and documented the fortune amassed by a single family—the Balls—from their business producing glass canning jars. The Lynds showed how the Ball family dominated many dimensions of the city's life. If anyone doubted the Balls' prominence, one only had to note

**TABLE 12–1  Three Models of Canadian Politics: A Summary**

| | Pluralist Model | Power-Elite Model | Marxist Model |
|---|---|---|---|
| **How is power distributed in Canadian society?** | Highly dispersed | Concentrated | Concentrated |
| **Is Canada basically democratic?** | Yes, because voting offers everyone a voice, and no one group or organization dominates society | No, because a small share of the people dominate the economy, government, and military | No, because the bias of the capitalist system is to concentrate both wealth and power |
| **How should we understand voter apathy?** | Apathy is indifference; after all, even poor people can organize for a greater voice if they wish | Apathy is understandable, given how difficult it is for ordinary people to oppose the rich and powerful | Apathy is alienation generated by a system that will always leave most people powerless |

that the local bank, a university, a hospital, and a department store all bore the family's name. In Muncie, according to the Lynds, the power elite more or less boiled down to a single family. Such influence of wealth is also observable in the province of New Brunswick, where the McCain and Irving families seem omnipotent.

From the Marxist perspective, the point is not to look at which individuals make decisions. Rather, as Alexander Liazos (1982:13) explains, "The basic tenets of capitalist society shape everyone's life: the inequalities of social classes and the importance of profits over people." As long as the basic institutions of society are organized to meet the needs of the few rather than the many, Liazos concludes, a truly democratic society is impossible.

Table 12–1 summarizes the three political models. Clearly, the Canadian political system gives almost everyone the right to participate in politics through elections. But, as the power-elite and Marxist models point out, at the very least the Canadian political system is far less democratic than most people think. Most citizens may have the right to vote, but the major political parties and their candidates typically support only those positions acceptable to the most powerful segments of society and consistent with the operation of our capitalist economy (Bachrach & Baratz, 1970).

Whatever the reasons, many people in Canada are losing confidence in their leaders. Canadians want more government transparency and greater accountability. Democracy Watch, a non-profit, non-partisan group, promotes civic input in public affairs. In 2000, it published a "report card" on the main Canadian political parties. All were found to fall short on promoting pro-democratic policies, such as proportional representation.

## POWER BEYOND THE RULES

Politics is always a matter of disagreement over a society's goals and the means to achieve them. A political system tries to resolve controversy within a system of rules. But political activity sometimes breaks the rules, or tries to do away with the entire system.

## REVOLUTION

**Political revolution** is *the overthrow of one political system in order to establish another.* Reform involves change *within* a system, modifying the law or, as an extreme case, a *coup d'état* (in French, literally "stroke of the state"), by which one leader topples another. Revolution, however, involves not just change at the top but a change *of the system itself.*

No type of political system is immune to revolution; nor does revolution produce any one kind of government. French revolutionaries in 1789 overthrew a monarch, only to set the stage for the return of a monarchy in the person of Napoleon. In 1917, the Russian Revolution replaced a monarchy with a socialist government built on the ideas of Karl Marx. In 1992, the Soviet Union was reborn as the Russian Federation, moving toward a market system and a greater political voice for its people.

Despite their striking variety, revolutions share a number of traits (Tocqueville, 1955, orig. 1856; Davies, 1962; Brinton, 1965; Skocpol, 1979; Lewis, 1984; Tilly, 1986):

1. **Rising expectations.** Common sense would suggest that revolution is more likely when people are grossly deprived, but history shows that most revolutions occur when people's lives are improving. Rising expectations, rather than bitter resignation, fuel revolutionary fervour.

2. **Unresponsive government.** Revolution becomes more likely when a government is unable or unwilling to reform, especially when demands for change are made by powerful segments of society. The October 1970 crisis in Quebec, when the Front de Liberation du Quebec (FLQ) adopted a violent strategy to realize its goal of political independence from the rest of Canada, serves as an example.

3. **Radical leadership by intellectuals.** The English philosopher Thomas Hobbes (1588–1679) claimed intellectuals provide the justification for revolution, and universities frequently are at the

*The first modern political revolution began in 1789 in France. This engraving,* titled To Versailles, To Versailles, *depicts the march of women to the king's palace in Versailles, on the outskirts of Paris, on October 5th, 1789, where they demanded more bread. The day after, the people forcibly led the royal family to Paris. Eventually, in October 1793, the royal family was executed by guillotine in a crowded public square.*

Source: *To Versailles, To Versailles,* March of the Women on Versailles, Paris, October 5, 1789, engraving by French School (18th century). Musée Carnavalet, Paris, France. Bulloz/The Bridgeman Art Library.

centre of political change. Students played a key role in China's pro-democracy movement and in the uprisings in Eastern Europe.

4. **Establishing a new legitimacy.** Overthrowing a political system is not easy, but more difficult still is ensuring a revolution's long-term success. Some revolutionary movements are unified merely by hatred of the past regime and fall apart once new leaders are installed. Revolutionaries must also guard against counterrevolutionary drives led by deposed leaders. This explains the speed and ruthlessness with which victorious revolutionaries typically dispose of former leaders.

Scientific research cannot declare that a revolution is good or bad. That judgment depends on one's values and, in any case, becomes evident only after many years. Ten years after its revolution, the future of the former Soviet Union remains unsettled.

## TERRORISM

**Terrorism** refers to *acts of violence or the threat of such violence used by an individual or a group as a political strategy.* Like revolution, terrorism falls outside the rules of established political systems. Paul Johnson (1981) offers three insights into terrorism.

First, terrorists consider violence a legitimate political tactic, despite the fact that such acts are condemned by virtually every nation. Terrorists also bypass (or are excluded from) established channels of political negotiation. Terrorism is, therefore, a weak organization's strategy to harm a stronger foe. The 1970 FLQ kidnapping and subsequent murder of then Quebec labour minister Pierre Laporte was strongly condemned in all of Canada. At the same time, it

served as a wake-up call for Canadians outside Quebec to the bitterness many Québécois feel about their position in Canada. Likewise, attacks against the U.S. embassies in Tanzania and Kenya in 1998 and the U.S.S. *Cole* in 2000 may have been morally wrong because they harmed innocent people, but they did raise the profile of organizations with grievances against the United States.

Second, terrorism is employed not just by groups but also by governments against their own people. *State terrorism* is the use of violence, usually beyond the rule of law, by government officials. State terrorism is common in some authoritarian and totalitarian states, which survive by inciting fear and intimidation. Saddam Hussein, for example, shores up his power in Iraq through state terrorism.

Third, democratic societies are especially vulnerable to terrorism because they afford extensive civil liberties to their people and have limited police networks. In contrast, while totalitarian regimes make widespread use of state terrorism, their extensive police power minimizes opportunities for individual terrorist acts.

Though taking hostages and killing innocent people provoke widespread anger, responding to terrorism is difficult. The immediate concern is identifying those responsible. Because terrorist groups are often shadowy organizations with no formal connection to any established state, a reprisal may be all but impossible. Then, too, a forcible military reaction may broaden the scope of violence, increasing the risk of confrontation with other governments.

Fourth and finally, terrorism is always a matter of definitions. Governments claim the right to maintain order, even by force, and may brand opponents who use violence as "terrorists." Political differences help explain why one person's "terrorist" is another's "freedom fighter."

# WAR AND PEACE

Perhaps the most critical political issue is **war,** *organized, armed conflict among the people of various societies, directed by their governments.* War is as old as humanity, of course, but understanding it is now an urgent matter since we possess the technological means to destroy ourselves.

For almost all of the 20th century, nations somewhere were in violent conflict. In the "Great War" (Second World War) alone, 56 500 Canadian soldiers lost their lives, and many more were injured. Other deadly conflicts throughout this century took the lives of countless Canadians and people from all corners of the globe. Domestic and international wars continue to be waged at this time, eating up a substantial portion of national budgets that could otherwise be used for more constructive purposes.

## THE CAUSES OF WAR

Wars occur so often that we might think there is something "natural" about armed conflict. But while many animals are naturally aggressive (Lorenz, 1966), research provides no evidence that human beings inevitably wage war under any particular circumstances. As Ashley Montagu (1976) observes, governments around the world usually have to force their people to mobilize for war.

Like other forms of social behaviour, warfare is a product of *society*—one that varies in purpose and intensity from place to place. The Semai of Malaysia, among the most peace loving of the world's peoples, rarely resort to violence. In contrast, the Yąnomamö, described in Chapter 2 (Culture), are quick to wage war.

If society holds the key to war or peace, under what circumstances *do* humans engage in warfare? Quincy Wright (1987) cites five factors that promote war:

1. **Perceived threats.** Societies mobilize in response to a perceived threat to their people, territory, or culture. The likelihood of armed conflict between the United States and the former Soviet Union, for example, has decreased as the two nations have become less fearful of each other.

2. **Social problems.** When internal problems cause widespread frustration at home, a nation's leaders may divert attention by attacking an external enemy as a form of scapegoating. Some analysts think the lack of economic development in the People's Republic of China, for example, led to hostility toward Vietnam, Tibet, and the former Soviet Union.

3. **Political objectives.** Poor nations, such as Vietnam, have used wars to end foreign domination. On the

*Not all terrorism is the work of individuals or groups. Since 1950, China has sought to maintain control of Tibet by force. This Tibetan refugee displays instruments of torture used against him by officials of the Chinese government.*

other hand, powerful countries such as the United States use a periodic "show of force" (such as the recent deployment of troops in Somalia, Haiti, and Bosnia) to enhance their global stature.

4. **Moral objectives.** Nations rarely claim to fight just to gain wealth and power. Instead, they infuse military campaigns with moral urgency, rallying their people around visions of "freedom" or "the fatherland." Although few doubt that the 1991 Persian Gulf War was largely about oil, some Western nations, especially the U.S., portrayed the mission as a drive to halt a Hitler-like Saddam Hussein.

5. **The absence of alternatives.** A fifth factor promoting war is the lack of alternatives. Although it is the United Nations's job to maintain international peace, the organization has had limited success in resolving tensions among nations.

## THE COSTS AND CAUSES OF MILITARISM

The costs of war extend far beyond battlefield casualties. Together, the world's nations spend $1 trillion annually (about $160 for every person on the planet) for military purposes. Such expenditures, of course, divert resources from the millions of poor people who desperately struggle for survival.

For years, defence has been the U.S. government's single biggest expenditure, accounting for 16 percent of all federal spending, or $277 billion in 1999 (by comparison, Canada spent about 1.7 percent of its GNP on the military). Some of this huge sum is the result of the *arms race*, a military spending spree carried on for decades by the United States and the former Soviet Union. Yet even after the collapse of the Soviet Union, military spending remains high. Thus, some analysts (allied with power-elite theory) claim that these countries are dominated by a **military-industrial complex,** *the close association of the federal government, the military, and defence industries.* The roots of militarism, then, lie not only in external threats to security but also in the institutional structures of a society (Marullo, 1987).

Another reason for continuing militarism is regional conflict. During the 1990s, localized wars broke out in Bosnia, Chechnya, and Zambia, and tensions run high in a host of other countries, including Ireland, Iraq, and a divided Korea. Even limited wars have the potential to escalate and involve other countries. In 1998, for example, India and Pakistan exploded nuclear bombs, raising fears of atomic war in that region. As more nations acquire nuclear weapons, the risk increases that regional conflict will erupt into deadly war.

## NUCLEAR WEAPONS

Despite the easing of superpower tensions, the world still contains almost 25 000 nuclear warheads, representing a destructive power equivalent to five tonnes of TNT for every person on the planet. Should even a small fraction of this arsenal be used in war, life as we know it would cease on much of the earth. Albert Einstein, whose genius contributed to the development of nuclear weapons, reflected, "The unleashed power of the atom has changed everything *save our modes of thinking,* and we thus drift toward unparalleled catastrophe." In short, nuclear weapons make full-scale war unthinkable in a world not yet capable of peace.

Great Britain, France, the People's Republic of China, Israel, India, and Pakistan are current members of the "nuclear club," but the vast majority of nuclear weapons are held by the United States and the Russian Federation. These two nations have agreed to reduce their stockpiles of nuclear weapons by 75 percent by 2003. But even so, the danger of catastrophic war increases with *nuclear proliferation,* the acquisition of nuclear weapons by other nations. Experts say Libya, Iran, Iraq, and North Korea have programs to develop nuclear weapons. While some nations have stopped the development of nuclear weapons—Argentina and Brazil halted work in 1990, and South Africa dismantled its arsenal in 1991—by 2010, as many as 50 countries could have the ability to fight a nuclear war. Such a trend makes any regional conflict far more dangerous (Thomas, Barry, & Liu, 1998).

## PURSUING PEACE

How can the world reduce the dangers of war? Here are the most recent approaches to peace:

1. **Deterrence.** The logic of the arms race holds that security derives from a balance of terror between the superpowers. Thus, the principle of *mutually assured destruction (MAD)* demands that either side launching a first strike against the other sustain massive retaliation. This deterrence policy kept the peace for almost 50 years during the cold war. Yet, it encouraged a massive arms race, and it cannot control nuclear proliferation, which poses a growing threat to peace.

2. **High-technology defence.** If technology created the weapons, perhaps it can also protect us from them—such is the claim of the *strategic defence initiative (SDI).* Under SDI, satellites and ground installations would destroy enemy missiles soon after they were launched. However, many analysts claim that "star wars" would be, at best, a leaky umbrella; others question the need for such an expensive scheme in light of the collapse of the Soviet Union.

   Worth noting, too, is that sophisticated technology raises not only new possibilities for defence but also new strategies for waging war. The Critical Thinking box takes a closer look at the possibilities for "information warfare."

3. **Diplomacy and disarmament.** Some analysts believe that the best road to peace is diplomacy rather than technology (Dedrick & Yinger, 1990). Diplomacy can enhance security by reducing, rather than building, weapons stockpiles.

   But disarmament, too, has limitations. No nation wishes to become vulnerable by eliminating its defences. Successful diplomacy, then, depends on everyone involved sharing responsibility for a common problem (Fisher & Ury, 1988). Furthermore, while the United States and the former Soviet Union have succeeded in negotiating arms reduction agreements, the threat from other nations such as Libya, North Korea, and Iraq—all of which desire to build nuclear arsenals—remains large.

4. **Resolving underlying conflict.** In the end, reducing the dangers of war may depend on resolving the issues that have fuelled the arms race. Even in the post–cold war era, regional conflicts remain in Latin America, Africa, Asia, and the Middle East. Is it sensible, some ask, for the world

## CRITICAL THINKING

# Information Warfare:
# Let Your Fingers Do the Fighting

For decades, scientists and military officials have studied how to use computers to defend against attacks by missiles and planes. Recently, however, the military has recognized that new information technology can fundamentally change the way war is waged. In place of rumbling tanks and screaming aircraft, electronic "smart bombs" can silently penetrate an enemy country's computer system and render it unable to transmit information.

In such "virtual wars," soldiers seated at workstation terminals would dispatch computer viruses to shut down the enemy's communication links, causing telephones to fall silent and air traffic control and railroad switching systems to fail. Computer systems would feed phony orders to field officers and televisions would broadcast "morphed"

news bulletins urging people to turn against their leaders.

Like the venom of a poisonous snake, the weapons of "information warfare" could paralyze an enemy prior to a conventional military attack. Another, more hopeful possibility is that new information technology might not set the stage for conventional fighting, but prevent it entirely. If, as in the old *Star Trek* episode, the "victims" of computer warfare could be limited to a nation's communications links—rather than its cities and people—wouldn't we all be more secure?

Yet so-called "info-war" also poses new dangers, since, presumably, a few highly skilled operators with sophisticated electronic equipment could also wreak communications havoc on Canada. The United States might be especially vulnerable to a cyber-attack

because of its military might. Perhaps not surprisingly, in 1996, the U.S. Central Intelligence Agency (CIA) began work on a defensive "cyber-war centre" to prevent what one official termed an "electronic Pearl Harbor."

*What do you think?*

1. *Do you think it is realistic to imagine that virtual warfare might replace conventional battlefield fighting? Why or why not?*

2. *Can you see ways in which new information technology might increase the chances to resolve disputes peacefully?*

3. *What about ways in which computer technology might increase dangers of war?*

Source: Waller (1995) and Weiner (1996).

---

to spend thousands of times more money on militarism than on peacekeeping? (Sivard, 1988).

## LOOKING AHEAD: POLITICS IN THE TWENTY-FIRST CENTURY

Just as economies are changing, so are political systems. As we enter the 21st century, several dilemmas and trends will likely command widespread attention.

One vexing problem in Canada is an inconsistency between our democratic ideals and our relatively low turnout at the polls. Perhaps, as the pluralists contend, many people do not bother to vote because they are basically content with their lives. But perhaps the power-elite theorists are right in saying that people withdraw from a system that concentrates wealth and power in the hands of so few people. Or, as Marxist critics contend, perhaps people find that our political system offers little real choice, tied as it is to our capitalist economic system. (The Controversy & Debate box on page 304 takes a look at our welfare

state, still an issue of contention.) In any case, it seems certain that we cannot endure a rising tide of apathy and falling confidence in government without moving toward real reform.

A second major trend is the global rethinking of political models. The cold war cast political debate in the form of two models, one based on capitalism, the other on socialism. But now analysts see a broader range of political systems, linking government to the economy in a variety of ways. "Welfare capitalism," as found in Sweden, or "state capitalism," as found in South Korea and Japan, are just two possibilities.

Third, we still face the danger of war in many parts of the world. Even as the United States and Russia dismantle some warheads, vast stockpiles of nuclear weapons remain, and nuclear technology continues to spread around the world. Moreover, new superpowers are likely to arise in the 21st century (the People's Republic of China and India are likely candidates), just as regional conflicts will surely continue to fester. One can only hope that our leaders will find nonviolent solutions to the age-old problems that provoke war.

# Is Canada's Welfare State a "Laggard"?

Many sociologists tend to place Canada in the same category as the United States when it comes to the welfare state. To both countries, the category of "liberal welfare state" has been applied. This implies, for example, similarities in regard to meagre public expenditure on social welfare, strict eligibility requirements for recipients of welfare benefits, and willingness to tolerate levels of income inequality that are high by international standards (Esping-Anderson, 1990). Some writers have gone so far as to portray the Canadian welfare state, and that of its neighbour to the south, as "laggards" (Kudrle & Marmor, 1981) that trail far behind the welfare states of continental Europe and especially the Nordic countries.

But how accurate is it to lump Canada with the U.S. when it comes to their social welfare states? Is Canada really a laggard, as many seem to believe? Perhaps it is, from a northern European perspective. Yet upon closer examination, the sentiment that these two countries are "country cousins," willing to provide assistance only to the deserving poor, becomes problematic. The evidence indicates, in fact, that whereas inequality in the U.S. has substantially worsened in recent years, Canada does comparatively well on this measure (Myles, 1996). This is less to do with relative equality of salaries and wages among workers than it is to do with the more equitable Canadian tax system, which redistributes wealth from the top to the bottom income groups in a way similar to welfare states of the Nordic countries. In other respects, though, Canada's welfare state remains minimal, particularly in the small number of subsidized child care places across the country (outside Quebec); as well, Canada offers a comparatively meagre income support system for poor families, and low unemployment insurance and parental benefits. Yet, on other counts, particularly in regard to health services and the new national child care benefit (July 1998), Canada does not fit the stereotype.

Canadian sociologists, in fact, have not been silent on the issue of the country's international position in regard to social welfare. John Myles and Denise Forcese (1981:24), for instance, point to a "clear division between the two North American countries on the one hand and Sweden on the other." Gregg Olsen (1994), in examining the same set of countries but focussing on public services in addition to income transfers, suggests that the Canadian welfare state may be stunted (similar to that of the U.S.) in respect to some income-transfer programs, while comprehensive (similar to Sweden) in health care services.

In brief, perhaps a better way to think of welfare states, including that of Canada, is as multidimensional, with policies that range in kind but also in degree, and that shape (for better or worse) individuals' relative situations as workers, family members, and citizens.

Sources: Kudrle & Marmor (1981), Myles & Forcese (1981), Esping-Andersen (1990), Olsen (1994), and Myles (1996).

# SUMMARY

## ECONOMICS

1. The economy is the major social institution by which a society produces, distributes, and consumes goods and services.

2. The primary sector of the economy generates raw materials and is largest in low-income, pre-industrial nations. The secondary, manufacturing sector is substantial in nations throughout the world. The tertiary, service sector dominates in post-industrial countries.

3. Capitalism is based on private ownership of productive property and the pursuit of profit in a competitive marketplace. Socialism is grounded in collective ownership of productive property through government control of the economy.

4. Capitalism's high productivity provides a high overall standard of living but with marked income inequality; socialism is less productive, generating lower living standards but with less economic inequality.

5. The emerging global economy links many nations, with little regard for national boundaries.

6. Canada is a post-industrial society where only a small percentage of workers hold agricultural jobs; a minority has blue-collar, industrial jobs; and three-quarters have white-collar, service jobs.

7. A profession is a special category of white-collar work based on theoretical knowledge, occupational autonomy, authority over clients, and emphasis on serving the community.

8. In 2000, 6.8 percent of Canadian workers were unemployed, with young people and minorities most likely to be jobless.

9. Women and other minorities represent an increasing share of all Canadian workers.

10. Corporations are the core of the Canadian economy. Most large conglomerates now operate in many countries.

## POLITICS

1. Politics is the major social institution by which a society distributes power and organizes decision making. Max Weber claimed that power is legitimized by tradition, rationally enacted rules and regulations, or the personal charisma of a leader.

2. Monarchy is common to pre-industrial societies; industrialization favours the development of democracy.

3. Authoritarian political systems deny popular participation in government. Totalitarian political systems go even further, controlling people's everyday lives.

4. The political spectrum—from the liberal left to the conservative right—involves attitudes on economic issues (such as the degree of government regulation of the economy) and social issues (including the rights and opportunities of various segments of the population).

5. Special-interest groups tend to be strong in countries such as Canada and the United States that have weak political parties. Only 63 percent of eligible Canadian voters cast ballots in the 2000 federal election.

6. The pluralist model of politics views power as widely dispersed; the power-elite model believes power is concentrated in a small, wealthy segment of our society; the Marxist political-economy model says the capitalist economy makes true democracy impossible.

7. Revolution radically transforms a political system. Terrorism employs violence in pursuit of a political goal.

8. War is armed conflict between governments. The development of nuclear weapons, as well as their proliferation, increases the threat of global catastrophe. World peace ultimately depends on resolving the tensions that underlie militarism.

9. New information technology is greatly expanding the flow of information across national boundaries as well as altering the nature of warfare.

## KEY CONCEPTS

### ECONOMICS

**social institution** (p. 278) an organized sphere of social life, or societal subsystem—such as the economy—designed to meet human needs

**economy** (p. 278) the social institution that organizes a society's production, distribution, and consumption of goods and services

**post-industrial economy** (p. 279) a productive system based on service work and high technology

**primary sector** (p. 279) the part of the economy that draws raw materials from the natural environment

**secondary sector** (p. 279) the part of the economy that transforms raw materials into manufactured goods

**tertiary sector** (p. 279) the part of the economy that involves services rather than goods

**global economy** (p. 279) expanding economic activity with little regard for national borders

**capitalism** (p. 280) an economic system in which natural resources and the means of producing goods and services are privately owned

**socialism** (p. 282) an economic system in which natural resources and the means of producing goods and services are collectively owned

**welfare capitalism (p.** 283) an economic and political system that combines a mostly market-based economy with extensive social welfare programs.

**state capitalism** (p. 283) an economic and political system in which companies are privately owned but cooperate closely with the government.

**profession** (p. 285) a prestigious, white-collar occupation that requires extensive formal education

**corporation** (p. 288) an organization with a legal existence, including rights and liabilities, apart from those of its members

**monopoly** (p. 288) domination of a market by a single producer

**oligopoly** (p. 288) domination of a market by a few producers

## POLITICS

**politics** (p. 290) the social institution that distributes power, sets a society's agenda, and makes decisions

**power** (p. 290) the ability to achieve desired ends despite resistance from others

**authority** (p. 291) power that people perceive as legitimate rather than coercive

**routinization of charisma** (p. 291) the transformation of charismatic authority into some combination of traditional and bureaucratic authority

**monarchy** (p. 291) a type of political system in which a single family rules from generation to generation

**democracy** (p. 292) a type of political system that gives power to people as a whole

**authoritarianism** (p. 292) a political system that denies popular participation in government

**totalitarianism** (p. 292) a highly centralized political system that extensively regulates people's lives

**welfare state** (p. 295) a range of government agencies and programs that provide benefits to the population

**pluralist model** (p. 298) an analysis of politics that sees power as dispersed among many competing interest groups

**power-elite model** (p. 298) an analysis of politics that sees power as concentrated among the rich

**Marxist political-economy model** (p. 298) an analysis that explains politics in terms of the operation of a society's economic system

**political revolution** (p. 299) the overthrow of one political system in order to establish another

**terrorism** (p. 300) acts of violence or the threat of such violence used by an individual or a group as a political strategy

**war** (p. 301) organized, armed conflict among the people of various societies, directed by their governments

**military-industrial complex** (p. 302) the close association of the federal government, the military, and defence industries

## CRITICAL-THINKING QUESTIONS

1. As social institutions, what are the economic and political systems supposed to do? How well, in your opinion, does each do its job?

2. How did the Industrial Revolution alter the economy of Canada? How is today's Information Revolution changing the economy?

3. Identify different positions on the political spectrum. How do economic issues differ from social issues? How is class position linked to people's political opinions on each kind of issue?

4. How are both the economy and politics becoming global in scope? Imagine changes in both that may occur by the end of the 21st century.

## APPLICATIONS AND EXERCISES

1. Aggregate data on the Canadian economy—about 75 percent of output in the service sector, 2 percent in the primary sector, and the remainder in the industrial sector—obscures great variety within this country. Visit the library and locate data that profiles your own city, region, and province.

2. Visit a discount store such as Wal-Mart or K-Mart and select an area of the store of interest to you. Do a little "fieldwork," inspecting products to see where they are made. Does your research support the existence of a global economy?

3. Do some research to trace the growth in the size of the federal government over the past 50 years.

Then try to discover how organizations at different points along the political spectrum (from socialist organizations on the left through the National Democrats, Liberals, Progressive Conservatives, Canadian Alliance to right-wing fringe groups) assess the size of the current welfare state.

4. Freedom House, the organization that studies civil rights and political liberty around the world, publishes an annual report, *Freedom in the World*. Find a copy in the library (or write to the organization at 1319 Eighteenth Street, Washington, DC 20036), and examine the trends or political profiles of countries of interest to you.

 SITES TO SEE

**www.pearsoned.ca/macionis**

Visit the interactive Web site that accompanies this text. Begin by clicking on the cover of your book. You will find a chapter-by-chapter study guide, practice tests, chat room, and many suggested Web links.

**www.statcan.ca/english/Pgdb/People/labour.htm**

Visit the Web site operated by Statistics Canada, where you will find a wide range of interesting data and reports on the Canadian labour market.

**www.clc-ctc.ca**

The Canadian Labour Congress unites 2.3 million Canadian workers promoting issues related to the social and economic justice of working peoples across the country.

**www.fao.org**

The Food and Agriculture Organization is a part of the United Nations concerned with how well the global economy meets the needs of the world's people. From its home page, look for the FAO's annual report, titled *State of Food Insecurity in the World*.

**www.nlc-bnc.ca/2/12/h12–275-e.html**

This Internet source provides key references for women in Canadian politics.

**www.amnesty.org**

Amnesty International operates an informative Web site that offers information about the state of human rights around the world.

**www.usis.usemb.se/terror/index.html**

This Web site provides information on global terrorism.

**www.dwatch.ca**

Visit the Web site for Democracy Watch, an independent, non-profit, non-partisan Canadian citizen advocacy organization based in Ottawa. The organization works with Canadian citizens and organizations in helping to reform Canadian government and business institutions to bring them in line with the realities of a modern, working democracy.

# FAMILY AND RELIGION

# CHAPTER OUTLINE

*T*he date is January 14, 2001. Two gay couples are pronounced married today—Joe Varnell to Kevin
Bourassa and Elaine Vautour to Anne Vautour—before
an elated church congregation of more than 600 in downtown Toronto. Rev. Brent Hawkes of the Metropolitan
Community Church called the ceremony an "historical
act" that will have repercussions around the globe. The
minister married the two couples under the authority of a
section of the Ontario Marriage Act that allows any adult
to be married and receive a marriage licence provided
that there is a "publication of banns" before those
gathered to witness the marriage. No legal reasons were
cited why the marriages of the two gay couples should
not be performed (though some conservative Christians
present at the ceremony did utter public protests). The
two gay marriages were the first wedding ceremonies in
Canada using banns.

The next step is to convince the Ontario government
to register the Bourassa-Varnell and Vautour marriages,
the end point in legalizing marriages in Canada. So far

**309**

*the province has refused to register the marriages, allegedly because the act would contravene federal marriage law. However, most federal as well as provincial legislation refers to marriage partners as "persons" rather than as "husband and wife." Should the Ontario government decide not to register the marriages, Rev. Brent Hawkes stated that he and the two couples will request that the courts issue a "writ of mandamus" demanding that the province "do its duty" and register the two gay marriages (Valpy, 2001).* ■

Should the law permit gay couples to marry? What exactly is a "family"? Are families disappearing? Such questions touch on many people's deeply held beliefs and are part of the current "family values" debate. To hear some tell it, the family is fast becoming an endangered species. Consider these statistics: The Canadian marriage rate today is down 20 percent from 1989. At the same time, for those who do marry, divorce rates have doubled over the past 25 years. The result is that about one-third of today's marriages end in divorce. Marital breakdown, coupled with the fact that about one in four children is born to an unmarried woman (though some of these women may have been living in a common-law relationship at the time their children were born), means that half of Canadian children born today will live with a single parent at some time before reaching age 18. This trend is one reason that the share of Canadian children living in poverty has been rising steadily (Statistics Canada, 2000m).

Together, these facts point to a basic truth: Families in Canada and in other high-income countries are changing, probably faster than any other social institution (Bianchi & Spain, 1996; Fox, 2001). Not long ago, the cultural ideal of the family consisted of a working husband, a homemaker wife, and their young children. Today, fewer people have such a singular vision of the family, and, at any given time, only about 15 percent of households fit that description.

This chapter examines the family and religion, closely linked as society's prominent *symbolic institutions*. Both help establish morality, maintain traditions, and join people together. Moreover, along with change in families, we have seen change in religion, as membership in long-established churches is declining and new sects are flourishing.

With an eye on Canada and making comparisons with other countries, we will examine why many people consider the family and religion to be bedrock foundations of social life, while others predict—and even encourage—the decline of both institutions.

## THE FAMILY: BASIC CONCEPTS

The **family** is *a social institution found in all societies that unites people in cooperative groups to oversee the bearing and raising of children*. Family ties are also called **kinship,** a *social bond based on blood, marriage, or adoption*. All societies have families, but exactly who people call their kin has varied through history, and varies today from one culture to another. In Canada, most people regard a **family unit** as *a social group of two or more people, related by blood, marriage, or adoption, who usually live together*. Here, as elsewhere, families form around **marriage,** *a legally sanctioned relationship usually involving economic cooperation, as well as sexual activity and childbearing, that people expect to be enduring.*

Today, some people object to defining only married couples and children as "families" because doing so implies a single standard of moral conduct. Also, because some business and government programs still use this conventional definition, unmarried but committed partners—whether heterosexual or homosexual—are excluded from health care and other benefits. More and more, however, organizations are coming to recognize *families of affinity*—that is, people with or without legal or blood ties who feel they belong together and want to define themselves as a family.

What does or does not constitute a family, then, is the central issue in the current "family values" debate. Statistics Canada also plays a role in this debate. Federal governmental officials no longer employ the traditional notion of family when collecting data on the Canadian "census family," which is currently defined as "a now-married couple (with or without never-married sons or daughters of either or both spouses), a couple living common-law (again with or without never-married sons or daughters of either or both partners), or a lone parent of any marital status, with at least one never-married son or daughter living in the same dwelling. Families of now-married and common-law couples together constitute "husband-wife families" (Statistics Canada, 1998i). Nevertheless, sociologists in Canada do not have access to accurate national data on gay families since, unlike Nordic countries such as Denmark and Sweden, Canada does not include gay families in its definition of "census families." On the other hand, Statistics Canada is planning to include a question on "sexual orientation" in the 2001 census. In short, the national and international trend is toward a wider definition of "family" (Fox & Luxton, 2001). In the near future a gay couple with or without children—like the two gay couples mentioned in the chapter opener—may count as a census family.

## THE FAMILY: GLOBAL VARIATIONS

In pre-industrial societies, people take a broad view of family ties, recognizing the **extended family,** *a family unit that includes parents and children, as well as other kin.* This group is also called the *consanguine family*, because

*When two same sex couples—Kevin Bourassa and Joe Varnell, and Anne Vautour and Elaine Vautour—were married at the Metropolitan Community Church of Toronto, on Sunday, January 14, 2001, the Ontario Government went on record stating that these church-sanctioned marriages would not be legally recognized. Yet many Canadians think this should be otherwise, including the large crowd of relatives and friends who attended the weddings of the two couples.*

it includes everyone with "shared blood." With industrialization, however, increasing social mobility and geographical migration give rise to the **nuclear family,** *a family unit composed of one or two parents and their children.* The nuclear family is also called the *conjugal family,* meaning "based on marriage." Although some members of our society live in extended families, the nuclear family has long been the most common in Canada.

## MARRIAGE PATTERNS

Cultural norms, and often laws, identify people as suitable or unsuitable marriage partners. Some norms promote **endogamy,** *marriage between people of the same social category.* Endogamy limits marriage prospects to others of the same age, village, race, religion, or social class. By contrast, **exogamy** refers to *marriage between people of different social categories.* In rural India, for example, a person is expected to marry someone from the same caste (endogamy) but from a different village (exogamy). The logic of endogamy is that people of similar position pass along their standing to their children, thereby maintaining the traditional social hierarchy. Exogamy, on the other hand, builds alliances and encourages cultural diffusion.

In high-income nations, laws prescribe **monogamy** (from the Greek, meaning "one union"), *marriage uniting two partners.* Global Map 13–1 on page 312 shows that while monogamy is the rule throughout the Americas and Europe, many low-income countries—especially in Africa and southern Asia—permit **polygamy** (from the Greek, meaning "many unions"), *marriage that unites three or more people.* Polygamy has two forms. By far the most common is *polygyny* (from the Greek, meaning "many women"), a form of marriage that unites one male and two or more females. Islamic

nations in the Middle East and Africa, for example, permit men up to four wives. Even so, most Islamic families are monogamous because few men can afford to support several wives and even more children. *Polyandry* (from the Greek, meaning "many men") unites one female and two or more males. One case of this rare pattern is in Tibet, a mountainous land where agriculture is difficult. There, polyandry discourages the division of land and allows several men to share the work.

Most of the world's societies have, at some time, permitted more than one marital pattern. Even so, as noted already, most marriages have been monogamous (Murdock, 1965). The historical preference for monogamy reflects two facts of life: Supporting several spouses is a heavy financial burden, and the number of men and women in most societies is roughly equal.

## RESIDENTIAL PATTERNS

Just as societies regulate mate selection, so they designate where a couple lives. In pre-industrial societies, most newlyweds live with one set of parents that offers them protection, support, and assistance. Most often, married couples live with or near the husband's family, termed *patrilocality* (Greek for "place of the father"). But in some societies (such as the North American Iroquois) couples live with or near the wife's family, called *matrilocality* (meaning "place of the mother"). Societies that engage in frequent local warfare tend toward patrilocality, so sons are close to home to offer protection. Societies that engage in distant warfare may be patrilocal or matrilocal, depending on whether sons or daughters have greater economic value (Ember & Ember, 1971, 1991).

Industrial societies show yet another pattern. Finances permitting, they favour *neolocality* (from

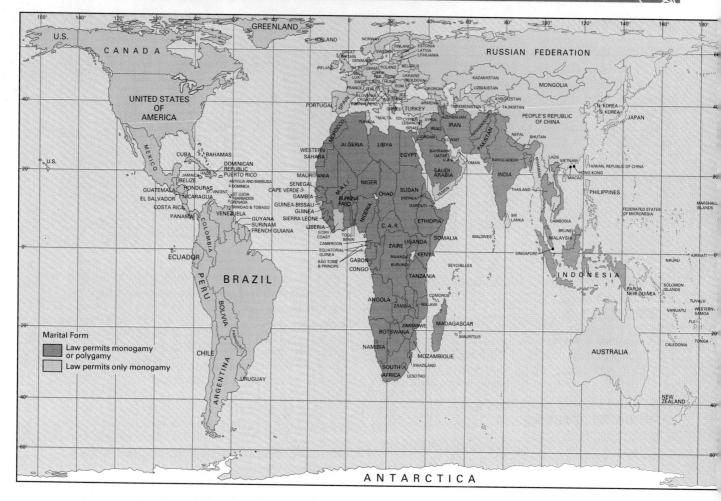

**GLOBAL MAP 13–1   Marital Form in Global Perspective**

Monogamy is the legally prescribed form of marriage in almost all high-income nations and throughout the Western Hemisphere. In most African nations and in southern Asia, however, polygamy is permitted by law. In many cases, this practice reflects the historic influence of Islam, a religion that allows a man to have up to four wives. Even so, most marriages in these traditional societies are monogamous, primarily for financial reasons.

Source: *Peters Atlas of the World* (1990).

Greek, meaning "new place"), by which a married couple lives apart from both sets of parents.

## PATTERNS OF DESCENT

**Descent** refers to *the system by which members of a society trace kinship over generations.* Most pre-industrial societies trace kinship through just the father's or the mother's side of the family. *Patrilineal descent,* the more common, traces kinship through males, so that prop-erty flows from fathers to sons. Patrilineal descent characterizes most pastoral and agrarian societies, where men produce the most valued resources. *Matrilineal descent,* by which people define only the mother's side as kin, and in which property passes from mothers to daughters, is found in horticultural societies where women are the primary food producers.

Industrial societies with greater gender equality recognize *bilateral descent* ("two-sided descent"). That is, children include as relatives people on both the father's side and on the mother's side of the family.

## PATTERNS OF AUTHORITY

The predominance of polygyny, patrilocality, and patrilineal descent reflects the global pattern of patriarchy. Indeed, as Chapter 10 (Gender Stratification) explains, no truly matriarchal society has ever existed.

In high-income countries such as Canada, more egalitarian families are evolving as the share of women in the labour force increases. However, even here, men are typically heads of households. Moreover, though children now more commonly take both of their parents' last names, children very rarely use only their mother's last name when both parents are married and living together.

# THEORETICAL ANALYSIS OF THE FAMILY

As in earlier chapters, several theoretical approaches offer a range of insights about the family.

## FUNCTIONS OF THE FAMILY: STRUCTURAL-FUNCTIONAL ANALYSIS

According to the structural-functional paradigm, the family performs many vital tasks. In fact, the family is "the backbone of society."

1. **Socialization.** As noted in Chapter 3 (Socialization: From Infancy to Old Age), the family is the first and most important setting for child rearing. Ideally, parents help children become well integrated and contributing members of society (Parsons & Bales, 1955). Of course, family socialization continues throughout the life cycle. Adults change within marriage and, as any parent knows, mothers and fathers learn as much from their children as the children learn from them.

2. **Regulation of sexual activity.** Every culture regulates sexual activity in the interest of maintaining kinship organization and property rights. The incest taboo, discussed in Chapter 7 (Sexuality), is a norm forbidding sexual relations or marriage between close kin. Although the incest taboo exists everywhere, precisely where one draws the line in defining incest varies from one culture to another (Murdock, 1965). Reproduction between close relatives can mentally and physically impair offspring. Yet only humans observe an incest taboo, suggesting that the key reason for controlling incest is social. Why? First, the incest taboo limits sexual competition in families by restricting sex to spouses. Second, since kinship defines people's rights and obligations toward each other, reproduction among close relatives would hopelessly confuse kinship ties and threaten the social order.

Third, forcing people to marry beyond their immediate families integrates the larger society.

3. **Social placement.** Families are not needed by people to reproduce, but they help maintain social organization. Parents confer their own social identity—in terms of race, ethnicity, religion, and social class—on children at birth.

4. **Material and emotional security.** Many people view the family as a "haven in a heartless world," offering physical protection, emotional support, and financial assistance. Thus, people living in families tend to be healthier than people living alone.

**Critical evaluation.** Structural-functional analysis explains why society, at least as we know it, depends on families. But this approach glosses over the diversity of Canadian family life and also ignores how other social institutions (say, government) could meet at least some of the same human needs. Finally, structural-functionalism overlooks negative aspects of family life, including patriarchy and family violence.

## INEQUALITY AND THE FAMILY: SOCIAL-CONFLICT ANALYSIS

The social-conflict paradigm also considers the family central to our way of life. But rather than focussing on ways that kinship benefits society, conflict theorists point out how the family perpetuates social inequality:

1. **Property and inheritance.** Friedrich Engels (1902; orig. 1884) traced the origin of the family to men's need (especially in the higher classes) to identify heirs so they could transmit property to their sons. Families thus concentrate wealth and reproduce the class structure in each succeeding generation (Mare, 1991).

2. **Patriarchy.** To know their heirs, men must control the sexuality of women. Families therefore transform women into the sexual and economic property of men. A century ago in Canada, most wives' earnings belonged to their husbands (Benoit, 2000a). Today, women still bear most responsibility for "mother work," that includes child rearing and housework (Fuchs, 1986; Hochschild, 1989; Presser, 1993; Keith & Schafer, 1994; Benokraitis & Feagin, 1995; Stapinski, 1998; Statistics Canada, 2000m; Rosenberg, 2001).

3. **Race and ethnicity.** Racial and ethnic categories persist over generations only to the degree that people marry others like themselves. Thus endogamous marriage shores up racial and ethnic hierarchies.

People in every society recognize the reality of physical attraction. But the power of romantic love, captured in Christian Pierre's painting, I Do, holds surprisingly little importance in traditional societies. In much of the world, it would be less correct to say that individuals marry individuals and more true to say that families marry families. In other words, parents arrange marriages for their children with an eye to the social position of the kin-groups involved.

**Critical evaluation.** Social-conflict analysis shows another side of family life: its role in social stratification. Engels criticized the family as part and parcel of capitalism. But noncapitalist societies have families (and family problems) all the same. The family may be linked to social inequality, as Engels argued, but the family carries out societal functions not easily accomplished by other means.

## CONSTRUCTING FAMILY LIFE: MICRO-LEVEL ANALYSIS

Both structural-functional and social-conflict analyses view the family as a structural system. Micro-level approaches, by contrast, explore how individuals shape and experience family life.

**Symbolic-interaction analysis.** Ideally, family living offers an opportunity for *intimacy*, a word with Latin roots that means "sharing fear." That is, as family members share many activities over time, they build emotional bonds. Of course, the fact that parents act as authority figures often limits their closeness with younger children. Only as young people reach adulthood do kinship ties "open up" to include sharing confidences as well as turning to one another for help with daily tasks and responsibilities (Macionis, 1978a).

**Social-exchange analysis.** Social-exchange analysis is another micro-level approach that depicts courtship and marriage as forms of negotiation (Blau, 1964). Dating allows each person to assess the advantages and disadvantages of taking another as a spouse, in light of what one has to offer in return. In essence, exchange analysts suggest, individuals "shop around" to make the best "deal" they can in a partner.

Physical attractiveness is one critical dimension of exchange. In patriarchal societies, men bring wealth

and power to the marriage marketplace, and women are expected to bring beauty. The importance of beauty explains women's traditional concern with their appearance and sensitivity about revealing their age. But as women have joined the labour force, they have become less dependent on men to support them, which indicates that the terms of exchange are converging for men and women.

**Critical evaluation.** Micro-level analysis offers a useful balance to structural-functional and social-conflict visions of the family as an institutional system. Both the interaction and exchange viewpoints show the individual experience of family life and how people shape it for themselves. This approach, however, misses the bigger picture: that family life is similar for people in the same social and economic categories. Canadian families vary in some predictable ways according to social class and ethnicity, and, as the next section explains, they typically evolve through distinct stages linked to the life course.

## STAGES OF FAMILY LIFE

Members of our society recognize several distinct stages of family life across the life course.

### COURTSHIP AND ROMANTIC LOVE

November 17, 2000—Victoria, B.C  It is a typical late fall Saturday in the city. We are at the Interfaith Chapel and attending the marriage of Jan and Nathan. Both are in their early twenties and beaming at their new status. On the surface, there is nothing at all

## Early to Wed: A Report from Rural India

Sumitra Jogi cries as her wedding is about to begin. Are they tears of joy? Not exactly. This "bride" is an 11-month-old squirming in the arms of her mother. The groom? A boy of six.

In a remote village in India's western state of Rajasthan, the two families gather at midnight to celebrate a traditional wedding ritual. It is May 2nd, in Hindu tradition an especially good day to marry. Sumitra's father smiles as the ceremony begins; her mother cradles the infant, who has fallen asleep. The groom, wearing a special costume and a red-and-gold turban on his head, gently reaches up and grasps the baby's hand. Then, as the ceremony ends, the young boy leads the child and mother around the wedding fire three-and-a-half times, while the audience beams at

the couple's first steps together as husband and wife.

Child weddings are illegal in India. But in rural regions, traditions are strong and marriage laws are hard to enforce. Thus, experts say, thousands of children marry each year. "In rural Rajasthan," explains one social worker, "all the girls are married by age 14. These are poor, illiterate families, and

they don't want to keep girls past their first menstrual cycle."

For a time, Sumitra Jogi will remain with her parents. But in eight or ten years, a second ceremony will send her to live with her husband's family, and her married life will begin.

If the reality of marriage is years in the future, why do families push their children to marry so early? Parents of girls know that the younger the bride, the smaller the dowry offered to the groom's family. Then, too, when girls marry this young, there is no question about their virginity, which raises their value on the marriage market. Overall, arranged marriages are an alliance between families. No one thinks about love or the fact that the children are too young to understand what is taking place.

Source: Based on Anderson (1995).

---

unusual about the young couple. Their relationship is based on romantic love rather than an arrangement struck between their parents or extended families, a practice still common in parts of the world. However, the new couple is different in at least one respect. Signifying the expanding role of the Internet in both Canada and England (where Nathan comes from), the couple's courtship spanning several months took place online. According to Jan, by that time she actually met Nathan in person, they were already planning their marriage.

Halfway across the globe, in rural Sri Lanka, and in pre-industrial societies throughout the world, most people consider courtship too important to be left to the young, let alone the Internet (Stone, 1977)!

*Arranged marriages* represent an alliance between two extended families of similar social standing and usually involve not just an exchange of children but also of wealth and favours. Romantic love has little to do with it, and parents may make such arrangements when their children are young. A century ago in Sri Lanka and India, half of all girls married before the age of 15 (Mayo, 1927; Mace & Mace, 1960). As the Global Sociology box explains, in some parts of rural India, child marriage persists today.

Industrialization erodes the importance of extended families as it weakens traditions. Young people who choose their own mates delay marriage until they gain the experience needed to select a suitable partner. Dating sharpens courtship skills and allows sexual experimentation.

Our culture celebrates *romantic love*—affection and sexual passion toward another person—as the basis for marriage. We find it hard to imagine marriage without love, and our popular culture—from fairy tales like "Cinderella" to today's paperback romance novels—

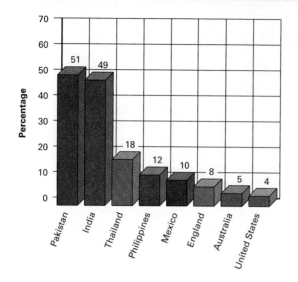

**FIGURE 13–1 Percentage of Post-secondary Students Who Express a Willingness to Marry without Romantic Love**

Source: Levine (1993).

portray love as the key to a successful marriage. However, as Figure 13–1 shows, in many countries romantic love plays a much smaller role in marriage.

Our society's emphasis on romantic love motivates young people to "leave the nest" to form families of their own; physical passion may also help a new couple through the difficult adjustments of living together (Goode, 1959). On the other hand, because feelings wax and wane, romantic love is a less stable foundation for marriage than are social and economic considerations—one reason that the divorce rate is much higher in Canada than in nations where culture limits choices in partners.

But even here, sociologists point out, society aims Cupid's arrow more than we like to think. Most people fall in love with others of the same race, comparable age, and similar social class. Our society "arranges" marriages by encouraging **homogamy** (literally, "like marrying like"), *marriage between people with the same social characteristics.*

### SETTLING IN: IDEAL AND REAL MARRIAGE

Our culture gives the young an idealized, "happily ever after" picture of marriage. Such optimism can lead to disappointment, especially for women, who are taught that marriage is the key to happiness. Then, too,

romantic love involves a lot of fantasy. We fall in love with others, not always as they are but as we want them to be (Berscheid & Hatfield, 1983).

Sexuality, too, can be a source of disappointment. In the romantic haze of falling in love, people may see marriage as an endless sexual honeymoon—only to realize that sex becomes less than all-consuming. About two in three married people report that they are satisfied with the sexual dimension of their relationship, although frequency of marital sex does decline over time. In general, couples with the best sexual relationships experience the most satisfaction in their marriages. Sex may not be the key to marital bliss, but good sex and good relationships often go together (Blumstein & Schwartz, 1983; Laumann et al., 1994).

*Infidelity*—sexual activity outside marriage—is another area where the reality of marriage does not coincide with our cultural ideal. Most Canadians adults do not approve of sex outside of marriage. Even so, the fact that a substantial minority of Canadian husbands and wives admit to having extramarital relations suggests that not everyone looks to marriage for sexual fulfillment in the long run (Angus Reid, 1997b).

### CHILD REARING

Despite the demands children make on us, a majority of adults in a recent international poll, including the majority of those surveyed in Canada (60 percent), identify raising children as integral to personal life fulfillment (The Gallup Organization,1997). However, because of the burden of child rearing, most Canadian adults, similar to their counterparts in a number of other countries, want no more than a few children, as Figure 13–2 documents. This represents a change from two centuries ago, when *eight* children was the Canadian average!

Big families pay off in pre-industrial societies because children supply needed labour. Thus people regard having children as a wife's duty, and, in the absence of effective birth control, childbearing is a regular event. Of course, a high death rate in pre-industrial societies prevents many children from reaching adulthood; as recently as 1921, Canada had a standardized death rate of 12.9 percent, compared to 4.8 percent in 1991. Neonatal death rates (deaths to infants under 28 days old) were 41.5 per 1000 live births in 1931; the rate in 1991 had fallen to 4.1 percent (McVey & Kalbach, 1995).

Industrialization transforms children, economically speaking, from a vital asset into a burdensome liability. Raising even one child to adulthood and helping to finance his or her education is exceedingly expensive in Canada. It has become even more so of late, owing to substantial increases in tuition fees at most Canadian colleges and universities. As a result,

Canadian family size has been dropping during this century. In 1996, there was an average of 1.2 children living at home per family in Canada. This is a decrease from 1.4 in 1981 and 1.8 in 1971 (Statistics Canada, 2000m).

The trend toward smaller families holds for all high-income nations. But the picture differs in low-income nations of Latin America, Asia, and especially Africa, where many women have few alternatives to bearing children. In such societies, four to six children is still the norm.

Parenting is not only expensive, but represents a lifetime commitment. As our society has given people greater choice about family life, more adults have opted to delay childbirth or to remain childless. The average age of women in Canada who gave birth to their first child in 1997 was just under 27, up from 26.0 in 1990 and 23 in the late 1960s (Statistics Canada, 2000m).

If Canadian parents are similar their U.S. counterparts, they would like to devote far more of their time to child rearing (Snell, 1990). But unless we accept a lower standard of living, economic realities demand that most parents pursue careers outside the home, even if that means giving less attention to their families (Fox, 2001).

In about 60 percent of two-parent families with children under the age of 15, both mothers and fathers are working (Statistics Canada, 1998k). Couples therefore have less time for parenting. Traditionalists in the "family values" debate caution that the trend toward more employed mothers may jeopardize the well-being of *latchkey kids* who are left fending for themselves. Progressives counter that such criticism seeks to penalize women for seeking the same career opportunities men have long enjoyed, and that, in any event, biological fathers are just as able to parent as their female counterparts.

Most northern European countries provide generous family leaves and benefits, as well as public child care, to help ease the conflict between family and work (Baker, 1995). Recent changes in the Canadian *Employment Insurance Act* have brought the length of the leave (12 months as of January 2001) within the range of that found in the Nordic countries. However, the Canadian leave is accompanied by comparatively low benefits (55 percent of previous wages), compared to 80 percent in Sweden (Benoit, 2000a). Even worse off are U.S. parents. It was not until 1993 that Congress passed the *Family and Medical Leave Act*, allowing up to 90 days' leave from work for a new child or serious family emergency. Still, most parents in the U.S. have to juggle parental and occupational responsibilities, and there are direct economic consequences because the U.S. leave has no monetary benefit unless parents belong to employer-sponsored parental programs.

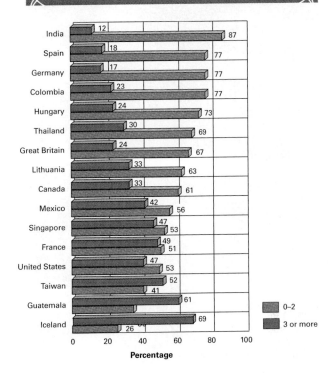

### GLOBAL SNAPSHOT

**FIGURE 13–2  Ideal Number of Children, Selected Countries, 1997**

*Question:* What do you think is the ideal number of children for a family to have?

**Note:** No opinion omitted.

Source: The Gallup Organization. *Special Reports: Global Study of Family Values* (Princeton, NJ: The Gallup Organization, 1997).

## THE FAMILY IN LATER LIFE

Increasing life expectancy in Canada means that, barring divorce, couples stay married for a long time. By age 60, most have completed the task of raising children. The remaining years of marriage bring a return to living with only one's spouse.

Like the birth of children, their departure—the "empty nest"—requires adjustments, although a marriage often becomes closer and more satisfying in midlife. Years of living together may have diminished a couple's sexual passion for each other, but understanding and commitment often increase.

Personal contact with children usually continues, since most older adults live a short distance from at least one of their children. Moreover, a substantial number of Canadian adults are grandparents, many of whom help

*Among Japanese, Korean, and Chinese women, the instance of lone parenthood is comparatively low.*

## CANADIAN FAMILIES: CLASS, RACE, AND GENDER

Dimensions of inequality—social class, ethnicity, race, and gender—are powerful forces that shape marriage and family life. This discussion addresses each factor in turn, but bear in mind that they overlap in our lives.

### SOCIAL CLASS

Social class frames a family's financial security and range of opportunities. Interviewing working-class women, Lillian Rubin (1976) found that wives thought a good husband was a man who held a steady job, did not drink too much, and was not violent. Rubin's middle-class informants, by contrast, never mentioned such things; these women simply *assumed* a husband would provide a safe and secure home. Their ideal husband was a man with whom they could communicate easily and share feelings and experiences. Clearly, what women (and men) feel they can hope for in marriage—and what they end up with—is linked to their social class. Much the same holds for children. Boys and girls lucky enough to be born into more affluent families enjoy better mental and physical health, develop more self-confidence, and go on to greater achievement than do children born to poor parents (Komarovsky, 1967; Bott, 1971, orig. 1957; Rubin, 1976; McLeod & Shanahan, 1993; Duncan et al., 1998).

### ETHNICITY AND RACE

Ethnicity and race, too, shape families. Analysis of Aboriginal and visible minority families must begin with the stark reality of economic disadvantage. Despite upward mobility over the generations, the incidence of low income among families of visible minorities is still significantly above the Canadian average. In 1995, about 36 percent of members of visible minorities lived on low incomes, compared with only 20 percent of the general population. About 45 percent of children under the age of six in the visible minority population were in low-income families in 1995, compared to 26 percent of all children. The incidence of low income was 32 percent among the visible minority population age 65 and over, while the national average was 19 percent (Statistics Canada, 1998i). Some visible minority groups are also more likely to be heads of households. Among females ages 15 to 44, black women (23 percent) were more than twice as likely in 1996 to be heading families on their own as were non-visible minority women (9 percent). Apart from blacks, females from Latin America (14 percent) and Southeast Asia (12 percent) were the next most likely to be lone parents. However, among

with child care and other responsibilities. Among Latin American, South Asian, and Aboriginal Canadians, in particular, grandmothers have a central position in family life (Statistics Canada, 2000m).

The other side of the coin is that adults in midlife now provide more care for aging parents. The "empty nest" may not be filled by a parent coming to live in the home, but many adults find caring for parents living to 80 and beyond to be more taxing than raising young children. The oldest of the "baby boomers"—now in their fifties—are called the "sandwich generation" because many (especially women) will spend as many years caring for their aging parents as they did caring for their children (Lund, 1993).

The final, and surely the most difficult, transition in married life comes with the death of a spouse. Wives typically outlive husbands because of women's greater life expectancy and the fact that women usually marry men several years older to begin with. Wives can thus expect to spend some years as widows. But the challenge of living alone following the death of a spouse is especially great for men, who usually have fewer friends than widows and may lack housekeeping skills.

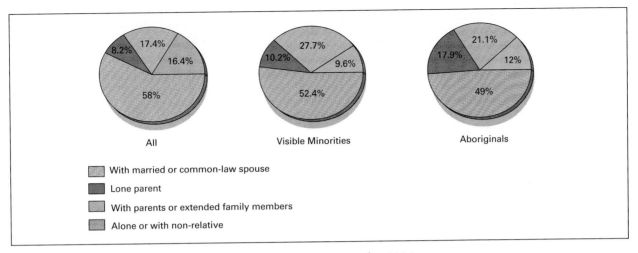

**FIGURE 13–3  Living Situation of Females Aged 15–64, Canada, 1996**

Source: Based on Statistics Canada (2000m).

Japanese, Korean, and Chinese women, the instance of lone parenthood is comparatively low (Statistics Canada, 2000a).

The patterns found among visible minority women are repeated for Aboriginal women. As explained in Chapter 9 (Race and Ethnicity), the personal incomes of Aboriginal men and women in Canada are substantially below the national incomes of non-Aboriginal men and women. People of Aboriginal ancestry are in fact twice as likely as non-Aboriginal people to have low incomes, so that family patterns reflect unemployment, underemployment, and, in some cases, physical environments replete with violence, alcoholism, and drug abuse.

Under these circumstances, maintaining stable family ties is difficult. Aboriginal lone mothers are especially marginalized economically. Almost three-quarters (73 percent) were living below Statistics Canada's low-income cut-offs in 1996, substantially more than the 43 percent for non-Aboriginal female lone parents (Statistics Canada, 2000m). Figure 13–3 shows that Aboriginal women are less likely to be living in husband–wife or common-law families than are their non-Aboriginal counterparts. Aboriginal women are more likely to be lone parents.

## GENDER

Regardless of race, Jessie Bernard (1982, orig. 1973) says every marriage is actually *two* different relationships: a woman's marriage and a man's marriage. Today, few marriages are composed of two equal partners. Patriarchy has diminished, but we still expect husbands to be older and taller than their wives and to have more important careers (McRae, 1986).

Why, then, do many people think that marriage benefits women more than it does men (Bernard, 1982)? The positive stereotype of the carefree bachelor contrasts sharply with the negative image of the lonely spinster, suggesting that women are fulfilled only through being wives and mothers.

But, Bernard claims, married women have poorer mental health, less happiness, and more passive attitudes toward life than single women do. Married men, on the other hand, generally live longer, are mentally better off, and report being happier than single men. These differences suggest why, after divorce, men are more eager than women to find a new partner.

Bernard concludes that there is no better guarantor of long life, health, and happiness for a man than having a woman well socialized to devote her life to taking care of him and providing the security of a well-ordered home. She is quick to add that marriage *could* be healthful for women if husbands did not dominate wives and expect them to do almost all the housework. Indeed, research confirms that the wives and husbands with the best mental health are those who share responsibilities for earning income, raising children, and keeping the home (Ross, Mirowsky, & Huber, 1983; Mirowsky & Ross, 1984; Leira, 1992; Eichler, 1997).

## TRANSITIONS AND PROBLEMS IN FAMILY LIFE

Ann Landers, a well-known observer of the North American scene, once said that one marriage in twenty is wonderful, five in twenty are good, ten in twenty are tolerable, and the remaining four are "pure hell." Families can be a source of joy, but the reality of family life often falls short of this ideal.

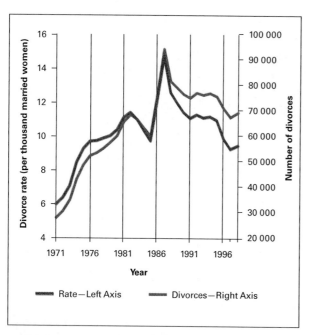

**FIGURE 13–4    Divorces in Canada, 1971–1998**
Source: Cansim, Tables D190, C241403.

## DIVORCE

Canadian society strongly supports marriage, and about nine out of ten people at some point "tie the knot." But many of today's marriages unravel. Figure 13–4 shows an increase in the Canadian divorce rate from the late 1960s (the date when the divorce laws were liberalized), peaking in 1987 (when restrictions were eased on marital dissolutions), and gradually levelling off by 1996. Based on 1998 divorce rates, 36 percent of Canadian marriages are expected to end in divorce.

This means that marriage in Canada is a fragile bond for most couples. Though only half that of the U.S. rate, where in 1997 more than four in ten marriages ended in divorce, Canada's divorce rate is still double that of Japan, and five times higher than in Italy (U.S. Census Bureau, 1998).

**Causes of divorce**  The comparatively high Canadian and U.S. divorce rates have many causes (Thornton, 1985; Waite, Haggstrom, & Kanouse, 1985; Weitzman, 1985; Gerstel, 1987; Furstenberg & Cherlin, 1991; Etzioni, 1993; Richardson, 1996; Luxton, 2001):

1.  **Individualism is on the rise.**  Members of families spend less time together than in the past. We have become more individualistic, more concerned with personal happiness than with the well-being of our families and children.

2.  **Romantic love often subsides.**  Because our culture bases marriage on romantic love, relation-

ships may fail as sexual passion fades. Many people end a marriage in favour of a new relationship that promises renewed excitement and romance.

3.  **Women are less dependent on men.**  Women's increasing participation in the labour force has reduced wives' financial dependency on husbands. Thus, women find it easier to leave unhappy marriages.

4.  **Many of today's marriages are stressful.**  With both partners working outside the home in most cases, jobs leave less time and energy for family life. This makes raising children harder than ever. Children do stabilize some marriages, but divorce is most common during the early years of marriage when many couples have young children.

5.  **Divorce is more socially acceptable.**  Divorce no longer carries the powerful stigma it did a century ago. Family and friends are now less likely to discourage couples in conflict from divorcing.

6.  **Legally, a divorce is easier to get.**  In the past, courts required divorcing couples to demonstrate that one or both were guilty of behaviour such as adultery or physical abuse. Today, divorce is legally permissible if a couple simply thinks their marriage has failed. Concern about easy divorce—voiced by many Canadians—has led some to advocate a rewriting of Canadian marriage law.

**Who divorces?**  At greatest risk of divorce are young couples—especially those who marry after a brief courtship—with little money, and who have yet to mature emotionally. The chance of divorce also rises if a couple marries after an unexpected pregnancy or if one or both partners have substance-abuse problems. People who are not religious are more likely to divorce than those who are.

Divorce also is more common if both partners have successful careers, perhaps due to the strains of a two-career marriage but also because financially secure people do not feel compelled to stay in an unhappy home. Finally, men and women who divorce once are more likely to divorce again, probably because problems follow them from one marriage to another (Booth & White, 1980; Yoder & Nichols, 1980; Glenn & Shelton, 1985).

Because over 80 percent of Canadian mothers gain custody of children, but fathers typically earn more income, the well-being of children often depends on fathers making court-ordered child-support payments (Statistics Canada, 1998k). Though Canadian courts tend to award child support in divorces involving children, in any given year, a significant number of children legally entitled to support receive only partial payments or no payments at all (Baker, 1995). Canadian data for 1994 to 1995 indicate that regular financial payments were received for about three-quarters of children whose parents reached an arrangement out of court; however, only just over half of children for whom financial support had been court ordered received regular custody payments (Statistics Canada, 1998k). In Canada, where children are seen as a private rather than a public responsibility, the failure of "deadbeat dads" to support their youngsters has prompted federal legislation: Employers must now withhold money from the earnings of parents who fail to pay up. Still, some fathers evade their responsibilities by moving or switching jobs, and many cannot afford to pay up even when they want to (Weitzman, 1985; Waldman, 1992). In contrast, Sweden has a publicly financed child-support payment system that provides a minimum guaranteed level of economic support for children following separation or divorce of their parents (Baker, 1995; Boje & Leira, 2000).

## REMARRIAGE

Four out of five people who divorce remarry, most within five years. In fact, about half of all marriages are now remarriages for at least one partner. Men, who derive greater benefits from wedlock, are more likely than women to remarry (McVey & Kalbach, 1995:237–38).

Remarriage often creates *blended families*, composed of children and some combination of biological parents and stepparents. Members of blended families thus have to define precisely who is part of the child's nuclear family. Adjustments are necessary; an only child, for example, may suddenly find that she now has two older brothers. Nevertheless, blended families offer both young and old the chance to relax rigid family roles.

## FAMILY VIOLENCE

The ideal family is a source of pleasure and support. The disturbing reality of many homes, however, is *family violence*—emotional, physical, or sexual abuse of one family member by another. Richard J. Gelles calls the family "the most violent group in society with the exception of the police and the military" (quoted in Roesch, 1984:75).

**Violence against women.** Family brutality often goes unreported to police, but results from the 1999 General Social Survey estimate that nearly 700 000 women who are married or in common-law relationships or in contact with their former partners were exposed to spousal violence over the five-year period predating the survey (Statistics Canada, 2000m). While men are also victims of spousal violence (at a rate of 7 percent compared to 8 percent for women), women (25 percent) are much more likely than are men

During her long career conducting sociological research, Jessie Bernard provided evidence that marriage is something of a surprise for women. Taught to see marriage as a solution to life's problems, Bernard explained, many women who enter traditional marriages soon face problems they did not expect. Susan Pyzow's painting, Bridal Bouquet, illustrates the idea.

Source: © Susan Pyzow, *Bridal Bouquet*, watercolour on paper, 10 × 13.5 in. Studio SPMInc.

(10 percent) to be severely abused by their partner. Women are also more likely to be victims of repeat spousal violence. In the 1999 survey, 65 percent of female victims (compared to 54 percent of males) experienced repeated instances of violence, with 25 percent of women and 13 percent of men having been exposed to spousal violence more than 10 times. Further, women who are victims of spousal abuse are more likely than men in comparable situations to need medical attention: 15 percent versus 3 percent. Finally, though the overall rate is decreasing, women are at a much greater risk for spousal homicide than are men. In other words, women are much more likely to be killed by a family member than are men: While only 18 percent of male homicide victims were murdered by a relative in 1998, the rate for female homicide victims was 58 percent. Overall, Canadian women are

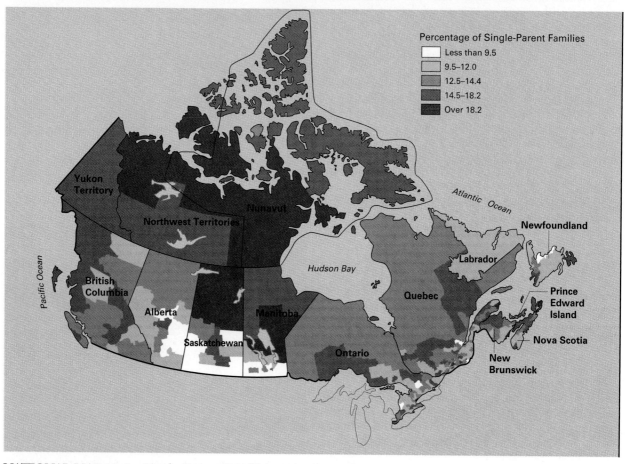

**NATIONAL MAP 13–1   Single-Parent Families across Canada**

Overall, about 14.5 percent of families were single-parent families in 1995. The number of single-parent families is greatest in urban areas, but such families are most concentrated in rural areas. With the limited social support available to single parents in rural areas, we can predict that many are largely relying on their extended families for support. What do you think explains the difference in proportion between rural and urban areas? Could it be that single parents in rural areas have more difficulty meeting new partners?

Source: Calculated based on data from Statistics Canada, Catalogue No. 95F018XDB96001 (1998b).

still more likely to be hurt by a family member than to be mugged or raped by a stranger or injured in an automobile accident (Statistics Canada, 2000m).

Historically, the law defined wives as the property of husbands, so that no man could be charged with raping his wife. In the past, too, the law regarded domestic violence as a private family matter, giving victims few options. Now, even without separation or divorce, a woman can at least obtain court protection from an abusive spouse. Bill C-126, known as the "Anti-Stalking Law," prohibits an ex-partner from following or otherwise threatening a woman (Statistics Canada, 1995). Further, communities across North

America have established domestic abuse shelters that provide counselling as well as temporary housing for women and children driven from their homes by domestic violence. While in 1975 there were only 15 shelters for abused women and children across the country, by 1998 this number had increased to 470 (Statistics Canada, 2000m). On the other hand, there still are no shelters for men and their children leaving abusive relationships.

**Violence against children.** Family violence also victimizes children. Figures for 1996 show that children under 18 years old were victims in 22 percent of the cases of violent crime reported to the police. Further, family members caused crimes against children in 20 percent of cases involving physical assaults and in 32 percent of cases involving sexual assaults (Statistics Canada, 1998j). Child abuse entails more than physical injury because abusive adults also violate trust to undermine a child's emotional well-being. Child abuse is most common among the youngest and most vulnerable children (Straus & Gelles, 1986; Van Biema, 1994).

Most child abusers are men; in 1996 fathers were the perpetrators of 73 percent of the reported physical assaults against children, and 98 percent of the sexual assaults (Statistics Canada, 1998j). These men do not conform to a simple stereotype, but most abusers do share one trait: having been abused themselves as children. Researchers have found that violent behaviour in close relationships is learned; in families, then, violence begets violence (Gwartney-Gibbs, Stockard, & Bohmer, 1987; Widom, 1996; Browning & Laumann, 1997).

## ALTERNATIVE FAMILY FORMS

The majority of Canadian families at mid-20th century were composed of a married couple who raised children. Such families dropped from 55 percent of all families in 1981. According to the 1996 census data, the figure is now 45 percent (Statistics Canada, 1999a).

### ONE-PARENT FAMILIES

Over 14 percent of Canadian families are one-parent families. National Map 13–1 shows the distribution of these families across Canada. In 1995, 22 percent of Canadian families with children under 18 years of age had only one parent in the household, up from 17 percent in 1981 (Statistics Canada, 1996a). Put another way, in less than a decade and a half, the number of lone-parent families in Canada grew from 712 000 to more than 1.1 million. *One-parent families*—83 percent of which in 1996 were headed by lone mothers, or four out of every five of such families—may result from divorce, death, or the decision of an unmarried woman to have a child (Statistics Canada, 2000m). Figure 13–5 compares the share of Canadian births outside of marriage with those for other high-income countries.

In 1996, nearly one-third of Aboriginal children under the age of 15 years lived in a one-parent family—twice the rate found in the population at large (Statistics Canada, 1998c). On the other hand, there is little difference in the probability of single parenthood for visible minorities and other women in Canada (Statistics Canada, 1995:135). Many one-parent families are multigenerational, with single parents (most of whom are mothers) turning to their own parents

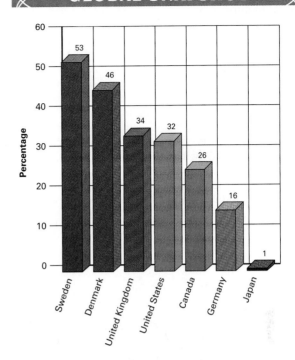

**FIGURE 13–5    Percentage of Births to Unmarried Women, 1995**

Source: U.S. Census Bureau (1998).

(again, typically mothers) for support. In countries such as Canada and the United States, then, the rise in single parenting is tied both to a declining role for fathers and the growing importance of grandparenting. By contrast, in countries such as Sweden and Finland, the increasing role of the welfare state in providing social services, such as public child care, significantly increases single parenthood (Macionis & Plummer, 1997:476–477).

Much research points to the conclusion that growing up in a one-parent family usually disadvantages children. According to some studies, a father and a mother each make a distinctive contribution to a child's social development, so it is unrealistic to expect a single parent to do as good a job. To make matters worse, most North American families with one parent—especially if that parent is a woman—contend with poverty. On average, children growing up in a single-parent family start out poorer, gain less schooling, and end up with lower incomes as adults. Such children are also more likely to be single parents themselves (Weisner & Eiduson, 1986; Wallerstein & Blakeslee, 1989; Astone & McLanahan, 1991; Li &

Wojtkiewicz, 1992; Biblarz & Raftery, 1993; Popenoe, 1993; Shapiro & Schrof, 1995; Webster, Orbuch, & House, 1995; Wu, 1996; Duncan et al., 1998). Other research suggests, however, that single parenting itself is not the problem, and that one caring parent is much better for a child than two uncaring ones. Further, in countries where the state has reduced poverty among one-parent families, children in these families appear to do as well as their counterparts in two-parent families (Sainsbury, 1996). Given the instability of common-law relationships, it is interesting to note that countries vary wildly in regard to their moral views on children being born outside marriage (see Figure 13–6); views diverge especially in regard to the growing trend in Canada and other industrial countries of never-married women having children (almost 24 percent of Canadian female lone parents in 1996 were of this type) (Statistics Canada, 1997b).

## COHABITATION

**Cohabitation** is *the sharing of a household by an unmarried couple.* The number of cohabiting couples in Canada increased substantially over the past two decades, so that by 1996, one Canadian couple out of seven was living in a common-law arrangement, up from one in nine in 1991. Nearly half of such unions involve children, sometimes born within the common-law union itself or otherwise from a former relationship (Statistics Canada, 1997b).

In global perspective, cohabitation is even more common in Sweden and the other Nordic countries as a long-term form of family life, and those who cohabit—with or without children—may count as a census family. By contrast, this family form is rare in more traditional (and Roman Catholic) nations such as Italy. On the other hand, Quebec currently has the highest cohabiting rate in Canada, with one in every four couples living in such a union (Turcotte & Bélanger, 1998). Cohabitation is gaining in popularity in Canada, and as this trend continues it may influence the future number of single-parent families because common-law unions have a higher probability of dis-solution than do formal marriages (Wu, 2000). According to a recent Statistics Canada study (2000d), women whose first marriage ended in divorce tend to enter a new union, but are likely to opt for common-law rather than marriage. The same holds true for women whose first union was common-law. They are also likely to form a new relationship but tend to con-tinue to live common-law. So, while marriage may be less popular, conjugal unions continue to be popular among Canadians.

## GAY AND LESBIAN COUPLES

In 1989, Denmark became the first country to lift the legal ban on homosexual marriages. This change extended social legitimacy to gay and lesbian couples, including advantages in inheritance, taxation, and joint property ownership. Norway (1993) and Sweden (1995) followed suit.

As noted in the chapter opener, it is still not possible in any Canadian province to register gay marriages, though some churches do sanction such marriages and may even use banns. Further, some provincial benefit plans and employers recognize same-sex unions in their private insurance plans. In 2000, the province of British Columbia changed a variety of provincial statutes granting same-sex couples the same rights and obliga-tions as common-law couples. At the same time, some gay couples with children are raising offspring from previous heterosexual unions, and some gay and lesbian couples have adopted children. Clearly, gay parenting challenges many traditional notions about families. It also indicates that many gay and lesbian couples derive the same rewards from child rearing as do "straight" couples (Bell, Weinberg & Kiefer-Hammersmith, 1981; Gross, 1991; Pressley & Andrews, 1992; Henry, 1993; Herman, 1994).

## SINGLEHOOD

Because most people in Canada marry at some point in their lives, we tend to see singlehood as a transitory stage of life that ends with marriage. In recent decades, however, more people have deliberately chosen to live alone. In the early 1950s, only one household in twelve contained a single person. By 1994, this proportion had risen to nearly one in four. In 1996, 2.6 million Canadians ages 15 and over lived alone, or about 12 percent of the population (Statistics Canada, 1997b). The figure for women was almost 1.5 million, or 13 percent of the total female population 15 years of age and up (Statistics Canada, 2000m). Most striking is the surging number of single *young* women. In 1960, approximately one in four Canadian women ages 20 to 24 were single; by 1994, the proportion had soared to about two-thirds. Underlying this trend is women's greater participation in the labour force. Women who are economically secure view a husband as a matter of choice rather than a financial necessity (Goldscheider & Waite, 1986).

Women ages 65 and over also are now much more likely to live alone—in fact, twice as likely as their male counterparts. In large part this is because women tend to survive their husbands and to subsequently remain unmarried (Statistics Canada, 2000m).

## NEW REPRODUCTIVE TECHNOLOGY

Recent medical advances, generally called *new reproductive technology (NRT)*, are changing families, too. In the 20 years since headlines proclaimed England's Louise Brown the world's first "test-tube" baby, thousands of people have been conceived in this way. Before too long, 2 or 3 percent of the population of industrial societies may be the result of new birth technologies.

Technically, test-tube babies result from *in vitro fertilization*, whereby doctors unite a woman's egg and a man's sperm "in glass," that is, in a laboratory dish. When successful, this complex medical procedure produces embryos, which doctors either implant in the womb of the woman who is to bear the child or freeze for use at a later time.

At present, *in vitro* fertilization helps some couples who cannot conceive normally to become parents. Yet numerous ethical issues remain unsolved in regard to NRT. Canada and the U.S. are almost alone among industrial nations in not adopting national regulations. Both countries leave up to medical experts such ethical issues as experimentation in the cloning of humans for body parts (for transplantation). Yet experts may not always be willing to place the public good ahead of their own self-interest. Canada has continued to resist regulating this area, even though a recent Angus Reid poll indicated that as much as 72 percent of the population finds cloning humans for body parts unacceptable (Angus Reid Group Inc., 1997a).

## LOOKING AHEAD: THE FAMILY IN THE TWENTY-FIRST CENTURY

Family life in Canada no doubt will continue to change in years to come, and change, of course, can cause controversy. In the case of the family, advocates of "traditional family values" line up against those who support greater personal choice; the Controversy & Debate box on page 328 sketches some of the issues. Sociologists cannot predict the outcome of this debate, but we can suggest five likely future trends.

First, the divorce rate is likely to remain high, even in the face of evidence that marital breakup harms children. Actually, today's marriages are about as durable as they were a century ago, when many were cut short by death (Kain, 1990); the difference is that now more couples *choose* to end marriages that fail to meet their expectations. Although the divorce rate declined slightly during the 1990s, it is unlikely that we will ever return to the low rates that marked the early decades of the 20th century.

Second, family life in the 21st century will be more diverse than ever. Cohabiting couples, one-parent fam-

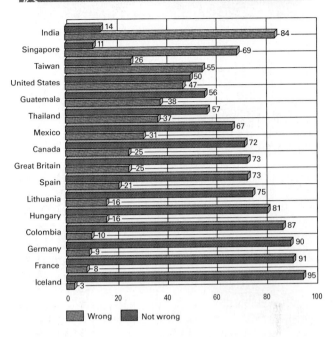

**Figure 13–6   Attitudes toward Children Being Born Outside of Marriage, Selected Countries, 1997**

*Question:* Do you think it is, or is not, morally wrong for a couple of have a baby if they are not married?

**Note:** No opinion omitted.

Source: The Gallup Organization. *Special Reports: Global Study of Family Values* (Princeton: NJ: The Gallup Organization, 1997).

ilies, gay and lesbian families, and blended families are all on the increase. Taken together, the diversity of family forms implies a trend toward more personal choice.

Third, men will play a limited role in child rearing. In the 1950s, a decade many people consider the "golden age" of families, men began to withdraw from active parenting (Snell, 1990; Stacey, 1990). A counter trend is now emerging as some men—older, on average, and more established in their careers—choose to devote more time to their children. But on balance, the relatively high Canadian divorce rate and the increase in single motherhood point to more children growing up with weaker ties to their fathers. However, in some countries where co-parenting is more common (such as Sweden), this trend is less apparent. In Canada,

*Although gay couples cannot legally marry in Canada, some are raising children from previous heterosexual unions, and some have adopted children.*

joint-custody arrangements are on the rise, with an increase from 1 percent in 1986, to 14 percent in the early 1990s, to 28 percent in 1997 (Statistics Canada, 2000m). Other evidence suggests as well that in countries with comprehensive welfare states and greater economic equality among social classes, men tend to play stronger roles in child rearing, and children in single-parent families do better (Boje & Leira, 2000).

Fourth, we will continue to feel the effects of economic change in our families (Hochschild, 1989; Benoit, 2000a). In many homes, both household partners work, rendering marriage the interaction of weary men and women who try to squeeze in a little "quality time" for their children (Dizard & Gadlin, 1990; Fox, 2001). Two-career couples may advance the goal of gender equality, but the long-term effects on families as we have known them are likely to be mixed.

Fifth and finally, the importance of new reproductive technology will increase. Ethical concerns about whether what *can* be done *should* be done will surely slow these developments, but new forms of reproduction will continue to alter the traditional meaning of parenthood.

Despite the change and controversies that have buffeted the family in Canada, most people still report being happy as partners and parents. Marriage and family life will likely remain a foundation of our society for some time to come.

## RELIGION: BASIC CONCEPTS

Like the family, religion has played a central part in the drama of human history. Families have long used religious rituals to celebrate birth, recognize adulthood, and mourn the dead.

French sociologist Emile Durkheim said religion involves "things that surpass the limits of our knowledge" (1965:62; orig. 1915). As human beings, we define most objects, events, and experiences as **profane** (from the Latin meaning "outside the temple"), *that which is an ordinary element of everyday life.* But we also consider some things **sacred,** *that which people set apart as extraordinary, inspiring a sense of awe and reverence.* Distinguishing the sacred from the profane is the essence of all religious belief. **Religion,** then, *is a social institution involving beliefs and practices based on a conception of the sacred.*

A global perspective reveals great variety in matters of faith, with no one thing sacred to everyone on earth. Although people regard most books as profane, Jews believe the Torah (the first five books of the Hebrew Bible or the Old Testament) is sacred, in the same way that Christians revere the Old and New Testaments of the Bible and Muslims exalt the Qur'an (Koran).

But no matter how a community of believers draws religious lines, Durkheim (1965:62) explained, people understand profane things in terms of everyday usefulness: We log on to the Internet with our computer or turn a key to start our car. What is sacred, however, we reverently set apart from daily life, giving it a "forbidden aura." For example, Muslims remove their shoes before entering a mosque to avoid defiling a sacred place with soles that have touched the profane ground outside. Similarly, Sikhs eat their ceremonial meal after temple prayers seated on the floor, rather than at (profane) tables. When moderate Sikhs in British Columbia recently defied traditionalists by sitting at tables to have their ceremonial meal after temple prayers, the Sikh religion's highest authority, the Akal Takhat, was called upon to reconfirm an edict banning tables and chairs from temples worldwide.

The sacred is embodied in *ritual,* or formal ceremonial behaviour. Holy Communion is the central ritual of Christianity; to the Christian faithful, the wafer and wine consumed during Communion are treated not in a profane way as food, but as the sacred symbols of the body and blood of Jesus Christ.

Since religion deals with ideas that transcend everyday experience, neither common sense nor sociology can verify or disprove religious doctrine. Religion is a matter of **faith**, *belief anchored in conviction rather than scientific evidence.* The New Testament of the Bible defines faith as "the conviction of things not seen" (Heb. 11:1) and exhorts Christians to "walk by faith, not by sight" (2 Cor. 5:7).

Some people with strong religious beliefs may be disturbed by the thought of sociologists turning a scientific eye on what they hold sacred. In truth, however, sociological study is no threat to anyone's faith. Sociologists study religion just as they study the family, to understand religious experiences around the world and how religion is tied to other social institutions. They make no judgments about whether a specific religion is right or wrong. Rather, sociological analysis takes a "worldly" approach by asking why religion takes a particular form in one society or another and how religious activity affects society as a whole.

## THEORETICAL ANALYSIS OF RELIGION

Sociologists have applied various theoretical paradigms to the study of religion. Each provides distinctive insights about religious life.

### FUNCTIONS OF RELIGION: STRUCTURAL-FUNCTIONAL ANALYSIS

According to Emile Durkheim, society has an existence and power of its own beyond the life of any individual. In other words, society itself is godlike, surviving the ultimate deaths of its members, whose lives it shapes. Thus, in religion, people celebrate the awesome power of their society (1965; orig. 1915).

No wonder, then, that people around the world transform everyday objects into sacred symbols of their collective life. Members of technologically simple societies, such as the fishing societies of the Northwest Pacific Coast, do this with a **totem**, *an object in the natural world collectively defined as sacred.* The totem—perhaps an animal or an elaborate work of art—becomes the centrepiece of ritual and symbolizes the power of collective life over any individual life (Dickason, 1992). In our society, the flag is a quasi-religious totem that is not to be used in a profane way (say, as clothing) or allowed to touch the ground.

Durkheim defined three major functions of religion that contribute to the operation of society:

1. **Social cohesion.** Religion unites people through shared symbolism, values, and norms. Religious thought and ritual establish morality and rules of fair play that make organized social life possible.

*For better or worse, the family is certainly changing. But the fact that young people still find marriage so attractive—even amid the most severe adversity—suggests that families will continue to play a central role in society for centuries to come.*

2. **Social control.** Society uses religious ideas to promote conformity. In medieval Europe, for example, monarchs claimed to rule by divine right. Even today, our leaders publicly ask for God's blessing, implying to audiences that the leaders' efforts are right and just.

3. **Providing meaning and purpose.** Religious belief offers the comforting sense that our brief lives serve some greater purpose. Strengthened by such beliefs, people are less likely to despair when one of life's calamities strikes. For this reason, we mark major life transitions—including birth, marriage, and death—with religious observances.

**Critical evaluation.** In Durkheim's structural-functional analysis, religion represents the collective life of society. The major weakness of this approach is that it downplays religion's dysfunctions—especially the fact that strongly held beliefs can generate social

# Should We Save the Traditional Family?

Are "traditional families" vital to our way of life? Or are they a barrier to progress? To begin, people typically use the term *traditional family* to refer to a married couple who, at some point in their lives, raise children. But the term is more than a description; it is also a moral statement. Those who support the traditional family generally place a high value on becoming and remaining married, urge parents to place children ahead of their own careers, and believe that society should accord special respect to two-parent families rather than various "alternative lifestyles."

On one side of the debate, conservative commentators note with alarm the rapid erosion of the traditional family (see, for example, Krueger, 1997; McLean, 1998). They point to at least four observations that are troublesome. First, the divorce rate has increased to the extent that 36 percent of today's marriages will end in divorce. Second, common-law unions have grown rapidly, from one in sixteen couples in 1981 to about one in seven in 1996. Third, an escalating number of children are being born outside marriage. Fourth, one-parent families have increased, from 8.4 percent of all families in 1961 to 14 percent in 1996. In light of these Canadian trends, which are similar to those found in other high-income countries, it is argued that the family is not just changing, it is falling apart. This breakdown is interpreted by the U.S. analyst David Popenoe as a fundamental shift from a "culture of marriage" to a "culture of divorce." Traditional vows of marital commitment—"till death us do part"—now amount to little more than "as long as I am happy." The increase in the divorce rate reveals the selfishness of men and women and their refusal to make the compromises inevitable in any marriage. Daniel Yankelovich (1994:20) sums up this cultural shift:

> The quest for greater individual choice clashed directly with the obligations and social norms that held families and communities together in earlier years. People came to feel that questions of how to live and with whom to live were a matter of individual choice not to be governed by restrictive norms.

According to Yankelovich and others sharing this viewpoint, the negative consequences of the cultural trend toward weaker families are obvious everywhere: without the care of a stay-at-home parent, more and more children become "latchkey kids"; the crime rate—especially among juveniles—increases, along with a host of other problematic behaviours, including underage smoking and drinking, premarital sex, and teenage pregnancies.

As Popenoe and popular opinion see it, we must work hard and quickly to reverse current trends. Government cannot be the solution and may even be part of the problem. Since 1960, as families have become weaker, government spending on social programs has soared. Popenoe calls for a cultural turnaround

---

conflict. Many nations have marched to war under the banner of their god; few people would dispute that religious beliefs have provoked more violence in the world than have differences of social class.

## CONSTRUCTING THE SACRED: SYMBOLIC-INTERACTION ANALYSIS

From a symbolic-interaction point of view, religion (like all of society) is socially constructed (although perhaps with divine inspiration). Through various rituals—from daily prayer to annual events such as Easter or Passover—people sharpen the distinction between sacred and profane. Further, says Peter Berger (1967:35–36), placing our fallible, brief lives within some "cosmic frame of reference" give us "the semblance of ultimate security and permanence."

Marriage is a good example. If two people look on marriage as simply a contract, they can end it whenever they want to. But defined as holy matrimony, their bond makes far stronger claims on them. This is surely why the divorce rate is lower among people who are religious. More generally, whenever humans face uncertainty or life-threatening situations—such as illness, war, and natural disaster—we embrace our sacred symbols.

**Critical evaluation.** In the symbolic-interaction approach, religion puts everyday life under a "sacred canopy" of meaning (Berger, 1967). Of course, Berger adds, the sacred's ability to give meaning and stabilize society depends on people ignoring its constructed character. After all, how much strength could we derive from sacred beliefs if we saw them as mere devices for coping with tragedy? Then, too, this micro-level view ignores religion's link to social inequality, to which we now turn.

by which we question and ultimately reject the recently popular "me first" view of our lives in favour of greater commitment to a spouse and children. (We have seen such a shift in attitudes in the case of cigarette smoking.) Yes, concludes Popenoe, we should save the traditional family, and that means we must publicly affirm the value of marital permanence as well as endorse the two-parent family as best for the well-being of children.

Judith Stacey, among others (Fox, 2001), says "good riddance" to the traditional family, offering a stark counterpoint to the conservative perspective presented above. To her, the traditional family is more problem than solution. Striking to the heart of the matter, Stacey writes (1990:269),

The family is not here to stay. Nor should we wish it were. On the contrary, I believe that all democratic people, whatever their kinship preferences, should work to hasten its demise.

Why reject the traditional family? Because, according to Stacey, it perpetuates and enhances social inequality. Families play a key role in maintaining the class hierarchy, transferring their wealth, education, and other forms of privilege (their "cultural capital") from one generation to another. Moreover, feminists criticize the traditional family's patriarchal form, which subjects wives to husbands' authority as well as saddling them with most of the responsibility for housework and child care. And from a gay rights perspective, she adds, a society that values traditional families inevitably denies homosexual men and women equal participation in social life.

Stacey thus applauds the breakdown of the family as a measure of social progress. Rather than viewing the family as a bedrock social institution, she blasts it as a political construction that serves to elevate one category of people—affluent white males—at the expense of women, homosexuals, and poor people who lack the resources to maintain middle-class respectability.

The concept of "traditional family" appears to be increasingly irrelevant to a diverse society in which people reject singular models of correct behaviour and in which both men and women must work for income. Canadian family sociologist Margit Eichler (1997) argues that the chief problem facing the Canadian family today is caring for dependent members while engaging in economic activities to maintain the family in the first place. If governments were really concerned about families, argues Eichler, they would take "public responsibility" for the nation's children, which would include providing generous parental benefits and subsidized, regulated child care.

*Continue the debate . . .*

1. *To strengthen families, Popenoe suggests that parents put children ahead of their own careers by limiting their joint work week to 60 hours. Do you agree? Why or why not?*

2. *Judith Stacey thinks that marriage is weaker today because women are rejecting patriarchal relationships. Do you agree? Why or why not?*

3. *Do you think we need to change family patterns for the well-being of our children? As you see it, what specific changes are called for?*

Sources: Stacey (1990, 1993), Beaujot (1991), Popenoe (1993), Council on Families in America (1995), Eichler (1997), Krueger (1997), Turcotte & Bélanger (1998), McLean (1998), and Fox (2001).

## INEQUALITY AND RELIGION: SOCIAL-CONFLICT ANALYSIS

The social-conflict paradigm highlights religion's support of social inequality. Religion, proclaimed Karl Marx, serves elites by legitimizing the status quo and diverting people's attention from social inequities.

Even today, the British monarch is the formal head of the Church of England, illustrating the close alliance between religious and political elites. In practical terms, working for political change may mean opposing the church—and, by implication, God. Religion also encourages people to endure without complaint the social problems of this world while they look hopefully to a "better world to come." In a well-known statement, Marx dismissed religion as "the sigh of the oppressed creature, the sentiment of a heartless world, and the soul of soulless conditions. It is the opium of the people" (1964b:27; orig. 1848).

Religion and social inequality are also linked through gender: Virtually all the world's major religions are patriarchal. For example, the Qur'an (Koran)—the sacred text of Islam—gives men social dominance over women:

Men are in charge of women. . . . Hence good women are obedient. . . . As for those whose rebelliousness you fear, admonish them, banish them from your bed, and scourge them (quoted in Kaufman, 1976:163).

Christianity—the major religion in the Western Hemisphere—has also supported patriarchy. Although Christians revere Mary, the mother of Jesus, the New Testament instructs us in this way:

A man . . . is the image and glory of God; but woman is the glory of man. For man was not made from woman, but woman from man. Neither was man created for woman, but woman for man (1 Cor. 11:7–9).

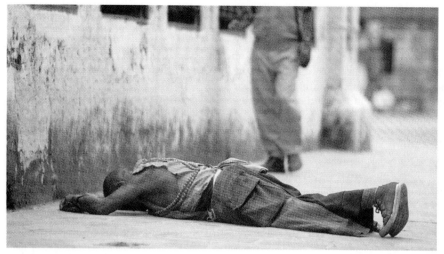

*Religion is founded on the concept of the sacred: that which is set apart as extraordinary and which demands our submission. Bowing, kneeling, or prostrating oneself are all ways of symbolically surrendering to a higher power. This monk is performing an act of prostration: circumambulation—that is, he falls flat on the ground every few steps as he moves around a holy shrine. In this way, he expresses his complete surrender to his faith.*

As in all the churches of the saints, the women should keep silence in the churches. For they are not permitted to speak, but should be subordinate, as even the law says. If there is anything they desire to know, let them ask their husbands at home. For it is shameful for a woman to speak in church (1 Cor. 14:33–35).

Wives, be subject to your husbands, as to the Lord. For the husband is the head of the wife as Christ is the head of the church. . . . As the church is subject to Christ, so let wives also be subject in everything to their husbands (Eph. 5:22–24).

Judaism, too, has traditionally supported patriarchy. Male Orthodox Jews include the following daily prayer:

Blessed art thou, O Lord our God, King of the Universe, that I was not born a gentile. Blessed art thou, O Lord our God, King of the Universe, that I was not born a slave. Blessed art thou, O Lord our God, King of the Universe, that I was not born a woman.

Despite patriarchal traditions, most religions now have women in leadership roles, and many are introducing more gender-neutral language in hymnals and prayer books. Such changes involve not just organizational patterns but conceptions of God. Theologian Mary Daly puts the matter bluntly: "If God is male, then male is God" (cited in Woodward, 1989:58).

**Critical evaluation.** Social-conflict analysis emphasizes the power of religion to legitimize social inequality. Yet religion also promotes change toward equality. Nineteenth-century religious groups in the United States, for example, played an important role in the movement to abolish slavery. During the 1950s and 1960s, religious organizations and their leaders were at the core of the civil rights movement. During the 1960s and 1970s, many clergy actively opposed the Vietnam War. As we will explain shortly, some religious leaders have supported social change in Latin America and elsewhere, including change for Aboriginal peoples in Canada.

## RELIGION AND SOCIAL CHANGE

Religion is not just the conservative force portrayed by Karl Marx. In fact, at some points in history, as Max Weber (1958; orig. 1904–5) explained, religion has promoted dramatic social change.

### MAX WEBER: PROTESTANTISM AND CAPITALISM

Weber contended that particular religious ideas set in motion a wave of change that brought about the industrialization of Western Europe. That is, industrial capitalism developed in the wake of Calvinism, a movement within the Protestant Reformation.

Central to the religious thought of John Calvin (1509–1564) is the doctrine of *predestination*: An all-knowing, all-powerful God has selected some people for salvation while condemning most to eternal damnation. Each individual's fate, sealed before birth and known only to God, is either eternal glory or endless hellfire.

Driven by anxiety over their fate, Calvinists understandably sought signs of God's favour in *this* world, and came to regard prosperity as a sign of divine blessing. Religious conviction and a rigid devotion to duty thus led Calvinists to work diligently, and many amassed great wealth. But money was not for self-indulgent spending or for sharing with the poor, whose plight they saw as a mark of God's rejection. As agents for God's work on earth, Calvinists believed that they could best fulfill their "calling" by reinvesting profits and reaping ever greater success in the process.

All the while, the Calvinists lived thrifty lives and embraced technological advances, thereby laying the groundwork for the rise of industrial capitalism. In time, the religious fervour that motivated early Calvinists weakened, leaving a profane "Protestant work ethic." To Max Weber, industrial capitalism itself was a "disenchanted" religion, further showing the power of religion to alter the shape of society.

## LIBERATION THEOLOGY

Historically, Christianity has reached out to suffering and oppressed people, urging all to strengthen their faith in a better life to come. In recent decades, however, some church leaders and theologians have taken a decidedly political approach and endorsed **liberation theology,** *a fusion of Christian principles with political activism, often Marxist in character.*

This social movement started in the late 1960s in Latin America's Roman Catholic church. Today, Christian activists continue to help people in low-income nations liberate themselves from abysmal poverty. Their message is simple: Social oppression runs counter to Christian morality, so, as a matter of faith and justice, Christians must promote greater social equality.

Despite liberal theology's Roman Catholic beginnings, Pope John Paul II condemns it for distorting church doctrine with left-wing politics. Nevertheless, the liberation theology movement has grown in Latin America, where many people find their Christian faith drives them to improve conditions for the world's poor (Boff, 1984; Neuhouser, 1989).

## CHURCH, SECT, AND CULT

Sociologists categorize the hundreds of different religious organizations found in Canada along a continuum, with *churches* at one end and *sects* at the other. Drawing on the ideas of his teacher Max Weber, Ernst Troeltsch (1931) defined a **church** as *a type of religious organization well integrated into the larger society.* Churchlike organizations typically persist for centuries and include generations of the same families. Churches have well-established rules and regulations and expect leaders to be formally trained and ordained.

While concerned with the sacred, a church accepts the ways of the profane world. Church members conceive of God in intellectual terms (say, as a force for good) and favour abstract moral standards ("Do unto others as you would have them do unto you"). By teaching morality in safely abstract terms, church leaders can avoid social controversy. For example, many churches that celebrate the unity of all peoples have all-white memberships. Such duality minimizes conflict between the church and political life (Troeltsch, 1931).

*Reverend Lois Mike is the first, and thus far the only, Inuit female priest in the 4 million square kilometres that make up the Anglican Church of Canada's Arctic Diocese. Reverend Mike, a 40-year-old mother of four, was ordained in 1994. She struggles daily to bring forth her pastoral message, which sometimes even the women in her church are not keen to accept from a female minister.*

December 11, 1994—Casablanca, Morocco
The waves of the Atlantic crash along the walls of Casablanca's magnificent coastline mosque, reputedly the largest in the world. From the top of the towering structure, a green laser cuts through the sky pointing to Mecca, the holy city of Islam, toward which the faithful bow in prayer. To pay for this monumental house of worship, King Hassam II, Morocco's head of state and religious leader, levied a tax on every citizen in his realm, all of whom are officially Muslim. This example of "government religion" contrasts sharply with our ideas about the separation of church and state.

*In global perspective, the range of religious activity is truly astonishing. Members of this Southeast Asian cult show their devotion to God by suspending themselves in the air using ropes and sharp hooks that pierce their skin.*

A church may operate as an arm of the state. A **state church** is *a church formally allied with the state*, as illustrated by Islam in Morocco. State churches have existed throughout human history; for centuries Roman Catholicism was the official religion of the Roman Empire, as was Confucianism in China until early in the 20th century. Today, the Anglican church is the official church of England, and Islam is the official religion of Pakistan and Iran. State churches count everyone in a society as a member, which sharply limits tolerance of religious differences.

A **denomination,** by contrast, is *a church independent of the state, which recognizes religious pluralism*. Denominations exist in nations that formally separate church and state, such as ours. Canada has dozens of Christian denominations—including Catholics, Baptists, Episcopalians, and Lutherans—as well as various categories of Judaism and other traditions. While members of any denomination hold to their own beliefs, they recognize the right of others to disagree.

Unlike a church, which tries to fit into the larger society, a **sect** is *a type of religious organization that stands apart from the larger society*. Sect members have rigid

religious convictions and deny the beliefs of others. In extreme cases, members of a sect may withdraw completely from society to practise their faith without interference. In Canada and the U.S., for example, the Amish and the Hutterities have long isolated themselves from modern life (Hostetler, 1980; Curtis & Lambert, 1990). Since North American culture holds up religious tolerance as a virtue, members of sects are sometimes accused of being dogmatic in their insistence that they alone follow the true religion.

In organizational terms, sects are less formal than churches. Thus, sect members may be highly spontaneous and emotional in worship, while members of churches tend to listen passively to their leader. Sects also reject the intellectualized religion of churches, stressing instead the personal experience of divine power. Rodney Stark (1985:314) contrasts a church's vision of a distant God—"Our Father, who art in Heaven"—with a sect's more immediate God—"Lord, bless this poor sinner kneeling before you now."

A further distinction between church and sect turns on patterns of leadership. The more churchlike an organization, the more likely that its leaders are formally trained and ordained. Sect-like organizations, which celebrate the personal presence of God, expect their leaders to exude divine inspiration in the form of **charisma** (from the Greek, meaning "divine favour"), *extraordinary personal qualities that can turn an audience into followers*, infusing them with an emotional experience.

Sects generally form as breakaway groups from established religious organizations (Stark & Bainbridge, 1979). Their psychic intensity and informal structure render them less stable than churches, and many sects blossom only to disappear soon after. The sects that do endure typically become more like churches, losing fervour as they become more bureaucratic and established.

To sustain their membership, many sects actively recruit, or *proselytize*, new members. Sects value highly the experience of *conversion*, or religious rebirth. Jehovah's Witnesses, for example, visit door to door to share their faith with others in the hope of attracting new members.

Finally, churches and sects differ in their social composition. Because they are more closely tied to the world, well-established churches tend to include people of high social standing. Sects, by contrast, attract more disadvantaged people. A sect's openness to new members and promise of salvation and personal fulfillment appeal to people who perceive themselves as social outsiders.

A **cult** is *a religious organization that is largely outside a society's cultural traditions*. Whereas most sects spin off from a conventional religious organization, a cult typically forms around a highly charismatic leader who offers a compelling message of a new and very different way of life. As many as 5000 cults exist in the

United States alone, and an unknown number exist in Canada (Marquand & Wood, 1997).

Because some cult principles or practices are unconventional, many people view cults as deviant or even evil. The suicides of 39 members of California's "Heaven's Gate" cult in 1997—people who claimed that dying was the doorway to a higher existence, perhaps in the company of aliens from outer space—confirmed the negative image the public holds of many cults. Also in 1997, the charred bodies of five people were found inside a house in Saint Casimir, Quebec. The three women and two men were members of the Solar Temple, an international cult professing the belief that such ritualized suicides lead to rebirth on a planet known as "Sirus." In short, say some scholars, calling a religious community a "cult" amounts to dismissing its members as crazy (Richardson, 1990; Shupe, 1995; Gleick, 1997).

This view of cults is unfortunate because there is nothing intrinsically wrong with this kind of religious organization. Many religions—Christianity, Islam, and Judaism included—began as cults. Of course, few cults exist for very long. One reason is that they are even more at odds with the larger society than are sects. Many cults demand that members not only accept their doctrine but embrace a radically new lifestyle. This is why people sometimes accuse cults of brainwashing their members, although research suggests that most people who join cults experience no psychological harm (Barker, 1981; Kilbourne, 1983).

# RELIGION IN HISTORY

Like the family, religion is a part of every known society. Also like the family, religion shows marked variation both historically and cross-culturally.

Early hunters and gatherers embraced **animism** (from the Latin, meaning "the breath of life"), *the belief that elements of the natural world are conscious life forms that affect humanity*. Animistic people view forests, oceans, mountains, and even the wind as spiritual forces. Many Native American societies are animistic, which accounts for their reverence for the natural environment.

Belief in a single divine power responsible for creating the world arose with pastoral and horticultural societies. Our conception of God as a "shepherd" should be no surprise since Christianity, Judaism, and Islam all had their beginnings among pastoral peoples.

In agrarian societies, religion becomes more important. The centrality of religion is evident in the huge cathedrals that dominated the towns of medieval Europe.

The Industrial Revolution ushered in a growing emphasis on science. More and more, people looked to physicians and scientists for the guidance and comfort they had earlier sought from priests. Even so, religion persists because science is powerless to address issues of ultimate meaning in human life. In other words, *how* this world works is a matter for scientists; but *why* we and the rest of the universe exist at all is a question for religion to answer.

# RELIGION IN CANADA

Just as people debate the health of family life in Canada, so analysts disagree about the strength of religion in our society. Research shows that changes are under way, but also confirms the ongoing role of religion in social life (Collins, 1982; Greeley, 1989; Woodward, 1992a; Hadaway, Marler, & Chaves, 1993; Bibby, 1993; Dawson, 1996).

## RELIGIOUS COMMITMENT

According to the 1996 General Social Survey, about 80 percent of Canadian adults identify with a particular religion (Statistics Canada, 1998a). Figure 13–7 on page 334 shows that 31.5 percent of Canadian adults identify with an established Protestant denomination or recent Protestant sect, another 44 percent identify themselves as Roman Catholics, and 5 percent say they belong to one of a variety of other faiths. These include Eastern Orthodox, Jewish, Islam, Hindu, Buddhist, and Sikh—making our society one of the most religiously diverse around the globe, though less so than the United States. Further, as illustrated in Figure 13–8 on page 335, Canada is one of the most religious of high-income countries, though again less so than the U.S.

Canada's religious diversity stems from a constitutional ban on any government-sponsored religion, as well as a high rate of immigration. At the national level, a greater number of Canadians identify themselves as Catholic, yet a substantial minority identify themselves as Protestant. At the provincial and territorial level, identification as Catholic stands out only in Quebec and New Brunswick. The opposite holds true in the other provinces and territories, where people are more likely to identify themselves as Protestant (Statistics Canada, 1993a).

**Religiosity** is *the importance of religion in a person's life*. By global standards, people in Canada and the U.S. are relatively religious; more so, for example, than the Japanese, British, and Swedes. Just how religious we are, however, depends on precisely how one operationalizes this concept. While the vast majority of Canadians (91 percent) claim to believe in God, only 61 percent believe in life after death (Campbell & Curtis, 1994). In 1946, 67 percent of Canadian adults attended weekly religious services. In 1998, the figure had dropped to a mere 22 percent (Clark, 2000). Further, as shown in Figure 13–9 on page 336, there is a notable pattern regarding people who attend religious services regularly. Married people are much

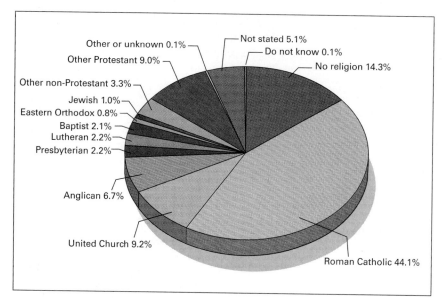

**FIGURE 13–7** Religious Identification in Canada, 1996

Source: Statistics Canada, 1996 General Social Survey, Electronic Data File (1998q).

more likely to do so, compared to single people and especially those living in common-law relationships.

On the other hand, a recent poll found that 63 percent of people in Ontario believed in miracles or divine intervention, and, perhaps surprisingly, 42 percent of them reported having personally experienced miracles or divine intervention. Finally, 54 percent of the Ontario population expressed a belief in angels (Angus Reid Group, Inc., 1996c).

Clearly the question "How religious are we?" yields no easy answers. Keep in mind, too, that people probably claim to be more religious than they really are. One team of researchers, which recently tallied actual church attendance in Ashtabula County in northeast Ohio, concluded that twice as many people said they attended church on a given Sunday as really did so. Strong religious values in U.S. society encouraged a "desirability" effect in the reporting of church attendance (Campbell & Curtis, 1994). In actuality, it is estimated that no more than 20 percent of the U.S. population attends worship services regularly—about the same as in Canada (Hadaway, Marler, & Chaves, 1993). Finally, religiosity varies among denominations. In Canada, weekly attendance at religious services has declined significantly for both Catholics and Protestants since the Second World War, though in the past decade attendance has increased slightly among fundamental Protestant sects, a phenomenon that is much more pronounced in the U.S.

## RELIGION: CLASS, ETHNICITY, AND RACE

Religious affiliation is related to a number of other factors. We shall consider three: social class, ethnicity, and race.

**Social class.** Protestants of European background have traditionally occupied a privileged place in Canadian society, while Catholics—the majority from French backgrounds and residing in the poorer regions of the country, such as Quebec and the Atlantic provinces—have tended to be of more moderate social standing (Porter, 1965). Yet circumstances have changed recently: Quebec society has become more secularized, and the population has experienced increased upward mobility, while at the same time the increasing religious diversity of Canadian society has challenged the once-dominant Protestant majority.

**Ethnicity.** Throughout the world, religion is closely allied with ethnicity, largely because one religion may predominate in a single region or society. The Arab cultures of the Middle East, for example, are mostly Islamic; Hinduism is tightly fused with the culture of India. Christianity and Judaism diverge from this pattern; while these religions are primarily Western, followers live in nations around the world (Riis, 1998).

The link between religion and ethnicity also comes through in Canada. Our society encompasses *Anglo-Saxon* Protestants, *Irish* Catholics, *Russian* Jews, and *Greek* Orthodox. This fusion of nationality and religion derives from an influx of immigrants from countries with a single major religion. Still, nearly every Canadian ethnic group incorporates at least some religious diversity. People of English ancestry, for instance, may Protestants, Roman Catholics, Jews, or affiliated with some other religion.

**Race.** Historically, the church has been central to the spiritual—and also political—lives of blacks living in Canada and the U.S. Transported to the Western

Hemisphere, most people of African descent became Christians—the dominant religion in the Americas—but they blended Christian belief and practice with elements of African tribal religions. Guided by this multicultural religious heritage, many people of colour participate in religious rituals that are—by European standards—both spontaneous and emotional (Frazier, 1965; Roberts, 1980).

As African Americans migrated from the rural South to the industrial cities of the North, and some as far afield as Eastern Canada, the church played a key role in addressing problems of dislocation, poverty, and prejudice. Further, black churches have provided an important avenue of achievement for talented men and women. Ralph Abernathy, Martin Luther King, Jr., and Jesse Jackson all gained world recognition as religious leaders.

## RELIGION IN A CHANGING SOCIETY

Just as we have seen change in family life, so we see that religion continues to change in Canada. Sociologists focus on the process of *secularization*.

## SECULARIZATION

**Secularization** refers to *the historical decline in the importance of the supernatural and the sacred*. Secularization (derived from the Latin, meaning "the present age") is commonly associated with modern, technologically advanced societies where science is the dominant mode of understanding.

Today, for example, we are more likely to experience the transitions of birth, illness, and death in the presence of physicians (with scientific knowledge) than church leaders (whose knowledge is based on faith). This shift alone suggests that religion's relevance for our everyday lives has declined. Harvey Cox elaborates:

> The world looks less and less to religious rules and rituals for its morality or its meanings. For some, religion provides a hobby, for others a mark of national or ethnic identification, for still others an aesthetic delight. For fewer and fewer does it provide an inclusive and commanding system of personal and cosmic values and explanations (1971:3; orig. 1965).

If Cox is right, should we expect religion someday to disappear? The consensus among sociologists is no. Recall that 90 percent of Canadians profess a belief in God, and more people claim to pray each day (75 percent) than voted in the 2000 federal election (63 percent).

Secularization does not, then, signal the death of religion. More correctly, some dimensions of religion (such as belief in life after death) may have declined, but others (such as the number of people declaring a religious affiliation) have increased. Moreover, people

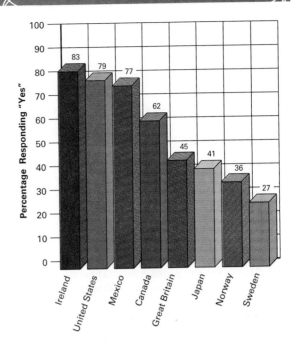

**FIGURE 13–8   Religiosity in Global Perspective**

*Survey Question:* Do you gain comfort and strength from religion?

Source: World Values Survey (1994).

are of two minds about whether secularization is good or bad. Conservatives see any weakening of religion as a mark of moral decline. Progressives, however, view secularization as liberation from the all-encompassing beliefs of the past, so people can choose what to believe. Secularization has also brought many religious practices (such as ordaining only men) into line with widespread social attitudes (including that of gender equality, exemplified by ordaining women as well as men).

## CIVIL RELIGION

One dimension of secularization is what Robert Bellah (1975) calls **civil religion,** *a quasi-religious loyalty based on citizenship*. Even in a basically secular society, in other words, citizenship may retain some religious qualities.

Many people in the U.S., for example, consider their way of life as moral and a force for good in the world. Some people in Canada express similar sentiments. And while Canadians and Americans differ as to what constitutes their nation's moral purpose, people at both ends of the political spectrum find religious qualities in political movements (Williams & Demerath, 1991).

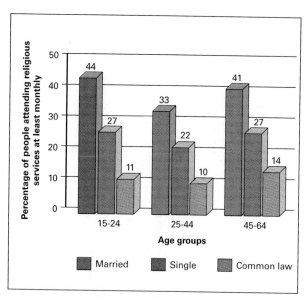

**FIGURE 13–9   Religious Attendance by Marital Status and Age Group, Canada, 1998**

As Figure 13–9 shows, formal marriage makes a difference in people's religiosity, as measured by higher regular attendance at religious services for married people as compared to single people and especially couples living in common-law relationships. Can you explain why this might be the case?

Source: Clark (2000).

Like its spiritual counterparts, civil religion involves a range of rituals from rising to sing the national anthem at sporting events to sitting down to watch public parades several times a year. And just as the Christian cross or the Jewish Star of David evokes a sense of spiritual affiliation, the flag serves as a sacred symbol of our national identity that we expect people to treat with reverence.

## RELIGIOUS REVIVAL

All things considered, religiosity in Canada has been stable in recent decades. Canada differs from the U.S., however, in that the declining membership in established "mainstream" churches—such as Anglican, Roman Catholic, and Presbyterian ones—has not corresponded to dramatically increased membership in other religious organizations (including the Mormons, Seventh-Day Adventists, and especially Christian sects) (Stark & Bainbridge, 1981; Roof & McKinney, 1987; Bedell, 1997).

One striking religious trend today has been **religious fundamentalism**, *a conservative doctrine that opposes intellectualism and worldly accommodation in favour of restoring traditional, otherworldly religion.* Fundamentalism

has developed in response to present-day secular institutions and the emergence of equality principles, including equality between the sexes. As a case in point, the fundamentalist Southern Baptists church (predominantly located in the southern U.S.) has emerged from the Protestant faith. The orthodoxy of their belief is evident in the recent declaration that a woman should "submit herself graciously" to her husband's leadership and a husband should "provide for, protect and lead his family" (Niebuhr, 1998:A6B). Fundamentalist groups have also proliferated among Roman Catholics and Jews across North America and around the globe.

In Canada, religious "fundamentalism" has mainly emerged in parts of Alberta, reflecting the somewhat moralistic social values (for example, anti-gay rights) and conservative political views articulated more often in Alberta than in other provinces. Yet this flavour of conservative Protestantism remains less evangelical and all-encompassing than the religious fundamentalism south of the Canadian border (Dawson, 1998).

In response to what they see as the growing influence of science and the weakening of the conventional family, religious fundamentalists defend what they call "traditional values." As they see it, liberal churches are simply too open to change. Religious fundamentalism is distinctive in five ways (Hunter, 1983, 1985, 1987):

1. **Fundamentalists interpret sacred texts literally.** Fundamentalists insist on a literal interpretation of the Bible and other sacred texts to counter what they consider excessive intellectualism among more liberal Christian organizations. Fundamentalist Christians, for example, believe God created the world in seven days precisely as described in Genesis.

2. **Fundamentalists reject religious pluralism.** Fundamentalists maintain that tolerance and relativism water down personal faith. They maintain, therefore, that their religious beliefs are true and other beliefs are not.

3. **Fundamentalists pursue the personal experience of God's presence.** In contrast to the worldliness and intellectualism of other religious organizations, fundamentalists seek to propagate "good old-time religion" and spiritual revival. Being "born again" and having a personal relationship with Jesus Christ should be evident in a person's everyday life.

4. **Fundamentalists oppose "secular humanism."** Fundamentalists believe accommodation to the changing world undermines religious conviction. *Secular humanism* is a general term that refers to our society's tendency to look to scientific experts rather than God for guidance about how to live.

5. **Fundamentalists endorse conservative political goals.** Although fundamentalism tends to back away from worldly concerns, some fundamentalist leaders in the U.S. (such as Ralph Reed, Pat Robertson, and Gary Bauer) have entered politics to oppose the "liberal agenda" that includes feminism and gay rights. Fundamentalists oppose abortion, gay marriage, and liberal bias in the media; they support the traditional two-parent family and seek a return of prayer in schools (Hunter, 1983; Speer, 1984; Ellison & Sherkat, 1993; Green, 1993; Manza & Brooks, 1997; Thomma, 1997; Rozell, Wilcox, & Green, 1998).

Opponents find fundamentalism rigid and self-righteous. But others find in fundamentalism—with its greater religious certainty and emphasis on experiencing God's presence—an appealing alternative to the more intellectual, tolerant, and worldly mainstream denominations (Marquand, 1997).

Which religious organizations are "fundamentalist"? This term is most correctly applied to conservative organizations in the larger evangelical tradition, including Pentecostals, Southern Baptists, Seventh-Day Adventists, and the Assemblies of God. Several religious movements taking hold in North American, including Promise Keepers for men and Chosen Women, have a fundamentalist orientation. In U.S. national surveys, 31 percent of adults describe their upbringing as "fundamentalist"; 39 percent claim a "moderate" religious upbringing; and 24 percent call their religious background "liberal" (NORC, 1999:143). As indicated in Figure 13–7 on p. 334, Canada differs from the U.S. in this regard, with less than 10 percent of the population claiming membership in "other" Protestant groups.

In contrast to local congregations of years past, some religious organizations—especially fundamentalist ones—have become *electronic churches* dominated by "prime-time preachers" (Hadden & Swain, 1981). Electronic religion, a pattern until recently found only in the U.S., has now found its way to Western Canada. It has propelled people such as Oral Roberts, Pat Robertson, and Robert Schuller to greater prominence than all but a few clergy in the past. Perhaps 5 percent of the U.S. television audience (about 10 million people) is regular viewers of religious television, while 20 percent (about 40 million) watches some religious programming every week (NORC, 1999). Again, the data from Canada show a different trend: Canadians appear to have much smaller appetites than do their southern neighbours for viewing evangelical services on television, with 1996 estimates of less than 1 percent of viewing time being spent on religious programming (Campbell & Curtis, 1994; Statistics Canada, 1998d). One explanation is that aggressive marketing of religion by sectarian competitors is much more

*Faith has a specific meaning for these individuals. For others, faith means something quite different. Do we need to separate religious from non-religious faiths?*

advanced in the U.S. than in other countries, including Canada and Britain (Bibby, 1987; Dawson, 1998).

## LOOKING AHEAD: RELIGION IN THE TWENTY-FIRST CENTURY

The popularity of media ministries, the emergence of religious fundamentalism, the continuing adherence of millions of people to the "mainstream" churches, the rise of liberation theology, and the belief in nontraditional religious forms, such as the cult of the individual and consumerism, show that "religion" will remain central to modern society. Moreover, high levels of immigration from many religious countries (in Latin America, the Middle East, and elsewhere) should both intensify and diversify the religious character of Canadian society in this new century.

The world is becoming more complex, and rapid social change seems to outstrip our capacity to make sense of it all. But rather than undermining religion, this process fires the religious imagination, as the Controversy & Debate box on page 338 argues. Moreover, new technology that can alter, sustain, and even create life confronts us with vexing moral dilemmas. Against this backdrop of uncertainty, it is little wonder that many people look to their faith for assurance and hope.

# Does Science Threaten Religion?

At the dawning of the modern age, the Italian physicist and astronomer Galileo (1564–1642) helped initiate the scientific revolution with a series of startling discoveries. Dropping objects from the Leaning Tower of Pisa, he discerned some of the laws of gravity. He also fashioned a telescope and surveyed the heavens, confirming a new proposition that the earth orbited the sun, rather than the other way around.

But his lively scientific imagination got him into trouble: Galileo was denounced by the Roman Catholic church, which had preached for centuries that the earth stood motionless at the centre of the universe. Galileo only

made matters worse by declaring that religious leaders and Biblical doctrine had no place in the building wave of science. Before long, he found his work banned and himself condemned to house arrest.

From its beginnings, science has maintained an uneasy relationship with religion. Indeed, as the course of Galileo's life makes clear, the claims of one sometimes infringe on the other's truth.

Through this century, too, science and religion have been at odds—this time over the issue of creation. In the wake of Charles Darwin's masterwork, *On the Origin of Species*, scientists concluded that humanity evolved from lower forms of life over the course of a

billion years. Yet the theory of evolution seems to fly in the face of the Biblical account of creation found in Genesis, which states that "God created the heavens and the earth," introducing the beginnings of life on the third day and then, on the fifth and sixth days, creating animal life, including human beings fashioned in God's own image.

Today—almost four centuries after the silencing of Galileo—many people still ponder the apparently conflicting claims of science and religion. But a middle ground is emerging, which acknowledges that Biblical accounts may be inspired by God and represent important philosophical truths without being literally correct in a scientific

## SUMMARY

### FAMILY

1. Although found everywhere in the world, the family varies across cultures and over time.

2. In high-income industrial countries such as Canada, marriage is monogamous. Many pre-industrial societies and some low-income countries even today, however, permit polygamy, of which there are two types: polygyny and polyandry.

3. In global perspective, patrilocal residence is more common than matrilocal residence. Industrial societies favour neolocality. Descent in pre-industrial societies tends to be either patrilineal or matrilineal; in industrial societies, descent is bilateral.

4. Structural-functional analysis identifies major family functions: socializing the young, regulating sexual activity, and providing social placement and emotional support. Social-conflict theories highlight how the family perpetuates inequality based on class, ethnicity, race, and gender. Symbolic-

interaction analysis highlights the dynamic and changeable experience of family life.

5. In Canada and elsewhere, family life evolves over the life course, beginning with courtship, extending through child rearing, and ending with the death of a spouse or partner, usually in old age.

6. Canadian families are diverse, with certain patterns linked to class position, ethnicity, race, and gender.

7. The divorce rate today is 10 times higher than it was a century ago; 36 percent of current marriages will end in divorce. Most people who divorce, especially men, remarry.

8. Women, men, and children are victims of family violence. Women suffer the most severe and repeated abuse.

9. Our society's family life is becoming more varied. Singlehood, cohabitation, and one-parent families are on the rise. While homosexual men and women cannot yet register their marriages with legal authorities, many form long-lasting relationships.

sense. That is, science and religion embody two different levels of understanding that respond to different kinds of questions. Both Galileo and Darwin devoted their lives to investigating *how* the natural world operates. Yet only religion can address *why* humans and the natural world exist in the first place.

The more scientists discover about the origins of the universe, the more overwhelming the entire process appears. Indeed, as one scientist recently noted, the mathematical odds that some cosmic "Big Bang" 12 billion years ago created the universe and led to the formation of life on earth as we know it today are utterly infinitesimal—surely much smaller than the chance of one person winning a state lottery for 20 weeks in a row. Doesn't such a scientific fact point to the operation of an intelligent and purposeful power underlying our creation? Can't one be both a scientific investigator and a religious believer?

There is another reason to acknowledge the importance of both scientific and religious thinking: Rapid scientific advances continue to leave in their wake vexing ethical dilemmas. Latter-day Galileos have unleashed the power of atomic energy, yet we still struggle to find its rightful use in the world. Similarly, unravelling the secrets of human genetics has now brought us to the threshold of manipulating life itself, a power that few have the moral confidence to use. In 1992, a Vatican commission created by Pope John Paul II conceded that the church's silencing of Galileo had been in error. Today, most scientific and religious leaders agree that even though science and religion represent distinctive truths, their teachings may be complementary. And many believe—in the rush to scientific discovery—that our world has never been in more need of the moral guidance afforded by religion.

*Continue the debate . . .*

1. *In what way are science and religion similar? In what way are they different?*

2. *Do you think that the sociological study of religion should also include the study of science as a belief system? Why or why not?*

3. *Do you think that ethics in scientific research should be given priority in Canadian universities? Why are why not?*

Source: Based on Gould (1981) and Huchingson (1994).

## RELIGION

1. Religion is a major social institution based on setting the sacred apart from the profane. Religion is grounded in faith, not scientific evidence. Sociologists study how religion affects society, but make no claims as to the truth of any particular religious belief.

2. Through religion, said Durkheim, people celebrate the power of their society. His structural-functional analysis suggests that religion promotes social cohesion and conformity, and confers meaning and purpose on life.

3. Using the symbolic-interaction paradigm, Peter Berger explains that people socially construct religious beliefs as a response to life's uncertainties and disruptions.

4. Social-conflict analyst Karl Marx claimed that religion supports inequality. On the other hand, Max Weber's analysis showed how religious ideas can trigger societal change.

5. Churches, which are religious organizations well integrated into their societies, fall into two categories—state churches and denominations. Sects, the result of religious division, are marked by charismatic leadership and suspicion of the larger society. Cults represent new and unconventional religious beliefs and practices.

6. How religious our society is depends on how we operationalize the concept of religiosity. The vast majority of people say they believe in God, but only about 22 percent of the Canadian population today reports attending religious services regularly.

7. The concept of secularization refers to the diminishing importance of religion. While some measures of religiosity (including church attendance) have declined, Canadians continue to identify with a mainstream church, and others express belief in nontraditional forms of religion, including cults of the individual and consumerism. It is unlikely, then, that religion will disappear.

8. Fundamentalism opposes religious accommodation to the world, advocates literal interpretation of sacred texts, and pursues the personal experience of God's presence. Some fundamentalist Christians have become a conservative force in politics.

# KEY CONCEPTS

## FAMILY

**family** (p. 310) a social institution found in all societies that unites people in cooperative groups to oversee the bearing and raising of children

**kinship** (p. 310) a social bond based on blood, marriage, or adoption

**family unit** (p. 310) a social group of two or more people, related by blood, marriage, or adoption, who usually live together

**marriage** (p. 310) a legally sanctioned relationship, usually involving economic cooperation as well as sexual activity and childbearing, that people expect to be enduring

**extended family** (consanguine family) (p. 310) a family unit that includes parents and children, as well as other kin

**nuclear family** (conjugal family) (p. 311) a family unit composed of one or two parents and their children

**endogamy** (p. 311) marriage between people of the same social category

**exogamy** (p. 311) marriage between people of different social categories

**monogamy** (p. 311) marriage uniting two partners at the same time

**polygamy** (p. 311) marriage that unites three or more people at the same time

**descent** (p. 312) the system by which members of a society trace kinship over generations

**homogamy** (p. 316) marriage between people with the same social characteristics

**cohabitation** (p. 324) the sharing of a household by an unmarried couple

## RELIGION

**profane** (p. 326) that which people define as an ordinary element of everyday life

**sacred** (p. 326) that which people set apart as extraordinary, inspiring a sense of awe and reverence

**religion** (p. 326) a social institution involving beliefs and practices based on a conception of the sacred

**faith** (p. 327) belief anchored in conviction rather than scientific evidence

**totem** (p. 327) an object in the natural world collectively defined as sacred

**liberation theology** (p. 331) a fusion of Christian principles with political activism, often Marxist in character

**church** (p. 331) a type of religious organization well integrated into the larger society

**state church** (p. 332) a church formally allied with the state

**denomination** (p. 332) a church, independent of the state, that recognizes religious pluralism

**sect** (p. 332) a type of religious organization that stands apart from the larger society

**charisma** (p. 332) extraordinary personal qualities that can turn an audience into followers

**cult** (p. 332) a religious organization that is largely outside a society's cultural traditions

**animism** (p. 333) the belief that elements of the natural world are conscious life forms that affect humanity

**religiosity** (p. 333) the importance of religion in a person's life

**secularization** (p. 335) the historical decline in the importance of the supernatural and the sacred

**civil religion** (p. 335) a quasi-religious loyalty based on citizenship

**religious fundamentalism** (p. 336) a conservative religious doctrine that opposes intellectualism and worldly accommodation in favour of restoring traditional, otherworldly religion

## CRITICAL-THINKING QUESTIONS

1. Identify several changes in the family since 1960. What factors are responsible for these changes?

2. On balance, are families in Canada becoming weaker, or simply different? What evidence supports your contention?

3. Explain Karl Marx's contention that religion tends to support the status quo. Develop a counterargument, based on Max Weber's analysis of Calvinism, that religion is a major force for social change.

4. What evidence suggests that religion has declining importance in Canada? In what ways does religion seem to be getting stronger?

## APPLICATIONS AND EXERCISES

1. Parents and grandparents can be a wonderful source of information about changes in marriage and the family. Spend an hour or two with couples of two different generations and ask about when they got together, what their lives together have been like, and what changes in family life today stand out to them.

2. Relationships with various family members differ. With which family member—mother, father, brother, sister—do you most readily, and least readily, share secrets? Why? Which family member would you turn to first in a crisis? Why?

3. Is religion getting weaker? To test the secularization thesis, go the library or local newspaper office and find an issue of your local newspaper published 50 years ago and, if possible, another from 100 years ago. Compare attention to religious issues then and now.

4. Research shows that religious people experience better emotional health and feel more content with their lives than non-religious people. Why do you think this might be the case?

 SITES TO SEE

www.pearsoned.ca/macionis
Visit the interactive Web site that accompanies this text. Begin by clicking on the cover of your book. You will find a chapter-by-chapter study guide, practice tests, chat room, and many suggested Web links.

www.cprn.com/cprn.html
Click on this site and it will take you to the Canadian Policy Research Network, which is dedicated to encouraging public debate on policy issues that affect the wide spectrum of Canadian family types.

web.uvic.ca/hrd/cfp
This is the site of the Canadian Families Project, an interdisciplinary research project based at the University of Victoria, B.C. The project team is researching Canadian families based on a special data set from the 1901 census. By the time you read this, the data set may be accessible to you.

www.fraserinstitute.ca
Browse through the various documents found at the Web site for the Fraser Institute, an independent public policy organization based in Vancouver, with offices in Calgary and Toronto. The Institute is well known for its conservative positions on the family and other social institutions.

www.polyamorysociety.org
Survey the increasing diversity of family life at the Web site for the Polyamory Society. What do you make of the society's views of family life?

www.bwanet.org
www.churchworldservice.org
www.catholicrelief.org
www.jdc.org
A number of religious organizations are involved in addressing hunger and other social problems. These are the Web sites that describe the activities of the Baptist World Alliance, Church World Service, Catholic Relief Services, and the American Jewish Joint Distribution Committee.

www.trinityumc.net/youth/cool.htm
This Web site is just for fun. Check it out!

# EDUCATION AND HEALTH

*Thirteen-year-old Naoko Matsuo has just returned from school to her home in suburban Yokohama, Japan. Instead of dropping off her books and beginning an afternoon of fun, she settles in to do her homework. Several hours later, her mother reminds her that it is time to leave for the juku, or "cram school," that she attends three evenings a week. After a short subway trip downtown, Naoko joins dozens of other girls and boys for intensive training in Japanese, English, math, and science.*

*Tuition for the juku costs the Matsuo family several hundred dollars a month. They hope, however, that the investment will pay off when Naoko begins a series of national examinations to determine her school placement, an ordeal culminating in the achievement test that determines whether she will attend an exclusive national university—the gateway to a high-paying, prestigious career (Simons, 1989).* ■

This chapter begins by exploring *education*, a vital social institution in industrial nations, including Canada and Japan. We shall explain *why* schooling is so important in modern societies, as well as *who* receives most educational benefits. The second half of the chapter examines *health and medicine*, another social institution with great importance in the modern world. Good health, like quality schooling, is distributed unequally throughout our society's population. In addition, like education, medicine reveals striking variation from society to society.

## EDUCATION: A GLOBAL SURVEY

**Education** is *the social institution through which society provides its members with important knowledge, including basic facts and job skills as well as cultural norms and values.*

343

Education takes place in a host of ways, some of them as informal as a family discussion. In industrial societies, as we shall see, education is largely a matter of **schooling**, *formal instruction under the direction of trained teachers.*

## SCHOOLING IN LOW-INCOME COUNTRIES

In agrarian countries, where most of the world's people live, families and local communities teach young people important knowledge and skills. Formal schooling, and especially learning that is not directly linked to work, is mostly available only to wealthy people. After all, the Greek root of the word *school* means "leisure." Thus, in ancient Greece, renowned teachers such as Plato, Socrates, and Aristotle taught aristocratic men; similarly, in ancient China, the famous philosopher K'ung Fu-tzu (Confucius) shared his wisdom with just a privileged few.

Schooling in low-income countries today is diverse because it reflects the local culture. In Iran, for example, schooling is closely tied to Islam. Similarly, schooling in Bangladesh (Asia), Zimbabwe (Africa), and Nicaragua (Latin America) has been molded by distinctive cultural traditions.

But all low-income countries have one trait in common when it comes to schooling—there is not very much of it. In the world as a whole, just half of all children reach the secondary grades; in the poorest nations (including several in central Africa), only half of all children ever get to school at all (Najafizadeh & Mennerick, 1992). As a result, one-fifth of Latin Americans, almost half of Asians, and nearly two-thirds of Africans are illiterate. Global Map 14–1 shows the extent of illiteracy around the world.

**A closer look: India.** India is a low-income country where people earn about 11 percent of the income standard in Canada, and most poor families depend on the earnings of children. Thus, even though India has outlawed child labour, many children work to help their families, which greatly limits their chances for schooling—almost 50 percent of children leave school before the fifth grade (UNESCO, 2000a). The result is that almost half the people in this vast country are illiterate.

Patriarchy also shapes Indian education. Indian parents rejoice at the birth of a boy, since he and his future wife both will contribute income to the family. But a girl is a financial liability, first, because parents must provide a dowry at the time of her marriage, and second, because after her marriage a daughter's work then benefits her husband's family. Thus, many Indians see little reason to invest in the schooling of girls, which is why only 39 percent of girls reach the secondary grades compared to 55 percent of boys (UNESCO, 2000b). The flip side of this pattern is that a large majority of the children working in Indian factories are girls—a family's way of benefitting from their daughters while they can.

## SCHOOLING IN HIGH-INCOME COUNTRIES

Ideally, industrial societies offer schooling to everyone. Industrial production demands that workers learn at least the basic "three Rs"—reading, 'riting, and 'rithmetic. Also, literate citizens are able to participate actively in political life.

**A closer look: The United States.** The United States was among the first countries to set a goal of mass public education. By 1850, half the U.S. population between the ages of 5 and 19 was enrolled in school. In 1918, the last of the U.S. states passed a *mandatory education law* requiring children to attend school until age 16 or completion of the eighth grade. A milestone was reached in the mid-1960s, when, for the first time, a majority of U.S. adults had high school diplomas. Today, more than four out of five adults have a high school education, and almost one in four has a four-year university or college degree.

**A closer look: Japan.** Before industrialization brought mandatory education to Japan in 1872, only a privileged few received schooling. Today, Japan's educational system is widely praised for producing some of the world's highest achievers.

The early grades concentrate on transmitting Japanese traditions, including obligation, to family. Starting in their early teens, students take a series of rigorous and highly competitive examinations. These tests, which resemble the Scholastic Aptitude Tests (SATs) used for college admissions in the United States, determine a Japanese student's future.

More men and women graduate from high school in Japan (96 percent) than in either Canada (72 percent) or the United States (74 percent). But competitive examinations after high school are used to limit admission to post-secondary institutions so that among those aged 25 to 64 only 18 percent have a post-secondary diploma or degree—compared to 39 percent in Canada and 35 percent in the United States (Statistics Canada, 2000g). Understandably, then, Japanese students take these examinations very seriously, and about half attend cram schools to prepare for them.

Japanese schooling produces impressive results. In a number of fields, notably mathematics and science, Japanese students outperform students in most other industrial societies, including Canada and the United States (OECD, 2000).

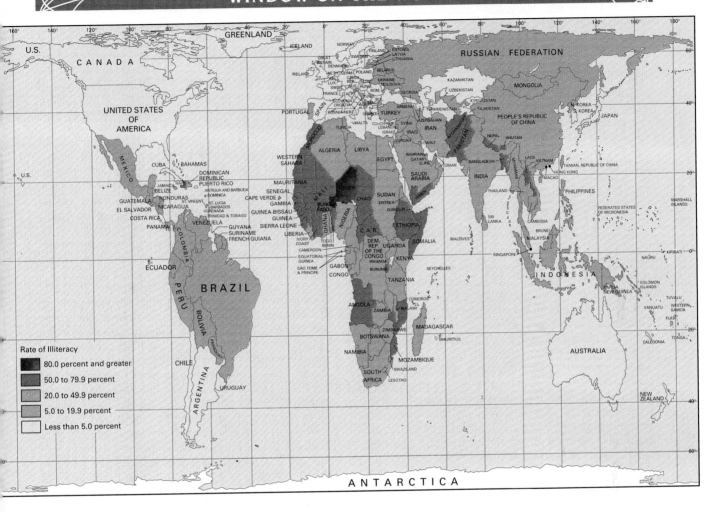

**GLOBAL MAP 14–1   Illiteracy in Global Perspective**

Reading and writing skills are widespread in every high-income country, with illiteracy rates generally below 5 percent. Throughout Latin America, however, illiteracy is more commonplace—one consequence of limited economic development. In about three dozen nations—many of them in Africa—illiteracy is the rule rather than the exception; there, people rely on "the oral tradition" of face-to-face communication rather than the written word.

Sources: United Nations Development Programme (2000); map projection from *Peters Atlas of the World* (1990).

## SCHOOLING IN CANADA

As in the U.S. and Japan, the educational system in Canada has been shaped by past traditions and cultural norms. The result is a mixture of public schools, elite private schools, and publicly funded Roman Catholic and Protestant schools. At the same time, a strong belief in equality between the sexes in regard to literacy and basic schooling has prevailed—a tradition, in fact, that predates the emergence of the modern education system as we have come to know it (Harrigan, 1990). Yet throughout the 20th century, educational participation was influenced by gender, geographic location, and social class. And, to some extent, it can be argued that this remains the case even today.

| TABLE 14–1 Educational Achievement in Canada, 1981–1996 | | | | |
|---|---|---|---|---|
| Population Ages 20 to 29 | Males | | Females | |
| | 1981 | 1996 | 1981 | 1996 |
| Less than high school | 30.6 | 20.7 | 28.3 | 15.7 |
| High school diploma | 15.4 | 15.6 | 20.9 | 13.0 |
| Some post-secondary | 16.9 | 21.6 | 14.2 | 20.8 |
| Completed non-university* | 25.5 | 25.9 | 25.5 | 29.9 |
| Completed university | 11.6 | 16.2 | 11.1 | 20.7 |

*"Completed non-university" refers to those who have received certificates or diplomas from technical schools or other non-academic institutions of higher education.

Source: Statistics Canada, The Daily, Tuesday, April 14 (1998i).

Nevertheless, in our country formal education for children of all social backgrounds has changed enormously since the mid-19th century. Prior to this time, education for most children—apart from those of the elite—was informal and unorganized (Prentice, 1977). Even by the turn of the 20th century, school attendance remained sporadic and most students—boys and girls in equal proportions—dropped out after the third grade (Harrigan, 1990; Baldus & Kassam, 1996). This was especially true for rural children. Further, schoolteachers were often ill-trained and poorly paid, typically receiving lower wages than day labourers of the time. Prejudice restricted females from public teaching until the second half of the 19th century, and even thereafter conditions were hardly equal between the sexes. For example, when Martha Hamm Lewis entered teachers' training school in the mid-19th century in New Brunswick, her principal required that she "enter the classroom 10 minutes before the male students, sit alone at the back of the room, always wear a veil, leave the classroom five minutes before the end of the lesson and leave the building without speaking to any of the young men" (MacLellan, 1972:6, cited in Wilson, 1996:99).

The early public schools in Canada did not champion class equality despite proclaiming an egalitarian ideology. Rather, they served to reproduce the existing social class system and to teach its validity to students in order to minimize conflict between the social classes (Curtis, 1988:370–371). Likewise, the early school books of Upper Canada were "infused with a hefty dose of class interest" (Baldus & Kassam, 1996:328), with their authors aiming mainly to curtail insubordination stemming from the "lower orders."

As the 20th century unfolded, women came to dominate the teaching profession, the quality of instruction greatly improved, and national legislation was passed requiring that children of both sexes across Canada remain in school until at least their mid-teens.

Increasingly, most groups embraced publicly funded education as a minimum requirement for future success in a modern industrial society.

Today, about 5 million students are enrolled full-time in Canada's 12 190 elementary schools and 3468 secondary schools. Many continue their educations: annually there are about 1 million full-time students attending 195 community colleges and 75 universities, which are partly supported by student tuition fees but mainly funded by public taxes (Statistics Canada, 2000h).

In 1997 Canada spent about 6.5 percent of the Canadian Gross Domestic Product (GDP) on education (World Bank, 1998). The comparable figures for the U.S. and Japan were 6.9 percent and 4.8 percent, respectively. These figures hide the fact that private spending makes up 25 percent of total spending in the U.S. compared to 11 percent in Canada (OECD, 2000). What this means is that the educational system in the U.S. is more dependent than our system on payments by students and their parents.

Table 14–1 shows that Canadians have recently made great strides in regard to educational attainment, accelerating the trend that has slowly been emerging over the past century or so. The increase for females is particularly impressive; in the 1996 census, more than 50 percent of females in their twenties had completed a post-secondary program, up from 37 percent in 1981. At the same time, the percentage of females in this age group who had not completed high school decreased from 28 to 16 percent in 1996.

Canada also compares well internationally in regard to educational attainment. The percentage of adults with post-secondary education is the highest in the world, as shown in Figure 14–1. It is noteworthy that in terms of percentage of citizens with university degrees, Canada is among the top five in the world. But what makes Canada stand out is the combination, with a large proportion of people with non-university post-secondary education. If programs shorter than two years are included, more than 50 percent of Canadian adults have some kind of post-secondary education.

As well as trying to make schooling more widely available, educational systems in industrial societies have also stressed the value of practical learning—that is, knowledge that has a direct bearing on people's work and interests. The educational philosopher John Dewey (1859–1952) championed progressive education, emphasizing practical skills rather than a fixed body of knowledge passed from generation to generation. This is a popular sentiment even in our society today, where 60 percent of decided respondents answered that young people should acquire a trade skill rather than a general university education (Angus Reid Group Inc., 1999a). Many of today's university students are selecting areas of major study with an eye toward future jobs. As a result of the Information Revolution, the top three fields in which males in Canada attained bachelor's degrees in 1997 were business, management, and commerce (14 percent); engineering (13 percent); and education (8 percent). For women acquiring bachelor's degrees, the leading areas were education (17 percent); business, management, and commerce (9 percent); and psychology (9 percent) (Statistics Canada, 2000h).

## THE FUNCTIONS OF SCHOOLING

Structural-functional analysis focusses on ways in which schooling enhances the operation and stability of society:

1. **Socialization.** Technologically simple societies look to families to transmit a way of life from one generation to another. As societies gain complex technology, they turn to trained teachers to convey specialized knowledge.

2. **Cultural innovation.** Schools create as well as transmit culture. Especially at centres of higher education, scholars conduct research that leads to discovery and changes our way of life.

3. **Social integration.** Schools mold a diverse population into a unified society sharing norms and values. Nineteenth-century Canadian educational reformer Egerton Ryerson argued that public schools could bring together children of all social classes under one roof, so that they could "imbibe the first elements of knowledge at the same fountain, commence the race of life upon equal terms, and cultivate the feelings of mutual respect and sympathy . . ." (Ryerson 1852, cited in Prentice, 1977:126). Canadian educational policies strive to balance this with some accommodation for our cultural, religious, and linguistic diversity.

4. **Social placement.** Schools identify talent and see that students receive instruction to meet their needs. Thus, schooling enhances meritocracy by rewarding talent and hard work regardless of social background, and provides a path to upward social mobility.

5. **Latent functions of schooling.** Schooling serves several less widely recognized functions. It provides child care for the growing number of one-parent and two-career families. In addition, it occupies thousands of young people in their twenties who otherwise would be competing for limited opportunities in the job market. High schools, colleges, and universities also bring together people of marriageable age. Last, school networks can be a valuable career resource throughout life.

**Critical evaluation.** Structural-functional analysis stresses ways that formal education supports the operation of a modern society. However, functionalism

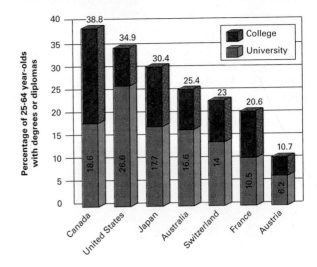

**GLOBAL SNAPSHOT**

**FIGURE 14–1** **Post-Secondary Education in Global Perspective**

**Note:** College education is defined as being two years or longer.
Source: OECD, 2000:33.

overlooks the problems inherent in our educational system and the way in which schooling helps to reproduce the class structure in each generation. In the next section, social-conflict analysis examines precisely these issues.

## SCHOOLING AND SOCIAL INEQUALITY

Social-conflict theory counters the functionalist idea that schooling develops everyone's talents and abilities. Rather, this approach studies how schooling causes and perpetuates social inequality:

1. **Social control.** As Samuel Bowles and Herbert Gintis (1976) see it, the clamour for public education in the late 19th century arose just as capitalists were demanding a docile and disciplined workforce. Once in school, immigrants learned not only the English language but also the importance of discipline and punctuality. Egerton Ryerson also saw this as a function for public schools because in the continuation of the short quote above he argues that public schools should "in no respect intrude upon the providential arrangements of order and rank in society, [but rather] divest poverty of its meanness and its hatreds, and wealth of its arrogance and selfishness" (Ryerson 1852, cited in Prentice, 1977:126).

*From a functionalist point of view, schooling provides children with the knowledge and skills they will need as adults. Conflict analysis adds that schooling differs according to the resources of the local community. When some schools offer children much more than others do, education perpetuates the class structure rather than increasing equality of opportunity.*

2. **Testing and social inequality.** Critics claim that the aptitude tests widely used by schools reflect our society's dominant culture, thereby placing working-class people, Aboriginal peoples, and visible minority students at a decided disadvantage. By defining majority students as smarter, standardized tests thus transform privilege into personal merit (Owen, 1985; Crouse & Trusheim, 1988; Putka, 1990). Scott McLean (1997) argues that even the very notion of an individual assessment measure, as well as our detailed statistical system for recording students' academic performance, holds little meaning among Inuit in the Canadian Arctic.

3. **Tracking and social inequality.** Despite controversy over tests and other quantitative measures, our educational system uses them for **streaming,** or **tracking,** *assigning students to different types of educational programs,* such as vocational or academic training. Tracking supposedly helps teachers meet a student's individual abilities and interests. Education critic Jonathan Kozol (1992), however, considers tracking one of the "savage inequalities" in our school system. Most students from privileged backgrounds get into higher tracks where they receive the best the school can offer. Students from disadvantaged backgrounds end up in lower tracks where teachers stress memorization and classroom drill (Bowles & Gintis, 1976; Persell, 1977; Davis & Haller, 1981; Oakes, 1982, 1985; Hallinan & Williams, 1989; Kilgore, 1991;

Gamoran, 1992). As a result of such criticisms, some Canadian schools have de-streamed their educational programs in recent years. Yet a variety of groups have opposed de-streaming, including school boards, teachers, and middle-class parents; the latter worry that without different tracks, their university-bound children will not have the required skills to successfully compete at university.

## PUBLIC AND PRIVATE EDUCATION

There has been a steady increase in private school enrollment to 288 174 during the 1997–1998 academic year—5.4 percent of the total elementary and secondary school enrollment in Canada (Statistics Canada, 2000h). When examined over time, private school enrollment in Canada shows a very gradual climb, from an all-time low in 1971 of only 2.41 percent to 5.4 percent of elementary and secondary students in 1997–1998—reflecting Canadian parents' growing dissatisfaction with the quality of public school education for their children (Statistics Canada, 1997e, Maxwell & Maxwell, 1995). Two recent Angus Reid polls attempted to capture Canadians' views on Canadian schools. These polls found, among other things, that 39 percent of respondents would seriously consider sending their child to a private school with an annual tuition fee of $5000 per student (Angus Reid Group Inc., 1996a) and over 60 percent thought that students in private schools "receive much better education than public school students" (Angus Reid Group Inc., 1999b).

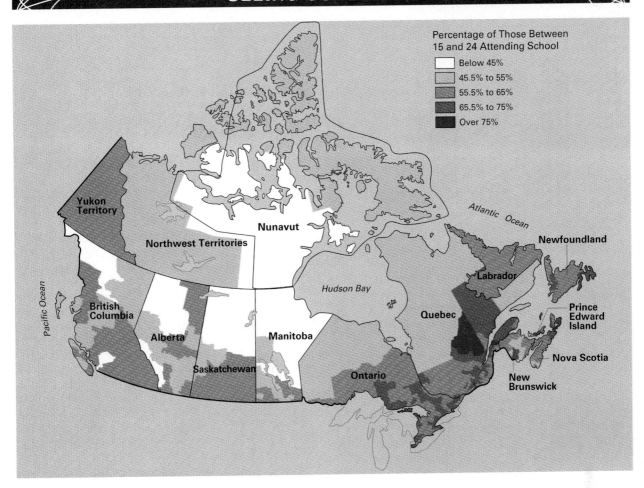

Percentage of Those Between
15 and 24 Attending School

☐ Below 45%
☐ 45.5% to 55%
☐ 55.5% to 65%
☐ 65.5% to 75%
☐ Over 75%

**NATIONAL MAP 14–1   School Attendance, Aged 15–24 Years, Canada, 1995–1996**

Generally speaking, school attendance is most common among youth and adults living in the urban south of the country. How would you explain this pattern? Income is one obvious consideration, but do you think that people's ideas about the importance of school attendance also vary depending on whether their environment is rural or urban?

**Note:** Educational participation is defined as full- or part-time attendance in courses that could be used as credits toward certificates, diplomas, or degrees.

Source: Based on Statistics Canada, Catalogue No. 95F0181XDB96001 (1998b).

The Canadian Association of Independent Schools (CAIS) is the association for elite private schools across the country. Its membership in 2001 comprised 71 "independent" (non-public) schools enrolling about 35 000 private school students (a little more than 10 percent of the total private school enrollment). According to Mary Percival Maxwell and James Maxwell (1995:335), "[d]espite their small numbers these schools have played a crucial role in the social reproduction of the upper classes . . . [and] their

graduates are disproportionately represented in the various institutional elites."

Over half of the CAIS private schools were established prior to 1920; 22 of them were founded in the 19th century. The original member CAIS schools were not only exclusive along class lines, but most were only open to a single sex. Before the First World War, upper-class Canadian families were likely to send both their daughters and sons to board at elite private schools. Worsening economic circumstances in

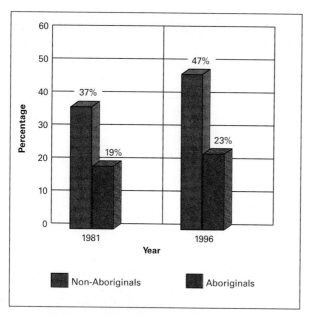

**FIGURE 14–2   Aboriginals and Non-Aboriginals, Ages 20 to 29, with Post-Secondary Degrees or Diplomas, Canada, 1981 and 1996**

Source: Statistics Canada, *The Daily*, Tuesday, April 14 (1998g).

subsequent decades meant that many families tended to commit their reduced resources to their sons' private school educations, while sending their daughters to less expensive local schools. As a result, by 1993 there remained only 16 private girls' schools (Maxwell & Maxwell, 1995). Yet even the single-sex private schools for boys have been forced to change with the times. During the 1970s, declining enrollments forced many of them to go "co-ed." At the same time, the ethnic makeup of these schools has become more diverse, reflecting the more heterogeneous ethnic makeup of the upper and upper-middle classes in present-day Canadian society. Despite their changing student populations, Canada's elite private schools continue to prepare their students for leadership positions in the various elites of the larger society, which does not differ significantly from what sociologists have observed in earlier generations (Porter, 1965; Clement, 1975; Newman, 1975). Public school financing does not differ very much across Canada, owing to the country's relative success in redistributing wealth through income tax. Nevertheless, Canadian data indicate that the provinces vary substantially in the number of years of education of the adult population, with people in Newfoundland having on average more than one year less education than people in Ontario, Alberta, and British Columbia (Statistics Canada, 2000h). Even if schools were exactly the same everywhere, students whose families value and encour-

age learning would still perform better since success in school is correlated with parents encouraging reading at home, buying books or borrowing them from public libraries, and enrolling children in extra-curricular activities (de Brouker & Lavalleé, 1998).

## ACCESS TO HIGHER EDUCATION

Schooling is the main path to high-paying jobs. For example, the average income for all women aged 25 to 34 who worked full-time in 1992 was about $28 000. Women who graduated two years earlier with bachelor's degrees earned $33 600 (Finnie, 2000).

In 1996, however, only 42 percent of males aged 20 to 29 years had attained post-secondary diplomas or university degrees, while just over half (51 percent) of females in this age group had done so (Statistics Canada, 1998g). National Map 14–1 on the previous page shows where in Canada school attendance of those aged 15 to 24 is more or less likely.

Figure 14–2 shows that even while more young people are accessing higher education today in Canada than ever before, those from less privileged family backgrounds—including a disproportionate number of Aboriginals—are not increasing their participation nearly to the extent that their more privileged friends are (Bouchard & Zhao, 2000). Post-secondary education in Canada is expensive. College and university revenue from government grants and contracts fell by 14.1 percent in 1996–1997 from five years earlier. In an attempt to offset this decline in institutional revenue, many colleges and universities have increased student tuition fees. For example, the average cost for tuition in an undergraduate arts program doubled from $1568 in 1988–1989 to $3199 in 1998–1999 (Statistics Canada, 2000i). At the same time, however, post-secondary students have gained from increased public expenditure on scholarships and bursaries, including most recently the 2.5-billion Millennium Scholarship Fund (MSF).

Nevertheless, the amount owing by those who take out student loans is increasing. Students who graduated with loans in 1995 still owed an average of $8300 in 1997—more than twice as much as the comparable figure for those who graduated in 1986 (Statistics Canada, 2000i). It is little wonder that the financial burdens of higher education discourage many young people from less privileged backgrounds from attending. For those who do complete post-secondary education, rewards include not just intellectual and personal growth but also increased opportunities for secure employment and higher income. This is especially the case for women. Looking at participants in the labour force—that is, either those who have jobs or are looking for them—we see that among women ages 24 to 34 (who were not enrolled in school) labour force participation increases with education; from

**TABLE 14–2 Average Income, by Gender and Educational Attainment, Canada, 1995**

| Education | Females | Males | Female Earnings as Percentage of Male Earnings |
|---|---|---|---|
| University degree | $43 337 | $60 870 | 71.2 |
| Less than university degree | 28 933 | 40 733 | 71.0 |
| Grades 9–13 with secondary school graduation certificate | 25 786 | 36 204 | 71.2 |
| Grades 9–13 without secondary school graduation certificate | 22 598 | 33 449 | 67.6 |
| Less than grade 9 | 19 254 | 29 795 | 64.6 |
| All levels of education | 30 130 | 42 488 | 70.9 |

**Note:** Persons working full-time, full-year in 1995.

Source: Statistics Canada, *The Nation: 1996 Census of Canada*, Electronic data file. Statistics Canada Catalogue No. 93F0029XDB96004, Table n04_1205.ivt. (1998q).

59 percent among those without high school diplomas, to 74 percent for those with high school diplomas, up to 90 percent for those with university degrees or certificates (Statistics Canada, 1998g).

In addition, education reduces unemployment. In 1998, the unemployment rate for those over 15 years of age was 8.3 percent overall. But there was a great difference between people according to their level of education. Those who had completed a diploma or degree had unemployment rates of 6.6 and 4.3 percent, respectively. Those who had not completed high school had unemployment rates higher than 14 percent. There is one interesting, and consistent, anomaly in these data—that between those who started but did not complete post-secondary education (9.5 percent), and those who completed high school but did not go on to further education (8.3 percent) (Statistics Canada, 2000h). It would appear that a little bit of post-secondary education is worse than none at all!

Table 14–2 shows the relationship between education and income for men and women of different age groups. In 1995, a woman with less than grade nine earned $19 254, while her counterpart with a university degree earned more than double, $43 337. Gender also counts significantly in this respect, however. A male with a university degree earned about $17 500 more than his female colleague.

## CREDENTIALISM

Sociologist Randall Collins (1979) used the label *credential society* to describe societies, such as Canada, where people regard diplomas and degrees highly. In modern, technologically advanced societies, credentials say "who you are" as much as does family background.

**Credentialism**, then, is evaluating a person on the basis of educational degrees. On the surface, credentialism is simply the way our modern society fills jobs with well-trained people. Collins explains, however, that credentials often bear little relation to the responsibilities of a specific job. In reality, advanced degrees often are an easy way to sort out people with the manners, attitudes, and even skin colour favoured by many employers. Credentialism is thus a gatekeeping strategy that restricts important occupations to a limited segment of the population.

## PRIVILEGE AND PERSONAL MERIT

If, as social-conflict analysis suggests, attending college is a rite of passage for affluent men and women, then *schooling transforms social privilege into personal merit.* But because of our cultural emphasis on individualism, we tend to see credentials as "badges of ability" rather than as symbols of family affluence (Sennett & Cobb, 1973). When we congratulate the new graduate, we rarely recognize the resources—both financial and cultural—that made this achievement possible. In the same way, we are quick to label the high school dropout "personally deficient," with little thought given to the social circumstances of that person's life that may have led to dropping out. The Social Diversity box on page 352 illustrates this process with the words of one bright but disillusioned child.

**Critical evaluation.** Social-conflict analysis links formal education to social inequality and shows how schooling transforms privilege into personal worthiness, and disadvantage into personal deficiency. However, critics say that the social-conflict approach minimizes the extent to which schooling provides upward mobility for talented women and men from all backgrounds. Further, despite claims that schooling supports the status quo, today's curricula challenge social inequality on many fronts.

# "Cooling Out" the Poor:
# Transforming Disadvantage into Deficiency

If schools paint disadvantaged students as "dumb," over time some of them come to believe it. This process of "cooling out" their ambitions sets into motion a self-fulfilling prophecy by which many students from low-income families end up settling for no more than what society handed them when they were born. Eleven-year-old Ollie Taylor describes the experience in these words:

The only thing that matters in my life is school and there they think I'm dumb and always will be. I'm starting to think they're right. Hell, I know they put all the black kids together in one group if they can, but that doesn't make any difference either. I'm

still dumb. Even if I look around and know that I'm the smartest in my group, all that means is that I'm the smartest of the dumbest, so I haven't got anywhere at all, have I? I'm right where I always was. Every word those teachers tell me, even the ones I like most, I can hear in their voice that what they're really saying is "All right you dumb kids. I'll make it as easy as I can, and if you don't get it then, you'll never get it. Ever." That's what I hear every day, man. From every one of them. Even the other kids talk that way to me too.

Source: Cottle (1974:22–24.)

## PROBLEMS IN THE SCHOOLS

An intense debate revolves around schooling in Canada. Because we expect schools to do so much—to equalize opportunity, instill discipline, and fire the individual imagination—few people think public schools are doing an excellent job. About two-thirds of Canadians say they believe high school graduates do not have strong reading and writing skills, and the same proportion do not think that our high schools do a good job of preparing students for today's workforce (Angus Reid Group Inc., 1999b).

### DISCIPLINE AND VIOLENCE

When many of today's older teachers think back to their own student days, school "problems" consisted of talking out of turn, chewing gum, breaking the dress code, or cutting class. But today's schools are also grappling with drug and alcohol abuse, teenage pregnancy, and outright violence.

While Canadians are used to hearing about violence in the United States, our collective conscience was shocked at the 1999 fatal shooting at the W.R. Myers school in Taber, Alberta. Moreover, in a survey conducted just prior to this shooting, one-third of Canadian teenagers under age 18 believed that

violence had increased in their school over the previous five years (Angus Reid Group Inc., 1999a).

### BUREAUCRACY AND STUDENT PASSIVITY

If some schools are plagued by violence, many more are filled with passive, bored students. Some of the blame for passivity can be placed on television (which now claims more of young people's time than does school), on parents (who are not involved enough with their children), and on the students themselves. But schools, too, must share the blame (Coleman, Hoffer, & Kilgore, 1981).

The small, personal schools that served local communities a century ago have evolved into huge educational factories. Theodore Sizer (1984) identified five ways in which large, bureaucratic schools undermine education (1984:207–9):

1. **Rigid uniformity.** Bureaucratic schools run by outside specialists (such as state education officials) generally ignore the cultural character of local communities and the personal needs of their children.

2. **Numerical ratings.** School officials focus on attendance rates, dropout rates, and achievement

test scores. They overlook dimensions of schooling that are difficult to quantify, such as creativity and enthusiasm.

3. **Rigid expectations.** Officials expect 15-year-olds to be in the tenth grade and eleventh graders to score at a certain level on a standardized verbal achievement test. Rarely are exceptionally bright and motivated students permitted to graduate early. Likewise, the system pushes poor performers on from grade to grade.

4. **Specialization.** High school students learn French from one teacher, receive guidance from another, and are coached in sports by still others. No school official comes to know the complete student. Students experience this division of labour as a continual shuffling among 50-minute periods throughout the school day.

5. **Little individual responsibility.** Highly bureaucratic schools do not empower students to learn on their own. Similarly, teachers have little say in what and how they teach their classes; they dare not accelerate learning for fear of disrupting "the system."

Of course, with more than 5.5 million elementary and secondary students in Canada, schools have to be bureaucratic to get the job done. But Sizer recommends that we "humanize" schools by eliminating rigid scheduling, reducing class size, and training teachers more broadly to make them more involved in the lives of their students. Moreover, James Coleman (1993) suggests that schools should be less "administratively driven" and more "output-driven." Perhaps this transformation could begin by ensuring that graduation from high school depends on what students have learned rather than how many years they have spent in the building.

## THE ACADEMY: THE SILENT CLASSROOM

Passivity is also common among college and university students (Gimenez, 1989). Sociologists rarely study the post-secondary classroom—a curious fact considering how much time they spend there. A fascinating exception is a study of a coeducational university where David Karp and William Yoels (1976) found that, even in small classes, only a few students speak up. Thus, passivity is a classroom norm, and students even become irritated if one of their number is especially talkative.

According to Karp and Yoels, most students think classroom passivity is their own fault. But as anyone who watches young people *outside* of class knows, they are usually active and vocal. Thus, it is schools that teach students to be passive, viewing instructors as

*Aboriginal students at this residential school in Port Alberni on Vancouver Island experienced rigid uniformity in the extreme. Twenty-five former students successfully sued the federal government and the United Church in 1998 for the abuse they suffered 30 years earlier.*

"experts" who serve up "truth." Students see their proper role as quietly listening and taking notes. As a result, the researchers estimate, just 10 percent of class time is used for discussion.

## DROPPING OUT

If many students are passive in class, others are not there at all. The problem of *dropping out*—quitting before earning a diploma, certificate or degree—leaves young people (many of whom are disadvantaged to begin with) ill-equipped for the world of work and at high risk for a life of poverty.

A recent study of high school dropouts by Canadian sociologist Scott Davies (1994) shows that social class is only weakly related to Canadian high school dropout rates. More important are such factors as streaming (mentioned above) and students' poor academic achievement—neither of which, notes Davies, is exclusive to lower-class and minority students.

Currently more than 20 percent of those who leave post-secondary schools have not finished their program requirement. Many of the problems that students have during their high school years follow them to college and university. Those that had difficulty attending, passing, and attaining high grades in high school are much more likely to drop out of their post-secondary school than are their colleagues who did not have these difficulties in high school (Butlin, 2000).

# Gender and Educational Achievement: Why Are the Boys No Longer at the Top of the Class?

Girls in Canada have made amazing strides in recent years, to the extent that they now top high school honour rolls (girls represented 60 percent of the honour rolls in Ontario and British Columbia in 1996) and are also getting top scholarships. They are confident, smart, and competitive—and determined to get ahead. The boys are nowhere to be seen. How do sociologists make sense of this discrepancy?

Our educational system devoted much attention in the past decade to making schools more "girl-friendly," by encouraging teachers to pay attention to gender bias in favour of boys, and to enhancing gender equality in education in general. The results are impressive: Girls have, in fact, made significant inroads, so that today they are surpassing boys in many academic achievement measures.

In a very short time, the gender equity concern among educators has been reversed. Now educators are worried about the relative under-achievement of the guys! In a recent seminar at the University of Victoria, education researcher Wes Imms's presentation was titled *Teaching the Boys: A New Agenda in Gender Equity*. And the problem is not just a home-grown Canadian one. A similar gender gap has been discussed of late in Britain, where girls are outperforming their male counterparts, especially in subjects such as English. According to Patrick Clarke, the former president of the B.C. Teachers' Federation, the boys have "retired to a leisured existence of watching sport and playing electronic games. They have been anesthetized by a boy culture that celebrates bravado, lassitude, and stupidity." With the obvious exception of "bravado," the above quote sounds remarkably similar to the explanations, of not so long ago, as to why *girls* did not do well in school.

To make matters worse, many of the traditional working-class jobs (such as logging and fishing) for boys who did not do well in school are no longer available. "Brawn" has by and large lost favour among Canadian employers. Boys, like girls themselves, have to use their "brains" if they are to succeed occupationally in later life.

Few sociologists studying education would argue that boys in Canada have fewer opportunities than girls. The cause of the reversal is puzzling, but some suggest that boys are less likely to think that it is "cool" or "manly" to read books or learn about literature and history. Though boys still outperform girls in science and mathematics, the gender gap is narrowing even for these subject areas. In fact, in 1998, there were more females than males enrolled in Canadian medical schools. Educators conclude that schools must develop new strategies to excite boys to learn. Some are even proposing all-boy classes to help them build up confidence in themselves and allow them to excel without worrying about the "gender thing." Sounds a lot like what feminists proposed for girls not so long ago—and look how well it worked!

Source: Based on Galt (1998).

## ACADEMIC STANDARDS

In Canada, as in many other countries, fears have been growing about the standard of education. According to the Conference Board of Canada, Canada's position as one of the strongest economic nations in the world is "at risk." Jim Nininger, the board's president, believes the country's high secondary school dropout rate, as well as a short supply of skilled labour and high public debt, is contributing to Canada's economic decline. Similar fears surround the alarming extent of **functional illiteracy**, *reading and writing skills inadequate for everyday living*. The extent of functional illiteracy in Canada is significantly lower than that of middle-income countries (such as Poland) but higher than in some other high-income countries (such as The Netherlands and Sweden). The Applying Sociology box shows that young boys are especially underperforming compared with their female counterparts.

A final concern is the mediocre performance of Canadian students in a global context. An international study of almost 40 countries showed that Canadian students in grade eight scored only slightly above average in their mathematical abilities (Beaton et al., 1996). Our students are generally less motivated than their counterparts in Japan, for example, and also do less homework. Moreover, Japanese young people, as well as their counterparts in Korea and Singapore—in fact, in most other countries—spend more days in school each year than Canadian students do.

## LOOKING AHEAD: SCHOOLING IN THE TWENTY-FIRST CENTURY

Despite the fact that Canada leads the world in sending people to post-secondary schools, the public school system struggles with serious problems, many of which have their roots in the larger society. Thus, during the 21st century, we cannot expect schools *by themselves* to provide high-quality education. Schools will only improve to the extent that students, teachers, parents, and local communities commit to educational excellence. In short, educational problems are *social* problems, and there is no "quick fix."

For much of the 20th century, there were just two models for education in Canada: public schools run by the government and private schools operated by nongovernmental organizations. In the past decade, however, many new ideas about schooling have come on the scene, including schooling for profit and a wide range of "choice" programs (Finn & Gau, 1998). In the decades ahead, we will likely see some significant changes in mass education guided, in part, by social science research pointing out the consequences of different strategies.

Another factor that will continue to shape schools is new information technology. Today almost all schools—and many day care centres—use computers to deliver some part of the curriculum. Unlike the human instructor, the computer is ready at the flick of a switch to teach students—again and again if necessary. This has tremendous potential to allow students to progress at their own pace. Even so, computers have their limitations; many argue—instructors in particular—that computers can never replace the personal insight or imagination of a motivated human teacher. Others argue that the limited amount of interaction possible in the many large classes in our schools today is perhaps not so different from watching the talented instructor on video delivered over the Internet.

Technology, however, is unlikely to solve the problems, including violence and bureaucratic rigidity, that plague our schools. What we need is a broad plan for social change that refires this country's early ambition to provide quality universal schooling to all—a goal that has so far eluded us.

# HEALTH

Another institution gaining importance in modern societies is **medicine,** *the social institution that focusses on combatting disease and improving health.* In ideal terms, according to the World Health Organization (1946:3), **health** is *a state of complete physical, mental, and social well-being.* This definition underscores an important idea: Health is as much a social issue as a biological one.

## HEALTH AND SOCIETY

Society affects health in four basic ways:

1. **Cultural patterns define health.** Standards of health vary from culture to culture. Early in this

*In the decades ahead, we will likely see some significant changes in mass education, guided in part by social science research pointing out the consequences of different strategies, such as educating children with disabilities, in order to provide quality universal schooling.*

century, for example, yaws, a contagious skin disease, was so common in tropical Africa that people there considered it normal (Dubos, 1980; orig. 1965). "Health," therefore, is relative—sometimes it is a matter of having the same diseases as one's neighbours (Pinhey, Rubenstein, & Colfax, 1997).

What people see as healthful also reflects what they think is morally good. People (especially men) in high-income countries such as Canada think a competitive way of life is "healthy" because it fits our cultural mores; however, stress contributes to heart disease and many other illnesses. On the other hand, people who object to homosexuality on moral grounds often call it "sick," even though it is natural from a biological point of view. Thus, ideas about health amount to a form of social control that encourages conformity to cultural norms.

2. **Cultural standards of health change over time.** Early in the 20th century, some physicians warned women not to go to university or college because higher education strained the female brain. Others denounced masturbation as a threat to health. Today, on both counts, we know differently. And 50 years ago, few physicians understood the dangers of cigarette smoking or too much sun exposure, practices that we now recognize as serious health risks.

3. **A society's technology affects people's health.** In low-income nations, infectious diseases are

**TABLE 14–3 Mortality Rates for Leading Causes of Death per 100 000 People, by Gender, Canada, 1993–1995**

|  | Females | Males |
|---|---|---|
| All causes | 844 | 521.6 |
| Cancers | 229.7 | 148.5 |
| Diseases of the heart | 230.8 | 129.7 |
| Cerebrovascular diseases | 52.8 | 43.9 |
| Chronic obstructive pulmonary diseases and allied conditions | 44.5 | 20.1 |
| Unintentional injuries | 37.8 | 17.9 |
| Pneumonia and influenza | 31.5 | 19.2 |
| Diabetes mellitus | 20.6 | 14.8 |

Source: Statistics Canada (2001b).

rampant because of malnutrition and poor sanitation. As industrialization raises living standards, people become more healthy. But industrial technology also creates new threats to health. As Chapter 15 (Population, Urbanization, and Environment) explains, high-income countries endanger health by overtaxing the world's resources and creating pollution.

4. **Social inequality affects people's health.** All societies distribute resources unequally. Overall, the rich have far better physical, mental, and emotional health than do the poor.

## HEALTH: A GLOBAL SURVEY

Because health is closely linked to social life, we find that human well-being has improved over the long course of history. For the same reason, we see striking differences in health around the world today.

### HEALTH IN LOW-INCOME COUNTRIES

With only simple technology, our ancestors could do little to improve health. Hunters and gatherers faced frequent food shortages, which sometimes forced mothers to abandon their children. Those lucky enough to survive infancy were still vulnerable to injury and illness, so half died by age 20 and few lived to age 40 (Lenski, Nolan, & Lenski, 1995).

As people developed agriculture, food became more plentiful. Yet social inequality, too, increased, so that elites enjoyed better health than peasants and slaves, who lived in crowded, unsanitary shelters and often went hungry. In the growing cities of medieval Europe, human waste and refuse piled up in the streets

spreading infectious diseases, and plagues periodically wiped out entire towns (Mumford, 1961).

`November 1, 1988—Central India` Poverty is not just a matter of what you have; it shapes what you are. Most of the people we see in the villages here have never had the benefit of a doctor or a dentist. The result is easy to see: People look old before their time.

In much of the world, poverty cuts decades off the life expectancy found in high-income countries. A look back at Global Map 9–1 on page 213 shows that in the poorest countries of the world, most people die even before reaching their teens. To make matters worse, medical personnel are few and far between, so that many of the world's poorest people never see a physician, nurse, or trained midwife.

The World Health Organization reports that 1 billion people around the world—one in six—suffer from serious illness due to poverty. Poor sanitation and malnutrition kill people of all ages. In a classic vicious circle, poverty breeds disease, which in turn reduces people's ability to work. Moreover, when medical technology does control infectious disease, the populations of low-income nations soar. But without resources to provide for the people they have now, these societies can ill afford population growth. Thus, programs to lower death rates in low-income countries must be coupled with programs to reduce birth rates.

### HEALTH IN HIGH-INCOME COUNTRIES

Industrialization dramatically changed patterns of health in Europe, although at first not for the better. By 1800, as the Industrial Revolution took hold, factory jobs drew people from the countryside. Cities became overcrowded, creating serious sanitation problems. Soon after, factories fouled the air with smoke, and workplace accidents became common.

But industrialization gradually began to improve health in Western Europe and North America as rising living standards translated into better nutrition and safer housing for most people. After 1850, medical advances also improved health, primarily by controlling infectious diseases. In 1854, for example, researcher John Snow mapped the street addresses of London's cholera victims and found they had all drunk contaminated water from the same well (Rockett, 1994). Such discoveries led scientists to link cholera to specific bacteria and, eventually, to develop a vaccine against the deadly disease. Armed with scientific knowledge, early environmentalists campaigned against common practices such as discharging raw sewage into

# Masculinity: A Threat to Health?

**D**octors call it "coronary-prone behaviour." Psychologists call it "Type A personality." Sociologists recognize it as our culture's conception of masculinity. It is a combination of attitudes and behaviour, common among men in our society, that includes (1) chronic impatience ("C'mon! Go faster or get outta my way!"), (2) uncontrolled ambition ("I've gotta have it . . . I *need* that!"), and (3) free-floating hostility ("Why are so many people *such idiots*?").

This pattern, although normal from a cultural point of view, is one major reason that men who are driven to succeed are at high risk for heart disease. By acting out the Type A personality, we may get the job done, but we set in motion complex biochemical processes that are very hard on the human heart.

Here are a few questions to help you assess your own degree of risk (or that of someone important to you):

1. *Do you believe that a person has to be aggressive to succeed?* For you, do "nice guys finish last"? For your heart's sake, try to remove hostility from your life. One starting point: How about eliminating profanity from your speech? Try replacing aggression with compassion, which can be surprisingly effective in dealing with other people. According to the latest health advice, compassion and humour—rather than irritation and aggravation—will enhance your life.

2. *How well do you handle uncertainty and opposition?* Do you have moments when you fume, "Why won't the waiter take my order?" or

"Environmentalists are plain nuts!" We all like to know what's going on and we want others to agree with us. But the world often doesn't work this way. Accepting uncertainty and opposition makes us more mature and certainly healthier.

3. *Are you uneasy showing positive emotion?* Many men think giving and accepting love from women, from children, and from other men is a sign of weakness. But the research shows that love supports health and hate damages it. As human beings, we have a great deal of choice about how we live. Think about the choices you make, and reflect on how our society's idea of masculinity often makes us hard on others (including those we love) and—just as important—hard on ourselves.

Sources: Based on Friedman & Rosenman (1974) and Levine (1990).

---

rivers used for drinking water. By the early 20th century, the death rate from infectious diseases had fallen sharply.

Thus, leading killers in 1900—influenza and pneumonia—account for just a small percentage of deaths today in Canada. As Table 14–3 shows, it is now chronic illnesses, such as heart disease, stroke, and cancer, that cause most deaths in Canada. Nothing alters the inevitability of death, but high-income countries at least manage to delay death until old age (Edmondson, 1997a).

## HEALTH IN CANADA

Because Canada is a high-income nation, health is generally good by global standards. Still, some categories of people have much better health than others.

## WHO IS HEALTHY? AGE, GENDER, CLASS, AND RACE

**Social epidemiology** is *the study of how health and disease are distributed throughout a society's population*. Social epidemiologists examine the origin and spread of epidemic diseases and show how people's health is tied to their physical and social environments.

**Age and gender.** Death is now rare among young people. Still, the young do fall victim to accidents and, more recently, to acquired immune deficiency syndrome (AIDS). Across the life course, women have better health than men. First, females are less likely than males to die before or immediately after birth. Then, as socialization begins, males become more aggressive and individualistic, which results in a higher

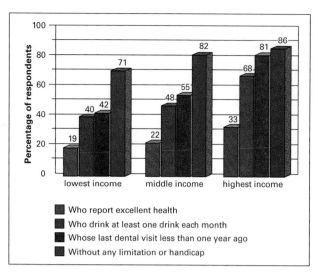

**FIGURE 14–3  Health Indicators by Income Group, Canada, 1996–1997**

**Note:** Lower middle- and higher middle-income groups omitted for clarity.

Source: Federal, Provincial and Territorial Advisory Committee on Population Health )1999).

rate of accidents, violence, and suicide. As the Social Diversity box on page 357 explains, the combination of chronic impatience, uncontrolled ambition, and frequent outbursts of hostility that doctors call "coronary-prone behaviour" closely matches our culture's definition of *masculinity*.

Canadian males have a 7.2-percent chance of dying violently, compared with 4.6 percent for females. Statistics Canada (2000g) reported that there were 555 homicides in Canada in 1998. The gender breakdown was 68 percent for men and 32 percent for women.

**Social class, ethnicity, and race.** Infant mortality—the death rate among newborns—is twice as high for Aboriginal children as for other Canadian children, and higher even than the infant mortality rates for children from the poorest neighbourhoods in urban pockets of the country. While children from our richest families have the best health in the world, children from our poorest families are as vulnerable to ill health as children in low-income countries. Figure 14–3 indicates the improvement in health associated with higher income—despite the higher incidence of alcohol consumption in the higher income groups.

Health, race, and ethnicity are also linked. As Figure 14–4 on page 360 shows, reported cases of tuberculosis are substantially higher for our foreign born and Aboriginal populations than for other Canadians.

Because Aboriginal Canadians are much more likely than other Canadians to be poor, they are more likely to die in infancy and to have shorter life expectancy. Studies show that life expectancy for Canada's Aboriginal population is five or more years less than that for the total Canadian population (Canadian Institute for Health Information, 2000). However, sex is an even stronger predictor of health than race, since Aboriginal women can expect to outlive males of either race (Statistics Canada, 2000m).

## CIGARETTE SMOKING

Cigarette smoking tops the list of preventable health hazards. Only after the First World War did smoking became popular in Canada, and despite growing evidence of its dangers, smoking remained fashionable even a generation ago. Today, however, most adults consider smoking a mild form of social deviance.

The popularity of cigarettes peaked in 1960, when almost 45 percent of Canadian adults smoked. By 1999, an estimated one-quarter of the population (6.1 million people) were smokers, a decrease from 30 percent in 1990 (Statistics Canada, 2000c). Quitting is difficult because cigarette smoke contains nicotine, a physically addictive drug. And many people smoke to cope with stress: Divorced and separated people are likely to smoke, as are the unemployed and people working in military services.

Generally speaking, the less schooling people have, the greater their chances of smoking. Moreover, a larger share of men (27 percent) than women (23 percent) smoked in 1999 (Statistics Canada, 2000c). But cigarettes—the only form of tobacco use to gain popularity among women—have taken a growing toll on women's health. By the early 1990s, lung cancer surpassed breast cancer as a cause of death among Canadian women.

In 1998, some 10 000 men and 6500 women died of lung cancer in Canada (Federal, Provincial and Territorial Advisory Committee on Population Health, 1999). Smokers also suffer more frequently from minor illnesses such as flu, and pregnant women who smoke increase the likelihood of spontaneous abortion, prenatal death, and low birth-weight babies. Even non-smokers exposed to cigarette smoke have a high risk of smoking-related diseases.

Tobacco is a billion-dollar industry in Canada. In 1997, the tobacco industry conceded that cigarette smoking is harmful to health, and agreed to stop marketing cigarettes to young people. But despite the anti-smoking trend in Canada, smoking among young adults (ages 20 to 24) remains very high: 39 percent for males and 29 percent for females. This was an increase for males in this age group from 1990 but a decrease for females over the same period (Federal, Provincial and Territorial Advisory Committee on Population Health, 1999). In addition, the use of chewing tobacco—also a threat to health—is increasing among the young.

Tobacco remains a billion-dollar business in Canada. The tobacco industry maintains that because the precise link between cigarettes and disease has not been specified, the health effects of smoking remain "an open question." But the tobacco industry is not breathing as easily today as it once did because laws mandating a smoke-free environment are spreading rapidly, and several jurisdictions—British Columbia most vocally—are contemplating following the U.S. lead of suing manufacturers for health care costs.

An unfortunate response to the anti-smoking trend in Canada and south of the border is that the tobacco industry has increased marketing abroad, where there is less regulation of sales and advertising (Scherer, 1996; Pollack, 1997). In many countries (especially in Asia) a large majority of men smoke. Worldwide, more than 1 billion adults (about 30 percent of the total) smoke, consuming some 6 trillion cigarettes annually—and smoking is on the rise. The good news is that about 10 years after quitting, an ex-smoker's health is about as good as that of someone who has never smoked at all.

## EATING DISORDERS

An *eating disorder* is an intense form of dieting or other unhealthy method of weight control. One eating disorder, anorexia nervosa, is characterized by dieting to the point of starvation; another is bulimia, which involves binge-eating followed by induced vomiting to avoid weight gain.

A clue to the fact that eating disorders have a significant cultural component is that 95 percent of people who suffer from anorexia nervosa or bulimia are women, mostly from white, affluent families. Only 5 percent of cases occur in males. The (Canadian) National Eating Disorders Information Centre estimates that anorexia nervosa occurs in approximately 1 to 2 percent of young women, and bulimia in approximately 2 to 3 percent of young women.

For women, Michael Levine (1987) explains, North American culture equates slenderness with being successful and attractive to men. On the flip side, we tend to stereotype overweight women (and, to a lesser extent, men) as "lazy," "sloppy," and even "stupid."

Research shows that most college- and university-age women believe (1) "guys like thin girls," (2) being thin is crucial to physical attractiveness, and (3) they are not as thin as men would like them to be. In fact, most college and university women want to be even thinner than most male fellow students say women should be. For their part, most men display far less dissatisfaction with their own body shape (Fallon & Rozin, 1985), though some research into young men has related body image dissatisfaction to unhealthy body-building practices, including the use of anabolic steroids (Canadian Centre for Drug-Free Sport, 1993).

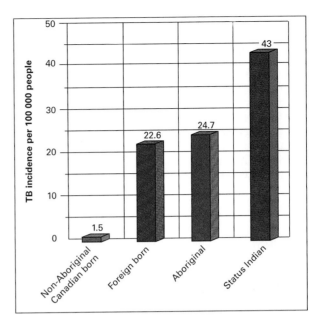

**FIGURE 14–4** **Reported Tuberculosis Cases, by Population Subgroup, Canada, 1996**

Source: Canadian Institute for Health Information (2000).

Since few women approach our culture's unrealistic standards of beauty, many develop a low self-image. Moreover, our idealized image of beauty leads many young women to diet to the point of risking their health.

## SEXUALLY TRANSMITTED DISEASES

Sexual activity, while both pleasurable and vital to the continuation of our species, can transmit more than 50 kinds of infection, or *venereal disease* (from Venus, the Roman goddess of love). Some people regard venereal diseases not only as illnesses but also as marks of immorality.

Sexually transmitted diseases (STDs) grabbed national attention during the "sexual revolution" of the 1960s, when infection rates rose as the result of people beginning sexual activity earlier and having a greater number of partners. As a result, STDs are an exception to the general decline in infectious diseases over the course of the past century. By the late 1980s, the rising danger of STDs, especially AIDS, generated a sexual counterrevolution against casual sex (Kain, 1987; Kain & Hart, 1987). The following sections briefly describe several common STDs.

**Gonorrhea and syphilis.** Gonorrhea and syphilis, among the oldest diseases known to humans, are caused by microscopic organisms that are almost always transmitted by sexual contact. Untreated, gonorrhea causes sterility, while syphilis can damage major organs and result in blindness, mental disorders, and death.

After a steady decline in gonorrhea rates since the early 1980s, there was an increase reported in 1998 (16.4 per 100 000), up from 14.9 per 100 000 in 1997 (Health Canada, 2000a). Syphilis rates have followed a similar pattern of significant decline over time, though there was an increase in 1996 due to an outbreak in Vancouver's downtown eastside. Both gonorrhea and syphilis can be easily cured with antibiotics such as penicillin. Thus, neither is currently a major health problem in Canada (Health Canada, 2000a).

**Genital herpes.** Genital herpes is not a reportable sexually transmitted disease in Canada. It is estimated, however, that the prevalence rate is in the range of the rate found in Sweden and the U.S. (Marc & Sacks, 1997). Though far less serious than gonorrhea and syphilis, herpes is incurable. People with genital herpes may exhibit no symptoms or they may experience periodic, painful blisters on the genitals accompanied by fever and headache. Although not fatal to adults, women with active genital herpes can transmit the disease during a vaginal delivery, and it can be deadly to newborns. Such women, therefore, are often forced to give birth by Caesarean section.

**AIDS.** The most serious of all sexually transmitted diseases is acquired immune deficiency syndrome, or AIDS. Identified in 1981, it is incurable and almost always fatal. AIDS is caused by the human immunodeficiency virus (HIV), which attacks white blood cells, weakening the immune system. AIDS thus renders a person vulnerable to a wide range of other diseases that eventually cause death.

By the beginning of 1998, a grand total of 15 528 cases of AIDS among Canadians had ever been reported to Health Canada. But because there is a considerable delay between the date when the illness is first diagnosed and the time this information reaches Health Canada, the figure is predicted to be revised to closer to 20 000. Even though 73 percent—11 000—of those who had ever been diagnosed with AIDS had died by 1998, the good news is that there has been a dramatic decrease in the number of new AIDS cases since 1995. This is good news because the decrease is partially attributable to the effectiveness of new treatment methods that delay or even may prevent HIV from causing AIDS. The Canadian incidence rate of just over 500 AIDS cases per 1 million Canadians means that our rate is only about a fifth of that in the U.S. (2400) but twice as high as that in Germany and the United Kingdom (Federal, Provincial and Territorial Advisory Committee on Population Health, 1999).

Globally, HIV infects some 40 million people—half of them under age 25—and the number is rising rapidly. Global Map 14–2 on page 363 shows that Africa (more specifically, countries south of the Sahara) has the highest HIV infection rate and accounts for two-thirds of all world cases. In the cities of African nations such as Zimbabwe, Botswana, Namibia, and Zambia, roughly one-fifth of all young adults are infected with HIV (Scommegna, 1996; United Nations Development Programme, 2000). It is in Asia, however, that this disease is spreading most quickly. North Americans account for less than 5 percent of global HIV cases.

Upon infection, people with HIV display no symptoms at all, so most are unaware of their condition. It takes one year or longer for AIDS symptoms to appear. Within 5 years, one-third of infected people develop full-blown AIDS; within 10 years, half develop it; and within 20 years, almost all become sick.

HIV is infectious but not contagious. That is, HIV is transmitted from person to person through blood, semen, or breast milk but *not* through casual contact such as shaking hands, hugging, sharing towels or dishes, swimming together, or even by coughing and sneezing. The risk of transmitting AIDS through saliva (as in kissing) is extremely low. Moreover, the risk of transmitting HIV through sexual activity is greatly reduced by the use of latex condoms. But in the age of AIDS, abstinence or an exclusive relationship with an uninfected person is the only sure way to avoid infection.

Specific behaviours place certain people at high risk for HIV infection. The first is *anal sex*, which can cause rectal bleeding, allowing easy transmission of HIV from one person to another. The practice of anal sex explains why men who have sex with men accounted for 50 percent of new AIDS cases in Canada in 1997 (Federal, Provincial and Territorial Advisory Committee on Population Health, 1999).

*Sharing needles* used to inject drugs is a second high-risk behaviour. Intravenous drug users accounted for 20 percent of new AIDS cases in 1997, a marked increase from 5 percent between in 1993 and less than 2 percent before 1990 (Federal, Provincial and Territorial Advisory Committee on Population Health, 1999). Sex with an intravenous drug user is also risky. Because intravenous drug use is more common among poor people in Canada, AIDS is now becoming a disease of the socially disadvantaged. Aboriginal people are doubly disadvantaged by poverty and race.

Using any drug, including alcohol, also increases the risk of being infected with HIV to the extent that it impairs judgment. In other words, even people who understand what places them at risk of infection may act less responsibly once they are under the influence of alcohol, marijuana, or some other drug.

While only about 7.2 percent of the people with AIDS in Canada in 1997 were women, there is an increasing trend toward positive HIV reports among heterosexuals (Health Canada, 1998). As Figure 14–5 shows, heterosexual activity does transmit HIV, and the danger rises with the number of sexual partners, especially if they fall into high-risk categories. In fact, worldwide, heterosexual relations are the primary means of HIV transmission, accounting for two-thirds of all infections.

Treating just one person with AIDS costs hundreds of thousands of dollars, and this figure may rise as new therapies appear. At present, government health programs, private insurance, and personal savings rarely cover more than a fraction of the cost of treatment. In addition, there is the mounting cost of caring for the children orphaned by AIDS. Overall, there is little doubt that AIDS represents both a medical and a social problem of monumental proportions.

The Canadian government responded slowly to the AIDS crisis, largely because gays and intravenous drug users are widely viewed as deviant. But funding allocated for AIDS research has increased, and researchers have identified some drugs, including protease inhibitors, that suppress the symptoms of the disease. But educational programs remain the most effective weapon against AIDS: prevention is the only way to stop a disease that has no cure.

## ETHICAL ISSUES SURROUNDING DEATH

Another new dimension of health and illness involves ethics. Now that technological advances have given human beings the power to draw the line separating life and death, people must decide how and when to do so.

**When does death occur?** Common sense suggests that life ceases when breathing and heartbeat stop. But the ability to revive or replace a heart and artificially sustain respiration makes this definition of death obsolete. Remember also that Erika—the toddler in Edmonton who wandered outside in March 2001 and was discovered frozen two hours later—had her heart restart spontaneously. Thus, medical and legal experts in North America define death as an *irreversible* state involving no response to stimulation, no movement or breathing, no reflexes, and no indication of brain activity (Ladd, 1979; Wall, 1980).

**Do people have a right to die?** Today, medical personnel, family members, and patients themselves bear the agonizing burden of deciding when a terminally ill person should die. Among the most difficult cases are people in a permanent vegetative state who cannot express their own desires about life and death. Generally speaking, the first duty of physicians and hospitals is to protect a patient's life. Even so, a mentally competent person in the process of dying can refuse medical treatment or even nutrition (either at

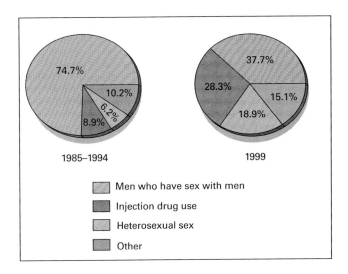

**FIGURE 14–5    Types of Transmission HIV/AIDS, Canada**

Based on those cases reporting exposure category.

Source: Health Canada (2000b).

the time or in advance, through a document called a "living will").

*Mercy killing* is the common term for **euthanasia,** *assisting in the death of a person suffering from an incurable disease.* Euthanasia (from the Greek, meaning "a good death") poses an ethical dilemma, being both an act of kindness and a form of killing.

Whether there is such a thing as a "right to die" is one of today's most difficult issues. All people with incurable diseases have a right to forgo treatment that might prolong their lives. But whether a doctor (or anyone else for that matter, including a parent) should be allowed to help bring about death is the heart of an ongoing debate. Though Parliament no longer views attempted suicide as a crime in Canada, it is still against the Criminal Code to *assist* a suicide. Still, many people in Canada are terminally ill, and some do express a wish for assistance to end their life. Such was the case for B.C. resident Sue Rodriguez, who in 1993 took her case all the way to the Supreme Court. The court did not rule in her favour, though Rodriguez ultimately got her wish through the assistance of an anonymous physician. A sympathetic B.C. member of Parliament, Svend Robinson, was also at her side. A special prosecutor later ruled against charging either party of wrongdoing.

Supporters of *active* euthanasia—allowing a dying person to enlist the services of a physician to bring on a quick death—argue that there are circumstances (such as when a dying person suffers from great pain) that make death preferable to life. Critics, however, counter that permitting active euthanasia invites abuse.

They fear that patients will feel pressure to end their lives to spare family members the burden of caring for them, and the high cost of hospitalization. Further, research in The Netherlands, where physician-assisted suicide is legal, indicates that about one-fifth of all such deaths have occurred without a patient explicitly requesting to die (Gillon, 1999).

In Canada, the Saskatchewan farmer Robert Latimer has been in and out of court for poisoning his disabled daughter, Tracey, in 1993. She had a severe case of cerebral palsy. In November 1998, the Saskatchewan Court of Appeal ruled that Latimer must return to prison to serve his life sentence, with no opportunity for parole for 10 years. Latimer's lawyers have since appealed the case to the Supreme Court of Canada but lost. Latimer is now back in jail, completing his sentence. The Canadian public remains torn over the case. The "right to die" debate is sure to continue.

# THE MEDICAL ESTABLISHMENT

Through most of human history, health care has been the responsibility of individuals and their families. Members of pre-industrial societies also turn to various health practitioners—including midwives, acupuncturists, and herbalists.

As a society industrializes, health care becomes the responsibility of specially trained and legally licensed healers. The medical establishment of modern, industrial societies took form over the past 150 years as healers and researchers applied the logic of science to their work.

## THE RISE OF SCIENTIFIC MEDICINE

In pre-Confederation Canada, herbalists, druggists, midwives, and ministers each practised various forms of the healing arts. But not all did so effectively: Unsanitary instruments, lack of anesthesia, and simple ignorance made surgery a terrible ordeal in which practitioners—including "learned physicians"—killed as many patients as they saved.

In 1795, in Upper Canada, the first *Medical Act* attempted to regulate the practices of "physic and surgery" by making it illegal for untrained healers to practise medicine without licences; only those with university degrees were exempted. The impracticality of the ruling soon became apparent, and the small degree-holding segment of the medical profession was left vulnerable to public critics. The original *Medical Act* was repealed in 1806, and traditional healers, including midwives, remained immune from the licensing laws of the Ontario Medical Board for the next half-century. In 1866, however, the government changed the law so that practitioners of midwifery and other healing arts, such as naturopathy, required medical degrees. As a result, by the time of Confederation in 1867, the predominantly male medical profession in the province enjoyed a legal monopoly over the birthing chamber (Benoit, 1998b). No female physicians were licensed in Ontario until the 1880s, and owing to continuing patriarchal traditions, few women entered this profession for many decades thereafter. Although some "traditionalist" physicians opposed this turn of events embraced by their "radical" colleagues, and called instead for formal training and legalization of lay healers, their efforts proved unsuccessful (Biggs, 1983).

The Canadian Medical Association (CMA), founded in 1867, also symbolized the growing acceptance of a scientific model of medicine. The CMA widely publicized the successes of its members in identifying the causes of life-threatening diseases—bacteria and viruses—and developing vaccines to prevent them. Still, other approaches to health care, such as regulating nutrition, also had defenders. But the CMA responded boldly—some thought arrogantly—to these alternative approaches, trumpeting the superiority of its practitioners.

The influential *Flexner Report* of 1910 highlighted the abysmal situation of Canadian (and U.S.) medical education, reporting that 90 percent of all physicians at the time received their training from profit-making schools that in many cases did not adequately train doctors. Abraham Flexner recommended the elimination of all "diploma mills," and the tightening of education and licensing standards for North American physicians. Traditional healers, as well as black and female physicians, became easy targets for the reformed medical profession.

The *Flexner Report* effectively led to the closing down of schools teaching other methods of healing (herbal medicine, homeopathy, and so on), limiting the practice of medicine to those with medical science degrees. These developments awarded medical doctors the primary role in the health care of the population, and gave social legitimacy to **scientific medicine**—*the social institution that focusses on combatting disease and improving health*. In the process, both the prestige and income of physicians rose dramatically; today, doctors are among the highest-paid workers in Canada.

Practitioners of other approaches, such as naturopathy, midwifery, and chiropractic medicine, for a short time continued to offer their traditional practices, but were then, and until very recently, relegated to the fringe of the medical profession. For example, chiropractic services have in the past decade gained partial coverage under some provincial health care systems, and even more recently, midwifery has gained coverage under the provincial health care systems of Ontario, British Columbia, Quebec, and Manitoba (DeVries et al., 2001).

Scientific medicine, taught in expensive, urban medical schools, also changed the social profile of

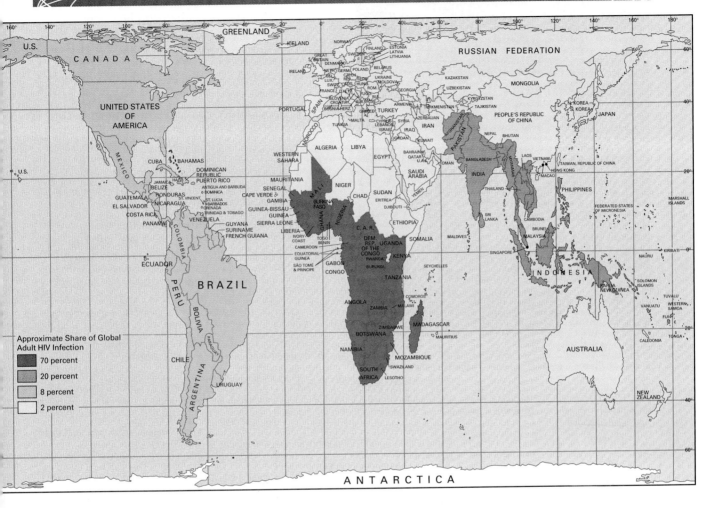

**GLOBAL MAP 14–2    HIV Infection of Adults in Global Perspective**

Almost 70 percent of all global HIV cases are recorded in sub-Saharan Africa. This high infection rate reflects the prevalence of other sexually transmitted diseases and infrequent use of condoms, factors that promote heterosexual transmission of HIV. Southeast Asia, where HIV is spreading most rapidly, accounts for another 20 percent of infections. South and North America together account for 8 percent of all cases. The incidence of infection is still low in the remaining regions of the world.

Sources: Population Reference Bureau (2000); map projection from *Peters Atlas of the World* (1990).

doctors. As the CMA standards took hold, more and more physicians came from privileged city backgrounds and, as a result, upon graduation chose to practise in cities. Furthermore, as mentioned above, women had figured prominently in many fields of healing denigrated by the CMA. Some early medical schools did train women, but, owing to the *Flexner Report* and declining financial resources, most of these schools soon closed. Only in recent decades have women increased their representation in the medical profes-

sion. In 1998, women accounted for 28 percent of Canada's practising physicians, up from 25 percent in 1993 (Canadian Institute for Health Information, 2000).

These female physicians in Canada, like their counterparts in most other high-income countries, remain clustered in the lower-ranking medical specialities, separated by a *glass ceiling* from their male colleagues in top administrative and specialty posts. Even in Finland, where more than half of all physicians are

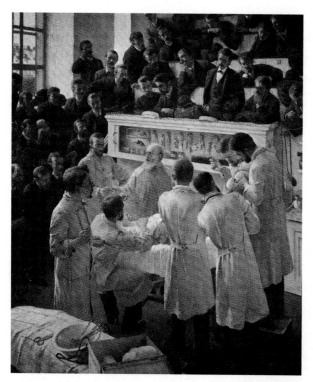

*The rise of scientific medicine during the 19th century resulted in new skills and technology for treating many common ailments that had afflicted humanity for centuries. At the same time, however, scientific medicine pushed forms of health care involving women to the margins, and placed medicine under the control of men living in cities. We see this pattern in the A.F. Seligmann painting* General Hospital, *showing an obviously all-male medical school class in Vienna in 1880.*

female, male physicians continue to view surgery as a male preserve. Gradually, however, they have opened the doors in medical administration and research to their female colleagues.

## HOLISTIC HEALTH

Recently, the scientific model of medicine has been tempered by the introduction of **holistic health,** *an approach to health care that emphasizes prevention of illness and takes into account a person's entire physical and social environment.* Alternative and complementary health practitioners—including massage therapists, Chinese and Aboriginal healers, homeopaths, chiropractors, and herbalists—agree on the need for drugs, surgery, artificial organs, and high technology, but they don't want high technology to turn medicine into narrow specialties concerned with symptoms rather than people, and with disease instead of health. Here are three foundations of holistic health care (Duhl, 1980; Ferguson, 1980; Gordon, 1980):

1. **Patients are people.** Alternative and complementary health practitioners are concerned not only with symptoms but with how people's environment and lifestyle affect health. These practitioners extend the bounds of conventional medicine, taking an active role in combatting poverty, environmental pollution, and other dangers to public health.

2. **Responsibility, not dependency.** In the scientific model, patients are dependent on physicians. Holistic health tries to shift some responsibility for health from physicians to people themselves by emphasizing health-promoting behaviour. Holistic health favours an *active* approach to *health*, rather than a *reactive* approach to *illness*.

3. **Personal treatment.** Scientific medicine treats patients in impersonal offices and hospitals, both settings where the disease and its symptoms are the focus. Alternative and complementary health practitioners favour, as much as possible, a personal and relaxed environment such as the home where the situation of the individual is taken into account.

In sum, holistic health does not oppose scientific medicine but shifts the emphasis from treating disease to achieving the greatest well-being for everyone. Considering that over the past few decades many Canadian provinces have decided to certify a number of alternative and complementary health practices, there is clearly a need for non-medical practitioners concerned with the "whole" patient.

## PAYING FOR HEALTH: A GLOBAL SURVEY

As medicine has come to rely on high technology, the cost of health care in high-income societies has skyrocketed. To meet these costs, various countries have adopted individual strategies.

**The People's Republic of China.** An agrarian society in the process of industrializing, the People's Republic of China faces the daunting task of providing for the health of more than 1 billion people. China has experimented with private medicine, but the government controls most health care.

China's "barefoot doctors," roughly comparable to Canadian paramedics, bring some modern methods of health care to peasants in rural villages. Traditional healing arts, involving acupuncture and medicinal herbs, are still widely practised. In addition, the Chinese approach to health is based on a holistic concern for the interplay of mind and body (Sidel & Sidel, 1982b; Kaptchuk, 1985).

Today, as China embraces a market economy, the country struggles to extend the formal social safety net

## When Health Fails: A Report from Russia

Night is falling in Pitkyaranta, a small town on the western edge of Russia, near the border with Finland. Andrei, a 30-year-old man with a round face and a long ponytail, weaves his way through the deepening shadows along a busy street. He has spent much of the afternoon in a bar with friends, watching music videos while drinking vodka and smoking cigarettes. Andrei is a railroad worker, but several months ago he was laid off. "Now," he explains bitterly, "I have nothing to do but drink and smoke." Andrei shrugs off a question about his health. "The only thing I care about is finding a job. I am a grown man. I don't want to be supported by my mother and father." Andrei still thinks of himself as young; yet, according to current health patterns in Russia, for a man of 30, life is more than half over.

After the collapse of the Soviet Union in 1991, living conditions began getting worse, year after year. One result, say doctors, is massive stress—especially on men who earn too little to

support their families or are out of work entirely. Few people eat well anymore, and rates of drinking and smoking among Russian men are among the highest in the world. The World Health Organization reports that alcohol abuse is Russia's number-one killer, with cigarette smoking not far behind.

In towns such as Pitkyaranta, the signs of poor health are everywhere:

Women no longer breast-feed their babies; the rate of accidents and illnesses among adults has soared; people look old before their time. Doctors are struggling to stop the health slide, but, with poorly equipped hospitals, they are simply overwhelmed. Statistically, while life expectancy dropped several years for women, men's went into free fall; some recent recovery has raised men's life expectancy to 61 years, about where it was half a century ago. Just 100 miles to the west, in Finland, where economic trends are far better, the comparable figure is 74 years. In global context, life expectancy for Russian women has fallen below that in other rich countries; for Russian men, life expectancy is only a little better than in some of the world's lowest-income nations.

A joke is making the rounds among young Russian men like Andrei. Their health may be failing, they say, but this cloud has a silver lining: At least they no longer have to worry about retirement.

Source: Adapted from Landsberg (1998).

---

beyond its urban pockets to include the rural labour force. Many among the increasing "floating population" of migrant workers heading for the urban areas are without any coverage at all (The World Bank, 1995).

**The Russian Federation.** The Russian Federation is struggling to transform a state-dominated economy into more of a market system. For this reason, health care is in transition. Nevertheless, the idea that everyone has a right to basic health care remains widespread. As in China, people in the Russian Federation do not choose a physician, but report to a local government health facility. Physicians have much lower income than their counterparts in Canada, earning about the same salary as skilled industrial workers (while Canadian physicians' salaries are roughly five times those of skilled industrial workers).

Funded by government taxes, health care in the Russian Federation has suffered setbacks in recent

years, partly due to a falling standard of living, as the Global Sociology box explains. Moreover, a rising demand for health care services has strained a bureaucratic system that, at best, provides highly standardized and impersonal care. The optimistic view is that as market reforms proceed, both living standards and the quality of health service will improve. In any case, what does seem certain is that disparities in medical care among various segments of the population will increase (Specter, 1995; Landsberg, 1998).

**Sweden.** In 1891, Sweden began a compulsory, comprehensive system of government health care. Typically, physicians, like nurses, midwives, and other health care workers, are government employees, and most health facilities are government-managed. Sweden's system is called **socialized health care**, *a health care system in which the government owns and operates most health care facilities and employs most physicians.*

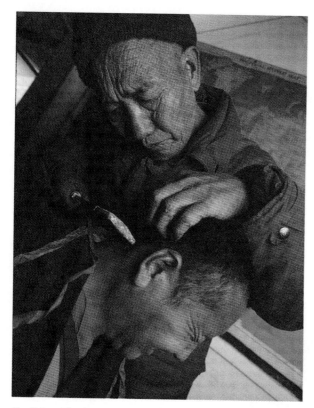

*Traditional healers work to improve people's health throughout the world, especially in low-income nations. Here, a Chinese practitioner treats a patient by burning rolled herbs into his scalp.*

Despite a strong government role, Sweden has a decentralized public health care system. Counties are responsible both for financing (through a high but progressive income tax on residents and with some central government economic support) and organizing health services for residents. Significantly, the Swedish health care system also has one of the highest ratios of nurses and midwives to citizens of any high-income country (Lassey et al., 1997:193). Figure 14–6 indicates the extent of socialized medicine in selected countries.

**The United States.** The United States is unique among high-income countries in having no universal, government-subsidized program of health care delivery. This is called a **direct-fee system**, *a health care system in which patients pay directly for the services of health providers (including physicians) and hospitals.* Thus, while Europeans look to government to fund 80 percent of medical costs, the U.S. government pays less than half of all medical costs (Lohr, 1988; U.S. Census Bureau, 1999).

In the United States, rich people can purchase the best health care in the world. Yet poor people fare worse than their counterparts in Europe. This disparity translates into relatively high death rates among both infants and adults in the United States compared to Canada and many European countries, even though that country spends more on health care, per person, than any other high-income nation (United Nations Development Programme, 2000).

Even though 84 percent of the U.S. population has some medical care coverage, most plans do not provide full coverage, so serious illness threatens even middle-class people with financial hardship. Worse, 44 million people (about 16 percent of the population) have no health insurance at all. Almost as many lose their coverage temporarily each year due to layoffs or job changes. Caught in the health care bind are mostly low- to moderate-income people: they cannot afford to become ill, but neither can they afford to pay for the care they need to stay healthy (Altman et al., 1989; Hersch & White-Means, 1993; Smith, 1993; U.S. Census Bureau, 1999).

## THE CANADIAN HEALTH CARE SYSTEM

Canada's "medicare" system is predominantly a publicly financed, privately delivered health care system. The system provides access to universal comprehensive coverage for hospital and in-patient and out-patient services that are deemed necessary by a physician. While the administration and delivery of health services is the responsibility of each individual province or territory, all areas of the country are expected to adhere to the national principles of universality, accessibility, portability, comprehensive coverage, and public administration.

Most Canadian physicians are private practitioners who work in independent or group practices and enjoy a high degree of autonomy. Private physicians are mainly paid on a fee-for-service basis and submit their service claims directly to the provincial health insurance plan for payment (Blishen, 1991; Segall & Chappell, 2000). Non-hospital dental care, many drugs, ambulance transport, private hospital beds, and other health services not covered by provincial health plans are either privately financed through employee benefit plans or paid for by individual Canadians. Such non-insured private health costs make up just under 30 percent of total health care costs (Canadian Institute for Health Information, 2000).

Health care in Canada is thus financed primarily by taxes. Under a new funding arrangement initiated in 1996–1997, the federal government's contribution to provincial health and social programs is now consolidated in a single block transfer, the Canada Health and Social Transfer. In 1999, total health expenditures (from personal and public sources) were 9.2 percent of Gross Domestic Product (GDP), a decrease from a peak in 1992 of 10.2 percent (Canadian Institute for Health Information, 2000). The new funding plan, along with recent provincial strategies to reform provincial health delivery systems, has stabilized public-sector spending—but escalated private-sector spending. The latter expanded by 5.5 percent in 1996, while public health expenditures declined by almost 1 percent.

Despite the many benefits of the Canadian health care system, there are problems that need addressing. Compared with the systems of other countries, including that of our neighbour to the south, the Canadian system makes less use of state-of-the-art technology. Some critics also point out that it responds slowly to people's needs, often requiring those facing major surgery to wait months for attention (Grant, 1984; Vayda & Deber, 1984; Rosenthal, 1991). Further, recent government cutbacks in health care funding have caused worry among Canadians that their much-admired health care system is in crisis. In fact, a recent Angus Reid poll (2000g) reported that Canadians think that health care is more important than all other issues on the Canadian agenda, including education, taxes, government, and unemployment.

## THEORETICAL ANALYSIS OF MEDICINE

Each of the theoretical paradigms in sociology helps us organize and understand facts and issues concerning human health.

### STRUCTURAL-FUNCTIONAL ANALYSIS

Talcott Parsons (1964; orig. 1951) viewed medicine as society's strategy to keep its members healthy. In this scheme, illness is dysfunctional because it reduces people's ability to perform their roles.

**The sick role.** Society responds to illness, Parsons argued, not only by providing physician-directed health care but also by affording people a **sick role,** *patterns of behaviour defined as appropriate for those who are ill.* Insofar as people suffer from poor health, the sick role exempts them from everyday responsibilities. However, people cannot simply declare themselves ill; this assessment falls to a recognized medical expert. Furthermore, upon assuming the sick role, the patient must do whatever is needed to regain good health, including cooperating with health professionals.

**The physicians' role.** Physicians evaluate people's claims of sickness and help restore the sick to normal routines. The physicians' role follows from their specialized knowledge; they expect patients to follow "doctor's orders" in order to complete treatment.

**Critical evaluation.** Parsons places illness and medicine within the broader organization of society. Others have extended the concept of the sick role to other situations such as pregnancy (Myers & Grasmick, 1989).

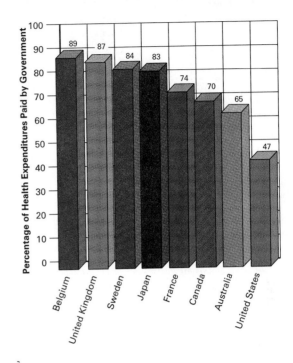

**FIGURE 14–6    Extent of "Socialized Medicine" in Selected Countries**

Source: The World Bank (2000).

One limitation of the sick role is that it applies to acute conditions (such as the flu) better than it does to chronic illness (such as heart disease), which may not be reversible. Moreover, a sick person's ability to take time off from work to regain health depends on the person's available resources.

### SYMBOLIC-INTERACTION ANALYSIS

According to the symbolic-interaction paradigm, society is less a grand system than a series of complex and changing realities. Health care, therefore, is socially constructed by people in everyday interaction.

**Socially constructing illness.** If we socially construct both health and illness, it follows that people in a poor society may view malnutrition as normal. Similarly, members of our own society give little thought to the harmful effects of a rich diet.

How we respond to illness, too, is based on social definitions that may or may not square with medical facts. For instance, people with AIDS may contend with prejudice that has no health basis. Likewise, students

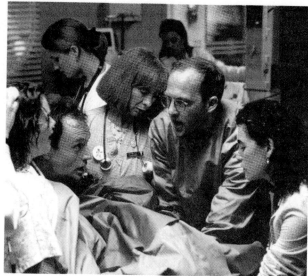

Our national view of health care has changed during the past several decades. Television viewers in the 1970s watched doctors such as Marcus Welby, M.D., confidently take charge of situations in a fatherly—and almost godlike—manner. By the 1990s, programs such as E.R. gave a more realistic view of the limitations of medicine to address illness, as well as the violence in our society.

may pay no attention to symptoms of illness on the eve of vacation, but dutifully report to the infirmary hours before a midterm examination. Health, in short, is less an objective fact than a negotiated outcome.

Indeed, how people define a health crisis may actually affect how they feel. Experts marvel at *psychosomatic* disorders (a fusion of the Greek words for "mind" and "body"), when state of mind guides physical sensations (Hamrick, Anspaugh, & Ezell, 1986). Applying sociologist W.I. Thomas's theorem (1966; orig. 1931), we can say that when health or illness is defined as real, it becomes real in its consequences.

**Socially constructing treatment.** In Chapter 4 (Social Interaction in Everyday Life), we used Erving Goffman's dramaturgical approach to explain how physicians tailor their physical surroundings (their office) and their behaviour (the "presentation of self") so that others see them as competent and in charge. Sociologist Joan Emerson (1970) further illustrates this process of reality construction in her analysis of the gynecological examination carried out by a male doctor. The situation is vulnerable to serious misinterpretation, since a man's touching a woman's genitals is conventionally viewed as a sexual act and possibly even an assault.

To ensure that the situation is defined as impersonal and professional, the health care staff wear uniforms, and the examination room is furnished with nothing but medical equipment. The doctor's manner is designed to make the patient feel that, to him [the gender of the physician in Emerson's research and the

norm of the time], examining the genital area is no different from treating any other part of the body. A female nurse is usually present during the examination not only to assist the physician, but to dispel any impression that a man and woman are "alone together."

The ability to manage situational definitions is not taught in medical schools. This is unfortunate because, as Emerson's analysis shows, understanding how medical personnel construct reality in the examination room is as important as mastering the medical skills required for effective treatment.

**Critical evaluation.** The symbolic-interaction paradigm reveals that what people view as healthful or harmful depends on a host of factors that are not, strictly speaking, medical. This approach also shows that in any medical procedure both patient and health care staff engage in a subtle process of reality construction.

Critics fault this approach for implying that there are no objective standards of well-being. Certain physical conditions do indeed cause specific changes in people, regardless of how we may view those conditions. People who lack sufficient nutrition and safe water, for example, suffer from their unhealthy environment, whether or not they define their surroundings as normal.

## SOCIAL-CONFLICT ANALYSIS

Social-conflict analysis points out the connection between health and social inequality and, taking a cue from Karl Marx, ties health care to the operation of capitalism. Researchers have focussed on three main issues: access to adequate health care, the effects of the profit motive, and the politics of health and medicine.

**Access to care.** Health is important to everyone. But by making health a commodity, capitalist societies allow health to follow wealth. As already noted, the access problem is more serious in the United States than in Canada. Yet even in our own country, as noted above, low-income people and Aboriginals are at a greater risk of mortality at birth and illness throughout their life cycle than are their better-off counterparts. Conflict theorists claim that while capitalism does provide excellent health care for the rich, it simply does not provide very well for the rest of the population.

**The profit motive.** Some social-conflict analysts go further, arguing that the real problem is not access to medical care but the character of capitalist medicine itself. The profit motive turns physicians, hospitals, and the pharmaceutical industry into multibillion-dollar corporate conglomerates. The quest for ever-increasing profits encourages unnecessary tests and surgery, and an over-reliance on drugs (Ehrenreich, 1978; Kaplan et al., 1985).

Most surgical operations performed in Canada each year are "elective," meaning that they are intended to promote long-term health rather than being prompted by a medical emergency. Social-conflict theorists charge that the decision to perform surgery reflects the financial interests of surgeons and hospitals, as well as the medical needs of patients (Illich, 1976). And, of course, any drugs or medical procedures subject patients to various risks, harming between 5 and 10 percent of them (Sidel & Sidel, 1982a; Cowley, 1995).

Finally, say conflict theorists, our society is all too tolerant of physicians having a direct financial interest in the tests and procedures they order for their patients (Pear & Eckholm, 1991). In short, health care should be motivated by a concern for people, not profits.

**Medicine as politics.** Although science declares itself to be politically neutral, scientific medicine frequently takes sides on significant social issues. For example, throughout most of this century, the Canadian medical establishment has mounted a strong and sustained campaign against the legalization and public funding of midwives—despite the fact that the World Health Organization recommends midwives as essential health care providers for women. The history of medicine, conflict theorists contend, is replete with sexual and racial discrimination justified by "scientific" facts (Leavitt, 1984). Consider the diagnosis of "hysteria," a term that has its origins in the Greek word *hyster*, meaning "uterus." In coining this word, medical professionals suggested that being a woman is somehow synonymous with being sick or crazy.

Even today, according to conflict theorists, scientific medicine explains illness in terms of bacteria and viruses rather than pointing up the damaging effects on health of social inequality. In this way, scientific medicine depoliticizes health in Canada by reducing social issues to simple biology.

**Critical evaluation.** Social-conflict analysis provides still another view of the relationships among health, medicine, and society. According to this paradigm, social inequality is the reason some people have better health than others.

The most common objection to the conflict approach is that it minimizes the advances in Canadian health that can be credited to scientific medicine and higher living standards. Though there is plenty of room for improvement, health indicators for our population as a whole rose steadily over the course of the 20th century, and we compare well on most measures with other high-income societies (Canadian Institute for Health Information, 2000).

In sum, sociology's three major theoretical paradigms explain why health and medicine are social issues. Indeed, as the Controversy & Debate box on page 370 explains, advancing technology has made this truer today than ever before. The famous French scientist Louis Pasteur (1822–1895), who spent much of his life studying how bacteria cause disease, said just before he died that health depends less on bacteria than on the social environment in which bacteria operate (Gordon, 1980:7). Explaining Pasteur's insight is sociology's contribution to human health.

## LOOKING AHEAD: HEALTH IN THE TWENTY-FIRST CENTURY

At the beginning of the 20th century, deaths from infectious diseases such as diphtheria and measles were widespread, and scientists had yet to develop penicillin and other antibiotics. Even a simple infection from a minor wound, therefore, was sometimes life threatening. Today, a century later, most members of our society take good health and long life for granted. It seems reasonable to expect improvements in Canadian health to continue throughout this new century.

Another encouraging trend is that more people are taking responsibility for their own health (Caplow et al., 1991; Segall & Chappell, 2000). Every one of us can live better and longer if we avoid tobacco, eat sensibly and in moderation, and exercise regularly.

Yet health problems will continue to plague Canadian society in the decades to come. The changing social profile of people with AIDS—which increasingly afflicts youth, the poor, and the marginalized—reminds us that Canada has much to do to improve the health of disadvantaged members of our society. Even

# The Genetic Crystal Ball: Do We Really Want to Look?

The liquid in the laboratory test tube seems ordinary enough, rather like a syrupy form of water. But this liquid is one of the greatest medical breakthroughs of all time; it may even hold the key to life itself. The liquid is deoxyribonucleic acid, or DNA, the spiralling molecule, found in every cell of the human body, that contains the blueprint for making each one of us human as well as different from every other person. The human body is composed of some 100 trillion cells, most of which contain a nucleus of 23 pairs of chromosomes (one of each pair comes from each parent). Each chromosome is packed with DNA in segments called genes. Genes guide the production of protein, the building block of the human body. If genetics sounds complicated (and it is), the social implications of genetic knowledge are even more complex. Scientists discovered the structure of the DNA molecule in 1952, and, in 2000, scientists reported that they had finally "mapped" our genetic landscape. Doing this may lead to understanding how each bit of DNA shapes our being. But do we really want to turn the key, to understand life itself?

In the Human Genome Project, many scientists see the chance to stop illness before it begins. Research, they point out, already has identified genetic abnormalities that cause some forms of cancer, sickle cell anemia, muscular dystrophy, Huntington's disease, cystic fibrosis, and other crippling and deadly afflictions. In the 21st century, genetic screening—a scientific "crystal ball"—could tell people their medical destiny and allow doctors to manipulate segments of DNA to prevent diseases before they appear.

But many people urge caution in such research, warning that genetic information can easily be abused. At its worst, genetic mapping opens the door to Nazi-like efforts to breed a "super-race." It seems inevitable that some parents will want to use genetic testing in order to predict the health (or even the eye colour) of their future child. What if they wish to abort a fetus because it falls short of their standards? Or, later, when genetic manipulations become possible, should parents be able to create "designer children"?

*Scientists are learning more and more about the genetic factors that prompt the eventual development of serious diseases. If offered the opportunity, would you want to undergo a genetic screening that would predict the long-term future of your own health?*

Then there is the issue of "genetic privacy." Can life insurance companies demand genetic testing before issuing policies? Can an employer screen job applicants to weed out those whose future illnesses might drain their health care funds? Clearly, what is scientifically possible is not always morally desirable. Society is already grappling with questions about the proper use of our expanding knowledge of human genetics. Such ethical dilemmas will only mount as genetic research moves forward.

*Continue the debate . . .*

1. *Traditional wedding vows join couples "in sickness and in health." Do you think individuals have a right to know the future health of their potential partner before tying the knot?*

2. *What about the desire of some parents to genetically design their children?*

3. *Is it right that private companies doing genetic work are able to patent their discoveries so that they alone can profit from the results?*

4. *Scientists are learning more and more about the genetic factors that prompt the eventual development of serious diseases. If offered the opportunity, would you want to undergo a genetic screening that would predict the long-term future of your own health?*

Sources: Elmer-Dewitt (1994a), L. Thompson (1994), Nash (1995), Golden (1999a), and D. Thompson (1999).

those among us who do not easily embrace the notion of serving as "our brother's keeper" should recognize our moral obligation to guarantee everyone the security of health care.

Finally, we find that health problems are far greater in low-income nations than in Canada. The good news is that life expectancy for the world as a whole has been rising—from 48 years in 1950 to 66 years today—and the biggest gains have been in low-income countries (Population Reference Bureau, 2000). But in much of Latin America, Asia, and especially Africa, hundreds of millions of adults and children lack not only access to health care services but even adequate food and safe water. Improving the health of the world's poorest people is a critical challenge in the 21st century.

# SUMMARY

## EDUCATION

1. Education is a major social institution for transmitting knowledge and skills as well as passing on norms and values. In pre-industrial societies, education occurs informally within the family; industrial societies develop formal systems of schooling.

2. Canada was among the first nations to institute compulsory mass public education, reflecting both democratic political ideals and the needs of an industrial-capitalist economy.

3. The structural-functional paradigm highlights the functions of schooling, including socialization, social placement, social integration, and innovation. Latent functions include child care and building social networks.

4. Social-conflict analysis links schooling to social hierarchies involving class, race, and gender. Formal education is seen as generating conformity in order to produce compliant adult workers.

5. The great majority of young people in Canada attend public-funded public schools. A small proportion of young people—generally the well-to-do—attend elite private schools.

6. Almost half of Canadian adults over the age of 25 hold post-secondary degrees or diplomas, marking the emergence of a credential society.

7. National opinion is critical of public schools. Violence permeates some Canadian schools, and educational bureaucracy fosters high dropout rates and widespread student passivity. Declining achievement test scores point to a slide in academic standards.

8. The school choice movement seeks to make educational systems more responsive to the public they serve.

## HEALTH

1. Health is a social issue because well-being depends on a society's technology and distribution of resources. Culture shapes definitions of health and patterns of health care.

2. Low-income nations suffer from inadequate sanitation, hunger, and other problems linked to poverty. Life expectancy is about 20 years less than in Canada; in some low-income countries half the children do not survive to adulthood.

3. Health improved dramatically in Western Europe and North America in the 19th century, first due to industrialization and later because of medical advances.

4. Infectious diseases were leading killers a century ago. Today, most people in Canada die in old age of chronic illnesses such as heart disease, cancer, or stroke.

5. More than three-fourths of Canadian children born today can expect to reach age 65. Throughout the life course, women have relatively better health than men, and people of high social position enjoy better health than others.

6. Cigarette smoking is the greatest preventable cause of death in Canada.

7. The incidence of sexually transmitted diseases has risen since 1960, an exception to the general decline in infectious disease.

8. Holistic health encourages people to assume greater responsibility for their own health, and encourages alternative and complementary healers to gain personal knowledge of patients and their environments.

9. Historically a family concern, health care is now the responsibility of trained specialists. The model of scientific medicine underlies the Canadian medical establishment. The holistic health approach seeks to give people greater responsibility for their own health.

10. Socialist societies define medical care as a right that governments offer equally to everyone. Yet strongly capitalist-oriented societies view health care as a commodity to be purchased. On the other hand, most capitalist governments (the United States being a significant exception) subsidize health care through socialized medicine or national health insurance.

11. Central to the structural-functional analysis of health is the concept of the sick role, which releases sick people from routine responsibilities. The symbolic-interaction paradigm investigates the social construction of both health and medical treatment. Social-conflict analysis focusses on unequal access to health care and criticizes our medical system for its profit orientation.

# KEY CONCEPTS

## EDUCATION

**education** (p. 343) the social institution through which society provides its members with important knowledge, including basic facts and job skills as well as cultural norms and values

**schooling** (p. 344) formal instruction under the direction of trained teachers

**streaming** or **tracking** (p. 348) the assignment of students to different types of educational programs

**credentialism** (p. 351) evaluating a person on the basis of educational degrees

**functional illiteracy** (p. 354) a lack of reading and writing skills needed for everyday living

## HEALTH

**medicine** (p. 355) the social institution that focusses on combatting disease and improving health

**health** (p. 355) a state of complete physical, mental, and social well-being

**social epidemiology** (p. 357) the study of how health and disease are distributed throughout a society's population

**euthanasia** (p. 361) (mercy killing) assisting in the death of a person suffering from an incurable illness

**scientific medicine** (p. 362) the social institution that focusses on combatting disease and improving health

**holistic health** (p. 364) an approach to health care that emphasizes prevention of illness and takes into account a person's entire physical and social environment

**socialized health care** (p. 365) a health care system in which the government owns and operates most medical facilities and employs most physicians.

**direct-fee system** (p. 366) a health care system in which patients pay directly for the services of physicians and hospitals

**sick role** (p. 367) patterns of behaviour defined as appropriate for those who are ill

# CRITICAL-THINKING QUESTIONS

1. Why does industrialization lead societies to expand their system of schooling?

2. Do you agree with research findings in this chapter that, by and large, college and university students are passive in class? How might students become more active participants in learning?

3. Explain why health is as much a social issue as a biological one.

4. Can you point to ways in which people can take responsibility for their own health? What traits of society as a whole shape patterns of health?

## APPLICATIONS AND EXERCISES

1. Arrange to visit a high school near your current school. Talk with an administrator to assess the extent of "tracking" the school uses. What seems to be the racial/economic/social background of most students in the higher-level and lower-level classes?

2. Most people agree that teaching our children is a vital task. Yet most teachers earn relatively low salaries. Check the prestige ranking for teachers back in Table 8–3 on page 192. What can you find out at the library (check with the government documents librarian) about the average salaries of teachers compared to other workers? Can you explain this pattern?

3. Arrange to speak with a midwife about her work helping women bear their babies. How do midwives differ in their approach from medical obstetricians?

4. In most communities, a trip to the cemetery is all it takes to see changes in mortality over time. Take a look at the headstones for people who lived in your community a century ago, and for more recent residents. What patterns in life expectancy emerge? How do you think the causes of death differ?

 ## SITES TO SEE

**www.pearsoned.ca/macionis**

Visit the interactive Web site that accompanies this text. Begin by clicking on the cover of your book. You will find a chapter-by-chapter study guide, practice tests, chat room, and many suggested Web links.

**www.nces.ed.gov/pubs98/violence/index.html**

School violence is the focus of this government Web site.

**www.chronicle.com**

This site provides general news and information about higher education.

**www.cdc.gov**

The Web site for the Centres for Disease Control and Prevention provides health news, statistical data, and even traveller's health advisories.

**www.who.int/**

The World Health Organization provides health indicators for many of the world's nations, as well as data profiling the health of the Canadian population.

**www.unaids.org**

Up-to-date information about the global AIDS epidemic can be found at this site, operated by the United Nations.

**www.doctorsoftheworld.org**
**www.imc-la.org**
**www.dwb.org**

Here are Web sites for several organizations of physicians involved in improving health around the world. The first is operated by Doctors of the World; the second presents the International Medical Corps; and the third profiles Doctors Without Borders.

**www.ph.ucla.edu/epi/snow.html**
**www.sph.unc.edu/courses/course_support/ case_studies/JohnSnow/episode1.htm**

Take a look at these sites at two schools of public health to learn a little about John Snow and epidemiology. These two sites offer examples of learning using the Internet. The first is an improvement over the straight text-based course in that there is audio added—you can listen to a person reading the material. This site is at University of North Carolina.

**stanford-online.stanford.edu/engelbart/**

This Stanford University site shows four hours of live video from a conference around the revolutionary ideas that Doug Engelbart sprung upon the world in 1968: the computer mouse, computer networks, and context-sensitive help— ideas that we take for granted today. While you are at this site, consider the possibility of delivering entire courses using this format.

# POPULATION, URBANIZATION, AND ENVIRONMENT

Pono Presse Internationale/Leopold Kram

*Two hundred years ago, Captain Vancouver first charted the Burrard Inlet. One hundred years later, Vancouver was home to fewer than 50 000 people. Today, with a population of more than 2 million, and as the city has expanded outward, commuting for an hour to work is commonplace.*

*Growth like this prompted experts to coin the term "urban sprawl." Such uncontrolled growth is the result of more and more people, all of whom want bigger houses, as well as the conveniences offered by roads, schools, recreation facilities, and, of course, superstores and shopping malls. No doubt, most people in Canada see growth like this as good—the product of prosperity.* ■

But is it that simple? This chapter examines three closely related processes: population increase, urbanization, and the state of the natural environment. As we shall see, population has soared during the past two centuries—in Canada but also around the world—and cities everywhere have grown rapidly. We shall consider how these changes have altered the shape of societies and what they mean for the future of the planet. We begin with population.

# DEMOGRAPHY: THE STUDY OF POPULATION

From the time people first walked the earth some 250 000 years ago until just 250 years ago, the earth's population was about 500 million—about the number of people in Europe today. Life for our ancestors was often short; people fell victim to diseases, frequent injury, and periodic natural disasters.

But about the year 1750, world population began to spike upward. We now add about 80 million people to the planet each year. In 1999, the number of people living on the earth passed the 6-billion mark.

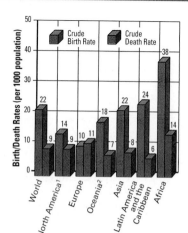

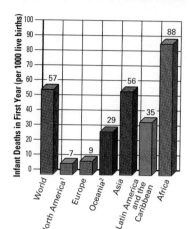

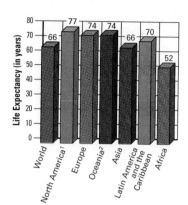

**FIGURE 15–1  Crude Birth Rates and Crude Death Rates, Infant Mortality Rates, and Life Expectancy, 2000**

[1] Canada and the United States

[2] Australia, New Zealand, and South Pacific Islands

Source: Population Reference Bureau (2000).

The causes and consequences of this drama are the focus of **demography**, *the study of human population.* Demography (from the Greek, meaning "description of people") is a specialty within sociology that analyzes the size and composition of a population and studies how people move from place to place. Demographers not only collect statistics, but also pose important questions about the effects of population growth and how population might be controlled. The following sections present basic demographic concepts.

## FERTILITY

The study of human population begins with how many people are born. **Fertility** is *the incidence of childbearing in a country's population.* During her childbearing years, from the onset of menstruation (typically in the early teens) to menopause (usually in the late forties), a woman is capable of bearing more than 20 children. But *fecundity*, or maximum possible childbearing, is sharply reduced by cultural norms, economic factors, and, in some societies, personal choice.

Demographers gauge fertility using the **crude birth rate**, *the number of live births in a given year for every 1000 people in a population.* To calculate a crude birth rate, divide the number of live births in a year by the society's total population and multiply the result by 1000. Canada's population on January 1, 2000, was 30.6 million. During the period July 1, 1999 to July 1, 2000, there were 334 000 births (Statistics Canada, 2000l; 2000r). That yields a crude birth rate of 10.9.

This birth rate is "crude" because it is based on the entire population—not just on women in their childbearing years. Comparing crude birth rates for various countries can be misleading, then, if one society has a larger share of women of childbearing age than another. A crude birth rate also ignores differences among various racial and ethnic categories. But this is easy to calculate and gives a good measure of a society's overall fertility. Figure 15–1 shows that, in global perspective, the crude birth rate of North Americans is low.

## MORTALITY

Population size also reflects **mortality**, *the incidence of death in a country's population.* To measure mortality, demographers use a **crude death rate**, *the number of deaths in a given year for every 1000 people in a population.* This time, we take the number of deaths in a year, divide by the total population, and multiply the result by 1000. Between July 1, 1999 and July 1, 2000, there were 229 000 deaths in the Canadian population of 30.6 million, yielding a crude death rate of 7.5. (Statistics Canada, 2000p). As Figure 15–1 shows, in global context this rate is about average.

A third useful demographic measure is the **infant mortality rate**, *the number of deaths among infants under one year of age for each 1000 live births in a given year.* To compute infant mortality, divide the number of deaths of children under one year of age by the number of live births during the same year and multiply the result by 1000. During the 12 months before July 1, 2000, there

*Migration is sometimes involuntary, and sometimes voluntary, as in the case of the many Albertans who left the Prairie dustbowl in the 1930s.*

were 1877 infant deaths and 334 000 births in Canada (Statistics Canada, 2000q; 2000r). Dividing the first number by the second and multiplying the result by 1000 yields an infant mortality rate of 5.6. The second part of Figure 15–1 indicates that, by world standards, North American infant mortality is low.

But remember the differences among various categories of people. For example, Aboriginals, who are twice as likely as non-Aboriginals to live below the poverty line, have an infant mortality rate almost twice as high as the national rate (Federal, Provincial, and Territorial Advisory Committee on Population Health, 1996).

Low infant mortality greatly raises **life expectancy**, *a synthetic measure of the average life span of a society's population.* Canadian males born in 1996 can expect to live 75.7 years, while females can look toward 81.4 years if the mortality rates observed in 1996 continue (Statistics Canada, 1998h). As the third part of Figure 15–1 shows, life expectancy for North Americans is more than 20 years greater than that typical of people living in low-income countries in Africa.

## MIGRATION

Population size is also affected by **migration**, *the movement of people into and out of a specified territory.* Migration is sometimes involuntary, such as the forcible transport of 10 million Africans to the Western Hemisphere as slaves during the early colonial period. Voluntary migration, however, usually results from several "push–pull" factors. Dissatisfaction with life on reserves may "push" Aboriginal peoples to move, while the opportunity for a better life may "pull" them to the city.

Movement into a nation—or *immigration*—is measured as an *immigration rate,* calculated as the number of people entering an area for every 1000 people in the population. Movement out of a nation—or *emigration*—

is measured in terms of an *emigration rate*, the number leaving for every 1000 people. Both types of migration usually occur at once; the difference is the *net migration rate.*

All nations also experience internal migration—that is, movement within their borders, from one region to another. We use the terms *in-migration* and *out-migration* to describe this movement. National Map 15–1 on page 378 shows where the Canadian population is moving, and the places left behind.

## POPULATION GROWTH

Fertility, mortality, and migration all affect the size of a society's population. In general, high-income nations (such as Canada) grow almost as much from immigration as from natural increase—51 percent of Canada's growth between the census years 1991 and 1996 came from migration—and low-income nations (such as India) grow almost entirely from natural increase.

To calculate a population's natural growth rate, demographers subtract the crude death rate from the crude birth rate. The natural growth rate of the Canadian population at the start of 2000 was 3.4 per 1000 (the crude birth rate of 10.9 minus the crude death rate of 7.5), or about 0.34 percent annual growth.

Global Map 15–1 on page 379 shows that population growth in Canada and other high-income countries is well below the world average of 1.4 percent. The earth's low-growth continents are Europe (currently posting a slight decline: expressed as –0.1 percent annual growth), North America (0.6 percent), and Oceania (1.1 percent). Close to the global average are Asia (1.5 percent) and Latin America (1.8 percent). The highest growth region of the world is Africa (2.5 percent).

A handy rule-of-thumb for estimating population growth is to divide a society's population growth rate

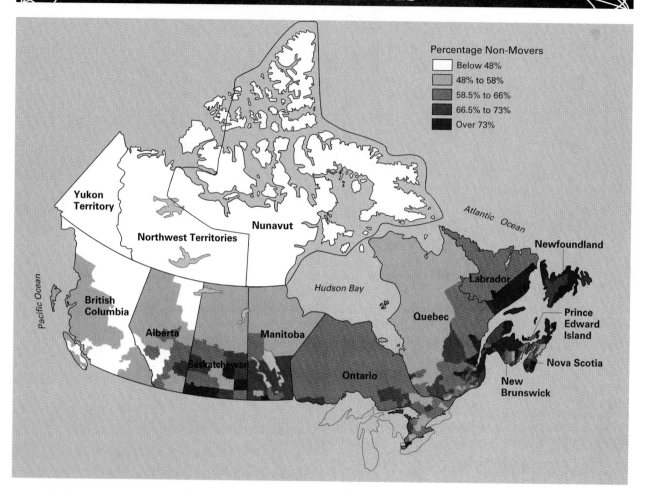

**NATIONAL MAP 15–1    Population Movement, Canada, 1991–1996**

The map shows the percentage of the population with the same address in 1996 as in 1991. Therefore, people living in the dark areas had not changed residence recently, nor had these areas received many migrants. In the light areas, on the other hand, either people had changed residence or these areas had received relatively many migrants. Overall, about 11.5 million Canadians had arrived at their 1996 address during the previous five years—6 million had moved within the same census subdivision, 3.5 million had moved within the province, 890 000 had moved between provinces, and 928 000 had immigrated. Based on this map, can you draw any conclusions about population movement in the early 1990s? Can you offer a demographic profile of the people who lived in the darker census divisions?

Source: Based on Statistics Canada, Catalogue No. 95F0181XDB96001 (1998b).

into the number 70 to calculate the *doubling time* in years. Thus, an annual growth of 2 percent (common in Latin America) doubles a population in 35 years, and a 3-percent growth rate (found in some African countries) drops the doubling time to just 24 years. The rapid population growth of the poorest countries is deeply troubling because they can barely support the populations they have now.

**POPULATION COMPOSITION**

Demographers also study the makeup of a society's population at a given point in time. One variable is the **sex ratio**, *the number of males for every 100 females in a given population*. In 1999 the sex ratio in Canada was 98, or 98 males for every 100 females (Statistics Canada, 2000a). Even though there are more males

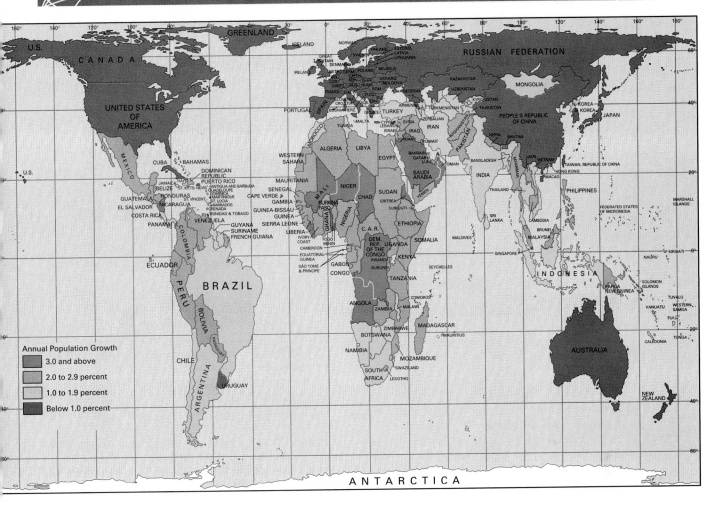

**GLOBAL MAP 15–1   Population Growth in Global Perspective**

The richest countries of the world—including Canada, and the United States, and the nations of Europe—have growth rates below 1 percent. The nations of Latin America and Asia typically have growth rates around 1.6 percent, which double a population in 44 years. Africa has an overall growth rate of 2.4 percent, which cuts the doubling time to 29 years. In global perspective, we see that a society's standard of living is closely related to its rate of population growth: Population is rising fastest in the world regions that can least afford to support more people.

Source: Population Reference Bureau (2000); map projection from *Peters Atlas of the World* (1990).

than females at birth, sex ratios are usually below 100 because, on average, women outlive men. In India, however, the sex ratio is 107, because parents value sons more than daughters and may either abort a female fetus, or, after birth, give more care to a male infant, raising the odds that a female child will die.

A more complex measure is the **age-sex pyramid**, *a graphic representation of the age and sex of a population.*

Figure 15–2 on page 380 presents the age-sex pyramids for the populations of Canada and Mexico. When these graphs were first developed, the number of births increased from year to year resulting in a roughly pyramid shape—hence the name. More recently, the number of births in many high-income countries has declined. For these nations, the population pyramid has a narrow base, as the Canadian pyramid illustrates.

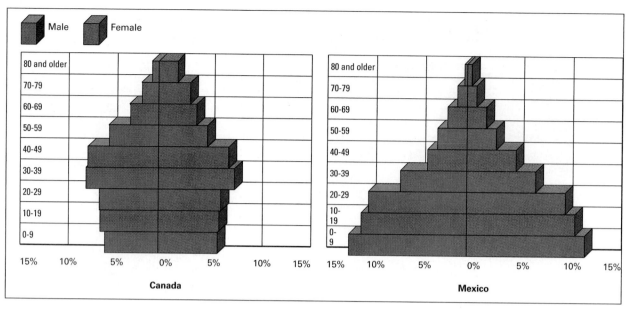

**FIGURE 15–2    Age–Sex Population Pyramids of Canada and Mexico, 2000.**

Source: Statistics Canada (2000a) and U.S. Census Bureau (2001) .

The bulge corresponding to ages 30 through the mid-50s reflects the high birth rates during the *baby boom* from the mid-1940s to the mid-1960s. The contraction just below—that is, people under age 30—reflects the subsequent *baby bust*, when the number of births declined from a high of 479 000 in 1959 to 343 000 in 1973.

Comparison of the Canadian and Mexican age-sex pyramids shows different demographic trends. The age-sex pyramid for Mexico, like that of other low-income nations, is wide at the bottom because the number of births increases every year. Mexico, in short, is a much younger society, with a median age of 20 compared to 36 in Canada. With a larger share of females still in their childbearing years, therefore, Mexico's crude birth rate (27) is, understandably, considerably higher than our own (10.9), and its annual rate of natural growth (1.8 percent) is more than five times the Canadian rate (0.34 percent).  This illustrates what demographers call *demographic momentum*—even with a sharp reduction in *fertility rates*, the large number of people in their childbearing years ensures a large *number of births*.

## HISTORY AND THEORY OF POPULATION GROWTH

In the past, people favoured large families since human labour was the key to productivity. Moreover, until rubber condoms appeared 150 years ago, preventing pregnancy was an uncertain proposition at best. But high death rates from widespread infectious diseases put a constant brake on population growth.

A major demographic shift (as shown in Figure 15–3), began about 1750 as the world's population turned upward, reaching the 1-billion mark by 1800. This milestone (which included the entire human history up to that point) was repeated by 1930—barely a century later—when a second billion people were added to the planet. In other words, not only was population increasing, but the *rate* of growth was accelerating. Global population reached 3 billion by 1962 (just 32 years later) and 4 billion by 1974 (a scant 12 years later). The rate of world population increase has slowed recently, but our planet passed the 5-billion mark in 1987 and the 6-billion mark late in 1999. In no previous century did the world's population even double. In the 20th century, it increased *fourfold*.

Currently, the world is gaining about 80 million people each year, with 95 percent of this increase in low-income countries. Experts predict that the earth's population will reach between 7.3 and 10.7 billion by 2050 (Gelbard, Haub, & Kent, 1999). Given the world's troubles feeding its current population, such an increase is a matter of urgent concern.

### MALTHUSIAN THEORY

It was the sudden population growth two centuries ago that sparked the development of demography. Thomas Robert Malthus (1766–1834), an English economist and clergyman, warned that population increase would soon lead to social chaos. Malthus (1926; orig. 1798) calculated that population would increase by what mathematicians call a *geometric progression*, illustrated by the series of numbers 2, 4, 8, 16, 32, and so on. At such a rate, Malthus concluded, world population would soon soar out of control.

Food production would also increase, Malthus explained, but only in *arithmetic progression* (as in the series 2, 3, 4, 5, 6) because, even with new agricultural technology, farmland is limited. Thus, Malthus presented a troubling vision of the future: people reproducing beyond what the planet could feed, leading ultimately to widespread starvation.

Malthus recognized that artificial birth control or abstinence might change the equation. But he found one morally wrong and the other quite unlikely. Thus, famine and war stalked humanity in Malthus's scheme, and he was justly known as "the dismal parson."

**Critical evaluation.** Fortunately, Malthus's prediction was flawed. First, by 1850 the European birth rate began to drop, partly because children were becoming an *economic liability* rather than an asset, and partly because people began using artificial birth control. Second, Malthus underestimated human ingenuity: Irrigation, fertilizers, and pesticides have increased farm production far more than he imagined.

Some criticized Malthus for ignoring the role of social inequality in world abundance and famine. For example, Karl Marx (1967; orig. 1867) objected to viewing suffering as a "law of nature" rather than the curse of capitalism.

Still, Malthus offered an important lesson. Habitable land, clean water, and fresh air are limited resources and, as we explain presently, greater economic productivity has taken a heavy toll on the natural environment. In addition, medical advances have lowered death rates, pushing up world population. In principle, of course, no level of population growth can go on forever. Thus, people everywhere must become aware of the dangers of population increase.

## DEMOGRAPHIC TRANSITION THEORY

A more complex analysis of population change is **demographic transition theory,** *a thesis linking demographic changes to a society's level of technological development.* Figure 15–4 on page 382 shows the demographic consequences at four levels of technological development.

**Stage 1.** Pre-industrial, agrarian societies have high birth rates because of the economic value of children and the absence of effective birth control. Death rates are also high due to low living standards and lack of medical technology. Outbreaks of disease neutralize

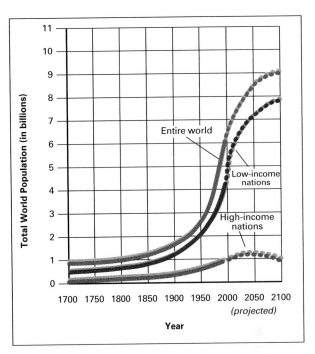

**FIGURE 15–3    The Increase in World Population, 1700–2100**

births, so population rises and falls with only a modest overall increase. This was the case for thousands of years in Europe before the Industrial Revolution.

**Stage 2.** The onset of industrialization brings a demographic transition as death rates fall due to greater food supplies and scientific medicine. But birth rates remain high, resulting in rapid population growth. It was during Europe's Stage 2 that Malthus formulated his ideas, which explains his pessimistic view of the future. Many of the world's low-income countries today are in this high-growth stage.

**Stage 3.** In a mature industrial economy, the birth rate drops, curbing population growth once again. Fertility falls, first, because most children survive to adulthood and, second, because high living standards make raising children expensive. Affluence, in short, transforms children from economic assets into economic liabilities. Smaller families, made possible by effective birth control, are also favoured by women working outside the home. As birth rates follow death rates downward, population growth slows further.

**Stage 4.** This stage corresponds to a post-industrial economy in which the demographic transition is complete. The birth rate keeps falling, partly because dual-income couples gradually become the norm and partly because the cost of raising children continues to rise. This trend, coupled with steady death rates, means that, at best, population grows only very slowly, or even decreases. This is case now in Japan, across European countries, and in Canada.

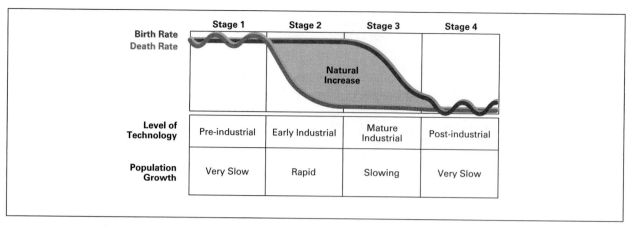

| | Stage 1 | Stage 2 | Stage 3 | Stage 4 |
|---|---|---|---|---|
| **Level of Technology** | Pre-industrial | Early Industrial | Mature Industrial | Post-industrial |
| **Population Growth** | Very Slow | Rapid | Slowing | Very Slow |

**FIGURE 15–4    Demographic Transition Theory**

**Critical evaluation.** Demographic transition theory suggests that the key to population control lies in technology. Instead of the runaway population increase feared by Malthus, this theory sees technology reining in growth and spreading material plenty.

Demographic transition theory dovetails with modernization theory, one approach to global development discussed in Chapter 9 (Global Stratification). Modernization theorists are optimistic that poor countries will solve their population problems as they industrialize. But critics—notably dependency theorists—strongly disagree. Unless there is a significant redistribution of global resources, they maintain, our planet will become increasingly divided into industrialized "haves," enjoying low population growth, and nonindustrialized "have-nots," struggling in vain to feed more and more people.

## GLOBAL POPULATION TODAY: A BRIEF SURVEY

What can we say about population in today's world? Drawing on the discussion so far, we can identify important patterns and reach several conclusions.

**The low-growth north.** When the Industrial Revolution began, population growth in Western Europe and North America peaked at 3 percent annually. But in the centuries since, the growth rate steadily declined, and in 1970 fell below 1 percent. As our post-industrial society enters Stage 4, the Canadian birth rate is less than the replacement level of 2.1 children per woman, a point demographers term **zero population growth,** *the level of reproduction that maintains population at a steady state.* Some 50 nations, almost all of them comparatively rich, have passed the point of zero population growth (World Bank, 2000).

Factors holding down population in these post-industrial societies include a high proportion of men and women in the labour force, rising costs of raising children, trends toward later marriage and singlehood, and widespread use of contraceptives and abortion.

In high-income nations, therefore, population increase is not the pressing problem that it is in low-income countries. Indeed, some analysts point to a future problem of *underpopulation* in countries such as Japan, Italy, and Canada, where the swelling ranks of the elderly have fewer and fewer young people to look to for support in old age (Chesnais, 1997).

**The high-growth south.** Population growth remains a serious threat to low-income nations of the Southern Hemisphere. Only a few societies lack industrial technology altogether, placing them in demographic transition theory's Stage 1. But much of Latin America, Africa, and Asia is at Stage 2, with agrarian economies and some industry. At the same time, advanced medical technology, supplied by high-income countries, has sharply reduced death rates, while birth rates remain high. This is why low-income societies now account for 40 percent of the earth's people and almost 60 percent of global population increase.

In low-income countries throughout the world, birth rates have fallen from an average of about six children per woman in 1950 to about three today. But fertility this high will only intensify global poverty. At a 1994 global population conference in Cairo, delegates from 180 nations agreed that a key element in controlling world population growth is raising the status of women. The Global Sociology box on page 384 takes a closer look.

In the past decade, the world has made significant progress in lowering fertility. But mortality, too, has come down. Although few would oppose medical programs that save lives—mostly those of children—

*The Getu family, on the left, lives in the low-income African nation of Ethiopia. The de Frutos family, to the right, lives in the high-income European nation of Spain. Comparing the two photographs, what can you learn about the relationship between a society's level of material affluence and family size? In fact, the fertility rate in Ethiopia is more than five times higher than that in Spain. Thus, while population levels are stable or declining in most of the world's richest countries, they are increasing in the world's poorest nations. This is why poor countries now account for 96 percent of global population increase.*

lower death rates mean an increasing population. In fact, population growth in most low-income regions of the world is due *mostly* to falling death rates. Around 1920, Europe and North America began to help spread scientific medicine and better nutrition around the world. Since then, inoculations against infectious diseases and the use of antibiotics and insecticides have pushed down death rates with stunning effectiveness. For example, in Sri Lanka, malaria caused half of all deaths in the 1930s; a decade later, use of insecticides to kill malaria-carrying mosquitoes had cut the death toll from this disease in half. Although this is a great medical achievement, Sri Lanka's population began to soar. Similarly, India's infant mortality rate slid from 130 in 1975 to less than 70 in 2000. This boosted India's population over the 1-billion mark in 1999—so that it joined China in this exclusive club that is unlikely ever to have any more members.

In short, in much of the world fertility rates are falling. But so is mortality, especially among children. The future rate of fertility decline will determine the size of the global populations.

## URBANIZATION: THE GROWTH OF CITIES

October 8, 1994—Hong Kong The cable train grinds to the top of Victoria Peak where we behold one of the world's most spectacular vistas: the city of Hong Kong at night! A million bright, colourful lights ring the harbour as ships, ferries, and traditional Chinese "junks" churn by. Few cities match Hong Kong for sheer energy: This small place is as economically productive as British Columbia, Alberta, and Saskatchewan combined, or as the entire nation of Finland. One could sit here for hours entranced by the spectacle of Hong Kong.

For most of human history, the sights and sounds of great cities such as Hong Kong, New York, or Toronto were simply unimaginable. Our distant ancestors lived in small, nomadic groups, moving as they depleted vegetation or hunted migratory game. The small settlements that marked the emergence of civilization in the Middle East some 12 000 years ago held only a small fraction of the earth's people. Today, the largest three or four cities of the world hold as many people as the entire planet did back then.

**Urbanization** is *the concentration of humanity into cities.* Urbanization both redistributes population within a society and transforms many patterns of social life. We will trace these changes in terms of three urban revolutions—the emergence of cities beginning 10 000 years ago, the development of industrial cities after 1750, and the explosive growth of cities in low-income countries today.

# Empowering Women:
# The Key to Controlling Population Growth

Sohad Ahmad lives with her husband in a farming village 75 kilometres south of Cairo, Egypt's capital city. Ahmad lives a poor life, like hundreds of millions of other women in the world. Yet her situation differs in an important respect: She has had only two children and will have no more.

Why do Sohad and her husband reject the conventional wisdom that children are an economic asset? One part of the answer is that Egypt's growing population has already created such a demand for land that her family could not afford more even if they had the children to farm it. But the main reason is that Sohad Ahmad does not want her life defined only by childbearing.

Like Ahmad, an increasing number of women in Egypt are taking control of their fertility and seeking more opportunities. Indeed, this country has made great progress in reducing its annual population growth from 2.8 percent annually during the 1980s to about 1.7 percent today (U.S. Bureau of the Census, 2001).

With its focus on raising the standing of women, the 1994 Cairo conference broke new ground. Past population control programs have simply tried to make birth control technology available to women. This is vital, since only half of the world's married women use effec-

*A simple truth: women who have more opportunity for schooling and paid work have fewer children. As more women attend school in traditional societies, the fertility rate in these countries is falling.*

tive birth control. But even with available birth control, population continues to expand in societies that define women's primary responsibility as raising children.

Dr. Nafis Sadik, an Egyptian woman who heads the United Nations' efforts at population control, sums up the new approach to lowering birth rates this way: *Give women more life choices and they will have fewer children.* In other words, women with access to schooling and jobs, who can decide when and if they wish to marry, and who bear children as a matter of choice, will limit their own fertility. Schooling must be available to older women too, Sadik adds, because they exercise great influence in local communities.

Evidence from countries around the world is that controlling population and raising the social standing of women are one and the same.

Source: Linden (1994); Ashford (1995).

## THE EVOLUTION OF CITIES

Cities are a relatively new phenomenon in human history. Only about 12 000 years ago did our ancestors begin founding permanent settlements, launching the *first urban revolution*.

**The first cities.** Hunting and gathering forced people to move all the time; once our ancestors discovered how to domesticate animals and cultivate crops, however, they were able to remain relatively stationary (Lenski, Nolan, & Lenski, 1995). Raising their own food also created a material surplus, which freed some people from food production and allowed them to build shelters, make tools, weave cloth, and take part in religious rituals. The emergence of cities, then, led to specialization and higher living standards.

The first city—Jericho, which lies to the north of the Dead Sea and dates back some 10 000 years—was home to only about 600 people. But as the century passed, cities grew to tens of thousands of people, and became the centres of vast empires. By 3000 B.C.E., Egyptian cities flourished, as did cities in China about 2000 B.C.E., and in Central and South America about 1500 B.C.E. In North America, however, only a few Aboriginal societies formed settlements, so that widespread urbanization had to await the arrival of European settlers in the 17th century (Lamberg-Karlovsky, 1973; Change, 1977; Coe & Diehl, 1980).

**Pre-industrial European cities.** European cities date back some 5000 years to the Greeks, and later the Romans, both of whom formed great empires and founded cities across Europe, including Vienna, Paris, and London. With the fall of the Roman Empire, the so-called "Dark Ages" began, as people withdrew within defensive walled settlements and warlords battled for territory. Only in the 11th century did trade flourish once again, allowing cities to grow.

Medieval cities were quite different from those familiar to us today. Beneath towering cathedrals, the narrow and winding streets of London, Brussels, and Florence teemed with merchants, artisans, priests, peddlers, jugglers, nobles, and servants. Occupational groups such as bakers, carpenters, and metalworkers clustered together in distinct sections or "quarters." Ethnicity also defined communities as people sought to keep out those who differed from themselves. The term "ghetto" (from the Italian word *borghetto*, meaning "outside the city walls") first described the segregation of Jews in Venice.

**Industrial European cities.** As the Middle Ages came to a close, steadily increasing commerce enriched a new urban middle class or *bourgeoisie* (French meaning "of the town"). With more and more money, the bourgeoisie soon rivalled the hereditary nobility.

By about 1750, the Industrial Revolution triggered a *second urban revolution*, first in Europe and then in North America. Factories unleashed tremendous productive power, causing cities to grow to unprecedented size. London, the largest European city, reached 550 000 people by 1700 and exploded to 6.5 million by 1900 (A. Weber, 1963, orig. 1899; Chandler & Fox, 1974).

Cities not only grew but changed shape as well. Older winding streets gave way to broad, straight boulevards that held the flow of commercial traffic and, eventually, motor vehicles. Steam and electric trolleys, too, crisscrossed the expanding cities. Since land was now a commodity to be bought and sold, developers divided cities into regular-size lots (Mumford, 1961). The centre of the city was no longer the cathedral; bustling central business districts arose, filled with banks, retail stores, and tall office buildings.

With a new focus on business, cities became ever more crowded and impersonal. Crime rates rose. Especially at the outset, a few industrialists lived in grand style, but most men, women, and children worked in factories for bare subsistence.

Organized efforts by workers to improve their lives eventually brought changes to the workplace, better housing, and the right to vote. Public services such as water, sewage, and electricity further improved urban living. Today, some urbanites still live in poverty, but a rising standard of living has partly fulfilled the city's historical promise of a better life.

## THE GROWTH OF NORTH AMERICAN CITIES

Most of the Aboriginals who inhabited North America for thousands of years before the arrival of Europeans

*Mont-St-Michel, a French town that rises against the Atlantic Ocean, is a wonderful example of a medieval settlement: small and walled, with narrow, irregular streets that even today make walking seem like a delightful stroll back in time.*

were migratory people, who formed few permanent settlements. The spread of villages and towns, then, came after European colonization.

**Colonial settlement: 1565–1800.** In 1565, the Spanish built a settlement at St. Augustine, Florida, and, in 1607, the English founded Jamestown, Virginia. The first lasting settlement, however, came in 1624 when the Dutch established New Amsterdam, later called New York. These settlements preceded those in Canada, where the first European did not reach the site that was to become Toronto until 1615.

New York, Boston (founded by the English in 1630), and Quebec City (where there was merely a trading post in 1608) started out as tiny villages in a vast wilderness. They resembled medieval towns in Europe, with narrow, winding streets that one can still see curving through lower Manhattan, downtown Boston, and parts of Quebec City.

But economic growth soon transformed these quiet villages into thriving towns with wide streets, usually built on a grid pattern. Even so, Montreal (founded in 1642) had grown to about 18 000 by the end of the 18th century, while Captain Vancouver had just explored and charted the Burrard Inlet in 1792. As the century closed, Canada, as we now know it, was still an overwhelmingly rural society.

**Urban expansion: 1800–1860.** Early in the 19th century, towns sprang up along the transportation routes that opened the Canadian West. First the cities along the major waterways connected to the Great Lakes emerged. By 1851, Quebec City had a population of 52 000, whereas the younger city of Montreal already had grown to 57 000.

*This satellite photo shows the Census Metropolitan Area of Vancouver. The mountains which surround the area are limiting future expansion.*

Progress was slow away from the waterways of the Great Lakes. It was only in 1860, for example, that New Westminster (now part of the greater Vancouver area) became the first incorporated municipality west of Ontario. It was not until the completion of the Canadian Pacific Railway in 1885 that urbanization spread to the western provinces.

**The metropolitan era: 1860–1950.** Industrialization also gave an enormous boost to urbanization, as factories strained to produce goods. Now waves of people fled the countryside for cities in hopes of obtaining better jobs. Soon after, tens of millions of immigrants—most from Europe—joined the surge to the cities to form a culturally diverse urban mix.

At the time of Canadian Confederation in 1867, less than 20 percent of the population lived in urban areas. By 1951 this proportion had grown to 63 percent. Individual cities grew accordingly—by 1911 the supremacy of Montreal and Toronto, with populations of 470 000 and 377 000 respectively, were well established. The next largest cities were Winnipeg (136 000) and Vancouver (100 000). These were still small cities compared to New York, which had already passed the 4-million mark. Such growth marked the era of the

**metropolis** (from Greek words meaning "mother city"), a *large city that socially and economically dominates an urban area*. Metropolises became the economic centres of Canada.

Industrial technology further changed the physical shape of cities, pushing buildings well above the three or four storeys common up to this point. By the 1880s, steel girders and mechanical elevators raised structures more than 10 storeys high. Railroads and highways drew cities outward. By 1931, pushing upward and outward, cities were home to a majority of the Canadian population.

**Urban decentralization: 1950–present.** The industrial metropolis reached its peak about 1950. Since then, something of a turnaround—termed *urban decentralization*—has occurred as people have deserted downtown areas for outlying **suburbs**, *urban areas beyond the political boundaries of a city* (Balakrishnan & Jarvis 1991). Thus the centres of the largest cities have actually experienced population decreases in the past few decades. Instead of densely packed central cities, the urban landscape has evolved into sprawling regions.

## SUBURBS AND URBAN DECLINE

Imitating European nobility, some of the rich always kept both "town" houses as well as "country" homes beyond the city limits (Baltzell, 1979). But not until after the Second World War did ordinary people find a suburban home within their reach. With more and more cars, new four-lane highways, affordable mortgages, and inexpensive homes, suburbs grew as never before. By 1981, most of the population in Canada's largest cities lived in suburbs outside the central city (McVey, Jr. & Kalbach, 1995).

Decentralization was not good news for everyone, however. Rapid suburban growth threw cities into financial chaos. Population decline meant reduced tax revenues. Further, cities that lost affluent people to the suburbs were left with the burden of providing expensive social programs to the poor who stayed behind. Inner-city decay has been particularly dramatic in the U.S., where deteriorating city centres have become synonymous with slum housing, crime, drugs, unemployment, poverty, and minority populations. There are similarities in Canada, Vancouver's downtown eastside being the most dramatic. However, marginalized populations are not as concentrated in other Canadian cities as they are in the cities of our neighbour to the south. Canadian inner cities have fared better in large part because of early adoption of urban renewal policies. Under this program, provincial and local governments have paid for the rebuilding of many inner cities—Montreal started this as early as 1966 (Wolfe, 1992). Yet critics of urban renewal charge that these

Peasant Dance *(above, c. 1565)*, by Pieter Breughel the Elder, *conveys the essential unity of rural life forged by generations of kinship and neighbourhood. By contrast, Ernest Fiene's* Nocturne *(right) communicates the impersonality common to urban areas. Taken together, these paintings capture Tönnies's distinction between* Gemeinschaft *and* Gesellschaft.

programs have benefitted business communities while not adequately addressing the housing needs of low-income residents (Jacobs, 1961; Greer, 1965; Gans, 1982).

## MEGALOPOLIS: REGIONAL CITIES

Another result of urban decentralization is urban regions. Statistics Canada recognizes about 140 regional cities, which are called **Census Agglomerations (CAs)**—*towns and surrounding areas where more than 10 000 people live in the urban core.* The smallest CA is Labrador city, with a 1996 population of 10 460 (Statistics Canada, 1998t). One-third of Canada's population lives in the three largest of the urban areas identified by Statistics Canada, the 25 **Census Metropolitan Areas (CMAs)**, *cities and surrounding areas where more than 100 000 people live in the urban core.* These CMAs range in size from Toronto at 4.7 million, to Thunder Bay at about 127 000 (Statistics Canada, 2000a).

As regional cities grow, they begin to overlap. There is now a continuous urban area from St. Catharines through Toronto to Oshawa, where about 6 million people live.

On an even larger scale, along the U.S. East Coast a 650-kilometre supercity stretches all the way from New England to Virginia. In the early 1960s, French geographer Jean Gottmann (1961) coined the term **megalopolis** to designate *a vast urban region containing a number of cities and their surrounding suburbs.* Although comprising hundreds of politically independent cities and suburbs, a megalopolis appears, from an airplane at night, to be a single continuous city.

## URBANISM AS A WAY OF LIFE

Early sociologists in Europe and North America analyzed the rise of cities. We briefly present their accounts of a way of life that almost all Canadians now take for granted.

### FERDINAND TÖNNIES: *GEMEINSCHAFT* AND *GESELLSCHAFT*

In the late-19th century, the German sociologist Ferdinand Tönnies (1855–1937) studied how life in the new industrial metropolis differed from life in rural villages. From this contrast, he developed two concepts that have become a lasting part of sociology's terminology.

Tönnies (1963; orig. 1887) used the German word **Gemeinschaft** (meaning roughly "community") to refer to *a type of social organization by which people are bound closely together by kinship and tradition.* The *Gemeinschaft* of the rural village, Tönnies explained, joins people in what amounts to a single primary group.

By and large, argued Tönnies, *Gemeinschaft* is absent in the modern city. On the contrary, urbanization fosters **Gesellschaft** (a German word meaning roughly "association"), *a type of social organization by which people come together only on the basis of individual self-interest.* In the *Gesellschaft* way of life, individuals are motivated by their own needs rather than a drive to enhance the well-being of everyone. By and large, city dwellers display little sense of community or common identity and look to others mostly as a means of advancing their individual goals. Thus, Tönnies saw in urbanization the erosion of close, enduring social relations in favour of the fleeting and impersonal ties typical of business.

## EMILE DURKHEIM: MECHANICAL AND ORGANIC SOLIDARITY

French sociologist Emile Durkheim agreed with much of Tönnies's thinking about cities. Yet, Durkheim countered, urbanites do not lack social bonds; they simply organize social life differently than do rural people.

Durkheim described traditional, rural life as *mechanical solidarity*, social bonds based on common sentiments and shared moral values. With its emphasis on tradition, Durkheim's concept of mechanical solidarity bears a striking similarity to Tönnies's *Gemeinschaft*. Urbanization erodes mechanical solidarity, Durkheim explained, but it also generates a new type of bonding, which he termed *organic solidarity*, social bonds based on specialization and interdependence. This concept, which parallels Tönnies's *Gesellschaft*, reveals an important difference between the two thinkers. Both thought the growth of industrial cities undermined tradition, but Durkheim optimistically pointed to a new kind of solidarity. Where societies had been built on *likeness*, Durkheim now saw social life based on *difference*.

For Durkheim, urban society offers more individual choice, moral tolerance, and personal privacy than people find in rural villages. In sum, Durkheim thought, something is lost in the process of urbanization, but much is gained.

## GEORG SIMMEL: THE BLASÉ URBANITE

German sociologist Georg Simmel (1858–1918) offered a micro-analysis of cities, studying how urban life shapes individual experience. According to Simmel,

individuals perceive the city as a crush of people, objects, and events. To prevent being overwhelmed by all this stimulation, urbanites develop a *blasé attitude*, tuning out much of what goes on around them. Such detachment does not mean that city dwellers lack compassion for others, but that they simply keep their distance as a survival strategy so they can focus their time and energy on those who really matter to them.

## ROBERT PARK AND LOUIS WIRTH: WALKING THE STREETS IN CHICAGO

Sociologists in North America soon joined in the study of rapidly growing cities. Robert Park, a leader of the first major North American sociology program at the University of Chicago, sought to add a street-level perspective by getting out and studying real cities. As he said of himself,

> "I suspect that I have actually covered more ground, tramping about in cities in different parts of the world, than any other living man" (1950:viii).

Walking the streets, Park found the city to be an organized mosaic of distinctive ethnic communities, commercial centres, and industrial districts. Over time, he observed, these "natural areas" develop and change in relation to one another. To Park, then, the city was a living organism.

Another major figure in the Chicago School of urban sociology was Louis Wirth (1897–1952). Wirth (1938) is best known for blending the ideas of Tönnies, Durkheim, Simmel, and Park into a comprehensive theory of urban life.

Wirth began by defining the city as a setting with a large, dense, and socially diverse population. These traits result in an impersonal, superficial, and transitory way of life. Living among millions of others, urbanites come into contact with many more people than rural residents do. Thus, when city people notice others at all, they usually know them not in terms of *who they are* but *what they do*: as, for instance, the bus driver, florist, or grocery store clerk. Specialized, urban relationships are sometimes pleasant for all concerned. But we should remember that self-interest rather than friendship is the main reason for the interaction.

Finally, limited social involvement coupled with great social diversity makes city dwellers more tolerant than rural villagers. Rural communities often jealously enforce their narrow traditions, but the heterogeneous population of a city rarely shares any single code of moral conduct (T. Wilson, 1985; Wilson, 1995).

**Critical evaluation.** Both in Europe and North America, early sociologists presented a mixed view of urban living. On the one hand, rapid urbanization was troubling. Tönnies and Wirth saw personal ties and traditional morality lost in the anonymous rush of the city. On the other hand, Durkheim and Park emphasized urbanism's positive face, pointing to greater personal autonomy and greater personal choice.

One problem is that Wirth and others painted urbanism in broad strokes that overlook the effects of class, race, and gender. There are many kinds of urbanites—rich and poor, black and white, Anglo and Aboriginals, women and men—all leading distinctive lives (Gans, 1968). In fact, cities can intensify these social differences. That is, we see the extent of social diversity most clearly in cities where various categories can form "critical masses" (Macionis & Parrillo, 2001).

## URBAN ECOLOGY

Sociologists (especially members of the Chicago School) also developed **urban ecology**, *the study of the link between the physical and social dimensions of cities.* Consider, for example, why cities are located where they are. The first cities emerged in fertile regions where the ecology favoured raising crops. Pre-industrial people, concerned with defence, built their cities on mountains (ancient Athens was perched on an outcropping of rock) or surrounded by water (Paris and Mexico City were founded on islands). With the Industrial Revolution, economic considerations situated all the major Canadian cities near waterways that facilitated trade.

Urban ecologists also study the physical design of cities. In 1925 Ernest W. Burgess, a student and colleague of Robert Park, described land use in Chicago in terms of *concentric zones.* City centres, Burgess observed, are business districts bordered by a ring of factories, followed by residential rings with housing that becomes more expensive the farther it is from the noise and pollution of the city's centre.

Homer Hoyt (1939) refined Burgess's observations, noting that distinctive districts sometimes form *wedge-shaped sectors.* For example, one fashionable area may develop next to another, or an industrial district may extend outward from a city's centre along a train or trolley line.

Chauncy Harris and Edward Ullman (1945) added yet another insight: As cities decentralize, they lose their single-centre form in favour of a *multicentered model.* As cities grow, residential areas, industrial parks, and shopping districts typically push away from one another. Few people wish to live close to industrial areas, for example, so the city becomes a mosaic of distinct districts.

*Social area analysis* investigates what people in particular neighbourhoods have in common. Three factors seem to explain most of the variation—family patterns, social class, and race and ethnicity (Shevky & Bell, 1955; Johnston, 1976; Balakrishnan & Jarvis, 1991). Families with children gravitate to areas with

*In low-income countries throughout the world, people are migrating from rural areas to cities in hope of a better life. The result is that many cities are overwhelmed with newcomers, who are forced to live wherever they can. Shanty settlements, such as this one in Manila, Philippines, pose obvious dangers to residents (and especially children) in terms of accidents and disease. What do you think would happen if heavy rains flooded this neighbourhood?*

large apartments or single-family homes and good schools. The rich seek high-prestige neighbourhoods, often in the central city near cultural attractions. People with a common social heritage cluster in distinctive communities.

Finally, Brian Berry and Philip Rees (1969) tied together many of these insights. They explain that distinct family types tend to settle in the concentric zones described by Ernest Burgess. Specifically, households with few children tend to cluster toward the city's centre, while those with more children live farther away. Social class differences are primarily responsible for the sector-shaped districts described by Homer Hoyt, as, for instance, the rich occupy one "side of the tracks" and the poor, the other. And racial and ethnic neighbourhoods are found at various points throughout the city, consistent with Harris and Ullman's multi-centred model.

## URBAN POLITICAL ECONOMY

In the late 1960s, many large North American cities were rocked by rioting. In the wake of this unrest, some analysts turned away from the ecological approach to a social-conflict understanding of city life. The *urban political economy* model applies Karl Marx's analysis of conflict in the workplace to conflict in the city (Lindstrom, 1995).

The ecological approach sees the city as a natural organism, with particular districts and neighbourhoods developing according to an internal logic. Political economists disagree. They claim that city life is defined by people with power: corporate leaders and political officials. Capitalism, which transforms the city into "real estate" traded for profit and concentrates wealth in the hands of the few, is the key to understanding city life. From this point of view, for example, the development of the West Edmonton Mall and the resulting decline in downtown Edmonton can only be understood by an analysis that includes looking at the close relationship that the developer (the Ghermezian family) had with provincial and municipal politicians.

**Critical evaluation.** Compared to the older urban ecology approach, the political economy view seems better able to address many recent changes in Canadian cities. But one criticism applies to both approaches: They focus on North American cities during a limited period of history. Much of what we know about industrial cities does not apply to pre-industrial towns in our own past or the rapidly growing cities in many low-income nations today. Therefore, it is unlikely that any single model of cities can account for the full range of urban diversity that we find in the world today.

## URBANIZATION IN LOW-INCOME COUNTRIES

November 16, 1988—Cairo, Egypt People call the vast Muslim cemetery in Old Cairo "The City of the Dead." In truth, it is very much alive: Tens of thousands of squatters have moved into the mausoleums, making this place an eerie mix of life and death. Children run across the stone floors, clothes lines stretch between the monuments, and an occasional television antenna protrudes from a tomb roof. With Cairo gaining 1000 people a day, families live where they can. . . .

Twice in human history the world has experienced a revolutionary expansion of cities. The first urban revolution began about 8000 B.C.E. with the first urban settlements, and continued until permanent settlements were in place on several continents. Then, about 1750, the second urban revolution took off and lasted for two centuries as the Industrial Revolution touched off rapid growth of cities in Europe and North America.

A third urban revolution is now under way. Today, 75 percent of people in industrial societies are already city dwellers. But extraordinary urban growth is occurring in low-income nations too—in 1950, about 25 percent of the people in these nations lived in cities; by 2005, the figure will exceed 50 percent. Moreover, in 1950, only seven cities in the world had populations over 5 million, and only two of these were in low-income countries. By 1999, 37 cities had passed this mark, and 26 of them were in low-income countries (*World Almanac 2000*, 1999).

This third urban revolution is taking place because many low-income nations have entered the high-growth Stage 2 of demographic transition theory. Falling death rates have fuelled population increase in Latin America, Asia, and, especially, Africa. For urban areas, the rate of increase is *twice* as high because, in addition to natural increase, millions of people leave the countryside each year in search of jobs, health care, education, and conveniences such as running water and electricity.

Cities do offer more opportunities than rural areas, but they provide no quick fix for the massive problems of escalating population and grinding poverty. Many cities in less well-off nations—including Mexico City, Egypt's Cairo, India's Calcutta, and Manila in The Philippines, are simply unable to meet the basic needs of much of their population. All these cities are surrounded by wretched shantytowns—settlements of makeshift homes built from discarded materials. As noted in Chapter 9 (Global Stratification), even city dumps are home to thousands of poor people, who pick through the waste hoping to find enough food to survive for another day.

## ENVIRONMENT AND SOCIETY

Our species has prospered, rapidly increasing the population of the planet. Moreover, an increasing share of humanity now lives in large, complex settlements that offer the promise of a better life than that found in rural villages.

But these advances have come at a high price. Never before in history have human beings placed such demands on the earth. This disturbing development brings us to the final section of this chapter: a look at the interplay of the natural environment and society. Like demography, **ecology** is another cousin of sociology, formally defined as *the study of the interaction of living organisms and the natural environment*. Ecology rests on the research of not only social scientists, but natural scientists as well. Here, however, we focus on aspects of ecology that involve now familiar sociological concepts and issues.

The **natural environment** refers to *the earth's surface and atmosphere, including living organisms, air, water, soil, and other resources necessary to sustain life*. Like every other species, humans depend on the natural environment to live. Yet, with our capacity for culture,

*The earth's rain forests—vital to the planet's ecology—are now half their original size and become smaller every year. Once the lush vegetation of such forests is lost, the soil is at risk of drying out and turning into a desert. Environmental damage is often irreversible.*

humans stand apart from other species as we alone take deliberate action to remake the world according to our own interests and desires. Thus human beings are unique in our capacity to transform the world, for better and worse.

Why is the environment of interest to sociologists? Simply because environmental problems—from pollution to acid rain to global warming—do not arise from the natural world operating on its own. Rather, as we shall explain, such problems result from the specific actions of human beings, making the problems *social* issues (Marx, 1994).

## THE GLOBAL DIMENSION

The study of the natural environment must be approached from a global perspective. The reason is that regardless of political divisions among nations, the planet is a single **ecosystem**, a *system composed of the interaction of all living organisms and their natural environment.*

The Greek meaning of *eco* is "house," reminding us that this planet is our home and that all living things and their natural environment are *interrelated.* In practice, any change in part of the natural environment ripples throughout the entire global ecosystem.

Consider, from an ecological point of view, our national love of eating hamburgers. People in North America (and, increasingly, around the world) have created a huge demand for beef, which has greatly expanded ranching in Brazil, Costa Rica, and other Latin American nations. To produce the lean meat sought by fast-food corporations, cattle in Latin America feed on grass, which uses a great deal of land. Latin American ranchers get the land for grazing by

clearing thousands of square kilometres of forests each year. These tropical forests, as we shall explain presently, are vital to maintaining the earth's atmosphere. Deforestation ends up threatening everyone, including people back in Canada who enjoy hamburgers without a thought to the environment (Myers, 1984a).

## TECHNOLOGY AND THE ENVIRONMENTAL DEFICIT

Our capacity for culture gives humans the power to alter the natural environment, to make and remake the world as we choose. Members of societies with simple, hunting and gathering technology have scarcely any ability to affect the environment. On the contrary, members of such societies are keenly dependent on nature, so that their lives are defined by the migration of game and the rhythm of the seasons. They are especially vulnerable to natural catastrophes, such as fires, floods, droughts, and storms.

Societies at intermediate stages of sociocultural evolution have a somewhat greater capacity to affect the environment. But the environmental impact of horticulture (small-scale farming), pastoralism (the herding of animals), and even agriculture (the use of animal-drawn plows) is limited because people still rely on muscle power for producing food and other goods.

Human control of the natural environment increased dramatically with the Industrial Revolution. Muscle power gave way to engines that burn fossil fuels: coal, at first, and then oil. Such machinery affects the environment in two ways, by consuming natural resources and by releasing pollutants into the atmosphere. Even more important, humans armed with

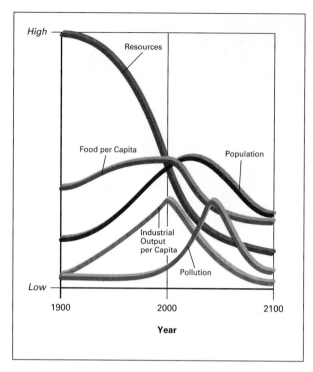

**FIGURE 15–5    The Limits to Growth: Projections**

Source: Based on Meadows et al. (1972).

industrial technology are able to bend nature to their will, tunnelling through mountains, damming rivers, irrigating deserts, and drilling for oil on the ocean floor. This is why people in high-income countries, who represent just 15 percent of humanity, use 80 percent of the world's energy (Connett, 1991; Miller, 1992).

The environmental impact of industrial technology goes beyond energy consumption. Just as important is the fact that members of industrial societies produce 100 times more goods than people in agrarian societies do. Higher living standards, in turn, increase the problem of solid waste (since people ultimately throw away most of what they produce) and pollution (since industrial production generates smoke and other toxic substances).

Right from the start, people recognized the material benefits of industrial technology. But only a century later did they begin to see the long-term effects on the natural environment. Indeed, one trait of the recent post-industrial era is a growing concern for environmental quality (Abrahamson, 1997; Kidd & Lee, 1997). Today, we realize that the technological power to make our lives better can also put the lives of future generations in jeopardy (Voight, cited in Bormann & Kellert, 1991:ix–x).

Evidence is mounting that we are running up an **environmental deficit**, *profound and negative long-term harm to the natural environment caused by humanity's focus on*

*short-term material affluence* (Bormann, 1990). The concept of environmental deficit is important for three reasons. First, it reminds us that the state of the environment is a *social issue*, reflecting choices people make about how to live. Second, it suggests that much environmental damage—to the air, land, or water—is *unintended*. By focussing on the short-term benefits of, say, cutting down forests, strip mining, or using throwaway packaging, we fail to see their long-term environmental effects. Third, in some respects, the environmental deficit is *reversible*. In other words, inasmuch as societies have created environmental problems, they can undo many of them.

## CULTURE: GROWTH AND LIMITS

Whether we recognize environmental dangers and decide to do something about them is a cultural matter. Thus, along with technology, culture has powerful environmental consequences.

**The logic of growth.** When this country sets aside specific areas as "parks" and "protected areas," we seem to be saying that except for these special areas, people can use natural resources freely for their own purposes (Myers, 1991). This aggressive approach to the natural environment has long been central to our way of life.

Chapter 2 (Culture) described many of the core values that underlie social life in Canada. We embrace the idea of *progress*, thinking that the future will be better than the present. Moreover, we look to *science* to make our lives easier and more rewarding. Taken together, such cultural values form *the logic of growth*.

The logic of growth is an optimistic view of the world. It holds that more powerful technology has improved our lives and new discoveries will continue to do so into the future. In simple terms, the logic of growth asserts that "people are clever," "having things is good," and "life gets better." A powerful force throughout the history of Canada and most other high-income, industrial societies, the logic of growth has driven individuals to settle the wilderness, build towns and roads, and pursue material affluence.

Even so, "progress" can lead to unexpected problems, including straining the environment. The logic of growth responds by arguing that people (especially scientists and other technology experts) will find a way out of any problem that growth places in our path. If, say, the world runs short of oil, scientists will come up with electric, solar, or nuclear engines or some as-yet-unknown technology to meet the world's energy needs.

But environmentalists counter that the logic of growth is flawed in assuming that natural resources such as oil, clean air, fresh water, and the earth's topsoil will always be plentiful. On the contrary, they claim, these are *finite* resources that we can and will exhaust if we continue to pursue growth at any cost. Echoing Malthus, environmentalists warn that if we call on the earth to support an increasing number of people, we will surely deplete finite resources, destroying the environment—and ourselves—in the process (Milbrath, 1989; Livernash & Rodenburg, 1998).

**The limits to growth.** If we cannot invent our way out of the problems created by the logic of growth, perhaps we need another way of thinking about the world. Environmentalists, therefore, counter that growth must have limits. Stated simply, the *limits to growth thesis* is that humanity must implement policies to control the growth of population, production, and use of resources in order to avoid environmental collapse.

In *The Limits to Growth*, a controversial book that had a large hand in launching the environmental movement, Donella Meadows and her colleagues (1972) used a computer model to calculate the planet's available resources, rates of population growth, amount of land available for cultivation, levels of industrial and food production, and amount of pollutants released into the atmosphere. The model reflects changes that have occurred since 1900, projecting forward to the end of the 21st century. The authors concede that such long-range predictions are speculative, and some critics think they are plain wrong (Simon, 1981). But right or wrong, the general conclusions of the study, shown in Figure 15–5, call for serious consideration.

According to the limits to growth thesis, we are quickly consuming the earth's finite resources. Supplies of oil, natural gas, and other energy sources are already falling sharply and will continue to drop, a little faster or slower depending on conservation policies in rich nations and how fast other nations industrialize. While food production per person will continue to rise into the next century, world hunger will persist because existing food supplies are so unequally distributed. By 2050, the model predicts, hunger will reach a crisis level, first stabilizing population and then sending it back downward. Eventually, depletion of resources will cripple industrial output as well. Only then will pollution rates fall.

Limits to growth theorists are also known as neo-Malthusians because they share Malthus's pessimism about the future. They doubt that current patterns of life are sustainable for even another century. If so, we face a fundamental choice: Either we make deliberate changes in how we live, or widespread calamity will force change upon us.

## SOLID WASTE: THE DISPOSABLE SOCIETY

As an interesting exercise, carry a trash bag around for a single day and collect everything you throw away. Most people are surprised to find that the average person in Canada discards about 1.8 kilograms of paper, metal, plastic, and other materials daily

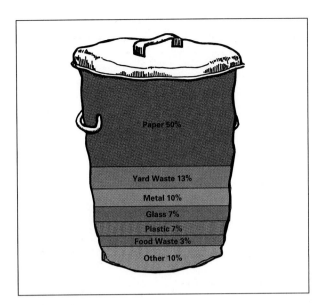

**FIGURE 15–6   Composition of Household Trash**
Sources: Based on Franklin Associates (1986) and Corley et al. (1993).

(*Canadian Geographic*, 1999). Figure 15–6 shows the composition of a normal household's trash.

As a rich nation of people who value convenience, Canada has become a *disposable society*. North Americans consume more products than people anywhere else on earth, and many of these products have throwaway packaging. The most familiar case is fast food, served with cardboard, plastic, and Styrofoam containers that we throw away within minutes. But countless other products—some of them wrapped inside two or even three layers—are elaborately packaged to make the product more attractive to the customer and to discourage tampering and theft.

Consider, too, that manufacturers market soft drinks, beer, and fruit juices in aluminum cans, glass jars, and plastic containers, which not only consume finite resources but also generate mountains of solid waste. Then there are countless items intentionally designed to be disposable: pens, razors, flashlights, batteries, even cameras. Other goods—from lightbulbs to automobiles—are designed to have a limited useful life, and then become unwanted junk. As Paul H. Connett (1991) points out, even the words we use to describe what we throw away—*waste, litter, trash, refuse, garbage, rubbish*—show how little we value what we cannot immediately use. But this was not always the case, as the Critical Thinking box on page 394 explains.

Living in a rich society, the average person in Canada or the U.S. consumes 50 times more steel, 170 times more newspaper, 250 times more gasoline, and 300 times more plastic each year than the typical individual in India (Miller, 1992). This high level of consumption means that we in Canada not only use a

# Why Grandmother Had No Trash

Grandma Macionis, we always used to say, never threw away anything. She was born and raised in Lithuania—the "old country"—where life in a poor village shaped her in ways that never changed even after she immigrated to the United States as a young woman.

After opening a birthday present, she would carefully save the box, wrapping paper, and ribbon, which meant as much to her as the gift they contained. Grandma never wore new clothes, her kitchen knives were worn narrow from decades of sharpening, and all her garbage was "recycled" as compost for her vegetable garden.

As strange as Grandma seemed to her grandchildren, she was a product of her

culture. A century ago, in fact, there was little "trash." If a pair of socks wore thin, Grandma mended them, probably more than once. When they were beyond repair, she used them as a rag for cleaning, or sewed them (with other old clothing) into a quilt. For her, everything had value—if not in one way, then in another.

During this century, as women joined men working out of the home, income went up and families began buying more and more "time-saving" products. Before long, few people cared about the home recycling that Grandma practised. Soon, cities sent crews from block to block to pick up truckloads of discarded material. The era of "trash" began.

---

disproportionate share of the planet's natural resources, but also generate a disproportionate share of the world's refuse.

We like to say that we "throw things away." But 80 percent of our solid waste is not burned or recycled, and never "goes away." Rather, it ends up in landfills, which are, literally, filling up. The city of Toronto is trying to deal with this issue now. After running out of space in its own landfills, it tried to ship garbage 600 kilometres north by rail to the abandoned Adams Lake mine close to the community of Kirkland Lake. Fierce opposition led to the garbage being shipped 400 kilometres west to Michigan instead. However, the controversy erupts again whenever an accident occurs that involves one of the hundreds of trucks that daily drive back and forth.

What can be discarded in a landfill is strictly regulated in most places; nevertheless, many dumpsites across Canada already contain hazardous materials that are polluting water both above and below the ground. In addition, what goes into landfills all too often stays there—sometimes for centuries. Millions of tires, diapers, and other items that we bury in landfills each year do not decompose and will be an unwelcome legacy for future generations.

Some environmentalists argue that we should address the problem of solid waste by doing what many of our grandparents did: Turn "waste" into a resource.

One way to do this is through *recycling*, reusing resources we would otherwise discard. Compared to a mere 20 years ago when only about 2 percent of our waste was recycled, recycling is now an accepted practice in the 52 percent of Canadian households that have curbside recycling. There are laws in many municipalities that mandate reuse of certain materials such as cardboard, glass bottles, and aluminum cans. In addition, on a purely economic basis recycling makes sense for some municipalities when we learn that Toronto spends $59 per tonne on the Blue Box materials sent to recyclers compared to the $87 it costs to send materials to the landfill (*Canadian Geographic*, 1999).

## WATER AND AIR

Oceans, lakes, and streams are the lifeblood of the global ecosystem. Humans depend on water for drinking, bathing, cooling, and cooking, for recreation, and a host of other activities.

According to what scientists call the *hydrological cycle*, the earth naturally recycles water and refreshes the land. The process begins as heat from the sun causes the earth's water, 97 percent of which is in the oceans, to evaporate and form clouds. Because water evaporates at lower temperatures than most pollutants, the water vapour that rises from the seas is relatively pure, leaving various contaminants behind. Water then falls to the earth as rain, which drains into streams and rivers, eventually returning to the sea. Two major concerns about water, then, are supply and pollution.

**Water supply.** For thousands of years, since the time of the ancient civilizations of China, Egypt, and Rome, water rights have figured prominently in codes of law. Today, as Global Map 15–2 on page 396 shows, some regions of the world, especially the tropics, enjoy a plentiful supply of water. High demand, coupled with modest reserves, make water supply a matter of concern in large parts of North America and Asia, where people look to rivers—rather than rainfall—for their water. In the Middle East, water supply has already reached a critical level. In Egypt, an arid region of the world, for instance, people depend on the Nile River for most of their water. But as the Egyptian population increases, shortages are becoming frequent. Egyptians today must make do with one-sixth the amount of water per person from the Nile compared to 1900. Within the next 30 years, across much of northern Africa and the Middle East, experts predict, as many as 1 billion people may lack the water they need for irrigation and drinking (Myers, 1984c; Postel, 1993).

But the world over, soaring population and complex technology have greatly increased societies' appetite for water. The global consumption of water (estimated at almost 4 quadrillion litres per year or 664 000 litres per capita) has tripled since 1950 and is expanding even faster than the world's population. As a result, even in parts of the world that receive plenty of rainfall, people are using groundwater faster than it can be naturally replenished. In the Tamil Nadu region of southern India, for example, people are drawing so much groundwater that the local water table has fallen 100 feet over the past several decades. Mexico City—which has sprawled to some 3600 square kilometres—has pumped so much water from its underground aquifer that the city has sunk 7.5 metres during the past century and is dropping about 6 cm per year. Farther north in the United States, pumping from the Ogallala aquifer, which lies below seven states from South Dakota to Texas, is now so rapid that some experts fear it could run dry within several decades. While we in Canada have access to a disproportionate share of the world's fresh water, we seem to realize the importance of our resource; whenever water exports have been proposed, a vigorous debate ensues.

In light of such developments, we must face the reality that water is a valuable, finite resource. Greater conservation of water by individuals (the average person consumes 45 million litres in a lifetime) is part of the answer. However, households around the world account for just 10 percent of water use. We need to curb water consumption by industry, which uses

*In Canada, most of us take safe water for granted. But people, and especially children, in low-income countries around the world are at high risk from infectious diseases that are spread by unclean water used for bathing, cooking, and drinking.*

20 percent of the global total, and farming, which consumes two-thirds of the total for irrigation (World Resources Institute, 2000).

New irrigation technology may reduce the demand for water in the future. But here again, we see how population increase, as well as economic growth, strains our ecosystem (Myers, 1984a; Goldfarb, 1991; Falkenmark & Widstrand, 1992; Postel, 1993).

**Water pollution.** In large cities—from Mexico City to Cairo to Shanghai—many people have no choice but to drink contaminated water. Infectious diseases such as typhoid, cholera, and dysentery, all caused by water-borne micro-organisms, spread rapidly through these populations (Clarke, 1984b; Falkenmark & Widstrand, 1992). As well as ensuring ample *supplies* of water, then, we must protect the *quality* of water.

Water quality in Canada is generally good by global standards. However, even here the problem of water pollution is growing steadily, as in the case of the raw sewage from St. John's and Victoria that goes straight into the ocean. Decades of heavy pollution of

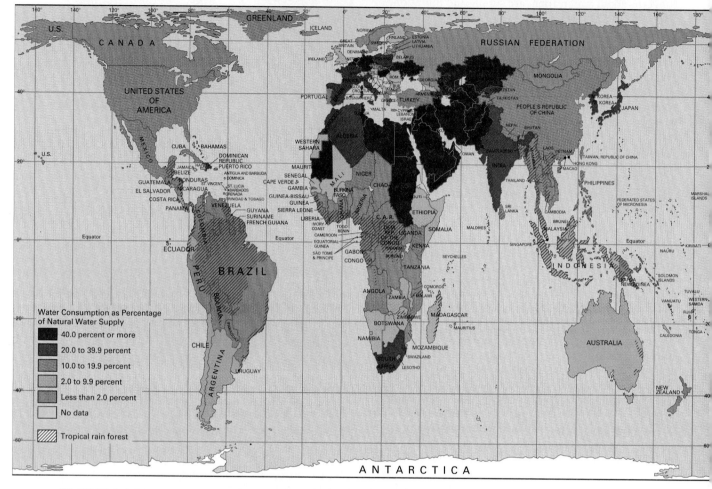

**GLOBAL MAP 15–2    Water Consumption in Global Perspective**

This map shows water consumption as a percentage of each country's renewable water resources. Nations near the equator consume only a tiny share of their available resources; indeed, much of this region is covered with rain forest. Northern Africa and the Middle East are a different story, however, with dense populations drawing on very limited water resources. As a result, in countries like Libya, Egypt, and Saudi Arabia, people (especially the poor) do not have as much water as they would like or, often, as they need.

Source: United Nations Development Programme (2000).

the Great Lakes, and of countless streams and rivers across the country, has seriously threatened plant and fish life, and for some species has resulted in extinction.

A special problem is *acid rain*, rain made acidic by air pollution that destroys plant and animal life. Acid rain (or snow) begins with power plants burning fossil fuels (oil and coal) to generate electricity; this burning releases sulphur and nitrogen oxides into the air. As the wind sweeps these gases into the atmosphere, they

react with the air to form sulfuric and nitric acid, which turns atmospheric moisture acidic.

This is a clear case of one type of pollution causing another: air pollution (from smokestacks) ends up contaminating water (in lakes and streams that collect acid rain). Moreover, acid rain is truly a global phenomenon because the regions that suffer the harmful effects may be thousands of kilometres from the original pollution. For instance, British power plants have caused

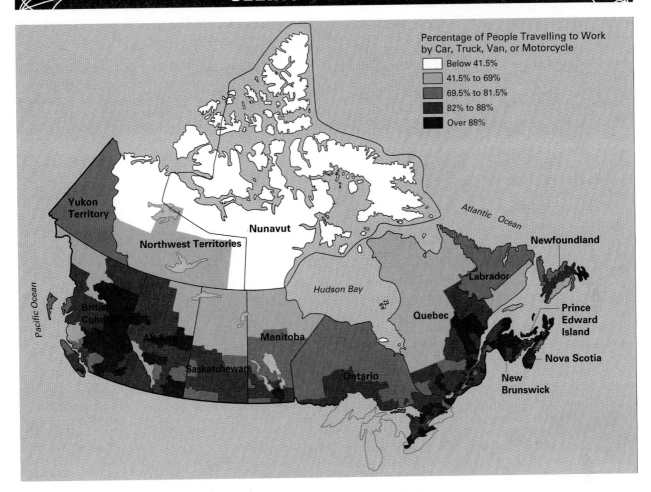

Percentage of People Travelling to Work by Car, Truck, Van, or Motorcycle

☐ Below 41.5%
☐ 41.5% to 69%
▨ 69.5% to 81.5%
▨ 82% to 88%
■ Over 88%

**NATIONAL MAP 15–2**  **Percentage of People Travelling to Work by Car, Truck, Van, or Motorcycle, Canada, 1996**

A very large percentage of Canada's population relies on cars, trucks, vans, and motorcycles to get to work. Is this something we can change? What patterns do you see in this map? Can we use this information to suggest ways to rely less on the internal combustion engine? Should we invest in further improvements in vehicle and engine design?

Source: Based on Statistics Canada, Catalogue No. 95F0181XDB96001 (1998b).

acid rain that has devastated forests and fish in Norway and Sweden up to 1500 kilometres to the northeast. Similarly, U.S. smokestacks have been accused of poisoning the forests in Eastern Canada.

**Air pollution.** Because we are surrounded by air, most people in Canada are more aware of air pollution than contaminated water. One of the unexpected consequences of industrial technology—especially the factory and the motor vehicle—has been a decline in air quality. By 1950, exhaust fumes from automobiles shrouded cities such as Vancouver, where the air is

trapped between the wind from the ocean and the postcard-pretty mountains. In London, factory smokestacks, automobiles, and coal fires used to heat households all added to what was probably the worst urban air quality of the past century. What some British jokingly called "pea soup" was, in reality, a deadly mix of pollution: During five days in 1952, an especially thick haze that hung over London killed 4000 people (Clarke, 1984a).

Air quality improved in the final decades of the past century. Rich nations passed laws that banned high-pollution heating, including the coal fires that choked

London 50 years ago. In addition, scientists devised ways to reduce the noxious output of factories as well as the growing number of automobiles and trucks. Nevertheless, even with improved technology, the impact of the internal combustion engine in significant. National Map 15–2 on page 397 shows that a large proportion of Canadians travel to work by car, truck, van, or motorcycle.

Though high-income countries can breathe a bit more easily than they once did, the problem of air pollution in poor societies is becoming more serious. One reason is that people in low-income countries still rely on wood, coal, peat, or other "dirty" fuels for cooking fires and to heat their homes. Moreover, nations eager to encourage short-term industrial development may pay little heed to the longer-term dangers of air pollution. As a result, many cities in Latin America, Eastern Europe, and Asia are plagued by air pollution as bad as London's was 50 years ago.

## THE RAIN FORESTS

**Rain forests** are *regions of dense forestation, most of which circles the globe close to the equator*. A glance back at Global Map 15–2 on page 396 shows that the largest tropical rain forests are in South America (notably Brazil), west central Africa, and southeast Asia. In all, the world's rain forests cover some 7 percent of the earth's total land surface.

Like other global resources, rain forests are falling victim to the needs and appetites of the surging world population. As noted earlier, to meet the demand for beef, ranchers in Latin America burn forested areas to increase their supply of grazing land. We are also losing rain forests to the hardwood trade. People in high-income nations pay exorbitant prices for mahogany and other woods because, as environmentalist Norman Myers (1984b:88) puts it, they have "a penchant for parquet floors, fine furniture, fancy panelling, week-end yachts, and high-grade coffins." Under such economic pressure, the world's rain forests are now just half their original size, and they continue to shrink by about 1 percent (170 000 square kilometres) annually. Unless we stop this loss, the rain forests will vanish before the end of the 21st century, and with them, protection for the earth's biodiversity and climate.

**Global warming.** Why are rain forests so important? One reason is that they cleanse the atmosphere of carbon dioxide ($CO_2$). Since the beginning of the Industrial Revolution, the amount of carbon dioxide produced by humans (mostly from factories and automobiles) has risen sharply. Much of this $CO_2$ is absorbed by the oceans. But plants take in carbon dioxide and expel oxygen. This is why the rain forests are vital to maintaining the chemical balance of the atmosphere.

The problem, then, is that production of carbon dioxide is rising while the amount of plant life on the earth is shrinking. To make matters worse, rain forests are being destroyed mostly by burning, which releases even more carbon dioxide into the atmosphere. Experts estimate the atmospheric concentration of carbon dioxide is now 20 to 30 percent higher than it was 150 years ago.

High above the earth, carbon dioxide acts like the glass roof of a greenhouse, letting heat from the sun pass through to the earth while preventing much of it from radiating back away from the planet. The result, say ecologists, is a **greenhouse effect**, *a rise in the earth's average temperature due to increasing concentration of carbon dioxide in the atmosphere*. Over the past century, the global temperature has risen about 1 degree Celsius.

Scientists warn that it could rise by 3 to 6 degrees during this century, which would melt vast areas of the polar ice caps and raise the sea level to cover low-lying land around the world. Were this to happen, water would cover all of Bangladesh, for example, and much of coastal Canada. On the other hand, the prairies—currently one of the most productive agricultural regions in the world—would likely become arid.

Not all scientists share this vision of future global warming. Some point out that global temperature changes have been taking place throughout history, apparently with little or nothing to do with rain forests. Moreover, higher concentrations of carbon dioxide in the atmosphere might speed up plant growth (since plants thrive on this gas), which would correct the imbalance and nudge the earth's temperature downward once again. Still other scientists think global warming might even have benefits, including longer growing seasons and lower food prices (Silverberg, 1991; Begley, 1997; McDonald, 1999).

**Declining biodiversity.** Clearing rain forests also reduces the earth's *biodiversity*. This is because rain forests are home to almost half of this planet's living species.

On earth, there are as many as 30 million species of animals, plants, and micro-organisms. Several dozen unique species of plants and animals cease to exist each day; but given the vast number of living species, why should we be concerned? Environmentalists give three reasons. First, our planet's biodiversity provides a varied source of human food. Using agricultural high-technology, scientists can "splice" familiar crops with more exotic plant life, making food more bountiful as well as more resistant to insects and disease. Thus, biodiversity is needed to feed our planet's rapidly increasing population.

Second, animal and plant biodiversity is a vital genetic resource. Medical and pharmaceutical researchers rely on it to provide hundreds of new compounds each year that cure disease and improve our lives. Children in Canada, for example, now have a good chance of surviving leukemia, a disease that was almost a sure killer two generations ago, because of a

*Members of small, simple societies, such as the Tan't Batu, who thrive in the Philippines, live in harmony with nature; such people do not have the technological means to greatly affect the natural world. Although we in complex societies like to think of ourselves as superior to such people, the truth is that there is much we can—and must—learn from them.*

compound derived from a pretty tropical flower called the rosy periwinkle. The oral birth control pill, used by millions of women in this country, is another product of plant research, this time involving the Mexican forest yam.

Third, with the loss of any species of life—whether it is one variety of ant, the spotted owl, the ancient Kootenay River white sturgeon, or the famed Chinese panda—the beauty and complexity of our natural environment is diminished. And there are clear warning signs: There are some 9000 different species of birds in the world and in three-quarters of these species we are seeing fewer and fewer birds.

Finally, note that, unlike pollution, the extinction of any species is irreversible and final. An important ethical question, then, is whether we who live today have the right to impoverish the world for those who live tomorrow (Myers, 1984b; Myers, 1991; Wilson, 1991; Brown et al., 1993).

### ENVIRONMENTAL RACISM

Conflict theory has given birth to the concept of **environmental racism**, *the pattern by which environmental hazards are greatest in proximity to poor people and especially minorities.* Historically, factories that spew pollution stand near neighbourhoods of the poor and minorities. Why? In part, because the poor themselves were drawn to factories in search of work, and once hired, their low incomes often meant they could afford housing only in undesirable neighbourhoods. Sometimes the only housing that fit their budgets stood in the very shadow of the plants and mills where they worked.

Nobody wants a factory or dump nearby, of course, but marginalized populations often are not successful when presenting their NIMBYism case (Not In My BackYard). Accordingly, landfills are more likely to be located in areas populated by Aboriginal peoples, visible minorities, and rural people (Ali, 1999).

## LOOKING AHEAD: TOWARD A SUSTAINABLE SOCIETY AND WORLD

The demographic analysis presented in this chapter points to some disturbing trends. We see, first, that the earth's population has reached record levels because birth rates remain high in poor nations and death rates have fallen just about everywhere. Lowering fertility will remain a pressing problem throughout this century. Even with some recent decline in population increase, the nightmare of Thomas Malthus is still a real possibility.

Further, population growth remains greatest in the poorest countries of the world, those without the means to support their present populations, much less their future ones. Supporting about 80 million additional people on our planet each year—most of whom are in poor societies—will require a global commitment to provide not only food but housing, schools, and employment. The well-being of the entire world may ultimately depend on resolving the economic and social problems of poor, overly populated countries and bridging the widening gulf between "have" and "have-not" societies.

*No one wants to live or work in a dangerous environment. But, in a world of political competition, it is the poor who often end up with the hazards in their backyards. Here, residents of this urban neighbourhood protest plans to construct a power plant in the area.*

Urbanization, too, is continuing, especially in low-income countries. Through human history, people have sought out cities with the hope that there they can find a better life. But the sheer number of people who now live in the emerging global supercities, including Mexico City, São Paulo (Brazil), Kinshasa (Zaire), Bombay (India), and Manila (the Philippines), have created urban problems on a massive scale.

Throughout the world, humanity is facing a serious environmental challenge. Part of this problem is population increase, which is greatest in poor societies. But part of the problem is also high levels of consumption, which mark rich nations such as our own. By increasing the planet's environmental deficit, our current way of life is borrowing against the well-being of our children and their children. Globally, members of rich societies, who currently consume so much of the earth's resources, are mortgaging the future security of the poor countries of the world.

The answer, in principle, is to form an **ecologically sustainable culture**, *a way of life that meets the needs of the current generation without threatening future generations.* Sustainable living depends on three strategies.

First, the world needs to bring population growth under control. The current population of more than 6 billion is already straining the natural environment. Clearly, the higher the world population climbs, the more difficult environmental problems will become. Even if the recent slowing of population growth continues, the world will have almost 8 billion people by 2050. Few analysts think that the earth can support this many people; most argue that we must hold the line at about 7 billion, and some argue that we must *decrease* population in the coming decades.

A second strategy is *conservation of finite resources.* This means meeting our needs with a responsible eye toward the future by using resources efficiently, seeking alternative resources of energy, and in some cases learning to live with less—the Controversy & Debate box questions whether our society is ready for this.

A third strategy is *reducing waste.* Whenever possible, simply using less is the best way to do this. But recycling programs, too, are part of the answer.

In the end, making all these strategies work depends on a more basic change in the way we think about ourselves and our world. Our *egocentric* outlook sets our own interests as standards for how to live; a sustainable environment demands an *ecocentric* outlook that helps us to see that the present is tied to the future and that everyone must work together. Most nations in the southern half of the world are *underdeveloped*, unable to meet the basic needs of their people. At the same time, most countries in the northern half of the world are *overdeveloped*, using more resources than the earth can sustain over time. Changes needed to create a sustainable ecosystem will not come easily. But the price of not responding to the growing environmental deficit will certainly be greater (Humphrey & Buttel, 1982; Burke, 1984; Kellert & Bormann, 1991; Brown et al., 1993).

In closing, consider that the great dinosaurs dominated this planet for some 160 million years and then perished forever. Humanity is far younger, having existed for a mere 250 000 years. Compared to the rather dim-witted dinosaurs, our species has the gift of great intelligence. But how will we use this ability? What are the chances that our species will continue to flourish 160 million years—or even 1000 years—from now? The shape of tomorrow's world depends on choices we make today.

# Reclaiming the Environment:
# What Are You Willing to Give Up?

Surveys tell us that many people in Canada describe themselves as sympathetic to environmentalism. Yet, we are unsure that we are willing to give up very much to reclaim the ecosystem.

At the outset, the environmental movement did not ask much of us. The "first wave" of environmentalism was little more than a conservation movement that focussed on protecting natural wilderness—such as the park in Banff, established in 1887—in the face of rapid economic development. Conservationists were responsible for pressing legislators to create scores of national parks and other protected areas where wildlife would be left undisturbed. Some Canadian conservationists became active in the U.S.-based Sierra Club and the National Audubon Society, both of which continue to monitor North American environmental issues today.

During the 1960s and early 1970s, a "second wave" of environmentalism took root, motivated predominantly by members of the upper-middle class, including university and college students and people from white-collar occupations.

In the 1990s, more members of the middle class, including artists and civil servants, have taken up the environmental cause (Hannigan, 1998). But how important is the environment today to the average Canadian citizen? As the figure shows, for most of the period between 1988 and 2001, Canadians were far more concerned about jobs than about the environment.

Canadian sociologist Shelley Ungar goes further and suggests that the environmental movements choose their agenda very carefully. The emphasis on recycling (rather than reducing and reusing), is a conscious choice taken by environmental groups. When faced with choosing between advocating car tune-up and proper tire pressure (rather than a reduction in driving), these movements choose the former because they "anticipated and actually encountered sufficient opposition from their middle-class constituency that they avoided taking challenging positions" (Ungar, 1998:269).

Perhaps our society has come to accept the idea that environmentalism is good in principle—but in reality, we are prepared to act on this idea only when other things, including jobs, are in place. It is far from clear that most people are willing to make the hard choices necessary to shift to a sustainable way of life.

*Continue the debate. . .*

1. *Do you think that limiting economic growth is necessary to secure our environmental future? Would you be willing to accept a lower standard of living to protect the natural environment?*

2. *What action have you ever taken (signing a petition, participating in a demonstration, modifying your consumption patterns) to safeguard the environment?*

3. *Where do you think the major Canadian political parties stand on environmental issues?*

Sources: Based on Angus Reid Group Inc. (1998d, 1998f, 1999c, 2000c, 2000d, 2000e, 2000f, 2000g, 2000h), Hannigan (1998), Ungar 1998).

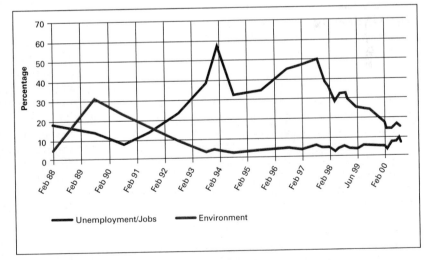

**Priorities for Government, Percentages Representing Poll Groups, Canada 1988–2000**

*Question:* When you think of issues presently confronting Canada, which one do you feel should receive the greatest attention from Canada's leaders?

**Note:** The percentages above represent the numbers of people who mentioned these topics among their top three issues.

Source: Angus Reid Group Inc. (1998d, 1998f, 1999c, 2000c, 2000d, 2000e, 2000f, 2000g, 2000h).

# SUMMARY

## POPULATION

1. Fertility and mortality, measured as crude birth rates and crude death rates, are major factors affecting population size.

2. Migration, another key demographic concept, has special importance to the historical growth of Canada and cities everywhere.

3. Demographers use age-sex pyramids to graphically show the composition of a population and to project population trends. Sex ratio refers to a society's balance of females and males.

4. Historically, world population grew slowly because high birth rates were largely offset by high death rates. About 1750, a demographic transition began as world population rose sharply, mostly due to falling death rates.

5. Thomas Robert Malthus warned that population growth would outpace food production, resulting in social calamity. Demographic transition theory, however, contends that technological advances gradually slow population increase.

6. World population is expected to reach between 7.3 and 10.7 billion by 2050. Such an increase will likely overwhelm many poor societies, where most of the increase will take place.

## URBANIZATION

1. The first urban revolution began with the appearance of cities about 8000 B.C.E. By the start of the common era, cities had emerged in most regions of the world except for North America.

2. Pre-industrial cities have low-rise buildings, narrow, winding streets, and personal social ties.

3. A second urban revolution began about 1750 as the Industrial Revolution propelled rapid urban growth in Europe. The physical form of cities changed, as planners created wide, regular streets to facilitate trade. The emphasis on commerce, as well as the increasing size of cities, made urban life more anonymous.

4. Urbanism came to North America with Europeans, who settled in a string of colonial towns dotting the Atlantic coastline. By 1850, hundreds of new cities were founded from coast to coast.

5. By 1931, most of the Canadian population lived in urban areas.

6. Rapid urbanization in Europe during the 19th century led early sociologists to contrast rural and urban life. Ferdinand Tönnies built his analysis on the concepts of *Gemeinshaft* and *Gesellschaft*, and Emile Durkheim devised parallel concepts of mechanical solidarity and organic solidarity. Georg Simmel claimed that the overstimulation of city life produced a blasé attitude in urbanites.

7. Robert Park, at the University of Chicago, believed cities permit greater social freedom. Louis Wirth saw large, dense, heterogeneous populations creating an impersonal and self-interested—though tolerant—way of life. Other researchers have explored urban ecology and urban political economy.

8. A third urban revolution is now occurring in low-income countries, where most of the world's largest cities will soon be found.

## ENVIRONMENT

1. A key factor affecting the natural environment is how human beings organize social life. Thus, ecologists study how living organisms interact with their environment.

2. Societies increase the environmental deficit by focussing on short-term benefits and ignoring the long-term consequences brought on by their way of life.

3. Our ability to alter the natural world lies in our capacity for culture. Humanity's effect on the environment has increased along with the development of complex technology.

4. The "logic of growth" supports economic development claiming that people can solve environmental problems as they arise. The opposing "limits to growth" thesis states that societies must curb development to prevent eventual environmental collapse.

5. Environmental issues include disposing of solid waste, as well as protecting the quality of air and water. The supply of clean water is already low in some parts of the world.

6. Rain forests help remove carbon dioxide from the atmosphere and are home to a large share of this planet's living species. Under pressure from commercial interests, the world's rain forests are now half their original size and are shrinking by about 1 percent annually.

7. Environmental racism refers to the pattern by which the poor—especially minorities—suffer most from environmental hazards.

8. A sustainable environment does not threaten the well-being of future generations. Achieving this goal requires controlling world population, conserving finite resources, and reducing waste and pollution.

## KEY CONCEPTS

### POPULATION

**demography** (p. 376) the study of human population

**fertility** (p. 376) the incidence of childbearing in a country's population

**crude birth rate** (p. 376) the number of live births in a given year for every 1000 people in a population

**mortality** (p. 376) the incidence of death in a society's population

**crude death rate** (p. 376) the number of deaths in a given year for every 1000 people in a population

**infant mortality rate** (p. 376) the number of deaths among infants under one year of age for each 1000 live births in a given year

**life expectancy** (p. 377) a synthetic measure of the average life span of a society's population

**migration** (p. 377) the movement of people into and out of a specified territory

**sex ratio** (p. 378) the number of males for every 100 females in a given population

**age-sex pyramid** (p. 379) a graphic representation of the age and sex of a population

**demographic transition theory** (p. 381) a thesis linking population patterns to a society's level of technological development

**zero population growth** (p. 382) the level of reproduction that maintains population at a steady state

### URBANIZATION

**urbanization** (p. 383) the concentration of humanity into cities

**metropolis** (p. 386) a large city that socially and economically dominates an urban area

**suburbs** (p. 386) urban areas beyond the political boundaries of a city

**Census Agglomerations (CAs)** (p. 387) towns and surrounding areas where more than 10 000 people live in the urban core

**Census Metropolitan Areas (CMAs)** (p. 387) cities and surrounding areas where more than 100 000 people live in the urban core

**megalopolis** (p. 387) a vast urban region containing a number of cities and their surrounding suburbs

*Gemeinschaft* (p. 388) a type of social organization by which people are bound closely together by kinship and tradition

*Gesellschaft* (p. 388) a type of social organization by which people have weak social ties and considerable self-interest

### ENVIRONMENT

**urban ecology** (p. 389) the study of the link between the physical and social dimensions of cities

**ecology** (p. 390) the study of the interaction of living organisms and the natural environment

**natural environment** (p. 390) the earth's surface and atmosphere including various living organisms and the air, water, soil, and other resources necessary to sustain life

**ecosystem** (p. 391) a system composed of the interaction of all living organisms and their natural environment

**environmental deficit** (p. 392) the situation in which our relation to the environment, while yielding short-term benefits, will have profound, negative long-term consequences

**rain forests** (p. 398) regions of dense forestation, most of which circle the globe close to the equator

**greenhouse effect** (p. 398) a rise in the earth's average temperature (global warming) due to an increasing concentration of carbon dioxide in the atmosphere

**environmental racism** (p. 399) the pattern by which environmental hazards are greatest in proximity to poor people—and especially minorities

**ecologically sustainable culture** (p. 400) a way of life that meets the needs of the current generation without threatening the environmental legacy of future generations

## CRITICAL-THINKING QUESTIONS

1. What are fertility and mortality rates? Which one has been more important in increasing global population?

2. How does demographic transition theory explain population patterns in terms of technological development?

3. According to Ferdinand Tönnies, Emile Durkheim, Georg Simmel, and Louis Wirth, what characterizes urbanism as a way of life? Note several differences in the ideas of these thinkers.

4. Evaluate the environmental prediction of Thomas Robert Malthus. On balance, do you think he was more wrong or more right? Why?

## APPLICATIONS AND EXERCISES

1. Here is an illustration of the problem of runaway growth (Milbrath, 1989:10): A pond has a single water lily growing on it. The lily doubles in size each day. In 30 days, it covers the entire pond. On which day does it cover half the pond? When you realize the answer, discuss the implications of this example for population increase.

2. Draw a "mental map" of a city familiar to you with as much detail of specific places, districts, roads, and transportation facilities as possible. Compare your map to a "real" one, or, better yet, a map drawn by someone else. Try to account for the differences.

3. Get a plastic trash bag and carry it around with you for one full day. Put everything you throw away in the bag. Afterward, weigh what you have; multiply this amount by 365 to estimate your yearly "trash factor." Multiple this amount by 30 million to estimate the annual waste of the entire Canadian population.

4. In the Bible, read Genesis, Chapter 1, especially verses 28–31. According to this account of creation, are humans empowered to do what we wish to the earth? Or are we charged to care for the earth? For more on this idea, see Wolkomir et al. (1997).

# SITES TO SEE

**www.pearsoned.ca/macionis**

Visit the interactive Web site that accompanies this text. Begin by clicking on the cover of your book. You will find a chapter-by-chapter study guide, practice tests, chat room, and many additional Web links.

**www.eclac.org**

This site, created by the Latin American and Caribbean Demographic Center (part of the United Nations), allows country-by-country analysis of population patterns for this region of the world.

**www.urban.nyu.edu**

New York University's Taub Urban Research Center is on the Internet. Visit this site to survey recent research on urban issues.

**www.mte.com/webcam**

Watch big-city life from the comfort of your own home: This site uses a cyber-view camera showing the action on New York City's Fifth Avenue and Forty-Fifth Street. What can you learn from "people watching" in this way? What does this observation *not* tell you about urban life?

**www.sierraclub.org**
**www.greenpeace.org**

Here are two environmental sites maintained by the Sierra Club and Greenpeace. Visit the two sites and see how these organizations are similar to one another as well as how they differ.

**www.kenyon.edu/projects/agri**

This site, constructed by college students, investigates how the way we live affects the planet and how the state of our planet affect our lives.

**www.rprogress.org**

Redefining Progress is a public policy organization that argues that we need to include both ecological sustainability and personal quality of life (such as the number of hours of leisure) when we estimate quality of life measures. The Genuine Progress Indicator attempts to do so.

On this site you can also estimate your ecological footprint—the amount of land required to sustain your current lifestyle—based on answers to 13 questions.

**www.census.gov/ipc/www**

The United States Census Bureau maintains a Web site where you can get basic demographic data for most countries. There is also a population watch on this site that shows the size of the global population. Most, if not all, publications released by the Census Bureau are freely available in electronic format.

**www.publications.worldbank.org**

One of the best-kept secrets is that the World Bank has the most recent *World Development Report* available in electronic format on their Web site.

**www.statcan.ca**

Statistics Canada keeps up-to-date information on the Canadian population. There are many free publications available, and you can sign up for the *Daily*—a daily e-mail from Statistics Canada that includes summaries of the most recently released publications.

# CHAPTER 16

# SOCIAL CHANGE: MODERN AND POSTMODERN SOCIETIES

*In 1900, people lined up at the Paris Exposition to catch a glimpse of some of the world's latest inventions, including something called a "voice recorder" and the Kodak company's first small camera, the "Brownie." The same year, not far away in Germany, a physicist named Max Planck had just discovered atomic radiation, although he was not sure exactly what it was and had little idea of what people might do with it. Another German, a doctor named Sigmund Freud, published a book on the interpretation of dreams, which few people found very convincing. Farther east in Russia, a young man named Vladimir Lenin published his first newspaper article calling for a people's revolution to overthrow the government. In China, a rebellion against exploitation by foreign powers started the world thinking about the evils of colonialism. Across the Atlantic Ocean in Newfoundland, 1901 saw Gugliemo Marconi receive the first wireless telegraph signal sent across the Atlantic from Cornwall, England. The young Marconi, then only 27 years of age, had amazed leading physicists all over the world.*

*It is scarcely possible for people today to imagine how different life was a century ago. Most people in Canada still lived in small towns and on farms. They had no computers, televisions, or even radios. Most homes did not even have electricity. There were no superhighways—only a few people had ever seen an automobile (known back then as a "horseless carriage"). Most people travelled around their communities by foot or on horseback, and a few went greater distances by railroad, in passenger cars pulled by steam-powered locomotives. Almost all women worked only in the home; none was permitted by law to vote. For both women and men, life was also much shorter: On average, people lived only about 50 years.* ■

It is easy to find ways in which life today seems better than it was a century ago. We now enjoy countless conveniences, travel farther and faster, and live longer than ever before. Yet, as this chapter explains, social change is a process with negative as well as positive consequences. Indeed, as we shall see, the founding thinkers of sociology were mixed in their assessment of *modernity*, changes brought about by the Industrial Revolution. Likewise, today's sociologists point to both good and bad qualities of *postmodernity*, the recent transformations caused by the Information Revolution and the post-industrial economy. What is clear—for better and worse—is that the rate of change has never been faster than it is now.

**407**

*Because change in industrial societies is so rapid, we can see differences in personal appearance—one important kind of fashion—over short periods of time. The five photographs (beginning with the top left) show hairstyles commonly worn by women in the 1950s, 1960s, 1970s, 1980s, and 1990s.*

## WHAT IS SOCIAL CHANGE?

In earlier chapters, we examined relatively *static* social patterns, including status and role, social stratification, and social institutions. We also looked at the *dynamic* forces that have shaped our way of life, ranging from innovations in technology to the growth of bureaucracy and the expansion of cities. These are all dimensions of **social change,** *the transformation of culture and social institutions over time.* This complex process has four major characteristics:

1. **Social change happens all the time.** "Nothing is certain except death and taxes," goes the old saying. Yet our thoughts about death have changed dramatically as life expectancy in Canada has doubled since 1850 (Beaujot, 1991). Taxes, meanwhile, were unknown through most of human history, beginning only as societies grew in size several thousand years ago. In short, virtually everything is subject to the twists and turns of change.

    Still, some societies change faster than others. As Chapter 2 (Culture) explained, hunting and gathering societies change quite slowly; members of technologically complex societies, on the other hand, can witness significant change within the space of a single lifetime.

    Moreover, in a given society, some cultural elements change faster than others. William Ogburn's (1964) theory of *cultural lag* (see Chapter 2) asserts that material culture (that is, things) usually changes faster than nonmaterial culture (ideas and attitudes). For example, medical technology that prolongs life has developed more rapidly than have ethical standards for deciding when and how to use it.

2. **Social change is sometimes intentional but often unplanned.** Industrial societies actively promote many kinds of change. For example, scientists seek more efficient forms of energy, and advertisers try to convince us that life is incomplete without this or that new gadget. Yet rarely can anyone envision all the consequences of the changes that are set in motion.

    Early automobile manufacturers understood that cars would allow people to travel in a single day distances that a century before had required weeks or months. But no one could see how much the mobility provided by automobiles would alter life in Canada, scattering family members, threatening the environment, and reshaping cities and suburbs. Neither could automotive pioneers have predicted the more than 3000 deaths each year in car accidents, or the 170 000 Canadians with disabilities due to motor vehicle accidents.

3. **Social change is controversial.** As the history of the automobile demonstrates, social change has both good and bad consequences. Capitalists welcomed the Industrial Revolution because advancing technology increased productivity and swelled profits. Many workers, however, feared that machines would make their skills obsolete and therefore resisted the push toward "progress." In Canada, changing patterns of social interaction between Aboriginals, visible minorities and other Canadians, women and men, and gays and heterosexuals, give rise to both celebration and backlash as people disagree about how we ought to live.

4. **Some changes matter more than others.** Some changes (such as clothing fads) have only passing significance, whereas other innovations (such as computers) last a long time and may change the entire world. Looking ahead, will the Information Revolution turn out to be as pivotal as was the Industrial Revolution? Like the automobile and television, computers will continue to have both positive and negative effects, providing new kinds of jobs while eliminating old ones, isolating some people in offices while linking others in global electronic networks, offering vast amounts of information while threatening personal privacy.

## CAUSES OF SOCIAL CHANGE

Social change has many causes. And in a world linked by sophisticated communication and transportation technology, change in one place often begets change elsewhere.

### CULTURE AND CHANGE

Chapter 2 (Culture) identified three important sources of cultural change. First, *invention* produces new objects, ideas, and social patterns. Rocket propulsion research, which began in the 1940s, has produced sophisticated spacecraft that can reach toward the stars. Today we take such technology for granted; during the 21st century, a significant number of people may well travel in space.

Second, *discovery* occurs as people take notice of existing elements of the world. Medical advances, for

*Today, most of the people with access to computers live in high-income countries such as Canada. But the number of people in agrarian societies going online is on the rise. How do you think the introduction of new information technology will change more traditional societies? Are all the changes likely to be for the good?*

example, offer a growing understanding of the human body. Beyond their direct effects on human health, medical discoveries have stretched life expectancy, setting in motion the "greying" of Canadian society (see Chapter 3, Socialization: From Infancy to Old Age).

Third, *diffusion* creates change as products, people, and information spread from one society to another. Ralph Linton (1937a) recognized that many familiar aspects of our culture came from other lands. For example, cloth (developed in Asia), clocks (invented in Europe), and coins (devised in Turkey) have all become part of our way of life. In general, material things diffuse more easily than cultural ideas. That is, new breakthroughs (such as the science of cloning) occur faster than our understanding of when—and even if—they are morally desirable.

### CONFLICT AND CHANGE

Tension and conflict within a society also produce change. Karl Marx saw class conflict as the engine that drives societies from one historical era to another. In industrial-capitalist societies, he maintained, the struggle between capitalists and workers propels society toward a socialist system of production.

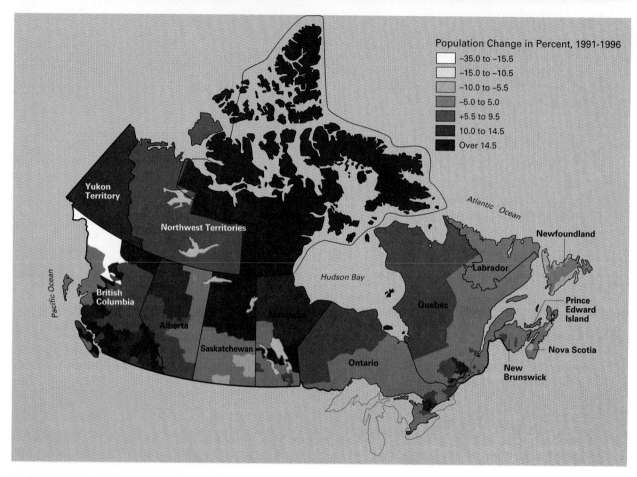

Population Change in Percent, 1991-1996
- −35.0 to −15.5
- −15.0 to −10.5
- −10.0 to −5.5
- −5.0 to 5.0
- +5.5 to 9.5
- 10.0 to 14.5
- Over 14.5

**NATIONAL MAP 16–1    Population Change, Canada, 1991–1996**

This map illustrates that population changes at different rates across Canada. The growth in our largest cities is evident in the map, but it also shows that there are many rural areas that are growing rapidly. What are the most important causes and consequences of the different rates of growth across Canada?

Source: Calculated based on data in Statistics Canada Catalogue No. 95F0181XDB96001 (1998b).

In more than a century since Marx's death, this model has proved to be simplistic. Yet Marx correctly foresaw that social conflict arising from inequality (involving not just class but race and gender) would force changes in every society, including our own.

### IDEAS AND CHANGE

Max Weber also contributed to our understanding of social change. While Weber acknowledged that conflict could bring about change, he traced the roots of most social changes to ideas. For example, people with charisma can carry a message that sometimes changes the world.

Weber highlighted the importance of ideas by revealing how the religious beliefs of early Protestants set the stage for the spread of industrial capitalism (see Chapter 13, Family and Religion). The fact that industrial capitalism developed primarily in areas of Western Europe where the Protestant work ethic was strong proved to Weber (1958; orig. 1904–5) the power of ideas to bring about change.

## DEMOGRAPHIC CHANGE

Population patterns can also transform a society. Profound change is taking place as our population, collectively speaking, grows older. As Chapter 3 (Socialization: From Infancy to Old Age) explained, 11 percent of the Canadian population is over age 65, triple the proportion in 1900. By the year 2030, seniors will account for 25 percent of the total. Medical research and health care services already focus extensively on the elderly, and life will change in countless additional ways as homes and household products are redesigned to meet the needs of growing ranks of older consumers.

Migration within and among societies is another demographic factor that promotes change. In Canada between 1870 and 1930, millions of immigrants entered industrial cities. Thousands more from rural areas joined the rush. As a result, farm communities declined, metropolises expanded, and Canada for the first time became a predominantly urban nation. Similar changes are taking place today as people moving from Moncton to Victoria mix with new immigrants from Latin America, Asia, and India.

Where in Canada have demographic changes been greatest? National Map 16–1 provides one answer, showing where the largest share of people do—and do not—move.

## SOCIAL MOVEMENTS AND CHANGE

A final cause of social change lies in our own efforts. People commonly band together to form **social movements,** *organized activity that encourages or discourages social change.* Our nation's history is the story of all kinds of social movements, from the colonial drive for independence to today's organizations supporting or opposing abortion, gay rights, and gun control.

**Types of social movements.** Researchers classify social movements according to the kind of change they seek (Aberle, 1966; Cameron, 1966; Blumer, 1969). One variable asks, *Who is changed?* Some movements target selected people while others try to change everyone. A second variable asks, *How much change?* Some movements attempt only superficial change, while others pursue a radical transformation of society. Combining these variables results in four types of social movements, as shown in Figure 16–1.

*Alternative social movements* are the least threatening to the status quo because they seek limited change in only some parts of the population. Promise Keepers, one example of an alternative social movement, encourages Christian men to be more spiritual and supportive of their families.

*Redemptive social movements* also have a selective focus, seeking radical change in some individuals. For

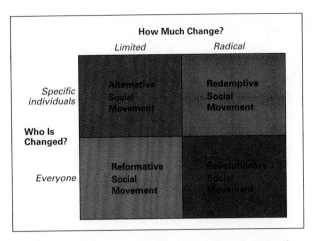

**FIGURE 16–1   Four Types of Social Movements**
Source: Based on Aberle (1966).

example, Alcoholics Anonymous is an organization that helps people with an alcohol addiction achieve a sober life.

*Reformative social movements* aim for only limited change, but target everyone. The environmental movement seeks to interest everyone in protecting the natural environment.

*Revolutionary social movements* are the most extreme of all, striving for major transformation of an entire society. Sometimes pursuing specific goals, sometimes spinning utopian dreams, these social movements (including both the left-wing Communist Party and right-wing militia organizations) seek to radically alter our social institutions.

**Explaining social movements.** Sociologists have devised several ways of looking at social movements. One approach, *deprivation theory*, holds that social movements arise among people who feel deprived of something—say, income, safe working conditions, or political rights. Whether one feels deprived or not, of course, depends on one's expectations. Thus, people mobilize in response to **relative deprivation,** *a perceived disadvantage arising from some specific comparison.* This concept helps explain why movements for change surface in both good and bad times: It is not people's absolute standing that counts but how they subjectively perceive their own situation (Tocqueville, 1955, orig. 1856; Davies, 1962; Merton, 1968).

*Mass-society theory*, a second approach, argues that social movements attract socially isolated people who seek, through their membership, a sense of identity and purpose. From this point of view, social movements have a personal as well as a political agenda (Kornhauser, 1959; Melucci, 1989).

*Resource-mobilization theory*, a third theoretical scheme, links the success of any social movement to

*One example of a new social movement is the worldwide effort to eliminate land mines. Years after hostilities cease, these mines still remain in place and take a staggering toll in civilian lives. At a protest in Berlin, Germany, a mountain of shoes stands as a memorial to the tens of thousands who have been crippled or died as a result of stepping on underground mines.*

available resources—including money, human labour, and access to the mass media. Since most social movements begin small, they must look beyond themselves to mobilize the resources needed to increase their chances for success (Killian, 1984; Snow et al., 1986; Baron, Mittman, & Newman, 1991; Burstein, 1991; Meyer & Whittier, 1994; Zhao, 1998).

Fourth, *culture theory* points out that social movements depend not only on material resources but also on cultural symbols. People must have a shared understanding of injustice in the world before they can mobilize to bring about change. In addition, specific symbols (such as mass media images of starving children around the world) can generate powerful feelings that motivate people to act (Giugni, 1998; Staggenborg, 1998).

Fifth, and finally, *new social movements theory* points out the distinctive character of recent social movements in post-industrial societies. Not only are these movements typically national or international in scope, but most focus on quality-of-life issues—including the natural environment, world peace, or animal rights—rather than the traditional concern with economic issues (Tindall, 1994; Tyyskä, 1998). This broader scope of contemporary social movements results from closer ties among governments and among ordinary people around the world, who are now linked by the mass media and new information technology (Melucci,

1980; McAdam, McCarthy, & Zald, 1988; Kriesi, 1989; Pakulski, 1993; Jenkins & Wallace, 1996).

**Stages in social movements.** Social movements typically unfold in stages. The *emergence* of social movements occurs when a small group believes society is flawed. Both the women's movement and the response to the AIDS crisis began with a small vanguard who tried to mobilize the public.

The *coalescence* of a social movement depends on available resources. A newly formed movement must clearly state its goal, recruit new members, and devise policies and tactics. Leaders must also gain access to the mass media and forge alliances with other organizations.

As it accumulates resources, a social movement may undergo *bureaucratization*. This means that a movement's becoming established depends less on the charisma and talents of a few leaders than on a professional staff, which increases the chances for the movement's long-term survival.

Finally, social movements *decline* as resources dry up, the group faces overwhelming opposition, or members achieve their goals and lose interest. Some well-established organizations outlive their original causes and move on to new crusades; others lose touch with the idea of changing society and choose, instead, to become part of the "system" (Piven & Cloward, 1977; Miller, 1983).

# MODERNITY

A central concept in the study of social change is **modernity**, *social patterns resulting from industrialization*. In everyday terms, modernity (its Latin root means "lately") refers to the present in relation to the past. Sociologists use this catchall concept to describe the many social patterns set in motion by the Industrial Revolution beginning in Western Europe in the mid-18th century. **Modernization**, then, is *the process of social change begun by industrialization*. Peter Berger (1977) identified four major characteristics of modernization:

1. **The decline of small, traditional communities.** Modernity involves "the progressive weakening, if not destruction, of the . . . relatively cohesive communities in which human beings have found solidarity and meaning throughout most of history" (Berger, 1977:72). For thousands of years, in the camps of hunters and gatherers and in the rural villages of Europe and North America, people lived in small-scale communities where life revolved around family and neighbourhood. Such traditional worlds give each person a well-defined place that, while limiting range of choice, offers a strong sense of identity, belonging, and purpose.

*George Tooker's 1950 painting* The Subway *depicts a common problem of modern life: Weakening social ties and eroding traditions create a generic humanity in which everyone is alike yet each person is an anxious stranger in the midst of others.*

Source: George Tooker, *The Subway*, 1950, egg tempera on composition board, 18 1/8 × 36 1/8", Whitney Museum of American Art, New York. Purchased with funds from the Julianna Force Purchase Award, 50.23.

Small, isolated communities still exist in Canada, of course, but they are now home to only a small percentage of our nation's people. These days, their isolation is only geographic: Cars, telephones, television, and, increasingly, computers, allow most rural families to take the pulse of the larger society, and connect them to the entire world.

2. **The expansion of personal choice.** People in traditional, pre-industrial societies view their lives as shaped by forces—gods, spirits, or, simply, fate—beyond human control. As the power of tradition erodes, people come to see their lives as an unending series of options, a process Berger calls *individualization.* It is not unusual for people in Canada, for instance, to show an openness to change by discarding one "lifestyle" and adopting another. Indeed, a common belief is that people *should* take control of their lives.

3. **Increasing social diversity.** In pre-industrial societies, strong family ties and powerful religious beliefs enforce conformity, and discourage diversity and change. Modernization promotes a more rational, scientific worldview, as tradition loses its hold and people gain more individual choice. The growth of cities, expansion of impersonal bureaucracy, and the social mix of people from various backgrounds combine to foster diverse beliefs and behaviour.

4. **Future orientation and growing awareness of time.** While premodern people focus on the past, people in modern societies think more about the future. Modern people are not only forward-looking but also optimistic that new inventions and discoveries will improve their lives.

Modern people also organize daily routines down to the very minute. With the introduction of clocks in the late Middle Ages, Europeans began to think not in terms of sunlight and seasons but in terms of hours and minutes. Preoccupied with personal gain, modern people demand precise measurement of time and are likely to agree that "Time is money." Berger points out that one indicator of a society's degree of industrialization is the proportion of people wearing wristwatches.

Finally, recall that modernization touched off the development of sociology itself. As Chapter 1 (Sociology: Perspective, Theory, and Method) explained, the discipline originated in the wake of the Industrial Revolution in Western Europe, a time and place where social change was proceeding most intensely. Early European and North American sociologists tried to analyze the rise of modern society and its consequences—both good and bad—for human beings.

## FERDINAND TÖNNIES: THE LOSS OF COMMUNITY

The German sociologist Ferdinand Tönnies (1855–1937) produced a lasting account of modernization in his theory of *Gemeinschaft* and *Gesellschaft* (see Chapter 15, Population, Urbanization, and Environment). Like Peter Berger, whose work he influenced, Tönnies (1963; orig. 1887) viewed modernization as the progressive loss of *Gemeinschaft,* or human community. As Tönnies saw it, the Industrial Revolution weakened the social fabric of family and tradition by introducing a businesslike emphasis on facts, efficiency, and money. European and North American societies gradually became rootless and impersonal as people came to associate with one another mostly on the basis of self-interest—the state Tönnies termed *Gesellschaft*.

Early in the 20th century, at least some of Canada approximated Tönnies's concept of *Gemeinschaft*. Families that had lived for many generations in small villages and towns were bound together in a hard-working, slow-moving way of life. Telephones (invented in 1876) were rare; it wasn't until the early decades of the century that people were able call coast-to-coast. Living without television (introduced in 1939 and widespread after 1950), families entertained themselves, often gathering with friends in the evening to share stories, sorrows, or song. Without rapid transportation (Henry Ford's assembly line began in 1908, but cars became common only after the Second World War), for many their own town was their entire world.

Inevitable tensions and conflicts divided these communities of the past. But, according to Tönnies, the traditional spirit of *Gemeinschaft* meant that people were "essentially united in spite of all separating factors" (1963:65; orig. 1887).

Modernity turns society inside out, so that, as Tönnies put it, people are "essentially separated in spite of uniting factors" (1963:65; orig. 1887). This is the world of *Gesellschaft*, where, especially in large cities, most people live among strangers and ignore those they pass on the street. Trust is hard to come by in a mobile and anonymous society in which, according to researchers, people tend to put their personal needs ahead of group loyalty and a majority of adults believe "you can't be too careful" in dealing with people (NORC, 1999:173). No wonder that millions of men and women attend weekly support groups (also made up of strangers) where they establish temporary emotional ties and find someone who simply is willing to listen (Leerhsen, 1990).

**Critical evaluation.** Tönnies's theory of *Gemeinschaft* and *Gesellschaft* is widely used to describe modernization. The theory's strength lies in its synthesis of various dimensions of change—growing population, the rise of cities, increasing impersonality in interaction. But modern life, while often impersonal, is not devoid of *Gemeinschaft*. Even in a world of strangers, modern friendships can be strong and lasting (Wellman, 1999). Moreover, some analysts think that Tönnies favoured—perhaps even romanticized—traditional societies, while overlooking bonds of family and friendship that continue to flourish in modern societies.

## EMILE DURKHEIM: THE DIVISION OF LABOUR

The French sociologist Emile Durkheim shared Tönnies's interest in the profound social changes wrought by the Industrial Revolution. For Durkheim, modernization was marked by increasing **division of labour**, or *specialized economic activity* (1964b; orig. 1893). Whereas every member of a traditional society performs more or less the same daily round of activities, modern societies function by having people perform highly specialized roles.

Durkheim explained that pre-industrial societies are held together by *mechanical solidarity*, or shared moral sentiments (see Chapter 15, Population, Urbanization, and Environment). Thus members of such societies view everyone as basically alike, doing the same work and belonging together. Durkheim's concept of mechanical solidarity is virtually the same as Tönnies's *Gemeinschaft*.

With modernization, the division of labour becomes more and more pronounced. To Durkheim, this change meant less mechanical solidarity, but more of another kind of tie: *organic solidarity*, or the mutual dependency among people engaged in specialized work. Put simply, modern societies are held together not by likeness but by difference: All of us must depend on others to meet most of our needs. Organic solidarity corresponds to Tönnies's concept of *Gesellschaft*.

Despite obvious similarities in their thinking, Durkheim and Tönnies viewed modernity somewhat differently. To Tönnies, modern *Gesellschaft* amounted to the loss of social solidarity because people lose the "natural" and "organic" bonds of the rural village, leaving only the "artificial" and "mechanical" ties of the big city. Durkheim had a different take on modernity, even reversing Tönnies's language to bring home the point. Durkheim labelled modern society "organic," arguing that modern society is no less natural than any other, and he described traditional societies as "mechanical" because they are so regimented. Thus, Durkheim viewed modernization not so much as a loss of community as a change from community based on bonds of likeness (kinship and neighbourhood) to community based on economic interdependence (the division of labour). Durkheim's view of modernity is thus both more complex and more positive than Tönnies's view.

**Critical evaluation.** Durkheim's work stands alongside that of Tönnies, which it closely resembles, as a highly influential analysis of modernity. Of the two, Durkheim was the more optimistic; still, he feared that modern societies might become so diverse that they would collapse into **anomie**, *a condition in which society provides little moral guidance to individuals*. Living with weak moral norms, modern people can become egocentric, placing their own needs above those of others and finding little purpose in life.

The suicide rate—which Durkheim considered a good index of anomie—did, in fact, increase in Canada over the course of the 20th century. Moreover, the vast

*Max Weber maintained that the distinctive character of modern society was its rational worldview. Virtually all of Weber's work on modernity centred on types of people he considered typical of their age: the scientist, the capitalist, and the bureaucrat. Each is rational to the core: The scientist is committed to the orderly discovery of truth; the capitalist to the orderly pursuit of profit; and the bureaucrat to orderly conformity to a system to rules.*

majority of North American adults report that they see moral questions not in clear terms of right and wrong but as confusing "shades of grey" (NORC, 1999:369). Yet, shared norms and values seem strong enough to give most people a sense of meaning and purpose. Moreover, whatever the hazards of anomie, most people value the personal freedom modern society affords.

## MAX WEBER: RATIONALIZATION

For Max Weber, modernity meant replacing a traditional worldview with a rational way of thinking. In pre-industrial societies, tradition acts as a constant brake to change. To traditional people, "truth" is roughly the same as "what has always been" (1978:36; orig. 1921). To modern people, by contrast, truth is the result of rational calculation. Because they value efficiency and have little reverence for the past, modern people will adopt whatever social patterns allow them to achieve their goals.

Echoing Tönnies's and Durkheim's assertion that industrialization weakens tradition, Weber declared modern society to be "disenchanted." The unquestioned truths of an earlier time have been challenged by rational thinking: In short, modern society turns away from the gods. Throughout his life, then, Weber studied various modern "types"— the scientist, the capitalist, the bureaucrat—all of whom share the detached worldview that he believed was coming to dominate humanity.

**Critical evaluation.** Compared with Tönnies, and especially Durkheim, Weber was critical of modern society. He knew that science could produce technological and organizational wonders, yet he worried that science was carrying us away from more basic questions about the meaning and purpose of human existence. Weber feared that rationalization, especially in bureaucracies, would erode the human spirit with endless rules and regulations.

Finally, some of Weber's critics think that the alienation Weber attributed to bureaucracy actually stemmed from social inequality. This criticism leads us to the ideas of Karl Marx.

## KARL MARX: CAPITALISM

For Karl Marx, modern society was synonymous with capitalism; he saw the Industrial Revolution primarily as a *capitalist revolution.* Marx traced the emergence of the bourgeoisie in medieval Europe to the expansion of commerce. The bourgeoisie gradually displaced a feudal aristocracy as the Industrial Revolution placed a powerful new productive system under its control.

Marx agreed that modernity weakened small-scale communities (as described by Tönnies), increased the division of labour (as noted by Durkheim), and fostered a rational worldview (as Weber claimed). But he saw these simply as conditions necessary for capitalism to flourish. Capitalism, according to Marx, draws population from farms and small towns into an ever-expanding market system centred in the cities;

specialization is needed for efficient factories; and rationality is exemplified by the capitalists' relentless pursuit of profit.

Earlier chapters have painted Marx as a spirited critic of capitalist society, but his vision of modernity also incorporates a considerable measure of optimism. Unlike Weber, who viewed modern society as an "iron cage" of bureaucracy, Marx believed that social conflict in capitalist societies would sow the seeds of revolutionary change, leading to an egalitarian socialism. Such a society, as he saw it, would harness the wonders of industrial technology to enrich people's lives and also rid the world of classes, the source of social conflict and so much suffering. While Marx's evaluation of modern capitalist society was highly negative, then, he imagined a future of human freedom, creativity, and community.

**Critical evaluation.** Marx's theory of modernization is a complex theory of capitalism. But he underestimated the dominance of bureaucracy in shaping modern societies. In socialist societies, in particular, the stifling effects of bureaucracy turned out to be as bad as, or even worse than, the dehumanizing aspects of capitalism. The recent upheavals in Eastern Europe and the former Soviet Union reveal the depth of popular opposition to oppressive state bureaucracies.

# STRUCTURAL-FUNCTIONAL ANALYSIS: THE THEORY OF MASS SOCIETY

The rise of modernity is a complex process involving many dimensions of change, described in previous chapters and summarized in Table 16–1. How can we make sense of so many changes going on at once? Sociologists have devised two broad explanations of modern society, one based on the structural-functional paradigm and the other based on social-conflict theory.

The first approach—guided by the structural-functional paradigm and drawing on the ideas of Tönnies, Durkheim, and Weber—understands modernity as the emergence of *mass society* (Dahrendorf, 1959; Kornhauser, 1959; Nisbet, 1966, 1969; Baltzell, 1968; Stein, 1972; Berger, Berger, & Kellner, 1974; Pearson, 1993). A **mass society** is *a society in which industry and bureaucracy have eroded traditional social ties*. A mass society is marked by weak kinship and impersonal neighbourhoods, so individuals are socially isolated. This isolation, in turn, leaves members of mass societies morally uncertain and personally powerlessness.

## THE MASS SCALE OF MODERN LIFE

Mass-society theory argues, first, that the complexity of modern life has increased by a magnitude unimaginable in earlier times. Before the Industrial Revolution, Europe and North America formed a mosaic of countless rural villages and small towns. In these local communities, which inspired Tönnies's concept of *Gemeinschaft*, people lived out their lives surrounded by kin and guided by a shared heritage. Gossip was an informal, yet highly effective, way of ensuring conformity to community standards. Such small communities tolerated little social diversity—the state of mechanical solidarity described by Durkheim.

For example, before 1690, English law demanded that everyone regularly participate in the Christian ritual of Holy Communion (Laslett, 1984). Because social differences were repressed, subcultures and countercultures were few, and change proceeded slowly.

Increasing population, the growth of cities, and specialized economic activity driven by the Industrial Revolution gradually altered this pattern. People came to know one another by their jobs (for example, as "the doctor" or "the bank clerk") rather than by their kinship group or hometown. People looked on most others simply as strangers. The face-to-face communication of the village was eventually replaced by the impersonal mass media—newspapers, radio, television, and, more recently, computer networks. Large organizations steadily assumed more responsibility for the daily needs that had once been fulfilled by family, friends, and neighbours; public education drew more people to schools; police, lawyers, and courts supervised a formal criminal justice system. Even charity became the work of faceless bureaucrats working for various social welfare agencies.

Geographic mobility, mass communications, and exposure to diverse ways of life all erode traditional values. People become more tolerant of social diversity, defending individual rights and freedom of choice. Subcultures and countercultures multiply. Treating people differently according to their race, sex, or religion comes to be defined as backward and unjust. In the process, minorities at the margins of society gain greater power and broader participation in public life. Yet, mass society theorists fear that transforming people of various backgrounds into a generic mass may end up dehumanizing everyone.

## THE EVER-EXPANDING STATE

In the small-scale, pre-industrial societies of Europe, government amounted to little more than a local noble. A royal family formally reigned over an entire nation, but in the absence of swift transportation and efficient communication, the power of even absolute monarchs fell far short of that wielded by today's political leaders.

As technological innovation allowed government to expand, the centralized state grew in size and importance. At the time of Confederation, the federal

TABLE 16–1 Traditional and Modern Societies: The Big Picture

| Elements of Society | Traditional Societies | Modern Societies |
|---|---|---|
| **Cultural Patterns** | | |
| Values | Homogeneous; sacred character; few subcultures and countercultures | Heterogeneous; secular character; many subcultures and countercultures |
| Norms | High moral significance; little tolerance of diversity | Variable moral significance; high tolerance of diversity |
| Time orientation | Present linked to past | Present linked to future |
| Technology | Preindustrial; human and animal energy | Industrial; advanced energy sources |
| **Social Structure** | | |
| Status and role | Few statuses, most ascribed; few specialized roles | Many statuses, some ascribed and some achieved; many specialized roles |
| Relationships | Typically primary; little anonymity or privacy | Typically secondary; considerable anonymity and privacy |
| Communication | Face to face | Face-to-face communication supplemented by mass media |
| Social control | Informal gossip | Formal police and legal system |
| Social stratification | Rigid patterns of social inequality; little mobility | Fluid patterns of social inequality; considerable mobility |
| Gender patterns | Pronounced patriarchy; women's lives centered on the home | Declining patriarchy; increasing number of women in the paid labor force |
| **Social Institutions** | | |
| Economy | Based on agriculture; some manufacturing in the home; little white-collar work | Based on industrial mass production; factories become centers of production; increasing white-collar work |
| State | Small-scale government; little state intervention in society | Large-scale government; considerable state intervention in society |
| Family | Extended family as the primary means of socialization and economic production | Nuclear family retains some socialization functions but is more a unit of consumption than of production |
| Religion | Religion guides worldview; little religious pluralism | Religion weakens with the rise of science; extensive religious pluralism |
| Education | Formal schooling limited to elites | Basic schooling becomes universal, with growing proportion receiving advanced education |
| Health | High birth and death rates; brief life expectancy because of low standard of living and simple medical technology | Low birth and death rates; longer life expectancy because of higher standard of living and sophisticated medical technology |
| Settlement patterns | Small scale; population typically small and widely dispersed in rural villages and small towns | Large scale; population typically large and concentrated in cities |
| **Social Change** | Slow; change evident over many generations | Rapid; change evident within a single generation |

government was a tiny organization whose prime function was collecting and allocating taxes to different regions of the country. Since then, government has assumed responsibility for more and more areas of social life—schooling the population, regulating wages and working conditions, establishing standards for products of all sorts, administering health care, and offering financial assistance to the ill and the unemployed. To pay for such programs, taxes have soared: Today's average Canadian worker labours more than six months a year just to pay for the broad array of services the government provides.

In a mass society, power resides in large bureaucracies, leaving people in local communities little control over their lives. For example, state officials mandate that local schools must meet educational standards, local products must be government certified, and every citizen must maintain extensive tax records. While such regulations may protect people and enhance social equality, they also force us to deal increasingly with nameless officials in distant and often unresponsive bureaucracies, and they undermine the autonomy of families and local communities.

The growing complexity of modern life may have positive aspects, but only at the cost of our losing our cultural heritage. Modern societies increase individual rights, tolerate social differences, and raise living standards. But they are prone to what Weber feared most—excessive bureaucracy—as well as to Tönnies's self-centredness and Durkheim's anomie. Their size,

*Many people marvelled at the industrial technology that was changing the world a century ago. But some critics pointed out that the social consequences of the Industrial Revolution were not all positive.*

complexity, and tolerance of diversity in modern societies all but doom traditional values and family patterns, leaving individuals isolated, powerless, and materialistic. As Chapter 12 (Economics and Politics) noted, voter apathy is a serious and growing problem in Canada. But should we be surprised that individuals in vast, impersonal societies end up thinking that no one person can make a difference?

**Critical evaluation.** Critics contend that mass-society theory romanticizes the past. They remind us that many people in the small towns of our past were eager to set out for a better standard of living in cities. Moreover, this approach ignores problems of social inequality. Critics say mass-society theory attracts social and economic conservatives who defend conventional morality and are indifferent to the historical plight of women and other minorities.

## SOCIAL-CONFLICT ANALYSIS: THE THEORY OF CLASS SOCIETY

The second interpretation of modernity derives mostly from the ideas of Karl Marx. From a social-conflict perspective, modernity takes the form of a **class society**, *a capitalist society with pronounced social stratification.* That is, while agreeing that modern societies have expanded to a mass scale, this approach views the heart of modernization as an expanding capitalist economy, rife with inequality (Miliband, 1969; Habermas, 1970; Polenberg, 1980; Blumberg, 1981; Harrington, 1984).

### CAPITALISM

Class-society theory follows Marx in claiming that the increasing complexity of social life in modern times has resulted from the insatiable appetite of capitalism. Because a capitalist economy pursues ever-increasing profits, both production and consumption steadily increase. According to Marx, capitalism rests on "naked self-interest" (1972:337; orig. 1848). This self-centredness erodes the social ties that once cemented small-scale communities. Capitalism also treats people as commodities: as a source of labour and a market for capitalist products.

Capitalism supports science not just as the key to greater productivity, but as an ideology that justifies the status quo. That is, modern societies encourage people to view human well-being as a *technical* puzzle to be solved by engineers and other experts, rather than through the pursuit of *social* justice (Habermas, 1970). A capitalist culture, for example, seeks to improve health through scientific medicine rather than by eliminating poverty, which is at the root of many health problems.

Businesses also raise the banner of scientific logic, trying to increase profits through greater efficiency. As Chapter 12 (Economics and Politics) explained, capitalist corporations have reached enormous size and control unimaginable wealth by "going global" as multinationals. From the class-society point of view, then, the expanding complexity of life is less a function of *Gesellschaft* than the inevitable and destructive consequence of capitalism.

### PERSISTENT INEQUALITY

Modernity has gradually worn away some of the rigid categorical distinctions that divided pre-industrial societies. But class-society theory maintains that elites persist—albeit now as capitalist millionaires rather than nobles born to wealth and power. Canada may have no hereditary monarchy, but the richest 20 percent of families own roughly four-fifths of the country's entire wealth, and the wealthiest 10 percent of families—the "very-rich"—control over half of all property.

What of the state? Mass-society theorists contend that the state works to increase equality and combat social problems. Marx was skeptical that the state could accomplish more than minor reforms because, as he saw it, real power lies mostly in the hands of capitalists who control the economy. Class-society theorists add that, to the extent that working people and minorities do have greater political rights and enjoy a higher standard of living today, these changes are the fruits of political struggle, not expressions of government goodwill. In short, they conclude, despite our pretensions of democracy, most people are still powerless in the face of wealthy elites.

Class-society theory also dismisses Durkheim's argument that people in modern societies suffer from anomie, claiming instead that people are able to contend with alienation and powerlessness. Not surprisingly, then, the class-society interpretation of modernity enjoys widespread support among social democrats (and radicals) who favour greater equality and seek extensive regulation (or abolition) of the capitalist marketplace. Table 16–2 summarizes the views of modern society offered by mass-society theory and class-society theory. While the former focusses on the increasing complexity of social life and growth of government, the latter stresses the expansion of capitalism and the persistence of inequality.

**Critical evaluation.** A basic criticism of class-society theory is that it overlooks the increasing prosperity of modern societies, as well as the fact that discrimination based on race, ethnicity, religion, and gender is now illegal and is widely regarded as a social problem. Further, a sizable number of Canadians do not want an egalitarian society—they prefer a system of unequal rewards that reflects personal differences in talent and effort.

Moreover, few observers think that a centralized economy would cure the ills of modernity in light of socialism's failure to generate a high overall standard of living. Many other problems in Canada—from unemployment, homelessness, and industrial pollution to unresponsive government—have also been commonplace in socialist nations such as the former Soviet Union.

## MODERNITY AND THE INDIVIDUAL

Both mass- and class-society theories focus on broad patterns of change since the Industrial Revolution. But from these macro-level approaches, we can also draw micro-level insights into how modernity shapes individual lives.

### TABLE 16–2 Two Interpretations of Modernity: A Summary

| | Process of Modernization | Effects of Modernization |
|---|---|---|
| **Mass-Society Theory** | Industrialization; growth of bureaucracy | Increasing scale of life; rise of the state and other formal organizations |
| **Class-Society Theory** | Rise of capitalism | Expansion of the capitalist economy; persistence of social inequality |

## MASS SOCIETY: PROBLEMS OF IDENTITY

Modernity liberated individuals from small, tightly knit communities of the past. Most members of modern societies have privacy and freedom to express their individuality. Mass society theory suggests, however, that extensive social diversity, isolation, and rapid social change make it difficult for many people to establish any coherent identity (Wheelis, 1958; Riesman, 1970; Berger, Berger, & Kellner, 1974).

Chapter 3 (Socialization: From Infancy to Old Age) explained that people's personalities are mostly a product of their social experiences. The small, homogeneous, and slowly changing societies of the past provided a firm (if narrow) foundation for building a personal identity. Even today, Hutterite communities that flourish in Canada teach young men and women "correct" ways to think and behave. Not everyone born into a Hutterite community can tolerate such rigid demands for conformity, but most members establish a well-integrated and satisfying personal identity (Curtis & Lambert, 1990).

Because mass societies are socially diverse and rapidly changing, they offer only shifting sands on which to build a personal identity. Left to make many life decisions on their own, people—especially those with greater affluence—face a bewildering range of options. The freedom to choose has little value without standards to guide the selection process, however, and in a tolerant mass society, people may find one path no more compelling than the next. Not surprisingly, many people shuttle from one identity to another, changing their lifestyle, relationships, and even religion in search of an elusive "true self." Beset by the widespread relativism of modern societies, people without a moral compass suffer a loss of civility and find little of the virtue, security, and certainty once provided by tradition.

To David Riesman (1970; orig. 1950), modernization brings changes in **social character**, *personality patterns common to members of a particular society.* Pre-industrial societies promote what Riesman calls

*Mass-society theory attributes feelings of anxiety, isolation, and lack of meaning in the modern world to rapid social change that washes away tradition. Edvard Munch captured this vision of modern emptiness in his painting* The Scream *(left). Class-society theory, by contrast, ties the experience of powerlessness to the poverty of many amidst the privilege of the few, a situation depicted in Paul Marcus's work* Dinner Is Served *(right).*

Source: Edvard Munch, *The Scream*, Oslo, National Gallery. © Paul Marcus, *Crossing the Rio Grande*, 1999, oil painting on canvas, 63 × 72 in. Studio SPM Inc.

**tradition-directedness**, *rigid conformity to time-honoured ways of living.* Members of such societies model their lives on those of their ancestors, so that "living the good life" amounts to "doing what people have always done."

Tradition-directedness corresponds to Tönnies's *Gemeinschaft* and Durkheim's mechanical solidarity. Culturally conservative, tradition-directed people think and act alike. Unlike the conformity often found in modern societies, the uniformity of tradition-directedness is not people's effort to mimic one another. Instead, people are alike because they all draw on the same solid cultural foundation. Hutterite women and men exemplify tradition-directedness; in the Hutterite culture, tradition ties everyone to ancestors and descendants in an unbroken chain of righteous living.

Members of diverse and rapidly changing societies define a tradition-directed personality as deviant because it seems so rigid. Modern people, by and large, prize personal flexibility, the capacity to adapt, and sen-

sitivity to others. Riesman calls this type of social character **other-directedness**, *a receptiveness to the latest trends and fashions, often expressed by imitating others.* Because their socialization occurs within societies that are continuously in flux, other-directed people develop fluid identities marked by superficiality, inconsistency, and change. They try on different "selves," almost like so many pieces of new clothing, seek out "role models," and engage in varied "performances" as they move from setting to setting (Goffman, 1959). In a traditional society, such "shiftiness" marks a person as untrustworthy; but in a changing, modern society, the chameleon-like ability to fit in virtually anywhere is very useful.

In societies that value the up-to-date rather than the traditional, people anxiously look to others for approval, using members of their own generation rather than elders as role models. "Peer pressure" can be irresistible to people without strong, enduring standards to guide them. Our society urges people to be true to themselves; but when social surroundings change so rapidly, how can people develop the self to which they should be true? This problem lies at the root of the identity crisis so widespread in industrial societies today. "Who am I?" and "What is right?" are nagging questions that many of us struggle to answer. In truth, this problem is not so much psychological as sociological, reflecting the cultural instability of modern mass society.

## CLASS SOCIETY: PROBLEMS OF POWERLESSNESS

Class-society theory paints a different picture of modernity's effects on individuals. This approach maintains that persistent inequality undermines modern society's promise of individual freedom. For some, modernity serves up great privilege, but for many, everyday life means coping with economic uncertainty and a gnawing sense of powerlessness (Newman, 1993).

For Aboriginal peoples and visible minorities, the problem of relative disadvantage looms even larger. Similarly, although women participate more broadly in modern societies, they continue to run up against traditional barriers of sexism. In short, this approach rejects mass-society theory's claim that people suffer from too much freedom. Instead, class-society theory holds that our society still denies a majority of people full participation in social life.

On a global scale, as Chapter 9 (Global Stratification) explained, the expanding scope of world capitalism has placed more of the earth's population under the influence of multinational corporations. As a result, 56 percent of the world's income is currently concentrated in high-income nations, where just 15 percent of its people live. Is it any wonder, class-society theorists ask, that people in low-income nations seek greater power to shape their own lives?

The problem of widespread powerlessness led Herbert Marcuse (1964) to challenge Max Weber's contention that modern society is rational. Marcuse condemned modern society as irrational for failing to meet the needs of so many people. While modern capitalist societies produce unparalleled wealth, poverty remains the daily plight of more than 1 billion people. Moreover, Marcuse argued, technological advances further reduce people's control over their own lives. The advent of high technology generally has conferred a great deal of power on a core of specialists—not the majority of people—who now dominate discussion of events such as computing, energy production, and health care. Countering the popular view that technology *solves* the world's problems, Marcuse suggested that it is more accurate to say that science *causes* them. In sum, class-society theory asserts that people suffer because modern societies have concentrated both wealth and power in the hands of a privileged few.

## MODERNITY AND PROGRESS

In modern societies, most people expect—and applaud—social change. We link modernity to the idea of *progress* (from the Latin, meaning "moving forward"), a state of continual improvement. By contrast, we see stability as stagnation.

Given our bias in favour of change, members of our society tend to look upon traditional cultures as backward. But change, particularly toward material affluence, is a mixed blessing. As the Global Sociology box on page 422 shows, social change is too complex to equate with progress. Even getting rich has its advantages and disadvantages, as the case of the Kaiapo illustrates.

Historically, among people in Canada, a rising standard of living has made lives longer and, in a material sense, more comfortable. At the same time, many people wonder if today's routines are too stressful, with families often having little time for relaxation or simply spending time together.

Science, too, has its pluses and minuses. As Figure 16–2 on page 423 shows, people in Canada have considerable confidence—more than those in most other industrial societies apart from the U.S.—that science improves our lives. But surveys also show that many North Americans feel that science "makes our way of life change too fast" (NORC, 1999:356).

New technology has always sparked controversy. A century ago, the introduction of automobiles and telephones allowed more rapid transportation and more efficient communication. But at the same time, such technology also weakened traditional attachments to hometowns and even to families. Today, people might well wonder if computer technology will do the same thing: giving us access to people around the world, but shielding us from the community right outside our doors; providing more information than ever before but, in the process, threatening personal privacy. In short, we all realize that social change comes faster all the time, but we may disagree about whether a particular change is progress or a step backward.

## MODERNITY: GLOBAL VARIATION

October 1, 1994—Kobe, Japan Riding the computer-controlled monorail high above the streets of Kobe or the 300-kilometre-per-hour bullet train to Tokyo, we see Japan as the society of the future, in love with high technology. Yet the Japanese remain strikingly traditional in other respects: Few corporate executives and almost no politicians are women; young people

# Does "Modern" Mean "Progress"?
## The Case of Brazil's Kaiapo

The firelight flickers in the gathering darkness as Chief Kanhonk sits, as he has done at the end of the day for many years, ready to begin an evening of animated talk and storytelling. This is the hour when the Kaiapo, a small society in Brazil's lush Amazon region, celebrate their heritage. Because the Kaiapo are a traditional people with no written language, the elders rely on evenings by the fire to pass along their culture to their children and grandchildren. In the past, evenings like this have been filled with tales of brave Kaiapo warriors fighting off Portuguese traders in pursuit of slaves and gold.

But as the minutes pass, only a few older villagers assemble for the evening ritual. "It is the Big Ghost," one man grumbles, explaining the poor turnout. The "Big Ghost" has indeed descended upon them; its bluish glow spills from windows throughout the village. The Kaiapo children—and many adults as well—are watching sitcoms on television. Installing a satellite dish in the village several years ago has had consequences greater than anyone imagined. In the end, what their enemies failed to do with guns,

the Kaiapo may well do to themselves with prime-time programming.

The Kaiapo are among the 230 000 native peoples who inhabit the country we call Brazil. They stand out because of their striking body paint and ornate ceremonial dress. Beginning in the 1980s, they became rich from gold mining and harvesting mahogany trees. Now they must decide if their newfound fortune is a blessing or a curse.

To some, affluence means the opportunity to learn about the outside world through travel and television. Others, like Chief Kanhonk, are not so sure. Sitting by the fire, he thinks aloud, "I have been saying that people must buy useful things

like knives and fishing hooks. Television does not fill the stomach. It only shows our children and grandchildren white people's things." Bebtopup, the oldest priest, nods in agreement, and says, "The night is the time the old people teach the young people. Television has stolen the night" (Simons, 2001:497).

The Kaiapo story shows us that change is not a simple path toward "progress." The Kaiapo are moving toward modernity, but this process will have both positive and negative consequences. On the one hand, they now enjoy a higher standard of living, with better shelters, more clothing, and new technology such as television to connect them to the larger world. On the other hand, this new affluence has greatly weakened Kaiapo traditions, so that many of their number now wonder—with good reason—who or what they have become. The drama of the Kaiapo is being played out around the world as more and more traditional cultures are being lured away from their heritage by the affluence and materialism of rich societies.

Source: Based on Simons (2001).

still accord seniors considerable respect; and public orderliness contrasts with the turmoil of Canadian cities.

Japan is a nation at once traditional and modern. This contradiction reminds us that, while it is useful to contrast traditional and modern social patterns, the old and the new often coexist in unexpected ways. In the People's Republic of China, ancient Confucian principles are mixed with contemporary socialist thinking. Similarly, in Mexico and much of Latin America, people observe centuries-old Christian rituals even as they struggle to move ahead economically. In short,

combinations of traditional and modern are far from unusual—indeed, they are found throughout the world.

## POSTMODERNITY

If modernity was the product of the Industrial Revolution, is the Information Revolution creating a postmodern era? A number of scholars think so, and use the term **postmodernity** to refer to *social patterns characteristic of post-industrial societies.*

Precisely what postmodernism is remains a matter of debate. This term has been used for decades in literary, philosophical, and even architectural circles. It has moved into sociology on a wave of social criticism that has been building since the spread of left-leaning politics in the 1960s. Although there are many variants of postmodern thinking, all share the following five themes (Bernstein, 1992; Borgmann, 1992; Crook, Pakulski, & Waters, 1992; Hall & Neitz, 1993; Inglehart, 1997; Rudel & Gerson, 1999).

1. **In important respects, modernity has failed.** The promise of modernity was a life free from want. As many postmodernist critics see it, however, the 20th century was unsuccessful in solving social problems such as poverty, since many people still lack financial security.

2. **The bright light of "progress" is fading.** Modern people look to the future expecting that their lives will improve in significant ways. Members (even leaders) of a postmodern society, however, have less confidence about what the future holds. Furthermore, the buoyant optimism that carried society into the modern era more than a century ago has given way to stark pessimism: many people in Canada and the U.S., for example, believe that life is getting worse (Angus Reid Group, Inc., 1998g; NORC, 1999:204).

3. **Science no longer holds the answers.** The defining trait of the modern era was a scientific outlook and a confident belief that technology would make life better. But postmodern critics contend that science has failed to solve many old problems (such as poor health) and has even created new problems (such as degrading the environment).

    More generally, postmodernist thinkers discredit science as a "metanarrative" that implies a singular truth. On the contrary, they maintain, objective reality and truth do not exist. Reality amounts to so much "social construction," they say; moreover, we can "deconstruct" science to see how it has been widely used for political purposes, especially by powerful segments of society.

4. **Cultural debates are intensifying.** As we have already explained, modernity represented an era of enhanced individuality and expanding tolerance. But feminists point out that patriarchy continues to limit the lives of women, and multiculturalists remind us that racial and ethnic minorities still live at the margins of society.

    Moreover, now that more people have all the material things they really need, ideas are taking on greater importance. Thus, postmodernity is also a postmaterialist era, in which issues such as social justice, as well as the environment and animal rights, command increasing public attention.

5. **Social institutions are changing.** Just as industrialization brought sweeping transformation

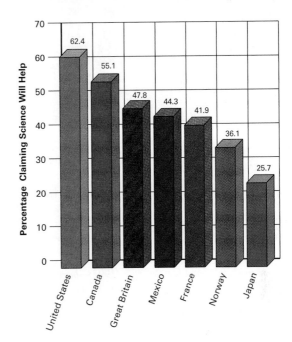

**FIGURE 16–2 Support for Science: A Global Survey**

*Survey Question*: "In the long run, do you think the scientific advances we are making will help or harm humankind?"

Source: World Values Survey (1994).

to social institutions, the rise of a post-industrial society is remaking society. For example, the Industrial Revolution placed material things at the centre of productive life; now, the Information Revolution emphasizes ideas. Similarly, the postmodern family no longer conforms to any one pattern; on the contrary, individuals are choosing among many family forms.

**Critical evaluation.** Analysts who claim that Canada and other high-income nations are entering a postmodern era criticize modernity for failing to meet human needs. Yet, in defence of modernity, we might note the marked increases in longevity and living standards over the course of the past century. Moreover, even if we were to accept postmodernist views that science is bankrupt and progress is a sham, what are the alternatives?

Finally, many voices offer different understandings of recent social trends. The Applying Sociology box on page 425 provides one case in point.

*Does advancing technology make society better? In some ways, perhaps. However, many films—including* Frankenstein *(1931) and* Jurassic Park *(1993)—have expressed the concern that new technology not only solves old problems but creates new ones. All the sociological theorists discussed in this chapter shared this ambivalent view of the modern world.*

## LOOKING AHEAD: MODERNIZATION AND OUR GLOBAL FUTURE

Imagine the entire world's population reduced to a single village of 100. The 15 richest people in the village earn 56 percent of all income. By contrast, the 41 poorest people (who together earn less than the village's richest person) lack secure housing and safe drinking water, so their lives are at risk.

The tragic plight of the world's poor shows that some desperately needed change has not yet occurred. Chapter 9 (Global Stratification) presented two competing views of why 1 billion people the world over are poor. Modernization theory claims that in the past the entire world was poor and that technological change, especially the Industrial Revolution, enhanced human productivity and raised living standards in many nations. From this point of view, the solution to global poverty is to promote technological development around the world.

For reasons suggested earlier, however, global modernization may be difficult to achieve. Recall that David Riesman portrayed pre-industrial people as *tradition-directed* and likely to resist change. So modernization theorists urge the world's rich societies to help low-income countries grow economically. Industrial nations can speed development by exporting technology to poor regions, welcoming students from these countries, and providing foreign aid to stimulate economic growth.

The review of modernization theory in Chapter 9 points to some success for these policies in Latin America and, especially, in the small Asian countries of Taiwan, South Korea, Singapore, and Hong Kong. But jump-starting development in the poorest countries of the world poses greater challenges. Moreover, even where dramatic change has occurred, modernization entails a trade-off. Traditional people, such as Brazil's Kaiapo, may acquire wealth through economic development, but only at the cost of losing their traditional identity and values as they are drawn into a global "McCulture" based on Western materialism, pop music, trendy clothes, and fast food. One Brazilian anthropologist expressed hope about the future of the Kaiapo: "At least they quickly understood the consequences of watching television. . . . Now [they] can make a choice" (Simons, 2001:497).

Not everyone thinks that modernization is really an option. According to a second approach to global stratification, *dependency theory*, today's poor societies have little ability to modernize, even if they want to. From this point of view, the major barrier to economic development is not traditionalism but global domination by rich capitalist societies. Initially, as Chapter 9 explains, this system took the form of colonialism, whereby European nations seized much of Latin America, Africa, and Asia. Trading relationships soon enriched England, Spain, and other colonial powers, while their colonies became poorer and poorer. Almost all societies subjected to this form of domination are now politically independent, but colonial-style ties

# Tracking Change:
# Is Life in Canada Getting Better or Worse?

We began this chapter with a look at what life was like in 1900—more than a century ago. It is easy to see that in many ways, life is far better today than it was for our grandparents and great-grandparents. But especially in recent decades, the indicators are not so clear-cut. Life may be improving in some respects, but in others it is getting worse. Here is a look at some trends shaping Canada since 1970.

First, the good news: By some measures life in this region is clearly improving. Infant mortality has fallen steadily, meaning that fewer children die soon after birth. In addition, an increasing share of people is reaching old age and, after reaching age 65, is living longer than ever. More good news: The poverty rate among the elderly is well below what it was in 1970. Schooling is another area of improvement: The share of people drop-ping out of high school is down, while the share completing university is up, compared to a generation ago. Finally, the *Human Development Report* for 2000 placed Canada at the top of its "human development index list" of 174 nations around the globe (United Nations Development Programme, 2000).

Now, the bad news: By some measures—several having to do with children—the quality of life in Canada has actually fallen in recent decades. The official rate of child abuse is up, as is the level of child poverty, and the rate of suicide among youths, especially males. Although the level of violent crime fell through most of the 1990s, it is still above the 1970 level. Average hourly wages—one measure of basic economic security—show a downward trend, so that families have had to rely on two or more wage-earners to maintain family income. Finally, economic inequality in this country has been increasing.

Overall, then, the evidence does not support any simple ideas about "progress over time." Social change has been—and probably will continue to be—a complex process that reflects the kinds of priorities we set for this nation as well as our will to achieve them.

*What do you think?*

1. *Based on material from earlier chapters, can you explain any of the trends described above? For example, why have suicide rates increased for youth, especially males? Which other trends can you explain?*

2. *Which of the trends mentioned above do you find most important? Why?*

3. *On balance, do you think the quality of life in Canada is improving or not? Why?*

*We tend to view tradition and modernity as opposites—the more of one found in a society, the less there is of the other. In reality, these concepts can operate independently, as we see in Japan, where traditional and modern aspects of life are often seen side by side.*

# Personal Freedom and Social Responsibility: Can We Have It Both Ways?

Shortly after midnight on a crisp March evening in 1964, a car pulled into the parking lot of a New York apartment complex. Kitty Genovese turned off the headlights, locked the doors of her vehicle, and headed across the blacktop toward the entrance to her building. Seconds later, a man wielding a knife lunged at her, and, as she shrieked in terror, he stabbed her repeatedly. Windows opened above as curious neighbours searched for the cause of the commotion. But the attack continued—for more than 30 minutes—until Genovese lay dead in the doorway. Subsequent investigation failed to identify the assailant but did confirm a stunning fact: Not one of dozens of neighbours who witnessed the attack on Kitty Genovese went to her aid or even called the police.

Decades later, people still recall the Genovese tragedy in discussions of what we "owe" others. As members of a modern society, we prize our individual rights and personal privacy, but we sometimes withdraw from public responsibility and turn a cold shoulder to people in need. When a cry for help is met by indifference, have we pushed our

modern idea of personal autonomy too far? In a cultural climate of ever more individual rights, can we keep a sense of human community?

These questions point up the tension between traditional and modern social systems, which is evident in the writings of all the sociologists discussed in this chapter. Tönnies, Durkheim, and others concluded that in some respects, traditional community and modern individualism don't go together. That is, society can unite its members in a moral community only to the extent that it limits their range of personal choices about how to live. In short, while we value both community and autonomy, we can't have it both ways.

Sociologist Amitai Etzioni (1993) has tried to strike a middle ground. The communitarian movement rests on the simple premise that "strong rights presume strong responsibilities." Or, put otherwise, an individual's pursuit of self-interest must be balanced by a commitment to the larger community.

Etzioni claims modern people have become too focussed on individual rights. That is, people expect the system

to provide for them, but they are reluctant to support the system. For example, while we believe in the principle of trial by a jury of one's peers, fewer and fewer people today are willing to perform jury duty; similarly, the public is quick to accept government services, but increasingly reluctant to pay the taxes that subsidize these services.

Communitarians advance four proposals aimed at balancing individual rights with public responsibilities. First, our society should halt the expanding "culture of rights" by which people have placed their own interests ahead of social involvement (after all, nothing in the Canadian Charter of Rights and Freedoms allows us to do whatever we want to). Second, communitarians remind us, all rights involve responsibilities (we cannot simply take from society without giving something back). Third, some responsibilities, such as upholding the law or protecting the natural environment, are too important for anyone to ignore. Fourth, defending legitimate community interests may mean limiting individual rights (protecting public

---

continue in the form of multinational corporations operating around the world.

In effect, dependency theory asserts, rich nations achieved their modernization at the expense of poor ones, which provided them with valuable natural resources and human labour. Even today, the world's poorest countries remain locked in a disadvantageous economic relationship with rich nations, dependent on wealthy countries to buy their raw materials and in return provide them with whatever manufactured products they can afford. Overall, dependency theorists conclude, continuing ties with rich societies will only perpetuate current patterns of global inequality.

Whichever approach one finds more convincing, we can no longer isolate the study of Canada from the study of the rest of the world. At the beginning of the 20th century, a majority of people in even today's high-income nations lived in relatively small settlements

with limited awareness of the larger world. Now, early in the 21st century, the entire world has become one human village because the lives of all people are increasingly linked.

The past century witnessed unprecedented human achievement. Yet solutions to many problems of human existence—including finding meaning in life, resolving conflicts among societies, and eradicating poverty— have eluded us. The Controversy & Debate box examines one dilemma: balancing individual freedom and personal responsibility. To the list of pressing matters, new concerns have been added, such as controlling population growth and establishing a sustainable natural environment. In the new century, we must be prepared to tackle such problems with imagination, compassion, and determination. Our unprecedented understanding of human society gives us reason to look to the task with optimism.

safety, for example, might mean subjecting workers to drug tests).

The communitarian movement appeals to many people who, along with Etzioni, seek to balance personal freedom with social responsibility. But critics have attacked this initiative from both sides of the political spectrum. To those on the left, problems ranging from voter apathy to street crime cannot be solved by some vague notion of "social reintegration." Instead, we need expanded government programs to increase social equality. Specifically, these critics say, we must curb the political influence of the rich and actively combat racism and sexism.

Conservatives on the political right also find fault with Etzioni's proposals, but for different reasons (Pearson, 1995). To these critics, the communitarian movement amounts to little more than a rerun of the 1960s leftist agenda. That is, the communitarian vision of a good society favours liberal goals (such as protecting the environment) but says little about conservative goals such as allowing prayer in school or restoring the strength of traditional families. Moreover, conservatives ask whether a free society should permit the kind of social engineering that Etzioni advocates (such as instituting anti-prejudice programs in schools and requiring people to perform a year of national service).

Perhaps, as Etzioni himself has suggested, the fact that both the left and the right find fault with his views indicates that he has identified a moderate, sensible answer to a serious problem. But it may also be the case that in a society as diverse as Canada, people will not readily agree about what they owe to themselves—and to each other.

Continue the debate . . .

1. *Have you ever chosen not to come to the aid of someone in need or danger? Why?*

2. *Some argue that young people today have a strong sense of "self-entitlement." Do you believe that you differ from your parents in this respect?*

3. *Do you agree or disagree that our society needs to balance rights with more responsibility? Explain your position.*

*In today's world, people can find new ways to express age-old virtues such as concern for their neighbours. Habitat for Humanity, an organization with chapters in cities and towns across North America, is made up of people who want to lend a helping hand to those in need. This chapter is helping local families realize their dream of owning a home.*

## SUMMARY

1. Every society changes continuously, although at varying speeds. Social change often generates controversy.

2. Social change is the result of invention, discovery, and cultural diffusion as well as social conflict.

3. Social movements are deliberate efforts to promote or resist change. Analysts link social movements to relative deprivation, the rootlessness of mass society, an organization's ability to muster resources, and cultural symbols that encourage change.

4. Modernity refers to the social consequences of industrialization, which, according to Peter Berger, include the erosion of traditional communities,

expansion of personal choice, increasingly diverse beliefs, and a keen awareness of the future.

5. Ferdinand Tönnies described modernization as the transition from *Gemeinschaft* to *Gesellschaft*, which signifies the progressive loss of community amid growing individualism.

6. Emile Durkheim saw modernization as a function of society's expanding division of labour. Mechanical solidarity, based on shared activities and beliefs, gradually gives way to organic solidarity, in which specialization makes people interdependent.

7. According to Max Weber, modernity replaces traditional thinking with rationality. Weber feared the dehumanizing effects of rational organization.

8. Karl Marx saw modernity as the triumph of capitalism over feudalism. Viewing capitalist societies as fraught with conflict, Marx advocated revolutionary change to achieve a more egalitarian, socialist society.

9. According to mass-society theory, modernity increases the scale of life, enlarging the role of government and other formal organizations in carrying out tasks previously performed by family members and neighbours. Cultural diversity and rapid social change make if difficult for people in modern societies to define virtue, develop stable identities, and find meaning in their lives.

10. Class-society theory states that capitalism is central to Western modernization. This approach charges that by concentrating wealth in the hands of a few, capitalism generates widespread feelings of powerlessness.

11. Social change is too complex and controversial to be equated simply with progress.

12. Postmodernity refers to cultural traits typical of post-industrial societies. Postmodern criticism of society centres on the failure of modernity, and especially science, to fulfill its promise of prosperity and well-being.

13. In a global context, modernization theory links global poverty to the power of tradition. Therefore, some modernization theorists advocate intentional intervention by rich societies to stimulate the economic development of poor nations.

14. Dependency theory explains global poverty as the product of the world economic system. The operation of multinational corporations ensures that poor nations will remain economically dependent on rich nations.

## KEY CONCEPTS

**social change** (p. 408) the transformation of culture and social institutions over time

**social movement** (p. 411) organized activity that encourages or discourages social change

**relative deprivation** (p. 411) a perceived disadvantage arising from some specific comparison

**modernity** (p. 412) social patterns resulting from industrialization

**modernization** (p. 412) the process of social change begun by industrialization

**division of labour** (p. 414) specialized economic activity

**anomie** (p. 414) Durkheim's designation of a condition in which society provides little moral guidance to individuals

**mass society** (p. 416) a society in which industry and bureaucracy have eroded traditional social ties

**class society** (p. 418) a capitalist society with pronounced social stratification

**social character** (p. 419) personality patterns common to members of a particular society

**tradition-directedness** (p. 420) rigid conformity to time-honoured ways of living

**other-directedness** (p. 420) a receptiveness to the latest trends and fashions, often expressed by imitating others

**postmodernity** (p. 422) social patterns characteristic of post-industrial societies.

## CRITICAL-THINKING QUESTIONS

1. How well do you think Tönnies, Durkheim, Weber, and Marx predicted the character of today's modern society? How are their visions of modernity the same? How do they differ?

2. What traits lead some to call Canada a "mass society"? Why do other analysts describe Canada as a "class society"?

3. What is the difference between anomie (a trait of mass society) and alienation (a characteristic of class society)? Among which categories of the Canadian population would you expect each trait to be more pronounced?

4. Why do some analysts believe that Canada has become a postmodern society? Do you agree? Why or why not?

## APPLICATIONS AND EXERCISES

1. Do you have an elderly relative or friend? If asked, most older people will be happy to tell you about the social changes they have seen in their lifetimes.

2. Ask people in your class or friendship group to make five predictions about Canadian society in the year 2050, when today's 20-year-olds will be senior citizens. Compare notes. On what issues is there agreement?

3. Has the rate of social change been increasing? Do some research about inventions over time and see for yourself. Consider, for example, modes of travel, including walking, riding animals, taking trains, cars or airplanes, and most recently riding rockets into space. The first two characterized society for tens of thousands of years; the last four emerged in barely two centuries.

 ## SITES TO SEE

**www.pearsoned.ca/macionis**

Visit the interactive Web site that accompanies this text. Begin by clicking on the cover of your book. You will find a chapter-by-chapter study guide, practice test, chat room, and many suggested Web links.

**www.canadians.org**

The Canadian Council of Canadians claims to be an independent non-partisan group providing a critical and progressive voice on key national issues.

**www.gwu.edu/~ccps**

This Web site describes the goals of the Communitarian Network.

**www.acdi-cida.gc.ca/index.htm**

The Canadian International Development Agency's purpose is to support sustainable development in low-income countries in order to reduce poverty, and contribute to a more equitable and prosperous world. The site offers extensive information on the agency's policies and projects.

**www.habitat.ca**

Habitat for Humanity Canada is a national affiliate of Habitat for Humanity, a non-profit, ecumenical Christian housing ministry dedicated to ending substandard housing and homelessness around the globe.

**www.utoronto.ca/utopia**

Deliberate change is sometimes inspired by visions of utopia—ideal societies that exist nowhere. Read about the Society for Utopian Studies at this Web site.

# G L O S S A R Y

**abortion** the deliberate termination of a pregnancy

**absolute poverty** a deprivation of resources that is life-threatening

**achieved status** a social position that a person assumes voluntarily and that reflects a significant measure of personal ability and choice

**ageism** prejudice and discrimination against the elderly

**age-sex pyramid** a graphic representation of the age and sex of a population

**agriculture** large-scale cultivation using plows harnessed to animals or more powerful energy sources

**alienation** the experience of powerlessness in social life

**animism** the belief that elements of the natural world are conscious life forms that affect humanity

**anomie** Durkheim's designation of a condition in which society provides little moral guidance to individuals

**anticipatory socialization** social learning directed toward gaining a desired position

**ascribed status** a social position that a person receives at birth or assumes involuntarily later in the life course

**asexuality** sexual attraction to people of either sex

**assimilation** the process by which minorities gradually adopt patterns of the dominant category

**authoritarianism** a political system that denies popular participation in government

**authority** power that people perceive as legitimate rather than coercive

**beliefs** specific statements people hold to be true

**bisexuality** sexual attraction to people of both sexes

**blue-collar occupation** lower-prestige work that involves mostly manual labour

**bureaucracy** an organizational model designed to perform tasks efficiently

**bureaucratic inertia** the tendency of bureaucratic organizations to perpetuate themselves

**bureaucratic ritualism** a preoccupation with rules and regulations to the point of obstructing an organization's goals

**capitalism** an economic system in which natural resources and the means of producing goods and services are privately owned

**capitalist** one who owns a factory or other productive enterprise in pursuit of profits

**caste system** social stratification based on ascription

**cause and effect** a relationship in which we know that change in one (independent) variable causes change in another (dependent) variable

**Census Agglomerations (CAs)** towns and surrounding areas where more than 10 000 people live in the urban core

**Census Metropolitan Areas (CMAs)** cities and surrounding areas where more than 100 000 people live in the urban core

**charisma** extraordinary personal qualities that can turn an audience into followers

**church** a type of religious organization well integrated into the larger society

**civil religion** a quasi-religious loyalty based on citizenship

**class society** a capitalist society with pronounced social stratification

**class system** social stratification based on both birth and individual achievement

**clearance rates** the rate at which police solve crime

**cohabitation** the sharing of a household by an unmarried couple

**cohort** a category of people with a common characteristic, usually their age

**colonialism** the process by which some nations enrich themselves through political and economic control of other nations

**concept** an abstract idea that represents some aspect of the world, inevitably in a somewhat simplified form

**concrete operational stage** Piaget's term for the level of development in which individuals perceive causal connections in their surroundings

**corporate crime** the illegal actions of a corporation or people acting on its behalf

**corporation** an organization with a legal existence, including rights and liabilities, apart from those of its members

**correlation** a relationship by which two (or more) variables change together

**counterculture** cultural patterns that strongly oppose conventional culture

**credentialism** evaluating a person on the basis of educational degrees

**crime** the violation of norms formally enacted into criminal law

**crimes against property** (property crimes) crimes that involve theft of goods belonging to others

**crimes against the person** (violent crimes) crimes that involve violence or the threat of violence

**criminal justice system** a formal response by police, courts, and prison officials to alleged crime

**criminal recidivism**  subsequent offences committed by people previously convicted of crimes

**critical sociology**  the study of society that focusses on the need for social change

**crude birth rate**  the number of live births in a given year for every 1000 people in a population

**crude death rate**  the number of deaths in a given year for every 1000 people in a population

**cult**  a religious organization that is largely outside a society's cultural traditions

**cultural integration**  the close relationship among various elements of a cultural system

**cultural lag**  the fact some cultural elements change more quickly than others, which may disrupt a cultural system

**cultural relativism**  the practice of evaluating any culture by its own standards

**cultural transmission**  the process by which one generation passes culture on to the next

**cultural universals**  traits that are part of every known culture

**culture**  the beliefs, values, behaviour, and material objects that constitute a people's way of life

**culture shock**  the personal disorientation accompanying exposure to an unfamiliar way of life

**Davis-Moore thesis**  the assertion that social stratification is universal because it benefits the operation of a society

**democracy**  a type of political system which gives power to people as a whole

**demographic transition theory**  a thesis linking population patterns to a society's level of technological development

**demography**  the study of human population

**denomination**  a church, independent of the state, that recognizes religious pluralism

**dependency theory**  a model of economic development that explains global inequality in terms of the historical exploitation of low-income societies by high-income ones

**descent**  the system by which members of a society trace kinship over generations

**deterrence**  the use of punishment to discourage criminality

**deviance**  the recognized violation of cultural norms

**direct-fee system**  a health care system in which patients pay directly for the services of physicians and hospitals

**discrimination**  treating various categories of people unequally

**division of labour**  specialized economic activity

**dramaturgical analysis**  the investigation of social interaction in terms of theatrical performance

**dyad**  a social group with two members

**ecologically sustainable culture**  a way of life that meets the needs of the current generation without threatening the environmental legacy of future generations

**ecology**  the study of the interaction of living organisms and the natural environment

**economy**  the social institution that organizes a society's production, distribution, and consumption of goods and services

**ecosystem**  a system composed of the interaction of all living organisms and their natural environment

**education**  the social institution through which society provides its members with important knowledge, including basic facts and job skills as well as cultural norms and values

**ego**  Freud's term for a person's conscious attempts to balance the pleasure-seeking drives of the human organism and the demands of society

**endogamy**  marriage between people of the same social category

**environmental deficit**  the situation in which our relation to the environment, while yielding short-term benefits, will have profound, negative long-term consequences

**environmental racism**  the pattern by which environmental hazards are greatest in proximity to poor people—and especially minorities

**ethnicity**  a shared cultural heritage

**ethnocentrism**  the practice of judging another culture by the standards of one's own culture

**ethnomethodology**  the study of the way people make sense of their everyday surroundings

**Eurocentrism**  the dominance of European (especially English) cultural patterns

**euthanasia**  (mercy killing) assisting in the death of a person suffering from an incurable illness

**exogamy**  marriage between people of different social categories

**experiment**  a research method used to investigate cause-and-effect relationships under highly controlled conditions

**expressive leadership**  group leadership that emphasizes collective well-being

**extended family**  (consanguine family) a family unit that includes parents and children, as well as other kin

**faith**  belief anchored in conviction rather than scientific evidence

**family unit**  a social group of two or more people, related by blood, marriage, or adoption, who usually live together

**family**  a social institution found in all societies that unites people in cooperative groups to oversee the bearing and raising of children

**feminism**  the advocacy of social equality for women and men, in opposition to patriarchy and sexism

**feminization of poverty**  the trend by which women are overrepresented among the poor

**fertility** the incidence of childbearing in a country's population

**folkways** less important norms that people apply with considerable individual discretion

**formal operational stage** Piaget's term for the level of development in which individuals think abstractly and critically

**formal organization** a large secondary group that is organized to achieve specific goals

**functional illiteracy** a lack of reading and writing skills needed for everyday living

*Gemeinschaft* a type of social organization by which people are bound closely together by kinship and tradition

**gender** the personal traits and social meanings that members of a society attach to being female and male

**gender** the significance that members of a society attach to being female or male

**gender roles** (sex roles) attitudes and activities that a society links to males and females

**gender stratification** the unequal distribution of wealth, power, and privilege between women and men

**genocide** the systematic killing of one category of people by another

**gerontocracy** a form of social organization in which the elderly have the most wealth, power, and privileges

**gerontology** the study of aging and the elderly

*Gesellschaft* a type of social organization by which people have weak social ties and considerable self-interest

**global economy** expanding economic activity with little regard for national borders

**global perspective** the study of the larger world and our society's place in it

**greenhouse effect** a rise in the earth's average temperature (global warming) due to an increasing concentration of carbon dioxide in the atmosphere

**groupthink** the tendency of group members to conform, resulting in a narrow view of some issue

**hate crime** a criminal act against a person or a person's property by an offender motivated by racial or other bias

**health** a state of complete physical, mental, and social well-being

**heterosexism** a view stigmatizing anyone who is not heterosexual as "queer"

**heterosexuality** sexual attraction to someone of the other sex

**hidden curriculum** subtle presentations of political or cultural ideas

**high culture** cultural patterns that distinguish a society's elite

**high-income countries** industrial nations in which most people are relatively rich

**holistic health** an approach to health care that emphasizes prevention of illness and takes into account a person's entire physical and social environment

**homogamy** marriage between people with the same social characteristics

**homophobia** the fear of close personal interaction with people thought to be gay, lesbian, or bisexual

**homosexuality** sexual attraction to someone of the same sex

**horticulture** a way of life based on the use of hand tools to raise crops

**hunting and gathering** a way of life based on the use of simple tools to hunt animals and gather vegetation

**id** Freud's term for the human being's basic drives

**ideology** cultural beliefs that justify social stratification

**incest taboo** cultural norms that forbid sex or marriage between certain relatives

**industry** the production of goods using advanced sources of energy to drive large machinery

**infant mortality rate** the number of deaths among infants under one year of age for each 1000 live births in a given year

**ingroup** an esteemed social group commanding a member's loyalty

**institutional prejudice and discrimination** bias inherent in the operation of society's institutions

**instrumental leaders** group leadership that emphasizes the completion of tasks

**intergenerational social mobility** the social standing of children in relation to their parents

**interpretive sociology** the study of society that focusses on the meanings people attach to their social world

**intersexed person** a human being with some combination of female and male genitalia

**intragenerational social mobility** a change in social position occurring during a person's lifetime

**kinship** a social bond based on blood, marriage, or adoption

**labelling theory** the assertion that deviance and conformity result not so much from what people do, as from the response of others to those actions

**language** a system of symbols that allows people to communicate with one another

**latent functions** the unrecognized and unintended consequences of any social pattern

**liberation theology** a fusion of Christian principles with political activism, often Marxist in character

**life expectancy** a synthetic measure of the average life span of a society's population

**looking-glass self** Charles Horton Cooley's term

referring to a conception of self based on how we suppose others see us

**low-income countries** nations with little industrialization in which most people are poor

**macro-level orientation** a concern with broad patterns that characterize society as a whole

**manifest functions** the recognized and intended consequences of any social pattern

**market income** wages or salary from work, earnings from investments and private pensions

**marriage** a legally sanctioned relationship, usually involving economic cooperation as well as sexual activity and childbearing, that people expect to be enduring

**Marxist political-economy model** an analysis that explains politics in terms of the operation of a society's economic system

**mass media** impersonal communications directed to a vast audience

**mass society** a society in which industry and bureaucracy have eroded traditional social ties

**master status** a social position with exceptional importance for identity, often shaping a person's entire life

**matriarchy** a form of social organization in which females dominate males

**measurement** the procedure for determining the value of a variable in a specific case

**medicalization of deviance** the transformation of moral and legal deviance into a medical condition

**medicine** the social institution that focusses on combatting disease and improving health

**megalopolis** a vast urban region containing a number of cities and their surrounding suburbs

**meritocracy** social stratification based on personal merit

**metropolis** a large city that socially and economically dominates an urban area

**micro-level orientation** a concern with small-scale patterns of social interaction in specific settings

**middle-income countries** nations with limited industrialization in which most people have moderate personal income

**migration** the movement of people into and out of a specified territory

**military-industrial complex** the close association of the federal government, the military, and defence industries

**minority** any category of people, distinguished by physical or cultural difference, that a society sets apart and subordinates

**miscegenation** biological reproduction by partners of different racial categories

**modernity** social patterns resulting from industrialization

**modernization** the process of social change begun by industrialization

**modernization theory** a model of economic and social development that explains global inequality in terms of technological and cultural differences among societies

**monarchy** a type of political system in which a single family rules from generation to generation

**monogamy** marriage uniting two partners at the same time

**monopoly** domination of a market by a single producer

**mores** norms that have great moral significance

**mortality** the incidence of death in a society's population

**multiculturalism** an educational program recognizing the cultural diversity of Canada and promoting the equality of all cultural traditions

**multinational corporation** a large business that operates in many countries

**natural environment** the earth's surface and atmosphere including various living organisms and the air, water, soil, and other resources necessary to sustain life

**neocolonialism** a new form of global power relationships that involves not direct political control but economic exploitation by multinational corporations

**network** a web of weak social ties

**nonverbal communication** communication using body movements, gestures, and facial expressions rather than speech

**norms** rules and expectations by which a society guides the behaviour of its members

**nuclear family** (conjugal family) a family unit composed of one or two parents and their children

**oligarchy** the rule of the many by the few

**oligopoly** domination of a market by a few producers

**organizational environment** a range of factors outside the organization that affects its operation

**organized crime** a business supplying illegal goods or services

**other-directedness** a receptiveness to the latest trends and fashions, often expressed by imitating others

**outgroup** a scorned social group toward which one feels competition or opposition

**participant observation** a research method by which investigators systematically observe people while joining in their routine activities

**pastoralism** a way of life based on the domestication of animals

**patriarchy** a form of social organization in which males dominate females

**peer group** a group whose members have interests, social position, and age in common

**personal space** the surrounding area over which a person makes some claim to privacy

**personality** a person's fairly consistent patterns of acting, thinking, and feeling

**plea bargaining** a legal negotiation in which the prosecutor reduces a charge in exchange for a defendant's guilty plea

**pluralism** a state in which people of all races and ethnicities are distinct but have social parity

**pluralist model** an analysis of politics that sees power as dispersed among many competing interest groups

**political revolution** the overthrow of one political system in order to establish another

**politics** the social institution that distributes power, sets a society's agenda, and makes decisions

**polygamy** marriage that unites three or more people at the same time

**popular culture** cultural patterns widespread among a society's people

**pornography** sexually explicit material that causes sexual arousal

**positivism** a way of understanding based on science

**post-industrial economy** a productive system based on service work and high technology

**postmodernity** social patterns characteristic of post-industrial societies.

**power** the ability to achieve desired ends despite resistance from others

**power-elite model** an analysis of politics that sees power as concentrated among the rich

**prejudice** a rigid and irrational generalization about an entire category of people

**preoperational stage** Piaget's term for the level of development in which individuals first use language and other symbols

**presentation of self** Goffman's term for the ways in which individuals, in various settings, try to create specific impressions in the minds of others

**primary group** a small social group whose members share personal and enduring relationships

**primary sector** the part of the economy that draws raw materials from the natural environment

**primary sex characteristics** the genitals, organs used for reproduction

**profane** that which people define as an ordinary element of everyday life

**profession** a prestigious, white-collar occupation that requires extensive formal education

**proletariat** people who sell their productive labour

**prostitution** the selling of sexual services

**queer theory** a growing body of knowledge that challenges an allegedly heterosexual bias in sociology

**race** a socially constructed category composed of men and women who share biologically transmitted traits that members of a society deem socially significant

**racism** the belief that one racial category is innately superior or inferior to another

**rain forests** regions of dense forestation, most of which circle the globe close to the equator

**rationality** deliberate, matter-of-fact calculation of the most efficient means to accomplish a particular task

**rationalization** Max Weber's term for the change from tradition to rationality as the dominant mode of human thought

**reference group** a social group that serves as a point of reference in making evaluations and decisions

**rehabilitation** reforming the offender to preclude further offences

**relative deprivation** a perceived disadvantage arising from some specific comparison

**relative poverty** the deprivation of some people in relation to others who have more

**reliability** consistency in measurement

**religion** a social institution involving beliefs and practices based on a conception of the sacred

**religiosity** the importance of religion in a person's life

**religious fundamentalism** a conservative religious doctrine that opposes intellectualism and worldly accommodation in favour of restoring traditional, otherworldly religion

**research method** a systematic plan for conducting research

**resocialization** deliberate socialization intended to radically alter an individual's personality

**retribution** inflicting suffering on an offender comparable to that caused by the offence

**role** normative patterns of behaviour for those holding a particular status

**role conflict** incompatibility among the roles corresponding to two or more statuses

**role set** a number of roles attached to a single status

**role strain** incompatibility among roles corresponding to a single status

**routinization of charisma** the transformation of charismatic authority into some combination of traditional and bureaucratic authority

**sacred** that which people set apart as extraordinary, inspiring a sense of awe and reverence

**Sapir-Whorf thesis** the assertion that people perceive the world only in terms of the symbols contained in their language

**schooling** formal instruction under the direction of specially trained teachers

**science** a logical system that bases knowledge on direct, systematic observation

**scientific management** Frederick Taylor's term for applying scientific principles to the operation of a business or other large organization

**secondary group** a large and impersonal social group whose members pursue a special interest or activity

**secondary sector** the part of the economy that transforms raw materials into manufactured goods

**secondary sex characteristics** bodily development, apart from the genitals, that distinguishes biologically mature females and males

**sect** a type of religious organization that stands apart from the larger society

**secularization** the historical decline in the importance of the supernatural and the sacred

**segregation** the physical and social separation of categories of people

**self** George Herbert Mead's term for that part of an individual's personality composed of self-awareness and self-image

**sensorimotor stage** Piaget's term for the level of development in which individuals experience the world only through sensory contact

**sex** the biological distinction between females and males

**sex ratio** the number of males for every 100 females in a given population

**sexism** the belief that one sex is innately superior to the other

**sexual harassment** comments, gestures, or physical contact of a sexual nature that are deliberate, repeated, and unwelcome

**sexual orientation** a person's preference in terms of sexual partners: same sex, other sex, either sex, neither sex

**sick role** patterns of behaviour defined as appropriate for those who are ill

**social change** the transformation of culture and social institutions over time

**social character** personality patterns common to members of a particular society

**social construction of reality** the process by which individuals creatively build reality through social interaction

**social control** attempts by society to regulate the thought and behaviour of individuals

**social dysfunction** the undesirable consequences of any social pattern for the operation of society

**social epidemiology** the study of how health and disease are distributed throughout a society's population

**social function** the consequences of any social pattern for the operation of society as a whole

**social group** two or more people who identify and interact with one another

**social institution** an organized sphere of social life, or societal subsystem—such as the economy—designed to meet human needs

**social interaction** the process by which people act and react in relation to others

**social mobility** a change of position in a stratification system

**social movement** organized activity that encourages or discourages social change

**social protection** rendering an offender incapable of further offences, either temporarily through incarceration or permanently by execution

**social stratification** a system by which a society ranks categories of people in a hierarchy

**social structure** any relatively stable pattern of social behaviour

**social-conflict paradigm** a framework for building theory that sees society as an arena of inequality that generates conflict and change

**socialism** an economic system in which natural resources and the means of producing goods and services are collectively owned

**socialization** the lifelong social experience by which individuals develop their human potential and learn culture

**socialized health care** a health care system in which the government owns and operates most medical facilities and employs most physicians.

**society** people interacting in a limited territory guided by their culture

**sociobiology** a theoretical paradigm that explains how biology affects how humans create culture

**socioeconomic status** a composite social ranking based on various dimensions of inequality

**sociology** the systematic study of human society

**state capitalism** an economic and political system in which companies are privately owned but cooperate closely with the government.

**state church** a church formally allied with the state

**status** a recognized social position that an individual occupies

**status consistency** the degree of consistency in a person's social standing across various dimensions of inequality

**status set** all the statuses a person holds at a particular time

**stereotype** an exaggerated description that one applies to all people in some category

**stigma** a powerfully negative label that radically changes a person's social identity and self-concept

**structural social mobility** a shift in the social position of a large number of people due to changes in society itself

**structural-functional paradigm** a framework for building theory that sees society as a complex system whose parts work together to promote stability

**subculture** cultural patterns that distinguish some segment of a society's population

**suburbs** urban areas beyond the political boundaries of a city

**superego** Freud's term for the presence of culture within the individual in the form of internalized values and norms

**survey** a research method in which participants respond to a series of statements or questions in a questionnaire or an interview

**symbol** anything that carries a particular meaning recognized by people who share a culture

**symbolic-interaction paradigm** a framework for building theory that sees society as the product of the everyday interaction of individuals

**technology** the knowledge that people apply to the practical tasks of living

**terrorism** acts of violence or the threat of such violence used by an individual or a group as a political strategy

**tertiary sector** the part of the economy that involves services rather than goods

**theoretical paradigm** a set of fundamental assumptions that guides thinking and research

**theory** a statement of how and why specific facts are related

**Thomas theorem** the assertion that situations defined as real become real in their consequences

**total institution** a setting in which individuals are isolated from the rest of society and manipulated by an administrative staff

**totalitarianism** a highly centralized political system that extensively regulates people's lives

**totem** an object in the natural world collectively defined as sacred

**tracking** the assignment of students to different types of educational programs

**tradition** sentiments and beliefs about the world that are passed from generation to generation

**tradition-directedness** rigid conformity to time-honoured ways of living

**transsexuals** people who feel they are one sex even though biologically they are the other

**tryad** a social group with three members

**urban ecology** the study of the link between the physical and social dimensions of cities

**urbanization** the concentration of humanity into cities

**validity** the quality of measuring precisely what one intends to measure

**values** culturally defined standards of desirability, goodness, and beauty that serve as broad guidelines for social living

**variable** a concept whose value changes from case to case

**victimless crime** violation of law in which there is no readily apparent victim

**war** organized, armed conflict among the people of various societies, directed by their governments

**wealth** the total value of money and other assets, minus outstanding debts

**welfare capitalism** an economic and political system that combines a mostly market-based economy with extensive social welfare programs.

**welfare state** a range of government agencies and programs that provide benefits to the population

**white-collar crime** crimes committed by people of high social position in the course of their occupations

**white-collar occupation** higher-prestige work that involves mostly mental activity

**zero population growth** the level of reproduction that maintains population at a steady state

# REFERENCES

Abbott, Andrew. *The System of Professions: An Essay on the Division of Expert Labor*. Chicago: University of Chicago Press, 1988.

Aberle, David F. *The Peyote Religion Among the Navaho*. Chicago: Aldine, 1966.

Abrahamson, Paul R. "Postmaterialism and Environmentalism: A Comment on an Analysis and a Reappraisal." *Social Science Quarterly*. Vol. 78, No. 1 (March 1997):21–23.

Abrahamson, Peter. "The Scandinavian Model of Welfare." Conference proceedings in *Comparing Social Welfare Systems in Nordic Europe and France*. Vol. 4 (1999):31–60.

Adler, Jerry. "When Harry Called Sally . . ." *Newsweek*. (October 1, 1990):74.

Adorno, T.W. et al. *The Authoritarian Personality*. New York: Harper & Brothers, 1950.

Akers, Ronald L., Marvin D. Krohn, Lonn Lanza-Kaduce, and Marcia Radosevich. "Social Learning and Deviant Behavior." *American Sociological Review*. Vol. 44, No. 4 (August 1979):636–55.

Alam, Sultana. "Women and Poverty in Bangladesh." Women's Studies International Forum. Vol. 8, No. 4 (1985):361–71.

Ali, S. Harris. "The Search for a Landfill Site in the Risk Society." *Canadian Review of Sociology and Anthropology*. Vol. 36, No. 1 (February 1999):1–19.

Allahar, Anton. "Race and Racism: Strategies of Resistance." In Vic Satzewich, ed. *Racism and Social Inequality in Canada: Concepts, Controversies & Strategies of Resistance*. Toronto: Thompson Educational Publishing, Inc., 1998:335–354.

Allan, Emilie Andersen, and Darrell J. Steffensmeier. "Youth, Underemployment, and Property Crime: Differential Effects of Job Availability and Job Quality on Juvenile and Young Adult Arrest Rates." *American Sociological Review*. Vol. 54, No. 1 (February 1989):107–23.

Allen, Thomas B., and Charles O. Hyman. *We Americans: Celebrating a Nation, Its People, and Its Past*. New York, NY: National Georgraphic Society, 1999.

Alphonso, Caroline. "Girl's Death to Escape Bullying Shocks Town." *Globe and Mail*. (November 17, 2000):A7.

Altman, Drew et al. "Health Care for the Homeless." *Society*. Vol. 26, No. 4 (May–June 1989):4–5.

Ambert, Anne-Marie. "Toward a Theory of Peer Abuse." *Sociological Studies of Children*. Vol. 7 (1995):177–205.

American Medical Association (AMA). *Executive Summary of Media Violence Survey Analysis*. [Online] http://www.ama-assn.org/ad-com/releases/1996/mvan1909.htm, 1997.

Amnesty International. "The Death Penalty: List of Abolitionist and Retentionist Countries." [Online] http://www.amnesty.org/ailib/intcam/dp/abrelist.htm, April 3, 2000.

Anderson, Elijah. "The Code of the Streets." *Atlantic Monthly*. Vol. 273 (May 1994):81–94.

Anderson, John Ward. "Early to Wed: The Child Brides of India." *Washington Post*. (May 24, 1995):A27, A30.

Anderson, Tammi L., and Lynn Bondi. "Exiting the Drug-Addict Role: Variations by Race and Gender." *Symbolic Interaction*. Vol. 21, No. 2 (1998):155–174.

Anderssen, Erin. "Native Women Launch Fight Over Divorce Law." *Globe and Mail*. (June 11, 1998):A3.

Ang, Ien. *Watching Dallas: Soap Opera and the Melodramatic Imagination*. London: Methuen, 1985.

Angier, Natalie. "Scientists, Finding Second Idiosyncrasy in Homosexuals' Brains, Suggest Orientation is Physiological." *New York Times*. (August 1, 1992):A7.

Angus Reid Group Inc. *Multiculturalism and Canadians: National Attitude Survey, 1991*. Ottawa: Multiculturalism and Citizenship Canada, 1991.

_____. *The Federal Political Scene*. Public release dated Thursday, December 28, 1995. [Online] http://www.angusreid.com/pressrel/DecFedPolScene.html

_____. *Canadian Views on the Public Education System*. Table accompanying public release dated Saturday, September 7, 1996a. [Online] http://www.angusreid.com/pressrel/pubedspt96.html

_____. *Federal Political Trends and the Public Agenda*. Public release dated Monday, December 9, 1996b. [Online] http://www.angusreid.com/pressrel/fedpoltrendsdec96.html

_____. *Ontarians' Belief in Miracles & Angels*. Public release dated Wednesday, December 25, 1996c. [Online] http://www.angusreid.com/pressrel/miraclesdec96.html

_____. *Public Attitudes on Some Specific Gay Rights Issues*. Public release dated Friday June 7, 1996d. [Online] http://www.angusreid.com/pressrel/gayrights.html

_____. *Public Support for the Federal Gun Control Legislation*. Public release dated Monday December 23, 1996e. [Online] http://www.angusreid.com/pressrel/guncontrol.html

_____. *Canadians' Attitudes Toward Cloning*. Public release dated Tuesday, December 16, 1997a. [Online] http://www.angusreid.com/pressrel/pr161297_2.html

_____. *Infidelity*. Public release dated September 14, 1997b. [Online] http://www.angusreid.com/pressrel/FIDEL1.html

_____. *The '97 Election: Late Campaign*. Public release dated Thursday, May 29, 1997c. [Online] http://www.angusreid.com/pressrel/97fedelect_latecampaign.htm

_____. *Women in Politics*. Special report dated May 13, 1997d. [Online] http://www.angusreid.com/wip/index.htm

_____. *Canadian Investors Suffered Losses during Stock Market Tumble*. Public Release dated October 5, 1998a.

_____. *Canadians' Views on Including Sexual Orientation in Human Rights Legislation*. Public release dated Sunday, May 10, 1998b. [Online] http://www.angusreid.com/pressrel/pr100598.html

_____. *Chrétien Continues to Ride High in Public Esteem, But Slight Majority (58%) Would Support Change in Party Leadership Before Next Election*. Tables accompanying press release dated July 10, 1998c. [Online] http://www.angusreid.com/pressrel/pr100798.html

_____. *Healthcare Overtakes All Issues on Public Agenda*. Tables accompanying public release dated July 11, 1998d. [Online] http://www.angusreid.com/pressrel/pr110798.html

_____. *Let's Talk About Sex, Tables*. Public release dated Tuesday, March 3, 1998e. [Online] http://www.ipsos-reid.com /media/content/pdf/pr030398tb.pdf

_____. *The Public Agenda*. Public release dated November 24, 1998f. [Online] http://www.ipsos-reid.com/media/content/pdf/pr241198_1.PDF

_____. *Six in Ten Canadians Believe That Younger Generations Will Be Worse Off Financially Than Their Own*. Public release dated Tuesday, August 4, 1998g. [Online] http://www.angusreid.com/pressrel/pr040898.html

_____. *Canadian Teens Voice Their Opinions on Violence in Their Schools*. Public Release Dated May 3, 1999a.

_____. *Canadians' Assessment and Views of the Educational System*. Public Release dated Tuesday, June 22, 1999b.

_____. *Liberals (47%) Still Tops in Federal Vote and Overall Performance Approval (62%)*. Public release dated June 17, 1999c, Table 2, [Online] http://www.ipsosreid.com/media/content/pdf/pr990617_t2.pdf

_____. "Click and Connect: New Study Shows that the Internet Has Re-Defined The Social Interactions Of Canadians, By Helping Start New Relationships." (October, 2000a).

_____. *Federal Election Poll: November 24, 2000*. Tables accompanying press release dated November 24, 2000b. [Online] http://www.ipsos-reid.com/media/content/pdf/mr001124_1t.pdf

_____. *Federal Political Scene March 2000*. Public release dated March 13, 2000c, Tables, [Online] http://www.ipsos-reid.com/media/content/pdf/mr000313tb.pdf

_____. *Federal Political Scene Late May 2000*. Public release dated June 2, 2000d, Tables, [Online] http://www.ipsosreid.com/media/content/pdf/mr0602tb.pdf

_____. *Federal Political Scene August 2000*. Public release dated August 18, 2000e, Tables, [Online] http://www.ipsos-reid.com/media/content/pdf/mr000818tb_2.PDF

_____. *Federal Political Scene Late August 2000*. Public release dated August 30, 2000f, Tables, [Online] http://www.ipsos-reid.com/media/content/pdf/mr000830_1t.pdf

_____. *Federal Political Scene Early October 2000*. Public release dated October 16, 2000g; Tables [Online] http://www.ipsos-reid.com/media/content/pdf/mr001016tb_2.PDF

_____. *Top Issues on the Public Agenda and Federal Voting Intentions*. Public release dated February 6, 2000h, Tables, [Online] http://www.ipsos-reid.com/media/content/pdf/mr000206_3tb.pdf

Annan, Kofi. "Astonishing Facts." *New York Times*. (September 27, 1998):16.

Annis, Robert C. "Effect of Test Language and Experimenter Race on Canadian Indian Children's Racial and Self-Identity." *Journal of Social Psychology*. Vol. 126, No. 6 (December 1986):761–73.

Applebaum, Eileen, and Rosemary Batt. *The New American Workplace: Transforming Work Systems in the United States*. Ithaca: ILR Press, 1994.

Arat-Koc, Sedef. "In the Privacy of Our Own Home: Foreign Domestic Workers as Solution to the Crisis in the Domestic Sphere in Canada." *Studies in Political Economy*. Vol. 28 (Spring 1989):33–58.

Ariès, Philippe. *Centuries of Childhood: A Social History of Family Life*. New York: Vintage Books, 1965.

Armstrong, Pat. "Caring and Women's Work." *Health and Canadian Society*. Vol. 2, No. 1 (1994):109–18.

Armstrong, Pat, and Hugh Armstrong. *Wasting Away: The Undermining of Canadian Health Care*. Toronto: Oxford University Press, 1996.

Artz, Sibylle. *Sex, Power, & the Violent School Girl*. Toronto: Trifolium Books, 1998.

Asante, Molefi Kete. *Afrocentricity*. Trenton, N.J.: Africa World Press, 1988.

Asch, Solomon. *Social Psychology*. Englewood Cliffs, N.J.: Prentice Hall, 1952.

Ashford, Lori S. "New Perspectives on Population: Lessons From Cairo." *Population Bulletin*. Vol. 50, No. 1 (March 1995).

Astone, Nan Marie, and Sara S. McLanahan. "Family Structure, Parental Practices and High School Completion." *American Sociological Review*. Vol. 56, No. 3 (June 1991):309–20.

Attorney General's Commission on Pornography. *Final Report*. Washington, D.C.: U.S. Dept. of Justice, 1986.

Bachrach, Peter, and Morton S. Baratz. *Power and Poverty*. New York: Oxford University Press, 1970.

Backman, Carl B., and Murray C. Adams. "Self-Perceived Physical Attractiveness, Self-Esteem, Race, and Gender." *Sociological Focus*. Vol. 24, No. 4 (October 1991):283–90.

Bagley, Robin. *Sexual Offences Against Children: Report of the Committee on Sexual Offences Against Children and Youth*. Ottawa: Canadian Government Publishing, 1984.

Baker, Mary Anne, Catherine White Berheide, Fay Ross Greckel, Linda Carstarphen Gugin, Marcia J. Lipetz, and Marcia Texler Segal. *Women Today: A Multidisciplinary Approach to Women's Studies*. Monterey, Calif.: Brooks/Cole, 1980.

Baker, Maureen. *Canadian Family Policies: Cross-National Comparisons*. Toronto: University of Toronto Press, 1995.

Baker, Ross. "Business as Usual." *American Demographics*. Vol. 19, No. 4 (April 1997):28.

Balakrishnan, T.R., and Feng Hou. *The Changing Patterns of Spatial Concentration and Residential Segregation of Ethnic Groups in Canada's Major Metropolitan Areas 1981–1991*. Discussion Paper No. 95-2. London: University of Western Ontario, Population Studies Centre, 1995.

Balakrishnan, T.R., E. Lapierre-Adamcyk and K.J. Krotki. *Family and Childbearing in Canada: A Demographic Analysis*. Toronto: University of Toronto Press, 1993.

Balakrishnan, T.R., and George K. Jarvis. "Is the Burgess Concentric Zonal Theory of Spatial Differentiation Still Applicable to Urban Canada?" *Canadian Review of Sociology and Anthropology*. Vol. 28, No. 4 (November 1991):527–40.

Baldus, Bernd, and Meenaz Kassam. "'Making Me Truthful and Mild:' Values in Nineteenth-Century Ontario Schoolbooks." *Canadian Journal of Sociology*. Vol. 21, No. 3 (1996):327–57.

Baldus, Bernd, and Verna Tribe. "Children's Perceptions of Inequality." In Lorne Tepperman and James Curtis, eds., *Everyday Life: A Reader*. Toronto: McGraw-Hill Ryerson Limited, 1992:88–97.

Baltzell, E. Digby. *The Protestant Establishment: Aristocracy and Caste in America*. New York: Vintage Books, 1964.

_____, ed. *The Search for Community in Modern America*. New York: Harper & Row, 1968.

_____. *Puritan Boston and Quaker Philadelphia*. New York: Free Press, 1979.

Barash, David. *The Whispering Within*. New York: Penguin Books, 1981.

Barker, Eileen. "Who'd Be a Moonie? A Comparative Study of Those Who Join the Unification Church in Britain." In Bryan Wilson, ed., *The Social Impact of New Religious Movements*. New York: The Rose of Sharon Press, 1981:59–96.

Baron, James N., Brian S. Mittman, and Andrew E. Newman. "Targets of Opportunity: Organizational and Environmental Determinants of Gender Integration Within the California Civil Service, 1979–1985." *American Journal of Sociology*. Vol. 96, No. 6 (May 1991):1362–1401.

Barry, Kathleen. "Feminist Theory: The Meaning of Women's Liberation." In Barbara Haber, ed., *The Women's Annual 1982–1983*. Boston: G. K. Hall, 1983:35–78.

Bartlett, Donald L., and James B. Steele. "Corporate Welfare." *Time*. Vol. 152, No. 19 (November 9, 1998):36–54.

Bassuk, Ellen J. "The Homelessness Problem." *Scientific American*. Vol. 251, No. 1 (July 1984):40–45.

Bauer, P.T. *Equality, the Third World, and Economic Delusion*. Cambridge, Mass.: Harvard University Press, 1981.

Baydar, Nazli, and Jeanne Brooks-Gunn. "Effect of Maternal Employment and Child-Care Arrangements on Preschoolers' Cognitive and Behavioral Outcomes: Evidence From Children From the National Longitudinal Survey of Youth." *Developmental Psychology*. Vol. 27 (1991):932–35.

Beaton, Albert E. et al. *Mathematics Achievement in the Middle School Years: IEA's Third International Mathematics and Science Study*. Chestnut Hill, MA: Center for the Study of Testing, Evaluation, and Educational Policy, Boston College, 1996.

Beaujot, Roderic. *Population Change in Canada: The Challenge of Policy Adaptation*. Toronto: McClelland Inc., 1991.

Becker, Howard S. *Outside: Studies in the Sociology of Deviance*. New York: Free Press, 1966.

Bedell, Kenneth B. *Yearbook of American and Canadian Churches 1997*. Nashville, Tenn.: Abingdon Press, 1997.

Beeghley, Leonard. *The Structure of Social Stratification in the United States*. Needham Heights, Mass.: Allyn & Bacon, 1989.

Begley, Sharon. "Gray Matters." *Newsweek*. (March 7, 1995):48–54.

———. "How to Beat the Heat." *Newsweek*. (December 8, 1997):34–38.

Bell, Alan P., Martin S. Weinberg, and Sue Kiefer-Hammersmith. *Sexual Preference: Its Development in Men and Women*. Bloomington: Indiana University Press, 1981.

Bell, Daniel. *The Coming of Post-Industrial Society: A Venture in Social Forecasting*. New York: Basic Books, 1973.

Bell, David, and Lorne Tepperman. *The Roots of Disunity: A Look at Canadian Political Culture*. Toronto: McClelland & Stewart Ltd, 1979.

Bellah, Robert N. *The Broken Covenant*. New York: Seabury Press, 1975.

Bellas, Marcia L. "Comparable Worth in Academia: The Effects on Faculty Salaries of the Sex Composition and Labor-Market Conditions of Academic Disciplines." *American Sociological Review*. Vol. 59, No. 6 (December 1994):807–21.

Beltrame, Julian, and Brenda Branswell. "The Enemy Within." *Maclean's*. Vol. 113, Issue 43 (October 23, 2000):36–38.

Bem, Sandra Lipsitz. *The Lenses of Gender: Transforming the Debate on Sexual Inequality*. New Haven, Conn.: Yale University Press, 1993.

Benedict, Ruth. "Continuities and Discontinuities in Cultural Conditioning." *Psychiatry*. Vol. 1 (May 1938):161–67.

Bennett, Stephen Earl. "Left Behind: Exploring Declining Turnout among Non-college Young Whites, 1964–1988." *Social Science Quarterly*. Vol. 72, No. 2 (June 1991):314–33.

Benoit, Cecilia. "Gender, Work and Social Rights: Canada, the United States and Sweden as Case Examples." Paper presented at the ISA 14th World Congress in Sociology, Montreal, Canada, July 28, 1998.

_____. "Rediscovering Appropriate Care: Maternity Traditions and Contemporary Issues in Canada." In David Coburn et al., eds., *Health and Canadian Society*. 3rd ed. Toronto: University of Toronto Press, 1998b.

_____. *Women, Work and Social Rights: Canada in Historical and Comparative Perspective*. Scarborough, Ontario: Prentice Hall Canada, 2000a.

_____. "Variation Within Post-Fordist and Liberal Welfare State Countries: Women's Work and Social Rights in Canada and the United States." In Thomas Boje, and Arnlaug Leira, eds. *Gender, Welfare State and the Market: Towards a New Division of Labour*. London: Routledge, 2000b: 71–88.

Benoit, Cecilia, and Alena Heitlinger. "Women's Health Caring Work in Comparative Perspective: Canada, Sweden and Czechoslovakia/Czech Republic as Case Examples." *Social Science and Medicine*. Vol. 47, No. 8 (August, 1998):1101–11.

Benoit, Cecilia, and Dena Carroll. "Aboriginal Midwifery in British Columbia: A Narrative Still Untold." *Western Geographic Series*. Vol. 30 (1995):221–46.

Benokraitis, Nijole, and Joe Feagin. *Modern Sexism: Blatant, Subtle, and Overt Discrimination*. 2nd ed. Englewood Cliffs, N.J.: Prentice Hall, 1995.

Benson, Michael L., and Francis T. Cullen. *Combating Corporate Crime*. Boston: Northeastern University Press, 1998.

Bergamo, Monica, and Gerson Camarotti. "Brazil's Landless Millions." *World Press Review*. Vol. 43, No. 7 (July 1996):46–47.

Berger, Peter L. *Invitation to Sociology*. New York: Anchor Books, 1963.

_____. *The Sacred Canopy: Elements of a Sociological Theory of Religion*. Garden City, N.Y.: Doubleday, 1967.

_____. *Facing Up to Modernity: Excursions in Society, Politics, and Religion*. New York: Basic Books, 1977.

_____. *The Capitalist Revolution: Fifty Propositions About Prosperity, Equality, and Liberty*. New York: Basic Books, 1986.

Berger, Peter, Brigitte Berger, and Hansfried Kellner. *The Homeless Mind: Modernization and Consciousness*. New York: Vintage Books, 1974.

Berger, Peter L., and Hansfried Kellner. *Sociology Reinterpreted: An Essay on Method and Vocation*. Garden City, N.Y.: Anchor Books, 1981.

Berger, Peter L., and Thomas Luckmann. *The Social Construction of Reality: A Treatise in the Sociology of Knowledge*. Garden City, N.Y.: Anchor Books, 1967.

Bergesen, Albert, ed. *Crises in the World-System*. Beverly Hills, Calif.: Sage, 1983.

Bernard, Jessie. *The Future of Marriage*. New Haven, Conn.: Yale University Press, 1982; orig. 1973.

_____. *The Female World*. New York: Free Press, 1981.

Bernard, Larry Craig. "Multivariate Analysis of New Sex Role Formulations and Personality." *Journal of Personality and Social Psychology*. Vol. 38, No. 2 (February 1980):323–36.

Bernstein, Richard J. *The New Constellation: The Ethical-Political Horizons of Modernity/Postmodernity*. Cambridge, Mass.: MIT Press, 1992.

Berry, Brian L., and Philip H. Rees. "The Factorial Ecology of Calcutta." *American Journal of Sociology*. Vol. 74, No. 5 (March 1969):445–91.

Berscheid, Ellen, and Elaine Hatfield. *Interpersonal Attraction*. 2nd ed. Reading, Mass.: Addison-Wesley, 1983.

Bertrand, Jane, Margaret McCain, J. Fraser Mustard, and J. Douglas Willms. "A First Tier for Canadian Children: Findings from the Early Years Study in Ontario." *Atlantic Centre for Policy Research*. New Brunswick: University of New Brunswick. No. 6 (July 1999):1–4.

Besserer, Sandra. "Criminal Victimization: An International Perspective." *Juristat*. Statistics Canada Catalogue No. 85-002-XIE. Vol. 18, No. 6 (March 1998):1–13.

Besserer, Sandra, and Catherine Trainor. "Criminal Victimization in Canada, 1999." *Juristat*. Statistics Canada Catalogue No. 85-002-XIE. Vol. 20, No. 10 (November, 2000):1–16.

Best, Raphaela. *We've All Got Scars: What Boys and Girls Learn in Elementary School*. Bloomington: Indiana University Press, 1983.

Bianchi, Suzanne M., and Daphne Spain. "Women, Work, and Family in America." *Population Bulletin*. Vol. 51, No. 3 (December 1996).

Bibby, Reginald W. *Fragmented Gods: The Poverty and Potential of Religion in Canada*. Toronto, Canada: Irwin Publishers, 1987.

_____. *Unknown Gods: The Ongoing Study of Religion in Canada*. Toronto: Stoddart, 1993.

Biblarz, Timothy J., and Adrian E. Raftery. "The Effects of Family Disruption on Social Mobility." *American Sociological Review*. Vol. 58, No. 1 (February 1993):97–109.

Biernacki, Patrick. *Pathways from Heroin Addiction: Recovery Without Treatment*. Philadelphia: Temple University Press, 1986.

Biggs, Lesley. "The Case of the Missing Midwives: A History of Midwifery in Ontario from 1795–1900." *Ontario History*. Vol. 75 (1983):21–35.

Billson Janet Mancini, and Bettina J. Huber. *Embarking Upon a Career with an Undergraduate Degree in Sociology*. 2nd ed. Washington, D.C.: American Sociological Association, 1993.

Blau, Judith R., and Peter M. Blau. "The Cost of Inequality: Metropolitan Structure and Violent Crime." *American Sociological Review*. Vol. 47, No. 1 (February 1982):114–29.

Blau, Peter M. *Exchange and Power in Social Life*. New York: Wiley, 1964.

_____. *Inequality and Heterogeneity: A Primitive Theory of Social Structure*. New York: Free Press, 1977.

Blau, Peter M., and Otis Dudley Duncan. *The American Occupational Structure*. New York: Wiley, 1967.

Blau, Peter M., Terry C. Blum, and Joseph E. Schwartz. "Heterogeneity and Intermarriage." *American Sociological Review*. Vol. 47, No. 1 (February 1982):45–62.

Blishen, Bernard. *Doctors in Canada*. Toronto: University of Toronto Press, 1991.

Blumberg, Paul. *Inequality in an Age of Decline*. New York: Oxford University Press, 1981.

Blumer, Herbert G. "Collective Behavior." In Alfred McClung Lee, ed., *Principles of Sociology*. 3rd ed. New York: Barnes & Noble Books, 1969:65–121.

Blumstein, Philip, and Pepper Schwartz. *American Couples*. New York: Wm. Morrow, 1983.

Bobo, Lawrence, and Vincent L. Hutchings. "Perceptions of Racial Group Competition: Extending Blumer's Theory of Group Position to a Multiracial Social Context." *American Sociological Review*. Vol. 61, No. 6 (December 1996):951–72.

Boethus, Maria-Pia. "The End of Prostitution in Sweden?" Stockholm: Swedish Institute. No. 426 (October), 1999. [Online] http://www.si.se/eng/esverige/cs426.html

Boff, Leonard and Clodovis. *Salvation and Liberation: In Search of a Balance between Faith and Politics*. Maryknoll, N.Y.: Orbis Books, 1984.

Bohannan, Cecil. "The Economic Correlates of Homelessness in Sixty Cities." *Social Science Quarterly*. Vol. 72, No. 4 (December 1991):817–25.

Bohlen, Celestine. "Facing Oblivion, Rust-Belt Giants Top Russian List of Vexing Crises." *New York Times* (November 8, 1998):1, 6.

Boje, Thomas, and Arnlaug Leira. *Gender, Welfare State and the Market: Towards a New Division of Labour*. London: Routledge, 2000.

Boli, John, and George M. Thomas. "World Culture in the World Polity: A Century of International Non-Governmental Organization." *American Sociological Review*. Vol. 62, No. 2 (April 1997):171–90.

Bonner, Jane. Research presented in "The Two Brains." Public Broadcasting System telecast, 1984.

Booth, Alan, and Lynn White. "Thinking About Divorce." *Journal of Marriage and the Family*. Vol. 42, No. 3 (August 1980):605–16.

Borgmann, Albert. *Crossing the Postmodern Divide*. Chicago: University of Chicago Press, 1992.

Boritch, Helen. *Fallen Women: Female Crime and the Criminal Justice System in Canada*. Toronto: ITP Nelson, 1997.

Bormann, F. Herbert. "The Global Environmental Deficit." *Bioscience*. Vol. 40 (1990):74.

Bormann, F. Herbert, and Stephen R. Kellert. "The Global Environmental Deficit." In Herbert F. Bormann, and Stephen R. Kellert, eds., *Ecology, Economics, and Ethics: The Broken Circle*. New Haven, Conn.: Yale University Press, 1991:ix–xviii.

Borovoy, A. Alan. "Racism Study Focuses Too Much on Feelings, Not Actions." *The Toronto Star*. (February 14, 1996, final ed.):A19.

Bott, Elizabeth. *Family and Social Network*. New York: Free Press, 1971; orig. 1957.

Bouchard, Brigitte, and John Zhao. "University Education: Recent Trends in Participation." *Education Quarterly Review*. Vol.6 No. 4 (August 2000):24–32.

Bowlby, Geoff. 2001. "The Labour Market Review." Perspectives on Labour and Income. Statistics Canada Catalogue No. 75-001-XIE. Vol. 2, No. 1 (January 2001):5–35.

Bowles, Samuel, and Herbert Gintis. *Schooling in Capitalist America: Educational Reform and the Contradictions of Economic Life*. New York: Basic Books, 1976.

Boyer, Debra. "Male Prostitution and Homosexual Identity." *Journal of Homosexuality*. Vol. 17, Nos. 1, 2 (1989):151–84.

Braithwaite, John. "The Myth of Social Class and Criminality Reconsidered." *American Sociological Review*. Vol. 46, No. 1 (February 1981):36–57.

Brand, Dionne. *No Burden to Carry: Narrative of Black Working Women in Ontario, 1920s to 1950s.* Toronto: Women's Press, 1992.

Brinton, Crane. *The Anatomy of Revolution.* New York: Vintage Books, 1965.

Brock, Deborah. *Making Work, Making Trouble: Prostitution as a Social Problem.* Toronto: University of Toronto Press, 1998.

Brodie, Janine, Shelley Gavigan, and Jane Jenson, eds. *The Politics of Abortion.* Toronto: Oxford University Press, 1992.

Brown, J. David. "The Professional Ex-: An Alternative for Exiting the Deviant Career." In E. Rubington, and M. Weinberg, eds., *Deviance: The Symbolic Interactionist Perspective.* 6th ed. Boston: Allyn and Bacon, 1996:439–456.

Brown, Lester R. et al., eds. *State of the World 1993: A Worldwatch Institute Report on Progress Toward a Sustainable Society.* New York: Norton, 1993.

Brown, Mary Ellen, ed. *Television and Women's Culture: The Politics of the Popular.* Newbury Park, Calif.: Sage, 1990.

Browning, Christopher R., and Edward O. Laumann. "Sexual Contact between Children and Adults: A Life Course Perspective." *American Sociological Review.* Vo. 62, No. 5 (August 1997):540–60.

Brym, Robert J., and Bonnie J. Fox. *From Culture to Power: The Sociology of English Canada.* Toronto: Oxford University Press, 1989.

Buraway, Michael. "Review Essay: The Soviet Descent into Capitalism." *American Journal of Sociology.* Vol. 102, No. 5 (March 1997):1430–44.

Burke, Tom. "The Future." In Sir Edmund Hillary, ed., *Ecology 2000: The Changing Face of the Earth.* New York: Beaufort Books, 1984:227–41.

Burkett, Elinor. "God Created Me to Be a Slave." *New York Times Sunday Magazine* (October 12, 1997):56–60.

Burr, Grant N., Stephen Wong, Sarah Vander Veen, and Deqiang Gu. "Three Strikes and You're Out: An Investigation of False Positive Rates Using a Canadian Sample." *Federal Probation.* Vol. 64, No. 1 (June 2000):3–6.

Burstein, Paul. "Legal Mobilization as a Social Movement Tactic: The Struggle for Equal Employment Opportunity." *American Journal of Sociology.* Vol. 96, No. 5 (March 1991):1201–25.

Butlin, George. "Determinants of University and Community College Leaving." *Education Quarterly Review.* Statistics Canada No. 81-003-XIE. Vol. 6, No. 4 (August 2000):8–23.

Callahan, Daniel. *Setting Limits: Medical Goals in an Aging Society.* New York: Simon & Shuster, 1987.

Cameron, William Bruce. *Modern Social Movements: A Sociological Outline.* New York: Random House, 1966.

Campbell, Robert A., and James E. Curtis. "Religious Involvement Across Societies." *Journal for the Scientific Study of Religion.* Vol.33, No. 3 (September 1994):217–29.

Canadian Centre for Drug-Free Sport. *Over 80,000 Young Canadians Using Anabolic Steroids.* Ottawa: News Release, 1993. [Online] http://www.hc-sc.gc.ca/main/hppb/nutrition/pube/vtlk/vitlk07.htm

*Canadian Geographic.* "Landfill Landscape." Vol. 111, No. 4, (May/June 1999):56–65.

Canadian Institute for Health Information, 2000. *Health Care in Canada: A First Annual Report.* Ottawa: Statistics Canada.

Canadian Press Newswire. *Reporter Recovering from Murder Attempt Says Tougher Biker Laws Needed.* October 21, 2000.

Canadian Radio-television and Telecommunications Commission. "New Violence Classification System for Television Programming: Another Mechanism to Protect Children Against TV Violence Ottawa-Hull." (June 18, 1997).

Canadian Sociology and Anthropology Association. [Online] http://www.arts.ubc.ca/csaa/eng/englcode.htm. 1994.

Cantor, Murial G., and Suzanne Pingree. *The Soap Opera.* Beverly Hills, Calif.: Sage, 1983.

Caplow, Theodore et al. *Middletown Families.* Minneapolis: University of Minnesota Press, 1982.

Caplow, Theodore, Howard M. Bahr, John Modell, and Bruce A. Chadwick. *Recent Social Trends in the United States, 1960–1990.* Montreal: McGill-Queen's University Press, 1991.

Carley, Kathleen. "A Theory of Group Stability." *American Sociological Review.* Vol. 56, No. 3 (June 1991):331–54.

Carlson, Norman A. "Corrections in the United States Today: A Balance Has Been Struck." *The American Criminal Law Review.* Vol. 13, No. 4 (Spring 1976):615–47.

Carmichael, Stokely, and Charles V. Hamilton. *Black Power: The Politics of Liberation in America.* New York: Vintage Books, 1967.

Carroll, James R. "Congress Is Told of Coal-Dust Fraud UMW; Senator from Minnesota Rebukes Industry." Louisville Courier Journal (Thursday, May 27, 1999):1A.

Cassidy, Barbara, Robina Lord, and Nancy Mandell. "Silenced and Forgotten Women: Race, Poverty, and Disability." In Nancy Mandell, ed., *Feminist Issues: Race, Class, and Sexuality.* Scarborough, Ontario: Prentice Hall Allyn and Bacon Canada, 1998:26–54.

*Catalyst.* "Catalyst Census Finds Few Women Corporate Officers." February 8, 2000. [Online] http://www.catalystwomen.org/press/release020800.html

Center for the Study of Sport in Society. *1998 Racial and Gender Report Card.* [Online] Available [Online] http://www.sportinsociety.org, February 19, 2000.

Chagnon, Napoleon A. *Yanomamö: The Fierce People.* 4th ed. New York: Holt, Rinehart & Winston, 1992.

Chandler, Tertius, and Gerald Fox. *3000 Years of Urban History.* New York: Academic Press, 1974.

Change, Kwang-Chih. *The Archaeology of Ancient China.* New Haven, Conn.: Yale University Press, 1977.

Chapkis, Wendy. *Live Sex Acts: Women Performing Erotic Labor.* New York: Routledge, 1997.

Charles, Maria. "Cross-National Variation in Occupational Segregation." *American Sociological Review.* Vol. 57, No. 4 (August 1992):483–502.

Chauncey, George. *Gay New York: Gender, Urban Culture, and the Making of the Gay Male World 1890-1940.* New York: Basic Books, 1994.

Cheney, Peter. "Is Pornography Out of Control?" *Globe and Mail.* Saturday, December 2, 2000:F4–5.

Chesnais, Jean-Claude. "The Demographic Sunset of the West?" *Population Today.* Vol. 25, No. 1 (January 1997):4–5.

Christie, Nancy. *Engendering the State: Family, Work, and Welfare in Canada.* Toronto: University of Toronto Press, 2000.

Chui, Tina W.L., James E. Curtis, and Ronald D. Lambert. "Immigrant Background and Political Participation: Examining

Generational Patterns." *Canadian Journal of Sociology.* Vol. 16, No. 4 (Fall 1991):375–96.

Church, George J. "Unions Arise—With New Tricks." *Time.* Vol. 143, No. 24 (June 13, 1994):56–58.

Citizens' Forum on Canada's Future. *Report to the People and Government of Canada.* Ottawa: Minister of Supply and Services Canada, 1991.

Clark, Margaret S., ed. *Prosocial Behavior.* Newbury Park, Calif.: Sage, 1991.

Clark, Warren. "Patterns of Religious Attendance." *Canadian Social Trends.* Ottawa: Statistics Canada. No. 59 (Winter 2000):23–27.

Clarke, Robin. "Atmospheric Pollution." In Sir Edmund Hillary, ed., *Ecology 2000: The Changing Face of the Earth.* New York: Beaufort Books, 1984a:130–48.

_____. "What's Happening to Our Water?" In Sir Edmund Hillary, ed., *Ecology 2000: The Changing Face of the Earth.* New York: Beaufort Books, 1984b:108–29.

Clement, Wallace. *The Canadian Corporate Elite.* Toronto: McClelland and Stewart, 1975.

Clinard, Marshall, and Daniel Abbott. *Crime in Developing Countries.* New York: Wiley, 1973.

Cloward, Richard A., and Lloyd E. Ohlin. *Delinquency and Opportunity: A Theory of Delinquent Gangs.* New York: Free Press, 1966.

Coe, Michael D., and Richard A. Diehl. *In the Land of the Olmec.* Austin: University of Texas Press, 1980.

Cohen, Albert K. *Delinquent Boys: The Culture of the Gang.* New York: Free Press, 1971; orig. 1955.

Cohen, Lloyd R. "Sexual Harassment and the Law." *Society.* Vol. 28, No. 4 (May–June 1991):8–13.

Cohen, Mark Nathan. *Health and the Rise of Civilization.* New Haven: Yale University Press, 1989.

Coleman, James S., and Thomas Hoffer. *Public and Private High Schools: The Impact of Communities.* New York: Basic Books, 1987.

Coleman, James, Thomas Hoffer, and Sally Kilgore. *Public and Private Schools: An Analysis of Public Schools and Beyond.* Washington, D.C.: National Center for Education Statistics, 1981.

Coleman, Richard P., and Lee Rainwater. *Social Standing in America.* New York: Basic Books, 1978.

Collins, Randall. "A Conflict Theory of Sexual Stratification." *Social Problems.* Vol. 19, No. 1 (Summer 1971):3–21.

_____. *The Credential Society: An Historical Sociology of Education and Stratification.* New York: Academic Press, 1979.

_____. *Sociological Insight: An Introduction to Nonobvious Sociology.* New York: Oxford University Press, 1982.

Colloway, N.O., and Paula L. Dollevoet. "Selected Tabular Material on Aging." In Caleb Finch, and Leonard Hayflick, eds., *Handbook of the Biology of Aging.* New York: Van Nostrand-Reinhold, 1977:666–708.

Colton, Helen. *The Gift of Touch: How Physical Contact Improves Communication, Pleasure, and Health.* New York: Seaview/Putnam, 1983.

The Commission on Systematic Racism in the Ontario Criminal Justice System. *Report.* Toronto: Queen's Printer for Ontario, 1995.

Computer Industry Almanac, Inc. *Finland Leading Country in Internet Users Per Capita.* Press release dated March 20, 1998.

Comte, Auguste. *Auguste Comte and Positivism: The Essential Writings.* Gertrud Lenzer, ed. New York: Harper Torchbooks, 1975.

Connett, Paul H. "The Disposable Society." In F. Herbert Bormann, and Stephen R. Kellert, eds., *Ecology, Economics, and Ethics: The Broken Circle.* New Haven, Conn.: Yale University Press, 1991:99–122.

Corelli, Rae. "Winter of Discontent: Welfare Cuts and Layoffs Add to the Ranks of Canada's Homeless." *Maclean's.* Toronto ed,. Vol. 109, No. 6 (February 5, 1996):46–48.

Corley, Robert N., O. Lee Reed, Peter J. Shedd, and Jere W. Morehead. *The Legal and Regulatory Environment of Business.* 9th ed. New York: McGraw-Hill, 1993.

Council on Families in America. *Marriage in America: A Report to the Nation.* New York: Institute for American Values, 1995.

Counts, G.S. "The Social Status of Occupations: A Problem in Vocational Guidance." *School Review.* Vol. 33 (January 1925):16–27.

"Court Rules French Can't Access Nazi Web Auction." *Times Colonist.* (November 21, 2000):A3.

Courtney, Alice E., and Thomas W. Whipple. *Sex Stereotyping in Advertising.* Lexington, Mass.: D.C. Heath, 1983.

Cowan, Carolyn Pope. *When Partners Become Parents.* New York: Basic Books, 1992.

Cowley, Geoffrey. "The Prescription That Kills." *Newsweek* (July 17, 1995):54.

Cox, Harvey. *The Secular City.* Rev. ed. New York: Macmillan, 1971; orig. 1965.

COYOTE (Call Off Your Old Tired Ethics). [Online] http://www.freedomusa.org/coyotela/what_is.html, April 2, 2000.

Crocker, Diane, and Valery Kalemba. "The Incidence and Impact of Women's Experiences of Sexual Harrassment in Canadian Workplaces." *The Canadian Review of Sociology and Anthropology.* Vol. 36, No. 4 (November 1999):541–558.

Crook, Stephan, Jan Pakulski, and Malcolm Waters. *Postmodernity: Change in Advanced Society.* Newbury Park, Calif.: Sage, 1992.

Crouse, James, and Dale Trusheim. *The Case Against the SAT.* Chicago: University of Chicago Press, 1988.

Currie, Elliott. *Confronting Crime: An American Challenge.* New York: Pantheon Books, 1985.

Curtis, Bruce. *Building the Educational State: Canada West, 1831–1871.* London, ON: Althouse Press, 1988.

Curtis, James E., Edward G. Grabb, and Douglas Baer. "Voluntary Association Membership in Fifteen Countries: A Comparative Analysis." *American Sociological Review.* Vol. 57, No. 2 (April 1992):139–52.

Curtis, James E., and Ronald D. Lambert. "Culture." In Robert Hagedorn, ed., *Sociology.* Toronto: Holt, Rinehart and Winston of Canada, 1990:21–59.

Curtiss, Susan. *Genie: A Psycholinguistic Study of a Modern-Day "Wild Child."* New York: Academic Press, 1977.

Dafoe, Chris. "The Resurrection of Big Bear." *Globe and Mail.* (Saturday, July 18, 1998): C1, C3.

Dahl, Robert A. *Who Governs?* New Haven, Conn.: Yale University Press, 1961.

_____. _Dilemmas of Pluralist Democracy: Autonomy vs. Control._ New Haven, Conn.: Yale University Press, 1982.

Dahrendorf, Ralf. _Class and Class Conflict in Industrial Society._ Stanford, Calif.: Stanford University Press, 1959.

Daly, Martin, and Margo Wilson. _Homicide._ New York: Aldine, 1988.

Davies, Christie. _Ethnic Humor Around the World: A Comparative Analysis._ Bloomington: Indiana University Press, 1990.

Davies, James C. "Toward a Theory of Revolution." _American Sociological Review._ Vol. 27, No. 1 (February 1962):5–19.

Davies, Mark, and Denise B. Kandel. "Parental and Peer Influences on Adolescents' Educational Plans: Some Further Evidence." _American Journal of Sociology._ Vol. 87, No. 2 (September 1981):363–87.

Davies, Scott. "In Search of Resistance and Rebellion among High School Dropouts." _Canadian Journal of Sociology._ Vol. 19, No. 3 (Summer 1994):331–50.

Davies, Scott, and Neil Guppy. "Race and Canadian Education" in Vic Satzewich, ed., _Racism & Social Inequality in Canada._ Toronto: Thompson Educational Publishing, Inc., 1998:131–155.

Davis, Donald M. Cited in "T.V. Is a Blonde, Blonde World." _American Demographics_, special issue: Women Change Places. Ithaca, NY: 1993.

Davis, Kingsley. "Extreme Social Isolation of a Child." _American Journal of Sociology._ Vol. 45, No. 4 (January 1940):554–65.

_____. "Final Note on a Case of Extreme Isolation." _American Journal of Sociology._ Vol. 52, No. 5 (March 1947):432–37.

_____. "Sexual Behavior." In Robert K. Merton, and Robert Nisbet, eds., _Contemporary Social Problems._ 3rd ed. New York: Harcourt Brace Jovanovich, 1971:313–60.

Davis, Kingsley, and Wilbert Moore. "Some Principles of Stratification." _American Sociological Review._ Vol. 10, No. 2 (April 1945):242–49.

Davis, Sharon A., and Emil J. Haller. "Tracking, Ability, and SES: Further Evidence on the 'Revisionist-Meritocratic Debate.'" _American Journal of Education._ Vol. 89 (May 1981):283–304.

Dawson, Lorne. _Comprehending Cults: The Sociology of New Religious Movements._ Toronto: University of Toronto Press, 1998.

Dawson, Lorne L., ed. _Cults in Context: Readings in the Study of New Religious Movements._ Toronto: Canadian Scholar's Press, 1996.

De Brouker, Patrice, and Laval Lavallée. "Getting Ahead: Does Your Parents' Education Count?" _Education Quarterly Review._ Statistics Canada Catalogue No. 81-003XIE. Vol. 5, No. 1 (August 1998):22–28.

De Tocqueville, Alexis. _The Old Regime and the French Revolution._ Stuart Gilbert, trans. Garden City, N.Y.: Anchor/Doubleday Books, 1955; orig. 1856.

Deckard, Barbara Sinclair. _The Women's Movement: Political, Socioeconomic, and Psychological Issues._ 2nd ed. New York: Harper & Row, 1979.

Dedrick, Dennis K., and Richard E. Yinger. "MAD, SDI, and the Nuclear Arms Race." Manuscript in development. Georgetown, Ky.: Georgetown College, 1990.

Delacroix, Jacques, and Charles C. Ragin. "Structural Blockage: A Cross-national Study of Economic Dependency, State Efficacy, and Underdevelopment." _American Journal of Sociology._ Vol. 86, No. 6 (May 1981):1311–47.

DeLuca, Tom. "Joe the Bookie and the Class Voting Gap." _American Demographics._ Vol. 20, No. 11 (November 1998):26–29.

Demerath, N.J., III. "Who Now Debates Functionalism? From System, Change, and Conflict to 'Culture, Choice, and Praxis.'" _Sociological Forum._ Vol. 11, No. 2 (June 1996):333–45.

Denis, Wilfred. "The Politics of Language." In Peter S. Li, ed., _Race and Ethnic Relations in Canada._ Toronto: Oxford University Press, 1990:148–185.

Department of Justice Canada. _Experience in British Columbia._ 1995.

_Der Spiegel._ "Third World Metropolises Are Becoming Monsters; Rural Poverty Drives Millions to the Slums." _World Press Review._ (October 1989).

Desmond, Bill. "Metro Racism Survey Rapped." _The Toronto Star,_ final ed. (January 11, 1996):A10.

Devine, Joel A. "State and State Expenditure: Determinants of Social Investment and Social Consumption Spending in the Postwar United States." _American Sociological Review._ Vol. 50, No. 2 (April 1985):150–65.

Devor, Holly. _FTM: Female-to-Male Transsexuals in Society._ Bloomington, IN: Indiana University Press, 1997.

DeVries, R., C. Benoit, E. Van Teijlingen, and Sirpa Wrede (eds.). _Birth by Design: The Social Shaping of Maternity Care in Northern Europe and North America._ London: Routledge, 2001.

Dickason, Olive Patricia. _Canada's First Nations: A History of Founding Peoples from Earliest Times._ Toronto: McClelland and Stewart Inc., 1992.

Dixon, William J., and Terry Boswell. "Dependency, Disarticulation, and Denominator Effects: Another Look at Foreign Capital Penetration." _American Journal of Sociology._ Vol. 102, No. 2 (September 1996):543–62.

Dizard, Jan E., and Howard Gadlin. _The Minimal Family._ Amherst: The University of Massachusetts Press, 1990.

Dobyns, Henry F. "An Appraisal of Techniques with a New Hemispheric Estimate." _Current Anthropology._ Vol. 7, No. 4 (October 1966):395–446.

Dollard, John et al. _Frustration and Aggression._ New Haven, Conn.: Yale University Press, 1939.

Domhoff, G. William. _Who Rules America Now? A View of the '80s._ Englewood Cliffs, N.J.: Prentice Hall, 1983.

Donald, Leland. _Aboriginal Slavery on the Northwest Coast of North America._ Berkeley: University of California Press, 1997.

Donovan, Virginia K., and Ronnie Littenberg. "Psychology of Women: Feminist Therapy." In Barbara Haber, ed., _The Women's Annual 1981: The Year in Review._ Boston: G. K. Hall, 1982:211–35.

Doob, Anthony N. "Transforming the Punishment Environment: Understanding Public Views of What Should Be Accomplished at Sentencing." _Canadian Journal of Criminology._ Vol. 42, No. 3 (July 2000): 323–347.

Downe, Pamela. "Selling Sex, Studying Sexuality: Voices of Costa Rican Prostitutes and Visions of Feminists." _Atlantis._ Vol. 23, No. 1 (Fall/Winter 1998): 60–68.

Doyle, James A. _The Male Experience._ Dubuque, Iowa: Wm. C. Brown, 1983.

Doyle, Richard F. _A Manifesto of Men's Liberation._ 2nd ed. Forest Lake, Minn.: Men's Rights Association, 1980.

Driedger, Leo. _Multi-Ethnic Canada: Identities and Inequalities._ Toronto: Oxford University Press, 1996.

Dryburgh, Heather. "Teenage Pregnancy." *Health Reports*. Statistics Canada Catalogue No. 92-003-XIE. Volume 12, No. 1 (October) 2000:9–19.

Dubos, René. *Man Adapting*. New Haven, Conn.: Yale University Press, 1980; orig. 1965.

Duffy, Ann. "The Feminist Challenge: Knowing and Ending the Violence." In Nancy Mandell, ed., *Feminist Issues: Race, Class, and Sexuality*. 2nd ed. Scarborough, Ontario: Prentice Hall Allyn and Bacon Canada, 1998:132–59.

Duhl, Leonard J. "The Social Context of Health." In Arthur C. Hastings et al., eds., *Health for the Whole Person: The Complete Guide to Holistic Medicine*. Boulder, Colo.: Westview Press, 1980:39–48.

Dull, M.W. "Gays and Mayor in Fight Over Rights." *The Globe and Mail*. December 23, 1997.

Dumas, Jean. *Report on the Demographic Situation in Canada 1993*. Statistics Canada Catalogue No. ASDF91-209E. Ottawa: Statistics Canada, Demography Division, 1994.

Durkheim, Emile. *The Division of Labor in Society*. New York: Free Press, 1964a; orig. 1895.

_____.*The Rules of Sociological Method*. New York: Free Press, 1964b; orig. 1893.

_____. *The Elementary Forms of Religious Life*. New York: Free Press, 1965; orig. 1915.

Dworkin, Andrea. *Intercourse*. New York: Free Press, 1987.

Ebaugh, Helen Rose Fuchs. *Becoming an EX: The Process of Role Exit*. Chicago: University of Chicabo Press, 1988.

*The Economist*. "Japan's Missing Children." Vol. 333, No. 7889 (November 12, 1994):46.

Edin, Kathryn, and Laura Lein. "Work, Welfare, and Single Mothers' Economic Survival Strategies." *American Sociological Review*. Vol. 62, No. 2 (April 1996):253–66.

Edwards, David V. *The American Political Experience*. 3rd ed. Englewood Cliffs, N.J.: Prentice Hall, 1985.

Edwards, Gary, and Josephine Mazzuca. "One-in-Four Canadians Favour Legalized Abortion Under Any Circumstance." *The Gallup Poll*. Vol. 59, No. 76 (December 13, 1999):1–2.

Edwards, Richard. *Contested Terrain: The Transformation of the Workplace in the Twentieth Century*. New York: Basic Books, 1979.

Ehrenreich, Barbara. The Hearts of Men: American Dreams and the Flight from Commitment. Garden City, N.Y.: Anchor Books, 1983.

———. "The Real Truth about the Female Body." *Time*. Vol. 153, No. 9 (March 15, 1999):56–65.

Ehrenreich, John. "Introduction." In John Ehrenreich, ed., *The Cultural Crisis of Modern Medicine*. New York: Monthly Review Press, 1978:1–35.

Eichler, Margrit. *Nonsexist Research Methods: A Practical Guide*. Winchester, Mass.: Unwin Hyman, 1988.

_____. *Family Shifts: Families, Policies, and Gender Equality*. Toronto: Oxford University Press, 1997.

Eisenberg, Daniel. "Rise of the Permatemp." *Time*. Vol. 154, No. 2 (July 12, 1999):48.

Eisenstadt, S.N. "Multiple Modernities in an Age of Globalization. *Canadian Journal of Sociology*. Vol. 24, No. 2 (1999):283–295.

Eisenstein, Zillah R., ed. *Capitalist Patriarchy and the Case for Socialist Feminism*. New York: Monthly Review Press, 1979.

Ekman, Paul. "Biological and Cultural Contributions to Body and Facial Movements in the Expression of Emotions." In A. Rory, ed., *Explaining Emotions*. Berkeley: University of California Press, 1980:73–101.

_____. *Telling Lies: Clues to Deceit in the Marketplace, Politics, and Marriage*. New York: Norton, 1985.

Elias, James, Vern Bullough, Veronica Elias, and Joycelyn Elders, eds. *Prostitution: On Whores, Hustlers, and Johns*. New York: Promethus Books, 1998.

Elias, Norbert. *The History of Manners: The Civilizing Process: Volume I*. New York: Pantheon Books, 1978.

Elias, Robert. *The Politics of Victimization: Victims, Victimology and Human Rights*. New York: Oxford University Press, 1986.

Ellingsaeter, Anne Lise. "Dual Breadwinner Societies: Provider Models in the Scandinavian Welfare States." *Acta Sociologica*. Vol. 41, No.1 (1998):59–73.

Elliot, Delbert S., and Suzanne S. Ageton. "Reconciling Race and Class Differences in Self-Reported and Official Estimates of Delinquency." *American Sociological Review*. Vol. 45, No. 1 (February 1980):95–110.

Ellison, Christopher G., and Darren E. Sherkat. "Conservative Protestantism and Support for Corporal Punishment." *American Sociological Review*. Vol. 58, No. 1 (February 1993):131–44.

Elmer-DeWitt, Philip. "First Nation in Cyberspace." *Time*. Vol. 142, No. 24 (December 6, 1993):62–64.

_____. "Battle for the Internet." *Time*. Vol. 144, No. 4 (July 25, 1994):50–56.

_____. "The Genetic Revolution." *Time*. Vol. 143, No. 3 (January 17, 1994a):46–53.

Ember, Melvin, and Carol R. Ember. "The Conditions Favoring Matrilocal Versus Patrilocal Residence." *American Anthropologist*. Vol. 73, No. 3 (June 1971):571–94.

_____. *Anthropology*. 6th ed. Englewood Cliffs, N.J.: Prentice Hall, 1991.

Emerson, Joan P. "Behavior in Private Places: Sustaining Definitions of Reality in Gynecological Examinations." In H. P. Dreitzel, ed., *Recent Sociology*. Vol. 2. New York: Collier, 1970:74–97.

Engels, Friedrich. *The Origin of the Family*. Chicago: Charles H. Kerr & Company, 1902; orig. 1884.

England, Paula. *Comparable Worth: Theories and Evidence*. Hawthorne, N.Y.: Aldine, 1992.

Erikson, Robert S., Norman R. Luttbeg, and Kent L. Tedin. *American Public Opinion: Its Origins, Content, and Impact*. 2nd ed. New York: Wiley, 1980.

Errington, Elizabeth Jane. 1995. *Wives and Mothers, School Mistresses and Scullery Maids: Working Women in Upper Canada, 1790–1840*. Montreal and Kingston: McGill-Queen's University Press.

Eshleman, J.R., and S.J. Wilson. *The Family*. Scarborough, Ontario: Prentice Hall, 1998.

Esping-Andersen, Gösta. *The Three Worlds of Welfare Capitalism*. Princeton: Princeton University Press, 1990.

Etzioni, Amitai. *A Comparative Analysis of Complex Organization: On Power, Involvement, and Their Correlates*. Rev. and enlarged ed. New York: Free Press, 1975.

_____. "How to Make Marriage Matter." *Time*. Vol. 142, No. 10 (September 6, 1993):76.

Etzioni-Halevy, Eva. *Bureaucracy and Democracy: A Political Dilemma.* Rev. ed. Boston: Routledge & Kegan Paul, 1985.

Falk, Gerhard. Personal communication, 1987.

Falkenmark, Malin, and Carl Widstrand. "Population and Water Resources: A Delicate Balance." *Population Bulletin.* Vol. 47, No. 3 (November 1992). Washington, D.C.: Population Reference Bureau.

Fallon, A.E., and P. Rozin. "Sex Differences in Perception of Desirable Body Shape." *Journal of Abnormal Psychology.* Vol. 94, No. 1 (1985):100–105.

Farrell, Michael P., and Stanley D. Rosenberg. *Men at Midlife.* Boston: Auburn House, 1981.

Featherman, David L., and Robert M. Hauser. *Opportunity and Change.* New York: Academic Press, 1978.

Featherstone, Mike, ed. *Global Culture: Nationalism, Globalization, and Modernity.* London: Sage, 1990.

Federal, Provincial and Territorial Advisory Committee on Population Health. *Report on the Health of Canadians.* Ottawa: Minister of Supply and Services Canada, 1996.

Federal, Provincial and Territorial Advisory Committee on Population Health. *Statistical Report on the Health of Canadians.* Revised Version (March 2000). Statistics Canada Catalogue No. 82-570-XIE. Ottawa: Minister of Public Works and Government Services Canada, 1999.

Federal, Provincial and Territorial Advisory Committee on Population Health. *Statistical Report on the Health of Canadians.* Health Canada: Ministry of Public Works and Government Services Canada, 1999. Catalogue No. H39-467/1999E.

Federal, Provincial and Territorial Advisory Committee on Population Health. *Statistical Report on the Health of Canadians.* Ottawa: Statistics Canada, 1999.

Federal, Provincial/Territorial Ministers Responsible for the Status of Women. *Economic Gender Equality Indicators.* Ottawa: Status of Women, 1997.

Fennell, Tom, and Sheng Xue. "The Smuggler's Slaves." *Maclean's.* Vol. 111, No. 50 (December 12, 2000):14–19.

Ferguson, Tom. "Medical Self-Care: Self Responsibility for Health." In Arthur C. Hastings et al., eds., *Health for the Whole Person: The Complete Guide to Holistic Medicine.* Boulder, Colo.: Westview Press, 1980:87–109.

Fernandez, Roberto M., and Nancy Weinberg. "Sifting and Sorting: Personal Contacts and Hiring in a Retail Bank." *American Sociological Review.* Vol. 62, No. 6 (December 1997):883–902.

Ferree, Myra Marx, and Elaine J. Hall. "Rethinking Stratification from a Feminist Perspective: Gender, Race, and Class in Mainstream Textbooks." *American Sociological Review.* Vol. 61, No. 6 (December 1996):929–50.

Fetto, John. "Down for the Count." *American Demographics.* Vol. 21, No. 11 (November 1999):46–47.

*Financial Post 500 Magazine.* "Special Report: The Financial Post 500 Magazine." (June 8, 1998).

Finkelstein, Neal W., and Ron Haskins. "Kindergarten Children Prefer Same-Color Peers." *Child Development.* Vol. 54, No. 2 (April 1983):502–508.

Finn, Chester E., Jr., and Rebecca L. Gau. "New Ways of Education." *The Public Interest.* Vol. 130 (Winter 1998):79–92.

Finnie, Ross. "Holding Their Own: Employment and Earnings of Postsecondary Graduates." *Education Quarterly Review.* Statistics

Canada Catalogue No. 81-003XIE. Vol. 7, No. 1 (November 2000):21–37.

Fiorentine, Robert. "Men, Women, and the Premed Persistence Gap: A Normative Alternatives Approach." *American Journal of Sociology.* Vol. 92, No. 5 (March 1987):1118–39.

Fiorentine, Robert, and Stephen Cole. "Why Fewer Women Become Physicians: Explaining the Premed Persistance Gap." *Sociological Forum.* Vol. 7, No. 3 (September 1992):469–96.

Firebaugh, Glenn. "Growth Effects of Foreign and Domestic Investment." *American Journal of Sociology.* Vol. 98, No. 1 (July 1992):105–30.

_____. "Does Foreign Capital Harm Poor Nations? New Estimates Based on Dixon and Boswell's Measures of Capital Penetration." *American Journal of Sociology.* Vol. 102, No. 2 (September 1996):563–75.

_____. "Empirics of World Income Inequality." *American Journal of Sociology.* Vol. 104, No. 6 (May 1999):1597–1630.

Firebaugh, Glenn, and Dumitru Sandu. "Who Supports Marketization and Democratization in Post-Communist Romania?" *Sociological Forum.* Vol. 13, No. 3 (September 1998):521–41.

Firebaugh, Glenn, and Frank D. Beck. "Does Economic Growth Benefit the Masses? Growth, Dependence, and Welfare in the Third World." *American Sociological Review.* Vol. 59, No. 5 (October 1994):631–53.

Fisher, Elizabeth. *Woman's Creation: Sexual Evolution and the Shaping of Society.* Garden City, N.Y.: Anchor/Doubleday, 1979.

Fisher, Roger, and William Ury. "Getting to YES." In William M. Evan and Stephen Hilgartner, eds., *The Arms Race and Nuclear War.* Englewood Cliffs, N.J.: Prentice Hall, 1988:261–68.

Fiske, Alan Paige. "The Cultural Relativity of Selfish Individualism: Anthropological Evidence that Humans Are Inherently Sociable." In Margaret S. Clark, ed., *Prosocial Behavior.* Newbury Park, Calif.: Sage, 1991:176–214.

Flaherty, Michael G. "A Formal Approach to the Study of Amusement in Social Interaction." *Studies in Symbolic Interaction.* Vol. 5. New York: JAI Press, 1984:71–82.

_____. "Two Conceptions of the Social Situation: Some Implications of Humor." *The Sociological Quarterly.* Vol. 31, No. 1 (Spring 1990).

"Forbes World's Richest People." [Online] http://www.forbes.com/worldsrichest. May 18, 2001.

Ford, Clellan S., and Frank A. Beach. *Patterns of Sexual Behavior.* New York: Harper & Row, 1951.

Foss, Krista. "Canadians at Forefront of Web Use in Schools." *Globe and Mail.* (September 11, 2000).

Foucault, Michel. *The History of Sexuality: An Introduction.* Vol. 1. Robert Hurley, trans. New York: Vintage, 1990; orig. 1978.

Fox, Bonnie, ed. *Family Patterns/Gender Relations.* Toronto: Oxford University Press, 2001.

Fox, Bonnie, and Meg Luxton. "Conceptualizing Family." In Bonnie Fox (ed.), *Family Patterns/Gender Relations.* Toronto: Oxford University Press, 2001:22–33.

Frager, Ruth A. *Sweatshop Strife: Class, Ethnicity, and Gender in the Jewish Labour Movement in Toronto, 1900–1939.* Toronto: University of Toronto Press, 1992.

Frank, André Gunder. *On Capitalist Underdevelopment.* Bombay: Oxford University Press, 1975.

_____. *Crisis: In the World Economy*. New York: Holmes & Meier, 1980.

_____. *Reflections on the World Economic Crisis*. New York: Monthly Review Press, 1981.

Franklin Associates. *Characterization of Municipal Solid Waste in the United States, 1960–2000*. Prairie Village, Kans.: Franklin Associates, 1986.

Frazier, E. Franklin. *Black Bourgeoisie: The Rise of a New Middle Class*. New York: Free Press, 1965.

Fredrickson, George M. *White Supremacy: A Comparative Study in American and South African History*. New York: Oxford University Press, 1981.

Free, Marvin D. "Religious Affiliation, Religiosity, and Impulsive and Intentional Deviance." *Sociological Focus*. Vol. 25, No. 1 (February 1992):77–91.

Freedom House. *Freedom in the World 1998–1999*. New York: Freedom House, 1999.

French, Marilyn. *Beyond Power: On Women, Men, and Morals*. New York: Summit Books, 1985.

Friedman, Meyer, and Ray H. Rosenman. *Type A Behavior and Your Heart*. New York: Fawcett Crest, 1974.

Fuchs, Victor R. "Sex Differences in Economic Well-Being." *Science*. Vol. 232 (April 25, 1986):459–64.

Fukuyama, F. *The End of History and the Last Man*. New York: The Free Press, 1992.

Fuller, Rex, and Richard Schoenberger. "The Gender Salary Gap: Do Academic Achievement, Intern Experience, and College Major Make a Difference?" *Social Science Quarterly*. Vol. 72, No. 4 (December 1991):715–26.

Furstenberg, Frank F., Jr., and Andrew Cherlin. *Divided Families: What Happens to Children When Parents Part*. Cambridge, Mass.: Harvard University Press, 1991.

Gagliani, Giorgio. "How Many Working Classes?" *American Journal of Sociology*. Vol. 87, No. 2 (September 1981):259–85.

Gagne, Patricia, Richard Tewksbury, and Deanna McGaughey. "Coming Out and Crossing Over: Identity Formation and Proclamation in a Transgender Community." *Gender and Society*. Vol. 11, No. 4 (August 1997):478–508.

Gallup Organization, The. *Special Reports: Global Study of Family Values*. Princeton, NJ: The Gallup Organization, November 7, 1997.

Gallup Organization, The. *The Gallup Poll Monthly*. December, 1993.

Galt, Virgina. "Where the Boys Aren't: At the Top of the Class." *Globe and Mail*. (February 26, 1998). [Online] http://www.theglobeandmail.com/NIF/19980226/USITUN.html

Gamson, William A. "Beyond the Science-versus-Advocacy Distinction." *Contemporary Sociology*. Vol. 28, No. 1 (January 1999):23–26.

Gans, Herbert J. *People and Plans: Essays on Urban Problems and Solutions*. New York: Basic Books, 1968.

_____. *The Urban Villagers: Group and Class in the Life of Italian-Americans*. New York: Free Press, 1982; orig. 1962.

Gardner, Arthur. "Their Own Boss: The Self-Employed in Canada." *Canadian Social Trends*. No. 37 (Summer 1995):26–29.

Gardner, Dan. "Immigration Ignored in Election Despite Its Impact on the Future: Polls Show Canadian Concern Over Immigration Levels, But the Political Debate on the Issue Is Missing." *Vancouver Sun* (May 31, 1997):A6.

Garfinkel, Harold. "Conditions of Successful Degradation Ceremonies." *American Journal of Sociology*. Vol. 61, No. 2 (March 1956):420–24.

_____. *Studies in Ethnomethodology*. Cambridge: Polity Press, 1967.

Gee, Ellen, and Gloria Gutman. *Overselling of Population Aging: Apocalyptic Demography, Intergenerational Challenges and Social Policy*. Toronto: Oxford University Press, 2000.

Gee, Marcus. "Born in 169 Other Countries." *Globe and Mail*. (June 10, 1998):A27.

Geertz, Clifford. "Common Sense as a Cultural System." *The Antioch Review*. Vol. 33, No. 1 (Spring 1975):5–26.

Gelbard, Alene, Carl Haub, and Mary M. Kent. "World Population Beyond Six Billion." *Population Bulletin*. Vol. 54, No. 1 (March 1999).

Gelles, Richard J., and Claire Pedrick Cornell. *Intimate Violence in Families*. 2nd ed. Newbury Park, Calif.: Sage, 1990.

Gelman, David. "Who's Taking Care of Our Parents?" *Newsweek*. (May 6, 1985):61–64, 67–68.

_____. "Born or Bred?" *Newsweek*. (February 24, 1992):46–53.

Gerber, Theodore P., and Michael Hout. "More Shock than Therapy: Market Transition, Employment, and Income in Russia, 1991–1995." *American Journal of Sociology*. Vol. 104, No. 1 (July 1998):1–50.

Gerlach, Michael L. *The Social Organization of Japanese Business*. Berkeley and Los Angeles: University of California Press, 1992.

Gerstel, Naomi. "Divorce and Stigma." *Social Problems*. Vol. 43, No. 2 (April 1987):172–86.

Geschwender, James A. *Racial Stratification in America*. Dubuque, Iowa: Wm. C. Brown, 1978.

Gewertz, Deborah. "A Historical Reconsideration of Female Dominance among the Chambri of Papua New Guinea." *American Ethnologist*. Vol. 8, No. 1 (1981):94–106.

Ghosh, Ratna. *Redefining Multicultural Education*. Toronto: Harcourt Brace Canada, 1996.

Gibbons, Don C., and Marvin D. Krohn. *Delinquent Behavior*. 4th ed. Englewood Cliffs, N.J.: Prentice Hall, 1986.

Gibbs, Nancy. "When Is It Rape?" *Time*. Vol. 137, No. 22 (June 3, 1991a):48–54.

_____. "The Clamor on Campus." *Time*. Vol. 137, No. 22 (June 3, 1991b):54–55.

_____. "How Much Should We Teach Our Children about Sex?" *Time*. Vol. 141, No. 21 (May 24, 1993):60–66.

_____. "Cause Celeb." *Time*. Vol. 147, No. 25 (June 17, 1996):28–30.

Giddens, Anthony. *Sociology: A Brief but Critical Introduction*. New York: Harcourt Brace Jovanovich, 1982.

———. *The Transformation of Intimacy*. Cambridge, UK: Polity Press, 1992.

Giele, Janet Z. "Gender and Sex Roles." In Neil J. Smelser, ed., *Handbook of Sociology*. Newbury Park, Calif.: Sage, 1988:291–323.

Gigliotti, Richard J., and Heather K. Huff. "Role Related Conflicts, Strains, and Stresses of Older-Adult College Students." *Sociological Focus*. Vol. 28, No. 3 (August 1995):329–42.

Gilbert, Neil. "Realities and Mythologies of Rape." *Society*. Vol. 29, No. 4 (May–June 1992):4–10.

Gilligan, Carol. *In a Different Voice: Psychological Theory and Women's Development*. Cambridge, Mass.: Harvard University Press, 1982.

Gillon, Raanan. "Euthanasia in the Netherlands—Down the Slippery Slope?" *Journal of Medical Ethics*. Vol. 25, No. 1 (February 1999):3–4.

Gimenez, Martha E. "Silence in the Classroom: Some Thoughts about Teaching in the 1980s." *Teaching Sociology*. Vol. 17, No. 2 (April 1989):184–91.

Ginsburg, Faye, and Anna Lowenhaupt Tsing, eds. *Uncertain Terms: Negotiating Gender in American Culture*. Boston: Beacon Press, 1990.

Giovannini, Maureen. "Female Anthropologist and Male Informant: Gender Conflict in a Sicilian Town." In John J. Macionis, and Nijole V. Benokraitis, eds., *Seeing Ourselves: Classic, Contemporary, and Cross-Cultural Readings in Sociology*. 2nd ed. Englewood Cliffs, N.J.: Prentice Hall, 1992:27–32.

Giugni, Marco G. "Structure and Culture in Social Movements Theory." *Sociological Forum*. Vol. 13, No. 2 (June 1998):365–75.

Gladue, Brian A., Richard Green, and Ronald E. Hellman. "Neuroendocrine Response to Estrogen and Sexual Orientation." *Science*. Vol. 225, No. 4669 (September 28, 1984):1496–99.

Glaser, Nona. Y. *Women's Paid and Unpaid Labour: The Work Transfer in Health Care and Retailing*. Philadelphia: Temple University Press, 1993.

Gleick, Elizabeth. "The Marker We've Been Waiting For." *Time*. Vol. 149, No. 14 (April 7, 1997):28–42.

Glenn, Norval D., and Beth Ann Shelton. "Regional Differences in Divorce in the United States." *Journal of Marriage and the Family*. Vol. 47, No. 3 (August 1985):641–52.

Glueck, Sheldon, and Eleanor Glueck. *Unraveling Juvenile Delinquency*. New York: Commonwealth Fund, 1950.

Gnida, John J. "Teaching 'Nature versus Nurture': The Case of African American Athletic Success." *Teaching Sociology*. Vol. 23, No. 4 (October 1995):389–95.

Goffman, Erving. *The Presentation of Self in Everyday Life*. Garden City, N.Y.: Anchor Books, 1959.

_____. *Asylums: Essays on the Social Situation of Mental Patients and Other Inmates*. Garden City, N.Y.: Anchor Books, 1961.

_____. *Stigma: Notes on the Management of Spoiled Identity*. Englewood Cliffs, N.J.: Prentice Hall, 1963.

_____. *Interactional Ritual: Essays on Face to Face Behavior*. Garden City, N.Y.: Anchor Books, 1967.

Goldberg, Steven. *The Inevitability of Patriarchy*. New York: Wm. Morrow, 1974.

_____. Personal communication, 1987.

Golden, Frederic. "Good Eggs, Bad Eggs." *Time*. Vol. 153, No. 1 (January 11, 1999a):56–59.

———. "Lying Faces Unmasked." *Time*. Vol. 153, No. 13 (April 5, 1999b):52.

Goldfarb, William. "Groundwater: The Buried Life." In F. Herbert Bormann, and Stephen R. Kellert, eds., *Ecology, Economics, and Ethics: The Broken Circle*. New Haven, Conn.: Yale University Press, 1991:123–35.

Goldscheider, Frances Kobrin, and Linda J. Waite. "Sex Differences in the Entry Into Marriage." *American Journal of Sociology*. Vol. 92, No. 1 (July, 1986):91–109.

Goldsmith, H.H. "Genetic Influences on Personality From Infancy." *Child Development*. Vol. 54, No. 2 (April 1983):331–35.

Goode, William J. "The Theoretical Importance of Love." *American Sociological Review*. Vol. 24, No. 1 (February 1959):38–47.

_____. "Encroachment, Charlatanism, and the Emerging Profession: Psychology, Sociology and Medicine." *American Sociological Review*. Vol. 25, No. 6 (December 1960):902–14.

Gordon, James S. "The Paradigm of Holistic Medicine." In Arthur C. Hastings et al., eds., *Health for the Whole Person: The Complete Guide to Holistic Medicine*. Boulder, Colo.: Westview Press, 1980:3–27.

Gordon, Sol, and Craig W. Snyder. *Personal Issues in Human Sexuality: A Guidebook for Better Sexual Health*. 2nd ed. Boston: Allyn & Bacon, 1989.

Goring, Charles Buckman. *The English Convict: A Statistical Study*. Montclair, N.J.: Patterson Smith, 1972; orig. 1913.

Gottfredson, Michael R., and Travis Hirschi. "National Crime Control Policies." *Society*. Vol. 32, No. 2 (January-February 1995):30–36.

Gottmann, Jean. *Megalopolis*. New York: Twentieth Century Fund, 1961.

Gough, Kathleen. "The Origin of the Family." *Journal of Marriage and the Family*. Vol. 33, No. 4 (November 1971):760–71.

Gould, Stephen J. "Evolution as Fact and Theory." *Discover*. (May 1981):35–37.

Grant, Karen R. "The Inverse Care Law in the Context of Universal Free Health Insurance in Canada: Toward Meeting Health Needs through Public Policy." *Sociological Focus*. Vol. 17, No. 2 (April 1984):137–55.

Gratzer, David. *Code Blue: Reviving the Canadian Health Care System*. Toronto: ECW Press, 1999.

Greeley, Andrew M. *Religious Change in America*. Cambridge, Mass.: Harvard University Press, 1989.

Green, John C. "Pat Robertson and the Latest Crusade: Resources and the 1988 Presidential Campaign." *Social Sciences Quarterly*. Vol. 74, No. 1 (March 1993):156–68.

Greenberg, David F. *The Construction of Homosexuality*. Chicago: University of Chicago Press, 1988.

Greenfield, Lawrence A. *Child Victimizers: Violent Offenders and their Victims*. Washington, D.C.: U.S. Bureau of Justice Statistics, 1996.

Greenspoon, Edward. "Pay-Equity Costs Too High: Chrétien." *Globe and Mail*. (August 18, 1998):A3.

Greer, Scott. *Urban Renewal and American Cities*. Indianapolis, Ind.: Bobbs-Merrill, 1965.

Gregory, Paul R., and Robert C. Stuart. *Comparative Economic Systems*. 2nd ed. Boston: Houghton Mifflin, 1985.

Gross, Jane. "New Challenge of Youth: Growing Up in a Gay Home." *New York Times*. (February 11, 1991):A1, B7.

Guindon, Hubert. "Quebec and the Canadian Question." In James Curtis and Lorne Tepperman, eds., *Images of Canada: The Sociological Tradition*. Scarborough, Ontario: Prentice-Hall, Inc., 1990:30–41.

Gwartney-Gibbs, Patricia A., Jean Stockard, and Susanne Bohmer. "Learning Courtship Agression: The Influence of Parents, Peers, and Personal Experiences." *Family Relations*. Vol. 36, No. 3 (July 1987):276–82.

Gwynne, S. C., and John F. Dickerson. "Lost in the E-Mail." *Time.* Vol. 149, No. 15 (April 21, 1997):88–90.

Habermas, Jürgen. *Toward a Rational Society: Student Protest, Science, and Politics.* Jeremy J. Shapiro, trans. Boston: Beacon Press, 1970.

Hacker, Helen Mayer. "Women as a Minority Group." *Social Forces.* Vol. 30 (October 1951):60–69.

_____. "Women as a Minority Group: 20 Years Later." In Florence Denmark, ed., *Who Discriminates Against Women?* Beverly Hills, Calif.: Sage, 1974:124–34.

Hackey, Robert B. "Competing Explanations of Voter Turnout among American Blacks." *Social Science Quarterly.* Vol. 73, No. 1 (March 1992):71–89.

Hackler, Jim. "Criminalizing Sex." In Jim Hackler, ed., *Canadian Criminology: Strategies and Perspectives.* Scarborough, Ontario: Prentice Hall Canada, 1999:254–67.

Hadaway, C. Kirk, Penny Long Marler, and Mark Chaves. "What the Polls Don't Show: A Closer Look at U.S. Church Attendance." *American Sociological Review.* Vol. 58, No. 6 (December 1993):741–52.

Hadden, Jeffrey K., and Charles E. Swain. *Prime-Time Preachers: The Rising Power of Televangelism.* Reading, Mass.: Addison-Wesley, 1981.

Hafner, Katie. "Making Sense of the Internet." *Newsweek.* (October 24, 1994):46–48.

Hagan, Jacqueline Maria. "Social Networks, Gender, and Immigrant Incorporation: Resources and Restraints." *American Sociological Review.* Vol. 63, No. 1 (February 1998):55–67.

Hagan, John, and Bill McCarthy. *Mean Streets: Youth Crime and Homelessness.* New York: Cambridge University Press, 1997.

Hagan, John, and Fiona Kay. *Gender in Practice : A Study of Lawyers' Lives.* New York Oxford University Press, 1995.

Hagan, John, and Patricia Parker. "White-Collar Crime and Punishment: The Class Structure and Legal Sanctioning of Securities Violations." *American Sociological Review.* Vol. 50, No. 3 (June 1985):302–16.

Haig, Robin Andrew. *The Anatomy of Humor: Biopsychosocial and Therapeutic Perspectives.* Springfield, Ill.: Charles C. Thomas, 1988.

Hall, Edward. *The Hidden Dimension.* New York: Doubleday, 1969.

Hall, John R., and Mary Jo Neitz. *Culture: Sociological Perspectives.* Englewood Cliffs, N.J.: Prentice Hall, 1993.

Hall, Kelley J., and Betsy Lucal. "Tapping in Parallel Universes: Using Superhero Comic Books in Sociology Courses." *Teaching Sociology.* Vol. 27, No. 1 (January 1999):60–66.

Hallinan, Maureen T., and Richard A. Williams. "Interracial Friendship Choices in Secondary Schools." *American Sociological Review.* Vol. 54, No. 1 (February 1989):67–78.

Hamer, Dean, and Peter Copeland. *The Science of Desire: The Search for the Gay Gene and the Biology of Behavior.* New York: Simon & Schuster, 1994.

Hamilton, Dwight. "It's Much Better to Be Rich." *The Financial Post.* (January 1, 1996):14.

Hamrick, Michael H., David J. Anspaugh, and Gene Ezell. *Health.* Columbus, Ohio: Merrill, 1986.

Handgun Control, Inc. Data cited in *Time* (December 20, 1993) and various newspaper reports (March 2, 6, 1994).

_____. [Online] http://www.handguncontrol.org/press/ archive/ march30-98.htm, April 3, 2000.

Hanson, R. Karl, Heather Scott, and Richard A. Steffy. "A Comparison of Child Molesters and Nonsexual Criminals: Risk Predictors and Long-term Recidivism." *Journal of Research in Crime and Delinquency.* Vol. 32, No. 3 (August 1995):327–337.

Hareven, Tamara K. "The Life Course and Aging in Historical Perspective." In Tamara K. Hareven, Tamara K., and Kathleen J. Adams, eds., *Aging and Life Course Transitions: An Interdisciplinary Perspective.* New York: Guilford Press, 1982:1–26.

Harlow, Harry F., and Margaret Kuenne Harlow. "Social Deprivation in Monkeys." *Scientific American.* Vol. 207 (November 1962):137–46.

Harpster, Paula, and Elizabeth Monk-Turner. "Why Men Do Housework: A Test of Gender Production and the Relative Resources Model." *Sociological Focus.* Vol. 31, No. 1 (February 1998):45–59.

Harries, Keith D. *Serious Violence: Patterns of Homicide and Assault in America.* Springfield, Ill.: Charles C. Thomas, 1990.

Harrigan, Patrick J. "The Schooling of Boys and Girls in Canada." *Journal of Social History.* Vol. 23, No. 4 (Summer 1990):803–26.

Harrington, Michael. *The New American Poverty.* New York: Penguin Books, 1984.

Harris, Chauncey D., and Edward L. Ullman. "The Nature of Cities." *The Annals.* Vol. 242 (November 1945):7–17.

Harris, Jack Dash. Lecture on cockfighting in the Philippines. Semester at Sea (October 27, 1994).

Harris, Marvin. "Why Men Dominate Women." *New York Times Magazine.* (November 13, 1977):46, 115–23.

_____. *Cultural Anthropology.* 1st ed., 1983; 2nd ed. New York: Harper & Row, 1987.

Harrison, Deborah, and Lucie Laliberté. *No Life Like It: Military Wives in Canada.* Toronto: James Lorimer & Company, Publishers, 1994.

Hawthorne, Peter. "South Africa's Makeover." *Time.* Vol. 154, No. 2 (July 12, 1999).

Health Canada. *HIV and AIDS in Canada: Surveillance Report to December 31, 1997.* Ottawa: Health Canada, 1998.

_____. *HIV and AIDS in Canada: Surveillance Report.* Ottawa: Health Canada, Laboratory Centre for Disease Control. (Dec. 1999)

_____. *1998–1999 Canadian Sexually Transmitted Diseases (STD) Surveillance Report.* Ottawa: Health Canada, Laboratory Centre for Disease Control. Volume 2656 (October 2000a).

_____. *HIV and AIDS in Canada: Surveillance Report to June 30, 2000.* Ottawa: Minister of Public Works and Government Services Canada. 2000b.

Heath, Julia A., and W. David Bourne. "Husbands and Housework: Parity or Parody?" *Social Science Quarterly.* Vol. 76, No. 1 (March 1995):195–202.

Hedley, Alan. "Convergence in Natural, Social, and Technical Systems: A Critique." *Current Science.* Vol. 79, No. 5 (September 2000):592–601.

Helgesen, Sally. *The Female Advantage: Women's Ways of Leadership.* New York: Doubleday, 1990.

Helin, David W. "When Slogans Go Wrong." *American Demographics.* Vol. 14, No. 2 (February 1992):14.

Henley, Nancy, Mykol Hamilton, and Barrie Thorne. "Womanspeak and Manspeak: Sex Differences in Communication, Verbal and Nonverbal." In John J. Macionis, and Nijole V. Benokraitis, eds., *Seeing Ourselves: Classic, Contemporary, and Cross-Cultural Readings in Sociology.* 2nd ed. Englewood Cliffs, N.J.: Prentice Hall, 1992:10–15.

Henry, Frances, Carol Tator, Winston Mattis, and Tim Rees. *The Colour of Democracy: Racism in Canadian Society.* Toronto: Harcourt Brace, 1995.

Henry, William A., III. "Gay Parents: Under Fire and On the Rise." *Time.* Vol. 142, No. 12 (September 20, 1993):66–71.

Herdt, Gilbert H. "Semen Transactions in Sambian Culture." In David N. Suggs, and Andrew W. Miracle, eds., *Culture and Human Sexuality.* Pacific Grove, Calif.: Brooks Cole, 1993:298–327.

Herek, Gregory M. "Myths about Sexual Orientation: A Lawyer's Guide to Social Science Research." *Law and Sexuality.* No. 1 (1991):133–72.

Herman, Dianne. "The Rape Culture." In John J. Macionis, and Nijole V. Benokraitis, eds., *Seeing Ourselves: Classic, Contemporary, and Cross-Cultural Readings in Sociology.* 5th ed. Upper Saddle River, NJ: Prentice Hall, 2001.

Herman, Didi. *Rights of Passage: Struggles for Lesbian and Gay Legal Rights.* Toronto: University of Toronto Press, 1994.

Herman, Edward S. *Corporate Control, Corporate Power: A Twentieth Century Fund Study.* New York: Cambridge University Press, 1981.

Herrnstein, Richard J., and Charles Murray. *The Bell Curve: Intelligence and Class Structure in American Life.* New York: Free Press, 1994.

Hersch, Joni, and Shelly White-Means. "Employer-Sponsored Health and Pension Benefits and the Gender/Race Wage Gap." *Social Science Quarterly.* Vol. 74, No. 4 (December 1993):850–66.

Hertz, R. *More Equal Than Others: Women and Men in Dual-Career Marriages.* Berkeley: University of California Press, 1986.

Hess, Beth B. "Breaking and Entering the Establishment: Committing Social Change and Confronting the Backlash." *Social Problems.* Vol. 46, No. 1 (February 1999):1–12.

Hirschi, Travis. *Causes of Delinquency.* Berkeley: University of California Press, 1969.

Hobart, Charles. *Premarital Sexual Standards among Canadian Students at the End of the Eighties.* Unpublished manuscript. Edmonton: University of Alberta, 1990.

Hoberman, John. *Darwin's Athletes: How Sport Has Damaged Black America and Preserved the Myth of Race.* Boston: Houghton Mifflin, 1997.

———. "Response to Three Reviews of Darwin's Athletes." *Social Science Quarterly.* Vol. 79, No. 4 (December 1998):898–903.

Hochschild, Arlie Russell. *The Managed Heart : Commercialization of Human Feeling.* Berkeley: University of California Press, 1983.

———. *The Time Bind: When Work Becomes Home and Home Becomes Work.* New York: Metropolitan Books, 1997.

Hodge, Robert W., Donald J. Treiman, and Peter H. Rossi. "A Comparative Study of Occupational Prestige." In Reinhard Bendix and Seymour Martin Lipset, eds., *Class, Status, and Power: Social Stratification in Comparative Perspective.* 2nd ed. New York: Free Press, 1966:309–21.

Holmes, Steven A. "U.S. Reports Drop in Rate of Births to Unwed Women." *New York Times.* (October 5, 1996a):1, 9.

———. "For Hispanic Poor, No Silver Lining." *New York Times.* (October 13, 1996b): sec. 4, p. 5.

Hostetler, John A. *Amish Society.* 3rd ed. Baltimore: Johns Hopkins University Press, 1980.

Hout, Michael. "More Universalism, Less Structural Mobility: The American Occupational Structure in the 1980s." *American Journal of Sociology.* Vol. 95, No. 6 (May 1998):1358–1400.

Hoyt, Homer. *The Structure and Growth of Residential Neighborhoods in American Cities.* Washington, D.C.: Federal Housing Administration, 1939.

Hsu, Francis L. K. *The Challenge of the American Dream: The Chinese in the United States.* Belmont, Calif.: Wadsworth, 1971.

Huchingson, James E. "Science and Religion." *The Herald.* (Dade County, Florida) (December 25, 1994):1M, 6M.

Huffman, Matt L., Steven C. Velasco, and William T. Bielby. "Where Sex Composition Matters Most: Comparing the Effects of Job versus Occupational Sex Composition of Earnings." *Sociological Focus.* Vol. 29, No. 3 (August 1996):189–207.

Hume, Stephen. "Our 'Dead Past,' Our Living Present: 'The Real History of B.C. . . . Racism, Official Oppression of Visible Minorities, . . . Hypocrisy.'" *The Vancouver Sun,* Final Edition. (September 13, 1995):A19.

Humphrey, Craig R., and Frederick R. Buttel. *Environment, Energy, and Society.* Belmont, Calif.: Wadsworth, 1982.

Humphries, Harry Leroy. *The Structure and Politics of Intermediary Class Positions: An Empirical Examination of Recent Theories of Class.* Unpublished PhD dissertation. Eugene: University of Oregon, 1984.

Hunter, James Davison. *American Evangelicalism: Conservative Religion and the Quandary of Modernity.* New Brunswick, N.J.: Rutgers University Press, 1983.

———. "Conservative Protestantism." In Philip E. Hammond, ed., *The Sacred in a Secular Age.* Berkeley: University of California Press, 1985:50–66.

———. *Evangelicalism: The Coming Generation.* Chicago: University of Chicago Press, 1987.

Huntington, S.P. *The Clash of Civilizations and the Future of the West.* New York: Simon & Schuster, 1996.

Hymowitz, Carol. "World's Poorest Women Advance by Entrepreneurship." *Wall Street Journal* (September 9, 1995):B1.

Iacovetta, Franca. "Remaking Their Lives: Immigrants, Survivors, and Refugees." In Joy Parr, ed., *A Diversity of Women: Ontario, 1945–1980.* Toronto: University of Toronto Press, 1995:135–167.

Ide, Thomas R., and Arthur J. Cordell. "Automating Work." *Society.* Vol. 31, No. 6 (September-October 1994):65–71.

Inglehart, Ronald. Modernization and Postmodernization: Cultural, Economic, and Political Change in 43 Societies. Princeton, N.J.: Princeton University Press, 1997.

Institute for Philosophy and Public Policy. "The Greying of America." Vol. 8, No. 2 (Spring 1988): 1–5.

Inter-Parliamentary Union. *Men and Women in Politics: Democracy Still in the Making–A World Comparative Study.* IPU: Geneva, 1997.

———. *Women In National Parliaments, Situation as of 15 January 2001.* [Online] http://www.ipu.org/wmn-e/classif.htm (January 4, 2001).

Isay, Richard A. *Being Homosexual: Gay Men and Their Development.* New York: Farrar, Straus & Giroux, 1989.

Jacobs, Jane. *The Death and Life of Great American Cities*. New York: Random House, 1961.

Jacoby, Russell, and Naomi Glauberman, eds. *The Bell Curve Debate*. New York: Random House, 1995.

Jaffe, A.J. *The First Immigrants from Asia: A Population History of the North American Indians*. New York and London: Plenum Press, 1992.

Jagger, Alison. "Political Philosophies of Women's Liberation." In Laurel Richardson, and Verta Taylor, eds., *Feminist Frontiers: Rethinking Sex, Gender, and Society*. Reading, Mass.: Addison-Wesley, 1983.

James, Carl E. "Up to No Good: Black on the Streets and Encountering Police." In Vic Satzewich, ed., *Racism & Social Inequality in Canada*. Toronto: Thompson Educational Publishing Inc. 1998:157–176.

Jamieson, Kathleen. "Sex Discrimination and the *Indian Act*." In J. Rick Ponting, ed., *Arduous Journey: Canadian Indians and Decolonialization*. Toronto: McClelland & Stewart, 1986:112–136.

Janis, Irving. *Victims of Groupthink*. Boston: Houghton Mifflin, 1972.

_____. *Crucial Decisions: Leadership in Policymaking and Crisis Management*. New York: Free Press, 1989.

Janus, Christopher G. "Slavery Abolished? Only Officially." *Christian Science Monitor*. (May 17, 1996):18.

Jeffries, T. "Sechelt Women and Self-Government." In Creese, G., and Strong-Boag, V., eds., *British Columbia Reconsidered: Essays on Women*. Vancouver: Press Gang Publishers, 1992:90–95.

Jencks, Christopher. "Genes and Crime." *New York Review*. (February 12, 1987):33–41.

Johnson, Holly. *Dangerous Domains: Violence Against Women in Canada*. Toronto: Nelson, 1996.

Johnson, Paul. "The Seven Deadly Sins of Terrorism." In Benjamin Netanyahu, ed., *International Terrorism*. New Brunswick, N.J.: Transaction Books, 1981:12–22.

Johnston, R.J. "Residential Area Characteristics." In D.T. Herbert and R.J. Johnston, eds., *Social Areas in Cities. Vol. 1: Spatial Processes and Form*. New York: Wiley, 1976:193–235.

Johnson, Roland. [Online] http://www.PersonalWebs.myriad.net/Roland. (1996).

Jones, Arthur. "Welfare Reform Makes Children Prime Victims." *National Catholic Reporter* (April 30, 1999):14–16.

Jones, Judy. "More Miners Will Be Offered Free X-Rays; Federal Agency Wants to Monitor Black-Lung Cases." *Louisville Courier Journal*. (Thursday, May 13, 1999):1A.

Josephy, Alvin M., Jr. *Now That the Buffalo's Gone: A Study of Today's American Indians*. New York: Alfred A. Knopf, 1982.

Kadushin, Charles. "Friendship among the French Financial Elite." *American Sociological Review*. Vol. 60, No. 2 (April 1995):202–21.

Kahne, Hilda, and Janet Giele, eds. *Women's Work and Women's Lives: The Continuing Struggle Worldwide*. Bounder: Westview Press, 1992.

Kain, Edward L. "A Note on the Integration of AIDS into the Sociology of Human Sexuality." *Teaching Sociology*. Vol. 15, No. 4 (July 1987):320–23.

_____. *The Myth of Family Decline: Understanding Families in a World of Rapid Social Change*. Lexington, Mass.: Lexington Books, 1990.

Kain, Edward L., and Shannon Hart. "AIDS and the Family: A Content Analysis of Media Coverage." Presented to National Council on Family Relations, Atlanta, 1987.

Kalbach, Warren E., and Wayne W. McVey. *The Demographic Basis of Canadian Society*. 2nd ed. Toronto: McGraw-Hill Ryerson, 1979.

Kamala, Kempadoo, and Jo Doezema. *Global Sex Workers: Rights, Resistence, and Redefinition*. New York and London: Routledge, 1998.

Kaminer, Wendy. "Volunteers: Who Knows What's in It for Them." *Ms.* (December 1984):93–94, 96, 126–28.

Kamiya, Gary. "Cablinasian Like Me." *Salon*. [Online] www.salon.com/april97/tiger970430.html (accessed March 5, 2001): 1997.

Kanter, Rosabeth Moss. *Men and Women of the Corporation*. New York: Basic Books, 1977.

Kanter, Rosabeth Moss, and Barry A. Stein. "The Gender Pioneers: Women in an Industrial Sales Force." In R.M. Kanter and B.A. Stein, eds., *Life in Organizations*. New York: Basic Books, 1979:134–60.

Kaplan, Eric B. et al. "The Usefulness of Preoperative Laboratory Screening." *JAMA, Journal of the American Medical Association*. Vol. 253, No. 24 (June 28, 1985):3576–81.

Kaptchuk, Ted. "The Holistic Logic of Chinese Medicine." In Shepard Bliss et al., eds., *The New Holistic Health Handbook*. Lexington, Mass.: The Steven Greene Press/Penguin Books, 1985:41.

Karp, David A., and William C. Yoels. "The College Classroom: Some Observations on the Meaning of Student Participation." *Sociology and Social Research*. Vol. 60, No. 4 (July 1976):421–39.

Kates, Robert W. "Ending Hunger: Current Status and Future Prospects." *Consequences*. Vol. 2, No. 2 (1996):3–11.

Kaufman, Walter. *Religions in Four Dimensions: Existential, Aesthetic, Historical and Comparative*. New York: Reader's Digest Press, 1976.

Keith, Pat M., and Robert B. Schafer. "They Hate to Cook: Patterns of Distress in an Ordinary Role." *Sociological Focus*. Vol. 27, No. 4 (October 1994):289–301.

Kellert, Stephen R., and F. Herbert Bormann. "Closing the Circle: Weaving Strands Among Ecology, Economics, and Ethics." In F. Herbert Bormann and Stephen R. Kellert, eds., *Ecology, Economics, and Ethics: The Broken Circle*. New Haven, Conn.: Yale University Press, 1991:205–10.

Kentor, Jeffrey. "The Long-Term Effects of Foreign Investment Dependence on Economic Growth, 1940–1990." *American Journal of Sociology*. Vol. 103, No. 4 (January 1998):1024–46.

Kerckhoff, Alan C., Richard T. Campbell, and Idee Winfield-Laird. "Social Mobility in Great Britain and the United States." *American Journal of Sociology*. Vol. 91, No. 2 (September 1985):281–308.

Kidd, Quentin, and Aie-Rie Lee. "Postmaterialist Values and the Environment: A Critique and Reappraisal." *Social Science Quarterly*. Vol. 78, No. 1 (March 1997):1–15.

Kidron, Michael, and Ronald Segal. *The New State of the World Atlas*. New York: Simon & Schuster, 1991.

Kiely, Ray. "Globalization, Post-Fordism and the Contemporary Context of Development." *International Sociology*. Vol. 13, No. 1 (March 1998):95–116.

Kilbourne, Brock K. "The Conway and Siegelman Claims Against Religious Cults: An Assessment of Their Data." *Journal for the Scientific Study of Religion*. Vol. 22, No. 4 (December 1983):380–85.

Kilbourne, Jean. *Slim Hopes: Advertising and the Obsession with Thinness*. Video presentation. Northampton, Mass.: The Media Education Foundation, 1995.

Kilgore, Sally B. "The Organizational Context of Tracking in Schools." *American Sociological Review*. Vol. 56, No. 2 (April 1991):189–203.

Killian, Lewis M. "Organization, Rationality and Spontaneity in the Civil Rights Movement." *American Sociological Review*. Vol. 49, No. 6 (December 1984):770–83.

King, Kathleen Piker, and Dennis E. Clayson. "The Differential Perceptions of Male and Female Deviants." *Sociological Focus*. Vol. 21, No. 2 (April 1988):153–64.

Kinsey, Alfred et al. *Sexual Behavior in the Human Male*. Philadelphia: Saunders, 1948.

_____. *Sexual Behavior in the Human Female*. Philadelphia: Saunders, 1953.

Kleinfeld, Judith. "Student Performance: Males versus Females." *The Public Interest*. No. 134 (Winter, 1999):3–20.

Kluckhohn, Clyde. "As An Anthropologist Views It." In Albert Deuth, ed., *Sex Habits of American Men*. New York: Prentice Hall, 1948.

Kogawa, Joy. *Obasan*. Markham: Penguin Books, 1981.

Kohlberg, Lawrence, and Carol Gilligan. "The Adolescent as Philosopher: The Discovery of Self in a Postconventional World." *Daedalus*. Vol. 100 (Fall 1971):1051–86.

Kohn, Melvin L. *Class and Conformity: A Study in Values*. 2nd ed. Homewood, Ill.: Dorsey Press, 1977.

Komarovsky, Mirra. *Blue Collar Marriage*. New York: Vintage Books, 1967.

_____. "Cultural Contradictions and Sex Roles: The Masculine Case." *American Journal of Sociology*. Vol. 78, No. 4 (January 1973):873–84.

Kono, Clifford, Donald Palmer, Roger Friedland, and Matthew Zafonte. "Lost in Space: The Geography of Corporate Interlocking Directorates." *American Journal of Sociology*. Vol. 103, No. 4 (January 1998):863–911.

Kornhauser, William. *The Politics of Mass Society*. New York: Free Press, 1959.

Kozol, Jonathan. *Rachel and Her Children: Homeless Families in America*. New York: Crown Publishers, 1988.

Krahn, Harvey J., and Graham S. Lowe. *Work, Industry, and Canadian Society*. 3rd ed. Toronto: ITP Nelson, 1998.

Kriesi, Hanspeter. "New Social Movements and the New Class in the Netherlands." *American Journal of Sociology*. Vol. 94, No. 5 (March 1989):1078–116.

Krueger, Ingrid. "Commitment Gives Way to Convenience." *Alberta Report/ Western Report*. Vol. 24, No. 46 (October 27, 1997):45–46.

Kruks, Gabriel N. "Gay and Lesbian Homeless/Street Youth: Special Issues and Concerns." *Journal of Adolescent Health*. Special Issue, No. 12 (1991):515–18.

Kudrle, Robert T., and Theodore R. Marmor. "The Development of the Welfare States in North America." In Peter Flora and Arnold J. Heidenheimer, eds., *The Development of Welfare States in North America*. London: Transaction Books, 1981.

Kuhn, Thomas. *The Structure of Scientific Revolutions*. 2nd ed. Chicago: University of Chicago Press, 1970.

Kuznets, Simon. "Economic Growth and Income Inequality." *The American Economic Review*. Vol. XLV, No. 1 (March 1955):1–28.

_____. *Modern Economic Growth: Rate, Structure, and Spread*. New Haven, Conn.: Yale University Press, 1966.

Ladd, John. "The Definition of Death and the Right to Die." In John Ladd, ed., *Ethical Issues Relating to Life and Death*. New York: Oxford University Press, 1979:118–45.

Lai, H. M. "Chinese." In *Harvard Encyclopedia of American Ethnic Groups*. Cambridge, Mass.: Harvard University Press, 1980:217–33.

Lamberg-Karlovsky, C.C., and Martha Lamberg-Karlovsky. "An Early City in Iran." In *Cities: Their Origin, Growth, and Human Impact*. San Francisco: Freeman, 1973:28–37.

Landers, Rene M. "Gender, Race, and the State Courts." *Radcliffe Quarterly*. Vol. 76, No. 4 (December 1990):6–9.

Landsberg, Mitchell. "Health Disaster Brings Early Death in Russia." *Washington Times* (March 15, 1998):A8.

Lappé, Frances Moore, and Joseph Collins. *World Hunger: Twelve Myths*. New York: Grove Press/Food First Books, 1986.

Lappé, Frances Moore, Joseph Collins, and David Kinley. *Aid as Obstacle: Twenty Questions about Our Foreign Policy and the Hungry*. San Francisco: Institute for Food and Development Policy, 1981.

LaPrairie, Carol. "The 'New' Justice: Some Implications for Aboriginal Communities." *Canadian Journal of Criminology*. Vol. 40, No. 1 (January 1998):61–79.

Larmer, Brook. "Dead End Kids." *Newsweek*. (May 25, 1992):38–40.

Larson, Lyle E., J. Walter Goltz, and Charles Hobart. *Families in Canada*. Scarborough: Prentice Hall Canada Inc., 1994.

Lasch, Christopher. *Haven in a Heartless World: The Family Besieged*. New York: Basic Books, 1977.

Laslett, Peter. *The World We Have Lost: England before the Industrial Age*. 3rd ed. New York: Charles Scribner's Sons, 1984.

Lassey, M., W. Lassey, and M. Jinks. *Health Care Systems around the World*. New Jersey: Prentice Hall, 1997.

Laumann, Edward O., John H. Gagnon, Robert T. Michael, and Stuart Michaels. *The Social Organization of Sexuality: Sexual Practices in the United States*. Chicago: University of Chicago Press, 1994.

Leacy, F.H. *Historical Statistics of Canada*. 2nd ed., electronic edition. Statistics Canada Catalogue No. 11-516-XIE. Ottawa: Statistics Canada, 1999.

Leadbeater, Bonnie J. Ross, and Niobe Way. *Urban Girls: Resisting Sterotypes, Creating Identities*. New York: New York University Press, 1996.

Leavitt, Judith Walzer. "Women and Health in America: An Overview." In Judith Walzer Leavitt, ed., *Women and Health in America*. Madison: University of Wisconsin Press, 1984:3–7.

Leerhsen, Charles. "Unite and Conquer." *Newsweek*. (February 5, 1990):50–55.

Leira, Arnlaug. *Welfare States and Working Mothers: The Scandinavian Experience*. New York: Cambridge University Press, 1992.

_____. "Combining Work and Family: Nordic Policy Reforms in the 1990s." In Thomas Boje, and Arnlaug Leira, eds., *Gender, Welfare State and the Market: Towards a New Division of Labour*. London: Routledge, 2000:157–174.

Leland, John. "Bisexuality." *Newsweek*. (July 17, 1995):44–49.

Lemert, Edwin M. *Social Pathology*. New York: McGraw-Hill, 1951.

_____. *Human Deviance, Social Problems, and Social Control*. 2nd ed. Englewood Cliffs, N.J.: Prentice Hall, 1972.

Lengermann, Patricia Madoo, and Ruth A. Wallace. *Gender in America: Social Control and Social Change*. Englewood Cliffs, N.J.: Prentice Hall, 1985.

Lennon, Mary Clare, and Sarah Rosenfeld. "Relative Fairness and the Doctrine of Housework: The Importance of Options." *American Journal of Sociology*. Vol. 100, No. 2 (September 1994):506–31.

Lenski, Gerhard and Jean, and Patrick Nolan. *Human Societies: An Introduction to Macrosociology*. 7th ed. New York: McGraw-Hill, 1995.

Leonard, Eileen B. *Women, Crime, and Society: A Critique of Theoretical Criminology*. New York: Longman, 1982.

LeVay, Simon. *The Sexual Brain*. Cambridge, Mass.: MIT Press, 1993.

Lever, Janet. "Sex Differences in the Complexity of Children's Play and Games." *American Sociological Review*. Vol. 43, No. 4 (August 1978):471–83.

Levine, Michael. *Student Eating Disorders: Anorexia Nervosa and Bulimia*. Washington, D.C.: National Educational Association, 1987.

_____. "Reducing Hostility Can Prevent Heart Disease." Mount Vernon News (August 7, 1990):4A.

Levine, Robert V. "Is Love a Luxury?" *American Demographics*. Vol. 15, No. 2 (February 1993):27–28.

Levinson, Daniel J., with Charlotte N. Darrow, Edward B. Klein, Maria H. Levinson, and Braxton McKee. *The Seasons of a Man's Life*. New York: Alfred A. Knopf, 1978.

Lévi-Strauss, Claude. *The Elementary Structures of Kinship*. London: Eyre and Spottiswoode, 1969.

Lewis, Flora. "The Roots of Revolution." *New York Times Magazine*. (November 11, 1984):70–71, 74, 77–78, 82, 84, 86.

Lewis, J., and E. Maticka-Tyndale. *Escort Services in a Border Town: Methodological Challenges Conducting Research Related to Sex Work*. Health Canada, Ottawa: Division of STD Prevention and Control, 1999.

Lewis, Oscar. *The Children of Sanchez*. New York: Random House, 1961.

Lewis, Pierce, Casey McCracken, and Roger Hunt. "Politics: Who Cares?" *American Demographics*. Vol. 16, No. 10 (October 1994):20–26.

Li, Jiang Hong, and Roger A. Wojtkiewicz. "A New Look at the Effects of Family Structure on Status Attainment." *Social Science Quarterly*. Vol. 73, No. 3 (September 1992):581–95.

Li, Peter. *The Chinese in Canada*. 2nd ed. Toronto: Oxford University Press, 1998.

Liazos, Alexander. "The Poverty of the Sociology of Deviance: Nuts, Sluts and Preverts." *Social Problems*. Vol. 20, No. 1 (Summer 1972):103–20.

_____. *People First: An Introduction to Social Problems*. Boston: Allyn and Bacon, 1982.

Lin, Nan, and Wen Xie. "Occupational Prestige in Urban China." *American Journal of Sociology*. Vol. 93, No. 4 (January 1988):793–832.

Linden, Eugene. "More Power to Women, Fewer Mouths to Feed." *Time*. Vol. 144, No. 13 (September 26, 1994):64–65.

Lindstrom, Bonnie. "Chicago's Post-Industrial Suburbs." *Sociological Focus*. Vol. 28, No. 4 (October 1995):399–412.

Linton, Ralph. "One Hundred Percent American." *The American Mercury*. Vol. 40, No. 160 (April 1937):427–29.

_____. *The Study of Man*. New York: D. Appleton-Century, 1937.

Lips, Hilary. *Sex and Gender: An Introduction*. 2nd ed. Mountain View, Calif.: Mayfield Publishing Co., 1993.

Liska, Allen E. *Perspectives on Deviance*. 3rd ed. Englewood Cliffs, N.J.: Prentice Hall, 1991.

Liska, Allen E., and Barbara D. Warner. "Functions of Crime: A Paradoxical Process." *American Journal of Sociology*. Vol. 96, No. 6 (May 1991):1441–63.

Livernash, Robert, and Eric Rodenburg. "Population Change, Resources, and the Environment." *Population Bulletin*. Vol. 53, No. 1 (March 1998).

Lohr, Steve. "British Health Service Faces a Crisis in Funds and Delays." *New York Times*. (August 7, 1988):1, 12.

Looker, E. Dianne, and Victor Thiessen. "Images of Work: Women's Work, Men's Work, Housework." *The Canadian Journal of Sociology*. Vol. 24, No. 2(Spring 1999):225–254.

Lorber, Judith. *Paradoxes of Gender*. New Haven, CT: Yale University Press, 1994.

Lord, Walter. *A Night to Remember*. Rev. ed. New York: Holt, Rinehart & Winston, 1976.

Lorenz, Konrad. *On Aggression*. New York: Harcourt, Brace & World, 1966.

Lowe, Graham. S. *The Quality of Work: A People-Centred Agenda*. Toronto: Oxford University Press, 2000.

Lowman, John. "Taking Young Prostitutes Seriously." *Canadian Review of Sociology and Anthropology*. Vol 24, No. 1 (1987):99–116.

_____. "Notions of Equality Before the Law: The Experience of Street Prostitutes and Their Customers." *Journal of Human Justice*. Vol. 1, No. 2 (1990):55–76.

Luker, Kristen. *Abortion and the Politics of Motherhood*. Berkeley: University of California Press, 1984.

Lund, Dale A. "Caregiving." *Encyclopedia of Adult Development*. Phoenix, Ariz.: Oryx Press, 1993:57–63.

Luo, Jar-Der. "The Significance of Networks in the Initiation of Small Businesses in Taiwan." *Sociological Focus*. Vol. 12, No. 2 (June 1997):297–317.

Lutz, Catherine A. *Unnatural Emotions: Everyday Sentiments on a Micronesia Atoll and Their Challenge to Western Theory*. Chicago: University of Chicago Press, 1988.

Lutz, Catherine A., and Geoffrey M. White. "The Anthropology of Emotions." *Annual Review of Anthropology*. Vol. 15 (1986):405–36.

Lutz, William. *The New Doublespeak: Why No One Knows What Anyone's Saying Anymore*. New York, NY: HarperCollins Publishers, 1996.

Luxton, Meg. *More Than a Labour of Love: Three Generations of Women in the Home*. Toronto: Women's Press, 1980.

_____. "Wives and Husbands." In Bonnie Fox, ed., *Family Patterns/Gender Relations*. Toronto: Oxford University Press, 2001:176–198.

Lynd, Robert S., and Helen Merrell Lynd. *Middletown in Transition*. New York: Harcourt, Brace & World, 1937.

Lynn, Marion, and Milana Todoroff. "Women's Work and Family Lives." In Nancy Mandell, ed., *Feminist Issues: Race, Class, and Sexuality*. 2nd edition. Scarborough, Ontario: Prentice Hall Allyn and Bacon Canada, 1998:208–32.

Ma, Li-Chen. Personal communication, 1987.

Mabry, Marcus. "New Hope for Old Unions?" *Newsweek*. (February 24, 1992):39.

Mabry, Marcus, and Tom Masland. "The Man after Mandela." *Newsweek*. (June 7, 1999):54–55.

Maccoby, Eleanor Emmons, and Carol Nagy Jacklin. *The Psychology of Sex Differences*. Palo Alto, Calif.: Stanford University Press, 1974.

Mace, David, and Vera Mace. *Marriage East and West*. Garden City, N.Y.: Doubleday (Dolphin), 1960.

Macionis, John J. "Intimacy: Structure and Process in Interpersonal Relationships." *Alternative Lifestyles*. Vol. 1, No. 1 (February 1978):113–30.

_____. "A Sociological Analysis of Humor." Presentation to the Texas Junior College Teachers Association, Houston, 1987.

_____. "Making Society (and, Increasingly, the World) Visible." In Earl Babbie, ed., *The Spirit of Sociology*. Belmont, Calif.: Wadsworth, 1993:221–24.

_____. *Sociology*. 8th ed. Upper Saddle River, New Jersey: Prentice-Hall, Inc., 2001.

Macionis, John J., and Ken Plummer. *Sociology: A Global Introduction*. New York: Prentice Hall Europe, 1997.

Macionis, John J., and Vincent R. Parrillo. *The Sociology of Cities*. 3rd ed. Upper Saddle River, N.J.:Prentice Hall, 1998.

_____. *Cities and Urban Life*. 2nd ed. Upper Saddle River, N.J.: Prentice Hall, 2001.

MacKay, Donald G. "Prescriptive Grammar and the Pronoun Problem." In Barrie Thorne, Cheris Kramarae, and Nancy Henley, eds., *Language, Gender and Society*. Rowley, Mass.: Newbury House, 1983:38–53.

Mackie, Marlene. *Constructing Women and Men: Gender Socialization*. Toronto: Holt, Rinehart and Winston, 1985.

Mackillop, Barry. *Alternative Measures in Canada—1998*. Statistics Canada Catalogue No. 85-5454-XIE. Ottawa: Minister of Industry, 1999.

MacKinnon, Catharine A. *Feminism Unmodified: Discourses on Life and Law*. Cambridge, Mass.: Harvard University Press, 1987.

Maddox, Setma. "Organizational Culture and Leadership Style: Factors Affecting Self-Managed Work Team Performance." Paper presented at the annual meeting of the Southwest Social Science Association, Dallas, February, 1994.

Madsen, Axel. *Private Power: Multinational Corporations for the Survival of Our Planet*. New York: Wm. Morrow, 1980.

Malamuth, N.M., and F. Donnerstein. *Pornography and Sexual Aggression*. Orlando, Florida: Academic Press, 1984.

Malthus, Thomas Robert. *First Essay on Population 1798*. London: Macmillan, 1926; orig. 1798.

Manza, Jeff, and Clem Brooks. "The Religious Factor in U.S. Presidential Elections, 1960–1992." *American Journal of Sociology*. Vol. 103, No. 1 (July 1997):38–81.

Marathon Records. [Online] http://www.marathonguide.com/history/index.cfm. May 8, 2001.

Marcuse, Herbert. *One-Dimensional Man*. Boston: Beacon Press, 1964.

Mare, Robert D. "Five Decades of Educational Assortative Mating." *American Sociological Review*. Vol. 56, No. 1 (February 1991):15–32.

Markoff, John. "Remember Big Brother? Now He's a Company Man." *New York Times*. (March 31, 1991):7.

Markovsky, Barry, John Skvoretz, David Willer, Michael J. Lovaglia, and Jeffrey Erger. "The Seeds of Weak Power: An Extension of Network Exchange Theory." *American Sociological Review*. Vol. 58, No. 2 (April 1993):197–209.

Marquand, Robert. "Worship Shift: Americans Seek Feeling of 'Awe.'" *Christian Science Monitor*. (May 28, 1997):1, 8.

Marquand, Robert, and Daniel B. Wood. "Rise in Cults as Millennium Approaches." *Christian Science Monitor*. (March 28, 1997):1, 18.

Marshall, Katherine. "Part-time by Choice." *Perspectives on Labour and Income*. Statistics Canada Catalogue No. 75-001-XIE. Vol. 1, No. 2 (November 2000):5–12.

Marshall, Susan E. "Ladies Against Women: Mobilization Dilemmas of Antifeminist Movements." *Social Problems*. Vol. 32, No. 4 (April 1985):348–62.

Martindale, Kathleen. "What Makes Lesbianism Thinkable?: Lesbianism from Adrienne Rich to Queer Theory." In Nancy Mandell, ed., *Feminist Issues: Race, Class, and Sexuality*. Scarborough, Ontario: Prentice Hall Allyn and Bacon Canada, 1998: 55–76.

Marullo, Sam. "The Functions and Dysfunctions of Preparations for Fighting Nuclear War." *Sociological Focus*. Vol. 20, No. 2 (April 1987):135–53.

Marx, Karl. *Karl Marx: Selected Writings in Sociology and Social Philosophy*. T. B. Bottomore, trans. New York: McGraw-Hill, 1964.

_____. *Capital*. Friedrich Engels, ed. New York: International Publishers, 1967; orig. 1867.

_____. "Critique of the Gotha Program." In Robert C. Tucker, ed., *The Marx-Engels Reader*. New York: Norton, 1972:388.

_____. "Theses on Feuer." In Robert C. Tucker, ed., *The Marx-Engels Reader*. New York: Norton, 1972:107–9; orig. 1845.

Marx, Karl, and Friedrich Engels. "Manifesto of the Communist Party." In Robert C. Tucker, ed., *The Marx-Engels Reader*. New York: Norton, 1972:331–62; orig. 1848.

Marx, Leo. "The Environment and the 'Two Cultures' Divide." In James Rodger Fleming, and Henry A. Gemery, eds., *Science, Technology, and the Environment: Multidisciplinary Perspectives*. Akron, Ohio: University of Akron Press, 1994:3–21.

Matas, Robert, and Craig McInnes. "Critics of Nisga'a Treaty Demand Referendum." *Globe and Mail*. (Thursday, July 23, 1998):A1, A5.

Matthiessen, Peter. *Indian Country*. New York: Viking Press, 1984.

Mauer, Marc. *Americans Behind Bars: The International Use of Incarceration, 1992–1993*. Washington, D.C.: The Sentencing Project, 1994.

Maxwell, Mary Percival, and James Maxwell. "Going Co-Ed: Elite Private Schools in Canada." *Canadian Journal of Sociology*. Vol. 20, No. 3 (Summer 1995):333–357.

Mayo, Katherine. *Mother India*. New York: Harcourt, Brace, 1927.

McAdam, Doug, John D. McCarthy, and Mayer N. Zald. "Social Movements." In Neil J. Smelser, ed., *Handbook of Sociology*. Newbury Park, Calif.: Sage, 1988:695–737.

McBroom, William H., and Fred W. Reed. "Recent Trends in Conservatism: Evidence of Non-Unitary Patterns." *Sociological Focus*. Vol. 23, No. 4 (October 1990):355–65.

McColm, R. Bruce, James Finn, Douglas W. Payne, Joseph E. Ryan, Leonard R. Sussman, and George Zarycky. *Freedom in the World: Political Rights & Civil Liberties, 1990–1991*. New York: Freedom House, 1991.

McCormick, Naomi B. *Sexual Salvation*. Westport, Conn.: Praeger, 1994.

MacDonald, Keith. *The Sociology of Professions*. London: Sage, 1995.

McDonald, Kim A. "Debate Over How to Gauge Global Warming Heats Up Meeting of Climatologists." *Chronicle of Higher Education*. Vol. XLV, No. 22 (February 5, 1999):A17.

McDonald, Marci. "Enemy Within: The Far Right's Racist War against Society is Opening New Fronts across Canada." *Maclean's*. Vol. 108, No. 19 (May 8, 1995):34–38.

McFarlane, Seth, Roderic Beaujot, and Tony Haddad. "Time Constraints and Relative Resources as Determinants of the Sexual Division of Domestic Work." *The Canadian Journal of Sociology*. Vol. 25, No. 1 (Winter 2000):61–82.

McKee, Victoria. "Blue Blood and the Color of Money." *New York Times*. (June 9, 1996):49–50.

McLaren, Angus, and Arlene Tigar McLaren. *The Bedroom and the State: The Changing Practices and Politics of Contraception and Abortion in Canada 1880–1980*. Toronto: McClelland and Stewart, 1986.

McLean, Candis. "Shacking Up and Breaking Down." *Alberta Report /Western Report*. Vol. 25, No. 27 (June 6, 1998):28–30.

McLean, Scott. "Objectifying and Naturalizing Individuality: A Study of Adult Education in the Canadian Arctic." *Canadian Journal of Sociology*. Vol. 22, No.1 (Winter 1997):1–30.

McLeod, Jane D., and Michael J. Shanahan. "Poverty, Parenting, and Children's Mental Health." *American Sociological Review*. Vol. 58, No. 3 (June 1993):351–66.

McLeod, Jay. *Ain't No Makin' It: Aspirations and Attainment in a Low-Income Neighborhood*. Boulder, Colo.: Westview Press, 1995.

McRae, Susan. *Cross-Class Families: A Study of Wives' Occupational Superiority*. New York: Oxford University Press, 1986.

McVey, Jr, Wayne W., and Warren E. Kalbach. *Canadian Population*. Toronto: Nelson Canada, 1995.Mead, George Herbert. *Mind, Self, and Society*. Charles W. Morris, ed. Chicago: University of Chicago Press, 1962; orig. 1934.

Mead, Margaret. *Sex and Temperament in Three Primitive Societies*. New York: William Morrow, 1963; orig. 1935.

Meadows, Donella H., Dennis L. Meadows, Jorgan Randers, and William W. Behrens, III. *The Limits to Growth: A Report on the Club of Rome's Project on the Predicament of Mankind*. New York: Universe, 1972.

Meek, James. "Blackshirts Don't Like the F-Word." *Guardian Weekly*. (July 12, 1998):5.

Meltzer, Bernard N. "Mead's Social Psychology." In Jerome G. Manis, and Bernard N. Meltzer, eds., *Symbolic Interaction: A Reader in Social Psychology*. 3rd ed. Needham Heights, Mass.: Allyn & Bacon, 1978.

_____. *Nomads of the Present: Social Movements and Individual Needs in Contemporary Society*. Philadelphia: Temple University Press, 1989.

Melucci, Alberto. "The New Social Movements: A Theoretical Approach." *Social Science Information*. Vol. 19, No. 2 (May 1980):199–226.

Merton, Robert K. "Social Structure and Anomie." *American Sociological Review*. Vol. 3, No. 6 (October 1938):672–82.

_____. *Social Theory and Social Structure*. New York: Free Press, 1968.

_____. "Discrimination and the American Creed." In *Sociological Ambivalence and Other Essays*. New York: Free Press, 1976:189–216.

Meyer, Davis S., and Nancy Whittier. "Social Movement Spillover." *Social Problems*. Vol. 41, No. 2 (May 1994):277–98.

Michels, Robert. *Political Parties*. Glencoe, Ill.: Free Press, 1949; orig. 1911.

Milbrath, Lester W. *Envisioning A Sustainable Society: Learning Our Way Out*. Albany: State University of New York Press, 1989.

Milgram, Stanley. "Behavioral Study of Obedience." *Journal of Abnormal and Social Psychology*. Vol. 67, No. 4 (1963):371–78.

_____. "Group Pressure and Action Against a Person." *Journal of Abnormal and Social Psychology*. Vol. 69, No. 2 (August 1964):137–43.

_____. "Some Conditions of Obedience and Disobedience to Authority." *Human Relations*. Vol. 18 (February 1965):57–76.

Miliband, Ralph. *The State in Capitalist Society*. London: Weidenfield and Nicolson, 1969.

Mill, Judy E. "HIV Risk Behaviors Become Survival Techniques for Aboriginal Women." *Western Journal of Nursing Research*. Vol. 19, No. 4 (August 1997):466–90.

Miller, Arthur G. *The Obedience Experiments: A Case of Controversy in Social Science*. New York: Praeger, 1986.

Miller, Frederick D. "The End of SDS and the Emergence of Weatherman: Demise through Success." In Jo Freeman, ed., *Social Movements of the Sixties and Seventies*. New York: Longman, 1983:279–97.

Miller, G. Tyler, Jr. *Living in the Environment: An Introduction to Environmental Science*. Belmont, Calif.: Wadsworth, 1992.

Miller, Jacquie. "Report Names Toronto as Canada's Racism Capital." *The Gazette* (Montreal), Final Edition. October 6, 1997:A8.

Miller, Walter B. "Lower Class Culture as a Generating Milieu of Gang Delinquency." In Marvin E. Wolfgang, Leonard Savitz, and Norman Johnston, eds., *The Sociology of Crime and Delinquency*. 2nd ed. New York: Wiley, 1970:351–63; orig. 1958.

Millet, Kate. *Sexual Politics*. Garden City, N.Y.: Doubleday, 1970.

Mink, Barbara. "How Modernization Affects Women." *Cornell Alumni News*. Vol. III, No. 3 (April 1989):10–11.

Mintz, Beth, and Michael Schwartz. "Interlocking Directorates and Interest Group Formation." *American Sociological Review*. Vol. 46, No. 6 (December 1981):851–69.

Mirowsky, John. "The Psycho-Economics of Feeling Underpaid: Distributive Justice and the Earnings of Husbands and Wives." *American Journal of Sociology*. Vol. 92, No. 6 (May 1987):1404–34.

Mirowsky, John, and Catherine Ross. "Working Wives and Mental Health." Presentation to the American Association for the Advancement of Science, New York, 1984.

Mofina, Rick. "Force Fights Racism: Survey Reveals Problems." *The Calgary Herald*, Final Edition. (September 27, 1996):A1.

Molm, Linda D. "Risk and Power Use: Constraints on the Use of Coercion in Exchange." *American Sociological Review*. Vol. 62, No. 1 (February 1997):113–33.

Montagu, Ashley. *The Nature of Human Aggression*. New York: Oxford University Press, 1976.

Mooney, Paul, and Sheng Xue. "*The Impossible Dream.*" *Maclean's.* Vol. 113, No. 50 (December 12, 2000):20–21.

Moore, Gwen. "Structural Determinants of Men's and Women's Personal Networks." *American Sociological Review.* Vol. 55, No. 5 (October 1991):726–35.

_____. "Gender and Informal Networks in State Government." *Social Science Quarterly.* Vol. 73, No. 1 (March 1992):46–61.

Moore, Wilbert E. "Modernization as Rationalization: Processes and Restraints." In Manning Nash, ed., *Essays on Economic Development and Cultural Change in Honor of Bert F. Hoselitz.* Chicago: University of Chicago Press, 1977:29–42.

_____. *World Modernization: The Limits of Convergence.* New York: Elsevier, 1979.

Morra, Norman, and Michael D. Smith. "Men in Feminism: Reinterpreting Masculinity and Femininity." In Nancy Mandell, ed., *Feminist Issues: Race, Class, and Sexuality.* 2nd ed. Scarborough, Ontario: Prentice Hall Allyn and Bacon Canada, 1998:160–178.

Morton, F.L. *Morgentaler v. Borowski: Abortion, the Charter, and the Courts.* Toronto: McClelland and Stewart, 1993.

Mulford, Matthew, John Orbell, Catherine Shatto, and Jean Stockard.
"Physical Attractiveness, Opportunity, and Success in Everyday Exchange." *American Journal of Sociology.* Vol. 106, No. 6 (May 1998):1565–92.

Mumford, Lewis. *The City in History: Its Origins, Its Transformations, and Its Prospects.* New York: Harcourt, Brace & World, 1961.

Murdock, George Peter. "Comparative Data on the Division of Labor by Sex." *Social Forces.* Vol. 15, No. 4 (May 1937):551–53.

_____. "The Common Denominator of Cultures." In Ralph Linton, ed., *The Science of Man in World Crisis.* New York: Columbia University Press, 1945:123–42.

_____. *Social Structure.* New York: Free Press, 1965; orig. 1949.

Myers, Norman. "Disappearing Cultures." In Sir Edmund Hillary, ed., *Ecology 2000: The Changing Face of the Earth.* New York: Beaufort Books, 1984c:162–69.

_____. "Humanity's Growth." In Sir Edmund Hillary, ed., *Ecology 2000: The Changing Face of the Earth.* New York: Beaufort Books, 1984a:16–35.

_____. "The Mega-Extinction of Animals and Plants." In Sir Edmund Hillary, ed., *Ecology 2000: The Changing Face of the Earth.* New York: Beaufort Books, 1984b:82–107.

_____. "Biological Diversity and Global Security." In F. Herbert Bormann, and Stephen R. Kellert, eds., *Ecology, Economics, and Ethics: The Broken Circle.* New Haven, Conn.: Yale University Press, 1991:11–25.

Myers, Sheila, and Harold G. Grasmick. "The Social Rights and Responsibilities of Pregnant Women: An Application of Parsons' Sick Role Model." Paper presented to Southwestern Sociological Association, Little Rock, Arkansas, March 1989.

Myles, John. "When Markets Fail: Social Welfare in Canada and the United States." In Esping-Andersen, Gösta, eds., *Welfare States in Transition: National Adaptations in Global Economies.* London: Sage Publications, 1996:116–40.

Myles, John, and Dennis Forcese. "Voting and Class Politics in Canada and the United States. " *Comparative Social Research.* Vol. 4 (1981):3–31.

Nagel, Joane. "Constructing Ethnicity: Creating and Recreating Ethnic Identity and Culture." *Social Problems.* Vol. 41, No. 1 (February 1994):152–76.

Najafizadeh, Mehrangiz, and Lewis A. Mennerick. "Sociology of Education or Sociology of Ethnocentrism: The Portrayal of Education in Introductory Sociology Textbooks." *Teaching Sociology.* Vol. 20, No. 3 (July 1992):215–21.

Nash, J. Madeleine. "To Know Your Own Fate." *Time.* Vol. 145, No. 14 (April 3, 1995):62.

National Council of Welfare. *Poverty Profile 1998.* Minister of Public Works and Government Services Canada, 2000. [Online] http://www.ncwcnbes.net/htmdocument/reportpovertypro98/Poverty98.html

Nelson, E.D., and B.W. Robinson. *Gender in Canada.* Scarborough: Prentice Hall, 1999.

Neuhouser, Kevin. "The Radicalization of the Brazilian Catholic Church in Comparative Perspective." *American Sociological Review.* Vol. 54, No. 2 (April 1989):233–44.

Neuman, W. Laurence. *Social Research Methods: Qualitative and Quantitative Approaches.* 3rd ed. Boston: Allyn and Bacon, 1997.

Newman, Katherine S. *Declining Fortunes: The Withering of the American Dream.* New York: Basic Books, 1993.

Newman, William M. *American Pluralism: A Study of Minority Groups and Social Theory.* New York: Harper & Row, 1973.

Ng, Roxanne. "Racism, Sexism and Immigrant Women." In Sandra Burt, Lorraine Code, and Lindsay Dorney, eds., *Changing Patterns: Women in Canada.* 2nd ed. Toronto: McClelland and Stewart, 1993:279–307.

Ng, Roxanne, and Tania Das Gupta. "Nation Builders? The Captive Labour Force of Non-English Speaking Immigrant Women." *Canadian Women's Studies.* Vol. 3, No. 1 (1993b):83–85.

Niebuhr, Gustav. "Southern Baptists say Husbands Should Lead Wives." *Globe & Mail.* (Thursday, June 11, 1998):A6B.

Nielsen, Francois, and Arthur S. Alderson. "The Kuznets Curve: The Great U-Turn: Income Inequality in U.S. Counties, 1970 to 1990." *American Sociological Review.* Vol. 62, No. 1 (February 1997):12–33.

Nielsen, Joyce McCarl, ed. *Feminist Research Methods: Exemplary Readings in the Social Sciences.* Boulder, Colo.: Westview, 1990.

*1991 Green Book.* U.S. House of Representatives. Washington, D.C.: U.S. Government Printing Office, 1991.

Nippert-Eng, Christena E. *Home and Work: Negotiating Boundaries Through Everyday Life.* Chicago: The University of Chicago Press, 1995.

Nisbet, Robert A. *The Sociological Tradition.* New York: Basic Books, 1966.

_____. *The Quest for Community.* New York: Oxford University Press, 1969.

Nocera, Joseph. "Microsoft Tries to Crack AOL's Case." *Fortune.* Vol. 139, No. 12 (June 21, 1999):175–77.

NORC. General Social Surveys, 1972–1998: Cumulative Codebook. Chicago: National Opinion Research Center, 1999.

Novak, Viveca. "The Cost of Poor Advice." *Time.* Vol. 154, No. 1 (July 5, 1999):38.

Nunn, Clyde Z., Harry J. Crockett, Jr., and J. Allen Williams, Jr. *Tolerance for Nonconformity.* San Francisco: Jossey-Bass, 1978.

Oakes, Jeannie. "Classroom Social Relationships: Exploring the Bowles and Gintis Hypothesis." *Sociology of Education.* Vol. 55, No. 4 (October 1982):197–212.

_____. *Keeping Track: How High Schools Structure Inequality.* New Haven, Conn.: Yale University Press, 1985.

O'Brien, David J., Edward W. Hassinger, and Larry Dershem. "Size of Place, Residential Stability, and Personal Social Networks." *Sociological Focus*. Vol. 29, No. 1 (February 1996):61–72.

O'Brien, Mary. *The Politics of Reproduction*. Boston: Routledge & Kegan Paul, 1983.

O'Connor, Rory J. "Internet Declared Protected Speech." *Post-Star*, Glens Fall, N.Y. (June 27, 1997):A1–A2.

OECD. *Education at a Glance: 2000 Edition*. Paris: OECD, 2000.

Offir, Carole Wade. *Human Sexuality*. New York: Harcourt Brace Jovanovich, 1982.

Ogburn, William F. *On Culture and Social Change*. Chicago: University of Chicago Press, 1964.

Ogmundson, R., and J. McLaughlin. "Changes in An Intellectual Elite 1960–1990: The Royal Society Revisited." *Canadian Review of Sociology & Anthropology*. Vol. 31, No. 1 (February 1994):1–13.

Ohmae, Kenichi. *The Borderless World*. London: Fontana, 1991.

Olsen, Denis. *The State Elite*. Toronto: McClelland and Stewart, 1980.

Olsen, Gregg M. "Locating the Canadian Welfare State: Family Policy and Health Care in Canada, Sweden, and the United States." *Canadian Journal of Sociology*. Vol 19, No. 1 (1994):1–20.

———. "Re-Modeling Sweden: The Rise and Demise of the Compromise in a Global Economy." *Social Problems*. Vol. 43, No. 1 (February 1996):1–20.

Olzak, Susan. "Labor Unrest, Immigration, and Ethnic Conflict in Urban America, 1880–1914." *American Journal of Sociology*. Vol. 94, No. 6 (May 1989):1303–33.

Omatsu, Maryka. *Bittersweet Passage: Redress and the Japanese Canadian Experience*. Toronto: Between the Lines, 1992.

One World. [Online] http://www.oneworld.org, November 15, 1998.

O'Neil, Peter. "Use of Pepper Spray Was Reasonable, Chrétien Says." *Montreal Gazette*. (November 28, 1997):A15.

O'Reilly, Finbarr, and Doug Saunders. "Lock Up Your Toddlers." *Globe and Mail*. (June 3, 1998):A13.

Orlansky, Michael D., and William L. Heward. *Voices: Interviews with Handicapped People*. Columbus, Ohio: Merrill, 1981:85, 92, 133–34, 172.

Osgood, D. Wayne, Janet K. Wilson, Patrick M. O'Malley, Jerald G. Bachman, and Lloyd D. Johnston. "Routine Activities and Individual Deviant Behavior." *American Sociological Review*. Vol. 61, No. 4 (August 1996):635–55.

Ostrander, Susan A. "Upper Class Women: The Feminine Side of Privilege." *Qualitative Sociology*. Vol. 3, No. 1 (Spring 1980):23–44.

———. *Women of the Upper Class*. Philadelphia: Temple University Press, 1984.

Ouchi, William. *Theory Z: How American Business Can Meet the Japanese Challenge*. Reading, Mass.: Addison-Wesley, 1981.

Owen, David. *None of the Above: Behind the Myth of Scholastic Aptitude*. Boston: Houghton Mifflin, 1985.

Pakulski, Jan. "Mass Social Movements and Social Class." *International Sociology*. Vol. 8, No. 2 (June 1993):131–58.

Park, Robert E. *Race and Culture*. Glencoe, Ill.: Free Press, 1950.

Parsons, Talcott. "Age and Sex in the Social Structure of the United States." *American Sociological Review*. Vol. 7, No. 4 (August 1942):604–16.

———. *Essays in Sociological Theory*. New York: Free Press, 1954.

———. *The Social System*. New York: Free Press, 1964; orig. 1951.

———. *Societies: Evolutionary and Comparative Perspectives*. Englewood Cliffs, N.J.: Prentice Hall, 1966.

Parsons, Talcott, and Robert F. Bales, eds. *Family, Socialization and Interaction Process*. New York: Free Press, 1955.

Pear, Robert. "Women Reduce Lag in Earnings, But Disparities with Men Remain." *New York Times*. (September 4, 1987):1, 7.

Pear, Robert, with Erik Eckholm. "When Healers are Entrepreneurs: A Debate Over Costs and Ethics." *New York Times*. (June 2, 1991):1, 17.

Pearson, David E. "Post-Mass Culture." *Society*. Vol. 30, No. 5 (July-August 1993):17–22.

Pease, John, and Lee Martin. "Want Ads and Jobs for the Poor: A Glaring Mismatch." *Sociological Forum*. Vol. 12. No. 4 (December 1997):545–64.

Peat Marwick and Partners. "Canadians' Attitudes Toward and Perceptions of Pornography and Prostitution." *Working Papers on Pornography and Prostitution #6*. Ottawa: Department of Justice, 1984.

Persell, Caroline Hodges. *Education and Inequality: A Theoretical and Empirical Synthesis*. New York: Free Press, 1977.

Pessen, Edward. *Riches, Class, and Power: America before the Civil War*. New Brunswick, N.J.: Transaction, 1990.

*Peters Atlas of the World*. New York: Harper & Row, 1990.

Pinchot, Gifford, and Elizabeth Pinchot. *The End of Bureaucracy and the Rise of the Intelligent Organization*. San Francisco: Berrett-Koehler, 1993.

Pines, Maya. "The Civilization of Genie." *Psychology Today*. Vol. 15 (September 1981):28–34.

Pinhey, Thomas K., Donald H. Rubinstein, and Richard S. Colfax. "Overweight and Happiness: The Reflected Self-Appraisal Hypothesis Reconsidered." *Social Science Quarterly*. Vol. 78, No. 3 (September 1997):747–55.

Pirandello, Luigi. "The Pleasure of Honesty." In *To Clothe the Naked and Two Other Plays*. New York: Dutton, 1962:143–98.

Piven, Frances Fox, and Richard A. Cloward. *Poor People's Movements: Why They Succeed, How They Fail*. New York: Pantheon Books, 1977.

Plomin, Robert, and Terryl T. Foch. "A Twin Study of Objectively Assessed Personality in Childhood." *Journal of Personality and Sociology Psychology*. Vol. 39, No. 4 (October 1980):680–88.

Podolny, Joel M., and James N. Baron. "Resources and Relationships: Social Networks and Mobility in the Workplace." *American Sociological Review*. Vol. 62, No. 5 (October 1997):673–93.

Pohl, Rudiger. "The Transition from Communism to Capitalism in East Germany." *Society*. Vol. 33, No. 4 (June 1996):62–65.

———. "Overseas, Smoking Is One of Life's Small Pleasures." *New York Times*. (August 17, 1997):E5.

Polenberg, Richard. *One Nation Divisible: Class, Race, and Ethnicity in the United States since 1938*. New York: Pelican Books, 1980.

Polsby, Nelson W. "Three Problems in the Analysis of Community Power." *American Sociological Review*. Vol. 24, No. 6 (December 1959):796–803.

Ponting, J. Rick. "Racial Conflict: Turning Up the Heat." In Dan Glenday, and Ann Duffy, eds., *Canadian Society: Understanding and Surviving the 1990s*. Toronto: McClelland and Stewart, 1994:86–118.

_____. *First Nations in Canada: Perspectives on Opportunity, Empowerment, and Self-determination*. Whitby, Ont.: McGraw-Hill Ryerson, 1997.

_____. "Racism and Stereotyping of First Nations." In Vic Satzewich, ed., *Racism and Social Inequality in Canada: Concepts, Controversies & Strategies of Resistance*. Toronto: Thompson Educational Publishing, Inc., 1998:269–298.

Popenoe, David. "American Family Decline, 1960–1990: A Review and Appraisal." *Journal of Marriage and the Family*. Vol. 55, No. 3 (August 1993):527–55.

_____. "Parental Androgyny." *Society*. Vol. 30, No. 6 (September-October 1993b):5–11.

Popkin, Susan J. "Welfare: Views from the Bottom." *Social Problems*. Vol. 17, No. 1 (February 1990):64–79.

Population Reference Bureau. *World Population Data Sheet 2000*. Washington, D.C.: The Bureau, 2000.

Porter, John. *The Vertical Mosaic*. Toronto: University of Toronto Press, 1965.

Postel, Sandra. "Facing Water Scarcity." In Lester R. Brown et al., eds., *State of the World 1993: A Worldwatch Institute Report on Progress Toward a Sustainable Society*. New York: Norton, 1993:22–41.

Powell, Chris, and George E.C. Paton, eds. *Humour in Society: Resistance and Control*. New York: St. Martin's Press, 1988.

Prentice, Alison. *The School Promoters*. Toronto: McClelland and Stewart, 1977.

Prentice, Alison, Paula Bourne, Gail Guthbert Brandt, Beth Light, Wendy Mitchinson, and Naomi Black. *Canadian Women: A History*. 2nd ed. Toronto: Harcourt Brace & Company, 1996.

Presser, Harriet B. "The Housework Gender Gap." *Population Today*. Vol. 21, No. 7/8 (July-August 1993):5.

Pressley, Sue Anne, and Nancy Andrews. "For Gay Couples, the Nursery Becomes the New Frontier." *Washington Post*. (December 20, 1992):A1, A22–23.

Primeggia, Salvatore, and Joseph A. Varacalli. "Southern Italian Comedy: Old to New World." In Joseph V. Scelsa, Salvatore J. LaGumina, and Lydio Tomasi, eds., *Italian Americans in Transition*. New York: The American Italian Historical Association, 1990:241–52.

Provincial Health Officer, British Columbia. *A Report on the Health of British Columbians: Provincial Health Officer's Annual Report 1996*. Victoria, BC: Ministry of Health and Ministry Responsible for Seniors, 1997.

Puterbaugh, Geoff, ed. *Twins and Homosexuality: A Casebook*. New York: Garland, 1990.

Putka, Gary. "SAT To Become A Better Gauge." *Wall Street Journal*. (November 1, 1990):B1.

*Quarterly Demographic Statistics, January–March 2000*. Ottawa: Ministry of Industry. Catalogue No. 91-002-XIB. 2000b.

Queenan, Joe. "The Many Paths to Riches." *Forbes*. Vol. 144, No. 9 (October 23, 1989):149.

Quinney, Richard. *Class, State and Crime: On the Theory and Practice of Criminal Justice*. New York: David McKay, 1977.

Raphael, Ray. *The Men from the Boys: Rites of Passage in Male America*. Lincoln and London: University of Nebraska Press, 1988.

Reckless, Walter C., and Simon Dinitz. "Pioneering With Self-Concept as a Vulnerability Factor in Delinquency." *Journal of Criminal Law, Criminology, and Police Science*. Vol. 58, No. 4 (December 1967):515–23.

Reid, Angus. *Shakedown: How the New Economy is Changing Our Lives*. Toronto: Doubleday Canada, 1996.

Reiman, Jeffrey. *The Rich Get Richer and the Poor Get Prison: Ideology, Class, and Criminal Justice*. Boston: Allyn and Bacon, 1998.

Reinharz, Shulamit. *Feminist Methods in Social Research*. New York: Oxford University Press, 1992.

Reitz, Jeffrey G. *The Survival of Ethnic Groups*. Toronto: McGraw-Hill Ryerson Ltd., 1980.

Reitz, Jeffrey, and Raymond Breton. *The Illusion of Difference: Realities of Ethnicity in Canada and the United States*. Toronto: C.D. Howe Institute, 1994.

Remoff, Heather Trexler. *Sexual Choice: A Woman's Decision*. New York: Dutton/Lewis, 1984.

Remy, Jacqueline. "Interview with Agnes Fournier de Saint-Maur, Interpol Police Lieutenant." For *L'Express*; reprinted in *World Press Review*. (November 1996):7.

Reskin, Barbara, and Irene Padavic. *Women and Men at Work*. Thousand Oaks, Calif.: Pine Forge Press, 1994.

Richardson, C.J. "Divorce and Remarriage." In *Families: Changing Trends in Canada*. 3rd ed. Maureen Baker, ed. Toronto: McGraw-Hill Ryerson:315–49.

Richardson, James T. "Definitions of Cult: From Sociological–Technical to Popular Negative." Paper presented to the American Psychological Association, Boston, August, 1990.

Richer, Stephen. "Sex-Role Socialization and Early Schooling." *Canadian Review of Sociology and Anthropology*. Vol. 16, No. 2 (1979):195–205.

Ridgeway, Cecilia L. *The Dynamics of Small Groups*. New York: St. Martin's Press, 1983.

Riesman, David. *The Lonely Crowd: A Study of the Changing American Character*. New Haven, Conn.: Yale University Press, 1970; orig. 1950.

Rifkin, Jeremy. *The End of Work*. New York: G.P. Putnam's Sons, 1995.

Riis, Ole. "Religion Re-Emerging: The Role of Religion in Legitimating Integration and Power in Modern Societies." *International Sociology*. Vol. 13, No. 2 (June 1998):249–72.

Riley, Matilda White, Anne Foner, and Joan Waring. "Sociology of Age." In Neil J. Smelser, ed., *Handbook of Sociology*. Newbury Park, Calif.: Sage, 1988:243–90.

Riley, Nancy E. "Gender, Power, and Population Change." *Population Bulletin*. Vol. 52, No. 1 (May 1997).

Riska, Elianne, and Katarina Wegar, eds. *Gender, Work, and Medicine: Women and the Medical Division of Labour*. Newbury Park, Calif.: Sage Publications, 1993.

Ritzer, George. *The McDonaldization of Society: An Investigation into the Changing Character of Contemporary Social Life*. Thousand Oaks, Calif.: Pine Forge Press, 1993.

———. *The McDonaldization Thesis: Explorations and Extensions*. Thousand Oaks, Calif.: Sage, 1998.

Ritzer, George, and David Walczak. *Working: Conflict and Change*. 4th ed. Englewood Cliffs, N.J.: Prentice Hall, 1990.

Roach, Kent. "Changing Punishment at the Turn of the Century: Restorative Justice on the Rise." *Canadian Journal of Criminology*. Vol. 42 No. 3 (July 2000):249–280.

Roberts, J. Deotis. *Roots of a Black Future: Family and Church*. Philadelphia: The Westminster Press, 1980.

Roberts, Julian V. *Disproportionate Harm: Hate Crime in Canada.* Working document prepared for Research, Statistics and Evaluation Directorate, Policy Sector, Justice Canada. Document No. WD1995-11e (1995). Ottawa: Justice Canada.

Roberts, Steven V. "Open Arms for Online Democracy." *U.S. News and World Report.* Vol. 118, No. 2 (January 16, 1995):10.

Robinson, Joyce, and Glenna Spitze. "Whistle While You Work? The Effect of Household Task Performance on Women's and Men's Well-Being." *Social Science Quarterly.* Vol. 73, No. 4 (December 1992):844–61.

Robinson, Vera M. "Humor and Health." In Paul E. McGhee, and Jeffrey H. Goldstein, eds., *Handbook of Humor Research. Vol. II. Applied Studies.* New York: Springer-Verlag, 1983:109–28.

Rocher, Guy. "The Quiet Revolution in Quebec." In James Curtis, and Lorne Tepperman, eds., *Images of Canada: The Sociological Tradition.* Scarborough, Ontario: Prentice Hall Canada, Inc., 1990:22–29.

Roesch, Roberta. "Violent Families." *Parents.* Vol. 59, No. 9 (September 1984):74–76, 150–52.

Róna-Tas, Ákos. "The First Shall Be Last? Entrepreneurship and Communist Cadres in the Transition from Socialism." *American Journal of Sociology.* Vol. 100, No. 1 (July 1994):40–69.

Roof, Wade Clark, and William McKinney. *American Mainline Religion: Its Changing Shape and Future.* New Brunswick, N.J.: Rutgers University Press, 1987.

Rosenberg, Harriet. "Motherwork, Stress, and Depression: The Costs of Privatized Social Reproduction." In Bonnie Fox, ed., *Family Patterns/Gender Relations.* 2nd ed. Toronto: Oxford University Press, 2001:303–316.

Rosendahl, Mona. *Inside the Revolution: Everyday Life in Socialist Cuba.* Ithaca, N.Y.: Cornell University Press, 1997.

Rosenfeld, Megan. "Little Boys Blue: Reexamining the Plight of Young Males." *Washington Post.* (March 26, 1998):A1, A17–A18.

Rosenfeld, Michael J. "Celebration, Politics, and Selective Looting and Riots: A Micro-Level Study of the Bulls Riot of 1992 in Chicago." *Social Problems.* Vol. 44, No. 4 (November 1997):483–502.

Rosenthal, Elizabeth. "Canada's National Health Plan Gives Care to All, With Limits." *New York Times.* (April 30, 1991):A1, A16.

Ross, Catherine E., John Mirowsky, and Joan Huber. "Dividing Work, Sharing Work, and In-Between: Marriage Patterns and Depression." *American Sociological Review.* Vol. 48, No. 6 (December 1983):809–23.

Ross, David, Katherine Scott, and Peter Smith. *The Canadian Fact Book on Poverty 2000.* Ottawa: Council on Social Development, 2000.

Ross, John. "To Die in the Street: Mexico City's Homeless Population Boom as Economic Crisis Shakes Social Protections." *SSSP Newsletter.* Vol. 27, No. 2 (Summer 1996):14–15.

Rossi, Alice S. "Gender and Parenthood." In Alice S. Rossi, ed., *Gender and the Life Course.* New York: Aldine, 1985:161–91.

Rostow, Walt W. *The Stages of Economic Growth: A Non-Communist Manifesto.* Cambridge: Cambridge University Press, 1960.

_____. *The World Economy: History and Prospect.* Austin: University of Texas Press, 1978.

Rothman, Stanley, and Amy E. Black. "Who Rules Now? American Elites in the 1990s." *Society.* Vol. 35, No. 6 (September-October 1998):17–20.

Rowe, David C. "Biometrical Genetic Models of Self-Reported Delinquent Behavior: A Twin Study." *Behavior Genetics.* Vol. 13, No. 5 (1983):473–89.

Rowe, David C., and D. Wayne Osgood. "Heredity and Sociological Theories of Delinquency: A Reconsideration." *American Sociological Review.* Vol. 49, No. 4 (August 1984):526–40.

Rozell, Mark J., Clyde Wilcox, and John C. Green. "Religious Constituencies and Support for the Christian Right in the 1990s." *Social Science Quarterly.* Vol. 79, No. 4 (December 1998):815–27.

Rubin, Lillian Breslow. *Worlds of Pain: Life in the Working-Class Family.* New York: Basic Books, 1976.

Rudel, Thomas K., and Judith M. Gerson. "Postmodernism, Institutional Change, and Academic Workers: A Sociology of Knowledge." *Social Science Quarterly.* Vol. 80, No. 2 (June 1999):213–28.

Rudmin, Floyd W. "Cross-Cultural Psycholinguistic Field Research: Verbs of Ownership and Possession." *Journal of Cross-Cultural Psychology.* Vol. 25, No. 1 (March 1994):118–32.

Rule, James, and Peter Brantley. "Computerized Surveillance in the Workplace: Forms and Delusions." *Sociological Forum.* Vol. 7, No. 3 (September 1992):405–23.

Rushton, Philippe, and Anthony Bogaert. "Race Differences in Sexual Behaviour: Testing an Evolutionary Hypothesis." *Journal of Research on Personality* 21 (1987):529–51.

Russell, Diana E. *The Secret Trauma: Incest in the Lives of Girls and Women.* New York: Basic Books, 1986.

_____. *Dangerous Relationships: Pornography, Misogyny, and Rape.* Thousand Oaks, Calif.: Sage Publications, 1998.

Ryan, William. *Blaming the Victim.* Rev. ed. New York: Vintage Books, 1976.

Rymer, Russ. *Genie.* New York: HarperPerennial, 1994.

Sainsbury, Diane. *Gender, Equality and Welfare States.* Cambridge, Mass.: Cambridge University Press, 1996.

St. Jean, Yanick, and Joe R. Feagin. *Double Burden: Black Women and Everyday Racism.* Armonk, N.Y.: M.E. Sharpe, 1998.

Saks, Mike. "Professionalism and Health Care. In David Field and Steve Taylor, eds., *Sociological Perspectives on Health, Illness and Health Care.* London: Blackwell, 1998:175–191.

Sale, Kirkpatrick. *The Conquest of Paradise: Christopher Columbus and the Columbian Legacy.* New York: Alfred A. Knopf, 1990.

Sampson, Robert J., and John H. Laub. "Crime and Deviance Over the Life Course: The Salience of Adult Social Bonds." *American Sociological Review.* Vol. 55, No. 5 (October 1990):609–27.

Samuel, John T. *Visible Minorities in Canada: A Projection.* Toronto: Canadian Advertising Foundation, Race Relations Advisory Council on Advertising, June 1992.

Sandberg, Åke, Gunnar Broms, Arne Grip, Lars Sundström, Jasper Steen, and Peter Ullmark. *Technological Change and Co-Determination in Sweden.* Philadelphia: Temple University Press, 1992.

Sanders, Trevor. "Sentencing of Young Offenders in Canada, 1998/99." *Juristat.* Statistics Canada Catalogue No. 85-002-XIE. Vol. 20, No. 7 (September 2000):1–15.

Santoli, Al. "Fighting Child Prostitution." *Freedom Review.* Vol. 25, No. 5 (September-October 1994):5–8.

Sapir, Edward. "The Status of Linguistics as a Science." *Language.* Vol. 5 (1929):207–14.

_____. *Selected Writings of Edward Sapir in Language, Culture, and Personality.* David G. Mandelbaum, ed. Berkeley: University of California Press, 1949.

Satzewich, Vic. "Race, Racism and Racialization: Contested Concepts." In Vic Satzewich, ed., *Racism and Social Inequality in Canada: Concepts, Controversies & Strategies of Resistance.* Toronto: Thompson Educational Publishing, Inc., 1998:25–46.

Scaff, Lawrence A. "Max Weber and Robert Michels." *American Journal of Sociology.* Vol. 86, No. 6 (May 1981):1269–86.

Scambler, Graham, and Annette Scambler. *Rethinking Prostitution: Purchasing in the 1990s.* London and N.Y.: Routledge, 1997.

Scanlon, James P. "The Curious Case of Affirmative Action for Women." *Society.* Vol. 29, No. 2 (January-February 1992):36–42.

Scheff, Thomas J. *Being Mentally Ill: A Sociological Theory.* 2nd ed. New York: Aldine, 1984.

Scherer, Ron. "Worldwide Trend: Tobacco Use Grows." *Christian Science Monitor.* (July 17, 1996):4, 8.

Schiller, Bradley. "Who Are the Working Poor?" *The Public Interest.* Vol. 155 (Spring 1994):61–71.

Schissel, Bernard. *Social Dimensions of Canadian Youth Justice.* Toronto: Oxford University Press, 1993.

Schlesinger, Arthur. "The Cult of Ethnicity: Good and Bad." *Time.* Vol. 137, No. 27 (July 8, 1991):21.

Schutt, Russell K. "Objectivity versus Outrage." *Society.* Vol. 26, No. 4 (May/June 1989):14–16.

Schwartz, Felice N. "Management, Women, and the New Facts of Life." *Harvard Business Review.* Vol. 89, No. 1 (January-February 1989):65–76.

Schwartz, Martin D. "Gender and Injury in Spousal Assault." *Sociological Focus.* Vol. 20, No. 1 (January 1987):61–75.

Scoffield, Heather. "World's Poorest get Canadian Debt Relief." *Globe and Mail.* (December 10, 2000):A1.

Scommegna, Paola. "Teens' Risk of AIDS, Unintended Pregnancies Examined." *Population Today.* Vol. 24, No. 8 (August 1996):1–2.

Scott, John, and Catherine Griff. *Directors of Industry: The British Corporate Network, 1904–1976.* New York: Blackwell, 1985.

Scott, Katherine. *The Progress of Canada's Children 1996.* Ottawa: Canadian Council on Social Development, 1996.

Segall, Alexander, and Neena Chappell. *Health and Health Care in Canada.* Toronto: Prentice Hall, 2000.

Sekulic, Dusko, Garth Massey, and Randy Hodson. "Who Were the Yugoslavs? Failed Sources of Common Identity in the Former Yugoslavia." *American Sociological Review.* Vol. 59, No. 1 (February 1994):83–97.

Sennett, Richard. *The Corrosion of Character: The Personal Consequences of Work in the New Capitalism.* New York: Norton, 1998.

Sennett, Richard, and Jonathan Cobb. *The Hidden Injuries of Class.* New York: Vintage Books, 1973.

Shapiro, Joseph P., and Joannie M. Schrof. "Honor Thy Children." *U.S. News and World Report.* Vol. 118, No. 8 (February 27, 1995):39–49.

Shaver, Frances. "Prostitution: A Female Crime?" In Ellen Adelberg, and Claudia Currie, eds., *In Conflict With the Law: Women and the Canadian Justice System.* Vancouver: Press Gang Publishers, 1993. Page nos.

Shawcross, William. *Sideshow: Kissinger, Nixon and the Destruction of Cambodia.* New York: Pocket Books, 1979.

Sheehan, Tom. "Senior Esteem as a Factor in Socioeconomic Complexity." *The Gerontologist.* Vol. 16, No. 5 (October 1976):433–40.

Sheehy, Gail. *Understanding Men's Passages: Discovering the New Map of Men's Lives.* Toronto: Random House of Canada, 1998.

Sheldon, William H., Emil M. Hartl, and Eugene McDermott. *Varieties of Delinquent Youth.* New York: Harper, 1949.

Sheley, James F., Joshua Zhang, Charles J. Brody, and James D. Wright. "Gang Organization, Gang Criminal Activity, and Individual Gang Members' Criminal Behavior." *Social Science Quarterly.* Vol. 76, No. 1 (March 1995):53–68.

Sherman, Lawrence W., and Douglas A. Smith. "Crime, Punishment, and Stake in Conformity: Legal and Informal Control of Domestic Violence." *American Sociological Review.* Vol. 57, No. 5 (October 1992):680–90.

Shevky, Eshref, and Wendell Bell. *Social Area Analysis.* Stanford, Calif.: Stanford University Press, 1955.

Shipley, Joseph T. *Dictionary of Word Origins.* Totowa, N.J.: Roman & Allanheld, 1985.

Shively, JoEllen. "Cowboys and Indians: Perceptions of Western Films among American Indians and Anglos." *American Sociological Review.* Vol. 57, No. 6 (December 1992):725–34.

Shupe, Anson. *In the Name of All That's Holy: A Theory of Clergy Malfeasance.* Westport, Conn.: Praeger, 1995.

Shupe, Anson, William A. Stacey, and Lonnie R. Hazlewood. *Violent Men, Violent Couples: The Dynamics of Domestic Violence.* Lexington, Mass.: Lexington Books, 1987.

Sidel, Ruth, and Victor W. Sidel. *A Healthy State: An International Perspective on the Crisis in United States Medical Care.* Rev. ed. New York: Pantheon Books, 1982a.

_____. *The Health Care of China.* Boston: Beacon Press, 1982b.

Silverberg, Robert. "The Greenhouse Effect: Apocalypse Now or Chicken Little?" *Omni.* (July 1991):50–54.

Silverstein, Michael. In Jon Snodgrass, ed., *A Book of Readings for Men against Sexism.* Albion, Calif.: Times Change Press, 1977:178–79.

Simmel, Georg. *The Sociology of Georg Simmel.* Kurt Wolff, ed. New York: Free Press, 1950:118–69.

Simon, Julian. *The Ultimate Resource.* Princeton, N.J.: Princeton University Press, 1981.

Simons, Carol. "Japan's *Kyoiku* Mamas." In John J. Macionis, and Nijole V. Benokraitis, eds., *Seeing Ourselves: Classic, Contemporary, and Cross-Cultural Readings in Sociology.* Englewood Cliffs, N.J.: Prentice Hall, 1989:281–86.

Simons, Marlise. "The Price of Modernization: The Case of Brazil's Kaiapo Indians." In John J. Macionis, and Nijole V. Benokraitis, eds., *Seeing Ourselves: Classic, Contemporary, and Cross-Cultural Readings in Sociology.* 5th ed. Upper Saddle River, N.J.: Prentice Hall, 2001:496–502.

Singh and Darroch. "Adolescent Pregnancy and Childbearing: Level and Trends in Developed Countries." *Family Planning Perspectives.* Vol. 32, No. 1 (February 2000):14–23.

Sivard, Ruth Leger. *World Military and Social Expenditures, 1987–88.* 12th ed. Washington, D.C.: World Priorities, 1988.

Skocpol, Theda. *States and Social Revolutions: A Comparative Analysis of France, Russia, and China.* Cambridge, U.K.: Cambridge University Press, 1979.

Skolnick, Arlene. *The Intimate Environment: Exploring Marriage and the Family.* 6th ed. New York: HarperCollins, 1996.

Smith, Adam. *An Inquiry Into the Nature and Causes of the Wealth of Nations*. New York: The Modern Library, 1937; orig. 1776.

Smith, Allan. "Seeing Things: Race, Image, and National Identity in Canadian and American Movies and Television." *Canadian Review of American Studies*. Vol. 26, No. 3 (Autumn 1996):367–91.

Smith, Dorothy. *The Everyday World as Problematic: A Feminist Sociology*. Toronto: University of Toronto Press, 1987.

_____. *Writing the Social: Critique, Theory and Investigations*. Toronto: University of Toronto Press, 1999.

Smith, Douglas A. "Police Response to Interpersonal Violence: Defining the Parameters of Legal Control." *Social Forces*. Vol. 65, No. 3 (March 1987):767–82.

Smith, Douglas A., and Christy A. Visher. "Street-Level Justice: Situational Determinants of Police Arrest Decisions." *Social Problems*. Vol. 29, No. 2 (December 1981):167–77.

Smith, Douglas A., and Patrick R. Gartin. "Specifying Specific Deterrence: The Influence of Arrest on Future Criminal Activity." *American Sociological Review*. Vol. 54, No. 1 (February 1989):94–105.

Smith, Earl, and Wilbert M. Leonard, II. "Twenty-Five Years of Stacking Research in Major League Baseball: An Attempt at Explaining this Re-Occurring Phenomenon." *Sociological Focus*. Vol. 30, No. 4 (October 1997):321–31.

Smith, Robert B. "Health Care Reform Now." *Society*. Vol. 30, No. 3 (March-April 1993):56–65.

Smith-Lovin, Lynn, and Charles Brody. "Interruptions in Group Discussions: The Effects of Gender and Group Composition." *American Journal of Sociology*. Vol. 54, No. 3 (June 1989):424–35.

Smolowe, Jill. "When Violence Hits Home." *Time*. Vol. 144, No. 1 (July 4, 1994):18–25.

Snell, Marilyn Berlin. "The Purge of Nurture." *New Perspectives Quarterly*. Vol. 7, No. 1 (Winter 1990):1–2.

Snow, David A., E. Burke Rochford, Jr., Steven K. Worden, and Robert D. Benford. "Frame Alignment Processes, Micromobilization, and Movement Participation." *American Sociological Review*. Vol. 51, No. 4 (August 1986):464–81.

South, Scott J., and Steven F. Messner. "Structural Determinants of Intergroup Association: Interracial Marriage and Crime." *American Journal of Sociology*. Vol. 91, No. 6 (May 1986):1409–30.

Sowell, Thomas. *Race and Culture*. New York: Basic Books, 1994.

_____. "Ethnicity and IQ." In Steven Fraser, ed., *The Bell Curve Wars: Race, Intelligence and the Future of America*. New York: Basic Books, 1995:70–79.

Spates, James L. "Counterculture and Dominant Culture Values: A Cross-National Analysis of the Underground Press and Dominant Culture Magazines." *American Sociological Review*. Vol. 41, No. 5 (October 1976):868–83.

Spates, James L., and H. Wesley Perkins. "American and English Student Values." *Comparative Social Research*. Vol. 5. Greenwich, Conn.: JAI Press, 1982:245–68.

Specter, Michael. "Plunging Life Expectancy Puzzles Russia." *New York Times*. (August 2, 1995):A1, A2.

_____. "Deep in the Russian Soul, a Lethal Darkness." *New York Times*. (June 8, 1997): sec. 4, pp. 1, 5.

Speer, James A. "The New Christian Right and Its Parent Company: A Study in Political Contrasts." In David G. Bromley, and Anson Shupe, eds., *New Christian Politics*. Macon, Ga.: Mercer University Press, 1984:19–40.

Speier, Hans. "Wit and Politics: An Essay on Laughter and Power." Robert Jackall, ed. and trans. *American Journal of Sociology*. Vol. 103, No. 5 (March 1998):1352–1401.

Spencer, Martin E. "Multiculturalism, 'Political Correctness,' and the Politics of Identity." *Sociological Forum*. Vol. 9, No. 4 (December 1994):547–67.

Spitzer, Steven. "Toward a Marxian Theory of Deviance." In Delos H. Kelly, ed., *Criminal Behavior: Readings in Criminology*. New York: St. Martin's Press, 1980:175–91.

Stacey, Judith. *Patriarchy and Socialist Revolution in China*. Berkeley: University of California Press, 1983.

_____. *Brave New Families: Stories of Domestic Upheaval in Late Twentieth-Century America*. New York: Basic Books, 1990.

Staggenborg, Suzanne. "Social Movement Communities and Cycles of Protest: The Emergence and Maintenance of a Local Women's Movement." *Social Problems*. Vol. 45, No. 2 (May 1998):180–204.

Stanley, Liz, ed. *Feminist Praxis: Research, Theory, and Epistemology in Feminist Sociology*. London: Routledge & Kegan Paul, 1990.

Stapinski, Helene. "Let's Talk Dirty." *American Demographics*. Vol. 20, No. 11 (November 1998):50–56.

Stark, Rodney. *Sociology*. Belmont, Calif.: Wadsworth, 1985.

Stark, Rodney, and William Sims Bainbridge. "Of Churches, Sects, and Cults: Preliminary Concepts for a Theory of Religious Movements." *Journal for the Scientific Study of Religion*. Vol. 18, No. 2 (June 1979):117–31.

_____. "Secularization and Cult Formation in the Jazz Age." *Journal for the Scientific Study of Religion*. Vol. 20, No. 4 (December 1981):360–73.

Statistics Canada. *Religions in Canada*. Catalogue No. 93-319-XPB. Ottawa: Minister of Industry, 1993a.

_____. "The Violence Against Women Survey: Highlights." *The Daily*. Ottawa: Minister of Industry, Science and Technology, 1993b.

_____. *Report on the Demographic Situation in Canada, 1994*. Catalogue No. 91-209- XPE. (November 1994a):111–35.

_____. *Women in the Labour Force*. 1994 ed. Catalogue No. 75-50X-XPB. Ottawa: Minister of Industry, 1994b.

_____. *Women in Canada: A Statistical Report*. 3rd ed. Ottawa: Minister of Industry, 1995.

_____. *National Population Health Survey Overview, 1994-95*. Ottawa: Minister of Industry, 1995b.

_____. *The Daily* (June 19, 1996). [Online] http://www.statcan.ca/Daily/English/960619/d960619.htm

_____. *Canada's Culture, Heritage and Identity: A Statistical Perspective*. 1997 ed. Catalogue No. 87-211-XIB. Ottawa: Minister of Industry, 1997a.

_____. *The Daily* (October 14, 1997b). [Online] http://www.statcan.ca/Daily/English/971014/d971014.htm

_____. *The Daily* (November 4, 1997c). [Online] http://www.statcan.ca/Daily/English/971104/d971104.htm.

_____. *The Daily* (November 27, 1997d). [Online] http://www.statcan.ca/Daily/English/971104/d971104.htm

_____. *Education in Canada, 1996*. Catalogue No. 81-229-XIB. Ottawa: Minister of Industry, 1997e.

_____. "Homicide in Canada 1996." *Juristat.* Catalogue No. 85-002-XPE. Vol. 17, No 9 (July, 1997f):1–14.

_____. "Street Prostitution in Canada." *Juristat.* Catalogue No. 85-002-XPE. Vol. 17, No. 2 (February, 1997g):1–12.

_____. *1996 General Social Survey.* [Electronic data file.] 1998a.

_____. *Area Profiles: 1996 Census of Population.* [Electronic data file.] Statistics Canada Catalogue No. 95F0181XDB96001, Table prcumcsd.ivt, 1998b.

_____. *The Daily* (January 13, 1998c). [Online] http://www.statcan.ca/Daily/English/980113/d980113.htm

_____. *The Daily* (February 5, 1998d). [Online] http://www.statcan.ca/Daily/English/980205/d980205.htm

_____. *The Daily* (February 17, 1998e). [Online] http://www.statcan.ca/Daily/English/980217/d980217.htm

_____. *The Daily* (March 17, 1998f). [Online] http://www.statcan.ca/Daily/English/980317/d980317.htm

_____. *The Daily* (April 14, 1998g). [Online] http://www.statcan.ca/Daily/English/980414/d980414.htm

_____. *The Daily* (April 16, 1998h). [Online] http://www.statcan.ca/Daily/English/980416/d980416.htm

_____. *The Daily* (May 12, 1998i). [Online] http://www.statcan.ca/Daily/English/980512/d980512.htm

_____. *The Daily* (May 28, 1998j). [Online] http://www.statcan.ca/Daily/English/980528/d980528.htm

_____. *The Daily* (June 2, 1998k). [Online] http://www.statcan.ca/Daily/English/980602/d980602.htm

_____. *The Daily* (September 4, 1998l). [Online] http://www.statcan.ca/Daily/English/980904/d980904.htm

_____. *The Daily* (September 17, 1998m). [Online] http://www.statcan.ca/Daily/English/980917/d980917.htm

_____. *Earnings of Men and Women, 1996.* Catalogue No. 13-217-XPB. Ottawa: Minister of Industry, 1998n.

_____. *Income after Tax, Distributions by Size in Canada, 1996.* Catalogue No. 13-210-XPB. Ottawa: Minister of Industry, 1998o.

_____. *The Nation: 1996 Census of Canada.* [Electronic data file.] Statistics Canada Catalogue No. 93F0027XDB96004, Table 7_T4.ivt, 1998p.

_____. *The Nation: 1996 Census of Canada.* [Electronic data file.] Statistics Canada Catalogue No. 93F0029XDB96005, Table n05_1205.ivt, 1998q.

_____. *The Nation: 1996 Census of Canada.* [Electronic data file.] Statistics Canada Catalogue No. 93F0027XDB96007, Table n07_T7.ivt, 1998r.

_____. *The Nation: 1996 Census of Canada.* [Electronic data file.] Statistics Canada Catalogue No. 93F0029XDB96007, Table n07_1205.ivt, 1998s.

_____. *The Nation: 1996 Census of Canada.* [Electronic data file.] Statistics Canada Catalogue No. 95F0182XDB-8, Table pr8cma.ivt, 1998t.

_____. "Census Families in Private Households by Family Structure, Presence of Children and Labour Force Activity." 1999a. [Online] http://www.statcan.ca/english/census96/june9/f3can.htm

_____. *The Daily* (January 29, 1999b). [Online] http://www.statcan.ca/Daily/English/990129/d990129.htm

_____. *Low Income Persons, 1980 to 1997.* Ottawa: Minister of Industry. Catalogue No. 13-569-XIB, 1999c.

_____. *Statistical Report on the Health of Canadians.* Federal, Provincial and Territorial Committee on Population Health, 1999d.

_____. *Statistics Canada's Survey of Financial Security: Update July 1999.* Ottawa: Income Statistics Division. Catalogue No. 13F0026MIE, 1999e.

_____. *Annual Demographic Statistics, 1999.* Ottawa: Ministry of Industry. Catalogue No. 91-213-XIB, 2000a.

_____. *Average Hours per Week of Television Viewing.* [Online] http://www.statcan.ca/english/Pgdb/People/Culture/arts23.htm, November 25, 2000b.

_____. *The Daily.* (January 20, 2000c). [Online] http://www.statcan.ca/Daily/English/000120/d000120.pdf

_____. *The Daily.* (Thursday, March 16, 2000d). [Online] http://www.statcan.ca/Daily/English/000316/d000316.pdf

_____. *The Daily.* (Friday, June 16, 2000e). "Exploring Patterns of Corporate Diversification in Canada." [Online] http://www.statcan.ca/Daily/English/000616/d000616c.htm

_____. *The Daily* (Thursday, September 28, 2000f). [Online] http://www.statcan.ca/Daily/English/000928/d000928.pd

_____. "Education at a Glance." *Education Quarterly Review.* Statistics Canada Catalogue No. 81-003-XIE. Vol. 7, No.1 (November 2000g):56–60.

_____. *Education in Canada, 1999.* Statistics Canada Catalogue No. 81-229-XIE, May 2000h.

_____. *Education Indicators in Canada: Report of the Pan-Canadian Education Indicators Program, 1999.* Statistics Canada Catalogue No. 81-582-XIE. Ottawa: Canadian Education Statistics Council, 2000i.

_____. *Education Quarterly Review.* Vol. 7, No. 1. Catalogue No. 81-003-XIE, 2000j.

_____. "The Justice Factfinder, 1998." *Juristat.* Statistics Canada Catalogue No. 85-002-XIE. Vol. 20, No. 4 (June 2000k):1–12.

_____. *Quarterly Demographic Statistics, January-March 2000.* Ottawa: Ministry of Industry. Catalogue No. 91-002-XIB, 2000l.

_____. *Women in Canada 2000: A Gender-based Statistical Report.* Ottawa: Housing, Family and Social Statistics Division. Catalogue No.89-503-XPE. Ottawa: Ministry of Industry, 2000m.

_____. "Teenage Pregnancy." *Health Reports.* Vol. 12, No. 1 (Summer 2000n):9–20. Ottawa: Health Statistics Division.

_____. *Income in Canada 1998.* Ottawa: Ministry of Industry. Catalogue No. 75-202-XIE, 2000o.

_____. CANSIM Data Base Retrieval Output, Series C115100. Ottawa: Statistics Canada, 2000p.

_____. CANSIM Data Base Retrieval Output, Series C115103. Ottawa: Statistics Canada, 2000q.

_____. CANSIM Data Base Retrieval Output, Series D125599. Ottawa: Statistics Canada, 2000r.

_____. *Perspectives on Labour and Income.* Vol. 2, No. 1 (January 2001a). [Online] http://www.statcan.ca/english/indepth/75-001/online/00101/kl-ic_a.html

_____. *Selected Leading Causes of Death by Sex.* [Online] http://www.statcan.ca/english/Pgdb/People/Health/health36.htm. Accessed February 8, 2001b.

Steben, Marc, and Stephen L. Sacks. "Genital Herpes: The Epidemiology and Control of a Common Sexually Transmitted

Disease." *The Canadian Journal of Human Sexuality.* Vol. 6, No. 2 (1997).

Steele, Shelby. *The Content of Our Character: A New Vision of Race in America.* New York: St. Martin's Press, 1990.

Stein, Maurice R. *The Eclipse of Community: An Interpretation of American Studies.* Princeton, N.J.: Princeton University Press, 1972.

Stephens, John D. *The Transition From Capitalism to Socialism.* Urbana: University of Illinois Press, 1986.

Stewart Millar, Melanie. *Cracking the Gender Code: Who Rules the Wired World.* Toronto: Second Story Press, 1998.

Stier, Haya. "Continuity and Change in Women's Occupations following First Childbirth." *Social Science Quarterly.* Vol. 77, No. 1 (March 1996):60–75.

Stinchcombe, Arthur L. "Some Empirical Consequences of the Davis-Moore Theory of Stratification," *American Sociological Review.* Vol. 28, No. 5 (October 1963):808.

Stodghill, Ron, II. "Where'd You Learn That?" *Time.* Vol. 151, No. 23 (1998).

Stone, Lawrence. *The Family, Sex and Marriage in England 1500–1800.* New York: Harper & Row, 1977.

Stone, Robyn, Gail Lee Cafferata, and Judith Sangl. *Caregivers of the Frail Elderly: A National Profile.* Washington, D.C.: U.S. Department of Health and Human Services, 1987.

Straus, Murray A., and Richard J. Gelles. "Societal Change and Change in Family Violence From 1975 to 1985 as Revealed by Two National Surveys." *Journal of Marriage and the Family.* Vol. 48, No. 4 (August 1986):465–79.

Sullivan, Barbara. "McDonald's Sees India as Golden Opportunity." *Chicago Tribune,* Business section (April 5, 1995):1.

Sumner, William Graham. *Folkways.* New York: Dover, 1959; orig. 1906.

Sung, Betty Lee. *Mountains of Gold: The Story of the Chinese in America.* New York: Macmillan, 1967.

Sutherland, Edwin H. "White Collar Criminality." *American Sociological Review.* Vol. 5, No. 1 (February 1940):1–12.

Sutherland, Edwin H., and Donald R. Cressey. *Criminology.* 10th ed. Philadelphia: J.B. Lippincott, 1978.

Synnott, Anthony. "Little Angels, Little Devils: A Sociology of Children." *Canadian Review of Sociology and Anthropology.* Vol. 20, No. 1 (February 1983):79–95.

Syzmanski, Albert. *Class Structure: A Critical Perspective.* New York: Praeger, 1983.

Szasz, Thomas S. *The Manufacturer of Madness: A Comparative Study of the Inquisition and the Mental Health Movement.* New York: Dell, 1961.

_____. *The Myth of Mental Illness: Foundations of a Theory of Personal Conduct.* New York: Harper & Row, 1970; orig. 1961.

_____. "Mental Illness Is Still a Myth." *Society.* Vol. 31, No. 4 (May–June 1994):34–39.

_____. "Idleness and Lawlessness in the Therapeutic State." *Society.* Vol. 32, No. 4 (May-June 1995):30–35.

Tajfel, Henri. "Social Psychology of Intergroup Relations." *Annual Review of Psychology.* Palo Alto, Calif.: Annual Reviews, 1982:1–39.

Tannahill, Reay. *Sex in History.* Scarborough House Publishers, 1992.

Tannen, Deborah. *You Just Don't Understand: Women and Men in Conversation.* New York: Wm. Morrow, 1990.

_____. *Talking From 9 to 5: How Women's and Men's Conversational Styles Affect Who Gets Heard, Who Gets Credit, and What Gets Done at Work.* New York: Wm. Morrow, 1994.

Tanner, Julian, Harvey Krahn, and Timothy F. Hartnagel. *Fractured Transitions from School to Work: Reviisting the Dropout Problem.* Toronto: Oxford University Press, 1995.

Taylor, Charles. *Multiculturalism and the "Politics of Recognition": An Essay.* Princeton: Princeton University Press, 1992.

Taylor, Frederick Winslow. *The Principles of Scientific Management.* New York: Harper & Brothers, 1911.

Thomas, Evan, John Barry, and Melinda Liu. "Ground Zero." *Newsweek.* (May 25, 1998):28–32A.

Thomas, Jennifer. "Adult Correctional Services in Canada, 1998–99." *Juristat.* Statistics Canada Catalogue No. 85-002-XIE. Vol. 20, No 3 (June 2000):1–16.

Thomas, W.I. "The Relation of Research to the Social Process." In Morris Janowitz, ed., *W.I. Thomas on Social Organization and Social Personality.* Chicago: University of Chicago Press, 1966:289–305; orig. 1931.

Thomma, Steven. "Christian Coalition Demands Action from GOP." *Philadelphia Inquirer.* (September 14, 1997):A2.

Thompson, Dick. "Gene Maverick." *Time.* Vol. 153, No. 1 (January 11, 1999):54–55.

Thompson, Larry. "Fertility with Less Fuss." *Time.* Vol. 144, No. 20 (November 14, 1994):79.

Thorlindsson, Thorolfleur, and Thoroddur Bjarnason. "Modeling Durkheim on the Micro Level: A Study of Youth Suicidality." *American Sociological Review.* Vol. 63, No. 1 (February 1998):94–110.

Thornberry, Terrance, and Margaret Farnsworth. "Social Correlates of Criminal Involvement: Further Evidence on the Relationship between Social Status and Criminal Behavior." *American Sociological Review.* Vol. 47, No. 4 (August 1982):505–18.

Thorne, Barrie. *Gender Play: Girls and Boys in School.* New Brunswick, N.J.: Rutgers University Press, 1993.

Thorne, Barrie, Cheris Kramarae, and Nancy Henley, eds. *Language, Gender and Society.* Rowley, Mass.: Newbury House, 1983.

Thornton, Arland. "Changing Attitudes toward Separation and Divorce: Causes and Consequences." *American Journal of Sociology.* Vol. 90, No. 4 (January 1985):856–72.

Thurow, Lester C. "A Surge in Inequality." *Scientific American.* Vol. 256, No. 5 (May 1987):30–37.

Tilly, Charles. "Does Modernization Breed Revolution?" In Jack A. Goldstone, ed., *Revolutions: Theoretical, Comparative, and Historical Studies.* New York: Harcourt Brace Jovanovich, 1986:47–57.

Tindall, David. *Collective Action in the Rain Forest: Personal Networks, Collective Identity, and Participation in the Vancouver Island Wilderness Preservation Movement.* PhD thesis, Department of Sociology, University of Toronto, 1994.

Tittle, Charles R., and Wayne J. Villemez. "Social Class and Criminality." *Social Forces.* Vol. 56, No. 22 (December 1977):474–502.

Tittle, Charles R., Wayne J. Villemez, and Douglas A. Smith. "The Myth of Social Class and Criminality: An Empirical Assessment of the Empirical Evidence." *American Sociological Review.* Vol. 43, No. 5 (October 1978):643–56.

Tolson, Jay. "The Trouble With Elites." *The Wilson Quarterly.* Vol. XIX, No. 1 (Winter 1995):6–8.

Tönnies, Ferdinand. *Community and Society (Gemeinschaft und Gesellschaft)*. New York: Harper & Row, 1963; orig. 1887.

Traynor, Ian. "Immigrants Targeted in Wake of Far-Right Win." *Guardian Weekly*. (May 10, 1998):4.

Treas, Judith. "Older Americans in the 1990s and Beyond." *Population Bulletin*. Vol. 50, No. 2 (May 1995). Washington, D.C.: Population Reference Bureau.

Treiman, Donald. *Occupational Prestige in Comparative Perspective*. New York: Academic Press, 1977.

Tremblay, Sylvain. "Crime Statistics in Canada, 1999." *Juristat*. Statistics Canada Catalogue No. 85-002-XIE. Vol. 20, No. 5 (July, 2000):1–23.

Troeltsch, Ernst. *The Social Teaching of the Christian Churches*. New York: Macmillan, 1931.

Troiden, Richard R. *Gay and Lesbian Identity: A Sociological Analysis*. Dix Hills, N.Y.: General Hall, 1988.

Tucker, Robert, ed. *The Marx-Engels Reader*. 2nd ed. New York: Norton, 1978.

Tumin, Melvin M. "Some Principles of Stratification: A Critical Analysis." *American Sociological Review*. Vol. 18, No. 4 (August 1953):387–94.

_____. *Social Stratification: The Forms and Functions of Inequality*. 2nd ed. Englewood Cliffs, N.J.: Prentice Hall, 1985.

Turcotte, Pierre, and Alain Bélanger. *The Dynamics of Formation and Dissolution of First Common-Law Unions in Canada*. Research report. Ottawa: Statistics Canada, 1998.

Tyler, S. Lyman. *A History of Indian Policy*. Washington, D.C.: U.S. Department of the Interior, Bureau of Indian Affairs, 1973.

Tyyskä, Vappu. "Insiders and Outsiders: Women's Movements and Organizational Effectiveness." *The Canadian Review of Sociology and Anthropology*. Vol. 35, No. 3 (August 1998):391–410.

UNESCO. *Education for All, Year 2000 Assessment*. Statistical Document. Paris: UNESCO Institute for Statistics, 2000a.

_____. *World Education Report 2000*. Paris: UNESCO, 2000b.

U.S. Bureau of the Census. *World Population Profile: 1996*. Washington: U.S. Government Printing Office, 1996.

_____. International Data Base. [Online] February 2, 2001.

_____. International Data Base. [Online] http://www.census.gov/cgi-bin/ipc/idbsum?cty=MX. May 12, 2001.

U.S. Bureau of Justice Statistics. *Violence against Women*. Washington, D.C.: U.S. Government Printing Office, 1994.

———. *Household and Family Characteristics: March 1998 (Update)*. Current Population Reports, P20-515. Washington, D.C.: U.S. Government Printing Office, 1998.

———. *Statistical Abstract of the United States 1998*. Washington, D.C.: U.S. Government Printing Office, 1998.

_____. *Criminal Victimization 1998: Changes 1997–98 with Trends 1993–98*. Washington, D.C.: The Bureau, 1999.

U.S. Census Bureau. *Health Insurance Coverage*. (P60-208.) Washington, D.C.: The Bureau, 1999.

U.S. Department of Labor. Bureau of Labor Statistics. *Employment and Earnings*. Vol. 47, No. 1 (January 2000).

_____. *International Comparisons of Hourly Compensation Costs for Production Workers in Manufacturing, 1975–1999*. Supplementary Tables for BLS News Release USDL 00-254, September 7, 2000. [Online] ftp.ftp.bls.gov/pub/special.requests/ForeignLabor/supptab.txt. May 11, 2001.

U.S. Federal Bureau of Investigation. *Crime in the United States 1998*. Washington, D.C.: The Bureau, 1999.

U.S. House of Representatives. "Street Children: A Global Disgrace." Hearing on November 7, 1991. Washington, D.C.: U.S. Government Printing Office, 1992.

Ungar, Shelley. "Recycling and the Dampening of Concern: Comparing the Roles of Large and Small Actors in Shaping the Environmental Discourse." *Canadian Review of Sociology and Anthropology*. Vol. 35, No. 2 (May 1998):253–276.

United Nations Development Programme. *Human Development Report 1990*. New York: Oxford University Press, 1990.

_____. *Human Development Report 1991*. New York: Oxford University Press, 1991.

_____. *Human Development Report 1994*. New York: Oxford University Press, 1994.

_____. *Human Development Report 1995*. New York: Oxford University Press, 1995.

_____. *Human Development Report 1996*. New York: Oxford University Press, 1996.

_____. *Human Development Report 1998*. New York: Oxford University Press, 1998.

_____. *Human Development Report 1999*. New York: Oxford University Press, 1999.

_____. *Human Development Report 2000*. New York: Oxford University Press, 2000.

"Universities 2000: Classes." *Maclean's*. Vol. 113, No. 47 (November 20, 2000):76–78.

Unruh, John D., Jr. *The Plains Across*. Urbana: University of Illinois Press, 1979.

Vallas, Stephen P., and John P. Beck. "The Transformation of Work Revisited: The Limits of Flexibility in American Manufacturing." *Social Problems*. Vol. 43, No. 3 (August 1996):339–61.

Valpy, Michael. "Gays Claim First Legal Marriages." *The Globe & Mail*. (January 15, 2001): A1, A6.

Van Biema, David. "Parents Who Kill." *Time*. Vol. 144, No. 20 (November 14, 1994):50–51.

Vaughan, Mary Kay. "Multinational Corporations: The World as a Company Town." In Ahamed Idris-Soven et al., eds., *The World as a Company Town: Multinational Corporations and Social Change*. The Hague: Mouton Publishers, 1978:15–35.

Vayda, Eugene, and Raisa B. Deber. "The Canadian Health Care System: An Overview." *Social Science and Medicine*. Vol. 18, No. 3 (1984):191–97.

Vogel, Ezra F. *The Four Little Dragons: The Spread of Industrialization in East Asia*. Cambridge, Mass.: Harvard University Press, 1991.

Vogel, Lise. *Marxism and the Oppression of Women: Toward a Unitary Theory*. New Brunswick, N.J.: Rutgers University Press, 1983.

Vold, George B., and Thomas J. Bernard. *Theoretical Criminology*. 3rd ed. New York: Oxford University Press, 1986.

von Hirsh, Andrew. *Past or Future Crimes: Deservedness and Dangerousness in the Sentencing of Criminals*. New Brunswick, N.J.: Rutgers University Press, 1986.

Voydanoff, Patricia, and Brenda W. Donnelly. *Adolescent Sexuality and Pregnancy*. Newbury Park, Calif.: Sage, 1990.

Wadhera, Surinder, and Wayne J. Millar. "Teenage Pregnancies, 1974 to 1994." *Health Reports*. Vol. 8, No. 3 (Winter 1996):9–17.

———. "Marital Status and Abortion." *Health Reports*. Vol. 9, No. 3 (Winter 1997):19–26.

Waite, Linda J., Gus W. Haggstrom, and David I. Kanouse. "The Consequences of Parenthood for the Marital Stability of Young Adults." *American Sociological Review*. Vol. 50, No. 6 (December 1985):850–57.

Waldfogel, Jane. "The Effect of Children on Women's Wages." *American Sociological Review*. Vol. 62, No. 2 (April 1997):209–17.

Waldman, Steven. "Deadbeat Dads." *Newsweek*. (May 4, 1992):46–52.

Waldram, James B. "Native Employment and Hydroelectric Development in Northern Manitoba." In Graham S. Lowe, and Harvy J. Krahn, eds., *Work in Canada: Readings in the Sociology of Work and Industry*. Scarborough, Ontario: Nelson Canada, 1993:172–180.

Walker, Karen. "'Always There For Me': Friendship Patterns and Expectations among Middle- and Working-Class Men and Women." *Sociological Forum*. Vol. 10, No. 2 (June 1995):273–96.

Wall, Thomas F. *Medical Ethics: Basic Moral Issues*. Washington, D.C.: University Press of America, 1980.

Waller, Douglas. "Onward Cyber Soldiers." *Time*. Vol. 146, No. 8 (August 21, 1995):38–44.

Wallerstein, Immanuel. *The Modern World-System: Capitalist Agriculture and the Origins of the European World-Economy in the Sixteenth Century*. New York: Academic Press, 1974.

———. *The Capitalist World-Economy*. New York: Cambridge University Press, 1979.

———. "Crises: The World Economy, the Movements, and the Ideologies." In Albert Bergesen, ed., *Crises in the World-System*. Beverly Hills, Calif.: Sage, 1983:21–36.

———. *The Politics of the World Economy: The States, the Movements, and the Civilizations*. Cambridge, UK: Cambridge University Press, 1984.

———. "Possible Rationality: A Reply to Archer." *International Sociology*. Vol. 13, No. 1 (March 1998):19–21.

Wallerstein, Judith S., and Sandra Blakeslee. *Second Chances: Men, Women, and Children a Decade after Divorce*. New York: Ticknor & Fields, 1989.

Walton, John, and Charles Ragin. "Global and National Sources of Political Protest: Third World Responses to the Debt Crisis." *American Sociological Review*. Vol. 55, No. 6 (December 1990):876–90.

Warner, Michael. "Fear of a Queer Planet." *Social Text*. Vol. 29 (1991):3–17.

Warner, W. Lloyd, and Paul S. Lunt. *The Social Life of a Modern Community*. New Haven, Conn.: Yale University Press, 1941.

Weber, Adna Ferrin. *The Growth of Cities*. New York: Columbia University Press, 1963; orig. 1899.

Weber, Max. *The Protestant Ethic and the Spirit of Capitalism*. New York: Charles Scribner's Sons, 1958; orig. 1904–5.

———. *Economy and Society*. G. Roth, and C. Wittich, eds. Berkeley: University of California Press, 1978.

Webster, Pamela S., Terri Orbuch, and James S. House. "Effects of Childhood Family Background on Adult Marital Quality and Perceived Stability." *American Journal of Sociology*. Vol. 101, No. 2 (September 1995):404–32.

Weeks, Jeffrey. *Sexuality and Its Discontent*. New York: Routledge, 1985.

Weidenbaum, Murray. "Beyond Handouts." *Across the Board* (April 1991). In Kurt Finsterbusch, and George McKenna, eds., *Taking Sides: Clashing Views on Controversial Social Issues*. 8th ed. Guilford, Conn.: Dushkin Publishing Group, 1994.

———. "The Evolving Corporate Board." *Society*. Vol. 32, No. 3 (March/April 1995):9–20.

Weinberg, George. *Society and the Healthy Homosexual*. Garden City, N.Y.: Anchor Books, 1973.

Weinberg, Martin, Frances Shaver, and Colin Williams. "Gendered Sex Work in the San Francisco Tenderloin." *Archives of Sexual Behaviour*.

Weiner, Tim. "Head of C.I.A. Plans Center to Protect U.S. Cyberspace." *New York Times*. (June 26, 1996):B7.

Weinrich, James D. *Sexual Landscapes: Why We Are What We Are, Why We Love Whom We Love*. New York: Charles Scribner's Sons, 1987.

Weisberg, D. Kelly. *Children of the Night: A Study of Adolescent Prostitution*. Lexington, Mass.: D.C. Heath, 1985.

Weisburd, David, Stanton Wheeler, Elin Waring, and Nancy Bode. *Crimes of the Middle Class: White Collar Defenders in the Courts*. New Haven, Conn.: Yale University Press, 1991.

Weisner, Thomas S., and Bernice T. Eiduson. "The Children of the '60s as Parents." *Psychology Today*. (January 1986):60–66.

Weitzman, Lenore J. *The Divorce Revolution: The Unexpected Social and Economic Consequences for Women and Children in America*. New York: Free Press, 1985.

———. "The Economic Consequences of Divorce Are Still Unequal: Comment on Peterson." *American Sociological Review*. Vol. 61, No. 3 (June 1996):537–38.

Wellford, Charles. "Labeling Theory and Criminology: An Assessment." In Delos H. Kelly, ed., *Criminal Behavior: Readings in Criminology*. New York: St. Martin's Press, 1980:234–47.

Wellman, Barry, ed. *Networks in the Global Village*. Boulder, CO: Westview Press, 1999.

Wellman, Barry, and Keith Hampton. "Living Networked On and Offline." *Contemporary Sociology*. Vol. 28, No. 6 (November, 1999):648–54.

Wellman, Barry, and Milena Guila. "New Surfers Don't Ride Alone: Virtual Communities as Communities." In Marc Smith, and Peter Kollock, eds., *Communities in Cyberspace*. London: Routledge, 1999:167–194.

Wells, Jennifer. "The Blame Game: Bre-X Collapses and the Police Move in." *Maclean's*. (May 19, 1997). [Online] http://www.macleans.ca/newsroom051997/biz1051997.html

Westerman, Marty. "Death of the Frito Bandito." *American Demographics*. Vol. 11, No. 3 (March 1989):28–32.

Western, Bruce. "Postwar Unionization in Eighteen Advanced Capitalist Countries." *American Sociological Review*. Vol. 58, No. 2 (April 1993):266–82.

———. "A Comparative Study of Working-Class Disorganization: Union Decline in Eighteen Advanced Capitalist Countries." *American Sociological Review*. Vol. 60, No. 2 (April 1995):179–201.

Wheelis, Allen. *The Quest for Identity*. New York: Norton, 1958.

White, Jack E. "I am just who I am." *Time*. Vol. 149, No. 18 (May 1997):32–37.

White, Ralph, and Ronald Lippitt. "Leader Behavior and Member Reaction in Three 'Social Climates.'" In Dorwin Cartwright, and Alvin Zander, eds., *Group Dynamics*. Evanston, Ill.: Row, Peterson, 1953:586–611.

Whitman, David. "Shattering Myths about the Homeless." *U.S. News & World Report* (March 20, 1989):26, 28.

Whorf, Benjamin Lee. "The Relation of Habitual Thought and Behavior to Language." In *Language, Thought, and Reality*. Cambridge, Mass.: The Technology Press of MIT/New York: Wiley, 1956:134–59; orig. 1941.

Wiarda, Howard J. "Ethnocentrism and Third World Development." *Society*. Vol. 24, No. 6 (September-October 1987):55–64.

Wiatrowski, Michael A., David B. Griswold, and Mary K. Roberts. "Social Control Theory and Delinquency." *American Sociological Review*. Vol. 46, No. 5 (October 1981):525–41.

Widom, Cathy Spatz. "Childhood Sexual Abuse and Its Criminal Consequences." *Society*. Vol. 33, No. 4 (May/June 1996):47–53.

Wiles, P.J.D. *Economic Institutions Compared*. New York: Halsted Press, 1977.

Williams, Rhys H., and N. J. Demerath, III. "Religion and Political Process in an American City." *American Sociological Review*. Vol. 56, No. 4 (August 1991):417–31.

Williams, Robin M., Jr. *American Society: A Sociological Interpretation*. 3rd ed. New York: Alfred A. Knopf, 1970.

Williamson, Jeffrey G., and Peter H. Lindert. *American Inequality: A Macroeconomic History*. New York: Academic Press, 1980.

Wilson, Barbara. "National Television Violence Study." Reported by Julia Duin, "Study Finds Cartoon Heroes Initiate Too Much Violence." *Washington Times*. (April 17, 1998):A4.

Wilson, Clint C., II, and Felix Gutierrez. *Minorities and Media: Diversity and the End of Mass Communication*. Beverly Hills, Calif.: Sage Publications, 1985.

Wilson, James Q. *Bureaucracy: What Government Agencies Do and Why They Do It*. New York: Basic Books, 1991.

Wilson, Logan. *American Academics Then and Now*. New York: Oxford University Press, 1979.

Wilson, Thomas C. "Urbanism and Tolerance: A Test of Some Hypotheses Drawn From Wirth and Stouffer." *American Sociological Review*. Vol. 50, No. 1 (February 1985):117–23.

_____. "Urbanism and Unconventionality: The Case of Sexual Behavior." *Social Science Quarterly*. Vol. 76, No. 2 (June 1995):346–63.

Wilson, William Julius. *When Work Disappears: The World of the New Urban Poor*. New York: Alfred A. Knopf, 1996a.

_____. "Work." *New York Times Magazine*. (August 18, 1996b):26–31, 40, 48, 52, 54.

Wirth, Louis. "Urbanism as a Way of Life." *American Journal of Sociology*. Vol. 44, No. 1 (July 1938):1–24.

Witkin-Lanoil, Georgia. *The Female Stress Syndrome: How to Recognize and Live With It*. New York: Newmarket Press, 1984.

Wolf, Diane L., ed. *Feminist Dilemma of Fieldwork*. Boulder, Colo.: Westview Press, 1996.

Wolf, Naomi. *The Beauty Myth: How Images of Beauty are Used against Women*. New York: Wm. Morrow, 1990.

Wolfe, Jeanne M. "Canada's Liveable Cities." *Social Policy*. Vol. 23, No. 1 (Summer 1992):56–65.

Wolfgang, Marvin E., Robert M. Figlio, and Thorsten Sellin. *Delinquency in a Birth Cohort*. Chicago: University of Chicago Press, 1972.

Wolfgang, Marvin E., Terrence P. Thornberry, and Robert M. Figlio. *From Boy to Man, From Delinquency to Crime*. Chicago: University of Chicago Press, 1987.

"Women and Power." *The Christian Science Monitor*. (September 6, 1995):1, 9, 10, 11.

Wood, Chris. "Crimes of Hate: Murder Charges Revive the B.C. Racism Debate." *Maclean's*. Vol. 111, No. 18 (May 4, 1998):26–27.

Woods, Tiger. Interview with Oprah Winfrey. [Online] http://www.salon.com/april97/tiger970430.html

Woodward, Kenneth L. "Feminism and the Churches." *Newsweek*. Vol. 13, No. 7 (February 13, 1989):58–61.

_____. "Talking to God." *Newsweek*. Vol. 119, No. 1 (January 6, 1992):38–44.

World Almanac, The. *The World Almanac and Book of Facts 1999*. Mahwah, N.J.: World Almanac Books, 1999.

_____. *The World Almanac and Book of Facts 2000*. Mahwah, N.J.: World Almanac Books, 1999.

World Bank, The. *World Development Report 1993*. New York: Oxford University Press, 1993.

_____. *World Development Report 1995: Workers in an Integrating World*. New York: Oxford University Press, 1995.

_____. *World Development Report 1997: The State in a Changing World*. New York: Oxford University Press, 1997.

_____. *World Development Report 1998/99*. New York: Oxford University Press, 1998.

_____. *World Development Report 1999/2000*. New York: Oxford University Press, 2000.

_____. *World Development Report 2000/2001*. New York: Oxford University Press, 2000.

World Health Organization (WHO). *Constitution of the World Health Organization*. New York: World Health Organization Interim Commission, 1946.

World Resources Institute. *World Resources 2000/2001*. Washington, DC : World Resources Institute, 2000.

*World Values Survey, 1990–1993*. Ann Arbor, Mich.: Inter-university Consortium for Political and Social Research, 1994.

Worsley, Peter. "Models of the World System." In Mike Featherstone, ed., *Global Culture: Nationalism, Globalization, and Modernity*. Newbury Park, Calif.: Sage, 1990:83–95.

Wren, Christopher S. "In Soweto-by-the-Sea, Misery Lives on as Apartheid Fades." *New York Times*. (June 9, 1991):1, 7.

Wright, Erik Olin, and Bill Martin. "The Transformation of the American Class Structure, 1960–1980." *American Journal of Sociology*. Vol. 93, No. 1 (July 1987):1–29.

Wright, James D. "Ten Essential Observations On Guns in America." *Society*. Vol. 32, No. 3 (March-April 1995):63–68.

Wright, Quincy. "Causes of War in the Atomic Age." In William M. Evan and Stephen Hilgartner, eds., *The Arms Race and Nuclear War*. Englewood Cliffs, N.J.: Prentice Hall, 1987:7–10.

Wright, Richard A. *In Defense of Prisons*. Westport, Conn.: Greenwood Press, 1994.

Wright, Robert. "Hyperdemocracy." *Time*. Vol. 145, No. 3 (January 23, 1995):15–21.

Wu, Lawrence L. "Effects of Family Instability, Income, and Income Instability on the Risk of a Premarital Birth." *American Sociological Review*. Vol. 61, No. 3 (June 1996):386–406.

Wu, Zheng. "Premartial Cohabitation and the Timing of First Marriage." *Canadian Review of Sociology and Anthropology.* Vol. 36, No. 1 (February 1999):109–127.

_____. *Cohabitation: An Alternative Form of Living.* Don Mills, Ontario: Oxford University Press, 2000.

Yakin, Ertuk. "Convergence and Divergence in the Status of Moslem Women: The Cases of Turkey and Saudi Arabia." *International Sociology.* Vol. 6, No. 3 (September 1991):307–320.

Yankelovich, Daniel. "How Changes in the Economy are Reshaping American Values." In Henry J. Aaron, Thomas E. Mann, and Timothy Taylor, eds., *Values and Public Policy.* Washington, D.C.: The Brookings Institution, 1994:20.

Yeatts, Dale E. "Self-Managed Work Teams: Innovation in Progress." *Business and Economic Quarterly.* (Fall-Winter 1991):2–6.

_____. "Creating the High Performance Self-Managed Work Team: A Review of Theoretical Perspectives." Paper presented at the annual meeting of the Social Science Association, Dallas, February, 1994.

Yee, M. "Chinese Canadian Women: Our Common Struggle." In Creese, G., and Strong-Boag, V., eds., *British Columbia Reconsidered: Essays on Women.* Vancouver: Press Gang Publishers, 1992.

Yenerall, Joseph, Richard A. Calignon, and Timothy Casey. "The Power of Lower Status Participants in Educational Organizations." *Sociological Focus.* Vol. 27, No. 2 (May 1994): 161–172.

Yoder, Jan D., and Robert C. Nichols. "A Life Perspective: Comparison of Married and Divorced Persons." *Journal of Marriage and the Family.* Vol. 42, No. 2 (May 1980):413–19.

Yoels, William C., and Jeffrey Michael Clair. "Laughter in the Clinic: Humor in Social Organization." *Symbolic Interaction.* Vol. 18, No. 1 (1995):39–58.

Zhao, Dingxin. "Ecologies of Social Movements: Student Mobilization during the 1989 Prodemocracy Movement in Beijing." *American Journal of Sociology.* Vol. 103, No. 6 (May 1998):1493–1529.

Zuboff, Shoshana. "New Worlds of Computer-Mediated Work." *Harvard Business Review.* Vol. 60, No. 5 (September-October 1982):142–52.

**Frontispiece:** Dilip Mehta/Contact Press Images Inc.

**Chapter 1:** The Image Bank, **2**; Caroline Penn/Corbis, **2** (top left); Paul Liebhardt, **2** (top center, bottom left, bottom center, bottom right); Minh-Thu Pham, **2** (top right); Paul W. Liebhardt, **5**; Louise Gubb/SABA Press Photos, Inc., **8**; The Stapleton Collection/The Bridgeman Art Library International Ltd., **11**; Corbis-Bettmann, **13** (left); National Archives of Canada, **13** (centre); Brown Brothers, **13** (right); © Paul Marcus, *Furnishings*, oil painting on canvas, 64 in. × 48 in. Studio SPM Inc., **14**; Paul Gauguin, France, 1848–1903, *Where Do We Come From? What Are We? Where Are We Going?*, 1897, oil on canvas, 139.1 x 374.6 cm. (543.4 × 147.2”). Tompkins Collection, Courtesy of Museum of Fine Arts, Boston, **19**; Woodfin Camp/ Eastcott/Momatiuk, **22**.

**Chapter 2:** Still Pictures/Peter Arnold, Inc., **28**; Dick Hemingway **31** (top left); Carlos Humberto/TDC/Contact/Corbis/Stock Market, **31** (top center); Doranne Jacobson/International Images, **31** (top right, bottom left); Paul W. Liebhardt, **31** (middle left); David Austen/Stock Boston, **31** (middle center); J. Du Boisberran/The Image Bank, **31** (middle right); Jack Fields/Photo Researchers, Inc., **31** (bottom right); G. Humer/Gamma-Liaison, Inc., **32**; Jeff Greenberg/Picture Cube, **33** (left); CLEO Photo/Jeroboam, **33**(center); David Young-Wolff/Photoedit, **33** (right); Canapress/Ryan Remiorz, **35**; Superstock, **39** (top left); James R. Holland/Stock Boston, **39** (top right); Paul W. Liebhardt, **39** (middle left); Rosenfeld Images Ltd./Science Photo Library/Photo Researchers, Inc., **39** (middle right); Cameramann/The Image Works, **39** (bottom right); John Marshall Mantel/Corbis, **40**; Canapress/R. Remiorz, **42** (left); Michael Cooper, **42** (right); Jesse Levine, Laguna Sales, Palo Alto, **47**; Photographer Bill Coleman, www.amishphoto.com (814) 238-8495 #174, *One Day's Work*, **49**.

**Chapter 3:** Telegraph Colour Library/FPG International LLC, **54**; Ted Horowitz/The Stock Market, **56** (left); Henley & Savage/The Stock Market, **56** (center); Tom Pollak/Monkmeyer Press, **56** (right); UPI/Corbis-Bettmann, **57**; Laura Dwight/PhotoEdit, **59**; Keith Jewell, **60**; Rimma Gerlovina & Valeriy Gerlovin, Manyness, 1990, **61**; Dick Hemingway, **63**; Courtesy Alberta Filmworks/Alliance Atlantis, **66**; Elliott Erwitt/Magnum Photos, Inc., **71** (left); AP/Wide World Photos, **71** (right); SuperStock, Inc., **72**; Eastcott/Momatiuk/ Woodfin Camp & Associates, **73**.

**Chapter 4:** Stone, **78**; Department of Defence "Canadian Forces Photo," **80**; AP/Wide World Photos, **81**; UPI/Heinz Ruckemann, **84**; Paul W. Liebhardt, **85, 89**; David Cooper/Liaison Agency, Inc., **91** (top left); Alan Weiner/Liaison Agency, Inc., **91** (top center); Lynn McLaren/Index Stock Imagery, Inc., **91** (top right); Guido Rossi/The Image Bank, **91** (bottom left); Richard Pan, **91** (bottom center); Costa Manos/Magnum Photos, Inc., **91** (bottom right); Duke University Hartman Center for Sales Advertising and Marketing History with permission of Pepsi-Cola Company, **92**; Paul W. Liebhardt, **93**; Angela Maynard/PhotoDisc, Inc., **94**; Tony Freeman/Photoedit, **95**; CBC, **97**.

**Chapter 5:** Peter Christopher/Masterfile Corporation, **100**; Christopher Brown/Stock Boston, **102**; Angela Fisher/Carol Beckwith/Robert Estall Photo Agency, **105**; Cecilia Benoit, **107**; Bibliotheque Nationale, Paris, from "The Horizon History of China," by the editors of Horizon Magazine, American Heritage Publishing Co., Inc., 551 5th Avenue, New York, NY 10017 ® 1969, **112**; Gerhard Steiner/Corbis/Stock Market, **114**; Paul W. Liebhardt, **115**; George Tooker, *Government Bureau*, 1956, egg tempera on gesso panel, 195.8 x 295.8 inches, The Metropolitan Museum of Art, George A. Hearn Fund, 1956 (56.78), **117**; Andrew Winton, **119**; Dick Hemingway, **122**.

**Chapter 6:** M. Siluk/The Image Works, **126**; Sipa Press, **129**; North Wind Picture Archives, **130**; Paul W. Liebhardt, **132**; Bushnell/Soifer/Stone, **133**; Edward Gargan/New York Times Pictures, **134**; Canapress/Calgary Herald/Larry MacDougal, **135**; P. Bregg/Canapress, **137**; J. Bryksa/Canapress, **142**; A. Cairns/Canapress, **148**.

**Chapter 7:** Andy Warhol, *Marilyn*, 1967, © 2001 Andy Warhol Foundation for the Visual Arts/Artists Rights Society (ARS), New York. Tate Gallery, London/Art Resource, NY, **152**; Andre Gallant/The Image Bank, **154** (top left); Pete Turner/The Image Bank, **154** (top centre); Brun/Photo Researchers, Inc., **154** (top right); Bruno Hadjih/Liaison Agency, Inc., **154** (middle left); Elliot Erwitt/Magnum Photos, Inc., **154** (middle centre); George Holton/Photo Researchers, Inc., **154** (middle right); First Light, **154** (bottom); R. Remiorz/ Canapress, **155**; Reproduced by special permission of *Playboy* magazine. Copyright ©1953, ©1981 by *Playboy*. All rights reserved, **157**; B. Weil/Canapress, **158**; Biophoto Associates/Science Source/Photo Researchers, Inc., **160a**; Robert Noonan/Photo Researchers, Inc., **160b**; Ray Ellis/Science Source/Photo Researchers, Inc., **160c**; SIU/Photo Researchers, Inc., **160d,e**; Scott Camazine/Sue Trainor/Photo Researchers, Inc., **160f**; Mark Richards/PhotoEdit, **160g**; Charlesworth/SABA Press Photos, Inc., **168**; Mark Peterson/SABA Press Photos, Inc., **169**; Jean-Baptiste Greuze (1725-1805), *The Broken Jug*, 1772-1773 (*le cruche cassee*), rococo painting, canvas, 85 x 86.5 cm. Louvre, Dpt. des Peintures, Paris, France. © Photograph by Erich Lessing/Art Resource, NY, **170**; Richard Lord Enterprises, Inc., **171**.

**Chapter 8:** Dick Hemingway, **176**; Sebastiao Salgado/Magnum Photos, **178**; Doranne Jacobson/International Images, **179**; Per-Anders Pettersson/Black Star, **180**; Alexander Zemlianichenko/ AP/Wide World Photos, **181**; September: Harvesting Grapes by the Limbourg Brothers. *Tres Riches Heures du Duc de Berry* (early 15th century). Victoria & Albert Museum, London, UK. The Bridgeman Art Library, **184**; SuperStock, Inc., **186**; Dick Hemingway, **194**; R. Remiorz/Canapress, **195, 198**; Al Harvey, **201**.

**Chapter 9:** D. Aubert/Corbis/Sygma, **206**; Martin Benjamin/The Image Works, **209** (top left); Peter Turnley/Corbis, **209** (top right); Pablo Bartholomew/Liaison Agency, Inc., **209** (bottom right); David Stewart-Smith/SABA Press Photos, Inc., **210**; Malcolm

# INDEX

## NAME INDEX

McLean, Scott, 348
Mead, George Herbert, 15, 60–61, 62, 74
Mead, Margaret, 74, 232–33
Meadows, Donella, 393
Mercer, Rick, 94, 96, 97
Merton, Robert K., 13, 114, 132, 130–31, 137, 139, 263
Milgaard, David, 127, 149
Milgram, Stanley, 104–05
Miller, Walter, 131, 132
Mills, C. Wright, 6, 298
Mintz, Beth, 288
Moffett, Jim Bob, 137
Montagu, Ashley, 301
Moore, Wilbert, 183
Morgan, J.P., 185
Morgentaler, Henry, 172
Morin, Guy Paul, 127
Mother Teresa, 217
Murdock, George, 48, 233
Murphy, Emily, 247
Murray, Charles, 202–03, 260
Myles, John, 304

Newton, Isaac, 10
Nininger, Jim, 354
Noriega, Manuel, 223

Ogburn, William, 5, 408
Ohlin, Lloyd, 131, 132
Olsen, Gregg, 304
O'Ree, Willie, 16
Ouchi, William, 117–18

Park, Robert, 388, 389
Parks, Rosa, 81
Parsons, Talcott, 246, 367
Pasteur, Louis, 369
Piaget, Jean, 58–59, 60

Pirandello, Luigi, 83
Planck, Max, 407
Plato, 10, 183, 344
Polsby, Nelson, 298
Popenoe, David, 328–29
Porter, John, 42
Pot, Pol, 266

Quinney, Richard, 136

Reckless, Walter, 129
Reed, Ralph, 337
Rees, Philip, 389
Richels, Robert, 115
Riesman, David, 419, 424
Ritzer, George, 120, 121
Roach, Kent, 149
Roberts, Oral, 337
Robertson, Pat, 337
Robinson, Jackie, 16, 17
Robinson, Svend, 361
Rockefeller, John D., 185
Rodriguez, Sue, 361
Rogers, Ted, 298
Rostow, W.W., 217, 219
Rubin, Lillian, 318
Rushton, Philippe, 260
Ryerson, Egerton, 347

Sadik, Nafis, 384
Sansom, William, 88
Sapir, Edward, 35
Schlesinger, Arthur, Jr., 44
Schuller, Robert, 337
Schwartz, Michael, 288
Seko, Mobutu Sese, 223
Shakespeare, William, 10, 92
Sheehy, Gail, 79, 95
Sheldon, William, 128
Shively, JoEllen, 86
Simmel, Georg, 107

Simmel, Georg, 388
Sizer, Theodore, 352–53
Smith, Adam, 11, 281
Smith, Allan, 66
Smith, Dorothy, 249
Smith, Douglas, 145
Smith, Goldwin, 231
Snow, John, 356
Socrates, 344
Sophonow, Thomas, 127
Sowell, Thomas, 261
Spencer, Earl, 181
Spencer, Herbert, 13, 183, 185
Spitzer, Steven, 136–37
Stacey, Judith, 329
Stalin, Josef, 266
Stark, Rodney, 332
Steele, Shelby, 262–63
Stouffer, Samuel A., 106
Suharto, 84
Sumner, William Graham, 36
Sutherland, Edwin, 135, 137
Sutton, Willy, 94
Synnott, Anthony, 65
Szasz, Thomas, 134

Tannen, Deborah, 95, 117
Taylor, Charles, 66
Taylor, Frederick Winslow, 115–16, 119, 121
Taylor, Ollie, 352
Thomas, W.I., 84–85
Thompson, Kenneth, 193, 298
Thorne, Barrie, 89
Tönnies, Ferdinand, 387–88, 413, 415, 416, 417, 420, 426
Tribe, Verna, 62
Troeltsch, Ernst, 331

Trudeau, Pierre Elliott, 157, 292
Tumin, Melvin, 184

Ullman, Edward, 389
Ungar, Shelley, 401

Varnell, Joe, 309
Vautour, Anne, 309
Vautour, Elaine, 309
Visher, Christy, 145

Walker, Karen, 195
Wallerstein, Immanuel, 20, 220–21, 223
Walsh, David, 137
Watson, John B., 56
Watt, James, 278
Way, Niobe, 74
Weber, Max, 15, 18, 121, 111–13, 114, 115, 187–88, 216, 284, 291, 330–31, 410, 415, 416, 417, 421
Wellman, Barry, 109
Wells, Jennifer, 137
Whorf, Benjamin, 35
Wilson, William Julius, 199–200
Wirth, Louis, 388, 389
Wolf, Naomi, 236, 237
Woods, Tiger, 257
Wright, Quincy, 301

Yankelovich, Daniel, 328–29
Yezierska, Anzia, 266–67

Yoels, William, 353

# SUBJECT INDEX

Democracy, 292
oligarchy and, 115
Democracy Watch, 299
Democratic leadership, 104
Demographic momentum, 380
Demographic transition theory, 381–82
Demography, 375–76. *See also* Population.
Denmark, 295, 310
family in, 323, 324
Denomination, 332, 334
Dependency theory, 224, 289–90, 424
global poverty in, 220–23
limitations of, 222–23
population in, 382
Dependent variable, 18
Deprivation theory, 411
Descent, 312
Descriptive statistics, 18
'Designer children,' 370
Deterrence, 147, 148
arms race as, 302
Development, 424
Mead's stages of, 61
moral, stages of, 59
nature/nurture and, 56–57
social experience and, 55–58
stages of, 58–59
*See also* Dependency theory; Modernization theory.
Deviance, 128–38. *See also* Crime; Criminals.
AIDS and, 361
biological context of, 128
capitalism and, 136–37
diversity and, 139–40
gender and, 139
inequality and, 136–38
medicalization of, 134–35
personality and, 128
'sexual,' 161
smoking as, 358
social foundations of, 129–30
social-conflict analysis of, 136–38
structural-functional analysis of, 130–32
symbolic-interaction analysis of, 132–36
Deviant career, 133
*Dharma,* 217
Differential association theory
deviance in, 135, 136
prisons in, 148
Diffusion, 46, 409
Digimon, 64
Diplomacy, 302
Direct-fee system, 366

Disabilities, 81
Disarmament, 302
Discovery, 46, 409
Discrimination, 241, 263. *See also* Prejudice; Racism; Sexism.
institutional prejudice and, 263–64
in sports, 16
vicious circle of, 263, 264
Disposable society, 393
Distinct identity, 258
Diversity, 36, 41–48. *See also* Gender; Minority(ies); Race.
Canadian languages and, 44, 45
change and, 44–46
counterculture and, 44
crime and, 143
deviance and, 139–40
ethnocentrism and, 46–47
global culture and, 47–48
groups and, 107–09
high culture and popular culture as, 41–42
identity in, 419
multiculturalism and, 43–44
subcultures and, 42–43
in workplace, 286
Division of labour, 414
Divorce, 310, 316, 317, 319, 320–21
Aboriginal women and, 264
in the future, 325
smoking and, 358
traditional family and, 328
women and, 68
DNA, 370
Double meanings, 94
Double standard, 20, 50–51, 158, 251
Doubling time, 378
'Down under,' view from, 46, 47
Downsizing, 223, 277, 286
Downward social mobility, 195
Dramaturgical analysis, 15, 87–92
Dropping out, 353, 425
Dyad, 107
Dysfunction(s), social, 13

Eastern Europe. *See* Europe, Eastern.
Eating disorders, 359
Ecocentric outlook, 400
Ecologically sustainable culture, 400
Ecology, 390
urban, 389
Economic immigration, 270
Economic liability, 381

Economic trends, organizations shaped by, 113
Economy(ies), 278–90, 417. *See also* Income.
capitalist, 280–82, 283
command or centrally controlled, 282
corporations and, 288–90
export, 221
future, 290
global, 216–23, 279–80
history of, 278–84
laissez-faire, 281
sectors of, 279
socialist, 282–84
work and, 284–88
Ecosystem, 391
Education, 218, 343–55. *See also* School(s).
Aboriginals and, 255
in Canada, 345–47
conflict analysis of, 14
functions of, 347
gender and, 236, 242
global systems of, 343–47
higher, 346, 347, 350–51
in high-income countries, 344, 417
income and, 191
inequality and, 347–51
in low-income countries, 344, 417
privilege, merit and, 351.
problems with, 352–55
public and private, 348–50
sex, 163, 166
Efficiency, 120, 122–23
Ego, 58
Egocentric outlook, 400
Egypt, 246, 395
Elderly. *See* Age; Aging.
Electronic churches, 337
Elites
'cultural,' 64
high culture, 41
Email, 113
Embarrassment, 91–92
Emergence, of social movements, 412
Emigration, 377
Emigration rate, 377
Emotions
expression and, 91
universality of, 88
Empty nest, 316, 317
Endogamous, 313
Endogamous marriage, 179
Endogamy, 311
Energy consumption, 392
England, 86, 111. *See also* Great Britain.
church in, 332
post-revolution, 11
Entrepreneurs, 238

Environment, 40
future of, 399–401
growth and, 392–93
hostile, 244
in modernization theory, 220
organizational, 113
population and, 381
racism and, 399
rain forests and, 398–99
reclaiming, 401
society and, 390, 412
technology and, 391–92
waste and, 393–94
water and air pollution and, 394–98
Environmental deficit, 391–92
Environmental racism, 399
Environmentalism, 356, 401, 412. *See also* Environment.
Equality. *See also* Inequality.
class and, 183, 184
economic, 283
gender, 249
victimization and, 145
in workforce, 249
Erika, 361
Eros, 58
Escort services, 165
Estates, 181
Estonia, 182–83
Ethics
genetics and, 370
research, 21
Ethiopia, 210, 211, 214, 383
Ethnicity, 257–58. *See also* Minority(ies); Race.
crime and, 142–43
family and, 313, 318–39
health and, 358
income and, 191
poverty and, 199
religion and, 334
'Ethnic villages,' 264
Ethnocentricity, 56, 220
Ethnocentrism, 46
Ethnomethodology, 85
Etiquette, 37
Eurocentricism, 43
Europe, 381, 416
cities in, 384–85
Europe, Eastern, 8, 290, 416
air quality in, 398
socialism in, 224, 225, 284
standard of living in, 284
Europe, Western, 8, 216, 410
standard of living in, 284
Euthanasia, 361
Evaluation research, 7
Everyday living, social structure and, 79–80
Evolution, sociocultural, 37
'Exes,' 82–83

Multinational corporations, 215, 220, 289–90
Mundugumor, 233
Mutually assured destruction (MAD), 302

NAACP. *See* National Association for the Advancement of Colored People.
NAFTA. *See* North American Free Trade Agreement.
'Nagging,' 95
Names, 6
National Association for the Advancement of Colored People, 12
National Audubon Society, 401
National Council of Welfare, 194
National Eating Disorders Information Centre, 359
National Firearms Association, 297
NATO, 114
Natural environment, 390. *See also* Environment.
Nature
    laws of, 10
    vs. nurture, 56–57
Navaho, 155, 156
Nazis, 294
NDP, 295
Needs, basic, 58
Negroid, 256–57
Neocolonialism, 220
Neolocality, 311–12
Neo-Nazis, 44, 272
Nepal, 214
Netherlands, 111, 143, 145, 163, 164, 208, 362
Net migration rate, 377
Networks, 109
    informal, 113
New Democratic Party (NDP), 295–96, 297
Newfoundland, 5, 7, 29, 350
New Guinea, 233
New reproductive technology (NRT), 325, 326
New rich, 193, 194
New Social movements theory, 412
New Zealand, 8, 30, 144
NGOs. *See* Non-governmental organizations.
Nike, child labour and, 65
Niger, 214
Nigeria, 30
NIMBYism, 399
Nisga'a, 270–71

Non-governmental organizations (NGOs), 294
Nonverbal communication, 33, 88–89, 91, 93
Normative organization, 110
Norms, 36
    caste system and, 179
    deviance and, 129, 130, 136
    group, 113
    in traditional and modern societies, 417
North America. *See also individual countries.*
    cities in, 385–86
    individualism in, 4
    water in, 395
North American Free Trade Agreement (NAFTA), 48, 223
North American Indians. *See* Aboriginals.
North Atlantic Treaty Organization (NATO), 114
North Korea, 294, 302
*North of 60*, 66
Northwest Territories, 5, 7
Norway, 248, 324, 335, 397, 423
*Nouveau traité de la civilité* (de Courtin), 29
NRT. *See* New reproductive technology.
'Nuclear club,' 302
Nuclear family, 311
Nuclear proliferation, 302
Nuclear weapons, 302
Numerical ratings, 352

Objectivity, 18–19
Observation, participant, 22–23
Occupation(s)
    gender and, 236–38
    income levels by, 241, 243
    mass society and, 416
    prestige and, 191, 192
    professional, 285
*Official Languages Act*, 43
Old age, 68–71. *See also* Aging.
'Old money,' 193
Old rich, 194
Oligarchy, 115
Oligopoly, 288
Ontario, 163, 350
'Open systems,' 178
Operationalization, of variables, 18
Organic solidarity, 388, 414
Organization(s), 109–22
    civil law and, 138
    coercive, 110

'flattened,' 113, 119
formal, 109–21
global membership in, 109
Japanese, 117
normative, 110
small, 113
utilitarian, 110
voluntary, 110
Organizational environment, 113
Organized crime, 138
Orientation
    macro- and micro-level, 14
    personal and goal, 103
Other-directedness, 420
Outgroups, 106
Out-migration, 377
Outsiders, 5
Overdeveloped countries, 400. *See also* High-income countries.
Overgeneralizing, 20
Ownership, 93

Pakistan, 302, 332
Paradigms, three types of, 12, 15. *See also* Social-conflict theory; Structural-functional theory Symbolic-interaction theory.
Paraprofessionals, 285
Parental leave, 241
Parenthood, 62
    gay, 324
    influence of, 63
Paris Exposition, 407
Parti Québécois, 296
Participant observation, 22–23, 24
Particular, general vs., 4
Parties, political, 295–96, 297
Passivity, of students, 352
Pastoral, 188
Pastoralism, 38, 391
Patriarchal societies, 103–04, 247
Patriarchy, 233–35 , 417
    authority and, 313
    in Bangladesh, 250
    divorce laws and, 264
    family and, 313, 314, 319
    in Indian education, 344
    medicine and, 362
    prostitution and, 165, 167
    religion and, 329–30
    sexuality and, 171
Patrilineal descent, 312
Patrilocality, 311
Pea soup fog, 397
Peace, 302–03
Pearl Harbor, 105, 255
    electronic, 303
Peer abuse, 63
Peer group

as agent of socialization, 63
gender and, 236
Peer pressure, 420–21
*Perestroika*, 182
Performance, 87
    body language and, 88–89
    gender and, 89–90
Periphery, of world economy, 220
Persian Gulf War, 116, 301
Personal distance, 90
Personality, 55
    in adulthood, 67
    authoritarian, 261
    deviance and, 128–29
    Type A, 235, 357
Personality model, Freud's, 58
Personal orientation, 103
Personal space, 89–90
Philippines, 214, 223, 399
    cities in, 389
    crime rates in, 144
Physicians, 367, 368
    female, 362–64
    performance and, 87
Pill, birth control, 158. *See also* Birth control.
Pimps, 165
Play, 61
Plea bargaining, 145
Pluralism, 264–65
Pluralistic model, of politics, 298
Pokémon, 64
Pokot, 155
Poland, 114
Police
    prejudice and, 262
    sex workers and, 171
Political elites, 284
Political parties, 295–96, 297
Political revolution, 299–300
Political spectrum, 295
Politics, 290–303. *See also* Government; Political parties.
    class and, 194–95
    democracy and, 292
    feminism and, 247
    future of, 303
    gender and, 242, 244
    global, 291–99
    history of, 11, 290–91
Marxist model of, 298–99
    medicine as, 369
    militarism and, 301–03
    monarchy and, 291–92
    organizations shaped by, 113
    pluralistic model of, 298–99
    poverty and, 224
    power and, 299–302

Social cohesion, religion and, 327
Social construction of reality, 83–84
Social-conflict theory, 13–14, 15
  cities in, 389–90
  class society, 187, 418–19
  crime in, 138, 139
  culture in, 49
  education in, 347–48
  family in, 313–14
  gender in, 246–47
  medicine in, 368–69
  religion in, 329–30
  sexuality in, 171–72
  sports in, 16
Social control, 128. *See also* Control; Patriarchy.
Social Darwinism, 185
Social deviance. *See* Deviance.
Social distance, 261, 90
Social diversity. *See* Diversity.
Social dysfunctions, 13
Social epidemiology, 357
Social equality. *See* Equality.
Social-exchange, analysis, 15
Social experience
  development and, 55–57
  self and, 60
Social functions, 12
'Social gospel,' 185
Social groups, 101–09. *See also* Group(s); Organization(s)
  conformity in, 104–05
  diversity in, 107–09
  leadership in, 103–04
  networks as, 109
  primary and secondary, 102–03
  reference groups as, 105–06
  size of, 106–07
Social inequality. *See* Inequality.
Social institutions, 278
  changes in, 423
Social integration, suicide and, 5
Social interaction, 79–98
  dramaturgical analysis of, 87–92
  humour in, 94–98
  language and gender in, 92–93
  reality and, 83–87
  role and, 81–82
  status and, 80–83
Socialism, 185, 282–84. *See also* Marxism.
  dependency theory and, 223

modernization theory and, 219
  recent changes to, 283–84
Socialist feminism, 248
Socialization, 55, 58–61
  agents of, 61–65
  anticipatory, 63, 106
  family and, 313
  Freudian theory of, 58
  gender and, 60, 235–36
  Gilligan's theory of, 59–60
  Kohlberg's theories of, 59
  life course and, 65–72
  Mead's theory of, 60–61
  Piaget's theory of, 58–59
  schooling and, 347
Social isolation, 57–58
Social issues, 295
Socialized medicine, 364–66, 367
Social marginality, 5–6
Social mobility, 178, 195–98
  structured, 182
Social movements
  social change and, 411–12
  stages in, 412
Social placement, 347
  family and, 313
Social protection, 147, 148
Social reintegration, 427
Social responsibility, 426–27
Social stratification, 177–203. *See also* Class.in
  Canada, 189–94, 198–203
  caste, class and, 178–83
  conflict and, 184–88
  functions of, 183–84
  global poverty and, 214
  resocialization and, 72–73
  social mobility and, 195–98
  technology and, 188–89
Social structure, 12, 79–80
Society(ies), 3, 30
  global interconnection of, 8
  war and, 301
  service, 123
  sexual orientation as product of, 161
  traditional vs. modern, 417
Sociobiology, 50–51
Sociocultural evolution, 37
Socioeconomic status (SES), 187
Sociological perspective, 3–6
  benefits of, 6–7
Sociological theory, 12
Sociologists, clinical, 7
Sociology
  applied, 7
  careers in, 7
Comte's stage theory of, 10
  critical, 19–20

interpretive, 19
  marginal voices and, 11–12
  origins of, 10–12
  scientific, 10, 15–24
  social change and, 10–11
  stereotypes and, 25
  three methodological approaches to, 19–20
Solar Temple, 333
Solid waste, 392, 393–94
South Africa, 179, 180, 302
  apartheid in, 265
South Korea, 111, 218, 283, 291
  state capitalism in, 303
Soviet Union, 182–83, 223, 290, 294, 301, 302, 416. *See also* Russian Federation.
Russian Revolution in, 299
  socialism in, 224, 283
Spain, 12, 111, 383
Special-interest groups, 296–97
Specialization, 112, 278, 353
Specialized economic activity, 414
Specific deterrence, 147
Sports
  discrimination in, 16
  gender and, 223
  sociology of, 16–17
Spouse, 157. *See also* Marriage.
  death of, 318
Spurious correlation, 18
Sri Lanka, 315, 383
Stacking, 16, 17
Standard of living. *See also* Global stratification; Income; Poverty; Wealth.
  technological maturity and, 218
  healthcare and, 356
  progress and, 421
Staring, 90
State, 417. *See also* Government.
State capitalism, 283, 303
State church, 332
State terrorism, 300
Statistics, 23
  criminal 140, 141
  descriptive, 18
Statistics Canada, 23, 198, 310, 324
Status consistency, 180–81
Status, 80–83
  ascribed and achieved, 80–81
  class power and, 187
  insider, 96
  master, 81

in traditional and modern societies, 417
Status set, 80, 82
Status symbols, 194
STDs. *See* Sexually transmitted diseases.
Stereotypes, 25. *See also* Prejudice.
Stigma, 133–34
  divorce and, 320
  in labelling theory, 136
  prisons and, 148
Stone Age, 32
Strain theory
  deviance in, 130
  limitations of, 139
Strange, familiar vs., 4–5
Strategic defence initiative (SDI), 302
Stratification
  global. *See* Global stratification
  social. *See* Social stratification.
Streaming, 348, 353
'Street code,' 132
'Street' criminal, 142–43
Streetwalkers, 165, 171. *See also* Prostitution.
Stress, family, 241
Structural social mobility, 195
Structural-functional theory, 12–13
  culture in, 48–49
  deviance in, 130–32
  deviance in, 139
  family in, 313
  gender in, 245–46
  mass society in, 416
  medicine in, 367
  religion in, 327–28
  sexuality in, 168–70
  social stratification in, 187
  sports in, 16
Structured social mobility, 182
Student loans, 350
Subculture, 42–43
  conflict, 131
  deviant, 131–32
  retreatist, 131
Sublimation, 58
Subordination, 258
Substance abuse, 140, 158, 319, 320, 352, 365
Suburbs, 386–87
Suicide, 63
  in Canada, 5, 7, 12
  modernity and, 414–15
  'race,' 172
Superego, 58, 129
Surveys, 21–22
Survival, culture and, 30, 32
Sustainability, 399–400
Swaziland, 105

Virtual culture, 40
Virtual office, 279
Virtual wars, 303
Virtue, 93
Visible minorities, 271, 272.
    *See also* Minority(ies);
    Race.
Voluntary organization, 110
Voter apathy, 297, 427
Voting
Aboriginals and, 267
    women and, 297

Wage labour, 278
War, 301–02
    information, 303
    virtual, 303
*War Measures Act*, 266
Waste, 392, 393–94
    reduction, 400
Water
    consumption, 396
    pollution, 395–97
    supply, 394–95
Wealth, 190. *See also* Global
        stratification; Income.
    in Canada, 192–93
    concentration of, 186
    disparity in, 188–89
    global, 211, 212, 225
    high-income countries
        and, 221
    politics and, 292
    suicide and, 5
Wedge-shaped sectors, 389
Weight, 237

Welfare, 137, 185, 283
Welfare capitalism, 283, 303
Welfare state, 295, 304, 323
West Edmonton Mall, 390
Western Europe. *See*
    Europe, Western.
White Anglo-Saxon
    Protestants (WASPs),
    268
White-collar crime, 137–38,
    142
White-collar occupations,
    186
Wodaabe, 236
Women, 223. *See also*
        Gender.
    aboriginal, 23
    abortion rights and,
        172–73
    in adulthood, 67–68
    aging, poverty and, 70, 71
    in Canadian politics, 36
    divorce and, 318, 319, 320
    double standard and,
        50–51
    education of, 346, 350
    family and, 313
    global poverty and, 212–14
    in horticultural and
        agricultural cultures,
        38
    income and, 191
    in management, 114–16
    medicine and, 362, 363
    as minority, 243
    minority, 243

modernization and, 219
on the *Titanic*, 177
performance and, 89
in politics and
        government, 36, 243,
        244
population and status of,
        382, 384
pornography and, 164
power of, 234
prestige and, 191
prostitution laws and, 165
self-employment and, 286
in service society, 122–23
social behaviour of, 15–16
in social history, 12
sports and, 16, 223
suicide and, 5, 7, 12
religion and, 329–30, 331
employment,
        unemployment and,
        286, 289
upper class, 193
violence against, 243–44,
        321–22
voting and, 297
work and, 284, 289
Women's power index, 234
Work teams, competitive,
    119
Work. *See also* Income;
        Occupations
    gender and, 236–38, 239,
        240, 249, 289
    in manufacturing, 291
    mothers and, 240

part-time, 277–78
in post-industrial economy,
    284–88
unpaid, 238, 242. *See also*
    Housework.
Working class, 181, 193–94.
        *See also* Class.
    family in, 62, 195, 318
'Working poor,' 194, 201
'Working rich,' 193
Workplace, 284
    diversity in, 286, 289
World Bank, 23
World economy, 220. *See also*
    Economy; Global
    stratification; High-
    income countries;
    Low-income
    countries.
World Health Organization,
    355, 369
Writ of mandamus, 310

Xenophobia, 272

Yanomamö, 30, 32, 37, 38,
    301
Young offenders, 148
Young Offender Act, 149
Youth culture, 157–58
Yugoslavia, 42
Yukon Territories, 5, 7

Zero population growth, 382
Zero-sum, wealth as, 222